# Communication and Disenfranchisement
## Social Health Issues and Implications

# Communication and Disenfranchisement
## Social Health Issues and Implications

Edited by
### Eileen Berlin Ray
*Cleveland State University*

**LEA** LAWRENCE ERLBAUM ASSOCIATES, PUBLISHERS
1996   Mahwah, New Jersey

Lawrence Erlbaum Associates, Inc., Publishers
10 Industrial Avenue
Mahwah, New Jersey 07430

Cover design by Gail Silverman

**Library of Congress Cataloging-in-Publication Data**

Communication and disenfranchisement : social health issues and
   implications / edited by Eileen Berlin Ray.
        p.    cm.
   Includes bibliographical references and index.
   ISBN 0-8058-1530-9 (c : alk. paper). — ISBN 0-8058-1531-7 (pbk. :
alk. paper).
   1. Marginality, Social—United States.  2. Socially handicapped—
United States.  3. Victims—United States.  4. Communication in
medicine—United States.  5. Social medicine—United States.
I. Ray, Eileen Berlin.
HN90.M26C66  1996
306.4′61—dc20                                                        96-827
                                                                     CIP

Books published by Lawrence Erlbaum Associates are printed on acid-free paper,
and their bindings are chosen for strength and durability.

Printed in the United States of America
10  9  8  7  6  5  4  3  2  1

*To my parents,
Paul and Dorris Berlin*

# Contents

# Contributors

Terrance L. Albrecht
Department of Communication/
  Family Health
College of Public Health
University of South Florida
Tampa, FL 33612

Fredi Avalos-C'deBaca
School of Communication
San Diego State University
San Diego, CA 92182

Betsy Wackernagel Bach
Department of Communication Studies
University of Montana
Missoula, MT 59812

Deborah S. Ballard-Reisch
Department of Communication
University of Nevada, Reno
Reno, NV 89557

Mark Bergstrom
Department of Communication
University of Utah
Salt Lake City, UT 84112

Dawn O. Braithwaite
Department of Communication Studies
Arizona State University West
Phoenix, AZ 85069

Connie Bullis
Department of Communication
University of Utah
Salt Lake City, UT 84112

Robin P. Clair
Department of Communication
Purdue University
West Lafayette, IN 47907

Rebecca J. Welch Cline
Department of Communication
  Processes & Disorders
University of Florida
Gainesville, FL 32611

Frederick C. Corey
Department of Communication
Arizona State University
Tempe, AZ 85287

Stanley Deetz
Department of Communication
Rutgers University
New Brunswick, NJ 08903

Lynette Seccombe Eastland
Department of Speech &
  Communication Studies
Clemson University
Clemson, SC 29634

Anne Eckman
Department of Speech Communication
University of Illinois at Urbana–
  Champaign
Urbana, IL 61801

Patricia Geist
School of Communication
San Diego State University
San Diego, CA 92182

Julie L. Gray
School of Communication
San Diego State University
San Diego, CA 92182

Ginger Hill
School of Communication
San Diego State University
San Diego, CA 92182

Gerianne M. Johnson
Department of Speech &
  Communication
San Francisco State University
San Francisco, CA 94132

John Kahler
Department of Family Practice
Cook County Hospital and
  Humana Health Care Plans
Chicago, IL 60615

Heather Manns
Department of Communication
Illinois State University
Normal, IL 61761

Alicia A. Marshall
Department of Speech Communication
Texas A&M University
College Station, TX 77843

Maria Mastronardi
Department of Speech Communication
University of Illinois at Urbana–
  Champaign
Urbana, IL 61801

Nelya J. McKenzie
Department of Communication
Auburn University at Montgomery
Montgomery, AL 36117

Janet K. McKeon
Department of Communication
Michigan State University
East Lansing, MI 48824

Sandra Metts
Department of Communication
Illinois State University
Normal, IL 61761

Katherine Miller
Department of Communication Studies
University of Kansas
Lawrence, KS 66045

Hartmut B. Mokros
Department of Communication
Rutgers University
New Brunswick, NJ 08903

Jon F. Nussbaum
Department of Communication
University of Oklahoma
Norman, OK 73019

Eileen Berlin Ray
Department of Communication
Cleveland State University
Cleveland, OH 44115

George B. Ray
Department of Communication
Cleveland State University
Cleveland, OH 44115

Jill E. Rudd
Department of Communication
Cleveland State University
Cleveland, OH 44115

David R. Seibold
Department of Communication
University of California, Santa Barbara
Santa Barbara, CA 93106

Barbara F. Sharf
Department of Medical Education
University of Illinois at Chicago
Chicago, IL 60612

Lisa Sparks
Department of Communication
University of Oklahoma
Norman, OK 73019

Richard W. Thomas
Department of Speech
  Communication & Dramatic Arts
Central Michigan University
Mt. Pleasant, MI 48859

Teresa L. Thompson
Department of Communication
University of Dayton
Dayton, OH 45469


James T. West
Honolulu, HI 96822


Ruth E. Zambrana
School of Social Welfare
University of California
Los Angeles, CA 90024

# Introduction

Eileen Berlin Ray
*Cleveland State University*

This book is about some of the people, groups, and classes who are disenfranchised in the United States. Whether through birth, life events, or unfortunate circumstances, they are denied full privileges, rights, and power within the existing societal structure.[1] They are the "other," the marginalized, the victimized. The chapters in this volume speak about their experience, their challenges, and their accomplishments. More important, the topics to which these authors give their attention are not far removed from our everyday lives. We are each equally vulnerable and likely to be affected in some way. We may find, after deciding to have children, that we are infertile. We may become suddenly homeless after leaving an abusive marriage, getting laid off, or working at a minimum wage job that does not cover our basic needs. We may find ourselves becoming suddenly disabled,

---

[1]It should be noted that there are many people working within the system in important ways to help enfranchise "others." The significance of their work cannot be ignored, for without them, for example, soup kitchens would be unstaffed, rape crisis centers would not exist, formerly taboo topics would remain taboo, new laws would not be passed, and access to health care for the indigent would not improve. These efforts are in tension with those who believe people are responsible for what happens to them, such as getting HIV/AIDS, being homeless, raped, molested, battered, alcoholic, and so on. If victims are *responsible*, then they *caused* their condition and if they so chose, they could change their situation. Among these believers, there is no acknowledgment, much less understanding, of the impact of the complex cultural, socioeconomic, and political forces that continue oppression. Rather, their goal is to intentionally keep the disenfranchised invisible, perhaps by silencing them or discrediting their claims, or by drawing "others" into the mainstream under the guise of enfranchisement while simultaneously perpetuating the very structure that enables the disenfranchisement in the first place.

diagnosed with HIV or AIDS, our child may contract cancer, or we may be diagnosed as terminally ill. It may be our sister or our mother who is being physically abused. It may be our child or grandchild who is being molested by a family member. We may find ourselves being sexually harassed, living with or becoming an alcoholic, facing a divorce, or having to move our aging parents into a nursing home. It may happen to us or to someone we care about. With a roll of the die, with great abruptness, anyone can become "them."

This volume examines the communication–disenfranchisement relationship, specifically how it is accomplished, managed, and overcome. Through interactions with family, friends, and institutions, and from the mass media, definitions of acceptable identities, acceptable behaviors, acceptable topics of discussion, and acceptable expectations are made clear as to who "fits" where in American society, who controls the resources, who makes the decisions, and who sets the social standards. It is the analysis and understanding of this communicative process across various social health issues that provides insight into disenfranchisement and is the focus of this book.

It should be noted that many of the disenfranchised are members in more than one group, such as women of color living in poverty (see Zambrana, chapter 7, and Marshall & McKeon, chapter 8), women who have been sexually and physically abused (see E. B. Ray, chapter 14, and West, chapter 15), women or gay men with HIV/AIDS (see Cline & McKenzie, chapter 19, and Metts & Manns, chapter 18), or persons of color living in the inner city (see Sharf & Kahler, chapter 6). Obviously, there are myriad other combinations that result in different, and complex, constructions of disenfranchisement despite some shared experiences.

Unfortunately, there is no shortage of persons who are disenfranchised and there is no shortage of those who could be included in this book. Chapters appearing in this volume are, in many cases, continuations of research agendas but with a refocus on disenfranchisement (e.g., Ballard-Reisch; Braithwaite; Clair; Cline & McKenzie; Nussbaum, Bergstrom, & Sparks; Thomas & Seibold; Thompson; Rudd; West). Others reflect new lines of inquiry contributors were previously interested in pursuing and this project provided an appropriate outlet for their work (e.g., Geist, Gray, Avalos-C'deBaca, & Hill; Miller; E. B. Ray). It was my intention to generate awareness and give voice to these issues, to legitimate the study of the relationship between communication and social health issues, and to recognize the significance of the pragmatic and theoretic implications. In retrospect, the field of health communication has taken a rather narrow approach to what comprises its domain, with many research agendas fitting within a traditional systems framework (see, e.g., Ray & Donohew, 1990) and emphasizing concerns related to physical health. Although this was no doubt necessary when the field began, what we gained in depth in these areas may have been at the sacrifice of breadth in others. By setting an arbitrary boundary around what fits conceptually under the rubric of health communication, we have inadvertently marginalized the "others." What is called for, then, is an expansion of the boundaries so that topics of study previously neglected or stigmatized become mainstream. This requires setting a new research agenda, a conscious effort toward inclusiveness (not continued marginalization through oversight), and an expansion of what is encompassed within the field of health communication. It is my hope that this book makes a contribution toward these efforts.

## ORGANIZATION OF THE BOOK

This book is organized around the social health issues of socioeconomic status, family, abuse, and health concerns. It should be noted that there are numerous ways to organize these chapters that make conceptual sense. This framework was chosen because chapters grouped together have at least one salient issue in common. However, across topics and groups, the common threads of emotional and physical isolation, and the magnitude of negative personal and societal messages, exemplify the perpetuation of the disenfranchisement process. For example, experiences of infertile women, adult incest survivors, and physically abused or sexually harassed women underscore their emotional isolation, as they struggle with others' invalidating their experiences and challenging the legitimacy of their pain. The impact of physical isolation is apparent for the disenfranchised, compounded by the reality that, whether they are indigent, homeless, gay males, persons with AIDS, cancer patients, terminally ill, or elderly, all commonly encounter further disenfranchisement by the medical establishment. Finally, the power of interpersonal and societal messages to marginalize or empower the disenfranchised is highlighted throughout the book.

Part I presents four conceptual overviews of disenfranchisement. In chapter 1, Bullis and Bach compare, contrast, and critique different feminist perspectives. They examine the processes of "othering," or disenfranchising, and how each perspective encourages enfranchisement. This definition of the disenfranchised as the "other" is what Mokros and Deetz (chapter 2) refer to as an informative view of communication, where reality is defined prior to communication. They argue that this view is an inadequate explanatory framework. Rather, a constitutive view of communication is more useful, where the "others" are not considered natural but instead are socially constructed, discursive ways of understanding experience. Both G. B. Ray and Eastland (chapters 3 & 4) consider the reconstruction of identity in postmodern society and its relationship to disenfranchisement. Through an analysis of the self-help movement, G. B. Ray (chapter 3) compares the postmodern crisis in identities with the United States' traditional belief in individualism and the resulting self-disenfranchisement that occurs. Eastland (chapter 4) continues this discussion on postmodernism, identity, and disenfranchisement through her examination of the reconstruction of identity for gay men and lesbians within the political arena. Her detailed account of the Oregon Citizens Alliance (an ultraconservative/religious right-wing group) delineates their attempt to discursively construct gay men and lesbians as "others" in their campaign to pass a state constitutional amendment denying homosexuals' civil rights.

Part II focuses on issues related to socioeconomic status. Miller (chapter 5) explicates how the homeless socially construct their identities through their interactions with each other, with domiciled persons, and with service providers. Then, from the perspective of the homeless person, she identifies communication and behaviors they perceive as being either supportive or marginalizing. In chapter 6, Sharf and Kahler illustrate how indigent persons are not disenfranchised from health care but are victims of a health care system that has developed to their disadvantage. Focusing on inner city public hospitals, they describe their Culturally Sensitive Model of patient–physician communication, its utility when training medical professionals, and how its application has the potential to enfranchise patients. Chapters 7 (Zambrana) and 8 (Marshall & McKeon) focus on the specific population of women living in poverty. Zambrana discusses the poorer health status of poor women and women of color and factors that contribute to it. She argues that research on the health needs of poor and racial/ethnic women must include the complex interactions of race, gender, and class. Zambrana focuses on their utilization of health care services, whereas Marshall and McKeon emphasize the dissemination of health-related information. In their examination of communicative and behavioral factors that may contribute to their poorer health status, they argue that these women are "unreached," not "unreachable." In order to reach them, health care providers must be sensitive to their unique concerns and involve them in developing outreach strategies.

Part III examines family-related issues. In chapter 9, Geist, Gray, Avalos-C'deBaca, and Hill discuss how messages from interpersonal, societal, religious, and health care sources disenfranchise infertile couples and how couples may negotiate enfranchised identities by pursuing alternative medicine, infertility clinics, adoption, or through participation in support groups. Ballard-Reisch, in chapter 10, describes the disenfranchisement experienced when an adolescent is diagnosed with cancer. Alienation because of the stigma surrounding cancer, fear about the uncertainty of the disease and prognosis, and isolation from important support networks while immersed in treatment all act to marginalize the entire family. In chapter 11, Rudd considers the dissolution of intact families through divorce mediation. The goal of mediation is to change the divorce process from adversarial to conciliatory. Although proponents claim it is a mechanism that empowers women, opponents argue that it retains traditional power inequities and is simply a new vehicle for maintaining the status quo. Nussbaum, Bergstrom, and Sparks (chapter 12) tackle the difficult issue of placing an aging relative in a nursing home. They underscore the institutional and interpersonal disenfranchisement that begins even before the formal admissions process. Once admitted, these elderly find themselves structurally and relationally isolated as the institution depends on enforcing conformity and discouraging individuality. Interaction with family, friends within and outside the home, and alternatives to institutionalization are discussed as ways of involving the elderly in mainstream society.

Part IV centers on the issues of sexual and physical abuse, with a focus on women as victims. That is not to say men are not recipients of these abuses but rather that the authors chose to confine their analyses to women. In chapter 13, Eckman and Mastronardi provide an in-depth feminist analysis of sexual violence. They argue that myths comprise dominant communication practices that disenfranchise women who experience sexual violence and review the history and emergence of different feminist perspectives on sexual violence. E. B. Ray (chapter 14) explicates the often long-term negative impact of messages from perpetrators, family and friends, and the mass media, and how those in power respond as incest survivors find their individual, collective, and political voices. West (chapter 15) explores how women are disenfranchised by physically abusive relationships. Drawing from women's narratives, he examines the set of complex ideological practices that keeps abused women silent and perpetuates their marginalization. In chapter 16, Clair uses patriarchy and the discourse of privilege to provide a critical analysis of women as a disenfranchised group who are the primary targets, victims, and survivors of sexual harassment.

Part V focuses on health-related issues. In his examination of the gay men–physician relationship, Corey (chapter 17) explores the historical construction of homosexual desire as illness, the equation of HIV/AIDS with gay men, the use of silence and invisibility as ways to avoid stigmatization, and the negotiation of power between the health care system and the disenfranchised gay population. Metts and Manns (chapter 18) examine persons, predominantly White gay males, with HIV/AIDS. Drawing from extant literature and their interviews with 87 participants, they discuss how, in the face of societal disenfranchisement, those with HIV/AIDS often become empowered by developing individual and community-wide enfranchising support systems. Examining HIV/AIDS within a different population, Cline and McKenzie (chapter 19) underscore how multiple membership in disenfranchised groups magnifies women with HIV/AIDS' stigmatization. These women also tend to be members of minority groups and generally contracted the virus either through IV drug use or unsafe sexual practices. Contrasted with those empowered in Metts and Manns' sample, these women do not have access to, or are denied, the interpersonal and institutional social support that could help ease the emotional and physical pain of their illness.

The final four chapters not only highlight issues related to health care, but also provide specific suggestions for changing communication patterns that are disenfranchising. Thompson (chapter 20) discusses how our fear of death marginalizes the terminally ill, regardless of their particular illness. Her literature review emphasizes the communicative needs of these patients from caregivers, family, and friends, and special needs for patients and their families when the person dying is a child. She then discusses specific communicative strategies that can enable care providers to minimize disenfranchising patients so that they can die with dignity. Thomas and Seibold (chapter 21) consider concerns related to alcohol abuse. Although there is debate as to whether or not alcoholism is a disease, clearly the outcomes of abusive drinking impact drinkers' health and through their actions may affect the health of others. Alcohol abusers may be disenfranchised by losing privileges (i.e., losing their licenses due to drunk driving) and being stigmatized as alcoholics. This chapter focuses on the role of personal influence in the identification-intervention-prevention of alcohol problems and how communication enacts or enables the disenfranchisement process. Johnson and Albrecht (chapter 22) and Braithwaite (chapter 23) examine issues related to persons with disabilities. Johnson and Albrecht explore the changing social and legal constructions of disability and work and their bearing on employment-related social support and communication network involvement. They urge communication scholars to address the challenges, through training and research, faced by persons with disabilities within the workplace setting. Finally, Braithwaite examines disability as a health issue, a stigmatizing condition, and a culture. Drawing from interview data in her own research, interviewees emphasize communicative choices they can make to empower themselves individually and collectively.

## ACKNOWLEDGMENTS

During a major portion of my work on this book, I was on sabbatical in the Education Centre at Lincoln University, Canterbury, New Zealand. Words are inadequate to express my thanks and appreciation to the director of the Centre, Neil Fleming, for his financial support and his encouragement of this project. Completing this work was made much simpler because of him. I also want to acknowledge Ruth Margerison for her helpful insights, and other members of the Centre, Nicola Cameron, Jenny Lee, and Carrie

Moore for their support and collegiality, and Paul Humphreys for proof-reading manuscript drafts.

I greatly appreciate the comments and support provided by Kathy Miller, Patricia Geist, and Sandra Metts during various stages of this project, Kathleen O'Malley, Barbara Wieghaus, Sharon Levy, Amy Olener and the staff at Lawrence Erlbaum Associates for their help throughout my work on this book, and Amy Capwell for her help with the author index. Special thanks go to Janet Goodman for her support and insights, at home and abroad. Finally, my most heartfelt gratitude goes to my husband, George, for his unwavering love, support, and humor, and to our children, Bryan and Lesley, for making sure I keep my priorities straight.

## REFERENCES

Ray, E. B., & Donohew, L. (1990). *Communication and health: Systems and applications.* Hillsdale, NJ: Lawrence Erlbaum Associates.

# PART I

# CONCEPTUAL ORIENTATIONS TO DISENFRANCHISEMENT

# 1 Feminism and the Disenfranchised: Listening Beyond the "Other"

Connie Bullis
*University of Utah*

Betsy Wackernagel Bach
*University of Montana*

In this chapter, we discuss several feminist theories as they consider the "other." Although feminist theories differ dramatically from one another, all are working to identify oppressive patterns so that they may be critiqued and changed to better the lives of women and all of the oppressed or subjugated. Feminist voices often assert that such change betters the lives of the oppressors as well.

The "other" is a central problem that frames the need for social change in each feminist theory. Feminist views are related to this book as the chapters invite us to confront various "others." The authors of each chapter either (a) reveal the lives of "others," (b) evoke critiques of the ways "others" are identified, or (c) imply processes for transforming the ways current (i.e., patriarchal) arrangements (or practices, processes, and institutions) work against "others."

In this chapter, we discuss feminist theorizing of the "other." We begin by defining the "other" and explaining its importance to feminist theory. The process of "othering" or disenfranchising, or marginalizing in its various forms, is a primary feminist concern. We summarize several different feminist approaches, focusing on their treatment of the "other," or disenfranchisement, and the unique ways in which each encourages enfranchisement (see Eckman & Mastronardi, chap. 13, for a discussion of feminist theories and sexual violence). We also summarize criticisms of each feminist theory. We consider our discussion of the "other" as it is related to several key feminist tensions: (a) the autonomous individual and the disappearance of human agency, (b) universality and localness, (c) objectivist assumptions and social constructionist assumptions, (d) stable order and changing disorder, and (e) unity and diversity. We order our discussion so that it begins with feminist approaches most reliant on the "subject" or the "self," and proceed through feminist approaches that increasingly question the "subject" or "self" to postmodern feminism that calls for more radical transformation of the "self," and hence, the "other." Finally, we posit ecological feminism as a useful voice that avoids the excesses and manages tensions among various feminist voices in its treatment of the "self" and the "other." Although we advocate ecological feminism and we posit a historically dynamic ordering to the feminisms we discuss, we take Ferguson's (1993) advice on irony seriously. All the feminist voices we discuss are both commitments we continue to hold *and* laden with assumptions we continue to question.

We are aware of the danger of summarizing a set of different and unique positions within each of the categories we discuss as well as the permeability of the "types" of feminism. Categorizing always distorts, and our attempts to order diverse voices into (partially) coherent accounts absence many feminist voices, alternative plausible accounts, and ways in which distinctions are often blurred. As such, we do not position ourselves as spokeswomen for the "other" nor do we claim a comprehensive or fixed position. We believe that in approaching the disenfranchised as this book does, our brief examination of several different feminisms is helpful in opening multiple possibilities for considering multiple disenfranchising processes, groups of the disenfranchised, and processes for transforming current oppressive conditions. At the same time, we plead guilty to the charge that we privilege an ecofeminist voice in our (necessarily partial and temporary) account. We believe that, whereas most feminist voices have assumed that the "other" is an inevitability to be addressed, ecofeminism enables a reframing of key feminist assumptions that challenges the inevitability of the "other."

## THEORIZING THE "OTHER"

Most generally, the "other" refers to a person or group who is objectified or disenfranchised by the dominant culture and is treated as a nonperson. Stewart and Logan (1993) summarized ways in which objectifying occurs when people are treated (a) as interchangeable parts (rather than as unique human beings), (b) as if they have no feelings and emotions, (c) as incapable of reflective thought, and (d) as passive and unable to make choices. Objectifying can lead to generalization and stereotypical thought; it often occurs when a dominant culture expects those of other cultures to adhere to the values and belief systems perpetuated by the dominant culture. However, adherence typically entails erasing the subordinate culture, adopting the status of the "outsider within" (Collins, 1986), wherein the subordinate culture is within the dominant culture but denied the status of true membership, and/or systematic exclusion from the culture to which the subordinate aspires. On the other hand, those who do not adhere are stereotyped by the dominant culture and labeled "other." They may be ignored and/or destroyed. Collins (1991) asserted that members of a dominant culture engage in "othering" when they treat oppressed groups as objects who lack full human subjectivity, and as objects who can be controlled. "Othering" occurs when oppressed groups are positioned in a distinct relationship to the dominant culture and, by the very nature of this relationship, become subordinate. Hence, the dominant culture is able to construct a sense of "self" through the denigration of "others" (Fine, 1994). This "self" pervades Western life from theorizing to institutional arrangements to personal reflections on the self. The prevalent conception of the "self" requires an "other" for its existence and expansion (cf. Hegel, 1967; Sartre, 1956). Moreover, as Hegel's description of the master–bondsman relationship implies, the "self" is oppressed through the relationship. Hence, the attempt to move beyond the "other" addressed by feminism is not only for the betterment of the oppressed but for their oppressors as well.

Within modern Western culture, women have long been objectified and defined as the "other." Coming to terms with this disenfranchisement has become a primary (and necessary) task of both the women's movement (Olesen, 1994) and related feminist theorizing (Ferguson, 1993). The women's movement has focused on revealing and transforming the multiple processes through which the "other" is constructed and maintained so that women need not continue to accept marginal or subordinate status. The difficulty of bringing about such change has been revealed through the history of this movement. "The" women's movement has evolved through fractionating, resisting, and critiquing processes into a loosely connected process characterized by enormous differences in local dynamics. This complexity and diversity is mirrored in feminist theorizing which is itself diverse. The commonality among different feminist perspectives of interest here is the understanding of the processes involved in creating and maintaining the "other." Each perspective focuses on overlapping but different processes and modes of revealing and transforming these processes.

## FEMINIST THEORIES

Although there are a number of useful feminist topologies (see Buzzanell, 1994; Donovan, 1985; Ferguson, 1993; Jaggar, 1983), we do not comprehensively review any of them here. Instead, we discuss only a few feminisms chosen from our own biases and for our own purposes.

## Theories Maintaining the Autonomous Self

*Liberal Feminism.* Grounded in the liberal tradition, liberal feminism has predominated in the history of American feminism (Merchant, 1991), as well as in feminist theorizing (Bowen & Wyatt, 1993). Liberalism assumes that human beings are autonomous "subjects" who possess natural rights. They make rational choices to maximize their self-interests. Societal progress is assured through individual evolution. Individual subjects are assumed to be unified as are societies. In other words, it is considered ideal when goals are clear and struggles bring greater unity. Liberal feminism argues that only men have been granted their natural rights. Women have been excluded from opportunities to make rational choices in their own self-interests. Women are excluded from the institutions through which individuals (in this case, men) gain the resources to fully participate in a capitalistic democracy.

This approach reveals ways in which women are excluded and treated as "other." In her classic work *The Second Sex* (1949/1953) de Beauvoir followed the existential philosophers' distinction between the transcendental consciousness and the immanent physical. She chronicled ways in which women are confined to the immanent realm whereas men define themselves against the immanent and within the transcendent. In order to define the self as fully human, or transcendent, one needs an "other" as an object of comparison. Through the conscious comparison of opposites, the self is constructed as spiritual, active, good, creative, and evolving; the other is considered as matter, passive, evil, mechanical, and stagnant. In order to attain transcendence, the mind and spirit are valorized whereas the body and the physical are denigrated. Women are responsible for the physical and for maintaining pleasant environments within which men are able to focus on the transcendent. In this manner, men's "selves" are cast in a positive light, whereas the "other" (e.g., woman) is cast negatively.

Liberal feminism advocates that women must gain entry into institutions to acquire the rights inherent in full human status. Women should not internalize negative definitions of themselves. Instead, they should seek to transcend their positions with the immanent, thus escaping their status as "object" (or "other") in favor of adopting a status of "subject" or "self" as men have traditionally done. By defining themselves as active, good, creative, and evolving, rather than accepting the passive, evil, and stagnant definitions foisted upon them, women can become free "subjects." The "excluded" or "erased" voice of the disenfranchised, then, should speak up for its rights. For example, after their requests for meetings were ignored, a group of Utah's poor women seeking their right to affordable housing recently occupied the governor's offices until he agreed to meet with them. In this way, they denied their invisibility. Positive change is enacted through gaining rights, benefits, and opportunities that are equal to those of men. In fact, civil rights have been of concern to many groups designated as "other." For disenfranchised and persecuted groups, the right to exist free of persecution may be an enormous and coveted advantage. Liberal feminism implies that those granted full rights should extend these rights to all people. The history of progress for women, people of color, the disabled, and children in America is largely attributable to liberalism. Liberal feminist arguments have been used to enhance women's lives in such varied matters as the right to vote, entry to educational systems, equal pay, and criminalizing marital rape and sexual harassment.

Although enjoying prominence, liberal feminism has also been severely criticized, primarily for its adoption of liberalism's assumptions of universals such as rights, selves, others, and liberal democracies. As we discuss later, liberal feminists frequently exclude the voices of women of "other" classes and races by assuming that the problems of exclusion faced by any single woman are the same exclusions faced by every woman. Furthermore, more radical feminists have indicted liberal feminists for failing to critique the institutions from which women are excluded. Instead, liberal feminism values the stability and order of the status quo. Liberal assumptions, then, go unquestioned. For example, the notion that people have natural rights is treated as an objective, neutral, universal truth. Science epitomizes the way in which objective truth is revealed by neutral scientists who objectively study the world (cf. Code, 1991). Similarly, the need for transcendence and self-development is unquestioned. Core assumptions are held to be objective "facts." As women are assimilated into the realm of the "self," or the "transcendent," the realm of the immanent, or the physical, remains as the "other." Women achieve their status as "self" or human in the same way men have—through defining themselves against the "object" or the "other." Women, like men, pursue careers and denigrate "homemaking" and "motherhood." The realm of the "other" or disenfranchised, then, is left to those who have not transcended the physical or immanent—those who maintain physical places such as domestic labor, and most problematically, those who are subhuman with no hope of transcending their status such as animals, plants, and the physical world.

*Cultural Feminism.* In contrast to liberal feminism's assumption that all people are similar, cultural feminism assumes natural gender differences. Emerging in the late 19th and early 20th centuries (cf. Fuller, 1845/1971; Gage, 1893/1980), cultural feminism is rooted in the romantic, transcendentalist, and, to some extent, anarchist traditions. Like these traditions, cultural feminism insists that people, if unimpeded, naturally evolve and develop, like seeds, to grow into their true individual potentialities or "selves." As they do so, they will fit in with the natural, organic, stable social order. This organic, harmonious order will be maintained and will also naturally grow and evolve.

If left alone, balance evolves between gender differences. Men, due to their prehistoric roles and/or their biology (depending on which particular theorist we read), develop into competitive, aggressive, and individualistic selves. Women naturally evolve into cooperative, intuitive, collectively oriented selves. The status of "subject" or "self" in this view comes from within. However, external conditions need to be conducive to this natural development.

Patriarchal culture has destroyed this natural process and has distorted both the individuals and the collectivities that emerge by suppressing the feminine in favor of the masculine. Feminine nature is devalued and left undeveloped, resulting in oppressed women and excessively masculine institutions. For example, Christianity relies exclusively on a male god who demands obedience, requires an exclusive place at the top of a hierarchy, and exerts authority over people. Christianity, as depicted in the Bible, considers women to be unclean and inferior. Similarly, institutions such as the home are organized so that women and the feminine are denigrated. Competition is valued over cooperation. The rational is valued over the intuitive. The individual is valued over the collective, and ultimately, war and death are valued over peace and life. In patriarchal culture, because the entire cultural arrangements eschew women and all that is naturally feminine, and because women are owned and controlled rather than free, women are unable to grow and develop into their true selves. The dangerous imbalance created by patriarchy is harmful to men as well as women. In order to transform current conditions, women and the feminine need to be rediscovered and reintegrated to regain balance and wholeness.

Notice that, in spite of their differences, cultural feminism, like liberal feminism, assumes that individuals and societies are naturally unified and clearly ordered. Although there are two essential genders instead of one universal human, the feminine and the masculine are assumed to be universal essences. Like liberal feminists, cultural feminists assume truth to be objective and universal. In other words, whatever distortions current arrangements may include, it is an objective fact that if societies accepted gender differences and became rebalanced by revaluing the feminine, they would be whole, unified, stable, and happy. This natural order is a universal one. In other words, it applies similarly to all societies.

Cultural feminism has drawn on its vision to advocate many changes. Martin Buber's (1970) classic discussion of transforming relationships from subject–object (or I–it) relationships to subject–subject (or I–thou) relationships partially summarizes the changes cultural feminism advocates. Respecting and honoring gender differences, in this view, provides a means for enfranchising the disenfranchised. Rather than advocating that women gain the benefits men have enjoyed as does liberal feminism, cultural feminism insists on transforming current institutions by drawing on the feminine. Women need to first rediscover their selves free of the barriers imposed by patriarchal patterns of oppression. Specifically, women need to work alone and with other women to find their natures outside of patriarchal distortions. This involves finding time, space, and living arrangements away from oppressive domestic, community, and religious arrangements. Once the feminine is rediscovered, women can transform patriarchal institutions by reintegrating the feminine into them. For example, the honoring of female deities who symbolize motherhood and community maintenance would transform Christianity. Transforming home and work arrangements so that men participate more fully in the home and women (with their feminine natures intact) participate more fully in economic and political institutions should transform the institutions so that they become more balanced by including pacifism, cooperation, love, birth, community, connection, organicism, and less competitive means of managing public life. In other words, transformation is wrought by valuing the feminine "other" and then using this "other" as a basis for changing institutions and social arrangements. Gender differences, then, are a source of transformation.

Donovan (1985) documented the many ways in which cultural feminists have worked for political change. Cultural feminist efforts have focused on envisioning feminist societies (cf. Gilman, 1923/1976), providing material relief to poor women, creating transformative visions of goddess cultures (Eisler, 1987), and encouraging women to value and honor their feminine qualities. They have sought and won legislation such as shorter work hours and maternity considerations. Unlike liberal feminists, cultural feminists opposed the Equal Rights Amendment and opposed allowing women to serve in the military. Cultural feminism advocates special consideration for premenstrual syndrome (PMS) whereas liberal feminism opposes such treatment.

The primary criticism of cultural feminism is that it is "essentialist." By assuming that gender differences are natural, cultural feminism draws the disdain of many feminists. Three key points account for this strong criticism. First, feminists point out that assumed natural gender differences have long been pretexts for excluding, ignoring, and disenfranchising women. If the male is taken as the superior of the two natural types, women are assumed to be inferior and can legitimately be treated as "other." Second, as we see later, feminism has increasingly trended away from assumptions that people are created by "nature" and toward assumptions that people are socially or culturally constructed. In the throes of this trend, cultural feminism is a most unwelcome instance of diversity among feminist voices. Finally, cultural feminism is criticized for its adoption of "binary" gendered assumptions. The logic of opposites, so central to disenfranchisement (through "subject" and "object" designations) is maintained. By focusing on gender, a heterosexual world is maintained (Butler, 1990). Alternative sexual preferences are ignored, maintaining an "other." Alternative oppressive categories such as class and race are ignored.

*Radical Feminism.* Although radical feminism is perhaps the most difficult to summarize because it is so diverse depending on specific feminists' roots, one commonality is the belief that existing societal arrangements cannot be improved by including women. Neither gaining rights nor revaluing the natural feminine will be adequate to change the status quo. Rather, more fundamental change is needed. Radical feminists are more critical of a wide variety of institutions for their psychological oppression of women (Donovan, 1985) than are liberal and cultural feminisms. For example, the institutions of love, marriage, incest taboos, patriarchal religions, and the development of manhood by defining "self" over woman are identified by radical feminists as ways in which patriarchal hegemony is sustained. Similarly, they note that the family is a place where women are socialized into oppressive gender roles and argue that it is an institution from which women need to be freed. Women's forced role in reproduction is a central source of psychological oppression.

Like liberal feminism, radical feminism implies that the construction of the "other" is inherent in the construction of the male "self" in patriarchal systems. That is, self-definition is based on the need to become separate from and above. In order to become separate from and above, identifying an "other" is required. To ensure that the male "self" can emerge, women and other "others" are socialized into oppressive gender roles so that men will have "others" to rise above. For example, young boys learn not to be "sissies" whereas young girls learn to serve as spectators and cheerleaders for boys' activities. Women, then, are made to serve as men's resources or complements (Daly, 1973).

Because the "other" is so fundamental to current society, the only alternative open to the disenfranchised is to escape by constructing separate institutions and societies. For example, Johnson (1989) called for women (and, by extension, "others") to leave patriarchal institutions and to live as separately from them as possible. The separation is necessary because current institutions—home, school, politics, work, and the economic system—define women as resources for men. These institutions are not transformable. Transformation occurs when current systems are rejected as women refuse to accept the roles of complement or resource. This refusal fundamentally destroys the patriarchal system and opens possibilities for new institutions grounded in feminist principles. Radical feminism, then, points out the hope of creating societies that do not inevitably rely on the disenfranchised.

In spite of its name, radical feminism is relatively conservative compared with contemporary feminist voices. It relies on the hope of a unified order constructed by unified selves. Radical feminism displays an urge toward a new and improved universal order that will replace the current patriarchy so damaging to the disenfranchised.

Radical feminists are criticized for their lack of realism. Creating separatist institutions and societies is difficult, particularly for those who lack resources. Separate societies are also problematic given the biological necessities of reproduction. Finally, new institutions would have to be created by people who have been heavily impacted by their experiences in current institutions. Presumably, these new institutions would be defined by their opposition to current institutions. They would not be new in the sense of being created from scratch on a clean slate. Rather, they would be colored by current arrangements.

## Theories of the Located Self

Standpoint feminism, as well as the Marxist, Black, and minority feminisms that follow, shift assumptions about the "self" and "other" by integrating contextual, historical differences in their analyses. Their emphasis on positionality enables more contextually specific analyses of disenfranchising processes and experiences. These analyses complicate theorizing about the construction of multiple "selves" and multiple "others" and, as such, open additional possibilities for transformation. This set of feminist voices may be compared with the previous set by examining shifts in key assumptions that accompany the notion of located, positioned selves. The "self," in these views, is neither fully autonomous nor universal. As we see later, "selves" and "others" differ from one another depending on where they are located in social systems. For example, a wealthy White woman may be a "subject" in terms of her class and race and an "object" in terms of her gender. Her position is both similar to and different from her poor Black housekeeper who is an "object" in terms of her gender, race, and class. In these views, then, there is no universal "self" or "other." Nor is there a universal or natural way in which societies are ordered. The clear, stable order of truth becomes muddled as multiple standpoints are revealed to include such different perspectives. It is difficult to know what is objectively given with an eye to diversity and different perspectives. As these feminists examine people's positions, they question the possibility of scientific objectivity as well (cf. Code, 1991; Harding, 1991). Science is positioned within human society and cannot be objectively observing the society in which it is participating. The scientist's neutral position is instead revealed as one standpoint among many. The unity of the whole and the "self" is similarly questioned in favor of an assumption of difference and change.

*Standpoint Feminism.* Standpoint feminism, drawing heavily on Marxism, initially attempted to articulate "the" woman's standpoint as a position from which to critique and transform the status quo. Women's experiences as marginalized "others," it was assumed, could become a common ground from which women could work for change much as Marxism relied on class consciousness to motivate change. By articulating these experiences, women could be empowered as a strong political force. Moreover, women's positions as the "outsider within" (Collins, 1986) meant that women, in order to deter abuse, exclusion, and lack of resources, had learned to understand men and current societal arrangements. Men had no reciprocal need to understand women because their selves were maintained by projecting onto women the qualities, work, and positions they did not want to confront. Women's double understandings, then, could serve as valuable resources in bringing about change. This project was dismantled, primarily by feminists of color as they insisted on refusing to accept accounts of "woman's" standpoint proffered by middle-class First-World White women. Instead, they pointed out the multiple axes of differences among women. Women are positioned as multiple "others" depending on many factors such as race, class, marital status, and sexual preference (Longino, 1993). Focusing only on a narrow group of women's experiences and not examining larger positioning processes that create different standpoints, then, was revealed to be a way in which feminism replicated patriarchy by excluding the "other." Standpoint feminism, then, has evolved to assume that standpoints include both everyday experiences and the locations, conditions, and shaping processes that produce those experiences (Smith, 1987, 1993). By understanding the standpoints of "others" and the conditions that lead to "othering," we are able to invoke critiques, provide alternative points of view, and make suggestions for change. As such, the "others" become valued for their standpoints and their potential for bringing about change.

To differ from patriarchy, standpoints must be "self-defined standpoints" (Collins, 1991). However, the processes and conditions that create their particular standpoints are often invisible to people. Therefore, providing a self-defined standpoint is difficult. Those most oppressed may be those most likely to accept the definitions of themselves as "others." The patriarchal nature of basic institutions such as science and the professions adds to this difficulty (see Code, 1991; Harding, 1986, 1991). Specifically, the assumption of the neutral, rational, observer who, from a distanced position observes the object, or "other," in order to explain, predict, and control what the object is unable to manage from its embedded position pervades our institutions. God, scientists, professional experts, and administrators take on the role of the objective observer who, because of "his" ability to see more clearly, is positioned as the authority, capable of knowing, controlling, and making decisions about the object. The object is passively gazed upon. Subjects and objects, then, are created through this structure that positions some as observers and others as objects. Authority over "others" lives is thus removed from them and positioned in the experts' base of knowledge. Because the distanced gaze reduces and simplifies, "others" are reduced to stereotypes. For example, an expert educator may give an IQ test and then stereotype people as high, average, or low. The people so stereotyped are then reduced to these categories whereas the complexities that constitute their uniqueness are ignored. People designated as low are then positioned in special classes and self-fulfilling prophecies repeat themselves through the years. Those positioned as "low" would be expected to have great difficulty expressing their "own" standpoints. Moreover, patriarchal control of language, media, ideology, and the like, suppresses the articulation and expression of experiences.

Standpoint feminism focuses on ways through which the oppressed may articulate their voices. For example, both Scott (1985, 1990) and Collins (1991) noted that resistance depends on the ability of the oppressed to share their experiences with each other. Scott (1990) referred to the creation of "hidden" transcripts, transcripts created by the oppressed that are different from the "public" transcripts controlled by those in power. When these hidden transcripts, or standpoints, are articulated, personal experiences are transformed to collective voices that are more prone to stimulate acts of resistance. For example, Murphy's (1993) study of flight attendants uncovered conversations that took place outside of public settings in which attendants complained about weight regulations. Such talk could pass as "mere" gossip. However, through sharing experiences of radical dieting, purging, and overuse of laxatives, as well as their anger with the system requiring this of them, the attendants eventually publicly challenged and changed the official policy.

French feminists LaClau and Mouffe (1985) clarified the idea that collective resistance does not imply a unified, coherent oppositional group or standpoint. The process of creating and maintaining a dominant (e.g., patriarchal) discourse simultaneously creates and maintains different positions of marginality (such as those we have reviewed throughout this chapter). Resistance and transformation rely on solidarity among different standpoints. In this view, multiple but differing standpoints link together but do not unify in order to resist and change the status quo. In other words, although poor mothers who are denied safe housing for themselves and their children are in a unique position vis-à-vis the political system, they are joining hands with other marginalized groups such as environmental groups and labor groups to work toward electing the kinds of candidates who will support all of the groups' agendas. This does not imply that the different voices and positions need to be merged into a unified voice but rather that they resist together to bring about change. Moreover, poor mothers differ from one another in many ways such as race, sexual preference, and political party affiliation. In some ways, poor mothers may also serve as oppressors of one another and they may not adopt a permanent identity of "poor mother." Therefore, this approach is inconsistent with the liberal assumption of the unified self. The multiplicity necessary to begin to reveal standpoints (as experiences and as structures and processes that produce those experiences) simply denies the possibility of unified selves as subjects or objects.

Standpoint feminism can be criticized for opposite excesses. First, standpoint feminist attempts to discover articulatable standpoints risk overemphasizing commonalities and stabilities while underemphasizing important differences and changes. On the other hand, efforts to avoid false commonalities may deteriorate into fragmentation. In order to fully understand various positions and their constructions, the need to articulate new unique standpoints for each individual at each new moment is implied. To avoid these extremes, sets of feminisms that emphasize specific categories of oppression are valuable. We summarize socialist and Black feminisms as examples.

*Socialist Feminism.*   Socialist feminism provides one specific set of analyses that focuses on the standpoints of women. Socialist feminism is rooted in Marxism and its variants, where class differences among group positions create subjects and objects. Socialist feminism extends this analysis to address women. Women's work, in this view, is devalued and women are alienated from the capitalist patriarchy. In this system, men participate in and are responsible for production in the marketplace. Some men act as owners of capitalist companies whereas others sell their labor where they are valued for their ability to produce commodities which are, in turn, valued for their exchange. Using commodities solely for their exchange value means that the profit potential of the commodity becomes more important than its use value. Capitalism, by nature, is oriented toward profit, or surplus value. Profit is created through providing workers what is necessary to produce commodities and charging more for the products than they cost in labor. By emphasizing profit and surplus value, women's work is ignored. Yet that work is necessary for the system to continue. In other words, women must produce children to provide laborers. Women must care for the home and laborers so that the laborers are available to provide the labor. Multiple alienations result. Women's work is devalued because it is work performed for its *use* rather than its exchange value. Women are isolated in the home in ways that men are not (Donovan, 1985) and are denied political control, forcing their economic dependency on men. We can understand, from this analysis, that women's experiences of isolation are created through their position in capitalist patriarchal society.

Socialist feminism has extended this analysis to consider others on whom the system depends but who remain invisible, yet serve as unacknowledged producers of use and surplus to create profit for capitalists (cf. Mies & Shiva, 1993; Shiva, 1988; Waring, 1988). Merchant (1992) discussed the unacknowledged uses to which Third-World groups are put in support of capitalist production and the First-World market. For example, workers are inadequately paid and work in unbearable conditions in order to provide products to the First World for our consumption. Producing nations are often left with deteriorated environments incapable of sustaining human life on the one hand while they are also inadequately paid for their products in a market controlled by the First World. Within the First World too, unemployment (which often translates into homelessness) is necessary so that the capitalist system may have an excess labor pool available to produce maximum profit.

Because capitalism needs "others," socialist feminists do not advocate inclusion in the capitalist system. Rather, they advocate the dismantling of capitalism and uphold replacing it with an egalitarian socialist system where men and women would be resocialized into nonsexist, nonracist, and anti-imperialistic ways of living (Merchant, 1991). Transformation occurs when consciousness raising leads to the creation of alternative institutions to improve conditions for the disenfranchised. Women would not be the sole producers of products for their use value while men would not be the sole producers of products for their exchange value. Owners would not purchase workers' labor nor destroy Third-World environments and people for their own profit in a transformed system.

Socialist feminism is critiqued by examining women's oppressions in societies that are not capitalist. For example, anarchist Bookchin (1982) examined the problems inherent in hierarchy. (However, socialist feminists argue that no societies are unaffected by world capitalism.) Another critique is that socialist feminists focus exclusively on material roots of oppression. Sanday (1981) traced gender myths as they oppress across many different societal forms. We also know that race, sexual orientation, and marital status are some additional sources of oppression that operate outside of capitalism.

*Black and Minority Feminisms.*  The trend in standpoint feminism from specifying "the" woman's standpoint toward acknowledging complexity and difference is largely due to Black and minority feminisms' successful indictments of feminism for its color blindness. Revealing feminism to be deeply racist and classist, Black feminism has insisted on understanding differences among women. For example, Black feminism reveals our positions as White middle-class women as oppressive in combining Black and minority feminisms together here. Were we not positioned as we are, we might better understand differences among the standpoints we combine here and we might see more similarities among feminist voices we treat as distinct here.

Black feminism has revealed that many definitions of women as "other" have failed to take into account the perspectives of women of color. White women academicians initially theorized about women as "other." These White women wrote from their perspectives, or standpoints, which unintentionally excluded the voices of women of color. In other words, White women of middle and upper classes were assuming that their experiences were universal and representative of all women. In advancing feminist theory from their standpoint, White feminist theorists soon learned that their ideas came from a point of privilege, were myopic, and placed women of color in a place of dual oppression. Whereas White women were gaining a voice, women of color continued to be cast as the "other" and remained objectified and disenfranchised.

Black and minority feminists pointed out that White women are more privileged because of our relationship to White men. White women are of higher class, because more complete college, and are groomed to raise the ruling class. Hurtado (1989) noted because of White women's structural position (e.g., more likely to make more money, more likely to finish college and go to graduate school) it was not surprising that much of the contemporary feminist theory was written by White, educated women. Feminist theory reflects this privileged social status and is perceived by feminists of color as reflecting the perspectives, values, and beliefs of the middle class. White feminist theorists have been critiqued for offering theory that is individualistic (see Harding, 1991), middle-class (Hurtado, 1989; Longino, 1993), and insensitive to racial and class oppression (Chow, 1987; Garcia, 1990; Green, 1990; Lugones & Spelman, 1983). Dill (1983) noted that many Black women believed that the women's movement existed merely to satisfy the needs of personal self-fulfillment of White, middle-class women.

Early feminist theory was advanced to focus on White women's issues, rather than those of race or social class. For example, White, liberal feminists focused on obtaining access to the labor force and in escaping from the confines of the home. Black women, at the same time, were more concerned about being raped by White colonizers and having to ignore their own Black children while working in the homes of White women (Beale, 1970). Ironically, many would have readily accepted the luxury of being a housewife (Dill, 1983). Even experiences of White working-class women were absent in much of the early White feminist theory.

At the same time, White feminists, because of our privileged status, have taken a disproportionate number of leadership roles within feminist politics. White feminist theorists are consulted on women's issues.

Latina feminist theorist Lugones expressed her feelings of exclusion and disenfranchisement by noting:

> We and you do not talk the same language. When we talk to you we use your language: the language of your experience and of your theories. We try to use it to communicate our world of experience. But since your language and your theories are inadequate in expressing our experiences, we only succeed in communicating our experience of exclusion. We cannot talk to you in our language because you do not understand it. (Lugones & Spelman, 1983, p. 577)

Chicana feminist Garcia (1990) pointed out that in addition to being excluded by mainstream feminists, Chicana feminists faced additional oppression from Chicano men. They were ostracized and harassed for wanting to assimilate into the feminist ideology of an alien (e.g., White) culture that actively sought cultural domination. Chicana (and other feminists of color) too often find themselves "between a rock and a hard place." Because of the importance of these experiences, hooks (1981, 1984, 1989) and Collins (1991) have successfully insisted on a feminist respect for differences among women; they have encouraged researchers to focus on the conditions of Black women's lives as a move away from academic theorizing.

Collins (1991) summarized some changes advocated by Black feminism. First, she argued that it is necessary for Black women to clarify their self-definition and to engage in self-valuing. She insisted that this is necessary to resist the dehumanization that is inevitably inherent in systems of domination. That is, clarifying one's self-definition is necessary for Black women's survival. If Black women refuse to accept their assigned status as "other," then the entire rationale for such domination is challenged (Collins, 1991). A second theme involves making clear the interlocking nature of oppression. Black women are victims of race, gender, and class oppression. Work to reduce gender oppression still leaves Black women battling with race and class oppression. A final theme in Black feminist thought involves championing the importance of African-American women's culture. Some Black feminists have turned to the culture of the mothers and have worked to celebrate and preserve specific women's cultures. Collins noted that this is significant because it draws relationships between the consciousness of those oppressed and the actions they take to cope with that oppression. Black feminists have tempered the radical feminist interest in separatist societies because of their need to struggle against racism with Black men. Collins noted further that "while Black feminist activists may work on behalf of Black women, they rarely project separatist solutions to Black female oppression. Rather, the vision is one that . . . takes its 'stand on the solidarity of humanity' " (p. 43).

Black feminists indict White feminists for treating women of color as the "other" by ignoring their different standpoints. This is a serious offense, particularly because feminists have struggled to reveal and change men's erasing of women's standpoints. Like standpoint feminism, Black feminism can be criticized for its fragmenting influence. However, Collins (1991) noted that Black feminist writings, despite their diversity, share the common theme of "the oneness of human life" (p. 39), and defined Black feminism as "a process of self-conscious struggle that empowers women and men to actualize a humanist vision of community" (p. 39). We expand upon this theme later.

## Postmodern Feminism

Postmodern feminism, following postmodernism, assumes that what we commonly refer to as "natural" or "objective reality" exists only by virtue of the discursive system through which it is named or constructed and maintained. Whereas standpoint, socialist, and Black feminisms loosened the assumption of the autonomous self of liberalism by insisting on the (asymmetrical) positionality of all selves, postmodern feminism goes further by more persistently questioning the "subject." Postmodernism assumes that "selves" are created and positioned within discursive systems or language systems. There are no free, autonomous subjects who have natural rights except as they are sustained through language. This is what is commonly referred to as the "death" of the subject. It is a shift from a view that language is a tool developed and used by acting people to a view that language actively constructs people as we perceive ourselves and others. Through language, categories such as "self" and "other" are maintained. Language actively constructs subjectivities, or perceptions of selves. Moreover, language patterns partially "fix" these categories through repeating them routinely and persistently so that they are treated as if they exist "naturally" and that language simply expresses what is the "true" nature of reality.

The "other," in this view, is constructed through being absenced, or not made a part of the discourse. Therefore, its focus is to persistently question and deconstruct patterns of discourse that attempt to "naturalize" socially constructed realities. One primary focus has been on questioning the "subject" or the "self" of liberalism. For example, one feminist struggle was against the linguistic practice of using *he* as meaning all people. This practice silenced women and instead enabled only the (White, middle-class) male experience to "count" as universal for all people. Consider recent revelations about medical research excluding women. For example, coronary research was conducted on men and findings were considered to generalize. Women were absenced. A lack of knowledge of women's coronary problems resulted. Moreover, physicians were advising men on avoiding heart attacks while ignoring women's risks. These problems were revealed after feminists questioned the ways in which language focused on *he* while ignoring *she*.

Postmodern feminism reveals categories of binary opposites, much like cultural feminism. Recall opposites such as mind/body, reason/emotion, active/passive. However, whereas cultural feminism revalues the denigrated feminine side of these pairs, postmodern feminism questions the linguistic construction of the pairs. The pairs themselves not only construct one half as inferior, but absence possibilities of constructing alternatives to the pairs. For example, by treating gender, or male/female, as an oppositional pair, gender becomes a "natural" difference and it is easy to forget that gender is a linguistic process. Instead we engage in debates about whether gender differences are due to socialization or nature. Postmodern feminism instead advocates questioning the construction of gender. It reveals ways in which this category ignores possibilities such as gay and lesbian lives and ways in which the category maintains a "heterosexual order" (Butler, 1990) in the face of many alternative possibilities that are silenced. Marriage as we know it is thus assumed to be natural and all "other" arrangements such as collective living are ignored or devalued. Only by questioning the category and revealing ways in which it is linguistically constructed can we change.

Postmodern feminism, however, is acutely sensitive to the need to apply its view to alternatives as well. In other words, although gender and the accompanying set of practices such as marriage need to be continually questioned and deconstructed, the purpose is not to create a new and improved set of categories and their accompanying practices. Postmodern feminism incorporates no goal of changing the social order so that marriage is replaced by a different institution. Instead, an endless questioning of language is advocated so that meanings remain open to continuously evolving possibilities (cf. Ferguson, 1993). Certainty, or partially "fixed, closed" meanings, needs to constantly be challenged. Postmodern feminism assumes the inevitability of the "other" as language constructs categories. This process necessarily creates meanings and absences possibilities (such as women's heart problems). But to assume that by focusing on the absenced (women's heart problems) a new and better reality will emerge and continue is a mistake according to postmodern feminism. When women's heart problems become a focus, there is a continuous need to search for possibilities that are absenced so that heart problems do not remain on center stage while issues such as prevention and gynecological problems are ignored. Through continuously shifting categories and attending to multiple shifting axes of meanings, such "closure" or "fixing" of meanings can be avoided (Haraway, 1989). The problem of the "other," then, is addressed by constant vigilance to the discursive practices that create the "other" so that specific "others" are not assumed to be natural beings.

Through continuously opening meanings and challenging constructions through which "others" are implied, then, postmodern feminism attempts to destabilize both the construction of specific "others" as well as the category "other." Postmodern feminism is at work in a multitude of dispersed specific moments when patriarchal language is challenged. For example, direct critiques as challenging the use of *he* to refer to women, playing with new language choices and ironizing language categories as the term *herstory,* and revealing absenced "others" such as the invisible "object" in discussions of "selves" are ways in which postmodern feminism works. Its strongest contribution may be its pressure to encourage women to question their complicity in reproducing oppressions through employing or accepting oppressive discourse in their daily language.

Postmodern feminism is criticized for its constant deconstructive approach. By constantly focusing on revealing and critiquing discursive constructions, postmodern feminism does not advocate clear transformative visions. Nor does it enable the creation of stable standpoints from which to launch transformative change. With no standpoints, no subjects, and no visions of a better order, postmodern feminism does not describe how women form political factions capable of acting toward improving conditions. Postmodern feminism is also criticized for its stance toward objectivity. Postmodern feminism is criticized for its assumption that there is no objective physical reality outside of discourse. When objectivity is completely eschewed, it becomes difficult for women to convincingly argue to a majority liberal audience that women's oppression is a "real" problem. Butler (1992, 1993) argued that these criticisms are misguided in their assumption that calling categories (such as gender and objectivity) into question is synonymous with calling for the end of the categories themselves. Rather, calling categories into question is useful for opening up their meanings and offering possibilities for ongoing evolutionary shifts. However, postmodern feminism makes no claim to define these shifts, but only to create possibilities. In response to a common criticism that deconstructed subjects are unable to form political factions to act toward improving conditions, postmodern feminists maintain that a feminist "we" will continue to be used. However, postmodern feminists warn that feminists need to be aware that to articulate a "we" is to engage in exclusionary politics. Each time a "we" is voiced, a multitude of "others" are silently defined by exclusion. To engage in postmodern feminism is to consistently attempt to recover these exclusions of "others" and to "redeploy" them (Butler, 1992).

Postmodern feminism, in our ordering, may be viewed as at the opposite end of several poles from the first set of feminisms we considered. We are aware of the irony of positioning postmodernism as one end of binary oppositions but make no claim to have successfully escaped binary categories ourselves. Table 1.1 summarizes our comparisons of feminist ap-

TABLE 1.1
Summary of Feminist Perspectives

| Feminist Perspectives | | |
| --- | --- | --- |
| Liberal Feminism | Standpoint Feminism | Postmodern Feminism |
| Cultural Feminism | Women of Color | |
| Radical Feminism | Socialist Feminism | |
| Comparative Assumptions | | |
| Automotive "Self" | Positioned "Self" | Death of the "Self" |
| Universal Experiences | Located Experiences | Discursive Experiences |
| Objective Reality | Multiple Realities | Constructed Realities |
| Stability, Order | Complexity, Multiplicity | Instability |
| Unity | Diversity | Fragmentation |

proaches we have discussed. Postmodern feminism, with its emphasis on discourse, intensifies the shift away from the predominant assumptions related to the "subject" on which liberal feminism is based.

In postmodern feminism, there are no "subjects" except as they are constructed by discourse. Discourse operates at a local level. In other words, "subjects" and "others" are created and absenced at specific moments and places through specific instances of language. Reality is constructed in discourse and shifts through discourse. Whereas the standpoint feminisms complicated objectivity by revealing multiple positions, postmodern feminism has instead adopted an assumption that objectivity itself is discursively constructed and does not exist outside of discourse. Rather than the liberal feminist assumption that there is stability, order, and unity in both the self and the world, so that change is a shift from one order to another, postmodern feminism assumes endless change and diversity not directed toward a new order, goal, or stable point. Instead, constant questioning and questioning of questions as the endless play of discourse continues is advocated.

Our discussion and chart both summarize several feminisms and depict a feminist dilemma to which we now turn. As feminists increasingly eschew the autonomous, rational "subject" that requires an "object" or "other" and accompanying assumptions we have summarized, and turn to the standpoint, socialist, and Black feminisms, it becomes increasingly obvious that to adequately describe a standpoint, multiple conditions need to be considered. As multiple conditions are considered, standpoints and categories used to describe them are also revealed to be continuously shifting and difficult to adequately describe and understand. Postmodern feminism illustrates the extreme case. The autonomous, permanent, and the positioned "subject" or "self" is dead and the accompanying assumptions we have summarized are transformed into a discourse that can only advocate endless revealing and critiquing of disenfranchising discourses. Postmodern feminism, however, retains the "other" or the "disenfranchised" in the form of "absenced" voices that need to constantly be revealed, although such revealing inherently "absences" "other" voices. (Hence the prescription to constantly question discourse to identify such absences.) We have shown that in eschewing the assumptions of the left side of Table 1.1, it is difficult to avoid sliding through the middle to the opposites depicted on the right side by postmodern feminism. Ecological feminism offers a perspective that instead posits a reframing of these characteristics.

## Ecological Feminism: Beyond the "Other"

*Ecological feminism* (*ecofeminism*) is a term coined by Francoise d'Eaubonne in 1974 to call attention to women's potential to bring about an ecological revolution (Warren, 1991). Ecological feminism argues that there are historical, experiential, symbolic, and theoretical connections between the patriarchal domination of women, indigenous peoples, and nonhuman nature (Warren, 1990). In other words, the disenfranchising of women, marginalized people, and nature are intimately connected and are mutually reinforcing. Therefore, they need to be understood as the same processes. Although frequently dismissed as "essentialist," we believe that ecofeminism's attention to the connections between humans and nonhuman nature are its primary strength because it focuses on the consequences of "othering." All human life on this planet is threatened by the dominations it reveals, critiques, and works to transform. Ecofeminists are concerned that while feminists ignore this material reality, they contribute to the domination of nature and contribute to the death of life itself. In other words, the processes of disenfranchisement, from an ecofeminist perspective, are of ultimate consequence to ourselves and the planet that provides the conditions for life. In focusing on the connections between human and nonhuman nature a reconsideration of the "self" and "other" is enabled.

With roots in both ecology and feminism, ecological feminism provides an alternative construction of the relational or connected "subject" that requires no "other." Ecological feminism provides a model of connected subjectivity such that relationships among and between take precedence over individual elements. A focus on interdependence, connection, and relationship precludes the denigration of one element in favor of the other. Instead, relationships become the focus of understanding. This simple view reconstructs the "other" by emphasizing the relational connections in the context of a larger whole.

An example of these important connections is highlighted by Shiva (1988). In her investigations of the patriarchal "maldevelopment" projects that have been carried out in India, she documented the connections between the destruction of nature and the impact of this destruction on the lives of women. She noticed that local (e.g., indigenous) people and their knowledge of the land have been displaced in favor of "expert" (e.g., outside) knowledge in order to gain "productivity." Shiva detailed the multiple ways in which the experts' idea of productivity is connected to destroying the long-term ability of the soil, forests, and waters to sustain life.

Unfortunately, the distrust of women's knowledge has been central to this destruction. For centuries, these women participated in, and understood, specific connections among nature, their own agricultural practices, and the sustenance of their communities. The government, in an effort to encourage "development," began to introduce "green revolution" agricultural methods so that crops could be exported. These so-called "green" methods replaced the traditional methods of growing and harvesting crops. Shiva (1988) documented the devastating effects the introduction of these new methods had on the nutritional yield of the land as the world market, rather than local conditions, determined which crops to grow. Deep plowing, the use of pesticides, and replacing traditional crops with non-native ones contributed to the degradation of the soil and low crop yields. Because women traditionally rely on the soil, forests, and water in their daily work, they are first and most directly affected by these changes. They must work harder to provide less food for their communities. Women have been more active in politically resisting these projects. The Chipko (e.g., tree-hugging) movement begun by women in India to preserve their forests is the best known instance. As the government sold the local forests and the loggers arrived, community women walked into the forest and hugged the trees, preventing the logging.

By focusing on connections and drawing on ecological thinking (e.g., Capra, 1982; Leopold, 1949) rather than "self" and "other," ecological feminism transforms the remaining characteristics we have discussed and charted in Table 1.1. Local, specific relationships are connected to larger, more universal patterns. The local and universal are intricately related and neither is privileged over the other. Experiences are related to connections between discursive and material conditions. Similarly, the objective, multiple, and social construction assumptions of reality cannot be separated from one another. For example, rape, the extinction of multitudes of species, and relationships between human treatment of land and its inability to support human life are objective facts. At the same time, our human perspectives and interests, as enabled through discursive systems, shape and focus our attentions on (or away from) these processes as we understand the objective threats they pose to our survival. Moreover, in cases such as this, to understand how to transform the status quo, our participation via social constructions (such as cultural patterns that enable destruction) must be included. A focus on patterns of dynamic interdependencies and connections assumes both that there is some stability or repetition to these patterns while there is also enormous local variation leading to uncertainty and change as well. Ecological systems do not remain stable over time. Instead, patterned dynamic interdependencies bring about change, some of which is ordered, or predictable, and some of which is uncertain, or inherently unpredictable. Diversity and fragmentation are highly valued as directly connected with prospects for survival and stability of the whole. For example, if forests including multiple (connected) species and ages of trees and plants are clearcut and replaced with tree farms where one type of tree is planted, the lack of diversity means that if a bug arrives that destroys the single type of tree, the entire crop will be destroyed. In a more diverse forest, it is more probable that the destruction would be limited or stopped, even though such a forest might also appear fragmented.

To illustrate ecofeminism's unique voice, we critique the feminisms outlined earlier for their treatment of nonhuman nature as the "other" against which women's struggles are defined. By excluding nonhuman nature in their critiques of the patriarchy, feminists frequently retain the practice of marking, and subsequently marginalizing, the "other."

Our first example comes from the perspective of liberal feminists, who argue that women are similar to men and deserve equal legal rights. By linking women with men, liberal feminists implicitly assert that women and nature are not related. The move to ignore the relationship between women and nature is often intentional, as the association of women and nature has been (and still is perceived as) a dangerous one. Historically, the association of women and nature and the subsequent exclusion and denigration of both has been well documented as related to the Enlightenment (Capra, 1982; Merchant, 1980). As the scientific method, the development of industrialism, and liberalism evolved, the need to control and subdue nature included the need to control and subdue women as well. The Salem witch trials, which clearly coincide with the rise of liberalism, are cited as a clear example of the need to control women (see Barstow, 1994; Griffin, 1978; Merchant, 1980). To claim human (and equal) status for women, liberal feminists argued to dislodge the connection between women and nature, opting instead to claim a connection between woman and human (cf. de Beauvoir, 1949/1953). The "progress" made by women, then, is made by casting nature as "other" in need of control. Hence, liberal feminism perpetuates the "other" in its expressed desire to disassociate from nature.

It is cultural feminism alone that celebrates a connection between women and nature, a claim that has brought feminisms ceaseless criticisms from other feminists. The status of nature as "other" is so deeply ingrained among feminists that to link women with nature is perceived as destructive due to the harm this connection caused women. Cultural feminists have frequently been denounced for their attempts to reclaim the connection that has been so successfully severed by liberal feminism (see Code, 1991; Ortner, 1974).

Radical feminists, in their desire to encompass a variety of feminist approaches (Donovan, 1985), do not always include nature in their definitions. Although some radical feminists focus on the body as nature and use this to essentialize gender differences, radical feminists typically emphasize the need for separate institutions and practices to build a feminine society. Unfortunately, the envisioning of a feminine society does not take into account the role of nature in the building of such a society. Instead, nature remains as an inert "stage" upon which the building occurs. As such, nature is an absenced "other."

Socialist feminists, in their emphasis on the importance of production, accepted the Marxist assumption of nature as "other," as raw material to be used to generate surplus value. Nature is seen as simply a set of resources to be dominated so that products, profits, and human freedom could be realized (Merchant, 1991). Socialist feminism, then, advocates advancing women's status by severing the connection between women and nature as resources. We should note that several socialist feminist writings (cf. Mellor, 1992) are advocating a more ecologically sensitive socialist feminism.

Black and standpoint feminists emphasize differences and advocate turning attention to previously ignored and absenced "others." They do this, unfortunately, at the expense of nature. Collins (1991) specifically called for honoring human differences. However, she noted that autonomous groups must enter into dialogue and coalition building with one another in order to create a more "humanist" society. Although these feminists encourage women from autonomous, yet collective, groups to articulate their own standpoints, they simultaneously absence nature, implicitly defining humans as separate from nature. Longino (1993) noted that "women's advantage, according to some standpoint feminists, comes not from a special relation to nature, but rather from a dual position as subject/object" (in the dominant culture; pp. 207–208).

Because of their emphasis on language to the exclusion of material, objective nature, postmodern feminists are frequently accused of denying nature a "voice" (cf. Butler, 1993). Ironically, because postmodern feminists encourage the questioning of all constructions, they also enable the questioning of various feminisms' constructions of nature.

With the questioning and opening of nature as a central term, ecological feminism draws upon ecology to produce a critique of other feminists for their anthropocentric, or human-centered, focus. Much of this focus is based on the general conception of the "other." Consider Stewart and Logan's (1993) definition of the "other" we reported in the beginning of this chapter. They argued that when people are objectified they are treated as "objects," where they are seen as being more like nature than like humans. Ecological feminism suggests this dichotomy sustains the "other." When we adopt ecology's view of humans as participants in interdependent webs of life, the dichotomy between subject and object disappears. By examining disenfranchisement as it is intricately connected with the web of life in which we all participate, ecofeminists work toward the health and well-being of the web.

By its emphasis on connection and the recognition of humans and nature as participants in webs of life, ecofeminism offers alternatives to present conceptualizations of the "other." We have attempted to give both a name and a face to the "other" by identifying the "other" as it is conceptualized in different feminist perspectives. It is our hope that we can promote the end of the "other" by encouraging ecofeminist voices and practices.

## REFERENCES

Barstow, A. (1994). *Witchcraze: A new history of the European witch hunts*. San Francisco: Pandora.

Beale, F. (1970). Double jeopardy: To be Black and female. In R. Morgan (Ed.), *Sisterhood is powerful: An anthology of writings from the women's liberation movement* (pp. 340–353). New York: Vintage.

Bookchin, M. (1982). *The ecology of freedom*. Palo Alto, CA: Cheshire Books.

Bowen, S. P., & Wyatt, N. (1993). *Transforming visions: Feminist critiques in communication studies*. Cresskill, NJ: Hampton Press.

Buber, M. (1970). *I and thou* (W. Kaufmann, Trans.). New York: Scribner's.

Butler, J. (1990). *Gender trouble*. New York: Routledge, Chapman & Hall.

Butler, J. (1992). Contingent foundations: Feminism and the question of "postmodernism." In J. Butler & J. Scott (Eds.), *Feminists theorize the political* (pp. 3–21). New York: Routledge.

Butler, J. (1993). *Bodies that matter*. New York: Routledge.

Buzzanell, P. (1994). Gaining a voice: Feminist organizational communication theorizing. *Management Communication Quarterly, 7*, 339–383.

Capra, F. (1982). *The turning point*. New York: Bantam.

Chow, E. N. (1987). The development of feminist consciousness among Asian American women. *Gender and Society, 1*, 284–299.

Code, L. (1991). *What can she know?* Ithaca, NY, & London: Cornell University Press.

Collins, P. H. (1986). Learning from the outsider within: The sociological significance of Black feminist thought. *Social Problems, 33*(6), 14–32.

Collins, P. H. (1991). *Black feminist thought: Knowledge, consciousness, and the politics of empowerment*. New York: Routledge.

Daly, M. (1973). *Beyond god the father: Toward a philosophy of women's liberation*. Boston: Beacon Press.

de Beauvoir, S. (1953). *The second sex* (H. M. Parshley, Trans.). New York: Knopf. (Original work published 1949)

Dill, B. T. (1983). Race, class, and gender: Perspectives for an all inclusive sisterhood. *Feminist Studies, 9*, 131–149.

Donovan, J. (1985). *Feminist theory: The intellectual traditions of American feminism.* New York: Ungar.

Eisler, R. (1987). *The chalice and the blade: Our history, our future.* San Francisco: Harper & Row.

Ferguson, K. (1993). *The man question: Visions of subjectivity in feminist theory.* Berkeley: University of California Press.

Fine, M. (1994). Working the hyphens. In N. Denzin & Y. Lincoln (Eds.), *Handbook of qualitative research* (pp. 70–82). Thousand Oaks, CA: Sage.

Fuller, M. (1971). *Woman in the nineteenth century.* New York: Norton. (Original work published 1845)

Gage, M. (1980). *Woman, church and state.* Watertown, MA: Persephone. (Original work published 1893)

Garcia, A. M. (1990). The development of Chicana feminist discourse, 1970–80. In E. C. DuBois & V. L. Ruiz (Eds.), *Unequal sisters: A multicultural reader in U.S. women's history* (pp. 418–431). New York: Routledge.

Gilman, C. P. (1976). *His religion and hers: A study of the faith of our fathers and the work of our mothers.* Westport, CT: Hyperion. (Original work published 1923)

Green, R. (1990). The Pocahontas perplex: The image of Indian women in American culture. In E. C. DuBois & V. L. Ruiz (Eds.), *Unequal sisters: A multicultural reader in U.S. women's history* (pp. 15–21). New York: Routledge.

Griffin, S. (1978). *Woman and nature: The roaring inside her.* New York: Harper & Row.

Haraway, D. (1989). *Primate visions: Gender, race, and nature in the world of modern science.* New York: Routledge.

Harding, S. (1986). *The science question in feminism.* Ithaca, NY: Cornell University Press.

Harding, S. (1991). *Whose science? Whose knowledge? Thinking from women's lives.* Ithaca, NY: Cornell University Press.

Hegel, G. W. F. (1967). *The phenomenology of mind* (J. B. Baillie, Trans.). New York: Harper & Row.

hooks, b. (1981). *Ain't I a woman: Black women and feminism.* Boston: South End Press.

hooks, b. (1984). *From margin to center.* Boston: South End Press.

hooks, b. (1989). *Talking back: Thinking feminist, thinking Black.* Boston: South End Press.

Hurtado, A. (1989). Relating to privilege: Seduction and rejection in the subordination of White women and women of color. *Signs: Journal of Women in Culture and Society, 14,* 833–855.

Jaggar, A. (1983). *Feminist politics and human nature.* Totowa, NY: Rowman & Allanheld.

Johnson, S. (1989). *Wildfire: Igniting the she/volution.* Albuquerque, NM: Wildfire Books.

LaClau, E., & Mouffe, C. (1985). *Hegemony and socialist strategy.* London: Verso.

Leopold, A. (1949). *A Sand County almanac.* New York: Oxford University Press.

Longino, H. E. (1993). Feminist standpoint theory and the problems of knowledge. *Signs: Journal of Women in Culture and Society, 19,* 201–212.

Lugones, M. C., & Spelman, E. V. (1983). Have we got a theory for you! Feminist theory, cultural imperialism and the demand for "The Women's Voice." *Women's Studies International Forum, 6,* 573–581.

Mellor, M. (1992). *Breaking the boundaries: Towards a feminist green socialism.* London: Virago Press.

Merchant, C. (1980). *The death of nature: Women, ecology, and the scientific revolution.* San Francisco: Harper & Row.

Merchant, C. (1991). Ecofeminism and feminist theory. In I. Diamond & G. F. Orenstein (Eds.), *Reweaving the world: The emergence of ecofeminism* (pp. 100–105). San Francisco: Sierra Club Books.

Merchant, C. (1992). *Radical ecology: The search for a livable world.* New York: Routledge.

Mies, M., & Shiva, V. (1993). *Ecofeminism.* London: Zed Books.

Murphy, A. (1993). *Hidden transcripts: A field investigation.* Unpublished master's thesis, University of Utah, Salt Lake City.

Olesen, V. (1994). Feminisms and models of qualitative research. In N. Denzin & Y. Lincoln (Eds.), *Handbook of qualitative research* (pp. 158–174). Thousand Oaks, CA: Sage.

Ortner, S. (1974). Is female to male as nature is to culture? In M. Rosaldo & L. Lamphere (Eds.), *Women, culture and society* (pp. 67–87). Stanford, CA: Stanford University Press.

Sanday, P. (1981). *Female power and male dominance: On the origins of sexual inequality.* Cambridge, England: Cambridge University Press.

Sartre, J. (1956). *Being and nothingness* (H. E. Barnes, Trans.). New York: Philosophical Library.

Scott, J. (1985). *Weapons of the weak: Everyday forms of peasant resistance.* New Haven, CT: Yale University Press.

Scott, J. (1990). *Domination and the arts of resistance: Hidden transcripts.* New Haven, CT: Yale University Press.

Shiva, V. (1988). *Staying alive: Women, ecology and survival.* London: Zed Books.

Smith, D. (1987). Women's perspective as a radical critique of sociology. In S. Harding (Ed.), *Feminism & methodology* (pp. 84–96). Bloomington: Indiana University Press.

Smith, D. E. (1993). High noon in textland: A critique of Clough. *Sociological Quarterly, 34,* 183–192.

Stewart, J., & Logan, C. (1993). *Together: Communicating interpersonally* (4th ed.). New York: McGraw-Hill.

Waring, M. (1988). *If women counted.* San Francisco: Harper.

Warren, K. (1990). The power and promise of ecological feminism. *Environmental Ethics, 12*(3), 87–102.

Warren, K. J. (1991). Introduction. *Hypatia, 6*(1), 1–2.

# 2 What Counts as Real?: A Constitutive View of Communication and the Disenfranchised in the Context of Health

Hartmut B. Mokros
Stanley Deetz
*Rutgers University*

> *Theories of the real . . . control the vocabularies of healing. . . . If one could construct a map to negotiate a way through rival beliefs on health and healing, its baseline would be ontology, what counts as real. From this line a path would lead to the status of individuals in competing realities, then to different understandings of therapy that follow from competing descriptions of the human person. Finally, the moral and political languages of liberty, privacy, competence, and authority would appear. The first position, though, is reality. It fixes directions for the traveller journeying through the languages of health and healing, and provides the baseline references to justify beliefs about health acts and possibilities.*
>
> —Frohock (1992, pp. 47–48)

The potential relations among communication and disenfranchisement in health care are many and complex. Some deal with access to health care services and means of improving access. Others deal with the way certain groups of people are listened to and responded to. And others, yet, deal with meanings of health, illness, and treatment. Much of the past work has seen these relations more simply. The identification and targeting of disenfranchised groups would appear to be a key, and seemingly unproblematic, step toward removing the conditions and consequences of their disenfranchisement. Women, children, gays, the elderly, and the poor are but some of the more prominent groups who might be identified as disenfranchised from health care services in our society.

Communication research might proceed from there to design communication campaigns (Rice & Atkin, 1989) that make publicly apparent the unique health needs of the disenfranchised or inform the disenfranchised of health-promoting opportunities available to them (e.g., Witte, 1995). However, this emphasizes communication's instrumentality and thereby fails to recognize communication's full explanatory possibilities. As Deetz (1994) put it, "*if we are to make our full social contribution* [as students of communication], *we have to move from studying 'communication' phenomena as formed and explained psychologically, sociologically, and economically, and produce studies that study psychological, sociological, and economic phenomena as formed and explained communicationally*" (p. 568).

To explain phenomena communicationally requires that we ask what counts as real. Concern with what counts as real, and why this concern should matter, represents the focus of this chapter. We approach this by first examining two theoretically distinct views of communication, referred to as the informative and constitutive views. We then examine three empirical cases to illustrate how the question "what counts as real" calls our attention to "the disenfranchised" and "health" not as natural categories of this world but as products of social construction (e.g., Berger & Luckmann, 1966; Shotter & Gergen, 1994) as constituted through communication.

The first case, a newspaper editorial, shows how the construction of a health care issue creates the conditions for social disenfranchisement. In the second, an interactive moment from a doctor–patient diagnostic encounter illustrates how a physician's imposition of an illness category as "natural" disconfirms and thereby has the potential of disenfranchising a person from their self-understanding of their illness experience. Finally, the third example, a narrative account of living with a life-threatening illness, examines disenfranchisement as an inevitable subjective by-product of the illness process.

Through the analysis of these case examples, we wish to make apparent the constitutive nature of communication practices and the power of communicational explanations when approached constitutively. In so doing we argue that the informative view is not only inadequate for the development of a unique communicational explanatory voice in the debate surrounding social health issues, or any other psychosocial issue for that matter, but is potentially politically repressive precisely because it presupposes the existence of that which counts as real.

## TWO VIEWS OF COMMUNICATION

### Communication as Information Exchange

Everyday as well as scholarly discussion typically understands communication as a tool persons employ to address the practical demands of everyday life. Consider how this is expressed in the opening sentence of a recent study of the impact of health risk messages (Griffin, Neuwirth, & Dunwoody, 1995): "Communication scholars have long wrestled with the question of how messages influence behavior" (p. 201). Viewed in this way, communication is a tool by which persons, as self-contained, autonomous agents, exchange conventionally defined linguistic and linguistic-like signs. These signs provide labels to an already extant universe of objects, reasons, motives, and affections so that we might say that these signs represent and thereby "reflect" reality "out there." Communication in this model is the conduit (Reddy, 1979) by which information, as expressions of personal needs and desires and responses to needs and desires, is transferred between persons, namely, "information processors." Communication is a phenomenon to be explained rather than a mode of explanation. And it is explained by appeal to models outside of communication. Thus, Griffin et al. addressed "the question of how messages influence behavior . . . [by applying] one of the more successful social psychological models to the task of understanding the influence of health risk messages on individuals" (p. 201).

It is important to recognize that what we call language within this model forefronts the representational and referential function of language as "the" function of language. To put this in the vocabulary of our contemporary "information" age, language captures information about the world, and language use informs others about the world. In this regard, consider how our views of language are guided by the model of the dictionary (Mokros, 1993). This focus on representation leads us to overlook other functional properties of language in use such as the poetic, emotive, phatic, and metalingual functions described by Jakobson (1985; cf. Halliday, 1973).

Everyday understanding of language use, within this framework, treats persons and things as prior to moments of communication. Communication transmits information about things and persons as things, such as, for example, the discussion of persons as disenfranchised. This view rests on the assumption that knowledge is discovered, with language the medium for describing these discoveries. Consider in this regard how the phrase "research findings," as this is encountered in scholarly discussion, reveals how we reinforce the truthfulness of this assumption through our communication practices.

Research within this tradition treats communication as a site for empirical investigation, with the aim typically being the optimization of communicative, that is to say informative impact. In the health context concerns with the maximization of patient compliance, satisfaction, or attitude change, what Zook (1994) referred to as administrative concerns, exemplify this. Communication is treated as a factor in such studies affecting patient compliance, satisfaction, or attitude change. To put this another way, communication research that prioritizes information defines its aims as, for example, increasing access to information, and ensuring efficient, personally satisfying, and effective information exchange. The priority of information in this framework is most clearly apparent when communication and information come to be interchangeable.

Such informational perspectives tend to perceive problems of persons in terms of deficits (cf. Gergen, 1991). The disenfranchised in relation to issues of health are thereby seen as lacking access to health care services, relevant information, social respect, or policy-guided concern, for example. Even the fashionable, seemingly anti-informational, perspective of giving voice to the disenfranchised may be seen to assume solutions based on ridding people of their deficits. Such presumed deficits are always overcome at some cost. To become "informed" means at the same time to become "in-formed," to have the self and everyday meanings configured in a code not of one's own making. The disenfranchised thus always face a dilemma. Acquiring agency in the dominant system to access services often requires suppressing alternative identities. The loss of self becomes the price of care. But this is not just a price paid by socially marginalized peoples. Care is so fully intertwined with expertise and control that deficiency, inarticulation, and loss of agency is characteristic of all health care interactions.

## Communication as Constitutive

Whereas the informative view of communication regards reality as prior to communication, the constitutive view sees our experiences of reality to be a product of communicative activity. To approach communication as constitutive is to throw into question persons, diseases, and health as natural categories and to instead view these categories as discursive ways of understanding experience, understandings that are socially constructed (Berger & Luckmann, 1966; Shotter & Gergen, 1989, 1994). Persons, as well as things, are seen to be constituted through, rather than being prior to, communication practices. A communicative situation is, therefore, not merely a moment of information or message exchange, but is a situation within which communicative activities constitute its participants and the situation they believe to be situated within. Treichler (1989) developed such a position in detail in her discussion of the conception of childbirth. Interaction is filled with contests for meaning. Euphemisms and definitions are used by individuals and groups to constitute their own preferred versions of reality in the face of alternatives that threaten them. In Treichler's analysis "linguistic processes intersect with social structures, professional authority, economic resources, and political activism to produce gendered representations of social life and specifically of childbirth and women's health" (p. 428).

By this we do not mean that each communicative situation is one of creative actualization disconnected from prior communicative situations.

Quite to the contrary, the constitutive work of communication is largely reproductive. That is to say, any given communicative situation is only possible through the transference of past communicative practices and understandings into the present. This transference places any communicative situation under the umbrella of those discursive formations (Foucault, 1972) that structure, and thereby define and restrict, what we perceive to be real and of value. And, because our capacity to communicate with one another is contingent on these shared discursive formations as resources of expression, their definitional qualities continuously work their way through us, and thereby become naturalized, as they enable us to engage with others. Persons and things as communicationally constituted in this sense must be recognized as constituted ideologically and politically because they are products of a continuously amended and contested world view grounded in human relations.

Communicational explanations, when viewed in this constitutive sense, necessarily involve the explication of the ideological values inherent in communication practices. The everyday and scholarly treatment of communication as an informative activity is perhaps the most pronounced inherent ideological valuation imbuing communicative activity and its products. Constitutive explanations, as a metatheoretical framework, as theory for the comparative evaluation of theory (in practice), make possible the critical appraisal of extant communication practices through comparison with imagined plausible alternative modes of communicative practice. It is in this sense that the question "what counts as real" may not only be explained communicationally; when approached from a constitutive stance, it is a question that can *only* be explained communicationally.

## DISENFRANCHISEMENT AS CONSTITUTIVE
## PROCESS: THREE EXAMPLES

In the remainder of this chapter we explore some ways in which communication practices are constituted and how therein they constitute health and the disenfranchised in three empirical contexts. These include a newspaper editorial about the virtues of contraception, a doctor–patient interaction involving the evaluation of a young suicidal patient's mood state, and a narrative account of living with cancer. We hope that through these examples we may better convey our sense of the theoretical advantages that a constitutive perspective offers for conceptualizing issues of health and their implications (cf. Pearce, 1994). We also hope that these examples suggest types of data, methods, and issues that health communication scholars may recognize as legitimate and productive contexts, approaches, and concerns within which to situate their scholarship.

## The Construction (and Symbolic Function) of a Disenfranchised Group in Public Discourse

Public policy statements and mass-media texts provide an important locus within which to examine what counts as real and how what is real is publicly constituted and legitimated. Recently teen pregnancy has been targeted as a national problem. This is evident in the Clinton administration's virtual declaration of war on teen pregnancy. The elevation of this issue to a level of national awareness has been motivated by a number of sectors within the society and has been linked to a variety of additional public concerns such as family values, right to life, and federal welfare and entitlement programs. This has been greatly accelerated since then Vice President Quayle's criticism of the television show "Murphy Brown" for its portrayal of single motherhood as "just another lifestyle choice." The socially perceived relevance of these issues is no doubt pivotal for making sense of what is being characterized as a revolutionary move to the right in the 1994 U.S. election.

In the late 1980s the American Medical Association, through its Healthy Youth 2000 project, was one of the first major institutional voices to call attention to the "problem" of teen pregnancy. For our purposes, what is of interest in their elevation of this issue to one of national concern is their definition of teen pregnancy as a "health" problem. This health characterization has also appeared in discussions of unplanned pregnancy in general. The editorial that follows, which appeared in *The New York Times* under the title "Safe Sex, Safe Contraception" (1991) provides one example of this:

> Although Americans are increasingly outspoken about sex, they remain *curiously uninformed* about birth control. Some 10 percent of American *women at risk of pregnancy* use no method of contraception. They trust to luck alone—and *are responsible* for over half of the country's 3.5 million *unplanned pregnancies*.
>
> Even many who do use some form of birth control become pregnant, because they use a contraceptive improperly or choose a comparatively ineffective one. *Women* in both camps—the nonusers and ineffective users of birth control—are often *sadly ignorant* about the risks and benefits of contraceptives. Many have *exaggerated fears* about side effects and are especially *misinformed* about the pill.
>
> A new study from the Alan Guttmacher Institute demonstrating that the health hazards of pregnancy and childbirth far outweigh any possible side effects of contraceptive use should go a long way toward easing those fears. Even more impressive is the emerging evidence that certain contraceptives protect against one of the major causes of infertility and several reproductive cancers. . . .
>
> *She's* also much less likely to develop pelvic inflammatory disease, a major cause of infertility. So is the *woman* who uses a barrier method like the

diaphragm and spermicides, and *encourages her partner to use a condom.* She's also far less apt to suffer an ectopic pregnancy, an extremely dangerous condition that is usually the result of a previous pelvic infection.

Not all women can use all contraceptives. Many should be avoided by those who smoke, or have high blood pressure, or are over 35. Still, *using a contraceptive consistently and correctly* is a far more certain way for a *sexually* active woman to maintain good health than not using one. *May that message be heard all over the world.* (italics added)

Debates over issues of reproductive rights have been approached from what Gergen (1991) called romanticist and modernist discourses of the self. The romanticist view and vocabulary emphasizes "personal depth: passion, soul, creativity, and moral fiber" (p. 6). In contrast, the modernist discourse rejects the emphasis on the "natural" basis of the self that is "at the heart" of the romanticist discourse, and instead emphasizes the role of the reason, knowledge, and education in the social environment's creation of the self. Thus, when approached within a family values framework, the appeal made through a romanticist discourse emphasizes the erosion and loss of traditional moral values. Modernist texts, rather than seeking a return to a more fundamentalist world, urge progress toward a better world, a world of information and reason. It is such a modernist world view that drives the preceding editorial. The editorial presupposes the rightness of its world view and legitimates this world view by appealing to science as authority, here the Alan Guttmacher Institute's study. Consider, however, what kind of reality is being constructed here by focusing on the italicized phrases in the editorial.

The rational, acultural, casualness with which "unplanned" pregnancy is constituted as a health issue is impressive. To be unaware of contraception and its benefits and to leave pregnancy to chance are clearly regarded to be moral failings of women that stem from informational deficits. The social construction of unplanned pregnancy as a health care problem, one not limited to teen pregnancy, disenfranchises on moral grounds those women who trust to luck alone. Thus, the more fundamental unhealthiness alluded to here is the failure to live one's life rationally according to the tenets offered by our science.

Although the judgmental and disconfirmatory tenor, and historical and cultural insensitivity of the text are readily apparent, there is an additional point to be made about this text that is less apparent. Consider, in this regard, who would read and reflect upon such an editorial? It is unlikely that the editorial targets "the curiously uninformed [women]" who "trust to luck alone" as either the virtual audience imagined by the text's author or the realized audience who read the text.

Instead, the most likely readers of the text are those who share the rational, modernist scientific elite perspectives the editorial valorizes. When read in this way, the editorial functions to affirm the identity, the moral superiority of the nonignorant by forefronting the moral failings of the uninformed. In this way those who are ignorant and suspicious of the scientific marvels of our time are treated as a source of social illness in the context of concerns with public health. Thus, an editorial that claims to inform and enlighten "individuals" (that is, of course, to say women) about health and health-promoting practices is instead easily interpretable as a hegemonic manifesto ("may that message be heard all over the world") of a rational, scientifically guided, progressive world order. The text legitimates a social structure within which those who ought to legitimately exercise control are constituted by referencing those who have difficulty controlling themselves.

The costs of such an approach are many. The discursive reproduction of a classed society—with the rational, educated, and healthy women on one side and religious, uninformed, and sometimes pregnant on the other—leads to a perpetuation of paternalism and lessens the likelihood that the disenfranchised will take control of their own lives and put science to use in helping them fulfill their own goals and needs. Further, the modernist discourse situates the failing at the level of individual instrumental choice. By doing so the entire matrix of social and affective conditions in which personal needs, interpersonal relationships, "undesired" pregnancies, and failure to provide adequate child care arise, is collapsed to the decision to use a contraceptive. This is roughly equivalent to the employer who upon finding employees highly stressed on the job asserts that well-informed, rational employees will take stress medication, thereby implicitly regarding the ignorance of others as responsible for their fate. An entire array of social, mental, and physical costs are reduced to the marginal improvement of one index. Social responsibility is reduced, the symptom of a social problem is masked as an uninformed individual choice, and the society is hampered in making inclusively responsible and sensible choices together.

### Estrangement From One's "Own" Understanding of an Illness Experience

Examination of the earlier editorial illustrates how public discourse, which purportedly aims to inform, provides the conditions for disenfranchisement through its constitution of an objectifiable health care concern, one that may be remedied through rational, informed behavior. In this second example we examine how a psychiatric diagnostic evaluation, aimed at promoting the health of a patient, has as a by-product of how it is discursively approached and guided, the potential to disenfranchise a person from his or her understanding of self.

The following transcript represents a portion of an interview conducted by Dr. Frank, a child psychiatrist, with Ann, a 13-year-old, who had attempted to kill herself by slitting her wrists. Following her suicide attempt Ann was hospitalized and placed in a child psychiatric inpatient unit. Ann had been diagnosed as depressed at the time of her hospitalization. The interview was designed to evaluate the child's current state of depression and to also provide Dr. Frank, who was joining the team caring for Ann, an opportunity to talk with Ann about her problems. The transcript is limited to some of the early moments of the interview during which Dr. Frank invites Ann to offer her understanding of the difficulties that have led to her hospitalization. Mokros (1993) offered a more extended discussion of this interaction and its implications:

13. Dr. Frank: How come you are here?
14. Ann: Because I'm depressed.
15. Dr. Frank: Ah-ha, what does that mean, you're depressed?
16. Ann: My, in my own words?
17. Dr. Frank: Ah-ha.
18. Ann: It means, I just felt like, umm, umm, I feel alone.
19. Dr. Frank: Mm-hm.
20. Ann: Now, I don't, I don't really know how to describe this, it's kind of hard, it's just that I don't feel like I'm needed anymore, why do I keep saying that, or no one cares about me.
21. Dr. Frank: Mm-hm.
22. Ann: I just, that's how I kind of feel.
23. Dr. Frank: Mm-hm. Have you been feeling that way for a long time?
24. Ann: Yeah, since ahm March, may, part of February, and February.
25. Dr. Frank: Ah-ha. Did something happen that you felt sad, or?
26. Ann: Ah, well uh, it's kind of like all my emotions went together anger, sad, happy . . .

In response to Dr. Frank's question in Turn 13, Ann represented herself as an objective category, in the vocabulary she had been defined since admission to the hospital. However, rather than accepting this representation at face value, Dr. Frank invites Ann to describe what she means by this in Turn 15. Ann's question, "in my own words?" in response reveals her surprise that Dr. Frank may truly wish to listen and that her story indeed has value. Dr. Frank's Turn 17 confirms that this is indeed what she is interested in, Ann's own story.

Ann's "own words" describe her problem in relational terms: She feels "alone," not "needed anymore," and that "no one cares." It is a sense of social isolation and alienation that Ann describes. The depth with which she describes her feeling of alienation surprises even Ann, as is seen in

Turn 20 where she parenthetically adds, in a softened and speeded voice, "why do I keep saying that?" (a parenthetical aside that is interestingly not pursued by Dr. Frank). By asking in Turn 23 how long she had experienced such feelings, Dr. Frank appears to confirm the validity of Ann's feelings as she had expressed them in her "own words." But this is clearly not the case as is apparent in Turn 25.

At this point, Dr. Frank asked Ann if she knew of any potential precipitant for her problems. Instead of using Ann's "own words," which reflected social disconnectedness, Dr. Frank instead substituted the term *sad*. By introducing the concept sadness, Dr. Frank reconstructed Ann's phenomenological experience to conform to the diagnostic model of depression (*Diagnostic and Statistical Manual of Mental Disorders*, 4th ed.) within which sadness is the essential feature of depressive disorder. What is of interest here is Dr. Frank's reconstruction of Ann's experience in terms of "Ann's initial characterization of herself as "depressed," a characterization that Dr. Frank had asked Ann to put aside when she invited her to account for why she was in the hospital in her "own words."

Dr. Frank favors understanding Ann in terms of sadness rather than alienation. This understanding is theoretically consistent with the diagnostic criteria defining depressive disorder. Yet these criteria apparently obscure Dr. Frank from viewing the meaningfulness of what Ann has said. Sadness is an intrapersonal experience. Yet Ann has described something quite the contrary. She does not define her experience "intrapersonally," but in interpersonal or relational terms.

In the next turn, 26, Ann referred for the first and only time during the interview (which lasted roughly 20 minutes) to herself as "sad." Two aspects of this turn stand out. First, although she applied the word *sad* to herself, she qualified this so as to convey a general sense of emotional turmoil. Second, by listing symptoms—"anger, sad, happy"—without verbally linking them, she in a sense returned to an objectifying account of herself. Resistance to being misunderstood and resignation to a mode of understanding that does not fit her are both implicated in Ann's utterance.

Although Ann continued throughout the interview to resist the conceptualization of herself as depressed in terms of a state of sadness, it is this understanding of Ann that guided Dr. Frank's evaluation. Turn 37, which followed Ann's account of a variety of precipitants to her hospitalization exemplifies this:

> 37. Dr. Frank: So, you've been feeling sad since all of that? Do you feel sad about the fact that they've been sick or there's other things that make you sad too?

Apparent here is that Dr. Frank had early on in the course of the interview, possibly even prior to the interview, defined Ann's phenomenological state.

Her formulation was one based on a standardized understanding of depression, which she knew was Ann's diagnosis. It was not based on what Ann experienced and expressed even though she elicited this from Ann.

What is of principal interest here is not just the invalidation and reconstruction of Ann based on the psychiatrically preferred account, though clearly we do not want to lose Ann in the generalization. To the extent that she accepts the reconstruction, Ann is left with "depression"—a state largely out of her potential control, requiring medication and doctors—rather than a reconnection with her family in which she can be a productive agent in building a better relational life. She is also subject to one more relational disqualification, affirming the relational disconnectedness of which the suicide was a material and discursive move—"if I don't exist, I might just as well not exist," or perhaps, "someone might listen to me now." We feel that the discursive moves displayed in this interview are routine and perhaps normative. The professionalized dialogue functions more to reproduce the identity of the professional and value of the profession (and disenfranchise others) than to provide useful diagnoses and co-construct positive interventions (see Townley, 1993). This is not to suggest a lack of personal involvement, caring, or goodwill on the part of professionals like Dr. Frank. The highly trained and committed professional enacts discursive routines with unintended consequences. The thousands upon thousands of repetitions of these routines daily foster community disconnectedness, undermine the relational coproduction of knowledge and identity, reproduce a disenfranchised patient, reaffirm a privileged profession, and lead to less than adequate care.

## The Disenfranchising Experiences of Living With Cancer

Experiences of life-threatening illness make "normal" everyday experience appear odd and distant. Suddenly, one is no longer engaged as a full unquestioning member of the everyday social world. The demands of a new way of life—the life of the seriously ill patient—preclude this possibility. These are highly self-reflexive moments made possible by the continuously experienced mismatch between one's virtual and actual existence (Goffman, 1963). This ongoing sense of existential mismatch is, we believe, characteristic of the natural history of serious illness, a disenfranchising characteristic.

In this empirical case we present an experience-near narrative account of a marital couple's life with cancer. What is of interest in this case is how it captures the disenfranchising process of the illness experience and how, through this process, faith and trust become consciously realized anchors in which to fix a sense of place within a world turned upside down.

*Life With Cancer: A Reflexive Relational Narrative.*  A young woman in her mid-30s discovers a lump on her neck yet otherwise feels fine. Concerned, she sees an internist who assures her that in all likelihood there is no problem, but that the lump needs to be removed for biopsy. Within weeks she has several exploratory surgeries that include incisions in her neck, abdomen, groin, feet, and hip. These incisions result in the removal of her spleen, and a sampling of lymph nodes and bone marrow. Selected lymph nodes remaining in her gut are tagged before the abdominal incision is sutured. Radioactive dyes are injected through the tops of her feet into her lymphatic system. These surgical procedures confirm a diagnosis of Hodgkin's disease and its stage of development. She is told that her cancer is treatable, has been caught at an early stage, and will therefore require only radiation therapy and not also chemotherapy. She is further told that she will die unless she undertakes treatment.

Shortly after her surgery she is sent to meet with a radiation oncologist to plan her course of treatment. With her husband she proceeds to an elevator in an isolated wing of the hospital, the only elevator providing access to the hospital's subbasement where the radiation clinic is located. The symbolism of descending into the underworld, outside of social sight lines, is apparent to both of them. No one, they come to understand, passes through the radiation clinic on their way to somewhere else. Only "the chosen" enter.

There, her body is "mapped" for treatment, front and back are tattooed with small black dots to aid in positioning protective shielding of body parts judged healthy. Her husband is outraged by the tattoos, seeing them as the consequence of one more invasive procedure they had not been informed about, one more step not chosen. He is further outraged that she is not. He perceives that she has resigned herself to the course of medical events as he, with increasing agitation, questions its authority and legitimacy. For her the tattoos mean that she can forego the demeaning rite of having her body outlined with markers each day and can forego the associated discomfort as the marker is drawn across her still healing surgical scars. She was given the choice, markers or tattoos. She chose the tattoo alternative on the third day of treatment and saw this, as she still does, as a moment of control, a point in the process where she had a sense that her decision made a difference in the quality of her everyday experience. In fact, for 10 years he was not able to hear, let alone appreciate her perspective. For him it remained another act of defilement. She, on the other hand, resented this reaction by him, as it denied her agency.

Her radiation treatment begins and continues for more than a month. Daily she rises and proceeds to what her husband comes to view as an underground bunker in a war zone. In the waiting room hatted and scarved heads identify the patients. Their "escorts" are seated nearby without head coverings. There is little talk among those waiting and, but for the occasional outburst of emotional indignation, with some phrase like "this is my life we are talking about" shouted at the clinic staff, there is a sense of resigned emptiness. Every morning they arrive to the sights and sounds of the same network morning news show. She has never watched the show, nor has her husband who accompanies her. Now they sense no choice but to watch just as they have perceived no choice other than the surgeries and now the treatment. They feel as if their lives have come to a halt and find themselves repulsed by the glib "info-tainment" world in motion that the television imposes.

Every day she returns home nauseated and tired by the treatment. Every day she falls asleep largely unaware of the world around her, vomits in agony crying at her inability to keep down any food, disgusted by the blender drinks that now define her meals. He watches her, cleans up the messes, blends the drinks and "insists" on their consumption, experiences her existential anger and resistance in response to his insistence, and finds himself very alone. Their everyday actions, it is quite clear, have become a matter of faith. They trust in medicine at this point in ways they had never imagined trusting, for they believe that all they have is their ability to trust. They attempt to buttress faith with reason, reading medical journals, texts, and self-help books to attempt to understand what has happened, what is happening, and what might happen in the future. Both of them attempt to maintain their involvements in their everyday worlds. But these worlds and the routines that give them their distinctive character now have the feel of foreign lands. Each now regards their former world as empty and shallow and each sees their experiential present and future as stigmatized and polluted.

"Why me? Am I really ill? Maybe this happened because. . . ." In the course of such thoughts she is able to fill in the blank each time with some other reason why this punishment she lives in now is her own doing, her responsibility for who she is. Her husband feels suspicious and judgmental of the process and irrationally resentful that she is putting him through this.

The cancer is arrested by the treatment and, although over the years scares occur requiring new biopsies, she lives on as does their marriage. Two decades earlier she would have died within 6 months to a year. She has now lived more than a decade since her treatment, surely a product of the miracle of modern medicine. They have come to live what they regard as a normal and fulfilling life. Yet, the illness experience remains inseparable from their daily lives. A look back returns the past vividly to the present. And in this moment of arrested time the strangeness of the experience reverberates: She found a small lump on her neck, yet otherwise felt fine. It was the medical procedures that made her ill, not the illness. And although they believe in the reality of the illness, they do so and did so as a matter of faith, a faith in medical authority. It could not have worked otherwise, they are quite convinced.

*The Disenfranchising By-Products of Illness.*   They had access to the finest health care available; she paid attention sufficiently to her body to catch the cancer at an early stage; she survived as did she and her husband as a couple. Yet, their narrative reveals that they have both been disenfranchised from the "subjective" social and psychological world they once occupied and are thereby disenfranchised from themselves, from who they were.

The security of the everyday was replaced by an alternative world where a healthy woman was made sick to determine what was wrong with her. Thereafter, a course of treatment that comes close to killing her must be made sensible with the claim that this is her only option. She endures this all even though she never directly experiences her illness, only the invasive consequences of the fear it garners. The willingness and ability to endure in the face of apparent absurdity, we wish to suggest, might be productively examined in relationship to the inevitable disenfranchisement that the illness process engenders. Faith emerges as a way of fixing some semblance of identity as one's self seems to come unglued. Its antecedents are unimportant, so long as this faith somehow enables the individual to trustingly accept the legitimacy and authority of the health practitioner and the practices and traditions he or she instantiates.

Across cultures, healing was originally the province of religious practice. In our Western tradition, medicine has increasingly separated itself from this heritage appealing to science rather than faith and belief in the definition and remediation of illness states. Yet for those directly affected by life-threatening illness, participation in the process, from diagnosis through treatment, requires an enormous investment of faith and enormous capacity to trust. This, we assume is, in part, what Gonzales (1994) had in mind when she "invites us to consider the spiritual dimension" in research of health communication (p. 379).

We feel that this third case displays the essential tensions and dialectic quality of control in medical care. Whereas the first two cases could be reduced to a consideration of how dominant groups maintain themselves through discursive micropractices of control with the consequence of reproducing disenfranchised individuals and groups, this case fills out the fuller dynamics. Illness itself in a segmented and instrumentalized world is a form of alienation, loss of control, and disenfranchisement. The body is separated from the mind itself. And in a world where one can get better, one wants to get better even at the loss of a more organic connectedness. The medical profession has done wonders in treatment and the patient solicits the control of others in hope of regaining self-control. The patient openly strategizes their own subordination and disenfranchisement in the hope of renewed power, only rarely is it forced on them. Although filled with the tensions and contradictions that make up our contemporary lives, the giving of control over to another, taking from modern medicine and medical research what one can even at the cost of self-instrumentalization and social relational disconfirmation, is probably more positive than problematic.

But, as in all of life, too much of a "good" thing can be as harmful as a "bad" thing. Unnecessary asymmetries, the rigidification of medical routines, the reduction of a full set of life concerns, and the fixing of social relations each are costly moves in contemporary health care. Our point here is not to offer a way out of these tensions, neither to hide nor resolve them nor to provide a utopian health care system, but to reclaim productive tensions as a critical aspect of all life and social relations—including health. Disenfranchisement is a horrible cost of fleeing the tensions of life, a false hope of wellness at no cost, that comes as an inevitable by-product when we surrender to an elite to fix our problems. The cost arises from an elite's promising too much, acts of self-reproduction, routines of disenfranchisement, and self-disenfranchisement. Communication analyses offer not a better delivery system, but new, more productive ways to articulate and work with these tensions for the self-improvement of community decisions and health.

## CONCLUSION

Scholarship and everyday communication practice, we have argued, are typically understood from a communication as informative perspective. This perspective leads us to perceive seemingly "natural" categories: communication, the disenfranchised, and health. Approaching from a constitutive perspective makes apparent the explanatory and emancipatory (see Zook, 1994) restrictions of this informative view.

When social issues are approached from a constitutive perspective our concern is to first address the question "what is real." It is this concern that we have focused on in this chapter. Thus, for example, to recognize disenfranchisement as a process makes it feasible to recognize that the category that makes possible discussion of "the disenfranchised" is not a category whose membership is reducible to some set of individuals who differ from the rest of us. That is, instead of regarding the disenfranchised and enfranchised as individuals and groups, a constitutive perspective brings into relief that these are mutually determining perspectives rather than attributes of individuals or groups. This then suggests that it is impossible to understand the enfranchised without reference to the disenfranchised. And similarly, because the key criterion around which we enter into a discussion of communication and the disenfranchised is that of health, it is then impossible to understand what it means to be disenfranchised without also examining the assumptions that underpin our conceptualizations of health and illness. These are categories of social meaning that are constituted through human relationships, through and in communication, that we tend to accept instead as descriptions of reality.

## REFERENCES

Berger, P., & Luckmann, T. (1966). *The social construction of reality.* New York: Doubleday.
Deetz, S. A. (1994). Future of the discipline: The challenges, the research, and the social contribution. In S. A. Deetz (Ed.), *Communication yearbook 17* (pp. 565–600). Thousand Oaks, CA: Sage.
Frohock, F. M. (1992). *Healing powers: Alternative medicine, spiritual communities, and the state.* Chicago: University of Chicago Press.
Foucault, M. (1972). *The archaeology of knowledge.* New York: Pantheon.
Gergen, K. J. (1991). *The saturated self: Dilemmas of identity in contemporary life.* New York: Basic Books.
Goffman, E. (1963). *Stigma: Notes on the management of spoiled identity.* Englewood Cliffs, NJ: Prentice-Hall.
Gonzales, M. C. (1994). An invitation to leap from a trinitarian ontology in health communication research to a spiritually inclusive quatrain. In S. A. Deetz (Ed.), *Communication yearbook 17* (pp. 378–387). Thousand Oaks, CA: Sage.
Griffin, R. J., Neuwirth, K., & Dunwoody, S. (1995). Using theory of reasoned action to examine the impact of health risk messages. In B. R. Burleson (Ed.), *Communication yearbook 18* (pp. 201–228). Thousand Oaks, CA: Sage.
Halliday, M. (1973). *Explorations in the functions of language.* London: Edward Arnold.
Jakobson, R. (1985). Metalanguage as a linguistic problem. In S. Rudy (Ed.), *Roman Jakobson selected writings VII* (pp. 113–121). Berlin: Mouton.
Mokros, H. B. (1993). The impact of a native theory of information on two privileged accounts of personhood. In J. Schement & B. Ruben (Eds.), *Between communication and information: Information and behavior IV* (pp. 57–79). New Brunswick, NJ: Transaction.
Pearce, W. B. (1994). Recovering agency. In S. Deetz (Ed.), *Communication yearbook 17* (pp. 34–41). Thousand Oaks, CA: Sage.
Reddy, M. (1979). The conduit metaphor. In A. Ortony (Ed.), *Scholarly communication and bibliometrics* (pp. 284–324). Cambridge, England: Cambridge University Press.
Rice, R. E., & Atkin, C. K. (Eds.). (1989). *Public communication campaigns.* Thousand Oaks, CA: Sage.
Safe sex, safe contraception. (1991, April 27). *The New York Times,* p. A29.
Shotter, J., & Gergen, K. J. (Eds.). (1989). *Texts of identity.* Newbury Park, CA: Sage.
Shotter, J., Gergen, K. J. (1994). Social construction: Knowledge, self, others, and continuing the conversation. In S. A. Deetz (Ed.), *Communication yearbook 17* (pp. 3–33). Thousand Oaks, CA: Sage.
Townley, B. (1993). Foucault, power/knowledge, and its relevance for human resource management. *Academy of Management Review, 18,* 518–545.
Treichler, P. A. (1989). What definitions do: Childbirth, cultural crisis, and the challenge to medical discourse. In B. Dervin, L. Grossberg, B. O'Keefe, & E. Wartella (Eds.), *Rethinking communication: Vol. 2. Paradigm exemplars* (pp. 424–453). Thousand Oaks, CA: Sage.
Witte, K. (1995). Generating effective risk messages: How scary should your risk communication be? In B. R. Burleson (Ed.), *Communication yearbook 18* (pp. 229–254). Thousand Oaks, CA: Sage.
Zook, E. G. (1994). Embodied health and constitutive communication: Toward an authentic conceptualization of health communication. In S. A. Deetz (Ed.), *Communication yearbook 17* (pp. 344–377). Thousand Oaks, CA: Sage.

# 3 Identities in Crisis: Individualism, Disenfranchisement, and the Self-Help Culture

George B. Ray
*Cleveland State University*

> *I started Zen to get something for myself, to stop suffering, to get enlightened. Whatever it was, I was doing it for myself. I had hold of myself and I was reaching for something. Then to do it, I found out I had to give up that hold on myself. Now, it has hold of me, whatever "it" is.*
>
> —Tipton (1982, p. 115)

The individual just quoted is struggling to achieve what constitutes the true meaning of life for most Americans: becoming one's own person (Bellah, Madsen, Sullivan, Swidler, & Tipton, 1985). In the individualistic and egalitarian United States it is important, even necessary, for persons to achieve selfhood and the autonomy that goes with it. Without selfhood and autonomy there is no true participation in American society:

> But the radical egalitarianism of an individualistic society has its own problems. For such a society is really constituted only of autonomous middle-class individuals. Those who for whatever reason do not meet the requirement for full membership are left out. . . . The very existence of groups who do not meet the criteria for full social participation is anomalous. There should be no such groups. Their existence must be someone's fault. . . . (Bellah et al., 1985, p. 206)

Without full participation, there is disenfranchisement and here we see a linkage asserted between autonomy and enfranchisement. But what happens

45

when one struggles with one's identity? What happens when one fails to achieve a stable selfhood? Can an identity crisis actually lead to disenfranchisement?

This chapter discusses the prominence of individualism in American culture and how individualism affects personal identity, with an analysis of how identity problems can lead to disenfranchisement. The self-help culture in the United States is examined as a case of identities in crisis, which are due in part to the effects of modernism. The chapter concludes with a brief discussion of the prospects for political action that may help restore identities and therefore reenfranchise Americans.

## HISTORICAL OVERVIEW OF INDIVIDUALISM IN AMERICA

Individualism in the United States has meant a sense of personal identity, a consciousness that sets one apart from others in an autonomous, self-willed existence. From the earliest days of the nation, through the 20th century, individualism has been one of the most noteworthy characteristics of American culture (see, e.g., Arieli, 1964; Bellah et al., 1985).

### Aspects of Individualism

One of the hallmarks of American individualism is the location of the self within one's personal identity, a self that is personally constructed to suit one's *own* preferences (Shafer, 1991). Independence and singularity both contribute strongly to American individualism, primarily conceptualized within the constructs of autonomy and equality.

*Autonomy.*  As far back as the 1830s, Alexis de Tocqueville (1945) captured the essence of the autonomous American:

> As social conditions become more equal, the number of persons increases who, although they are neither rich nor powerful enough to exercise any great influence over their fellows, have nevertheless acquired or retained sufficient education and fortune to satisfy their wants. They owe nothing to any man [sic]; they acquire the habit of always considering themselves as standing alone, and they are apt to imagine that their whole destiny is in their hands. (p. 99)

The sense of the American individual emerges here as a person who thinks and acts alone. Observations such as these in the early 1800s often impressed visitors who saw contrasts with European society in which group ties and group identities were more common (Lipset, 1991). Embedded in autonomy has clearly been the idea of self-determination, as Americans have tended to view themselves as actors in a life that presents them with opportunities and choices (Carbaugh, 1988). It remains the choice of individuals to identify and select the most promising options for themselves. With an emphasis on self-reflection and self-determination, Americans have characteristically displayed their autonomous selves, resulting in some far-reaching implications.

In earlier times, such as 19th-century America, autonomy coincided with the tremendous economic expansion the United States underwent. Rapid industrialization resulted in a dynamic economy, which provided widespread growth in labor opportunities as well as increasing opportunities for entrepreneurs. These opportunities also proved attractive to immigrants who came to the United States. The main point was that individuals had opportunities. What they did with them was up to the individuals. Those who seemed not to share in the otherwise abundant life within the United States were thought to be unwilling to take advantage of opportunities. Thus, the autonomous, opportunistic individual was supposed to succeed in American life, whereas those who were not succeeding were assumed to be laggards, unmotivated to achieve, and deserving of whatever resulted from their little efforts (Lipset, 1991; Merton, 1957). One significant aspect of autonomy, then, is its orientation toward personal objectives and the exercise of individual action.

A second important aspect of a traditional view of autonomy is a strong sense of liberty. At times, liberty can result in self-interest being placed ahead of the common good, in what might be called "rampant individualism" (Glazer, 1979, p. 129). American history is replete with eras in which persons and organizations gained unfair advantage over others. Selfishness may often be in competition with altruism, and in any given case, selfishness may win out. What Americans have come to understand is that their personal freedoms may be pursued so long as there is no infringement on someone else's freedoms. Americans do not believe they possess unrestricted liberty; however, they believe that they are entitled to the pursuit of their self-interests if such pursuit is unchallenged. As Seymour Lipset (1991) observed, America has an emphasis on individual rights and guarantees them through due process. For example, such an emphasis has limited the power of the police and public prosecutors, and has provided civil liberties for criminals and suspects beyond the rights for such persons in existence elsewhere.

Thus, American individualism has a strong element of autonomy, which includes personal choice and liberty. The concept of autonomy is essential to understanding American individualism because it clarifies and underscores self-determination. The American self looks within and constructs a personal view of what is wanted or needed. The tendency for the individual is to consider what one alone can do to advance one's self-interest and take action.

## Equality

A second major feature of individualism in the United States is equality (Glazer, 1979; Myrdal, 1962). At once a cornerstone of American democracy and a constant source of tension, equality and all the discussions surrounding it have long been regarded as fundamental to the American experience.

The U.S. Constitution provides for equal rights to all citizens. Theoretically, no U.S. citizen has greater civil rights than anyone else. The fact that unequal rights have been the reality throughout the entire history of the United States simply is evidence that the Constitution is a document over which people can argue, and rights have had to be claimed, not automatically exercised. As Gunnar Myrdal (1962) found in his massive study on race relations, American society was characterized by the American creed, a set of beliefs, chief among which were liberty and equality. The creed is an ideology, and this, more than shared history or cultural heritage, is what unites Americans (Bercovitch, 1981; Lipset, 1991). However, as an ideology, belief in equality is more often professed than practiced. Americans are willing to overlook discrepancies in equality, even while maintaining belief in the ideology.

Supported by autonomy and equality, American individualism has thrived throughout American history. The society and its individualistic citizens seemed to mutually support each other in a healthy fashion well into the 20th century. Increasingly, though, there are concerns for the future of the traditional American individual.

## MODERN IDENTITY ISSUES

In his penetrating analysis of American culture in the 1950s, *The Lonely Crowd*, David Riesman (1961) discerned what to him was a disturbing pattern. In his analysis of the relationship between societal development and character, he hypothesized that Americans were drifting toward an other-directedness. Life in nonindustrialized cultures is characterized as tradition oriented, where food supplies limit population growth and most efforts are devoted to day-to-day living. Tradition-directed persons respect the time-honored customs of the family, caste, or clan to which they belong. The social order is relatively unchanging, and there is no long-range planning or accumulation of wealth. In contrast, in nations with expanding populations, economic opportunities are available for economic gain and self-development. An inner-directed character develops. Unlike the tradition-directed society, important activities take place outside of the family or primary group. Individuals look beyond tradition for ways of exercising options and taking advantage of opportunities. With important elements of social life occurring outside of the family or primary group, individuals need newer, more flexible methods of living. Riesman hypothesized that inner-directed individuals are guided by instructions instilled by parents early in life, and then manage to live socially without strict traditions.

It is in societies experiencing population decline where the third character type, the other-directed individual, is found. Riesman (1961) argued that as fewer and fewer people are engaged in agriculture, and even workers in manufacturing become fewer in number, these societies' economies become more service oriented and government becomes more centralized and bureaucratized. Taking advantage of economic opportunities for material gain is less of a problem in life, whereas human relations problems increase due to greater intercultural contact. Where traditional patterns of behavior are no longer useful and the internal compass may not be flexible enough, there is a need for a new psychological mechanism. The new mechanism is social approval and the other-directed person is forever looking to her or his social environment for signs of it. Conforming to the peer group's judgment is the new norm, and to Riesman this is most likely an insatiable need. Constant efforts to satisfy this need result in anxiety, insecurity, and concerns for self-esteem (Riesman, 1961). Riesman feared for the future of the United States in which a majority of other-directed persons will result in a leaderless society accompanied by a withdrawal from public life.

Although writing mainly on the three character types, Riesman (1961) denoted a fourth type of character, the autonomous individual. Like the other-directed individual, the autonomous person is capable of conforming to society's norms. However, unlike other-directedness, autonomy means one can choose not to conform. What matters most is whether or not the conformity is due to individual behavior, or a character form of behavior. If society can recognize nonconformity as deviance, but not maladjustment, then the character form is functional. To the extent society recognizes nonconformist behavior as maladjustment, the behavior is dysfunctional.

Concern about the nature of modern identity has continued into the late 20th century. Two of the more current writers on modern identity problems are Kenneth Gergen (*The Saturated Self*, 1991) and Anthony Giddens (*Modernity and Self-Identity*, 1991). One of their main themes is that modern (or, for Gergen, postmodern) society confronts individuals with vast amounts of information and a decontextualization of experience, both of which lead to a pervasive uncertainty and anxiety over who one is and how to maintain an identity. It is not the sheer amount of information that is most significant, but rather the information available that causes people to constantly rethink the connections between the self, social situations, relationships, roles, and events.

For Gergen (1991) the postmodern identity is not a problem per se. Western civilization has had at least three periods in which cultural notions of an individual self emerged. First was the romantic period, which occurred during the 17th and 18th centuries. Then, self was conceptualized as emotional, having deep or hidden aspects, and was revealed through passion, imagination, and deeds. In the 19th and 20th centuries emerged the modern self. In this era, which still prevails, self is rational and logical, has enduring traits, and is knowable. Now, according to Gergen and others, we have entered the postmodern condition, in which the self is fragmented, multi-faceted, and must be flexible enough to meet the ever-changing demands of contemporary social life. As eras overlap, interpretations of what constitutes a viable self may become problematic, as may be the case presently with the emergence of a postmodern self.

It must be emphasized that the postmodern identity is not a problem per se. According to Gergen (1991), there are identity problems only when one compares the postmodern self with the modern or romantic self. Compared to the romantic self, the postmodern self (or the modern self, for that matter) is arguably bereft of emotion. Or, compared to the modern self, the postmodern self is inconsistent, with no stable, logical point of view. A major difficulty, therefore, is that selfhood is discussed with vocabularies that apply to particular periods, and a given vocabulary may not apply to another period or conceptualization of selfhood. Indeed, there is no significant vocabulary for the postmodern self and it can only be discussed in terms that privilege other conceptualizations. Thus, there is a major dilemma; namely, that our current vocabulary of self stresses the modern notion and against this mode of thinking, the postmodern self is fragmented, fragile, and unstable. Even if such evaluations are obtained only though the modern-postmodern comparison, many people are too immersed in the modern vocabulary to discover anything other than the defective nature of postmodern identities, including their own.

Giddens (1991) stated that society is now in high or late modernity, during which individuals construct their self-identities through a reflexive understanding of their own biographies. Self-identity requires an ongoing interpretation or narrative of one's life, a "story" about oneself (p. 54). Through what Giddens called the reflexive project of the self, one continually redevelops one's narrative and self-identity emerges; however, identity problems occur when it becomes difficult for one to keep his or her narrative going. Effects of institutions such as mass media have been to remove events from their particular places and times and register them more or less generally present in everyone's consciousness. Modernity has also produced grave social, environmental, political, and economic problems, all of which make us feel we must live with risk in our lives. Risk extends to interpersonal trust and commitment, resulting in the anxious, uncertain, and powerless mood so characteristic of contemporary selfhood.

What Gergen (1991) and Giddens (1991) both described is potentially a major fault line in American individualism. Individuals feel they are entering new territories of identity, but the territory is uncharted. A large-scale identity search looms. It is at this point that the self-help movement becomes particularly attractive to those whose identities are in crisis.

## THE SELF-HELP MOVEMENT

Self-help refers to information that offers instruction or assistance in remedying personal problems (Simonds, 1992). The information should be intended for a lay audience, and should be presented for immediate and practical use (Starker, 1989). Although self-help is available on a multitude of topics, this discussion focuses on self-help in the areas of personal problems and development (e.g., psychological self-improvement, relationship enhancement, and sexuality). Those who actively use self-help materials are members of the self-help culture.

The self-help movement is an enormous culture, based on its size, activity, and prevalence on television and in bookstores. Daytime television everywhere in the United States is peppered with so-called talk shows. The names of the hosts are well known to many of us: Oprah, Donahue, Geraldo, Sally Jesse, Montel, and Ricki. Talk shows are also popular on radio. To be sure, many topics and programs on the talk shows are not about people with personal problems, but the personal problem category is common. As Wendy Kaminer (1993) pointed out, persons appearing on a talk show like "Donahue" can use phrases such as "12-step program" or "in recovery" and studio audience members nod knowingly, apparently familiar with the language and the culture. That these television talk shows are popular, have increased in number over the last 20 years, and now constitute a considerable portion of the daytime television format, all attest to the widespread interest in self-help. Certainly not all the viewers of these programs are themselves experiencing the problems of those appearing on the shows. However, the large audiences are indicative of interest in the self-help culture and its widespread presence in American life.

Consider also the phenomenon of self-help books in the United States. According to Wendy Simonds (1992), from 1963 to 1991, 114 different self-help books made it to *The New York Times* bestseller list. Kaminer (1993) provided data on the popularity of self-help books, including *Co-*

*Dependent No More* by Melody Beattie, which appeared on *The New York Times* bestseller list for over 100 weeks and in 1991 sold over 2 million copies. Kaminer also reported that the sales of Janet Woitetz's book, *Adult Children of Alcoholics*, were 2 million in 1991. As Simonds pointed out, one could consider the sales of self-help books as part of a general consumer culture in which more and more services, such as self-help, become marketable commodities. Simonds reported that in the United States prior to 1939 when paperback books first appeared, there were only about 4,000 businesses selling books and of these only 500 were legitimate bookstores. This was for the entire United States. With the advent of the shopping mall, bookstores and bookstore chains became much more visible and accessible to the mass consumer (Simonds, 1992). Now, of course, the retailing of books has been extended into other types of outlets. In addition to bookstores, drugstores, and newsstands, books are now available through various discount retailers and supermarkets, not to mention mail order sales and, of course, public libraries.

Of particular interest is why the self-help culture is so widespread. In part, it can be traced back to American individualism. As Kaminer (1993) noted, the early Americans 200 years ago were interested in making life better for themselves. At the time Tocqueville visited the United States in the early 1800s, it was clear to him that there was a self-improvement streak in Americans (Simonds, 1992), not unlike the emphasis on choice within the autonomy issue already discussed. Over the span of American history, there have been many writers on self-improvement, some of the more noteworthy being Mary Baker Eddy, Norman Vincent Peale, Dale Carnegie, and even Benjamin Franklin (Kaminer, 1993). The terminology of the earlier era may be different, but many of the same themes that appealed to readers 100 or more years ago are still found in today's self-help literature.

Thus, in one sense, there is nothing new about self-help in American culture. However, there are trends that suggest there may be something different about the current appeal of self-help.

## The Appeal of the Self-Help Movement

Over time, new and different maladies hit the bookstores and talk shows. In what Gergen (1991) called the "cycle of infirmity" (p. 15), a 20th-century trend has been for undesirable behavior to be diagnosed as a psychological disorder. The "new" disorders are discussed through a human deficit vocabulary which then shapes perceptions and attributions, all of which further establish the nature and extent of the disorder. As the new disorders (e.g., attention deficit disorder, seasonal affective disorder, and numerous addictive behaviors) become more widely referred to in the culture, it becomes more and more acceptable for individuals to be suffering from the effects of, and therefore be victimized by, the disorder. Behaviors now defined as disorders had not been diagnosed, let alone thought of, 100 or even 50 years ago. It is through the arbitrariness of cultural and political forces that they become officially recognized, and identified as dysfunctional. People with such disorders then become motivated to treat them and seek help in doing so.

*The Commodification of Self-Help.*    That so many people are consumers of self-help is clearly due in part to the marketing of the books. Along with radio, audio- and videotapes, television, and seminars, books represent an important medium for the selling of self-help. There is also a great deal of marketing done through magazines whose covers and stories inside tell about ways to do this or that, suggesting your life will be better if you follow the advice. It is not difficult to see how all of these media are mutually reinforcing. As a marketable commodity, self-help books can fulfill various needs and serve various functions in the marketplace just as other commodities do. Thus, mass marketing has been a factor in the current appeal of self-help.

In a deeper sense, however, mass marketing has not only advertised and promoted self-help, but it has instilled the values and behaviors that self-help is supposed to eradicate. One of the main effects of capitalism is modernity and the consumption of commodities in capitalistic systems tends to be based on appearances and images of use, rather than intrinsic value (Giddens, 1991). Marketing stimulates needs and desires that are processed on the individual level. Satisfying these needs is useful in maintaining one's personal autonomy. In this regard, self-help appeals to traditionally individualistic Americans who want to act autonomously in their self-interest. Yet mass-produced commodities are prepackaged, "one-size-fits-all" goods and it is only in the minds of consumers that individual preferences are evident. Furthermore, the consumption itself becomes more important than the commodity:

> To a greater or lesser degree, the project of the self becomes translated into one of possession of desired goods and the pursuit of artificially framed styles of life. The consumption of ever-novel goods becomes in some part a substitute for the genuine development of self; appearance replaces essence as the visible signs of successful consumption come actually to outweigh the use-values of the goods and services in question themselves. (Giddens, 1991, p. 198)

Authors, television producers, advertisers, editors, booksellers—all are agents in the self-help commodification process. To successfully market a commodity requires stimulating a need and delivering the product. Remaining successful requires never ultimately satisfying the need upon which its appeal is based. The delivery of self-help profits its producers far more than its receipt benefits its consumers.

Self-help offers the apparent opportunity for, and the illusion of, acquiring the means to change one's identity for the better. While consumers attempt to detach or establish independence from some condition that is interfering with their healthy selves, self-help therapy can actually substitute or add a new dependency: continued self-help. Consumers are always in the process of "becoming"; they never "become." And if consumers ever think they have "become," they are likely to be labeled as "in denial" (Kaminer, 1993, p. 26). Thus, consumers never quite satisfy their need for ongoing self-help resources, and it is extremely lucrative for self-help agents to maintain the dependence.

*Individualism Through Conformity.*   Self-help seekers are supposed to admit that there is something wrong with them, whether this be not reaching their goals in life, not being in fulfilling relationships, addictive behaviors, and so forth. Within the self-help movement, all disorders are common to everyone while being simultaneously unique to each individual. Their seriousness is not hierarchically arranged; all problems are relative. If it is a concern to you, it is important, valid, and a worthy candidate for self-help. If you disagree, you are in denial (Kaminer, 1993, p. 26).

Although it may be autonomous selves seeking help, self-help programs are most often organized through conformity (Kaminer, 1993; Simonds, 1992). Readers, support group members, seminar attendees, and so on, are urged to follow certain steps, rules, or various prescriptions. Prescriptive behaviors and attitudes are then adopted to enable the help seekers to realize a new identity, meaning that they can then be in recovery and become part of a group of "normal" or "functional" or "thriving" persons. An act of individual autonomy (choosing self-help) gets converted into a collectivist enterprise. At its best, self-help can assist people in developing a new way of seeing events and themselves; at its worst, it becomes groupthink.

What must be stressed at this point is the importance of autonomy in the context of enfranchisement in American culture. As noted earlier, autonomy is a key element in individualism. When American culture celebrates the individual, it recognizes a personal agent acting freely and intentionally out of self-interest in pursuit of self-development. These are basic tenets of autonomy and freedom (Lukes, 1973). In addition, it is assumed that individuals are performing this way because they have the capacity for autonomy. Accordingly, for acting autonomously, they receive respect as persons.

To be engaged in the self-help movement, as discussed here, is to consider oneself a victim. However, with the commodification of self-help, victimhood becomes self-perpetuating. Individuals find it easier and easier to see themselves as victims of one or another disorder, and recovery seems to be an ongoing process with no end state. Autonomous individuals are critical thinkers who plan and act intentionally with knowledge of alternatives. Self-help victims are asked to adopt someone else's plans and ways of thinking, and thus, give up their autonomy. As far as American culture is concerned, enfranchisement is significant because of the fundamental belief in self-determination. Without autonomy there is no self-determination, and without self-determination there is no enfranchisement.

## CONCLUSION

The idea of disenfranchisement implies a prior enfranchisement, which is entirely consistent with American culture. An important belief for Americans is an ideology of individualism based on autonomy and equality. Although professing strong belief in the ideology, many Americans find it convenient to overlook inconsistencies and dilemmas in putting the ideology into practice. The Constitution provides for equal rights for all citizens—not only the wealthy, or the young, or the intellectual elite, or any other class of persons. The rights are there for *all individuals*. But what is guaranteed at birth may not be available in adulthood. There is no shortage of examples, as this book's contents show, of how prior enfranchisement can be limited, and persons later become disenfranchised. Thus, the creed of individualism with its emphasis on equality and autonomy should be viewed as the ideological basis for a struggle in claiming and asserting rights. This chapter has hailed individualism as the independent, self-reliant manner with which Americans have characteristically approached life. The question, however, is whether or not individualism still dominates the American ethos.

The self-help movement represents an interesting case for considering the vitality of American individualism. In the last 35 years, Americans have been exposed increasingly to commodified self-help. However, it must be recognized that there have been authors and therapists who have genuinely helped individuals through sincere efforts, and this is not in the same category as the commodified self-help. Although discussing primarily commodified self-help, this chapter addresses the question of whether or not there are proportionately more people in the United States today using self-help than in the past.

It seems clear that traditional American individualism is showing signs of stress that could develop into major fractures. The American individual has always felt a degree of choice and control: Self-determination has been one of the foundations of American culture. Now, in the late modern or postmodern condition, a disorientation may be occurring. As Giddens

(1991) noted: "If there is one theme which unites nearly all authors who have written on the self in modern society, it is the assertion that the individual experiences feelings of powerlessness in relation to a diverse and large-scale social universe" (p. 191). If powerlessness is becoming a reality, then one of its most probable effects will be to undermine the sense of self-determination in American individualism. Perhaps this is what we witness now with the enormous numbers of persons seeking self-help, not to mention other sorts of help through private therapy, public agencies, charitable organizations, organized religion, and volunteer groups. Many of these persons are disenfranchised because they feel alienated from active participation in American society. They feel unsure of their reasoning, their mental stability, and their identities. This form of disenfranchisement is not necessarily due to an actual loss of personal, social, or political capabilities. Rather, there is a perceived sense of inadequacy, a doubting of confidence, and a confusion over who one is and what it means to be a fully functioning member of society. Instead of the traditional variety of economic, social, or political issues, identity problems may be said to be part of quality of life issues.

The gradual achievements in civil rights have made important differences for individuals and groups in America. But what can be said about persons who feel powerless because of quality of life issues? Can the political process help people reconstruct their identities? Giddens (1991) observed that the late modern era may see the beginnings of a life politics. In addition to continuing political and legal action to emancipate people, the goal of life politics is to raise political discussions to a level that will include morals. This agenda will face enormous resistance and will carry risks. But the modern condition has squelched discussions of moral implications of policy, with one important effect being problems in achieving authenticity in selfhood and constructing a viable self-identity. Constructing authentic selves is, according to Giddens, a moral issue that cannot be addressed under the traditional politics of modernity. As for American individualism, a 225-year tradition is not likely to be undone or revolutionized soon. In the United States it is still most common to think of oneself as a lone, autonomous individual. Presently, individualism is overemphasized in what Bellah et al. (1985) called radical individualism. However, with individualism existing in dialectical tension with populism (Shafer, 1991), the character pendulum only swings so far in one direction, and then starts a return, in this case to populism.

As Bell (1991) concluded, the distinguishing feature of the United States is that it has been the complete civil society, perhaps the only one in political history. By this he meant that in America, people have been placed ahead of the state. The modern era has greatly expanded the state, but there may be a return now to a more civil society with a decentralization of government and an emphasis on community and human relations. It is at the local level that individuals will address future issues in the spirit of autonomy, regaining some semblance of power in their identities and reenfranchising themselves.

# REFERENCES

Arieli, Y. (1964). *Individualism and nationalism in American ideology.* Cambridge, MA: Harvard University Press.

Bell, D. (1991). The "Hegelian" secret: Civil society and American exceptionalism. In B. E. Shafer (Ed.), *Is America different?: A new look at American exceptionalism* (pp. 46–70). Oxford, England: Clarendon.

Bellah, R. N., Madsen, R., Sullivan, W. M., Swidler, A., & Tipton, S. M. (1985). *Habits of the heart: Individualism and commitment in American life.* Berkeley: University of California Press.

Bercovitch, S. (1981). The rites of assent: Rhetoric, ritual, and the ideology of American consensus. In S. B. Girgus (Ed.), *The American self: Myth, ideology and popular culture* (pp. 5–42). Albuquerque: University of New Mexico Press.

Carbaugh, D. (1988). *Talking American: Cultural discourses on "Donahue."* Norwood, NJ: Ablex.

Gergen, K. (1991). *The saturated self: Dilemmas of identity in contemporary life.* New York: Basic Books.

Giddens, A. (1991). *Modernity and self-identity: Self and society in the late modern age.* Cambridge, England: Polity Press.

Glazer, N. (1979). Individualism and equality in the United States. In H. J. Gans, N. Glazer, J. R. Gusfield, & C. Jencks (Eds.), *On the making of Americans: Essays in honor of David Riesman* (pp. 127–142). Philadelphia: University of Pennsylvania Press.

Kaminer, W. (1993). *I'm dysfunctional, you're dysfunctional: The recovery movement and other self-help fashions.* New York: Vantage.

Lipset, S. (1991). American exceptionalism reaffirmed. In B. E. Shafer (Ed.), *Is America different?: A new look at American exceptionalism* (pp. 1–45). Oxford, England: Clarendon.

Lukes, S. (1973). *Individualism.* Oxford, England: Basil Blackwell.

Merton, R. (1957). *Social theory and social structure.* Glenco, IL: The Free Press.

Myrdal, G. (1962). *The American dilemma* (2nd ed.). New York: Harper & Row.

Riesman, D. (1961). *The lonely crowd: A study of the changing American character.* New Haven, CT: Yale University Press.

Shafer, B. E. (1991). What is the American way?: Four themes in search of their next incarnation. In B. E. Shafer (Ed.), *Is America different?: A new look at American exceptionalism* (pp. 222–261). Oxford, England: Clarendon.

Simonds, W. (1992). *Women and self-help culture: Reading between the lines.* New Brunswick, NJ: Rutgers University Press.

Starker, S. (1989). *Oracle at the supermarket: The American preoccupation with self-help books.* New Brunswick, NJ: Transaction.

Tipton, S. M. (1982). *Getting saved from the sixties.* Berkeley: University of California Press.

Tocqueville, A. de (1945). *Democracy in America.* New York: Knopf.

# 4 The Reconstruction of Identity: Strategies of the Oregon Citizens Alliance

Lynette Seccombe Eastland
*Clemson University*

*They are trying to tell us that we are not who we think we are; that we want special treatment. It isn't a matter of special rights, it's a matter of whether we have the same basic rights as everyone else in this society.*

—Anonymous Interviewee, age 34

Disenfranchisement is at the heart of the current struggle between gay men and lesbians and their opponents. The crux of the matter is very basically whether they are a disenfranchised group or a privileged one; whether the discrimination they experience has to do with "who they are" or the "bad behaviors" in which they elect to engage. It is essentially an issue of identity.

Identities, social constructionists claim, are formed through social processes and "maintained, modified, or even reshaped by social relations" (Berger & Luckmann, 1967, p. 173). Gergen (1991) talked about identity *production*. We are entering, he said, a new era of self-conception: "We bid adieu to the modernist concept of the concrete self and move into the postmodern reconstruction of self as relationship" (p. 145). As a relational construction, self is embedded in relations of power. There are, he contended, an ever increasing array of potential selves, "ersatz being." Choice, both our own and the choices of others, becomes a central element in the process. The ability to choose and the existence of more options constitutes a major threat to traditional modes of being. In fact, Gergen viewed us involved in a *war* of self-definition, for if the "other" is not who you thought they were, then you may not be who you thought you were. This "social" nature of identity is a major assumption of this chapter.

A second, but closely related assumption is that the primary medium within which identities are created and have their currency is textual. That is, "persons are largely ascribed identities according to the manner of their embedding within a discourse—in their own or in the discourse of others" (Shotter & Gergen, 1989, p. ix). Parker (1989) pointed out that the self is constructed in discourse and then "re-experienced within all the texts of everyday life" (p. 56). Cultural texts, then, furnish the resources for the formation of selves. They "lay out an array of enabling potentials, while simultaneously establishing a set of constraining boundaries beyond which selves cannot be easily made" (Shotter & Gergen, 1989, p. ix).

This war of self-definition is nowhere more evident or bitter than in the efforts of the ultraconservative and religious right to construct gay men and lesbians as "other" and thereby to distance them through discourse and law. In this chapter, I discuss several aspects of this nationwide campaign within the context of the efforts of one specific group, the Oregon Citizens Alliance (OCA). The Alliance, founded in 1986, is a family of separate organizations that share a common goal. Their statement of principles emphasizes conservative religious values and limited, constitutional government. They oppose welfare, gun control, and higher taxes, in addition to gay rights and abortion, and support "traditional family values" and the free-enterprise system. The strategies I discuss are drawn from their campaign in Oregon, but are more widely applicable because the OCA serves as a model for many such efforts.[1]

My objective is to explicate the harmful aspects of the conceptual processes and strategies at work in this campaign as they are revealed in the discourse. It is important because of the implications for the individual lives of gay men and lesbians, inasmuch as Berger and Luckmann (1967) contended that "To be given an identity involves being assigned a specific place in the world" (p. 132). In this chapter, I discuss (a) the historical, conceptual, social, and political context in which the campaign takes place, and (b) specific campaign strategies that call into question the identity of gay men and lesbians and thereby contribute to their disenfranchisement. Berger and Luckmann's concept of "conceptual liquidation" provides a framework for this examination.

In writing this chapter, I have considered OCA literature distributed to the public between 1991 and 1994,[2] the voter's pamphlet for the 1992

---

[1]One recent figure places the number of campaigns in the United States at 16, and the OCA has assisted in many of these efforts, as well as developing their own satellite organizations in Idaho and Washington.

[2]OCA literature reviewed include (beginning title words follow): "Catholic Politics," 1992; "Homosexual Bill," 1992; "Homosexuality, the Classroom," 1992; "Privacy or Promotion," 1992; "Pro-family answers," 1992; "Vote Yes," 1992; and "Why 'Gay Rights,' " 1992.

political campaign ("Vote Yes," 1992), two local town hall (open-forum) television programs aired in 1992, and two antihomosexual videotapes distributed by the OCA. The videos, titled *The Gay Agenda* and *Dangerous Behaviors: A Growing Pattern of Abuse*, were both produced by a religious group called The Report. Also taken into account are newspaper stories[3] on the campaign and interviews/discussions with key players.

## HISTORICAL CONTEXT

The current campaign can be seen within the context of the evolving re-positioning of homosexuals in relation to heterosexual society. Several dif-fering constructions of homosexuality are relevant. Prior to the 1970s, homosexuality was largely pathologized (Morin, 1977; Szasz, 1971) and therefore the boundaries between heterosexual and homosexual were clear. The same was true of the politicized construction of the 1970s and early 1980s (Freedman, Gelphi, Johnson, & Weston, 1982; Frye, 1983), which defined homosexuality as a challenge to an institutionalized heterosexual and patriarchal society. A more recent construction is what Kitzinger (1987) referred to as the liberal humanistic approach, which involves "gay affirm-ative" constructions. From this perspective homosexuality is "an alternative lifestyle, a way of loving, a sexual preference, a route to personal fulfillment or a form of self-actualization" (p. vii). Dannecker referred to the notion that gays are just the same as straights as the "dehomosexualizing of homosexuals" (in Kitzinger, 1987, p. 171). This view depoliticizes gay identity; the differences fade and the similarities are emphasized. Because it has created a more tolerant atmosphere in some quarters, liberal human-ism has resulted in what the OCA refers to as the "mainstreaming" of homosexuality. OCA founder, Lon Mabon, cited a visit to a lesbian bar on the "Roseanne" TV show and the appearance of a gay male couple in an Ikea furniture advertisement as evidence of this mainstreaming (Ruben-stein, 1994a).

Mainstreaming has certainly taken place in Oregon where increasing tolerance has seen the integration of gay men and lesbians into the political, civic, and cultural life of the state. A safer atmosphere has led to more visibility. Many openly gay businesses and cultural organizations are visible and thriving in the city, and community news is often featured on local networks and in local newspapers. An example of this is an evening news series run during the summer of 1992 on the local NBC affiliate. The series, on single social life in Portland, focused on the dating struggles of a het-

---

[3]Newspaper articles included in this chapter include Graves, 1992; Meehan, 1992a, 1992b, 1992c, 1994; Rubenstein, 1993a, 1993b, 1994; Sullivan, 1992; and Veermann, 1994.

erosexual man, a heterosexual woman, and a lesbian. Homosexuals are also visible in seeking and obtaining the same rights as other citizens. For example, in 1992 Multnomah County instituted spousal benefits for gay and lesbian employees. The state Bureau of Human Services runs ads seeking gay male and lesbian foster parents, and gay people in the state have been adopting children for a decade. To ultraconservatives these constitute "in your face" tactics.

Many see the campaign in terms of an urban–rural split. Over half the state's residents live in the area that begins with the city of Portland and extends 100 miles down the freeway to the university town of Eugene. Residents in these areas celebrate diversity and tolerance in public festivals and neighborhood activities and their liberal attitudes are reflected in voting behavior. To many rural Oregonians, Portland, with its large Asian and Russian immigrant population, racially mixed neighborhoods, and gay district, is a powerful haven of liberalism, and residents here to a great extent control state politics.

In 1988 the first OCA initiative was voted into law and overturned by then-governor Neil Goldschmidt's executive order banning discrimination based on sexual orientation, both in state employment and in the delivery of state services. The basic rallying cry of the OCA was that this granted "special rights" to homosexuals, who were *not* victims of discrimination, but had attained both prominence and visibility in the life of the state. The Oregon Court of Appeals overturned the initiative, but the conceptualization of "special" versus "basic" rights has been a major focal point of the OCA campaign ever since.

In 1992, the OCA's No Special Rights Committee sponsored a second measure, which focused on the passage of a state constitutional amendment that would equate homosexual behavior with pedophilia, sadism, and masochism, and require schools and agencies to set a standard that recognizes homosexuality as "abnormal, wrong, unnatural and perverse" ("Vote Yes," 1992, p. 93). The measure would have barred the state from extending antidiscrimination laws to homosexuals and prohibited government from "promoting, encouraging or facilitating homosexuality" ("Vote Yes," 1992). It was defeated November 3, 1992, by a vote of 57% to 43%.

The OCA immediately began to work on local ordinances in targeted Oregon towns, to work on a revised version of the measure for the next election, and to help other states organize similar efforts. Some communities adopted their own antidiscrimination decrees, but by April of 1994, 20 cities and counties had passed local measures (termed Sons of Measure 9 by the press) that prevent laws from specifically protecting gay males and lesbians from discrimination. To counter their efforts, the state legislature passed House Bill 3500, which bars enforcement of the OCA measures.

A new measure, "The Minority Status and Child Protection Act," which removes the controversial references to pedophilia and sadomasochism and focuses more on schools and what schools should teach is on the 1994 ballot. The implication of a threat to children remains intact.

## THE OCA CAMPAIGN AS A RELIGIOUS WAR

The metaphor of war is an apt one here. The campaign is clearly seen as such by both participants and observers. The OCA characterizes the campaign as "a holy war against the hordes of Satan." OCA founder, Lon Mabon, laces his language with frequent military metaphors. The OCA, he said, doesn't ". . . back off from tough fights. Our mission is to crash the barricades first. We're like the Marines, the 82nd Airborne and the cavalry. Our motivation is to get in the arena and start duking it out" (Rubenstein, 1993b, p. B4).

Not surprisingly, homosexuals see themselves as under attack: "We are under siege here in Oregon," declares a workshop moderator at a college-sponsored gender symposium, "and the attackers are not going to go away." Further allusions to the war metaphor appear in personal interaction, "I spent the whole weekend out there on the front lines," and in newspaper coverage. A series of editorials in *The Oregonian*, Oregon's largest daily, described the OCA efforts in the 1992 election as an "inquisition" and linked the measure to the "burning of heretics at the stake" (Editorial series, 1992, p. D10). The "war" has been bitter with a marked increase in hate crimes against gay men and lesbians (Rubenstein, 1994b, p. A32).

It is clearly recognized that this war is taking place at the level of language, and persuasive strategies are often explicitly discussed. Will Perkins, founder of the OCA's sister organization which spearheaded the Colorado campaign, recognized this when he said, "Language doesn't shape the campaign—it *is* the campaign" (Ingrasia, 1993, p. A1). In fact, part of the strategy is about discrediting the rhetoric of the other side. One OCA promotional piece aimed at liberals proclaims, " 'Gay Rights' Rhetoric Deceives the Public." Similarly, efforts at changing language lie at the heart of the anti-OCA effort. Rhetoricians Stewart, Smith, and Denton (1993) contended that the gay rights movement of the 1990s "is struggling to replace sexual 'preference' with sexual 'orientation,' 'special rights' with 'civil rights,' and 'agenda' with 'goals' " (p. 13).

Visibility is a central issue. Drawing attention to one's homosexuality violates an implied agreement. This issue of visibility is exemplified by the "in your face" tactics of radical groups, against which the OCA rails; but it is most threatening when the person working at the next desk "comes out" to you. The distance lessens considerably. In this context, "coming out" is seen as an aggressive act. It is clear that nothing less than invisibility is acceptable; anything more is aggressive. "Pro-family people," one hand-out maintains, "are willing to allow people the right to decide to be ho-mosexual as long as they keep it to themselves" ("Pro-Family Answers," 1992). The current campaign can be seen as an effort to both "silence" homosexuals, thereby rendering them invisible, and to restore "appropriate distance" by "rehomosexualizing" them. It does this by constructing ho-mosexuals as "the same as," but "different from" normal people. OCA strategy begins with "the same as" assumption of liberal humanism because many Oregonians already fit into this category, and focuses heavily on the "different from" aspect. Emphasizing just how different is what most of the OCA promotional literature aims at doing. This is accomplished es-sentially by repathologizing homosexuality within the conceptual universe of fundamentalist Christianity. The aim inherent in the strategies employed is not merely to distance homosexuals, but to "conceptually liquidate" them. It is a shift that attempts to at last deal with the homosexual "prob-lem," a sort of "conceptual" final solution. This is not lost on OCA opponents, who have run ads and written articles during the campaign likening the strategies of the campaign with prewar constructions of Jews in Nazi Germany (see, e.g., Quindlen, 1992).

So visibility is a vital aspect of the issues, with one group favoring the mainstream visibility of openly homosexual people and the other, outraged by that visibility, demanding their invisibility. What is lost in the debate is the fact that being visible, coming out, serves an empowering function for gay men and lesbians; and that imposed invisibility keeps them disenfran-chised and powerless. The OCA campaign is designed to restore that invisibility.

## STEPS AND STRATEGIES

Berger and Luckmann's (1967) notion of *conceptual liquidation* provides a useful framework within which to examine the OCA campaign. A part of the conceptual machinery that maintains our universe, conceptual liq-uidation operates through therapeutic processes to keep everyone within the universe in question and, through processes of nihilation, to liquidate everything outside it. Its use is particularly valuable here because it high-lights the relational aspects of self-definition, and provides a glimpse of the potential impact of the current campaign on the lives of lesbians and gay men. Taken as a whole, the OCA campaign can be seen as an effort to define homosexuals as "other," to account for that "otherness" in terms belonging to the conceptual universe of the average OCA member, and ultimately "to incorporate the deviant conceptions . . . and thereby to liquidate them ultimately" (Berger & Luckmann, 1967, p. 115). We conceptually liquidate others, Berger and Luckmann contended, when we "look upon these neighbors as less than human, congenitally befuddled about the right order of things, dwellers in a hopeless cognitive [and in this case, spiritual] darkness" (p. 115).

In this analysis, I demonstrate how the conceptual processes and strategies used by the OCA amount to conceptual liquidation and result in the continued disenfranchisement of gay men and lesbians.

Berger and Luckmann (1967) detailed the elements of conceptual liquidation, all of which can be found in the OCA's strategy. Deviations from "official" definitions of reality require a conceptual machinery to account for such deviations and to maintain the realities thus challenged. In the terms of this campaign, there must first be a body of knowledge (fundamentalist Christianity or "profamily" ideology) that includes a theory of deviance ("sin" or the changing nature of family) that is seen as constituting a threat to traditional modes of being (heterosexuality, the nuclear family). Second, there must be a theory that accounts for the deviance (having been lured into the lifestyle by others) and third, the prompt adoption of preventative measures (obliteration of diversity training, the removal of openly gay men and lesbians from educational systems, etc.). Finally, there is a conceptual system for the "cure of souls" (salvation or groups for "recovering" homosexuals), which integrates the deviants back into the accepted realms of being. I organize my discussion around these elements, which I articulate as "steps" in the conceptual process, discussing the relevant strategies that work to accomplish each step.

### Step One: The Construction of Homosexuality as "Threat"

"The appearance of an alternative symbol universe," Berger and Luckmann (1967) contended, "poses a threat because its very existence demonstrates empirically that one's own universe is less than inevitable" (p. 108). If homosexuality is a visible, legitimate alternative, then it constitutes a possible choice for normal human beings.

Much of the OCA's promotional material evidences a fear that homosexuality will get out of hand. Allusions to the biblical cities of Sodom and Gomorrah are frequent. OCA officials often claim that Measure 9 will act to stem an inevitable wave of perversion. "The state of Oregon," says one official, "will get more homosexuality and sadomasochism than they ever thought was out there" (Meehan, 1992a, p. A2).

That this fear is a prime motivator in antihomosexual campaigns is an often expressed opinion. Judith Barrington (1994), writing in *The Oregonian*, stated that the campaign "seems to assume that if we were to make the lives of gays and lesbians safe and free from discrimination, that lifestyle would be so appealing that large numbers might defect to the enemy camp" (p. D1). A similar point was also made by columnist Linda Ellerbee (1992) in regard to the question of gays in the military: "People aren't afraid of gays serving in the military. They're afraid of *gays serving with straight people* in the military . . . They are at heart, although they will not admit it, afraid homosexuality will rub off" (p. A31). The notion of "out of control" homosexuality is consistent with the nature of sin and temptation within this particular conceptual universe. If too many people give in to temptation, then we will be left with a "godless" society. L. Sheldon, founder of the Traditional Values Coalition, warned that because of homosexuality, the country is heading into a "post-Christian" era: "The churches are under attack because they are the last solid ground that holds true to the Adam and Eve narrative and not the Adam and Steve narrative" (Meehan, 1992b, p. D2).

The relational conception of self is clearly evident on both the social and personal levels. Berger and Luckmann (1967) maintained that in a collectivity that institutionalizes heterosexuality, the stubbornly homosexual individual is a candidate for therapy, "because this behavior is seen as constituting an obvious threat to the social norms and because [his] deviance is psychologically subversive to the masculinity of the majority" (p. 115). After all, Berger and Luckmann pointed out, some of them, "perhaps subconsciously, might be tempted to follow [his] example" (p. 113) or even worse "to change the old order in the image of the new" (p. 108). Although my discussion includes both lesbians and gay men, OCA printed material and videos focus most heavily on men because the "threat" is, to a great degree, perceived to be to conceptions of masculinity.

Some theorists draw a connection between discrimination against homosexuals and discrimination against women. Prejudice against homosexuality, Kitzinger (1987) claimed, "is caused by fear of blurring gender divisions" (p. 158). A threat of homosexuality is that it turns men into women—and thereby blurs the category. Men are only "real" men when they can see women as the other. Gergen (1991) also emphasized this in his relational view of identity: "The homosexual challenges a second critical criterion for determining gender: sexual preference. Precisely who one is, the culture is informed, cannot be determined by the object of one's attraction" (p. 144).

## Step Two: The Construction of Pathology

Threats to one's conceptual universe call for the construction of a conceptual machinery to keep actual or potential deviants within the institutionalized definitions of reality, or, in other words, "to prevent the inhabitants of a given universe from 'emigrating' " (Berger & Luckmann, 1967, p. 112). This conceptual machinery sets deviants apart from "normal" people by constructing their behavior as "pathological" in relation to a particular body of knowledge, in this case, ultraconservative Christianity.

Different aspects of OCA strategy emphasize that homosexuals are "the same as," but also "different from" other "normal" people. This apparent opposition is essential to locate the pathology, not in identity, but in behavior. Within their universe, human beings are created equal, but capable of sinful behavior. A person cannot "be" sin, but can indeed "commit" sin. As a consequence, a major thrust of the campaign is in efforts at constructing homosexuality as a *behavior* rather than an identity, and then in labeling the behavior as sinful (pathological). Constructing gays as just the same as straights reduces homosexuality to a simple behavioral choice. Within that universe, it could not be otherwise. Thus, the homosexual is defined in OCA literature as:

> A person who defines himself by his preference for sexual relations with a person or persons of the same gender. There are no other defining characteristics of a homosexual besides his choice of sexual behavior. The fact that many thousands of homosexuals have successfully left the lifestyle is proof that homosexuals can and do change. ("Pro-Family Answers," 1992)

What makes this particular construction harmful is the association of deviance with sinfulness and eternal damnation. Buying into it from the perspective of gay men and lesbians requires a denial of one's identity (inasmuch as homosexuals tend to believe they were "born that way"), and a labeling of one's personal affectional and sexual feelings as "sinful." For the homosexual who relates to this body of knowledge, this accomplishes a sense that she or he *is* sin. A second harmful aspect of this construction is the contradiction between theory and practice, between the OCA's campaign rhetoric and the way many of their supporters "talk" about, or to, homosexuals. "Pro-family people do not hate homosexuals," one handout proclaims, "in most cases the opposite is true. Pro-family people have compassion for people they believe trapped in a dysfunctional lifestyle" ("Pro-Family Answers," 1992). Yet, on the "battle front," encounters between the two groups are often hostile and tense. In talking to reporters, one OCA supporter revealed, "Well, they're no better than animals, are they?"

Some researchers, Kitzinger (1987) claimed, have equated "moral disapproval" of homosexuality based on religious objections with "disgust." The most extreme expressions of disapproval, she suggested, come not from mainstream Christians, who place an "emphasis on repentance, compassion, forgiveness," but from fundamentalist evangelical Christians, who discuss homosexuality in terms of "demonic activity" or "dark forces" (p. 176).

Constructing homosexual behavior as a matter of choice, rather than a matter of being, legitimizes the attempt to have homosexuality declared "abnormal and perverse," and to equate homosexual behavior with behaviors already regarded as pathological (such as pedophilia and sadism). This type of construction accomplishes two purposes. First, it renders the politicized aspects of gay male and lesbian identity harmless. Kitzinger (1987) pointed out that the use of disease terms to characterize socially and politically deviant behaviors functions as a powerful form of social control that "serves to invalidate and depoliticize incipient challenges to the dominant version of realty" and to "punish and control those who fail to conform to the dominant group's expectations" (p. 32).[4]

Second, because it denies identity, it isolates gay men and lesbians from their most probable allies and reference groups—racial and ethnic minorities and liberals—by suggesting that gay men and lesbians are a group defined by what they do rather than who they are, and are therefore seeking "special" as opposed to "basic" rights. This is reflected in the primary slogan of the 1992 campaign, which emphasized the "same as, yet different from" contention. "No Special Rights" (or "Equal Rights for All, Special Rights for None") is both a rallying cry and the name of the organized arm of the OCA that conducted the campaign (The No Special Rights Committee). This slogan creates what Stewart et al. (1994) referred to as a "blindering" effect by preventing audiences from considering alternative ways of thinking.

"Legitimate" minority groups, the OCA maintains, are "born" into their minority status and have suffered historically accepted evidences of discrimination, such as being denied the right to vote, being subjected to official segregation, being denied access by law to businesses, and suffering verifiable economic hardship. On the other hand, homosexuals are a very powerful special interest group that represents itself as a discriminated minority. Granting civil rights protection to them would be like "granting affirmative action quotas to celibates or polygamists just because they claimed to be born that way" ("Pro-Family Answers," 1992).

Although this strategy has cut off some minority support, most ethnic minority groups have rejected the argument. Virtually all African-American civil rights groups in the area came out in opposition to the measure and NAACP president, L. Richardson, warned African Americans that they were "being programmed to be used."

---

[4]This would include, for example, the characterization of menopause as a deficiency disease (McCrea, 1983), the pathology of "masturbatory insanity" (Szasz, 1980), "reformist delusions" (a Soviet diagnostic category discussed by Stone & Faberman, 1981), and "state benefit neurosis," an illness characterized by refusing to take poorly paid employment when more money is available through state benefits (Price, 1972).

Finally, the portrayal of homosexuals as a wealthy, privileged group serves up homosexuals as an economic scapegoat, alienating them from just about everyone else. "The average homosexual," the OCA contends, "has an income 70% higher than the average American and 49% of homosexuals hold professional or management positions" ("Pro-Family Answers," 1992). The "different than" construction isolates the group and significantly reduces the forces that must be dealt with in this war of identity.

### Step Three: The Construction of a Militant Homosexual Agenda

The deviant, Berger and Luckmann (1967) contended, "stands as a living insult to 'normal [men],' so there must be a theory, a 'pathology' that accounts for this shocking condition" (p. 113). Thus, the next step to conceptual liquidation is the construction of an explanation for homosexuality. The OCA finds this in their belief that homosexuals "recruit" others through both promotional efforts and personal pressure tactics. Clearly important here is the construction of "intent." This is accomplished through the creation of a homosexual agenda, which has as two of its purposes (a) the seduction of children into the homosexual lifestyle, and (b) the right to display extreme sexual practices publicly, including sadomasochism and pedophilia. This agenda, the OCA contends, has as its aim the creation of an army of converts. "Conversion" is a concept with which many OCA members can relate, because it is a reflection of their own methods for the growth of fundamental Christianity—the conversion of sinners. "Militant homosexuals are trying to force *their* perverse behavior on everyone else," the OCA claims, "it is not that we are trying to force our Christian beliefs on everyone else." In fact, the OCA contends, the campaign is simply "a response" to this militant agenda. Although it is not explicitly mentioned, addiction is an underlying metaphor in this construction. Like drugs, once tried, homosexual behavior is irresistible, but can be overcome with perseverance. Thus, homosexuals are the equivalent of "pushers," ever vigilant in their efforts to "hook" the potential young addict. This plays on the fears parents already have in regard to drugs.

The effort at recruitment is centered, the OCA maintains, in the public school system, and school administrators are seen as willing accomplices. AIDS education efforts, homosexual teachers, and programs aimed at helping gay youths are all targeted in OCA literature. The fact that most AIDS education is done by gay organizations is not lost on the OCA, who targets these organizations as primary recruiters of young people. Copies of handouts designed by AIDS organizations for the use of gay men, and containing explicit suggestions for "Great and Healthy Sex," are sent out with OCA literature. A handwritten note suggests that the flyer is distributed in elementary schools: "We don't find this appropriate for kindergarten through grammar school. Do you? I don't think so."

OCA promotional literature often lifts gay materials and behaviors out of the context in which they occur, presents them as representative, and then correlates them with efforts to endanger children. The most controversial instance of this is the use by the Alliance of the North American Man/Boy Love Association (NAMBLA). This organization is well-suited to the purposes of the constructed agenda in that it enables the OCA to make the jump from one "deviant" behavior (homosexuality) to another (pedophilia). That it is frequently cited as "representative" of the gay community causes much distress because most lesbians and gay men strongly disapprove of the organization. In OCA videos, this and other extremist groups are the focus of selected cuts from a San Francisco Gay Pride Parade. Cuts focusing on the NAMBLA contingency, as well as other politically unpopular groups, are juxtaposed with other scenes from the parade, which include crying children being carried or wheeled along by an adult.

Isolated quotes from protest rhetoric are used frequently as evidence of a carefully constructed and heavily financed homosexual agenda. One example is the use of "The Overhauling of Straight America," an article written by and for homosexuals that suggests strategies for desensitizing the American public to gays and gay rights. The article by Kirk and Pill, appearing in the now-defunct *Guide Magazine*, was published in 1987. The OCA interpreted the intent of this article to be the training of an actual army of militant gays supposedly already organized and ready to march. A few quotes are used to support specific OCA contentions. Other quotes, such as "people helping instead of hating, that's what America is all about" (p. 12) are omitted. A similar instance is the use of *The Homosexual Agenda* by Michael Swift. The piece, first published in the *Gay Community News* and reprinted in *The Congressional Record*, begins with a self-definition: "This essay is outre (passing the bounds of what is usual or proper), madness, a tragic, cruel fantasy, an eruption of inner rage, on how the oppressed desperately dream of being the oppressor."

The more sensational parts of the essay were picked up by the Concerned Women of America and quoted in advertisements they sponsored and in interviews with the press. One oft-used quote included this excerpt: "All laws banning homosexual activity will be revoked. All churches who condemn us will be closed. Our only gods are handsome young men."

In part, the OCA campaign can be regarded as a response to "gay style," particularly the "in your face" political techniques often employed as a means of protest and empowerment. The key here is visibility. Some tactics cannot be ignored. They command attention by their very outrageousness and they empower by making disenfranchised groups very visible. Groups, such as Queer Nation and Act-Up, believe that ". . . behaving well doesn't always work. We don't ask for attention; we demand it. Most gay and lesbian groups use straight lobbying techniques and dress in suits. We do it our way and use Queer culture, which includes camp and drag and all-out street fighting."

At a speech given by the OCA Communication Director, 100 Queer Nation supporters showed up wearing hot-pink gags, and others laughed, hissed, and held up signs reading "Shame" and "He's lying." These kinds of tactics signal a willingness on the part of those constructed as "deviant" to flaunt their deviance, rather than try to hide it, rendering them more visible and hence, from the OCA perspective much more dangerous. The OCA focuses heavily on such outrageous tactics and uses them to bolster their creation of a political and social agenda and to justify their campaign as a simple response to a militant homosexual agenda.

Conceptualizing homosexuals as an enemy of the family and a particular danger to children allows the OCA to call for the prompt adoption of preventative measures. That children are being pressured into homosexuality is a recurring theme in the campaign. Richard Weller, a "cured" homosexual and OCA spokesperson contends, "Fatherless children are being bought with drugs and money. They're being told they were born that way. I believe that boys with good, sober, loving and supportive fathers won't be victimized so easily" (Lydgate, 1994, p. 16). This contention is so crucial to the campaign that the new statewide initiative is named "The Minority Status and Child Protection Act." It calls for the adoption of programs that explicitly teach the dangers of homosexual behavior. Recruitment, the OCA contends, is not just sexual but includes "homopromo," everything that makes homosexuality visible and therefore an option. Diversity seminars, AIDS education, and books that portray homosexuals as normal people all qualify as recruitment.

### Step Four: The Construction of a Cure for Sick Souls

The final step of conceptual liquidation is the development of a conceptual system for the "cure of souls" (Berger & Luckmann, 1967, p. 113), the goal of which is "to incorporate the deviant concept within one's own universe and thereby to liquidate them ultimately" (p. 115). This is evident in "the ultimate OCA strategy," the cure of homosexuality (Lydgate, 1994, p. 14). This strategy is accomplished through the voices of "ultimate authorities"—several exhomosexual crusaders. Although the notion of the "cured" homosexual appeared early in the campaign with the inclusion of a cured homosexual in the video, *The Gay Agenda* (Report, 1992), it was not adopted as an organized aspect of the campaign until 1994. The use of this strategy is characterized as a significant shift that relies on more sophisticated understandings of the importance of the biology/behavior factor to most heterosexuals. It reinforces efforts to construct a theory that accounts for homosexuality as a behavioral choice, and it works hand-in-hand with the notion of "runaway homosexuality." Lydgate (1994) put it this way:

> By advertising that gay men and lesbians can escape, it also suggests something more sinister—that heterosexuals can get "trapped." If that is true, you could go the other way, from being heterosexual to being homosexual. So much of the OCA's work is based on the fear people have that homosexuals are going to recruit them. (p. 16)

The incorporation that is the goal here is accomplished through "therapy," which Berger and Luckmann (1967) assumed exists in some form whenever societies face the danger of individual deviance. Specific institutional arrangements may vary from psychoanalysis to exorcism. In this case the therapizing force is characterized by Lydgate (1994) as "a new gospel of 'personal salvation,' the resistance of 'ungodly' feelings and influences; and the preacher is an ex-homosexual" (p. 15).

In January of 1994, Project HOPE (Help One Person Escape) was instituted by the OCA to assist in perpetuating and reinforcing this "new gospel." A support group for gays and lesbians who want to escape their "lifestyle," HOPE provides an avenue for the deviant to integrate into the conceptual universe of the ultraconservative and to thereby become invisible. Interestingly, the metaphor of addiction emerges again in this notion of the "recovering" homosexual. In fact, one such recovery group sponsored by the Catholic Church, Courage, is based on the 12 steps of Alcoholics Anonymous. Comparing homosexuality to alcoholism is a popular technique of the OCA, which local newspapers attribute to the personal problems with alcohol and drugs experienced by the OCA's two founders. One exhomosexual likened his experience to "that of a drunk who gives up his booze": "To people who have forsaken their vices in their quest for born-again spiritual purity, homosexuality fits neatly into a litany of sins that includes alcoholism, gambling and drug abuse." Many exhomosexual crusaders have similar stories beginning with child abuse or teenage experiences with same-gender partners. All of them are men. The story of one such crusader was chronicled by Lydgate (1994):

> Weller's story is certainly chilling. He was just 17 when he had his first homosexual encounter . . . One out of nine children from a troubled family in Kelso, Wash., Weller was naive: He agreed to spend the night at the man's house. As he describes the scene, his hands tremble . . . He stayed with an older man for nine years because, he says, "I needed a daddy" . . . Suffering

bouts of depression, he became suicidal and wound up in the hospital after trying to kill himself . . . Time and time again, he repeats the phrase "good-sober-loving-and-supportive-father," stringing the words together like the names of partners in a law firm. (p. 17)

Weller's story reinforces that aspect of the constructed agenda, which casts children and young adults as victims of homosexual predators. Many of the OCA's exhomosexual crusaders have similar stories, and their real passion is saving young boys from the attentions of older homosexual men.

Although Project HOPE has drawn only a few participants, and no practicing gays or lesbians, it is symbolically very significant. Its existence shores up the concerns of those voters who might support the campaign, but have "some nagging doubts about fairness" (Lydgate, 1994, p. 18). Furthermore, it reinforces the existence of options for doing otherwise that legitimizes the efforts of the OCA in the first place.

## CONCLUSION

Not surprisingly, the strategy used by the OCA emerges from their own conceptual universe and projects onto homosexuals as a group similar intents and methods. Homosexuals, as well as conservative Christians, seek out the uninitiated, and work to convert them to their way of thinking. The distinction, however, is very clear. Christians work to convert others for "pure," righteous motives, whereas homosexuals do it to "satisfy" their own lust and gain for themselves an army of converts. Because within their own universe recruitment is a strategy that accomplishes community, it seems reasonable to them to assume that this is how others go about building community.

The effects of the campaign on gay men and lesbians can be assessed on both the community and the individual level. In some respects, the community has been empowered. In fact, Rubenstein (1994a) noted that "Oregon's gay and lesbian activists have forged one of the country's strongest political alliances" (p. A1). Strong connections have been made between the gay community and the African-American, Jewish, and mainstream Christian communities. Heterosexuals and homosexuals have come together to "fight" the OCA. During the campaign, many heterosexuals wore buttons that proclaimed them to be "straight, but not narrow." "The ballot measure," Rubenstein suggested, "mobilized those favoring gay rights in a way they never would have done on their own" (p. D4).

On the individual level, however, the effects have not been as positive. Antigay violence has increased 22% as has the severity of the crimes. Churches and offices of groups opposing the OCA have been vandalized.

The most devastating effects have been emotional. The community is developing its own "war stories." Stress-related disease has increased dramatically among gay men and lesbians and their supporters. "You're having an entire state discussing whether your humanity is as high as someone else's. It really grinds you down, whether you're way out there or locked in your closet" (Gallagher, 1993, p. 38).

Lakoff and Johnson (1980) discussed conceptual systems as metaphorical. We experience things in terms of the way we think about them. The OCA campaign and others like it are clearly being experienced as they are conceptualized—as war. "We are exhausted and stressed out. We're in an emotional Sarajevo" (Gallagher, 1993, p. 37). Gergen's (1991) war of self-definition is not necessarily one that is either lost or won. Definitions of identity are continually in flux, and disenfranchised groups may find their fight an ongoing battle.

# REFERENCES

Barrington, J. (1994, October 27). What is the homosexual agenda. *The Oregonian*, pp. D1, D12.

Berger, P., & Luckmann, T. (1967). *The social construction of reality*. New York: Anchor.

*Catholic politics and measure 9*. (1992). OCA promotional tabloid.

Editorial Series. (1992, October 29–November 4). Oregon's Inquisition I-XII. *The Oregonian*, p. D1.

Ellerbee, L. (1992, December 1). Hey, gays can kill people, too. *The Oregonian*, p. D5.

Freedman, E., Gelphi, B., Johnson, S., & Weston, K. (1982). *The lesbian issue: Essays from signs*. Chicago: University of Chicago Press.

Frye, M. (1983). *The politics of reality: Essays in feminist theory*. New York: The Crossing Press.

Gallagher, J. (1993, January). The rise of fascism in America. *The Advocate*, pp. 37–43.

Gergen, K. (1991). *The saturated self: Dilemmas of identity in contemporary life*. New York: Basic Books.

Graves, B. (1992, October 25). Founder says Project 10 tries to help gay teenagers. *The Oregonian*, p. D8.

*Homosexual bill threatens family values*. (1992). OCA promotional tabloid.

*Homosexuality, the classroom, and your children*. (1992). OCA promotional tabloid. (Available from NSR-PAC, P.O. Box 407, Wilsonville, OR)

Ingrasia, L. (1993, May 3). Fighting words. *The Wall Street Journal*, p. A1.

Kirk, M., & Pill, E. (1987, November). The overhauling of straight America. *Guide Magazine*, pp. 7–14.

Kitzinger, C. (1987). *The social construction of lesbianism*. London: Sage.

Lakoff, G., & Johnson, M. (1980). *Metaphors we live by*. Chicago: University of Chicago Press.

Lydgate, C. (1994, March 16). Queer cure. *Willamette Week*, pp. 14–18.

McCrea, F. B. (1983). The politics of menopause: The discovery of deficiency disease. *Social Problems, 31*, 111–123.

Meehan, B. (1992a, October 8). Scholars dispute accuracy of OCA's anti-gay video. *The Oregonian*, pp. A1–A2, A16–A17.

Meehan, B. (1992b, October 25). Founder of traditional values coalition appears for Measure 9. *The Oregonian*, p. D2.

Meehan, B. (1992c, November 1). The question: What is 9's fate? *The Oregonian*, pp. A1, A31.

Meehan, B. (1994, October 25). Measure 9 produces heated "town hall" debate. *The Oregonian*, p. D3.

Morin, S. F. (1977). Heterosexual bias in psychological research on lesbianism and male homosexuality. *The American Psychologist, 19*, 629–637.

Parker, I. (1989). Discourse and power. In J. Shotter & K. Gergen (Eds.), *Tests of identity* (pp. 56–69). London: Sage.

Price, J. H. (1972). *Psychiatric investigations*. London: Butterworth.

*Privacy or promotion: Gay rights rhetoric deceives the public*. (1992). OCA promotional tabloid.

*Pro-family answers to pro-gay questions*. (1992). OCA promotional tabloid.

Quindlen, A. (1992, October 29). In Oregon, bigotry will be on the ballot. *The Oregonian*, p. B2.

The Report (Producer). (1992). *The gay agenda* [Video]. (Available from "The Report," 42640 N. 10th St. West, Lancaster, CA 93534)

Rubenstein, S. (1993a, June 20). Increasingly, Christian right becomes a power in politics. *The Oregonian*, pp. A1, A22–A23.

Rubenstein, S. (1993b, June 21). OCA's rise meteoric since start-up in 1986. *The Oregonian*, pp. B1, B4.

Rubenstein, S. (1994a, April 11). Gays in politics: Uncommon clout. *The Oregonian*, p. A1.

Rubenstein, S. (1994b, November 1). Hate crimes increase in Northwest. *The Oregonian*, p. A32.

Shotter, J., & Gergen, K. (Eds.). (1989). *Texts of identity*. London: Sage.

Stewart, C., Smith, C., & Denton, R. (1993). *Persuasion and social movements*. Prospect Heights, IL: Waveland.

Stone, G. P., & Faberman, H. A. (1981). *Social psychology through symbolic interaction* (2nd ed.). Chichester, England: Wiley.

Sullivan, R. (1992, November 9). Postcard from Oregon: Revolution number 9. *The New Yorker*, pp. 67–79.

Szasz, T. (1971) *The manufacture of madness*. London: Routledge & Kegan Paul.

Szasz, T. (1980). *Sex: Facts, frauds and follies*. Oxford, England: Basil Blackwell.

Veermann, G. (1994, October 29). Measured words: A top Clinton aide discusses Measure 9 and the politics of AIDS. *Willamette Week*, p. 14.

*Vote yes on measure 9*. (1992). Oregon Citizens Alliance promotional tabloid.

Why "gay rights" are NOT civil rights. (1992). OCA promotional tabloid.

# PART II

# ISSUES RELATED TO SOCIOECONOMIC STATUS

# 5 Gimme Shelter: The Communication of America's Homeless

Katherine Miller
*University of Kansas*

> *Up close and in context, [the homeless] are remarkably like most of us in their basic needs, their dreams and desires, their interpersonal strategies, and their proclivity to account for their situation in a fashion that attempts to salvage the self. There are differences, to be sure, but . . . in most instances, these differences . . . are rooted in the profoundly dismal situation in which the homeless find themselves. Confronted with a similar set of circumstances, the behaviors, cognitions, and faces of most citizens would, no doubt, be much the same.*
> —Snow & Anderson (1993, pp. 314–315)

For many years, students in communication and other social science disciplines have been introduced early on to Abraham Maslow's (1943) hierarchy of needs theory. We learn that, according to Maslow, humans have a set of needs ranging from basic physiological and safety needs through "higher order" needs such as affiliation, esteem, and self-actualization. We also learn that these needs are arranged in a "hierarchy of prepotency" such that lower order needs such as food and shelter must be satisfied before an individual can move on to the satisfaction of the higher order needs. Although empirical research has not been highly supportive of the details of Maslow's theory (see, e.g., Miner, 1980), the basic gist of the hierarchy of needs rings true for both academics and the general public.

Homeless people in America today serve both as confirmation and disconfirmation of Maslow's theory. In our interactions with and studies of the homeless, we find that basic needs such as food and shelter are, indeed, driving forces that can leave devastation if withdrawn. However, we also learn that these lower order needs are not all-consuming. The homeless in America, struggling to meet basic needs for sustenance and protection from the elements, also strive to fulfill higher order needs of affiliation and esteem. Their messages serve as an attempt to shape lives that make sense both at an individual level and in connection to others.

In this chapter, I consider communication and homeless people primarily from the perspective of homeless individuals. In the first few sections, I build a framework for understanding homelessness by providing a historical backdrop, discussing the nature of America's homeless population, and considering several positions regarding the causes of homelessness. Then, I discuss the communication of homeless people at a variety of levels. I begin with a look at communication as a social process through which the homeless create and maintain an identity on the street. I then consider the social networks of homeless people both on the street and with family and friends off the street. Then, I review findings regarding homeless people's communication with service providers and with domiciled "citizens" within the community.

## UNDERSTANDING HOMELESSNESS

### Historical Backdrop

According to Baum and Burnes (1993), "homelessness has always been part of the American social experience. The homeless were the rejects of the colonies, the rugged explorers of the frontier, the tragic wreckage of the Civil War, the hoboes, tramps, and bums of the late nineteenth century, the denizens of the skid rows, . . . the products of the depression" (p. 107). As the preceding quotation elaborates, homelessness is clearly not a new phenomenon on the American scene. Rather, the homeless have been with us "ever since war and famine have occurred" (Handler, 1992, p. 35). In America, the first homeless were probably individuals who opted for the colonies over European jail. Since then, the American homeless population has at various times swelled as a result of industrialization, urbanization, the exploration of the frontier, war, and economic downturns. Throughout our history, there have also been various "types" of homeless people. For example, in the late 19th century, the traveling homeless who worked as itinerant ranchers, miners, or farmers were known as hobos. The traveling homeless who survived by panhandling and stealing were known as tramps. When these travelers settled in urban areas, they became the bums of skid row.

Throughout history, however, a distinction between the "deserving" and "undeserving" poor has served as a guidepost for social policy regarding the homeless. In the 18th and 19th centuries, this distinction was made between "poverty" and "pauperism." As Katz (1986), quoting an analysis written in 1834, wrote:

> Poverty resulted not from "our faults" but from "our misfortunes," and the poor should "claim our tenderest commiseration, our most liberal relief." But pauperism was a different story. "Pauperism is the consequence of willful error, of shameful indolence, of vicious habits. It is a misery of human creation, the pernicious work of man, the lamentable consequence of bad principles and morals." Relief to the poor was charity; relief to paupers increased "the evil in a tenfold degree." (p. 19)

During the 20th century, social programs arose to help deal with America's poor. Two of the earliest programs to arise were Aid to the Blind and Aid to Dependent Children (now called Aid to Families with Dependent Children). As Handler (1992) pointed out, these two programs illustrate the distinction that was typically made between programs for the "deserving" and "undeserving" poor. The blind were regarded as clearly "deserving"—there was nothing they could do to change the objective fact of blindness, and aid for this category of individuals was routine and automatic. In contrast, poor families were less clearly "deserving." Hence, Aid to Dependent Children included much stricter eligibility requirements and more discretion was provided to local authorities in providing benefits. Today, the general relief program in the United States is the clearest example of welfare provided for what many consider the "undeserving" poor.

Thus, throughout America's history, there has been a homeless population that has swelled and contracted with economic and historical events. Many scholars, however, argue that the homeless of today are qualitatively different from the homeless of the past. The "new homeless" of the 1980s and 1990s have been created as the safety net of state and federal social programs has frayed. However, the realization that homelessness persists in the United States has sometimes been met with resistance by the general public and policymakers. As Barak (1991) noted, "[e]arly on in the Reagan administration, when catsup was being counted as a vegetable in school children's lunches, there was an effort to dismiss the problem of homelessness, followed by efforts to minimize the size of the homeless population, and finally by the reluctant admissions that something should be done about the problem" (p. 25). Thus, today, policymakers and the general public are just beginning to come to grips with the implications of the "new homeless" population. In the next two sections of this chapter, I discuss the nature of homelessness in today's America by considering both who the homeless are and the constellation of causes that account for their situation.

## Who Are the Homeless in America?

In identifying the homeless population in America, a first logical step is to define the size of that population. How many people in America are homeless? This seemingly simple question has turned out to be extremely difficult to answer. Much of this difficulty is methodological in nature as there are few good ways to "count" the homeless (see Jencks, 1994). Individuals in shelters can be accounted for, but many homeless people do not use shelter services. And if a researcher attempts to do a count of the homeless at any given time, there are the dangers of missing people, counting twice, misestimating the vagaries of seasonal variations, and so on. The operational picture gets even cloudier if the researcher attempts to estimate the "near homeless," individuals who are just a paycheck away from the street. These methodological difficulties undoubtedly account for the large discrepancies in estimates of the homeless population in the United States. As Barak (1991) noted, estimates range from a low of about 300,000 with high estimates coming in at close to 3 million. Despite this inexactness, however, the recent trends regarding the number of homeless are clear. Homelessness in America increased substantially during the 1980s (Jencks, 1994). And, although improved employment may have abated the increase to some extent, there is little evidence that a substantial decline in the homeless population is occurring.

The composition of the homeless population today is somewhat at odds with the classical stereotypes of skid row bums and traveling vagrants (see Morse, 1992). The new homeless of the late 20th century are more likely to include women, children, and intact families. The new homeless tend to be younger and better educated than the homeless of the past. The new homeless are substantially poorer than their counterparts from earlier decades. The new homeless reside not just in large cities, but in suburban and rural areas as well. The new homeless represent the varied racial and ethnic backgrounds of America—they are White, African American, Hispanic, Asian, and Native American. But the new homeless are in some ways similar to the old homeless—many are single White men, many are suffering from alcoholism, drug addiction, or mental illness. In short, the homeless population in America today is a heterogeneous one. In spite of their heterogeneity, however, they are joined by their lack of consistent shelter and by other factors that have led to homelessness. These factors are considered in the next section of this chapter.

## Causes of Homelessness

The most proximate cause of homelessness is a lack of shelter, and this lack of shelter can almost always be traced to the gap between the cost of housing and the economic resources of the individual seeking housing. In other words, as Blau (1987) noted, "[p]overty has always been the first cause of homelessness" (p. 143). In most analyses, however, an attempt is made to go beyond this most proximate cause to uncover underlying factors that lead to life on the streets. In this vein, two general classes of factors are often proposed to account for homelessness in America.

The first set of factors, generally favored by conservative observers of the social scene, centers on the individual characteristics of homeless people. This does not suggest that these observers would all agree with Ronald Reagan's assessment that "the homeless are homeless, you might say, by choice" (Bassuk, 1984). However, as Barak (1991) noted, "conservative accounts of the homeless have tended to blame the victim for homelessness and to identify the homeless person as someone suffering from some kind of impaired capacity" (p. 54). The most often-cited individual causes of homelessness are alcoholism, poor physical health, mental illness, and defective personalities (see Morse, 1992, for review). Indeed, one critical account of current homelessness policy maintains that over 85% of the homeless suffer from some combination of alcoholism, drug addiction, and mental illness (Baum & Burnes, 1993), though most commentators would put the figure as significantly lower (e.g., Burt & Cohen, 1989).

A second class of explanatory factors is favored by liberal commentators. These observers believe that homelessness can be traced to structural explanations. That is, individuals are homeless not because of any inherent defect, but because of flaws in the economic and social systems that surround them. Coons (1987) enumerated many of these structural causes of homelessness: "drastic cuts in federal housing programs and social services, housing policies that encourage urban renewal and 'gentrification' without creating low-cost replacement housing, unemployment, the deinstitutionalization of mental patients without provision of much-needed community mental health services, and the breakdown of traditionally supportive social structures such as the family and community" (p. 5).

The truth regarding the cause of homelessness is probably to be found in an interaction between these two classes of factors. First, although individual characteristics such as alcoholism, drug abuse, and mental illness may not always precipitate a fall into homelessness, these illnesses and behavioral patterns may be the result of homelessness. Second, it is probable that individuals most likely to land on the street are those whose personal characteristics do not facilitate coping with the vagaries of the system that confronts them. As Redburn and Buss (1986) argued, "[m]ost people become homeless not as a result of a single catastrophic event, but at the end of a series of misfortunes . . . Their present condition reflects not only their inability to earn income by working, but also a social welfare system that provides haphazard and often inadequate coverage of those unable to support themselves" (p. 77). Finally, some critical scholars (e.g., Barak, 1991) are now arguing that an analysis of homelessness should transcend both the conservative explanation of individual differences and the liberal explanation of a flawed social system. Barak asserted that our attention should instead be directed to the distribution of power and the prevailing contradictions of postindustrial society.

## COMMUNICATION OF HOMELESS PEOPLE

### Creating Identity on the Street

One of the most fundamental functions of communication is the creation and maintenance of social reality and personal identity (Berger & Luckmann, 1966). Our traditional research in health communication has viewed interaction in a largely instrumental sense. That is, we communicate with others in order to accomplish health. However, a recent critique by Zook (1994) suggests that such an approach overlooks the important ontological functions of health communication. Zook argued that communication serves not just to manage health, but also to define health and to define ourselves as healthy or not healthy (see Mokros & Deetz, chap. 2 of this volume, for an in-depth discussion of this issue). The same argument can be made with regard to homeless people (see Snow & Anderson, 1987). That is, one of the primary functions of communication for these individuals is to define who they are and define what it means to be homeless.

A number of recent ethnographies have investigated the talk of homeless individuals, and through these ethnographies we get a glimpse of how the homeless in America define themselves through interaction. One of the most complete accounts of this process was presented by Snow and Anderson (1993). These scholars conducted a long-term ethnographic study of homeless street life in Austin, Texas, during the mid-1980s. The stories and conversations of their informants on the street created a revealing tapestry of how street people "salvage the self" through interaction. Snow and Anderson first noted that many homeless people invoke their own causal explanations for how they landed on the street. These accounts, summarized by the sayings, "I'm down on my luck," "I've paid my dues," and "What goes around comes around," create an identity that to a large extent exempts them from personal responsibility for homelessness and also holds the door open for a positive change in circumstances.

Further, Snow and Anderson (1993) noted that different types of homeless individuals use different types of identity statements. For example, these researchers found that people who had been homeless for a long period of time often embraced their identity through self-labeling and identification with roles such as "expert dumpster diver." In contrast, individuals who were new to the streets often attempted to distance themselves from individuals, roles, and institutions associated with street life. For example, one informant, talking about the clientele at the Salvation Army ("the Sally") explained: "I'm not like the other guys who hang out down at the Sally. If you want to know about street people, I can tell you about them; but you can't really learn about street people from studying me, because I'm different" (Snow & Anderson, 1993, p. 215).

Other ethnographic studies of the homeless have also described the ways in which identity is constructed through labeling and stories. Liebow's (1993) ethnographic account of women in an emergency shelter recounts the ways in which women use religion and each other in order to construct a day-to-day identity that is bearable. Walsh's (1992) interviews with children in a homeless shelter also provides poignant accounts of how children used interaction to understand the past and construct the future in order to make sense of situations that were largely beyond their control.

### Social Networks on the Street

The traditional view of homeless people depicts them as isolated from the general public and from each other. The stereotypical homeless person stands alone on a street corner or pushes a loaded shopping cart through the park in search of a solitary bench. This view of homeless people as "fundamentally detached from social life" (Levinson, 1963, p. 596) has been debunked by recent investigations of social ties among homeless people. For example, LaGory, Ritchey, and Fitzpatrick (1991) and Cohen and Sokolovsky (1981) used relatively sophisticated techniques to investigate the social ties of the homeless and found that these individuals are far from isolated. However, the nature of social ties among the homeless tend to be different from the ties of the domiciled in a number of important respects.

First, the social ties of the homeless are often contradictory in nature. As Snow and Anderson (1993) noted, "[q]uick and easy conviviality and an ethos supporting the sharing of modest resources are counterbalanced by chronic distrust of peers and fragility and impermanence of social bonds" (p. 194). That is, in the parlance of social network analysis, the homeless tend to have a great many weak ties and very few strong ties (Granovetter, 1973). Indeed, Snow and Anderson found that though their informants regarded many individuals as friends or even "close friends" they often did not even know these acquaintances' last names. The transitory nature of the bonds of the homeless suggests that they can provide support that is accommodative but not curative. As LaGory et al. (1991) noted, though these "social ties yield a sense of personal efficacy, they cannot resolve the severe impoverishment of homelessness" (p. 213).

Second, the social networks of the homeless vary a great deal with individuals' amount of time on the street and their role identification. Individuals who are recently dislocated try to avoid social contacts with other homeless, but the day-to-day needs of street life are often facilitated by such ties. Individuals who have been homeless for a longer period of time often form more "stable" social networks, though there are, of course, isolates among these groups. Similarly, the nature of interaction varies with different types of homeless. Snow and Anderson (1993) found that for some groups of "bums" and "tramps," interaction revolved around street survival activities and the procurement and consumption of alcohol. These groups, sometimes called "bottle gangs," consisted of a shifting group of individuals attached by relatively tenuous ties. In contrast, the raison d'être for contact between the recently dislocated tended to be job hunting and the sharing of information and resources for getting off the street and surviving while on the street. For many who have become somewhat adapted to street life, interaction revolves around the creation of detailed stories and scenarios about past experiences and future plans.

In short, both ethnographic and network-based accounts of interaction among the homeless suggest a complex interactional system of individuals who rely on each other for both instrumental and emotional support. Though ties on the street and in the shelter can often be fleeting, while they exist, those ties are critical for the day-to-day survival of homeless individuals. As Liebow (1993) wrote about homeless women in a Washington, DC, shelter: "For friendships the women could draw on—the mutual support that is exchanged among equals, that builds on both giving and taking, on shared life circumstances and perhaps shared fates—the women had to turn to one another" (pp. 161–162).

## Social Networks off the Street

As noted in the discussion of causes of homelessness, many homeless people come to shelters or to the streets because of crises with social contacts off the street (e.g., divorce, domestic violence) or when avenues of shelter and support through family and friends have been exhausted. This pattern is particularly true of women and families who are homeless. For example, McChesney (1992) detailed four "patterns of poverty" among homeless families. These were (a) unemployed couples who had no shelter opportunities with family or friends, (b) mothers leaving relationships (often abusive) who did not have the means to support themselves and their children, (c) mothers receiving Aid to Families with Dependent Children (AFDC) with no male family head and who could not make ends meet on public support, and (d) mothers who had been homeless teenagers. In all of these situations, homelessness is precipitated by a lack of social support from family and friends or a breakdown in a support system that had existed. Bassuk's (1992) study of women and children without shelter uncovered similar findings. Indeed, she reported that "[h]istorically, family relationships had been unstable" (p. 259) and that "relationships with men were characterized by instability, conflict, and violence" (p. 259).

Ethnographies of homeless people living on the street or in shelters have revealed the same general pattern with regard to social ties with domiciled family and friends. As Liebow (1993) summarized, "[f]or the great majority of women, friendships that pre-dated their homelessness might just as well have not existed" (p. 161). Similarly, Snow and Anderson's (1993) ethnography of homeless street people found that about two thirds of their informants traced their homelessness—at least in part—to family-related problems. Snow and Anderson noted, however, that there are several ways in which these findings can be interpreted. First, it is possible that homeless people have finally "worn out their welcome" with family and friends and have landed on the street (see also Jencks, 1994). Second, the problems of homeless people might be the result of family situations that have become so dysfunctional that they have sought refuge on the street. Third, it is possible that homeless individuals never had a stable family system to begin with. For individuals with dysfunctional families of origin, there is no social support buffer to rely on in times of need. In evaluating these three explanations, Snow and Anderson largely rejected the first, and found more support for the third than they originally anticipated. They summarized their data from a variety of informants:

> In all of these cases we see the same link between family and homelessness, a link that points to a seemingly inescapable conclusion: many of the homeless are on the street because they have no viable familial support network to tap when they are victimized by one or more of the structural forces . . . or by some other misfortune. . . . To attribute homelessness to personal disabilities in these and other such cases is not only to engage in victim-blaming, but it is to obfuscate the family dynamics that render some people especially vulnerable to homelessness. (pp. 264–265)

## Interaction With Service Providers

When most people think about services for the homeless, they think about shelters and soup kitchens. Indeed, these types of agencies are critical to the survival of those on the street, and it is not surprising that most research on service provision has concentrated on such organizations (see, e.g., Burt & Cohen, 1989). However, shelters and soup kitchens are only one level of service provision organizations. In delineating the range of services necessary for dealing with homelessness, it is instructive to look at programs authorized by the McKinley Homeless Assistance Act of 1987. This act is the major legislation designed to deal with homelessness in the United States, and according to Burt and Cohen:

> The McKinley Act also authorized and appropriated money for a wide range of other programs designed to assist homeless persons with emergency needs and also to provide necessary support and training to help them make the transition out of homelessness. These programs cover primary health care, mental health care, alcohol and other drug abuse services, education for both adults and children, job training, community services, and programs specifically for homeless veterans. (p. 12)

Thus, homeless people in America are dealing with workers in soup kitchens and shelters, government agencies and health clinics, transitional housing programs and job training agencies, 12-step programs and religious organizations. Of course, not all of the organizational personnel in contact with the homeless are there to "help" the homeless. Indeed, agencies such as plasma centers, day-labor agencies, and low-cost motels are often in business to make a profit from the homeless population.

In considering the variety of organizations in contact with the homeless, it is instructive to consider Snow and Anderson's (1993) typology of institutional response patterns toward the homeless. These researchers categorized organizational stances toward the homeless as either accommodative (work that helps the homeless survive in the short term), restorative (work that promotes an improved quality of life for the homeless over the long run), exploitative (work that provides a financial gain for the organization in serving the homeless population), exclusionist (work that serves to isolate the homeless from other segments of society), or containment (work that serves to keep the homeless "in their place"). In both ethnographic work (Snow & Anderson, 1993) and in a study involving extensive interviews and surveys (Miller, Birkholt, Scott, Stage, & Knelange, 1994) this typology provided an accurate representation of the variety of approaches taken by service providers.

But what are interactions with service providers like from the perspective of the homeless person? From most accounts, despite the usually good intentions of service providers, these interactions are seen as always frustrating and often demeaning. The maze of red tape surrounding the provision of service to the homeless provides most of the frustration. Homeless people are faced with a plethora of complicated—and often paradoxical—requirements for the receipt of services. Consider just a few examples. In most states, an individual must have a permanent address in order to receive government benefits such as AFDC. Thus, when a young mother is barely surviving on these benefits and finally goes over the edge into homelessness, she is likely to lose the very source of support that might serve as a bridge off the street (see Bassuk, 1992). Similarly, many government programs are earmarked for certain subpopulations of the homeless (e.g., families, the mentally ill, veterans). Thus, extensive records and application materials must accompany many requests for support. This is obviously a frustrating roadblock for most individuals on the street. Or, consider the requirement of many shelters that boys over a certain age (often 12) not be housed with women and female children or the requirement that men and women must live in separate quarters. These requirements mean that a homeless family seeking shelter must be "broken up" in order to find a place to sleep for the night. In short, these (and many other) institutional requirements for service make communication between the homeless and service providers an extremely frustrating experience.

From the perspective of the homeless person, interaction with service providers is also often highly demeaning. As Ferraro (1994) noted, "[s]helters are dehumanizing in that the things that provide identity and pride are stripped and controlled by the institution" (p. 5). When dealing with service providers, homeless individuals must follow the rules of the agency and hence they lose what little autonomy they have. Consider the following sign prominently displayed at a soup kitchen:

A person who comes to Angels House for help should realize that he or she has a serious life problem including bad habits, some of which are willful idleness, lack of self-discipline at the job site, alcoholism, drug abuse including nicotine addiction, chronic faultfinding with others and general unruliness. ANGELS HOUSE DOES NOT EXIST TO SUPPORT PEOPLE WHO WILLFULLY AND CONSISTENTLY INDULGE ANY OF THESE BAD HABITS. (Snow & Anderson, 1993, p. 85)

Similarly, the interpersonal interactions with service providers can also be demeaning. Often the contact between the homeless person and the service provider is a sanitized one that occurs across a desk or on opposite sides of a food-serving line. There is little time for the service provider to get to know people on an individual basis, and "fraternizing" is often discouraged (Snow & Anderson, 1993). Of course, these interactions are highly frustrating to service personnel, as well. As Ferraro (1994) noted, "[f]rontline workers in agencies are not given the time, flexibility, or re-sources to deal with the detailed problems of each person they encounter" (p. 11). Indeed, one of the most prevalent findings in Miller et al.'s (1994) study of service providers was their desire to be "more than a band-aid" and to treat clients with a full measure of dignity and respect. Unfortunately, the constraints of human service work often lead to interactions in which respect and dignity take a backseat to bureaucracy and expedience. This causes stress for individuals on both sides of the service provision equation.

### Interactions With the Domiciled Community

A final category of interactions engaged in by homeless people are those with housed individuals in the community. To a large extent, these inter-actions serve as a reminder of the homeless person's social status and serve to enhance feelings of self-doubt and inferiority. These messages of social status are communicated both in terms of interaction that occurs and interaction that does not occur. Although large-scale research on this issue is lacking, several ethnographies paint poignant pictures of how interaction with "citizens" can be horribly demeaning. For example, Snow and An-derson (1993) watched as children on a school bus threw coins at a group of homeless individuals, made obscene gestures, and shouted "Get a job." Walsh (1992) recounted how homeless children hide their homeless status from others at school lest they be teased or ostracized. Liebow (1993) shared the story of a woman who was told by an old acquaintance that, "[y]ou're homeless and in the shelter because that's where you want to be . . . You're just like all the other women there, and you're a fat slob to boot" (p. 161). In short, many interactions with the housed public serve to erode the often fragile self-concepts of homeless individuals.

Lack of communication with the homeless can also be devastating. As Derber (1979) commented, "members of the subordinate classes are re-garded as less worthy of attention in relations with members of dominant classes and so are subjected to subtle yet systematic face-to-face deprivation" (p. 42). Thus, when individuals walk on the other side of the street to avoid a street person, or avert their gaze from a sign announcing "Homeless Veteran—Will Work for Food," this lack of communication also serves to convey a disdain for those who are homeless.

This is not to suggest that all interaction with the domiciled community is negative. Indeed, there are many housed individuals who attempt to help the homeless, either by providing money or food to individuals on the street, or by volunteering their time, skills, or money to agencies that provide services to the homeless (see Miller et al., 1994). However, like communication with professional service providers, these interactions with members of the housed community are often highly sanitized. Further, many offers of help by the domiciled are made within specific temporal or spatial constraints. Temporally, media coverage of the homeless and offers to help with labor and funds typically peak during November and December. However, as a yuletide editorial in the *Los Angeles Times* indicated, "[c]ome January, when most people go back to their normal routines, the hunger and homelessness recognized in the holiday season will remain" ("If Only the Spirit," 1988). Spatially, many individuals only want to deal with the problems of the homeless when they are confined to the skid row areas of a city. When homelessness spreads to the suburbs or other more desirable neighborhoods, the NIMBY (not in my backyard) perspective sets in, and individuals are more likely to take an exclusionist stance than one guided by a restorative or accommodative motivation.

## CONCLUSION

The image of the homeless held by many Americans is an inaccurate one. Research on a variety of fronts clearly indicates that the homeless are a heterogeneous group. No doubt, some homeless individuals would match the stereotypes of an alcoholic tramp, a mentally ill bag lady, or a lazy drug addict. But there are also homeless individuals on the street who have simply been pushed over the edge by an abusive marriage, unemployment, or a minimum-wage job that does not cover minimum subsistence needs. Our vision of the social and inner lives of the homeless also tends to be a caricature of reality. The homeless are not all lonely—many have rich social lives on the street or in the shelter. And many homeless individuals maintain a great deal of human dignity in the face of situations that would leave most of us in despair. Homeless people, like everyone else, cannot and should not be reduced to stereotypes simply to enhance our own sense of control over the social world.

From this review, it is also clear that communication can be indicted for contributing to many problems of the homeless. Many individuals fall into homelessness because of a lack of social support. That central institution of American life touted by both conservative and liberal politicians—the family—has failed these people. Once individuals fall into homelessness, the bureaucratic red tape characteristic of much organizational communication hampers the homeless from marshaling the resources they need. Further, the messages and averted gazes of many in the general public eats away at the sense of self-efficacy many homeless are determined to maintain.

But if communication can be indicted for many of the problems faced by the homeless, communication professionals should also be in an ideal position to begin rectifying these problems. Scholars and practitioners in interpersonal and family communication can help us to better understand how dysfunctional systems of social support fail individuals living "on the fringes." With a better understanding of the dynamics of social support, we should be able to design educational and intervention programs that catch people before they fall over the edge. Health communication professionals could use their expertise in addressing the problems of health care access, mental health care, and substance abuse faced by many homeless individuals. Organizational communication scholars and practitioners could help in understanding both the interpersonal and the interorganizational processes through which service is provided to the homeless. By investigating both the systemic and cultural aspects of service provision, we could eliminate some of the frustrating and dehumanizing aspects of life on the street. Finally, as communication professionals, we could all help to boost awareness of how everyday interaction and media depictions help to shape the lives of the homeless. It is only by moving beyond our one-dimensional conception of the homeless that we can help these individuals to establish lives that are meaningful and rewarding.

# REFERENCES

Barak, G. (1991). *Gimme shelter: A social history of homelessness in contemporary America.* New York: Praeger.

Bassuk, E. L. (1984). The homelessness problem. *Scientific American, 251,* 40–45.

Bassuk, E. L. (1992). Women and children without shelter: The characteristics of homeless families. In M. J. Robertson & M. Greenblatt (Eds.), *Homelessness: A national perspective* (pp. 257–264). New York: Plenum.

Baum, A. S., & Burnes, D. W. (1993). *A nation in denial: The truth about homelessness.* Boulder, CO: Westview Press.

Berger, P. L., & Luckmann, T. (1966). *The social construction of reality: A treatise in the sociology of knowledge.* New York: Anchor.

Blau, J. S. (1987). *The homeless of New York: A case study in social welfare policy.* (Doctoral dissertation, Columbia University, 1987). University Microfilms International, No. AAC8723988.

Burt, M. R., & Cohen, B. E. (1989). *America's homeless: Numbers, characteristics and the programs that serve them.* Washington, DC: Urban Institute Press.

Cohen, C. I., & Sokolovsky, J. (1981). A reassessment of the sociability of long-term skid row residents: A social network approach. *Social Networks, 3,* 93–105.

Coons, C. (1987). The causes and history of homelessness. In *Resources guide: The national teach-in on homelessness.* New Haven, CT: Student Homeless Action Campaign.

Derber, C. (1979). *The pursuit of attention: Power and individualism in everyday life.* New York: Oxford University Press.

Ferraro, K. J. (1994). Not that easy: Stories from the streets and shelters. In *Reflections on homelessness in Maricopa County: Preliminary report of the research project for homeless people* (pp. 1–16). Tempe: Arizona State University, College of Public Programs.

Granovetter, M. (1973). The strength of weak ties. *American Journal of Sociology, 78,* 1360–1380.

Handler, J. F. (1992). The modern pauper: The homeless in welfare history. In M. J. Robertson & M. Greenblatt (Eds.), *Homelessness: A national perspective* (pp. 35–46). New York: Plenum.

If only the spirit of giving could continue. (1988, December 25). *Los Angeles Times.*

Jencks, C. (1994). *The homeless.* Cambridge, MA: Harvard University Press.

Katz, M. B. (1986). *In the shadow of the poorhouse: A social history of welfare in America.* New York: Basic Books.

LaGory, M., Ritchey, F. J., & Fitzpatrick, K. (1991). Homelessness and affiliation. *Sociological Quarterly, 32,* 201–218.

Levinson, B. M. (1963). The homeless man: A psychological enigma. *Mental Hygiene, 47,* 590–601.

Liebow, E. (1993). *Tell them who I am: The lives of homeless women.* New York: The Free Press.

Maslow, A. H. (1943). A theory of human motivation. *Psychology Review, 50,* 370–396.

McChesney, K. Y. (1992). Homeless families: Four patterns of poverty. In M. J. Robertson & M. Greenblatt (Eds.), *Homelessness: A national perspective* (pp. 245–256). New York: Plenum.

Miller, K. I., Birkholt, M., Scott, C., Stage, C., Knelange, L. (1994). Service provision to homeless people. In *Reflections on homelessness in Maricopa County: Preliminary report of the research project for homeless people* (pp. 33–56). Tempe: Arizona State University, College of Public Programs.

Miner, J. B. (1980). *Theories of organizational behavior.* New York: Dryden Press.

Morse, G. A. (1992). Causes of homelessness. In M. J. Robertson & M. Greenblatt (Eds.), *Homelessness: A national perspective* (pp. 3–17). New York: Plenum.

Redburn, F. S., & Buss, T. F. (1986). *Responding to America's homeless: Public policy alternatives.* New York: Praeger.

Snow, D. A., & Anderson, L. (1987). Identity work among the homeless: The verbal construction and avowal of personal identities. *American Journal of Sociology, 92,* 1336–1371.

Snow, D. A., & Anderson, L. (1993). *Down on their luck: A study of homeless street people.* Berkeley: University of California Press.

Walsh, M. E. (1992). *Moving to nowhere: Children's stories of homelessness.* New York: Auburn House.

Zook, E. G. (1994). Embodied health and constitutive communication: Toward an authentic conceptualization of health communication. In S. Deetz (Ed.), *Communication yearbook 17* (pp. 344–377). Newbury Park, CA: Sage.

# 6 Victims of the Franchise: A Culturally Sensitive Model of Teaching Patient–Doctor Communication in the Inner City

Barbara F. Sharf
*University of Illinois, Chicago*

John Kahler
*Cook County Hospital and Humana Health Care Plans, Chicago*

> *What is the "franchise" with regard to health care?* Webster's *(1989)
> defines franchise as ". . . a privilege of a public nature conferred on
> an individual or body of individuals by a governmental grant" (p. 563).
> Surely, everyone in this fine country of ours has access to health care.
> We have established safety nets for those who either temporarily, due
> to circumstance, or permanently, due to inherent moral weakness, find
> themselves without quality health insurance. They might not get "Cadil-
> lac care" from some of the finest private institutions (unless, of course,
> they are lucky enough to have an interesting and rare disease). But,
> they do have access to public sector health care and will receive their
> care and medications free.*

Although the preceding commentary is a fabrication, it could easily be a
transcript of currently popular talk radio or of conversations from many
middle-class living rooms. Yet recent ethnographic and sociological reports
make it abundantly clear that the social welfare systems established to
service at-risk communities make health care difficult to obtain at a minimum and sometimes even make medical problems worse.[1] We believe that
the majority of economically disadvantaged citizens in this society are not
"disenfranchised," that is, deprived of health care, but rather can be con-

---

[1]Two of the best examples of this type of work were written by journalists and are based
on observations of African-American families who live on the west side of Chicago. See
Kotlowitz (1991) and Abraham (1993).

sidered victims of this franchise, in terms of how they experience the systems that provide it.

We are well aware that the problems and practices to which we refer are systemic on a grand scale. However, because our professional responsibilities center on medical education, our focus is the individual patient–doctor interaction, with special attention to how we might better prepare primary care practitioners. Furthermore, we concern ourselves with the milieu with which we are most familiar, the public hospitals of the inner city.[2] We draw our examples from the teaching and research we have been doing with the Family Practice residency program at Cook County Hospital. The outpatient service that these residents staff at Fantus Clinic on Chicago's west side has a patient population that is predominantly composed of lower income African Americans, many of whom are late middle-aged to elderly individuals. The resident physicians are culturally diverse, but generally come from middle- to upper-class backgrounds.[3]

What we wish to explore in this chapter is how the interpersonal communication between patients and doctors may contribute to or guard against victimage of indigent patients within the health care franchise.

## HIDDEN AND NOT-SO-HIDDEN PREJUDICE

He was one of those fresh Jewish types you want to kill at sight, the presuming poor whose looks change the minute cash is mentioned. . . . She, on the other hand looked Italian, a goaty slant to her eyes, . . . she looked dirty.

---

[2]Public hospitals in this context are defined as those subsidized and administered through government-related bodies and financed with public monies. Such institutions have traditionally been the major source of health care to the poor and/or uninsured, though certainly some private, voluntary hospitals located in inner-city neighborhoods have served similar functions. Our respective experiences in medical education have been centered at two public hospitals: the University of Illinois Hospital, which is state supported with a predominantly academic mission, and Cook County Hospital, regulated by the Cook County Board of Commissioners with a predominantly public service mission to the people of Chicago. One of us (J.K.) is also a primary-care practitioner at an HMO office administered by the Humana Health Care Plans, a for-profit corporation. All three facilities are located among some of the neediest neighborhoods in Chicago.

[3]Of the 400 residents currently employed at Cook County Hospital, only 10% are graduates of American medical schools. International medical residents come from 15 different countries, the largest numbers from Pakistan, India, and the Philippines. The Department of Family Practice, although culturally diverse, does not reflect the same mix characteristic of the hospital generally. During the 1995–1996 residency year, of the 41 residents within the department, 18 or nearly half are American medical graduates; these residents include 7 African Americans and 3 Mexican Americans. Most of the U.S. medical school graduates select Cook County for residency training because of service-related ideals whereas the majority of the international medical school graduates come to this hospital because this is the best placement they can achieve.

So did he. Her hands were definitely grimy, with black nails. And she smelled.
. . . People like that belong in clinics, I thought to myself. I wasn't putting
myself out for them, not that day anyhow. (Williams, 1961, p. 167)

As a general practitioner in post-World War II Passaic, New Jersey, William
Carlos Williams' recollections reflect many of the attitudes toward the
indigent users of the health care systems of that time period. His narrator's
stereotypes of these individuals according to ethnicity and income levels
were the result of the prevailing sociocultural assumptions of his day. In
this character's mind, their claim for health care was more appropriate for
the public clinic than his own private practice. He decided to exert less
effort on them than on more desirable patients.[4] The candor of Williams'
narrator in reporting his thoughts sounds jarring in the current era where
out-and-out discrimination against Italians and Jews is not so prevalent;
replace those groups with Blacks and Mexicans and the same scenario is
not an anachronism, but still very real.

Many circumstances have changed since Dr. Williams practiced. Afri-
can-Americans have come to be a much more sizable minority or even the
predominant group in many large cities. The current immigrant populations
are different, fewer Europeans with many more Asians and Latinos. Doctors
may also be recent arrivals from other countries, bringing with them cultural
beliefs and attitudes that may differ from those of their patients and their
colleagues. Lone general practitioners who can be accessed by anyone are
becoming less prevalent. Uninsured people, unemployed and working poor,
of all ethnic and racial backgrounds, continue to be disadvantaged within
an increasingly costly health care system, and their numbers have swelled.

What remains painfully familiar are problems at the level of the patient–
physician relationship, the context in which Williams (1961) was writing.
These include misunderstandings and pejorative judgments about people
whose beliefs and practices, based on culture and life situation, run counter
to mainstream medical care. Patients who are less well educated, and thus
often more reticent about asking questions or seeking choices, are, not
surprisingly, less frequently provided information by practitioners (Abraham, 1993; Waitzkin & Stoeckle, 1972), the assumption being that if
people do not ask, they do not want to know. The social bases of such
clearly definable medical problems as substance abuse, improper diet and
exercise, trauma due to domestic violence and unsafe living environments
have been demonstrated to be relegated by physicians to the "margins" of

---

[4]To Williams' credit, within this story, the narrator confronts his prejudices and finds out
that the woman is not Italian, but a Polish Jew who had suffered immensely during the war.
Her life experiences help to shed new light for the doctor on what he had presumed was
inappropriate appearance, ignorant noncompliance regarding infant care, and her husband's
aggressive actions to ensure his family received good medical care.

their conversations with patients (Waitzkin, 1991) or disappear altogether from discourse (Warshaw, 1989), and therefore can never be dealt with as co-related factors.

Thus, to be a victim of the American health care franchise has to do with unequal access to primary and tertiary services, information, and choice; having to balance health-related priorities against those related to tremendously difficult aspects of everyday living; and impaired patient–doctor communication due to cultural differences and unchecked assumptions by both parties about the other.[5]

## HISTORICAL AND CONTEXTUAL CONSIDERATIONS

> The attitude prevailed that abject poverty was caused either by laziness or wickedness. . . . Almshouse hospitals were thought of as houses of refuge for the immoral. (Dowling, 1982, p. 81)[6]

Governmentally supported general hospitals in large metropolitan areas of this country function as the main health care facilities for urban indigent populations. Although individuals who can pay may use city hospitals for a variety of reasons (e.g., at Cook County Hospital, many African-American patients indicate that this is the place their families have used for several generations), these are also the facilities of last resort from which no one may be turned away. Additionally, these hospitals serve as major training sites for postgraduate (residency) education.

The historical analogue of the current two-tiered system of health care was present in the United States during colonial times. Prototypes of city hospitals originated in the American colonies as replicas of British almshouses in which the aged, homeless, insane, chronically ill, disabled, orphans, alcoholics, and criminals were placed in the same institution. "More respectable" citizens with means were treated at voluntary hospitals that were supported by private charities and run by independent boards, and generally received better care. By the time of the Civil War, the general hospitals had become separate from institutions such as workhouses, old-age homes, and insane asylums. Nonetheless, patients treated at these facilities were branded by the historically associated stigmas of "pauper" and "criminal."

Several additional developments contributed to the essential character and particular difficulties of city hospitals. Burgeoning waves of immigrant

---

[5]This kind of victimage is certainly not limited to urban environments. The same issues can be found among migrant farm workers, Appalachian miners, and other rural populations (Flannery, 1982).

[6]We are indebted to Dowling's (1982) account of the development of American city hospitals in the abbreviated historical summary that follows in this section.

populations, including the migration of rural Southern Black people to Northern cities during the first part of the 20th century, have created ongoing masses of people without sources of payment. Discrimination against certain categories of patients, including racial minorities and those with infectious diseases and substance-abuse problems, in other hospital settings meant that public hospitals became the refuge for these people (a pattern that is reflected today in the leadership role assumed by many public hospitals in the care of HIV-infected patients). Following the escalating flight of middle-class people out of the cities, many private hospitals have moved their facilities to the suburbs, creating an enlarged burden on the city hospitals.[7] In contemporary language, public hospitals are the recipients of patients who have been "dumped" from other sectors of the health care system. Whereas New York and Los Angeles each developed a system of multiple municipal hospitals geographically spread throughout the city, politicians in Chicago consolidated power in the original Cook County Hospital (at its current site since 1876), which remains a huge, largely unmanageable institution in a central location, with outmoded facilities, to which citizens throughout the greater metropolitan area must travel often lengthy distances and wait long hours for medical, laboratory, and pharmaceutical services.

City hospitals have always been able to offer doctors-in-training an abundance of patients and ample hands-on experience with a wide variety of diseases, albeit working in a deteriorated physical plant and cumbersome political bureaucracy, without many of the supporting services and resources available at better endowed hospitals. Following the 1910 Flexner Report, a Carnegie-funded national review of medical education, the quality of residency training programs in public hospitals improved, many through affiliations with university medical schools. Because the majority of patients who are treated at these hospitals do not have an ongoing relationship with an established physician, direct daily patient care in these institutions is primarily the responsibility of the house staff (interns and residents), under the supervision of attending physicians. Coupled with an advanced educational mission, also came increased interest in clinical research that has yielded significant scientific contributions. Unfortunately, some celebrated incidents in which there have been breeches of informed consent with public hospital patients have generated an ongoing air of suspicion that poor people may be used as scientific guinea pigs.[8]

---

[7]In Chicago, private hospitals maintaining their city-based locations have dropped out of the metropolitan trauma network at an alarming rate, again increasing the burden on Cook County and the few other remaining hospitals (Abraham, 1993).

[8]The best known of these cases is the infamous Tuskegee experiments (Jones, 1981), but a recent incident at Cook County Hospital (Locke, 1988; Rose, 1989) has heightened suspicion at the local level.

How then do these historical, structural, and organizational circumstances impact on the patient–physician relationship? Mizrahi's (1986) longitudinal study of an internal medicine residency yielded a harsh view of the impact of training in a public hospital setting. In addition to the conditions described above, she identified a set of intrinsic, ongoing tensions that result in a general resident perspective in which patients are viewed as "the enemy," and the goal of the house staff is to get rid of them.[9] Doctors-in-training are striving to see sufficient numbers of patients to gain a broad base of medical knowledge and competence, while simultaneously fending off the immense workload that expands every time they receive a new "hit" or patient admission. Objectification of patients is exacerbated by such factors as an emphasis on understanding pathology, pressure to be time efficient and contain costs, and rotation and call schedules that mitigate against continuity of care and relationships.

Thus, an implicit priority system that includes moral and social judgments becomes operant in terms of which patients to get rid of. The "ideal" patient has an interesting ailment; is compliant with doctors' directives; is intelligent, or at least an accurate historian; *and* of high moral quality. Undesirable patients are those who abuse themselves (and are thus held responsible for their diseases), the health care system, and the care providers.

Mizrahi (1984) also found that valued even less than the residents' inpatient assignments is the time spent in the outpatient clinics, the site of most primary and preventive care. Chronic conditions, such as obesity, diabetes, hypertension, and addiction, prevalent among indigent populations are viewed as uninteresting, morally unacceptable, and less conducive to learning. Supervision of clinic encounters is felt to be time consuming and residents feel overwhelmed by the psychosocial circumstances that compound their patients' medical problems. Mizrahi (1986) concluded:

> A public system of . . . medicine that relies . . . principally on provision of adult general medical care by novice internists who characterize themselves as harassed, oppressed, overworked, and underpaid, and whose personal goals and professional orientation to medicine are often opposed to the needs of the basic [patient] population, is programmed to produce profound deficiencies in the doctor–patient relationship. (p. 125)

Our experience with the residents in the Cook County Hospital setting confirms many of these observations, yet is somewhat more optimistic. Our residents can speak sincerely and humanistically about what they regard an effective patient–doctor relationship to be. They are also astute and aware of the barriers that get in the way of actualizing such relation-

---

[9]Many of Mizrahi's observations are corroborated in Samuel Shem's (1980) celebrated autobiographical novel, *The House of God*.

ships. What they suffer from is the inability to actualize this knowledge in practice. It is in the context of finding "teachable moments," ones that facilitate a breakthrough in a clinical impasse with implications for future insights, that we have developed the following model and sought ways to incorporate and apply it within our pedagogy.

## THE CULTURALLY SENSITIVE MODEL
## OF PATIENT–PHYSICIAN COMMUNICATION

Differences in race, ethnicity, socioeconomic status, and/or education have tended to characterize communication between doctors and patients in inner city settings. Although goodwill between individuals at times can go a long way toward ameliorating some of the distance created through these disparities, it is often insufficient to fully address functional and relational problems that arise between people who ordinarily would not be in contact outside the clinical context. In order to study and teach about interpersonal relationships of individual patient–doctor dyads, the concept of "patient–doctor communication" needs to be understood within a much broader context. To this end, we have chosen a systemic model of organizing the complex layers of meaning acting upon this relationship at any one time.

### Meaning-Centeredness

We begin with the premise that human communication is the attempt to create meaning with others. Because each person operates out of individual experience, the enterprise of conjoint meaning making can never be perfect or complete. The best we can aim for is a degree of shared understanding, the greater, the better. However, the more dissimilar we view another's experience from our own, the more decreased the possibilities for shared understanding. Although the traditional biomedical model gives little emphasis to "meaning," particular problems in meaning creation engendered in patient–doctor talk have been examined from many vantage points, including language (Barnlund, 1976; Mintz, 1992), power dynamics (Brody, 1992; Waitzkin, 1991; West, 1984), cultural frameworks (Kleinman, 1978, 1988), and narrativity (Sharf, 1990; Vanderford, Smith, & Harris, 1992).

   The Culturally Sensitive Model (see Fig. 6.1) is a meta-view that encompasses all these factors and others. It is an attempt to identify the range of sources for meanings that simultaneously inform individual transactions. Each time a physician and patient sit down to discuss the patient's presenting concerns, they bring to that conversation assumptions about the other and the world in which they both operate that may come from

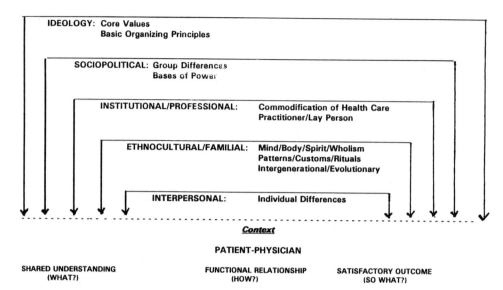

FIG. 6.1.   Culturally Sensitive Model of Patient–Physician Communication.

sources far removed from the medical context. Engel's (1977) well-known biopsychosocial model makes use of systems theory to incorporate recognition of psychological and social/community aspects of medical history taking and management, yet in both our experience and that of others (Miller, 1992), the biopsychosocial model may be difficult to put into clinical practice. Furthermore, both Engel's model and Kleinman's cultural/ethnographic approach remain "doctor-driven"; that is, better understanding the patient's perspective becomes a means of the physician's gaining patient cooperation (Taussig, 1980).

The multilayers of the Culturally Sensitive Model explore sources of meaning that impact both patient and physician. Identifying the complex layering of ideas that undergirds how each participant attempts to make sense of the interaction helps us to better understand what happens when the larger social world intrudes upon the intimate talk of patient and doctor, resulting in dynamics that may not be immediately apparent.

## The Ideological Layer of Meaning[10]

There are certain assumptions that are so basic we do not even question their veracity. The ideological level of meaning is the crucible from which

---

[10]For a discussion of ideology applied to medical practice based on an analysis of critical theories, see Waitzkin (1991).

the philosophical "truths," the ethical underpinnings of the society, are generated. American legal and ethical proceedings have provided us with a very stable society. The basic organizing principles—primacy of personal property, the rule of secular contractual law, the import of protecting the individual from the capriciousness of the government, and the accumulation of wealth as an emblem of success—have remained remarkably unchanged over 200 years. To those of us at this millennium, it seems to have always been so, but history records that at the time of the writing of the Constitution, these truths were far from self-evident (Bowen, 1986; Morris, 1989; Van Doren, 1982). It is from this source of meaning that the remainder of the levels in the model are energized. Societal changes of such magnitude to actually affect this level are improbable so that American doctrine has continued to remain intact. Witness the difference between the United States pre- and post-Civil War and the Soviet Union pre- and post-*glasnost* and *perestroika*. This country was stronger for our struggles, but the Soviet Union disintegrated as an entity.

Deeply ingrained ideologic values inform our interpersonal dealings, including enactments of inequality and stigma that become institutionalized as racism, sexism, and other negative treatments of "the other." Looking back at the earlier excerpt from Dr. Williams (1961), it seems overly simplistic to assume that only the particular ethnicities of these patients drove his basic distrust and dislike. His more basic concern with their perceived lack of personal worth was generated from core assumptions about people whose attributes and circumstances set them apart from the group of White, male property owners of Northern European descent of which he was a member.

## The Sociopolitical Layer of Meaning

From what origins do perceptions of "otherness" or distancing from people seen as different from ourselves come? This question is at the crux of understanding problems in cross-cultural communication, generally. Social and political forces form the backdrop and operant patterns for all human interactions. As the name implies, it is at this level of meaning that the politics or power structure of a country is formulated on the basis of social groupings, differentiated by a variety of demographic factors, and to which are ascribed commonly acknowledged comparative values.

In the contemporary United States, arguably the most prominent group differences that form the primary bases of social power include race, class, and gender; race and class have been particularly vivid markers within inner cities. Within these social categories, certain groups of Americans have traditionally enjoyed privileged status, the cumulative effect of which has been correlated with increased employment advantage, higher economic status, and access to positions of influence. Conversely, individuals who are members of other groupings, in particular racial minorities, have been marginalized in regard to the same opportunities (at times, regardless of educational preparation). In recent decades, of course, some of the marginalized voices have come to the forefront of social attention to challenge the established meanings attached to demographic categories, and yet the implicit value system of the sociopolitical structure has responded to change at a very slow pace.

How do we tease out the influence of these broad trends within specific contexts and relationships? Race seems inextricably linked to socioeconomic status (Pettigrew, 1981). For instance, certainly not all African Americans are poor or unhealthy, but, relative to all other social groups, they are disproportionately at risk for both conditions. Ethnicity and class to a large extent influence the communities in which people reside and, therefore, with whom they will come to associate. Until direct interaction teaches us about the uniqueness of an other and the amount of variability within any one sociopolitically defined group, stereotypes and generalized impressions may be the only information available to us as we enter into unfamiliar situations. Our knowledge and experience with sociopolitical meanings color relationships with, and responses to, others, including those in the medical context.

## The Institutional/Professional Layer of Meaning

Whereas the sociopolitical level focuses on the organization of individuals into broad social categories, the institutional subsystem looks at the organization of health care and related services by professional and corporate categories. The American Medical Association, various companies constituting the pharmaceutical industry, and hospital and health maintenance organization networks are each an example of such institutionalization. At this level of conceptualization, health-related meanings are understood in terms of an economic, marketplace perspective: Health care is a commodity that trained practitioners provide to paying or subsidized consumers. The current discourse on health care reform is, in large part, dominated by issues of finance (as opposed to justice or compassion, e.g.). Thus, sociopolitical concerns such as economic status and privileged position are, in fact, intertwined within the fabric of the health care system.

Poorer "consumers," such as the patients of publicly supported health facilities, have fewer choices, longer waits, and more restricted access to available resources. Their health and well-being is closely tied to institutions other than medical care facilities, including the welfare and social service systems, the public health department, the immigration service, the courts, churches, and schools. This interinstitutional significance, which is so essential in the day-to-day lives of many patients, is often overlooked by physicians whose gaze is much more narrowly focused (Saba & Rodgers, 1989).

Professional schools, societies, and associations are forms of health care institutions through which physicians and other health care practitioners are socialized into distinct subcultures, characterized not only by technical skills and knowledge, but also by occupational hierarchy, norms, and ethical standards. Such distinctions create both interprofessional (e.g., doctors and nurses) and intraprofessional (e.g., internists and surgeons) divergence and specialization.

Most of all, professionalization distances practitioners from laypersons in ways that are sometimes necessary, but that also may become dysfunctional. In general, physicians tend to be more empirical, technological, and focused on the medical problem itself and its objective manifestations in the form of clinical findings and laboratory results, a stance that Kleinman (1978, 1988) called the "disease" perspective and Mishler (1984) dubbed the "voice of medicine." In contrast, patients have an "illness perspective" and speak with the "voice of the life-world." That is, they are focused on their subjective experiences of feeling un-well (or "dis-eased") and the impact of those feelings on day-to-day living in the larger contexts of family, work, and recreation. Bringing the physician's expertise in disease and the patient's expertise in personal experience into partnership can be an effective approach toward solving, or at least caring for, problems of sickness and disability.

Quite often, however, such collaboration does not occur; the two voices talk past one another, such that the issues that brought the patient to the doctor are not really addressed. The further the professional medical voice is anchored from the voice of the layperson's life-world, be that through differences in education, language, class, ethnicity, or a myriad of other factors, the more likely it is that communication difficulties will result.

### The Ethnocultural/Familial Layer of Meaning

The issue of professional distance between Western practitioners and their patients is, in fact, one of the key factors posited as a reason for the current upsurge in the popularity of so-called alternative or unorthodox healers. Although some of the alternate pathways include different theories of somatic healing (e.g., homeopathic, osteopathic, chiropractic), several others (e.g., acupuncture, therapeutic massage, macrobiotic diets, herbal remedies), including many labeled as "New Age," are rooted in cultural traditions.

For generations, the United States promoted the national melting pot image, which promoted cultural assimilation. In recent decades, cultural diversity has come to be celebrated. Culture, in this sense, refers to patterns of everyday living, including forms of expression and social interaction, which tend to be implicit and assumed as "normal" until someone from outside a particular culture violates its norms; when called into question, social "rules," styles, and values can be identified. Cultural affinity may be rooted in common language, religion, national origin, geographic location, and/or historical experience. Typically, cultural groups develop customs or rituals to mark major life events, such as births, deaths, transitions into adulthood, marriages, and so forth. Although families are certainly unique entities with their own idiosyncratic myths and modus operandi, the family is usually the main conduit through which an individual learns cultural heritage. Thus, cultural knowledge is at once intergenerationally conveyed and evolutionary in terms of its adaptation to new environments and situations.

Ethnocultural conceptions of health and illness explain or discount the associations among body, mind, and spirit. In the United States, mainstream medicine has succeeded in trifurcating these elements of human well-being with an almost single-minded emphasis on the body, relegating mind to the specialty of psychiatry, which is often depicted as less scientific (Sharf, 1986), and spiritual matters almost entirely outside the practice of health care. Only recently have serious efforts been made to explore mind–body connections (Cousins, 1989; Siegel, 1986) and integrate the biopsychosocial aspects into clinical practice (Engel, 1980). The still predominant separate focus on body contrasts with many other cultural theories of health and illness found in disparate geographic areas (Snow, 1974) that emphasize the balance of energies involving mind, spirit, and body, and which may account for forces both internal and external to the individual.

The extremely diverse patient populations seen in urban public hospitals not only attribute a variety of explanatory models, which may blend elements of biomedicine and folk beliefs, to their health problems, but they often use a range of remedies that may include and combine physician-prescribed medications, over-the-counter products, traditional home remedies, and items obtained from the local herbalist or botánica, root doctor, curandero, and so on. Only very recently are Western medical educators coming to recognize the significant role that culture plays in attempted physician–patient negotiations and the potential value alternative healing practices may have in addressing problems that have not been responsive to biomedical interventions. Furthermore, the identification of conflicts among cultural and religious values exercised by both health professionals and patients are the bases for many major bioethical dilemmas occurring with increasing frequency within health care settings, the discussion of which impacts public policy decisions (Meleis & Jonsen, 1983; Veatch, 1989).

## The Interpersonal Level of Meaning

In any human transaction, the uniqueness of the individuals participating at a particular point in time create a dynamic that is not interchangeable or reproducible (Stewart, 1990). Although we are socialized in terms of expected role behaviors that we associated with "patient" and "doctor," the styles and sensibilities of specific people filling these roles with one another is the foundation of that often difficult-to-define quality called "rapport" or "connection" (or lack thereof).

The degree of intimacy, in terms of touch and personal disclosure, that tends to characterize the primary care patient–physician relationship sets it apart from almost all other kinds of professional relationships. That intimacy does not necessarily entail interpersonal liking. Both parties make use of a continuum of intimacy within the relationship to accomplish their respective goals, which may or may not be mutually negotiated.

Although the interpersonal level is continuously and overtly present during the course of the medical encounter, it may be subtly superseded by meanings derived from other levels. For example, it is not unusual for patients at Cook County to feel more familiarity and allegiance to the hospital and its institutional system in which they have learned how to function over a long period of time than to the continuous stream of young doctors-in-training with whom they have a relationship for 3 years at best.

## APPLYING THE MODEL IN REAL TIME

In our experience in teaching communication to residents, one of the benefits of using the Culturally Sensitive Model is to clarify how several layers of meaning are operational simultaneously, though one or more may predominate throughout the conversation; furthermore, the layer(s) of meaning most salient for one person may not be the same for the other.

To illustrate how the model can work to explain the subtleties and complexities that characterize physician–patient interaction in an inner-city clinic, we examine in detail two medical interviews that were videotaped as part of the Cook County Hospital Family Practice residency training. The interviews were routinely taped with the consent of both patient and doctor for purposes of the educational program. Residents typically review these videotapes with a faculty member. Neither of the two interviews was unusual in content or format; we selected them because we feel they are interesting illustrations of the different levels of the model in practice.

## Deciding What's "Normal"

In this interview, a 50-year-old African-American grandmother, Mrs. Betty Page, who is the sole caretaker of her 5-year-old granddaughter Lasheeka, brought her to see Dr. Wilmer, a 28-year-old, White male, first-year resident.[11] He first saw the little girl in the hospital for a lung infection 5 months prior; this was her second clinic appointment since then. A problem list in the typical medical format would probably have sounded like this: (a) presents with fever and wheezing due to asthma, (b) frequent lung and respiratory infections, (c) hyperactivity, (d) reported learning disabilities, (e) thinness, (f) regression to uncontrolled urination, and (g) eye muscle weakness; but the grandmother's overwhelming concern was quickly and simply stated: "Will she be able to be like a normal child?"

As Mrs. Page filled in some history, sociopolitical sources of meaning added to an understanding of Lasheeka's medical problems. She was born prematurely to a drug-addicted mother, weighing 1.5 lb and "had to be on a machine for 5 months." According to Dr. Wilmer, her lung infections and asthma were probably due to her underdeveloped lungs at birth.

Differences in professional and layperson understandings of illness came into play around the issue of Lasheeka's "normality." Despite Mrs. Page's claim that her granddaughter "acts more like a 2-year-old . . . jumps around while other children are reading . . . catches a cold every time she goes outside, . . . [and] doesn't have a lot of weight on her," Dr. Wilmer was not sure the girl was so different from her peers. He explained that many children this age catch colds easily and are within the same weight range. When asked, the child demonstrated an understanding of concepts that her grandmother did not think she knew.

Dr. Wilmer's approach was to prescribe a developmental evaluation as the first step of a long-term plan to assess and deal with possible problems. Despite three separate attempts by Dr. Wilmer to define what he meant by the term "developmental evaluation," which he indicated would be done by a psychologist, within her cultural framework, Mrs. Page struggled with the concept. She needed to be reassured that Lasheeka was not crazy, would

---

[11]This interview was part of a 1988–1989, funded study of cross-cultural doctor–patient communication at Cook County Hospital using interviews between first-year residents and their scheduled clinic patients (Sharf et al., 1990). As part of the protocol, Mrs. Page was asked to stay after her visit with the doctor to review and discuss the tape of the medical interview with an African-American, female, nonphysician interviewer. As usual, Dr. Wilmer reviewed the session at a separate time with a faculty member. Both resident and patient review sessions were videotaped as well.

not be put on psychiatric medications or be involved in a long series of meetings with the psychologist, and that the result would not be an immediate change. Still, in discussing the tape after her visit with the doctor, Mrs. Page stated that the result of the assessment would be to "make [Lasheeka] better" and that the doctor agreed she "will be like a normal child."

As Dr. Wilmer reviewed the tape, he did not stand in judgment of Mrs. Page, but was a little surprised about her inaccurate reporting of the child's capabilities. Some of the family history, which Mrs. Page later admitted she chose not to share with him, might have affected the doctor's capacity for understanding Mrs. Page's extreme concerns about her granddaughter. Unbeknownst to the physician, Mrs. Page also took care of a 14-year-old girl with developmental problems ("worse than Sheeka")[12], which meant that she had to divide her attention and had reason to be wary of Lasheeka's future development. Mrs. Page also confided to the patient interviewer that Lasheeka, who is her son's child, was unwanted by both her own mother and the woman her son eventually married. It is at once interesting and telling that Mrs. Page revealed to the doctor that Lasheeka's mother was a drug addict, but that she did not want him, or almost anyone else, to know that the little girl was unwanted. This aspect of her story appeared both hurtful and shameful: "It's something only a grandmother understands and I want this child to feel she is loved." Nonetheless, she told this family secret in front of Lasheeka, apparently assuming that the child was not paying attention or understanding what was being said.

In response to a number of questions by the patient interviewer, Mrs. Page expressed several times her satisfaction with Dr. Wilmer, presumably an interpersonal issue: "The child feels comfortable with this doctor, 'cause he takes the time with her." However, a sociopolitical edge surprisingly cut into this interchange when Mrs. Page was asked if she would prefer a Black doctor. She replied that she definitely would not and proceeded to tell of two very negative experiences she had with African-American physicians, including one who sexually abused her daughter.

This conversation between physician and patient was invested with meanings derived from every level of our model, especially for Mrs. Page. Dr. Wilmer acknowledged the unfortunate circumstances of Lasheeka's birth, but did not dwell on them as her grandmother did. Although the physician understood the grandmother's concern for "normality," which he defined as "free of asthma and on a developmental par with other kids," he focused on the importance of taking a baseline assessment of Lasheeka. What he could not understand, in part because he was not permitted to hear them,

---

[12]It is not clear from this conversation whether the older child is a daughter, granddaughter, or other relative.

were the many circumstances that prompted Mrs. Page to be so worried about this child. Neither was he aware of factors beyond his own experience with this family that caused him to be more trusted than some other practitioners. Although the mutual respect and interpersonal rapport that this doctor and patients had for one another was evident, Mrs. Page's expectations that Lasheeka needed to "learn to be normal" remained an ongoing issue in this relationship.

## Beyond That, I'm Doing Damn Good!

Mr. Johnson is a feisty 80-year-old African American seen by Dr. Ibo, a 28-year-old, first-year resident from Nigeria. This 45-minute interview was filled with emotion, animus, and misunderstanding, with expert knowledge of the young doctor pitted against the experienced, street-wise patient, who reported first coming for treatment in this hospital in 1931.

Early in the interview, Mr. Johnson described his primary complaints as numerous pains, mainly in his chest and knees: "They used to call it rheumatism when I was a kid . . . Now they call it arthritis." In attempting to conduct a thorough medical history, Dr. Ibo elicited from Mr. Johnson's chart a number of other health problems (high blood pressure and cholesterol), as well as risk factors including a pack-a-day smoking habit and a history of family heart disease. Although admitting that his chest pain "slows me down, man," Mr. Johnson argued he is doing well for his age. He talked of driving "a '60 GTO" and not feeling much in common with people his age ("I am up on current events, so I'm in a different category than they are").

Though Mr. Johnson was concerned with his arthritic pains, Dr. Ibo chose to make hypertension a major focus in this encounter, a conflict that raised several issues from the standpoint of the Culturally Sensitive Model. Perhaps most obvious were institutional/professional-based meanings. The differing priorities of doctor and patient was only one indicator of an ongoing struggle for control throughout the interview. Interspersed throughout Mr. Johnson's comments were phrases and idioms that had clearly originated from the medical context, with which he had many years of experience. While reviewing the tape of this interview, Dr. Ibo remarked about the "misuse" of this technical language by the patient. He felt that these words had specific meanings that Mr. Johnson misunderstood and therefore misused.

There was confusion between the professional and ethnocultural levels as well. When Dr. Ibo noted, "I understand you've been hypertensive for a long time," Mr. Johnson answered, "High blood tension, so that's gonna make me hypertensive, hyperactive." In this instance, a medical diagnosis, increased blood pressure, was imbued with the cultural sense of being "hyper," tense, and nervous. Through this usage, Dr. Ibo was offered a view of Mr. Johnson's world, which he neglected to pursue because of his fixed attention to the medical meaning.

In one particularly charged interchange regarding smoking, Dr. Ibo questioned, "You've been advised and told about how it affects your health?" to which Mr. Johnson replied, "Yeah, I understand. It's right on the packet." In a didactic tone, the physician asked the patient what he understood of the dangers, then explained how smoking affects the patient's other health problems. Mr. Johnson responded, "Yeah, but smokin' ain't gonna stop arthritis; *that's* my main problem!" At the professional level, Dr. Ibo was trying to provide guidance and health education, yet at the interpersonal level, Mr. Johnson experienced this behavior as the doctor exerting control, which the patient resisted. In fact, from a sociopolitical perspective it is well established that in the United States, African-American men have higher morbidity and mortality from hypertension than the population as a whole, even when other factors such as smoking and obesity are controlled.

This struggle escalated during a discussion about hypertension control, when Dr. Ibo tried to change two of the medications Mr. Johnson had been taking. The patient would have none of it: "Look man, I'll tell you what you can do. Give me the same medicines I've got here and I'll be fine." From an institutional standpoint, Mr. Johnson's many years of dealing with public health care were obvious: "That shit don't wash with me. You just got here, but I've been taking [these medications] for 10 years. . . . I'm getting disgusted. You give me some bullshit and sure enough my blood pressure will shoot up." If public sector patients do not have a primary-care provider with whom to identify, they are left to the whims of whomever they see. During 60 years of coming to "the County," Mr. Johnson had listened to many well-meaning, young physicians who felt they had the right answers to most questions. Mr. Johnson continued, "I'll have to come down [to the emergency room] and wait, 5, 10 hours to be seen. You won't be there. I will."

Mr. Johnson's reactions were reflective of the sociopolitical context in which this hospital functions: "Just give me my medicine and I'll get out of here. You can't cut me off of something that's helping me. If it's working, don't fix it!" Health care is similar to the other systems (e.g., public aid, the schools, Medicaid) with which this patient population interacts, insofar as the less contact the better. Such institutions are viewed as necessary evils rather than useful points of service.

The influence of the interpersonal layer became most obvious during Dr. Ibo's videotape review of this encounter, during which he stated that he did not like Mr. Johnson and felt sorry for him. He was understandably angry with this patient for negating his advice: "He didn't need the potassium chloride, but he wouldn't listen to me." But why did Dr. Ibo feel sorry for Mr. Johnson? The physician's answer was instructive with regard to the importance of ethnocultural and familial differences. In the society that Dr. Ibo comes from, one's family is the primary anchor to well-being. During the interview, Mr. Johnson revealed that his wife had died several years earlier (he was unable to specify how many years), and that he had one son from whom he was estranged. When Dr. Ibo stated he felt badly for this man not having any family on which to depend, it was pointed out that Mr. Johnson did not give any evidence of wanting things to be different, and, in fact, said that he liked to be "a loner." Nonetheless, Dr. Ibo contended that this "couldn't be true" because "every man needs" his family around him.

The struggle between this doctor and patient ended when Dr. Ibo's supervisor was consulted and agreed that Mr. Johnson's medications should not be changed. Left alone again, Dr. Ibo brought the interview to a conclusion by asking Mr. Johnson, "Are you happy now?"

## CONCLUSION: PUTTING THE MODEL IN PERSPECTIVE

From the perspective of communication theory, interpersonal interactions are to be assessed in terms of content and relationship (Watzlawick, Beavin, & Jackson, 1967). These parameters apply to patient–doctor communication as well. Both *shared understanding* and *functional relationship* are components we strive to include in teaching clinical competency to residents. At least one other dimension needs to be taken into account within medical interactions, namely in what ways communication affects the accomplishment of *health care outcomes*, which may range from continuity of a professional relationship over time or a mutually negotiated plan of management to provision of emotional support, lessening discomfort of, or increasing adjustment to, a chronic condition, or curing an acute medical problem (Beckman, Kaplan, & Frankel, 1989). It is the assessment of outcome(s) that is most likely to draw the attention of practitioners, so in reflecting on the utility of the Culturally Sensitive Model, we ask what is its impact on the teaching of medical residents, as well as their own clinical practices.

### As a Teaching Model

Physicians-in-training look for simple rules of thumb to guide them with their clinical encounters. They embrace clinical algorithms for the common problems they see. However, by its very nature, meaning generation cannot be reduced to an algorithm.

The subsystem identified within the model that is most accessible to change is the dyadic communication taking place at the interpersonal level. By working with residents, both in small-group seminars and individualized feedback sessions in which their videotaped encounters with patients are reviewed, our goals are to make doctors-in-training aware of how and why their patients' perspectives may differ from their own, identify ways of approaching these recognized differences, and enable practitioners to perceive how their patients' experiences of the health care enfranchisement may be enhanced or limited by the patient–doctor relationship—in short, to shape expectations of the house staff about the cultural context of medical practice and how they may expect to operate within it. This model has become the framework for organizing these teaching concepts and providing explanatory feedback that allows residents to rethink previous clinical difficulties and think about alternative strategies for future ones.

## As a Clinical Practice Model

We are the first to admit that for the most part this is a postdictive instrument, a method for gaining insight from events that have occurred. We *do not* expect practitioners will organize their patient encounters or substitute a clinical problem-solving approach with this schema. Yet we are also hopeful that as the elements of the model become more familiar to our learners, it can become a *diagnostic* tool they will access in moments of difficulty with their patients, one that will permit them to acknowledge differing vantage points as sources of meaning and misunderstandings, while they are still in the exam room, without becoming overwhelmed and stymied.

## As a Model of Patient Empowerment

We have focused on enhancing the patient–doctor relationship as a strategy for ultimate improvement of medical outcomes and patients' experiences of the health care options open to them. We also have strived to impact the institutional/professional level in a limited sense. Over the past decade, dozens of family practice residents, fellows, and faculty have been exposed to some phase of our training programs; most of these physicians have gone on to practice in the city of Chicago, and so we hope we have had a small role in shaping primary care as it has developed here.

Nonetheless, the Culturally Sensitive Model is limited by its rootedness in the health care status quo. We began this chapter with the thesis that the inner-city citizens who are forced to use public institutions are not disenfranchised from health care, but instead are victims of a franchise that has developed to their disadvantage in multiple ways. Although our perspective accounts for patient-derived meanings, it has no direct applicability for use by patients in its current form. As we work on future development and expansion of the model and its conceptual and practical implications, we hope to incorporate such ideas as community-based primary care and prevention with patient/citizens sharing participatory and decision-making roles, alongside government, health care corporations, and health professionals.

# REFERENCES

Abraham, L. K. (1993). *Mama might be better off dead: The failure of health care in urban America*. Chicago: University of Chicago Press.

Barnlund, D. (1976). The mystification of meaning: Doctor–patient encounters. *Journal of Medical Education, 51*, 716–725.

Beckman, H., Kaplan, S. H., & Frankel, R. (1989). Outcome based research on doctor–patient communications: A review. In M. Stewart & D. Roter (Eds.), *Communicating with medical patients* (pp. 223–227). Beverly Hills, CA: Sage.

Bowen, C. D. (1986). *Miracle at Philadelphia: The story of the constitutional convention May to September 1987*. New York: Little, Brown.

Brody, H. (1992). *The healer's power*. New Haven, CT: Yale University Press.

Cousins, N. (1989). *Head first: The biology of hope*. New York: Dutton.

Dowling, H. F. (1982). *City hospitals: The undercare of the underprivileged*. Cambridge, MA: Harvard University Press.

Engel, G. (1977). The need for a new medical model: A challenge for biomedicine. *Science, 196*, 129–136.

Engel, G. (1980). The clinical application of the biopsychosocial model. *American Journal of Psychiatry, 137*, 535–544.

Flannery, M. A. (1982). Simple living and hard choices. *The Hastings Center Report*, pp. 9–12.

Jones, J. (1981). *Bad blood: The Tuskegee syphilis experiment—A tragedy of race and medicine*. New York: The Free Press.

Kleinman, A. (1978). Culture, illness, and care: Clinical lessons from anthropologic and cross-cultural research. *Annals of Internal Medicine, 88*, 251–258.

Kleinman, A. (1988). *The illness narratives: Suffering, healing, and the human condition*. New York: Basic Books.

Kotlowitz, A. (1991). *There are no children here: The story of two boys growing up in the other America*. New York: Doubleday.

Locke, H. (1988, May 28). Dead infants trigger probe. *Chicago Defender*, p. 1.

Meleis, A. F., & Jonsen, A. R. (1983). Ethical crises and cultural differences. *Western Journal of Medicine, 138*, 889–893.

Miller, W. L. (1992). Routine, ceremony, or drama: An explanatory field study of the primary care clinical encounter. *Journal of Family Practice, 34*, 289–296.

Mintz, D. (1992). What's in a word: The distancing function of language in medicine. *The Journal of Medical Humanities, 13*, 223–233.

Mishler, E. G. (1984). *The discourse of medicine: Dialectics of medical interviews*. Norwood, NJ: Ablex.

Mizrahi, T. (1984, May). The outpatient clinic: The crucible of the physician-patient relationship in graduate medical training. *Journal of Ambulatory Care Management*, pp. 51–68.

Mizrahi, T. (1986). *Getting rid of patients: Contradictions in the socialization of physicians.* New Brunswick, NJ: Rutgers University Press.

Morris, R. B. (1989). *Witness at the creation.* New York: NAL-Dutton.

Pettigrew, T. F. (1981, Spring). Race and class in the 1980s: An interactive view. *Daedalus,* pp. 233–255.

Rose, S. (1989, February 18). Unauthorized CCH experiments probed. *Chicago Defender,* p. 1.

Saba, G. W., & Rodgers, D. V. (1989). Discrimination in urban family practice: Lessons from minority poor families. In G. W. Saba, B. M. Karrer, & K. V. Hardy (Eds.), *Minorities and family therapy* (pp. 177–207). New York: Haworth.

Sharf, B. F. (1986). Send in the clowns: The image of psychiatry during the Hinckley trial. *Journal of Communication, 36*(4), 80–93.

Sharf, B. F. (1990). Physician–patient communication as interpersonal rhetoric: A narrative approach. *Health Communication, 2,* 217–231.

Sharf, B. F., Kahler, J., Foley, R., Bomgaars, M., Grant, D., & Harper, S. (1990). *A shared understanding: Bridging racial and class differences in patient-doctor communication* (video and instructors' manual). Chapel Hill, NC: Health Sciences Consortium.

Shem, S. (1980). *The house of God.* New York: Dell.

Siegel, B. S. (1986). *Love, medicine, and miracles: Lessons learned about self-healing from a surgeon's experience with exceptional patients.* New York: Harper & Row.

Snow, L. P. (1974). Folk medical beliefs and their implications for care of patients. *Annals of Internal Medicine, 81,* 82–96.

Stewart, J. (1990). *Bridges not walls: a book about interpersonal communication* (5th ed.). Reading, MA: Addison-Wesley.

Taussig, M. T. (1980). Reification and the consciousness of the patient. *Social Science and Medicine, 14,* 3–13.

Vanderford, M. L., Smith, D. H., & Harris, W. S. (1992). Value identification in narrative discourse: Evaluation of an HIV education-demonstration project. *Journal of Applied Communication Research, 20,* 123–160.

Van Doren, C. (1982). *The great rehearsal.* Westport, CT: Greenwood.

Veatch, R. M. (Ed.). (1989). *Cross cultural perspectives in medical ethics: Readings.* Boston: Jones & Bartlett.

Waitzkin, H. (1991). *The politics of medical encounters: How patients and doctors deal with social problems.* New Haven, CT: Yale University Press.

Waitzkin, H., & Stoeckle, J. D. (1972). The communication of information about illness: Clinical, sociological, and methodological considerations. *Advances in Psychosomatic Medicine, 8,* 180–215.

Warshaw, C. (1989). Limitations of the medical model in the care of battered women. *Gender & Society, 3,* 506–517.

Watzlawick, P., Beavin, J. H., & Jackson, D. D. (1967). *Pragmatics of human communication: A study of interactional patterns, pathologies, and paradoxes.* New York: Norton.

*Webster's unabridged dictionary of the English language.* (1989). New York: Portland House.

West, C. (1984). *Routine complications: Trouble with talk between doctors and patients.* Bloomington: Indiana University Press.

Williams, W. C. (1961). A face of stone. In *The farmers' daughters: The collected stories of William Carlos Williams* (pp. 167–176). New York: New Directions.

# 7 A Research Agenda on Issues Affecting Poor and Minority Women: A Model for Understanding Their Health Needs

Ruth E. Zambrana
*University of California, Los Angeles*

The major purposes of this chapter are threefold: to provide an assessment of current knowledge on the health of poor and racial/ethnic women, to present an overview of the context of their use of health services, and to propose a research agenda and a model for understanding their health needs. Although the particular needs of women in general have generated serious concern and stimulated research on women's issues in the last decade, the needs of the most disadvantaged sectors of the population, poor women and women of color[1] have not received as extensive attention. The quality of life of poor and minority women, with specific reference to their health, mental health, and family roles, has been a low research priority. Rather, the majority of studies have focused either on the cultural consequences of their behavior or on issues related to acculturation into the dominant society (see reviews by Andrade, 1983; Baca-Zinn, 1982). Most studies also have tended to ignore issues of class (Nelson, 1982). Only a limited number of studies, mainly qualitative or of small sample size, and essays have attempted to identify special health needs of Latina and Black women (Boone, 1982; Jackson, 1981).

Although research has suggested that poor and racial/ethnic women face many social and economic barriers in their attempts to integrate into the dominant culture and that their health status is poor, the interpretations of the findings have led to explanations such as culture as an explanatory

---

[1]Throughout this article, the terms *women of color*, *minority women*, and *racial/ethnic women* are used interchangeably.

variable that have not significantly contributed to our knowledge of this group. Traditional, rigid demarcations between investigations of health and mental status and those of work and family roles have generated a limited model of women's health. More recently, researchers have developed a keener awareness of the relationship between work and family roles and health and mental health status (Kanter, 1977; Nathanson, 1980). For poor and racial/ethnic women in particular, these relationships have become strikingly clear as women's role responsibilities have increased. The socio-economic dimensions, including multiple role responsibilities within the family and psychosocial factors such as chronic life stress and forms of social support, are critical to an understanding of the health status of poor and minority women.

## BACKGROUND CHARACTERISTICS OF POOR
## AND MINORITY WOMEN

A review of the socio-demographic characteristics of the poor[2] and racial/ethnic[3] populations helps to explain some of the socioeconomic realities that influence their health status and other quality-of-life indicators. Blacks and Hispanics in the United States constitute about 18% of the total U.S. population. Blacks, the largest racial/ethnic minority group in the United States, are predominately concentrated in the South (53%) and in large urban centers in the Northeast and Northcentral regions of the United States. Seventy-nine percent of Blacks have completed high school and 13% are college graduates. The median income of Black families in 1981 was $13,270. Blacks are highly concentrated in service occupations (23%), as operators and laborers (27%), and as administrative support staff (24%). The Black unemployment rate is currently 18.9% (U.S. Department of Health & Human Services [USDHHS], 1985a).

The 14.6 million Hispanics in the United States represent 6.4% of the total U.S. population.[4] The largest group is comprised of Mexican-Ameri-

---

[2]There are very limited data on low-income White women. National data are aggregated by White, Black, and Other, and therefore do not reflect class distinctions.

[3]The major focus of data presented is in reference to Black, Mexican-American, and Puerto Rican subgroups. These are the largest racial/ethnic minority groups in the United States. However, it is recognized that other recent-immigrant groups from the Caribbean and Central America are at an economic disadvantage and have special health needs. The estimates of the number of undocumented workers in the United States range from 3 million to 12 million. Native Americans and Asian groups also represent distinct racial/ethnic populations and share a number of common conditions that contribute to poorer health status.

[4]There is tremendous diversity among and within the Hispanic population. This diversity is related in part to class position, cultural differences based on country of origin, generational differences in the United States, and regional/geographic distribution. Generalizations based on national data must be made with caution and understanding of the domains of diversity.

cans (60%), concentrated in the Southwest, followed by Puerto Ricans (14%) in the Northeast. In the past 15 years there has been a large influx of immigrants from Cuba (6%), South America, and most recently, Central America (20%). Geographically, 86% of all Hispanics live within 10 states and 63% are concentrated in three states: California, Texas, and New York. The great majority live in urban areas (U.S. Subcommittee on Census & Population, 1983).

Income potential is greatly affected by education. Lack of education clearly diminishes opportunities in the labor market. Hispanics tend to have completed fewer median school years than the general population. They also tend to be concentrated in lower-status blue-collar and white-collar occupations. Fifty-eight percent of Hispanics have completed a high school education. The median number of school years completed for Mexican-American women is 8.8 years; for Puerto Rican women it is 9.9 years; and for other Hispanics it is 12.2 years. For Black women, the median number of school years completed is 12.1 years. Education trends today for Black and Latina women continue to lag far behind White women (Massey, 1982).

Black, Mexican-American, and Puerto Rican women also tend to have more children at earlier ages than Anglo women and women in other Hispanic groups. The fertility rates for Puerto Rican, Mexican-American, and Black women are the same, 2.3 births per woman, compared to a rate of 1.7 for nonminority women. Just over half (51%) of Spanish-origin women and nearly half of Black women (49.4%) have incomes below the poverty level, compared with one fourth (25.7%) of Anglo women. The poverty rate for Latino heads of household is 3.4 times greater than that for Whites. For Puerto Rican, 40% of families are headed by women, compared to 37.7% of Blacks. For Mexican-Americans and other Hispanic families, the female head-of-household rates are about one-half these figures: 16% and 18%, respectively. The real income of Hispanic female-headed families declined during the 1970s (U.S. Commission on Civil Rights, 1982).

Women, especially racial/ethnic women, are also at a disadvantage because of the inability to find work and lower earnings. If wives and female heads of household were paid the wages that similarly qualified men received, about half of the families now living in poverty would no longer be poor. Currently, the incomes of more than one third of single mothers with children under 6 who work full time at paid labor are still below the poverty line.

## FACTORS THAT CONTRIBUTE TO HEALTH STATUS: CURRENT KNOWLEDGE

A major effort to address substantive and research issues in the area of women's health was realized at a conference sponsored by the National Center for Health Services Research. One major theme of the presented papers was:

... the worlds of women as relatives of the ill, as patients themselves or as decision-makers in situations influencing the health and health care of workers should be analyzed with respect to and for the meanings held by women in those worlds. In sum, research about women must be grounded in women's views, definitions, and concerns lest health care research continue to render inaccurate and biased views of those worlds based on the inappropriate categories generated at second hand by persons not a part of those worlds. (Olesen, 1977, p. 2)

Unfortunately, conference participants limited themselves to addressing a homogeneous population. As one commentator aptly pointed out, "we spent relatively little time delineating in specific terms the kinds of research needed to identify the needs of different segments of the female population—the racial segments, the ethnic segments, the children, the older women" (Olesen, 1977, p. 87).

A later analysis of "areas of deficient data collection and integration," related to women's health failed to even mention the need to collect data on minority women or other subpopulations (Muller, 1979). Information on the health status of poor and minority women, particularly their utilization patterns and help-seeking behaviors, are sorely lacking. A review of data in *Women and Health, U.S. 1980* (Moore, 1980) advised, in one paragraph, that data on minority women are needed.

Since the late 1970s there have been a number of data-collection efforts that have provided national data on racial/ethnic minorities. The undercount of the Black and Hispanic populations in the 1970 Census led to political advocacy by representatives of these groups to obtain national data. The 1978 National Health Interview Survey was the first effort to obtain data on a representative sample of the Black population. The National Health Interview Survey (Trevino & Moss, 1984) and the Hispanic Health and Nutrition Examination Survey (HHANES) represent national data-collection efforts resulting from several years of political advocacy on the part of Hispanic organizations.

During the last decade there have been three major government reports on the health status of low-income and minority populations. Health status trends among these groups were first substantively addressed in 1979. Racial minorities were found to have almost twice the infant mortality of Whites, a higher proportion of maternity-related and other reproductive health problems, and the highest incidence of acute conditions among lowest income females (U.S. Department of Health, Education, & Welfare, 1979). Minorities and low-income groups had higher death rates than the general population for four of the five leading causes of death: heart disease, cancer, stroke, and diabetes. These reports, however, provided only limited information on the specific health needs of women.

The two most recent government reports on racial/ethnic minorities are *Black and Minority Health* (USDHHS, 1985a) and *Women's Health* (USDHHS, 1985b). Several areas were identified as common to all of the groups and as contributing to poorer health status:

1. Ethnic minority women experience higher infant mortality rates, higher neonatal death rates, and higher postneonatal death rates. Low birthweight, which accounts for 60% of infant deaths, is higher among racial/ethnic minorities, especially Black women (12.4%) and Puerto Ricans (9.1%).

2. There is a greater prevalence of some chronic diseases among racial/ethnic minority women, such as diabetes, hypertension, cardiovascular diseases, and certain types of cancer such as cervical cancer.

3. There is a lower life expectancy of 5–7 years among racial/ethnic women than among their White counterparts, attributable to higher rates of chronic disease and less access to medical care systems, particularly for early detection and prevention of disease (USDHHS, 1985a).

In general, there is now a consensus among researchers that poor and racial/ethnic women are at a disadvantage in terms of their health status (e.g., Institute of Medicine, 1985). Overall assessments of the nature and types of disease patterns among the populations with respect to poor Black, Puerto Rican, and Mexican-American women and immigrant women are available. The difficulty, however, lies in assessing health problems among different racial and ethnic subgroups, especially poor White women and women of racial/ethnic minority backgrounds because of the failure to control for the socioeconomic status and other quality-of-life indicators of the groups under study (see, e.g., Camasso & Camasso, 1986). The changing composition of the family and the increasing numbers of employed women heads of households, with the anticipated adverse effect on their health status, make such information even more vital.

Of course, the health needs of low-income women are not necessarily distinct from her higher income racial or ethnic peers, but the combination of her disadvantages of gender, class, and racial/ethnic status increases the likelihood that she will have serious health needs and the probable likelihood that those needs will not be adequately met. Finally, although national health statistics are increasingly being compiled and reported by ethnicity, race, and gender, local health statistics generally are not. Most hospitals and health service agencies usually do not systematically report health information by ethnicity or class background. Without such basic data on health status and health-seeking behavior among these populations, in-depth study and analysis of local trends are seriously limited.

The methodological limitations of the studies that have been conducted are most clearly illustrated in the area of reproductive health. Two areas of particular concern are adolescent mothers and women of childbearing age. Although our knowledge has increased in the areas of adolescent childbearing and maternal and child health, there are still many gaps with reference to poor and racial/ethnic minority women.

## ADOLESCENT CHILDBEARING

Over the past 20 years a national decline in fertility levels has characterized a broad range of social groups within the United States, including women at all socioeconomic levels, racial/ethnic backgrounds, and religious groups (Gibson, 1976; Rindfuss & Sweet, 1978). In contrast, the number of pregnancies and births among unmarried adolescent girls has recently increased. The percentage of teen pregnancies has risen over the last 10 years from 8.5% of 15- to 19-year-olds in 1971 to 16.2% in 1979. In their study of sexually active teenage girls, Zelnik and Kantner (1980) found an increase of 50% among those who had never used contraceptives. The percentage of unwed births within the adolescent population has risen 60% since 1965 and 300% since 1942 (Bolton, 1982; Zelnik, Kantner, & Ford, 1981).

Teenage pregnancy and childbearing are now viewed as significant problems with negative psychological, social, medical, educational, and economic impact. Adolescent pregnancy and parenthood have been found to carry a high risk of adverse consequences, both short- and long-term, for mother, child, and family, leading Furstenburg (1976) to label it a "syndrome of defeat." Pregnant adolescents have been found to be obstetrically at risk, with maternal and infant mortality higher among teen mothers than among other groups. Nonfatal health complications have been found to be more common for teen mothers than for the population at large as well. Adolescent mothers are less likely to finish high school than other adolescents, which, combined with lack of child care, severely limits occupational opportunities (Guttmacher Institute, 1981).

With few exceptions, empirical research on adolescent sexuality and pregnancy has focused on Black and Anglo populations. Black adolescents were found to be more likely than Anglos to have nonmarital coitus without use of contraception, more likely to become pregnant, and more likely to keep their babies (Zelnik et al., 1981). Early inquiries have focused on the negative outcomes, and have relied on explanations based only on race and socioeconomic background. Not until the late 1970s was attention focused more extensively on the nature of the problem (e.g., socioeconomic antecedents), consequences, and intervention strategies. Even now, however, the national concern with adolescent reproductive behavior has almost totally neglected the large Latino population, an exception being the recent work by Becerra and de Anda (1984).

Latinos are one of the fastest growing ethnic groups in the United States. Research indicates that they will become the largest racial/ethnic minority group in the country during the first decade of the 21st century (Hayes-Bautista, Schink, & Chapa, 1986). Almost half of the Mexican-Americans, who make up 60% of the Latino population, are under 20 years of age (U.S. Bureau of the Census, 1984). For many years Latinos have had the highest fertility rate of any group identified in census data (Ventura & Heuser, 1981). The 1980 statistics show that a relatively large proportion, nearly one in five, of Latino births are to teenagers. Although interest in and use of contraceptives by Latinas have been reported in some studies to be high, unmarried Latina adolescents have far fewer rates of contraceptive use than adolescents from other ethnic groups (Becerra & de Anda, 1984; Rochat, 1981; Stein, 1985; U.S. Department of Health, Education, & Welfare, 1979).

Adolescent sexuality and fertility behavior are influenced by experiences within the family, peer group, school, media, and other institutions. Historical background, sociocultural values and norms, socioeconomic status, ethnicity, and religion have all been found to contribute to the development and expression of adolescent sexuality (Chilman, 1983). These are critical social variables that suggest an interactive model of developmental, cultural, and environmental forces that affects adolescent decision making and behaviors. This perspective suggests that relevant directions for the prevention of the syndrome of defeat associated with adolescent childbearing may be found. In conducting research that is sensitive to this constellation of factors, women's strengths in their sexual decision making also may be more fully appreciated.

## MATERNAL AND CHILD HEALTH

There is important evidence that points to ethnic variation in pregnancy outcomes for mothers and infants, with Black and Latina women placed at higher risk than women in most other ethnic groups. Mexican-American women between the ages of 15 and 29 have a higher percentage of deaths from complications of pregnancy than do Anglos (U.S. Subcommittee on Census & Population, 1983). Birthweights are 2.3 times lower for babies born to Black women in California than for Whites, and are also lower for Latinas (Williams, 1980). In a recent analysis of perinatal outcomes among Medicaid recipients in California, Norris and Williams (1984) found that White non-Hispanic women had the highest absolute and proportional decreases in the percentage of low-weight (less than 2,500 grams) births, whereas Blacks had the lowest decrease. In 1978, nearly 80% of White mothers began prenatal care in the first trimester compared with 60% of Black mothers (USDHHS, 1981). National data are not readily available for Latinas.

Several investigators have noted the relationship between late or no prenatal care and poorer pregnancy outcomes (Boone, 1982; Jackson, 1981; Norris & Williams, 1984; Showstack, Budetti, & Minkler, 1984). All of these authors also suggested that research and development of reasonable solutions and interventions are needed to improve maternal and child health. Despite these recommendations, there remains a significant gap in the maternal and child health literature for poor and racial/ethnic groups, and particularly around factors of class and ethnicity as they affect utilization of prenatal care.

In the last decade, two major questions have guided the study of prenatal care and outcome: the aspects of care that make a difference and the characteristics of the populations who seek care. The mechanisms whereby the mother's emotional state influences progress during the pregnancy and course of delivery are not known. Some studies, however, have identified nonmedical factors such as education, social support, and improved nutrition as contributing to more positive pregnancy outcomes (Barnard & Sumner, 1981). Differences in birth outcomes among different racial/ethnic groups seem to be related to social class and to lack of early initiation of prenatal care or no prenatal care (Boone, 1982; Jackson, 1981; Norris & Williams, 1984; Showstack et al., 1984). At present, little information is available on factors that contribute to the late initiation of prenatal care, either within racial/ethnic groups or between groups.

Maternal and child well-being are also influenced by psychosocial factors such as chronic stress and social support, and by breastfeeding practices, which are in turn reflective of social factors. Life stress has been examined as a factor in obstetrical complications. Gorsuch and Key (1974) found that major life events occurring 6 months prior to the pregnancy or during the second and third trimesters were associated with abnormalities. Social support has been shown to be an important factor in the maintenance of well-being and in decisions regarding help-seeking behaviors (Dohrenwend & Dohrenwend, 1978). Research on social support and health more broadly strengthens the evidence that support may be an important factor in pregnancy, labor, delivery, and prematurity (Cobb, 1976; Heller, 1979; House, 1981). Nuckolls, Cassell, and Kaplan (1972) found that women with high life change and low psychosocial assets (i.e., social support, positive attitudes toward pregnancy) suffered more complications at delivery than women with more assets or fewer life changes. Similarly, Lewis and Jones (1980) found that adolescents who had high stress and low social support also had more problems in delivery than other groups with stronger social support or less stress.

Race, ethnicity, and class may be discriminators of breastfeeding behavior, which is considered an important factor in both the physical and emotional development of the infant (Jeliffe & Jeliffe, 1982). In recent years, breastfeeding behavior has become more common among well-educated, high-socioeconomic status women, particularly Whites, than among lower income women, particularly Latinas and Blacks. In part, this phenomenon is related to education, participation in childbirth education, and a supportive family and institutional environment. Many middle-class women now select physicians and birth settings based on compatible values, such as environments supportive of breastfeeding. In a recent review of the literature on breastfeeding, Scrimshaw, Engle, Arnold, and Haynes (1984) concluded that very little empirical evidence is available on the factors influencing low-income Black and Latina women in their infant feeding decisions. Furthermore, Scrimshaw, Engle, and Horseley's (1985) work with Mexican-American women in Los Angeles identified institutional barriers to breastfeeding, particularly in the hospital of delivery. Molina (1983) stated that breastfeeding behavior requires active encouragement among Latina women, who tend to rely on bottle formulas because they believe this method is more nourishing. The need "to identify and reduce barriers which keep women from beginning or continuing to breastfeed their infants" was also noted by the U.S. Surgeon General, as was the need to encourage such breastfeeding in the Latina and Black population as a whole (USDHHS, 1984).

To date, few studies have examined the importance of social class as a variable, and the most recent work in the field of childbirth has minimized this factor (Nelson, 1982). According to Nelson, the majority of studies in reproductive health have been conducted on Anglo middle-class women who have education, knowledge, and familiarity with the health care system. Nelson also concluded with the precaution that a study that ignores social class as a variable may well lead to unsound generalizations.

## THE CONTEXT OF HEALTH STATUS AND FUNCTIONING

The low-income woman has basic primary and preventive health needs for herself and her family. She must address these needs using a male-dominated, affluent health care delivery system oriented toward tertiary care. At each step of the way the woman is faced with complex responsibilities and encounters multiple barriers, while being responsible for maintaining wellness and preventing illness for her family under socioeconomic conditions that promote mental and physical illness. She must sort out those health concerns that are most appropriately alleviated through traditional support, such as information and assistance from family and community, and those that are best served by modern medicine and institutional providers. She must learn how the health care system is organized, where to seek appropriate care, and how to linguistically and culturally translate their concerns into information that will be meaningful to health professionals. She bears the burden of evaluating prescribed treatment, both in terms of modern medical risk and in terms of congruence with her own culture and lifestyle. At the same time, poor and racial/ethnic women are most likely to be heads of households, to have larger families, to bear the heaviest burden of caring for the health and well-being of all family members, to be in the poorest health themselves, to experience the greatest psychologically induced symptoms or illnesses, and to be at highest medical risk, particularly during pregnancy and childbirth (Hurst & Zambrana, 1980; Marieskind, 1980; USDHHS, 1985a).

Racial/ethnic women share a disproportionately large responsibility not only for the care and nurturing of the children but also for their support. This responsibility is particularly striking given the increase in families headed by women and their disproportionate stratification in the labor force. A study of single parents found that poor health, personal illness, or the illness of a child or relative prevented a number of respondents from entering the labor market (Morgan, 1981). Hurst and Zambrana (1980) also found that poor health, particularly after childbirth, was a major factor in accounting for the discontinuous work histories among Puerto Rican women in New York.

Understanding access issues among poor and minority women requires consideration of economic, cultural, and systemic factors (Dutton, 1978). Whereas middle-class women are at least able to enter the health care system via a personal physician who can act as buffer, link, and translator, poor women confront impersonal institutions on their own. Minority women, particularly Hispanics, may also be handicapped by language, in addition to lack of education, information, and insurance.

Insurance coverage is a major barrier. Blacks and Puerto Ricans were twice as likely as Whites not to have health insurance. Among Mexican-Americans the noninsured rate is three and one-half times greater than that of White non-Hispanics. Individuals with low family income were found to be less likely to have health insurance. The most frequent reason cited for lack of health insurance reported by all racial/ethnic groups was inability to pay. Among Mexican-Americans, low rates of insurance coverage may also be accounted for by employers who generally do not provide such coverage as an employment benefit (Trevino & Moss, 1983).

Although increasing numbers of studies point to a relationship between health status and social roles, class and cultural variables as causal factors remain a poorly understood aspect of the health of low-income and minority women. Although cultural practices of Hispanic groups are related to family life and beliefs in nontraditional sources of health care, class and institutional barriers may be stronger predictors of health care-seeking behavior and health status (Chesney, Chavira, Hall, & Gary, 1982). As is true in many areas, the existence of cultural determinants of health behaviors tends to vary inversely with social-class standing.

Language and educational barriers prevent the poor, Hispanic, and minority woman from receiving most of the public health education that the middle class now takes for granted. She is not exposed to the controversies surrounding unnecessary surgery, informed consent, and sterilization reported regularly in the English-language press, which would make her a more discerning health "consumer." She has limited access to evaluations of potentially dangerous products conducted by such consumer organizations as the Consumer's Union or by the Food and Drug Administration. Books about family care, female health-related concerns, or how to be an active health consumer are rarely translated to Spanish and, even when they are, the information is not accessible to women who have little formal education, money, or exposure to bookstores and libraries.

Although studies of the health needs of poor and racial/ethnic women are important, it is most critical that these studies be sensitive to historical, cultural, and socioeconomic factors. Poor women have been subjected to persistent degrading treatment by the medical care system (Corea, 1977; Shaw, 1974). Researchers need to become aware of the situational factors that affect poor and minority women's health care status to avoid the perpetuation of stereotypes and nonconstructive labeling.

## A MODEL FOR UNDERSTANDING THEIR HEALTH NEEDS

Data and a research agenda would be meaningless without a context in which to interpret them (Becerra & Zambrana, 1985). Thus the health status of poor and minority women should be understood in relation to their race, class, and gender. Existing models and analyses can only provide limited explanatory power if directly applied to poor and racial/ethnic populations. For example, the analytic frameworks that have been developed, such as Becker's (1974) Health Belief Model and Aday and colleagues' (1980) Access to Care Model, have emerged from the study of dominant-culture middle-class populations. In a recent review by Verbrugge (1985) on gender and health, the author failed to address differential risks among women due to race and class.

A model that seeks to interpret data on these groups in a meaningful way must expand its parameters to take into account clearly defined socioeconomic, racial, cultural, and regional variables that have a particular relationship with access to health care resources, and psychosocial variables that address the relationship between health status and functioning, chronic life stress, sources of social support, work status, and occupational history. It has been suggested that the "mere struggle to provide for one's family causes half of all Black female adults to live in psychological stress" (*Health Factsheet on Black Women*, 1983). Occupational history may also be an important determinant of the health status of poor and racial/ethnic women who work (Mullings, 1984). Black women have a 39% greater chance of sustaining job-related disease and serious work-related injuries than non-minorities. Hispanics are overrepresented in such high-risk industries as construction, the garment industry, and metal mining (USDHHS, 1985a).

The ethnic and class differences within racial/ethnic groups must be carefully controlled for. A number of researchers have argued that hetero-geneity within Hispanic and Black groups by both class and country of origin must be recognized, particularly among the Hispanic population, which varies along the three parameters of race, ethnicity, and class. Data on Hispanics must be analyzed by region and cultural background (e.g., Puerto Rican, Mexican-American, and Cuban). Socio-demographic charac-teristics among these subgroups will also vary, together with health indi-cators. For individuals of Hispanic origin, the concept of acculturation needs close evaluation. In this author's opinion, the measurement of accul-turation is a proxy for social class, which must be understood within the context both of the recency of arrival (if an immigrant) and of language proficiency as a measure of an individual's familiarity with dominant-cul-ture systems. One recent study found that low acculturation was highly correlated with low social class and lower use of health services (Chesney et al., 1982).

This interactive model requires that social, behavioral, and environ-mental variables be clearly defined and examined both in designing studies and in interpreting data on poor and racial/ethnic populations (see, e.g., Carr & Wolfe, 1979). Dill (1983) aptly stated the importance of a more comprehensive perspective on racial/ethnic women:

> Concretely, and from a research perspective this suggests the importance of looking at both the structures which shape women's lives and their self-pre-sentations. This would provide us not only with a means of gaining insight into the ways in which racial, class and sexual oppression are viewed but with a means of generating conceptual categories that will aid us in extending our knowledge of their situation. At the same time, this new knowledge will broaden and even reform our conceptualization of women's situation. (p. 139)

## A RESEARCH AGENDA: BEGINNING DIRECTIONS
## FOR FUTURE RESEARCH

The recognition that poor and minority female populations have special needs is not a novel idea. Many of the initial public health endeavors in the late 19th and early 20th centuries, such as milk stations and neighborhood health centers, were aimed at women and children. Endeavors in the 1960s such as the "War on Poverty" programs were also geared to services for poor and minority women and their families (Davis & Schoen, 1978).

This section proposes a selective research agenda in the areas of reproductive health, health practices and cancer, poor and racial/ethnic minority women and aging, and the relationship between chronic life stress, social support, and health status and functioning. It should be recognized, however, that there are many other areas in which significant gaps in knowledge severely limit our understanding of minority health needs. For example, one rapidly escalating public health problem is the incidence of AIDS among minority women and children. It has been shown that increasing numbers of new pediatric AIDS cases are among Hispanic and Black children. The agenda is proposed within the context of a model that recognizes the plurality and interactive nature of factors influencing health status.

### Reproductive Health

Reproductive health represents a critical area of health care for poor and minority women because it includes those aspects of reproduction currently subject to public legislation and political action. Abortion, sterilization, and contraception are issues important to all women, but in many ways policy and practice, coupled with historic class and race inequalities, have made these particularly significant subjects for minority women, who have the least knowledge and are the most vulnerable population groups. A number of critical research areas that require attention are the relationship between occupational hazards and reproductive outcome, the prevalence of Caesarian section and hysterectomy, studies on the effects and context of materials presented in family life/sex education classes in schools, efficacy of informed consent procedures currently in use (with comparisons of experiences of different ethnic and social groups), studies of providers and recipients of genetic counseling, and amniocentesis and women of color.[5]

---

[5]A detailed research agenda has been developed by the Women's Rights Litigation Clinic and the Institute for Research on Women at Rutgers University in their project on "Reproductive Laws for the 1990s." The major areas identified are: social, economic, and technical aspects of infertility; use of reproductive services; and protections for choice and prenatal screening. The research agenda calls for a particular focus on how these issues affect women of color.

## Health Practices and Cancer

An important area of investigation includes health practices such as nutrition, substance use, and exercise, and their relationship to socioeconomic status and influence on health status and functioning. Mounting evidence suggests that poor health practices, or behavioral risks among lower socioeconomic groups, may contribute to their higher health risks. A number of studies have shown a relationship between health practices, ethnicity, and social class (Hamburg, Elliot, & Parron, 1982; Marcus & Crane, 1985). These preliminary findings need further investigation, using larger samples and including questions about drinking and smoking practices among poor and racial/ethnic women. Does lower use of alcohol and nicotine among Latina women contribute to more favorable birth outcomes, for example?

Major risk factors such as use of alcohol and tobacco, nutritional and dietary factors, and occupation are thought to account for approximately 72% of cancer mortality and 69% of incidence. Socioeconomic status also has been correlated with poorer survival from cancer and increased incidence of lung, breast, and cervical cancers among poor and minority women (USDHHS, 1985a). Again, there is limited information on poor and minority women, especially Hispanic women.

In response to the lack of data on Hispanics, the National Cancer Institute (NCI), Division of Cancer Prevention and Control has developed an Hispanic Cancer Control Program (HCCP). In the last year the HCCP has completed an annotated bibliography of literature on cancer and Hispanics (NCI, 1986a, 1986b). A research agenda developed by NCI in April 1986 defined the need for the collection of data locally and nationally using ethnic identifiers to develop cancer control interventions that address interethnic differences in cancer incidence, mortality, and survival, and to conduct research that examines basic risk factors in relationship to cancer incidence (NCI, 1986c), all virtually unexplored areas.

## Aging of Poor and Racial/Ethnic Women

There is a dearth of information about aging in the racial/ethnic subgroup, although it is known that these women become poorer earlier and at a greater rate. Understanding the qualitative experiences of these women will require investigating their labor market experiences, the types and nature of benefits accrued over time, if any, and the influence of their work experiences on their health status. The subjective meaning of aging among the different cohorts of poor and racial/ethnic women is also an important issue. Exploration of the meaning and quality of aging necessitates exam-

ining their educational and work backgrounds and whether these contribute
to a sense of life satisfaction. The economic and social options open to
these women after rearing their families, particularly if they are divorced
or widowed and have not had continuous work participation outside the
home, are other issues.

## Chronic Life Stress and Health Status and Functioning

The inquiry into stress must assess the nature and extent of chronic stress
over time and its impact on health status and functioning. It must conceptualize stress in relation to the quality of life issues of being poor, female,
and of color (see, e.g., Vega & Miranda, 1985). Analysis of social support,
a buffering factor in most stress models, is often fraught with methodological difficulties and rarely focuses on poor and minority women. In a
recent review, Vaux (1985) emphasized the lack of comparative research
on social support and how "relatively little is known about how it varies
across subgroups in the population" (p. 89). Refinement of these conceptual
areas and cross-validation of instruments to assure that they indeed measure
these concepts for poor and racial/ethnic women needs research. One important direction may be to explore the relationship between nature and
types of stress, sources of social support, and chronic illness. In a cross-
cultural study, it would be important to examine the differential impact of
these variables on the various groups.

## IMPLEMENTING THE AGENDA

Formulation of a model and a research agenda for poor and racial/ethnic
women is an important step toward achieving the goal of improved quality
of life for low-income and racial/ethnic individuals. The issues and agenda
developed in the several reports and policy statements discussed here clearly
point in the same direction. Given such agreement on issues and agenda,
an equally significant question arises: Who is responsible for seeking further
understanding of the problems and for proposing and implementing policy
solutions that are both relevant and appropriate?

    The answer to this question is both simple and complex. It is simple in
that the major health care needs of poor and racial/ethnic populations are
generally known, namely, better preventive and primary health care services.
The major issue for poor and racial/ethnic populations, especially the
women, is access and availability of services. It is also complex in that the
link between needs identification, policy formulation, and the development
of social welfare programs is problematic at best. An example is the move

for cost-containment in medical care that has led to the closure, defunding, and underfunding of public health facilities and to decreases in medical care benefits for the indigent. Thus, whatever the merits of the economic debate, the already underserved segment of the population is accumulating the disadvantages of increased health care costs and reduced services. In this author's opinion, a solution is to develop and implement a national health insurance program geared to respond to identified needs and to provide services to local communities, with community-level research supported as an integral part of all community-based health care services. This will assure the ongoing assessment of needs as the basis for future social welfare policy formulation and planning. The preeminent need is to lower the barriers that continue to limit access of the poor and of racial/ethnic populations to essential human services.

## ACKNOWLEDGMENTS

The author acknowledges the support of a UCLA Faculty Career Development award during the fall 1986 for preparation of this manuscript. Further acknowledgment is made to the research and editorial assistance of Laura Cummins and Robert Wymss. This chapter is a revised version of Zambrana (1988).

## REFERENCES

Andrade, S. J. (Ed.). (1983). *Latino families in the United States: A resourcebook for family education.* Education Department, Planned Parenthood Federation of America, New York.

Baca-Zinn, M. (1982). Review essay: Mexican-American women in the social sciences. *Signs, 8,* 259–272.

Barnard, K. E., & Sumner, G. A. (1981). The health of women with fertility-related needs. In L. V. Klerman (Ed.), *Research priorities in maternal and child health: Report of a conference June 9–10, 1981* (pp. 7–21). Washington, DC: Office of Maternal and Child Health, HSA, PHS, U.S. Department of Health and Human Services.

Becerra, R. M., & de Anda, D. (1984). Pregnancy and motherhood among Mexican American adolescents. *Health and Social Work, 9*(2), 106–123.

Becerra, R. M., & Zambrana, R. E. (1985). Methodological approaches to research on Hispanics. *Social Work Research and Abstracts, 21*(2), 42–49.

Becker, M. H. (1974). *The health belief model and personal health behavior.* San Francisco: Charles B. Slack.

Bolton, F. G. (1982). *The pregnant adolescent: Problems of premature parenthood.* Beverly Hills, CA: Sage.

Boone, M. S. (1982). A socio-medical study of infant mortality among disadvantaged Blacks. *Human Organization, 41*(3), 227–236.

Camasso, M. J., & Camasso, A. E. (1986). Social supports, undesirable life events and psychological distress in a disadvantaged population. *Social Service Review,* September, 378–394.

Carr, W., & Wolfe, S. (1979). Unmet needs as sociomedical indicators. In J. Elinson & A. Siegmann (Eds.), *Sociomedical health indicators* (pp. 33–46). Farmingdale, NY: Baywood.

Chesney, A. P., Chavira, J. A., Hall, R. P., & Gary, H. E., Jr. (1982). Barriers to medical care of Mexican-Americans: The role of social class, acculturation, and social isolation. *Medical Care, 20*(9), 883–891.

Chilman, C. (1983). *Adolescent sexuality in a changing American society.* New York: Wiley.

Cobb, S. (1976). Social support as a moderator of life stress. *Psychosomatic Medicine, 38*(5), 300–314.

Corea, G. (1977). *The hidden malpractice: How American medicine treats women as patients and professionals.* New York: Morrow.

Davis, K., & Schoen, C. (1978). *Health and the war on poverty: A ten-year appraisal.* Washington, DC: Brookings.

Dill, B. T. (1983). Race, class and gender: Prospects for an all-inclusive sisterhood. *Feminist Studies, 9*(Spring), 131–150.

Dohrenwend, D. B., & Dohrenwend, B. P. (1978). Some issues in research on stressful life events. *Journal of Nervous and Mental Disorders, 166,* 7–15.

Dutton, D. B. (1978). Explaining the low use of health services by the poor: Costs, attitudes or delivery systems? *American Sociological Review, 43,* 348–368.

Furstenburg, F. F. (1976). *Unplanned parenthood: The social consequences of teenage childbearing.* New York: The Free Press.

Gibson, C. (1976). The U.S. fertility decline, 1961–1975: The contribution of changes in marital status and marital fertility. *Family Planning Perspectives, 8,* 249–252.

Gorsuch, R. I., & Key, M. K. (1974). Abnormalities of pregnancy as a function of anxiety and life stress. *Psychosomatic Medicine, 36,* 352–361.

Guttmacher Institute. (1981). *Teenage pregnancy: The problem hasn't gone away.* New York: Author.

Hamburg, D. A., Elliot, G. R., & Parron, D. L. (1982). *Health and behavior frontiers of research in the biobehavioral sciences.* Institute of Medicine. Washington, DC: National Academy Press.

Hayes-Bautista, D. E., Schink, W. O., & Chapa, J. (1986). *The burden of support: The young Latino population in an aging American society.* Palo Alto, CA: Stanford University Press.

*Health factsheet on Black women.* (1983, Winter). National Women's Health Project, National Women's Health Network.

Heller, K. (1979). The effect of social support: Prevention of treatment implications. In A. P. Goldstein & F. H. Kanfer (Eds.), *Maximizing treatment gains in transfer enhancement in psychotherapy* (pp. 353–382). New York: Academic Press.

House, J. S. (1981). *Work, stress and social support.* Reading, MA: Addison-Wesley.

Hurst, M., & Zambrana, R. E. (1980). The health careers of urban women: A study in East Harlem. *Signs, 5*(3), 112–126. (Reprinted in C. R. Stimpson, E. Dixler, M. J. Nelson, & K. B. Jatrakis [Eds.], *Women and the American cities* [pp. 109–123]. Chicago: University of Chicago Press, 1980)

Institute of Medicine, Division of Health Promotion & Disease Prevention. (1985, January). *The prevention of low birthweight.* Washington, DC: National Academy Press.

Jackson, J. J. (1981). Urban Black Americans. In A. Harwood (Ed.), *Ethnicity and medical care.* Cambridge, MA: Harvard University Press.

Jeliffe, D. B., & Jeliffe, E. F. P. (1982). Cultural traditions and nutritional practices related to pregnancy and lactation. *Symposium Swedish Nutritional Foundation,* 48–61.

Kanter, R. (1977). *Work and family in the United States: A critical review and agenda for research and policy.* New York: Russell Sage Foundation.

Lewis, J. D., & Jones, A. C. (1980, September). *Psychological stress, social support systems and pregnancy complications in adolescents.* Paper presented at the annual meeting of the American Psychological Association, Montreal.

Marcus, A. C., & Crane, L. A. (1985). Smoking behavior among U.S. Latinos: An emerging challenge for public health. *American Journal of Public Health, 75*(2), 169–172.

Marieskind, H. I. (1980). *Women in the health system.* St. Louis, MO: Mosby.

Massey, D. (1982, March). *The demographic and economic position of Hispanics in the United States: 1980.* Report to the National Commission for Employment Policy.

Molina, C. (1983). Family health promotion: A conceptual framework for "La Salud" and "El Bienestar" in Latino communities. In S. J. Andrade (Ed.), *Latino families in the United States: A resourcebook for family life education* (pp. 35–42). New York: Education Department, Planned Parenthood Federation of America.

Moore, E. (1980). Women and health: United States. *Public Health Reports,* September–October supplement.

Morgan, L. A. (1981, August). *Access to training programs: Barriers encountered by Hispanic female heads-of-household in New York City.* New York: Puerto Rican Legal Defense and Education Fund.

Muller, C. (1979). Women and health statistics. *Women and Health, 4*(1), 37–59.

Mullings, L. (1984). Minority women, work and health. In W. Chavkin (Ed.), *Double exposure: Women's health hazards on the job and at home* (pp. 121–138). New York: Monthly Review Press.

Nathanson, C. A. (1980). Social roles and health status among women: The significance of employment. *Social Science and Medicine, 14A,* 463–471.

National Cancer Institute. (1986a). *Annotated bibliography of the literature on cancer in Hispanics.* Rockville, MD: NCI, Division of Cancer Prevention and Control, Hispanic Cancer Control Program.

National Cancer Institute. (1986b). *Information systems and data sources related to surveillance indicators for monitoring the progress of Hispanics toward achieving the cancer control national objectives.* Rockville, MD: NCI, Division of Cancer Prevention and Control, Hispanic Cancer Control Program.

National Cancer Institute. (1986c). *Proceedings summary of the Hispanic cancer control program workshop* (April 17–18). Rockville, MD: NCI, Division of Cancer Prevention and Control, Hispanic Cancer Control Program.

Nelson, M. K. (Ed.). (1982). The effect of childbirth preparation on women of different social classes. *Journal of Health and Social Behavior, 23*(4), 339–352.

Norris, F. D., & Williams, R. (1984). Perinatal outcomes among Medicaid recipients in California. *American Journal of Public Health, 74*(10).

Nuckolls, K. B., Cassell, J., & Kaplan, B. H. (1972). Psychosocial assets, life crises, and the prognosis of pregnancy. *American Journal of Epidemiology, 95,* 431–441.

Olesen, V. (Ed.). (1977). *Women and their health: Research implications for a new era.* Springfield, VA: National Technical Information Service.

Rindfuss, R., & Sweet, J. (1978). The pervasiveness of postwar fertility trends in the United States. In K. Taeuber, L. Bumpas, & J. Sweet (Eds.), *Social demography* (pp. 15–41). New York: Academic Press.

Rochat, R. (1981). Family planning practices among Anglo and Hispanic women in the U.S. counties bordering Mexico. *Family Planning Perspectives, 13,* 176–180.

Scrimshaw, S. C. M., Engle, P. L., Arnold, A., & Haynes, K. (1984). *The cultural context of breastfeeding in the United States.* Paper presented at the Surgeon General's Workshop on Breastfeeding and Human Lactation, Rochester, New York. Summarized in the *Report of the Surgeon General's Workshop on Breastfeeding and Human Lactation,* U.S. Department of Health and Human Services, DHHS Publication No. HRS-D-MC, 84-2 (1984).

Scrimshaw, S. C. M., Engle, P. L., & Horseley, K. (1985). Use of prenatal services by women of Mexican origin and descent in Los Angeles. *Prevention in Human Services,* Spring.

Shaw, N. S. (1974). *Forced labor: Maternity care in the U.S.* New York: Pergamon.

Showstack, J. A., Budetti, P. P., & Minkler, D. (1984). Factors associated with birthweight: An exploration of the roles of prenatal care and length of gestation. *American Journal of Public Health, 74*(9), 1003–1008.

Stein, S. J. (1985). *Factors related to contraceptive use among Mexican-American adolescents.* Unpublished doctoral dissertation, Wright Institute, Los Angeles.

Trevino, F. M., & Moss, A. J. (1983). Health insurance coverage and physician visits among Hispanic and non-Hispanic people. In *Health: United States, 1983.* Washington, DC: U.S. Public Health Service, National Center for Health Statistics, DHHS Publication No. (PHS) 84-1232.

Trevino, F. M., & Moss, A. J. (1984). Health insurance for Hispanic, Black and White Americans. *Vital and Health Statistics* (Series 10, No. 148). Washington, DC: U.S. Public Health Service, National Center for Health Statistics, DHHS Publication No. (PHS) 84-1576.

U.S. Bureau of the Census. (1984, July). *Population division.* Washington, DC: U.S. Government Printing Office.

U.S. Commission on Civil Rights. (1982). *Unemployment and underemployment among Blacks, Hispanics and women.* Washington, DC: U.S. Government Printing Office.

U.S. Department of Health, Education, & Welfare. (1979). (M. Rudov & N. Santangelo, preparers.) *Health status of low-income groups.* Washington, DC: U.S. Government Printing Office. DHEW Publication No. (HRA) 79-627.

U.S. Department of Health & Human Services. (1981). *Health: United States 1981.* Hyattsville, MD: U.S. Public Health Service, Publication No. (PHS) 82-1232.

U.S. Department of Health & Human Services. (1984). *Report of the Surgeon General's workshop on breastfeeding and human lactation.* DHHS Publication No. HRS-D-MC 84-2.

U.S. Department of Health & Human Services. (1985a). *Black and minority health.* Report of the Secretary's Task Force, Executive Summary (Vol. I), Washington, DC.

U.S. Department of Health & Human Services. (1985b). *Women's health.* Report of the Public Service Task Force on Women's Health Issues (Vol. II), Washington, DC.

U.S. Subcommittee on Census & Population. (1983). *The Hispanic population of the U.S.: An overview.* Washington, DC: U.S. Government Printing Office.

Vaux, A. (1985). Variations in social support associated with gender, ethnicity and age. *Journal of Social Issues, 41*(1), 89–110.

Vega, W. M., & Miranda, M. R. (1985). *Stress and Hispanic mental health.* Washington, DC: U.S. DHHS, National Institute of Mental Health.

Ventura, S., & Heuser, R. (1981). Births of Hispanic parentage, 1978. *Monthly Vital Statistics Report, 32* (supplement). Hyattsville, MD: National Center for Health Services Research, Public Health Service.

Verbrugge, L. M. (1985). Gender and health: An update on the hypotheses and evidence. *Journal of Health and Social Behavior, 26,* 156–182.

Williams, R. (1980). Monitoring perinatal mortality rates: California, 1970 to 1976. *American Journal of Obstetrics and Gynecology, 136*(5), 559–568.

Zambrana, R. E. (1988). A research agenda on issues affecting poor and minority women: A model for understanding their health needs. In C. A. Perales & L. S. Young (Eds.), *Too little, too late: Dealing with the health needs of women in poverty* (pp. 137–160). Binghamton, NY: Haworth Press.

Zelnik, M., & Kantner, J. (1980). Sexual activity, contraceptive use and pregnancy among metropolitan area teenagers: 1971–1979. *Family Planning Perspectives, 12,* 230–237.

Zelnik, M., Kantner, J., & Ford, K. (1981). *Sex and pregnancy in adolescence.* Beverly Hills, CA: Sage.

# 8 Reaching the "Unreachables": Educating and Motivating Women Living in Poverty

Alicia A. Marshall
*Texas A&M University*

Janet K. McKeon
*Michigan State University*

For decades, health communicators have recognized the need to devote attention to disseminating health-related information to the public and motivating them to engage in a variety of healthy behaviors. Health communicators have also long acknowledged the importance of giving special attention to limited-resource individuals as they traditionally are less informed than the general populace and equally less likely to engage in such desired behaviors (Bergner & Yerby, 1968; Childers & Post, 1975; Freimuth, 1990; Hoff, 1966). Despite this recognition of needed educational and outreach efforts, there exists a level of resignation that these individuals have become disenfranchised within our society, that is, isolated or distanced from the mainstream population. Labels such as unreachable, disenfranchised, indigent, hard-to-reach, and chronically uninformed (Bazzoli, 1986; Childers & Post, 1975; Freimuth, 1990; Hoff, 1966) serve to perpetuate the notion that attempting to reach individuals living in poverty may be a fruitless endeavor. As Hoff (1966) suggested years ago perhaps the more appropriate label to use for this target population is "unreached" rather than "unreachable." Such a linguistic change emphasizes the potential for reaching these individuals.

Over time one fact has become painfully clear: Members of this unreached population generally are in poorer health than individuals of higher socioeconomic status. Although true of men, women, and children facing the economic challenges, the present chapter devotes most of its attention to women specifically that have been disenfranchised from health-related services and information. The goal of the chapter is to examine various factors that have contributed to the lower health status of impoverished women, and then to postulate ways in which health communicators may be able to begin to narrow this health status margin.


## THE DISENFRANCHISED AND HEALTH STATUS, BEHAVIOR, AND KNOWLEDGE


### Health Status of the Disenfranchised

*Healthy People 2000*, a comprehensive statement of national health promotion and disease prevention objectives prepared by the U.S. Department of Health and Human Services (1990), has identified poor people as a specific target group to focus on prior to the year 2000. Given approximately one in every eight Americans are living on incomes below the federal guidelines for poverty, this focus certainly seems warranted. According to *Healthy People 2000*: "Health disparities between poor people and those with higher incomes are almost universal for all dimensions of health. Those disparities may be summarized by the finding that people with low income have death rates that are twice the rates for people with incomes above the poverty level" (Amler & Dull, 1987, p. 29).

The National Heart, Lung, and Blood Institute reports that limited-resource individuals experience a 25% greater risk of death from heart disease than for the overall population (U.S. Department of Health and Human Services, 1990). Likewise, the incidence of cancer is markedly greater, and the survival of cancer significantly lower, among individuals living in poverty (U.S. Department of Health and Human Services, 1985). Additional indicators of poor health status, such as hospitalization and restricted activities, also indicate significant disparities between lower socioeconomic status (SES) individuals versus individuals with higher SES. Individuals living in poverty have significantly higher rates of hospitalization and longer lengths of stay (Dutton, 1986). Struggling with restricted activities is also far more common among these individuals. The U.S. National Center for Health Statistics (1983) reported that limited-resource individuals spend more than 2 months a year with restricted activity (often resulting in the inability to work), which exceeds the typical amount of restricted activity experienced by individuals with middle or upper incomes by four times. Finally, individuals living in poverty are four and a half times more likely to view themselves as being in only fair or poor health than individuals living on more stable and substantial incomes (U.S. National Center for Health Statistics, 1991).

When considering health challenges facing women specifically, the data are even more troublesome. Perhaps most startling is the gradual decrease in the discrepancy in life expectancy between men and women. For generations, women have had an average life expectancy of 8 to 10 years longer than men. However, over the last two decades this range has been on a gradual decline (U.S. National Center for Health Statistics, 1985). Women are now more likely than men to fall below 50% of the poverty threshold, thus representing the poorest of the poor (Zopf, 1989). As a result, women are more likely to face the accompanying health-related problems, thus explaining the decrease in life expectancy. The rate of lung cancer in women, for example, has significantly increased over the past 30 years (U.S. National Center for Health Statistics, 1985). A similar alarming trend exists in the incidence of breast cancer which, over recent years, has risen from striking approximately 1 in 12 women to striking 1 in 8 women in their lifetime (American Cancer Society, 1994). Finally, higher birth rates among young girls living in poverty also contributes to the overall poorer health facing these disenfranchised women. Childbirth at a young age, with an immature reproductive system and typically with insufficient prenatal care, results in increased health risks.

All told, the data just presented certainly paint a bleak picture of the overall health status of individuals, particularly women, living in poverty. Countless sociopolitical, financial, and nutritional explanations have been posited for this relationship between health and poverty. What follows is a communication-based explanation, arguing that these disenfranchised women have not been sufficiently educated or motivated to engage in desirable health behaviors or to take advantage of available health-related services.

## Utilization of Health-Related Services and Practices

Certainly, one of the most striking factors contributing to the poor health status of poor women is their underutilization of available health care services. As Bergner and Yerby (1968) summarized:

> The poor are less inclined to take preventative measures, and delay longer in seeking medical care. When they do approach health practitioners, they are more likely to select subprofessionals or the marginal practitioners often found in their neighborhoods. It appears that the people most in need of medical services are the ones who least often obtain them. (p. 543)

As this suggests, these individuals are far less likely to seek out medical attention, particularly for acute and relatively mild conditions, due to their limited resources (Dutton, 1986).

Women are particularly less likely to engage in annual check-ups and early disease detection screening. Breast cancer in the United States has reached epic proportions. To date the best known defense against this disease is early detection through regular self breast exams, clinical breast exams, and mammography screening. Approximately 90% of women diagnosed with breast cancer when the cancer is still localized reach the critical 5-year survival mark (U.S. National Center for Health Statistics, 1991). Yet, less than 30% of poor women ever have a mammogram. Unfortunately, given few women living in poverty have regular mammograms, the chance of early detection and survival is virtually eliminated for these individuals (U.S. National Center for Health Statistics, 1991). Increasing the use of mammography screening among this population of women has become a priority in the United States in recent years. However, despite intensive efforts, there still exists a dramatic underutilization of mammograms among older, poorer, and less educated women (AMC Cancer Research Center, 1992).

The preceding examples suggest that the poorer health status of women living in poverty may be a result of women not taking advantage of available health services and/or engaging in regular preventive behaviors such as early detection cancer screenings. A second, equally important contributing factor may be their limited knowledge about issues related to health and illness. The apparent gap in health-related knowledge between lower SES individuals and those of higher SES is considered next.

## Health-Related Knowledge Among Women Living in Poverty

Beyond being less likely to take advantage of health care services, these disenfranchised women are also generally less knowledgeable about diseases, symptoms, warning signs, and the communicability of disease (Childers & Post, 1975). Sadly, they also tend to know significantly less about preventive health services and fundamental health practices. Even more troublesome is the fact that these individuals tend to not know what specific health-related services are available to them (Childers & Post, 1975).

In considering the health-related information deficit clearly evident among individuals living in poverty, Donohue, Tichenor, and Olien (1975) posited what is known as the knowledge gap hypothesis. These authors argued that "as the infusion of mass media information into a social system increases, segments of the population with higher socioeconomic status tend to acquire this information at a faster rate than the lower status segments, so that the gap in knowledge between these segments tends to increase rather than decrease" (p. 159). These authors would maintain that as more and more health-related information is made available to individuals through the media (e.g., factors contributing to cancer and innovative treatments now available) limited-resource individuals would take in this information at a significantly slower rate than those of higher socioeconomic status. As Dervin (1980) explained, these "[gaps] exist . . . because some people are less able and less willing to take in information than others" (p. 77). In reviewing numerous studies testing the knowledge gap hypothesis, Gaziano (1983) concluded that despite a uniform interest in health across all socioeconomic strata, there still exists a significant knowledge gap between lower SES individuals and those of higher SES.

Part of the explanation for this knowledge gap rests in the authors' assumption of a high correlation between SES and level of education; those with a higher SES tend to be better educated, and better educated individuals tend to be better able to comprehend health-related information. Moreover, those who have achieved higher educational levels tend to actively seek out more information.

In sum, strong evidence exists that impoverished women, and thus disenfranchised from the general population, experience poorer health than individuals living under more financially stable conditions. Two explanations for this discrepancy in health status are (a) limited-resource individuals are not taking advantage of available services or engaging in critical preventive behaviors, and (b) these individuals are generally less informed about health care issues. Before attempting further to educate and motivate these women to alter their health-related behaviors through the use of revised communication strategies, we must first have a clearer understanding of some of the critical factors contributing to the existing levels of knowledge and desire to act.

## FACTORS CONTRIBUTING TO UNDERUTILIZATION OF SERVICES AND LIMITED HEALTH-RELATED KNOWLEDGE

### Utilization of Available Services

McGuire and Popkin (1990) argued that poor women living in today's society are playing a zero-sum game; that is, to take advantage of social services that are available to improve their nutrition and general health requires an investment of time, energy, and other precious resources that the women may not be able to expend. As one woman facing cancer explained: "[my] husband couldn't afford insurance and paying the rent and buying food, so we had to let the insurance go. I could tell them that I have cancer and I am paying for insurance, but they would not accept that. If you're not able to pay the rent on time or you go to some of the grocery stores they don't want to hear that sad story" (American Cancer Society, 1989, p. 20).

Overall, these women tend to exhibit a focus on the "here and now." For most, the immediate need of placing food on the table tonight for their family far outweighs the need for an annual check-up screening for diseases that may afflict them in the distant and unpredictable future. A national survey conducted by the Center for Disease Control and Prevention reported that approximately half of the women surveyed said they would not pay $150 a year for a mammogram and nearly 40% said they believed mammograms to be too expensive and thus were unlikely to have one (AMC Cancer Research Center, 1992). At a regional hearing conducted by the American Cancer Society (1989) one woman summed it up best:

> To go to the doctor is $50. To get a mammogram is $100 because it's on sale this month at the local hospital. To get it read is another $50 to $100 dollars; and then my doctor said I need a biopsy if it's suspicious for cancer. I don't have any money. If I quit my job and wait until Welfare approves me so I can get a medical card it's going to be months. Meanwhile, how do I feed my children? (p. 21)

It is clear that the struggle to manage very limited resources, coupled with the inherent focus on the present rather than on the future, functions as a critical barrier to taking advantage of numerous future-oriented social services and preventive screening opportunities.

Other structural variables conspire to prevent women from taking advantage of health-related services as well. Bergner and Yerby (1968) suggested that in fact individuals living in poverty have numerous barriers to overcome in order to take advantage of health-related services supposedly designed expressly for them. Structural barriers constructed by the programs themselves are particularly troublesome and surprising. Often features such as the location of the clinic, times of the available appointments, and the availability of transportation and child care seem to reflect more the needs of the providers than the needs of the potential clients. In many instances it would appear that the lifestyle of the target population is not taken into account when health services and programs are being developed and established.

Finally, every day we hear through the media the challenges facing the poor as they attempt to enter the health care system and to survive on limited or no health insurance. Most frustrating and frightening is the realization that due to limitations in space, personnel, and resources the poor are actually being discouraged from engaging in critical preventive behaviors such as early detection cancer screening. Testimony presented during hearings conducted by the American Cancer Society (1989) indicates

that "[the current health care system] is a system which discourages preventive healthcare, which encourages patients to wait until their health
problems are virtually unbearable before seeking care, and which imposes
unnecessary delays in diagnosis and treatment" (p. 15). An OB/GYN nurse
practitioner who cares for poor women in San Francisco perhaps voiced
the frustration clearest when she testified that:

> I am continually frustrated by the inaccessibility of services for poor women.
> At times I am told to call back in two months to make an appointment for
> a mammogram that will be scheduled another two to three months later.
> Within this time span I have lost my patient for follow-up; another high risk
> poor woman is unable to receive early detection and screening services.
> (American Cancer Society, 1989, p. 18)

In sum, numerous factors may be contributing to women not taking
advantage of health-related services established specifically to meet their
needs. Three such factors presented here are facing the challenges of living
on limited resources, as well as coping with obstacles erected by the programs' designs and by the current health care system. Numerous other
factors not attributable to the programs or health care system themselves
are also contributing to women not engaging in a host of preventive health
behaviors. Many have argued that factors intrinsic to the individuals themselves, such as locus of control or general health beliefs, are even more
powerful determinants of health behaviors. The roles of such beliefs and
orientations are examined next.

## Engaging in Preventive Health Behaviors

*Orientation.*   One factor preventing these disenfranchised women from
engaging in desirable preventive health behaviors relates to their general
orientation or outlook on life events. One's orientation, known as locus
of control, rests at the very core of every individual. Within everyone there
exists some personal explanation for why certain things happen. For some,
explanations for why things happen revolve around internal factors. Individuals exhibiting such an internal locus of control take more personal
responsibility for events they experience in their lives (Rotter, 1966). They
are more likely to blame themselves, for example, for being unemployed.
With respect to their own health or illness, individuals with an internal
orientation believe that if sickness occurs it is because of something they
did to cause it or failed to do something to avoid it. As such, these individuals would be more likely to engage in preventive health behaviors, such
as going for regular early-detection cancer screenings, in order to assert
this control over their own health. Thus, these individuals with an internal

health locus of control overall tend to engage in more preventive health behaviors, and are more likely to keep scheduled appointments and return for additional needed treatment (see Wallston & Wallston, 1978). With respect to knowledge and information seeking, they tend to know more about their condition if they are sick, are generally more inquisitive of health care providers, are more prone to be dissatisfied with the information available to them related to their health, are more likely to attend to and recall general health information, and are generally more active in seeking out health-related information (Quadrel & Lau, 1989; Wallston, Maides, & Wallston, 1976; Wallston & Wallston, 1978). With such knowledge comes a greater probability of acting in particularly healthy ways due to the increased understanding of the consequences of unhealthy acts and the benefits of healthy behaviors.

In contrast, other individuals have what is known as an external locus of control (Rotter, 1966). These individuals believe that life events are beyond their control. An individual with an external locus of control might claim that she or he is unemployed because it is fate, God's will, or the fault of some powerful other (e.g., "those politicians running this country").

Individuals maintaining an external health locus of control believe that no matter what they do, they will become ill if it is "meant to be." These individuals tend to act much more passively with regard to health-related behaviors given their lack of confidence in the significance of such behaviors. For example, externals are more likely to smoke and are less likely to attempt to quit smoking, tend to have more difficulty with weight loss, and generally are less likely to engage in preventive behaviors (see Wallston & Wallston, 1978). Likewise, externals are less likely to attend to, recall, or seek out health-related information that might serve to persuade them to engage in healthy behaviors (Quadrel & Lau, 1989; Wallston & Wallston, 1978).

Unfortunately, the poor tend to be more likely to exhibit an external locus of control as well as be a more "despairing, fatalistic people with a pervasive sense of helplessness" (Freimuth, 1990, p. 176). It may well be that this external orientation is adopted or acquired due to the circumstances surrounding these individuals. Regardless of its origin, this external and pessimistic orientation has been found to be widespread among limited-resource individuals.

With respect to cancer beliefs in particular, individuals living in poverty typically maintain a belief of cancer as a death sentence. As the director of the Richard Cabot Clinic in Kansas City explained: "There's a fatalistic attitude, but there's a reason for that attitude . . . their realities are that people do die from cancers. Their realities are that if you don't have money, you're not going to get treated and you are gonna die" (American Cancer Society, 1989, p. 32). Certainly, this fatalistic attitude, coupled with the external orientation, explains why few poor women seek out cancer-screening opportunities. From their perspective, there is little value in being informed of the presence of a disease where death is almost certain and the individual feels little can be done to alter that course. Thus, not only do they tend to believe there is little they can do to control their own health, but they also hold onto a fairly gloomy picture concerning their future prospects. Given this orientation, it is not surprising to find that many of these disenfranchised women are less likely to engage in a variety of preventive health behaviors given their disbelief in their utility.

*Self-Efficacy.* Another factor that certainly may be functioning to inhibit women is their sense of self-efficacy. First introduced by Bandura (1977), self-efficacy refers to one's belief or confidence in his or her ability to engage in a particular behavior. People are only likely to exhibit a particular behavior if they think they are personally capable of doing or adopting the new behavior. For example, a woman is not likely to conduct regular self breast exams if she feels unable to do them adequately.

In combination, self-efficacy and locus of control are quite powerful predictors of individuals' behavior. Rosenstock, Strecher, and Becker (1988) illustrated the relative relationship between locus of control and self-efficacy as they relate to the probability of following through with a recommended health-related behavior. These authors suggested that an individual with an internal locus of control and high self-efficacy is most likely to follow through with a recommended behavior. For example, a person who (a) believes stopping smoking will decrease his or her chances of getting lung cancer (thus internally oriented), and (b) believes she or he can successfully quit smoking (therefore high self-efficacy) is most likely to actually attempt to quit smoking. Those individuals who believe they will get lung cancer regardless of whether or not they quit smoking (thus externally oriented) and have little confidence in their actual ability to quit (thus low self-efficacy) are the least likely to attempt to stop smoking. Unfortunately, as discussed earlier, limited-resource individuals are more likely to fit the latter description. Thus, women living in poverty, for example, may be less likely to get regular cancer screening as they are less likely to see the value of the screening and are less confident in their ability to emotionally and physically handle the actual screening.

*Health Beliefs.* One final, and perhaps most powerful, factor contributing to whether or not individuals engage in various healthy behaviors is their personal health belief system. The Health Belief Model (HBM), first posited in the 1950s by a group of social psychologists, was developed to explain the types of motivation that influence decision making and lead to individuals engaging in particular healthy behaviors (Rosenstock, 1974). Essentially, the model hypothesizes that the likelihood of engaging in a particular health-related behavior is a function of an individual's internal assessments of threat, benefits of the behavior, and costs of the behavior.

The HBM suggests that individuals first assess the extent to which a particular disease or ailment is a threat to them; that is, how susceptible are they to getting the disease, and how serious would it be if they were to contract the disease. If, for example, Joe is operating on the assumption that men do not get breast cancer,[1] or is unaware of the serious nature of breast cancer, then his assessment of threat would be relatively low. In this instance Joe would not be likely to engage in early detection screening. In contrast, Joanne, a woman who has a history of breast cancer in her family and who recognizes the seriousness of breast cancer, is more likely to assess the threat of breast cancer as very high. In this particular scenario, Joanne would be much more likely to engage in recommended early-detection screening.

The model suggests, however, that additional assessments and beliefs would enter into Joanne's internal equation prior to her deciding whether or not to have regular mammograms. Beyond assessing the potential threat of the disease, individuals are also believed to evaluate the potential benefits of engaging in the recommended behavior as well as the costs or disadvantages in engaging in the behavior. Consider Joe and Joanne described previously. Joe might understand the benefits of having a mammogram as it relates to early detection of breast cancer, but might well view the potential physical pain brought on by the procedure and the financial cost of the procedure (typically not covered by insurance, particularly for men) as outweighing the benefits. In this case, in light of the accompanying low threat of the disease, Joe is likely to opt not to have the screening. Likewise, despite the perception of high threat for the woman, Joanne might believe the procedure to be too costly or potentially too painful, or may be too frightened of the potential results to warrant having the screening done. In this case as well we might find Joanne not engaging in the desired behavior (i.e., having a mammogram). Overall this model suggests that the likelihood of engaging in a desired preventive behavior is a direct result of whether or not the perceived threat of the disease is high and the perceived benefits of the preventive action outweigh the perceived barriers or costs of the action.

The HBM is useful when attempting to understand why women living in poverty are less likely to engage in various preventive behaviors, particularly early cancer detection screening. First, numerous researchers have found that many women do not see the need for regular screening as they

---

[1]In fact, 1,000 new cases of breast cancer in men are detected each year according to the American Cancer Society (1994).

do not perceive their own susceptibility to breast cancer (particularly among women with no familial history of the disease; AMC Cancer Research Center, 1992). This would suggest that women in general are likely to see their personal threat of the disease to be low. Second, women (particularly women living in poverty) have reported numerous powerful barriers that act to prevent them from engaging in regular screening. Such barriers include cost of the screening, fear of the results, apprehension of the exam or procedure itself, and embarrassment (AMC Cancer Research Center, 1992). Such disadvantages or barriers are likely to outweigh the perceived benefits of the screening, particularly given the poor tend to possess a limited knowledge of the benefits of cancer screening and early detection.

Thus, the HBM would lead us to conclude that women living in poverty are less likely to engage in a particular preventive behavior such as early detection cancer screening. Although not a component of the HBM specifically, health locus of control and self-efficacy are important factors to consider as well as discussed previously. Given these women are more likely to be externally oriented and are likely to have a lower sense of self-efficacy, it is not surprising to find that many of them are not engaging in desirable, healthy behaviors.

## Health-Related Knowledge

One final factor contributing to the poorer health status of disenfranchised women is the limited knowledge they possess with respect to health-related issues, services, and desirable behaviors. Numerous factors are likely to be contributing to the existing knowledge gap described previously. Here, the role the currently used strategies for disseminating health-related information play in the knowledge gap are considered. Generally, the typical modes used to attempt to educate women living in poverty are ineffective and act to further isolate these women within society. Specifically, the sources and channels often used to disseminate health-related information, and the messages themselves, are inappropriate and thus often ineffective in reaching the members of this "unreachable" population. Each of these factors (i.e., source, message, and channel) are considered in turn next.

*Message Source.* In their book *The Information Poor*, Childers and Post (1975) argued that the poor live in an "information ghetto" that functions as a closed system, allowing little information in, and "harboring an inordinate amount of unawareness and misinformation" (p. 32). Individuals living in poverty, as most people, often rely on neighbors, friends, and family members as their principal sources for health-related information. It has been argued that these individuals rely more heavily on informal sources of health-related information than do individuals living in more affluent communities (Freimuth, 1990). Unfortunately, these local informal sources tend to be relatively uninformed and less knowledgeable due to the ineffectiveness of strategies to disseminate accurate information into these impoverished communities and neighborhoods. Often opinion leaders or informal leaders emerge in neighborhoods and take on the role of seeking out and sharing information with other community members. Although their efforts and motivation are genuine, by virtue of being members of an isolated community they still face the social barriers that hinder their ability to obtain relevant and easy to comprehend health-related information.

Information that does successfully filter into the information ghetto often comes through impersonal sources, such as through mass media channels. Mass media attempts have historically tended to rely on seemingly inappropriate spokespersons or sources of information. It has long been held that in order to be appropriate, sources of information must be viewed by the target audience as credible; one of the most critical components of source credibility is perceived similarity with the target audience (O'Keefe, 1990). This principle is frequently overlooked when attempting to reach individuals living in poverty. For example, one recent statewide campaign attempting to encourage limited-resource women to engage in regular mammography screening used the current governor as the spokesperson. Unfortunately, it was widely known that the governor had recently cut funding to a variety of social welfare programs during his term of office. Not only was it difficult for the members of the target audience to identify with this spokesperson as he sat in the plush setting of his home, but they already held a resentment and distrust of the individual thus making him a source with virtually no credibility.

*Message Characteristics.*   As stated earlier, information that filters into the information ghetto from the outside is typically impersonal in nature brought in through mass media channels (e.g., television, radio, magazines, and newspapers). Although quite effective for reaching the general public, mass media messages generally have been argued to be less effective in reaching those living in poverty. Overall, many of the messages being transmitted through these impersonal channels tend to not take into account the frame of reference of this particular target audience. That is, messages encouraging women to have regular cancer screening, or to take children in for vaccinations, or encouraging men to have prostate cancer screenings are in essence encouraging a population struggling to survive day to day to engage in behaviors that require a future orientation. In essence, many of the behaviors being advocated are seen by the members of the target audience as irrelevant or as an unobtainable and/or unaffordable luxury because of their overriding need to meet basic day-to-day needs first.

*Message Channels.* One additional factor to consider that significantly contributes to the level of health-related knowledge represented among individuals living in poverty is how information is actually being distributed to the target audience. That is, what channels are typically used to disseminate health-related information, and are these channels necessarily the most appropriate? All too often such information is disseminated through written advertisements, brochures, or flyers (thus assuming reading comprehension). Moreover, there is a predominant utilization of English as the sole language of these materials. Unfortunately, when considering individuals living in poverty, one often finds lower reading ability, as well as lower proficiency with the English language as it is often a second language (Childers & Post, 1975). Understanding technical information such as health-related information is likely to be particularly challenging given these circumstances.

Although commonly held, these assumptions are not always an accurate reflection of lower SES individuals. Sadly, today we find more and more individuals who are "suddenly poor"; competent, educated individuals who because of a variety of circumstances (e.g., the death of the sole breadwinner, the loss of a long-standing job) suddenly find themselves with limited resources and job skills. These individuals, faced with the new and unforeseen challenges of living on limited resources, may not struggle with these barriers due to limited literacy or language proficiency, but nonetheless face many of the other challenges described here.

The actual medium typically used to disseminate health-related information also contributes to the limited health-related knowledge possessed by the poor. For example, information is often included in outlets not commonly used by the target audience, such as specialized magazines. The use of magazines and other print media in general should be called into question given the numerous investigations that have indicated the relatively low reliance on print media among those living in poverty for information (Childers & Post, 1975). Generally, disadvantaged individuals rely more on electronic media as their principal source of information, more so than more financially and/or educationally privileged individuals (Dervin & Greenberg, 1972). Unfortunately, as Childers and Post argued, the electronic media tends to present "ends"-oriented information, that is related to the importance of engaging in a particular behavior, and leave the "means"-oriented information (i.e., the how-to information) to the print media. Thus, it could be argued that individuals relying predominantly on electronic media as their information source are getting only half of the relevant health-related information, what is important to do but not how to do it or where to go for assistance.

In sum, several components of the information dissemination strategies often used are contributing to these individuals' limited health-related knowledge. Among them is the reliance on the part of the target audience on local and potentially uninformed sources of information, as well as the reliance on the part of health educators on less than reliable or credible sources of information through mass media. Moreover, the media appeals for proactive health behavior may not be appealing to the target audience's frame of reference and priorities. Finally, the channels selected to transmit such information may not be the most effective for reaching into these "unreached" communities.

Overall, several factors have been posited as contributing to the significantly lower health status of disenfranchised women living in poverty. The underutilization of health-related services may well be due to the women's day-to-day struggles with managing limited resources, along with the structural barriers erected by the facilities and programs themselves. Maintaining an external orientation along with a low sense of self-efficacy strongly contribute to women not engaging in desirable health behaviors. In addition, having limited knowledge concerning the benefits of proactive health behaviors, as well as their personal susceptibility to a variety of diseases such as breast cancer, also helps explain why these women tend to not engage in desirable behaviors such as regular cancer screenings. Finally, the limited level of health-related knowledge evident among the women has been fostered by ineffective media strategies. When considered in combination, it is not surprising that there exists a poorer health status among these disenfranchised women.

Health communicators and educators may not be able to overcome the structural barriers contributing to the underutilization of health services. Nonetheless, they can certainly tackle the second two factors, increasing women's knowledge about health-related issues and motivating them to engage in more desirable health behaviors. Recommendations for such efforts are discussed in the final section of this chapter.

## RECOMMENDATIONS FOR REACHING THE "UNREACHABLES"

Above all else, the goal of health communicators should be to involve the disenfranchised in the development of any strategies specifically geared to increase their knowledge and motivation to act. Women living in poverty will continue to be disenfranchised and marginalized from the general public as long as their unique perspectives and viewpoints are ignored. Taking into account their perspective can be accomplished if, and only if, these women's expertise is acknowledged and "harvested." Who best to develop strategies for educating and motivating disenfranchised women with respect to health-related issues than representatives from that very community?

One widely used technique for accessing the perspectives or viewpoints of a select group of individuals is focus group interviewing. The focus group interview is "a qualitative research technique used to obtain data about feelings and opinions of small groups of participants about a given problem, experience, service, or other phenomenon" (Basch, 1987, p. 414). In essence, a focus group interview consists of bringing together a small group of representatives (i.e., typically 7–10 individuals per group) from a particular target community or group (e.g., women living in poverty) to participate in a focused discussion around a select topic (e.g., barriers to health care).

In an attempt to elicit the viewpoints of disenfranchised women living in poverty the authors of the present chapter conducted 13 focus groups with a total of 85 women living in poverty. The purpose of these discussions specifically was to elicit recommendations from these women regarding more effective sources and channels of health-related information, as well as more appropriate messages, that might ultimately motivate them to engage in more desirable health behaviors. The results of those discussions are used as the foundation for the recommendations given next.

## Preferred Sources and Channels of Health-Related Information

Consistent with Childers and Post's (1975) observations, the members of women's immediate friendship and family network were seen as having the most influence over the women. These interpersonal sources were reported as being the most likely to be able to motivate the women to engage in a desirable health behavior. Additional interpersonal strategies, such as getting telephone calls from health program volunteers and/or personal letters or post cards from health agencies, were also seen as effective. Underlying this preference was the sense of accessibility through the directness of the contact. The personal appeal held more power for the women through the implied message of "we care" or "you, as an individual, are important."

Second, the majority of women preferred talking to other women about their unique health concerns. Women are best able to relate to the issues of concern and would be seen as genuine. Bringing together small groups of neighborhood women for informal discussions was encouraged. The presence of knowledgeable, female peer educators to answer questions was also viewed as desirable. The focus group experience itself was reported by numerous discussants as being educational and motivating, even though not designed with such a purpose in mind.

Third, women who had engaged in the specific desired behaviors were seen as particularly valuable sources of information due to their direct experience. That is, the women suggested that talking to another woman who had recently had a mammogram, and could answer their questions from direct personal experience, would be seen as a more valuable source of information than perhaps a health care provider.

Finally, the women strongly believed that distant sources such as celebrities or politicians were ineffective and not motivating as they are not able to relate to the women's experiences nor can they identify with the target population. Other impersonal channels, such as the mass media, were also seen as ineffective by many of the discussants. Television commercials, newspaper ads, and flyers distributed in local businesses were generally unremarkable and often disregarded or ignored.

These observations would suggest several issues to consider when developing new strategies for educating and motivating disenfranchised women. Certainly these observations suggest that the perceived credibility of the source rests in the extent to which the source is seen as an "insider" to the community, someone with direct experience and understanding of the unique concerns and issues facing these women. The discussions also verified the observation that local opinion leaders and personal network links are the most influential when it comes to persuading these women to engage in a desirable health behavior. Finally, credibility also rests more in personal experience with the issues at hand rather than through formal education and subsequent expertise.

Based on these observations and recommendations, designers of health communication or education strategies should tap into the powerful local networks for disseminating health-related information. Rather than relying on outsiders to educate and motivate, turn to insiders as educators and advocates for healthier behaviors. Developing peer education-training programs, for example, that educate small groups of local women with the expectation that they would pass along the information to their friends were frequently suggested by the discussants. It was also suggested that locally held educational programs for small groups of women should feature speakers from their community or neighborhood that had direct experience with the targeted behavior, rather than relying solely on local health department officials or physicians to talk.

## Preferred Health-Related Information

With respect to the development of effective messages specifically, two issues were considered: (a) the content specifically, and (b) the general appeal or focus of the message. First, sadly, the women demonstrated the hypothesized limited health-related knowledge. Across all 13 groups, the women recognized their limited knowledge and desired greater access to detailed but easy to understand information concerning women's unique health issues. Specifically, they clearly needed to be better educated on health-related programs available to them. One explanation for the underutilization of health programs that emerged from these discussions was simply lack of awareness of the programs' existence. Information on cost of the programs, availability of transportation and child care, and qualifications for the programs would potentially increase the utilization of the available services. Such information would also acknowledge the struggles with managing limited resources as discussed earlier.

The discussants also wanted access to clearer and more specific information as to what to expect from the examinations, procedures, or behaviors being advocated. One clear barrier preventing women from taking advantage of opportunities and engaging in desirable behaviors revolved around the fear of the unknown. Any efforts to take the mystique out of unfamiliar procedures and/or behaviors was seen as useful and valuable. For example, simply telling women exactly what to expect when they have a mammogram and what it is likely to feel like would go a long way toward demystifying the procedure and encouraging women to have the screening. Likewise, the women suggested providing information that directly addressed other commonly held barriers or fears (e.g., dispel the fear that exposure to the radiation from the mammography is dangerous).

The discussants wanted additional information concerning why they should engage in the behaviors being advocated. Given the reported minimal perception of susceptibility to disease and the accompanying limited understanding of the short-term and long-term benefits of various desirable behaviors, it is not surprising that the women voiced a need for additional information to convince them to engage in the behaviors being advocated.

With respect to recommendations for the general appeals that would be more effective, the women were in agreement. First and foremost, use positive messages that convey hope and self-confidence to the women. Personal stories of women who succeeded were seen as very motivational. The use of negative messages or strong fear appeals were seen as ineffective. The use of abstract information such as statistics was also seen as ineffective as they were not meaningful and "hard to relate to." A combination of educational information with positive emotional appeals was seen as potentially most effective and motivational. Overall, the messages should function to increase perceptions of susceptibility of disease, the benefits of action, and confidence in ability to engage in the behaviors, and to decrease the sense of hopelessness, fears, and the belief that health is out of their control.

Finally, the discussants emphasized the importance of designing the general educational materials sensitively. That is, the women felt very strongly that often the brochures and information available to them was insensitive to the possible reading or language difficulties facing many members of their community. Using language that is straightforward and easy to understand was strongly advocated. In addition, the discussants felt strongly about making all materials available in a variety of languages, thus more effectively reaching into the Hispanic or Arab or Asian communities.

## SUMMARY

The purpose of this chapter was to explore behavioral and communicative factors that may be contributing to disenfranchised women living in poverty experiencing poorer health than more affluent individuals. Health communicators and educators need to address more explicitly the factors that are contributing to women not engaging in desirable health behaviors or possessing sufficient health-related information. Factors such as orientation, self-efficacy, beliefs about health and illness, and general understanding of health have been presented as significantly contributing to the poor health status facing these disenfranchised women. In order to more effectively educate and motivate these women, they should be integrally involved in the process of developing outreach strategies. Only through this increased involvement, and a heightened awareness and sensitivity to the unique issues and concerns facing these women, will health communicators be able to reach the yet unreached and motivate them to engage in desirable health behaviors in hopes of improving their health and well-being.

## REFERENCES

AMC Cancer Research Center. (1992). *Breast and cervical screening: Barriers and use among specific populations.* Denver, CO: Author.

American Cancer Society. (1989). *Cancer and the poor: A report to the nation.* Atlanta: Author.

American Cancer Society. (1994). *Cancer facts and figures: 1994.* Atlanta: Author.

Amler, R. W., & Dull, H. B. (1987). *Closing the gap: The burden of unnecessary illness.* New York: Oxford University Press.

Bandura, A. (1977). *Social learning theory.* Englewood Cliffs, NJ: Prentice-Hall.

Basch, C. E. (1987). Focus group interview: An underutilized research technique for improving theory and practice in health education. *Health Education Quarterly, 14,* 411–448.

Bazzoli, G. J. (1986). Health care for the indigent: Overview of critical issues. *Health Services Research, 21,* 353–393.

Bergner, L., & Yerby, A. S. (1968). Low income and barriers to use of health services. *The New England Journal of Medicine, 278,* 541–546.

Childers, T., & Post, J. A. (1975). *The information poor in America.* Metuchen, NJ: Scarecrow Press.

Dervin, B. (1980). Communication gaps and inequities: Moving toward a reconceptualization. In B. Dervin & M. Voigt (Eds.), *Progress in communication science* (pp. 73–112). Norwood, NJ: Ablex.

Dervin, B., & Greenberg, B. S. (1972). *The communication environment of the urban poor* (CUP Report No. 15). East Lansing: Michigan State University.

Donohue, G. A., Tichenor, P. J., & Olien, C. N. (1975). Mass media and the knowledge gap: A hypothesis reconsidered. *Communication Research, 2,* 3–23.

Dutton, D. B. (1986). Social class, health, and illness. In L. Aiken & D. Mechanic (Eds.), *Applications of social science to clinical medicine and health policy* (pp. 31–62). New Brunswick, NJ: Rutgers University Press.

Freimuth, V. S. (1990). The chronically uninformed: Closing the knowledge gap in health. In E. B. Ray & L. Donohew (Eds.), *Communication and health: Systems and applications* (pp. 171–186). Hillsdale, NJ: Lawrence Erlbaum Associates.

Gaziano, C. (1983). The knowledge gap: An analytical review of media effects. *Communication Research, 10,* 447–486.

Hoff, W. (1966). Why health programs are not reaching the unresponsive in our communities. *Public Health Reports, 81,* 654–658.

McGuire, J. S., & Popkin, B. M. (1990). *Helping women improve nutrition in the developing world* (World Bank Tech. Rep. No. 114). Washington, DC: The World Bank.

O'Keefe, D. J. (1990). *Persuasion: Theory and research.* Newbury Park, CA: Sage.

Quadrel, M. J., & Lau, R. R. (1989). Health promotion, health locus of control, and health behavior: Two field experiments. *Journal of Applied Social Psychology, 19,* 1497–1521.

Rosenstock, I. M. (1974). Historic origins of the health belief model. *Health Education Monographs, 2,* 328–335.

Rosenstock, I. M., Strecher, V. J., & Becker, M. H. (1988). Social learning theory and the health belief model. *Health Education Quarterly, 15,* 175–183.

Rotter, J. B. (1966). Generalized expectancies for internal versus external control of reinforcement. *Psychological Monographs, 80,* 1–28.

U.S. Department of Health and Human Services. (1985). *Report of the Secretary's Task Force on Black and Minority Health.* Washington, DC: U.S. Government Printing Office.

U.S. Department of Health and Human Services. (1990). *Healthy People 2000: National health promotion and disease prevention objectives.* Washington, DC: U.S. Government Printing Office.

U.S. National Center for Health Statistics. (1983). *Disability days: United States, 1980* (Series 10, 143). Washington, DC: Public Health Service.

U.S. National Center for Health Statistics. (1985). *Health promotion and disease prevention: United States, 1985.* Washington, DC: U.S. Department of Health and Human Services.

U.S. National Center for Health Statistics. (1991). *Health, United States, 1991.* Hyattsville, MD: U.S. Department of Health and Human Services.

Wallston, K. A., Maides, S., & Wallston, B. S. (1976). Health-related information seeking as a function of health-related locus of control and health value. *Journal of Research in Personality, 10,* 215–222.

Wallston, B. S., & Wallston, K. A. (1978). Locus of control and health: A review of literature. *Health Education Monographs, 6,* 107–117.

Zopf, P. E., Jr. (1989). *American women in poverty.* New York: Greenwood.

# PART III

# ISSUES RELATED
# TO FAMILY

# 9 Silent Tragedy/Social Stigma: Coping With the Pain of Infertility

Patricia Geist
Julie L. Gray
Fredi Avalos-C'deBaca
Ginger Hill
*San Diego State University*

*The problem of infertility is as old as human civilization. All cultures, from ancient times to the present, have had their fertility rites and practices, dolls and amulets, herbs and folk medicines to ensure that there would indeed be a new generation to carry on the culture. Traditionally, the woman was held responsible for whether or not offspring were produced, and in most societies, the "barren woman" was, and still is, a tragic figure. The woman's worth was perceived largely in terms of childbearing and childrearing abilities; the man had other important roles in the economy and defense of the community. Some notions of the male role in reproduction existed in ancient times, as evidenced by the existence of phallic cults and paraphernalia. However, it was not until the seventeenth century that spermatozoa were observed under the microscope, and not until the eighteenth century that their role in fertilization was discovered. For a while the "homunculus" theory prevailed, which held that a sperm contained a fully formed miniature person, and that the womb provided an incubator in which it could grow. By the nineteenth century, early workers in genetics found that both parents contributed equally to the genetic makeup of the new individual, except for sex differentiation which is mediated exclusively by the male, and the mammalian ovum was observed. The twentieth century brought great strides in the understanding of reproductive physiology, the complex events occurring within the menstrual cycle, and the multiplicity of factors in both male and female that could enhance or impair conception and the carriage of a pregnancy to term.*
—Mazor & Simons (1984, pp. xv–xvi)

159

As this concise history of the problem of infertility reveals, our knowledge and understanding of reproduction and infertility has increased substantially, and as a result we have gained clearer insight into both men's and women's responsibility for fertility or infertility. However, even with this advanced understanding, our society and culture, our families, our religions, and our health care system communicate disenfranchising messages to individuals and couples who face infertility.

The definition of infertility offered by the American Fertility Society states that "a marriage is to be considered barren after a year of coitus without contraception" (Thompson, 1984, p. 3). Even though there are over 10 million infertile people in our society, they are often invisible and do not know how to contact or support one another (Menning, 1984). Americans, in defining infertility as a medical problem, turn to the medical profession for an explanation and a solution (Greil, 1991).

A dramatic increase in the use of medical services for infertility has occurred during the last two decades. A 1988 congressional document on infertility reported that "the estimated number of visits to private physicians for infertility-related consultation rose from approximately 600,000 in 1968 to 1.6 million in 1984" (Stanton & Dunkel-Schetter, 1991, p. 5). And the treatment of infertility has become an increasingly large business, accounting for $2 billion in total annual revenues (DeWitt, 1993).

This chapter explores the silent tragedy and social stigma faced by people who are coping with the pain of infertility. Disenfranchising messages regarding infertility surround all of us, but the individual or couple who are unable, for whatever reason, to conceive or bear children are haunted, even pursued, by these painful messages. These messages come from a multitude of directions: from the media, from the church, from the legal system, from the government, from the health care system, and frequently from the couple's own family and friends. The deleterious impact of this disenfranchisement is felt deeply within individuals' self-image and carries over to their relationships with those closest to them.

This chapter is organized around the sources of disenfranchising messages—four origins of messages communicated to infertile couples. First, we examine the role that society and culture play in communicating these messages. Second, we consider how these messages are translated into our definitions of self through interactions with family members. Third, we describe the emphasis that four religions place on fertility and how they communicate explanations and consequences for infertility. Fourth, our attention is turned to the infertility experience in the health care system—diagnosis, treatment, and ideologies of the medical community. The final section of the chapter explores the avenues for negotiating an empowered identity in the face of childlessness.

## INFERTILITY, SOCIETY, AND CULTURE

In the United States, one out of every six couples has some difficulty in conceiving or carrying a pregnancy to term (Menning, 1977). The National Center for Health Statistics reveals that in 1988, 11% of married couples, a total of 3.1 million couples, had trouble conceiving or giving birth to a child (DeWitt, 1993). The increasing numbers of women and men who are experiencing the pain of infertility has created a need to understand the ways in which this group of people has become disenfranchised.

Society and culture play a major role in the disenfranchisement of infertile men and women. On a day-to-day basis our society disenfranchises infertile individuals by stigmatizing their inability to procreate, often blaming women's new role in society, sensationalizing the issue of infertility in the media, and negatively scrutinizing their lifestyle choices (see Faludi, 1991). Society continues to glorify parenthood even as it confronts a rapidly changing social environment that is struggling to include alternative attitudes and lifestyles.

The last two decades have seen an increase in the rise of childlessness. Society, and the institutions that sustain it, create an environment that rejects and alienates the infertile by virtually ignoring their condition and by offering little emotional support. Daniluk (1991) described infertility as a kind of "death for which there are no rituals and little public acknowledgement" (p. 318). Infertile individuals feel invisible in a society that remains insensitive to their pain.

Regardless of the reasons for not having children, childless couples receive stigmatizing messages, often negating their sense of masculinity and femininity. A frequently heard piece of advice is "adopt and you'll get pregnant," as if infertility is just a psychological barrier (Greil, 1991). Even couples who have solved their infertility problem through adoption continue to experience disenfranchising messages. One woman recounted the painful situation at a baby shower as guests were telling their labor and delivery stories when her friend spoke up and said, "Jean had it easy. She just had to drive downtown" (p. 130). Upsetting incidents such as this discount the difficulty of infertility, often even implying couples are lucky to be infertile. In addition, because they are unable to conceive, they are seen as not fulfilling their biological destinies (Berg, Wilson, & Weingartner, 1991; Lorber & Bandlamudi, 1993). "The infertile couple receives the additional stress of societal and cultural messages that they are somehow unfulfilled, lacking in adult adequacy, unnatural or selfish" (Valentine, 1986, p. 66).

Women, in particular, experience covert and overt retaliation from a society that refuses, or is unable, to cope with the reality of two-income families and the aspirations of many young women to pursue professional goals (Faludi, 1991; J. Schwartz, 1993). In the last few years, there has been a moralistic crusade in the United States to return to "traditional" family values. This crusade has been supported directly by right-wing conservative religious factions and indirectly by so-called "objective" sources such as *The New England Journal of Medicine* (D. Schwartz & Mayaux, 1982) and *The New York Times* (Webster, 1982). According to *The New England Journal of Medicine* (D. Schwartz & Mayaux, 1982), there was a significant increase of infertility in women over the age of 30; women in their early to mid-30s had a 40% probability of being infertile. It was often suggested that women need to take responsibility for this "epidemic" and reconsider career plans and personal goals. This perspective is reinforced by the print media and television, giving this issue both front-page and prime-time coverage (Faludi, 1991).

In contrast, a report by the U.S. National Center for Health Statistics (1985) found only a 13.6%, not a 40%, probability of infertility for women between the ages of 30 and 34. And even though studies existed to confirm that infertility was greater for women in their early 20s than it was for women in their 30s, Americans became preoccupied with reproductive issues and the "choices" couples were making about careers and parenthood (Faludi, 1991).

In the 1980s, the film industry jumped on the "baby bandwagon." Movies such as *Baby Boom*, *Raising Arizona*, *She's Having a Baby*, and *Three Men and a Baby* served to create, and give credence to, society's modern-day obsession with parenthood (Faludi, 1991; J. Schwartz, 1993). In a society that is heavily influenced by media, these images are powerful in the propagandizement of parenthood as the key to maturity and success. The nation seemed to be swept up in a collective wave of sentimentality, reinforcing the urgency of the infertility "epidemic" that has continued into the 1990s (J. Schwartz, 1993). This "sentimentality" was responsible for the rebirth of traditional family ideals: "The values of this movement have reinforced the social image of infertility as a major health problem—sometimes with moralistic overtones" (Aral & Cates, 1983, p. 2330). This line of "moralist" thinking is particularly harmful to infertile individuals because traditionalist values are often implicit in infertility counseling (Valentine, 1986). As their personal and medical histories are exposed, infertile individuals are often made to feel guilty for past behaviors: sexual conduct, the decision to delay childbirth, their choice of birth control methods, the contraction of sexually transmitted diseases, and abortions (Valentine, 1986).

It is especially difficult for infertile women to find emotional support. They are criticized by both feminist *and* conservative peers (Houghton & Houghton, 1984; J. Schwartz, 1993), finding themselves in a Catch-22 position. A woman seeking medical help is criticized by feminists for falling victim to a male-dominated medical profession (Faludi, 1991). Some feminists view women who are willing to carry the burden for both infertility treatment and the maintenance of a heterosexual relationship as "too willing victims" (Corea et al., 1987; Klein, 1989; Overall, 1987; Spallone & Steinberg, 1988; Stanworth, 1987).

Conversely, women who do not attempt treatment are stigmatized for not trying hard enough by conservatives. Marshner (1982) summarized the conservative view this way: "A woman's nature is, simply, other oriented. . . . Women are ordained by their nature to spend themselves in meeting the needs of others" (p. 12). A "real woman" will go to any length necessary to have a child.

Even women who do not necessarily identify with Marshner's (1982) description of womanhood unknowingly contribute to the ostracism of childless women. Miall (1985) stated that childlessness disqualifies infertile women from being part of the "in-group of mothers" (p. 391). They are frequently treated by women with children as second-class citizens who cannot contribute to conversations about childbearing (Miall, 1985). According to Abbey, Andrews, and Halman (1991), "[i]nfertile women may feel more isolated and in need of emotional support than their partners if their lack of children makes it more difficult for them to maintain their same-sex friendships" (p. 297). Childless women may feel disconnected from other women and female friends, increasing their desire to reproduce.

For many infertile people, the ability to have children is extremely important and is intricately enmeshed with their goals of fulfillment and happiness in life. This would explain why threats to one's fertility can be so devastating. Subtle and overt forms of disenfranchising messages are communicated to infertile couples every day as they participate in a society that expects them to become parents (Faludi, 1991; J. Schwartz, 1993). Society transmits these powerful messages through its various institutions, one of the most influential being the family.

## INFERTILITY AND FAMILY

An individual's family of origin is the most critical factor in determining his or her self-concept and worldview (Berg et al., 1991; Stanton & Dunkel-Schetter, 1991). As a large part of our socialization process, the intense biological instinct to reproduce is reinforced by cultural expectations transmitted through familial experiences (Houghton & Houghton, 1984). Although families may be more accepting of alternative lifestyles than ever before, they continue to communicate powerful negative messages to infertile individuals (J. Schwartz, 1993), so that infertile individuals often feel alienated from the people they love the most. Thus, their own family may be the primary source of their feelings of inadequacy and disenfranchisement.

For the family, reproduction may be seen as the replenishment of generations, representing a small piece of immortality—an extension into the future (McDaniel, Hepworth, & Doherty, 1992). Implicit in the reproductive process is this notion of immortality through the distribution of the familial genetic pool. This is demonstrated overtly by older family members encouraging couples to have children in order to "pass on" the family name. Infertility interrupts this "continuity," preventing regeneration. Becker and Nachtigall (1991) explained reproduction as "the march of generations, the renewal of life. Infertility thus constitutes a major loss" (p. 876). Infertile couples may feel as if they have failed their families by their inability to continue the family line.

In addition to family continuation, many people see the reproductive stage of the life cycle as a prominent marker of adulthood, and childbearing as full membership into the family system. Boszormenyi-Nagy and Sparks (1973) stated that family loyalty is typically based on biological hereditary kinship. Emotional and biological continuity from generation to generation forms family identity, family legacy, and family myths. Events and rituals such as birthdays, weddings, christenings, and funerals provide the foundation for both familial and social alliances. Individuals may view reproduction as admission into this family system (Houghton & Houghton, 1984).

Parents of infertile children frequently internalize the pain and shame that their son or daughter is experiencing. They may assume the blame based on past behaviors and feel responsible for giving their child defective genes or sexual organs. In a small percentage of cases, parents *have* unintentionally caused infertility in their children, such as mothers who took diethylstilbestrol (DES) between 1941 and 1971 to prevent their own miscarriages. This drug resulted in pregnancy loss and/or congenital malformations in the reproductive tracts of the children (Burns, 1987).

Although family members may empathize and even internalize the pain of the infertile couple, they are often insensitive to their emotional needs. In times of crisis, many individuals turn to their families for emotional support. However, infertile couples do not always find the understanding they are seeking. Interactions with family members may be a tremendous source of confusion and pain as infertile couples struggle to find significant roles within the family unit (Houghton & Houghton, 1984).

Parents of infertile couples also may feel humiliation/alienation within their own social groups when they are unable to share common experiences, such as becoming grandparents. They too are excluded from conversations and social activities that center on grandparenting (Houghton & Houghton, 1984). This shame may be communicated in the form of additional pressure on their children to procreate.

Many infertile couples feel an obligation to provide grandchildren as a "token" of appreciation for their own positive childhood experiences. Providing grandchildren becomes a way of repaying parents for a good child-hood—rebalancing the family ledger (Boszormenyi-Nagy & Sparks, 1973). Grandchildren can be a source of comfort and purpose to aging parents and often can help in alleviating tensions within the family unit by acting as a reuniting force within the family. Providing grandchildren can be a positive and healing experience by "offering opportunities for reparation or reconciliation after the turbulence of adolescent separation" (McDaniel et al., 1992, p. 104). The exclusion from contributing to, and benefiting from, this mode of cohesion communicates to infertile couples that they are not valued members of the family unit.

The impact of these issues on family members is often expressed through their messages to infertile couples. Miscommunication and animosity may emerge from remarks made by family members directed toward the infertile couple and their situation. Comments from others, such as "just relax" or "adopt and you will get pregnant" are particularly hurtful, evoking feelings of anger and anxiety directed at family members who attempt to minimize their situation. Coupled with these feelings of animosity are feelings of jealousy toward fertile family members (Honea-Flemming, 1986). Accord-ing to Dunkel-Schetter and Lobel (1991), "because family members are biologically similar and yet able to have children" (p. 37), resentments may be amplified. Infertile women may be particularly affected by this division.

For infertile women, tensions may exist between themselves and sisters or sisters-in-law. Motherhood is often infused with power and status within the family unit. There can be a sense of competition in terms of fertility and the number of children conceived. This fertility "power play" is fueled by emotions of jealousy and a sense of personal failure (McDaniel et al., 1992). Coupled with the sense of failure associated with the experience of infertility is an additional layer of guilt for having negative feelings toward loved ones. Jealousy and guilt result in further estrangement from fertile family members.

Feelings of alienation often seem to spiral and perpetuate themselves. For example, to avoid awkward situations, family members are reluctant to include the infertile couple in social events that center on children (Coates & Wortman, 1980; Wortman & Dunkel-Schetter, 1979). Conversely, it is difficult for the infertile couple to communicate and identify with family members who do not share their dilemma: "Significant others unintention-ally say and do things which upset the individual in need of support, who in turn withdraws. This response causes potential supporters to feel unap-preciated and unwanted, so they withdraw. Thus, the infertile individual becomes even more isolated" (Coates & Wortman, p. 158). This pattern of isolation may be difficult to break.

The family unit is a microcosm of a society where motherhood is tra-ditionally regarded as an achievement. Both the family and society have a vested interest in the propagation of the human race. Childbearing is both socially and biologically significant. Families, like society at large, continue to struggle with new societal roles and expectations. Only recently have women been given the opportunity to seek fulfillment outside the role of motherhood (Faludi, 1991). Clearly, there is a need for family members to become more sensitive to the issues surrounding infertility (Houghton & Houghton, 1984). As a result of disenfranchising messages, the infertile couple often find the need to reposition themselves and redefine their roles within the family structure. This repositioning often involves other institutions. Although the family is central in the transmission of value systems, particularly concerning reproduction, religious institutions can create additional psychological social barriers for infertile individuals.

## INFERTILITY AND RELIGION

Religion plays a central role in many people's lives. It shapes world views and often provides explanations for life occurrences. Despite potential support from religious institutions and their members, infertile couples often receive disenfranchising messages from the beliefs of their religion. For instance, many religious foundations and beliefs place a strong emphasis on childbearing. A religious institution that has a strong family emphasis can be alienating to couples who do not or can not have children. This section explores the Catholic, Mormon, Islamic, and Jewish religions, revealing the messages these institutions often send to infertile couples.

### Catholicism

Catholicism is known for its emphasis on the importance of children in marriage and the family (Poston & Kramer, 1984). Poston and Kramer reported that the catechism taught to Catholic children before 1962 specified the purposes of marriage as twofold: "[T]he primary purpose was the procreation and rearing of children; the secondary purpose was the mutual satisfaction and support of the husband and wife, along with the satisfaction of their sexual desires. . . . Childlessness was, at best, frowned upon by the Catholic Church, if not discouraged" (pp. 5–6). For Catholics raised in the Church since 1962, little has changed. Poston and Kramer explained that with the end of the Vatican II, the goals of marriage have been redefined with the two purposes being equal. However, despite this dramatic change in definition, having children is still considered one of the major objectives of marriage. Young Catholics are still taught through the catechism that having children is central to married life.

The Catholic Church continues their strong pronatalistic message in the rites of marriage. When a couple wishes to be married in the Catholic Church, they must meet with a priest or a deacon for at least three separate marriage sessions. Before the first session, the bride and groom are asked to answer six questions under oath, outside of each other's presence: "The fourth question asks, 'God willing, do both of you intend to have children in this marriage?' If both parties respond negatively and insist that they do not plan to have children, then it is doubtful that they could be married in the [Catholic] Church" (Poston & Kramer, 1984, pp. 6–7). The wedding ceremony continues the emphasis on the importance of the woman's role as a mother. A woman's life role is seen as mother and wife first, and individual second. These messages from the catechism, marriage preparation, and the marriage ceremony tell couples that having children is of utmost importance to their roles as "good" Catholics. When couples cannot conceive, they may feel like they have failed in the roles expected of them by their religion.

In addition to the messages directly from the Church, in the Old Testament, infertility is presented as a curse. In Genesis 30:1, 22–23, Rachel's infertility is portrayed as being forgotten by God: "When Rachel saw that she was not bearing Jacob any children, she became jealous of her sister. So she said to Jacob, 'Give me children, or I'll die!' Then God remembered Rachel; he listened to her and opened her womb. She became pregnant and gave birth to a son and said, 'God has taken away my disgrace' " (The Thompson, 1983, pp. 30–31). Even the New Testament repeats the stories of infertile women: Luke 1:7, 24–25: "But [Zechariah and Elizabeth] had no children, and they were both well along in years. . . . After this, his wife Elizabeth became pregnant and for five months remained in seclusion. 'The Lord has done this for me,' she said. 'In these days he has shown his favor and taken away my disgrace among the people' " (The Thompson, 1983, p. 1044).

For infertile couples, religious stories such as these present their infertility as "God's will" (Greil, 1991). Indeed, according to Greil, "many infertile individuals try to bargain with God. A participant in Greil's study reported saying 'If you just let me have a baby, I'll go to church for the next fifty years' " (p. 162). The idea of infertility as God's will leads individuals to feel like God is punishing them. As another one of Greil's participants expressed: "We're not a very religious family. We go to church. We were both brought up in church. But it was like, if there is this God who's this wonderful person, why is he doing this to us? We've been good people, we've played by the rules, and we've done what we should have done all of our lives. Why is he punishing us? was how I felt" (p. 160). The messages from the Catholic Church and the Bible, the foundation of the Catholic Church, tell of the importance of having children. Infertile couples may naturally feel separated from the Church by not being able to fulfill their required roles as parents. In addition, they may feel "out of favor" with God, and infertility is presented as a curse on them. However, the Catholic Church is not the only religion to send such powerful pronatalistic messages to its followers.

## Mormonism

As Wilcox (1987) explained, "Many of the rituals of the Mormon religion center on the importance of having children. Being a mother is considered the pinnacle of female achievement, the most significant work and the most exalted role a Mormon woman can have—more primary (though perhaps just barely) than that of a wife" (pp. 208–209). Mormonism rests on the belief that "As man is, God once was; as God is, man may become" (Young, 1954, p. 30). According to Mormon theology, a host of other worlds exist for habitation by men who have been advanced to divine status: "Thus if a good Latter-day Saint were faithful and married a wife or wives under the 'celestial marriage system' for time and eternity, he might advance to be a god over his own world with its inhabitants from his own family. . . . To these believers, then, the more children they had the better" (p. 30). Marriage is required for the full salvation of Mormon men (Charles, 1987). Charles explained the foundation of this belief using the Mormon text of the Doctrine and Covenants. According to Section 131, there are three heavens or degrees. For a man to advance to the highest degree he must enter the "new and everlasting covenant of marriage. And if he does not, he cannot obtain it. He may enter into the other but that is the end of his kingdom; he cannot have an increase" (p. 46).

The next section of the Doctrine and Covenants, Section 132, explains that the new covenant of marriage is polygyny or polygamy. Women are seen as instruments for their husbands' using. The system of polygamy was created to facilitate the advancement of the man into his reward in the afterlife.

Although men are "saved" by marrying and being "righteous," Mormon women are in a completely different circumstance. As Young (1954) explained, "A woman's salvation here and hereafter was completely dependent upon her being married to a man who held the divine keys of admission into heaven" (p. 33). The pressure to have children is very intense for the Mormon woman:

A woman's main function was to bear children for her husband. If a man had no progeny he was forgettable, not "immortal" at all. Childbirth was thus the key to a woman's worth, and infertility was always seen as caused by a defect in a wife, never in a husband. Even though a man might already have children by another wife, a wife who was barren still felt a desperate need to provide her husband with children. The stories of Sarah, Rachael,

Samson's mother, and Hannah all manifest the stigma and disgrace associated with barrenness. The jealousy of Sarah toward Hagar, of Rachael toward Leah, and the pride of Hagar and Leah in their own fertility, show that women evaluated themselves and each other by their ability to bear children. (Charles, 1987, p. 40)

Although the pressure is on the couple to have children, it is more focused on the woman. After all, a polygamous man could find another wife to bear him children. Infertility on the part of the man is not addressed in the literature.

Although polygamy is no longer widely practiced among Mormons (Shipps, 1987), its roots in the history of Mormonism are still felt among Mormon women today. "In early Utah much of the focus of the mother's influence was directed toward her power to 'build up the kingdom' through her children" (Wilcox, 1987, p. 209). Wilcox quoted a typical 1867 sermon from then apostle George Q. Cannon: "A great glory is bestowed on woman, for she is permitted to bring forth the souls of men. . . . It is a glorious mission which God has assigned to his daughters, and they should be correspondingly proud of it" (pp. 209–210). For the Mormons, a man's children and descendants will form his "kingdom." This explains why men are "anxious to have numerous families, as the more children a man has, the greater will be his power and glory hereafter, as their patriarch and monarch" (Stenhouse, 1872, p. 186). Infertility is seen as a barrier to achieving salvation in the Mormon perspective.

Although "subordination and inferiority of women is no longer explicitly preached in the Mormon church" (Charles, 1987, p. 57), women still occupy a lesser role. "Partnership in marriage is still a hierarchy in which each person assumes her or his proper and essential role" (p. 57). For women, this role has changed little. According to Wilcox (1987), "In the last twenty years, much of the Mormon rhetoric about mothers has remained virtually indistinguishable from that of the previous thirty or forty years. . . . The glorification of motherhood has continued with little or no change" (p. 216). Like the Catholic couple, a Mormon couple's infertility is seen as destroying their traditional role in the Mormon religion. However, for the Mormon couple, their salvation virtually depends on their fertility, adding a greater threat to an already painful situation. In contrast to the overwhelmingly strong messages of the Mormon religion, Islam contains a slightly different message.

## Islam

Muslims, whatever their religious group, firmly believe in the Quran as the only divine scripture of Islam and they must follow the guidelines of the Quran in all aspects of their lives (Mahmood, 1977). A Muslim will consult the Quran in all matters, including those of fertility. The family is the basic social unit in Muslim society, with marriage the fundamental Islamic institution. Marriage and family formation are seen as grave responsibilities with many specific regulations (Omran, 1992). However, unlike the Mormons, Muslims are not under intense pressure to have large families (Mahmood). The law of Islam indicates that Muslims are under many familial obligations, to their children, their parents, their siblings, and other extended family members. Therefore, Muslims are encouraged to have only as many children as they can support (Mahmood).

In addition, childbearing does not play as central a role in the institution of marriage. Procreation in Islamic marriages is not the sole purpose of marital sexual relations: "Dwelling together in tranquility is an overall purpose in marriage. This is more equitable because 'all couples can achieve tranquility, but not all couples are fertile. . . . While procreation is an expectation in marriage, it is not its exclusive purpose' " (Omran, 1992, p. 15). It is this expectation that adds pressure for the infertile couple. As Omran asserted, "Children are highly valued in many societies, but particularly so for the Muslims. . . . Muslims believe that children are gifts of Allah" (pp. 30–31). Additionally, children are seen as "proof of a wife's fertility and a husband's virility" (p. 31).

Children also carry an economic, as well as social, value. Children constitute a built-in social security system for parents in old age, in crippling sickness, and in case of unemployment. Pride in having a large family is a feature of traditional societies where numbers are equated with power. This stems from tribal beliefs that having many children, particularly sons, was a prerequisite for protecting family wealth, property, honor, and social functions (Omran, 1992). The messages from the Muslim religion are mixed, acknowledging that children are not the only reason for marriage, but placing a value on them socially and economically. The more informal messages from the Muslim culture are more strongly pronatalistic. This can lead to feelings of separation from their faith and culture by the infertile Muslim couple.

Omran (1992) recognized the dilemma these messages pose for the infertile couple and supported help for them from the medical community: "The treatment of infertility is the complement of family planning. Having children is one of the joys of life and those who have no children should be assisted to have some. Services to control infertility should therefore be provided as an integral part of family planning services" (p. 184). However, these treatments are limited by the Quran:

> The treatment of infertility is not only allowed but recommended. There is no problem with chemical or surgical therapy as long as it is performed by honest, experienced specialists. . . . Although surrogate motherhood is not specifically mentioned in the *fatwa,* it is understood from other evidence that

it is forbidden. Adoption is also forbidden because of the deception involved. Caring for a child and treating him or her as kin is allowed but no false family name is provided. (Omran, p. 186)

Thus, adoption and surrogacy are not options for the infertile couple. Other methods are preferred and acceptable in the Muslim religion. Although the acceptance of these treatments is encouraging for the infertile couple, the restrictions on adoption and surrogacy limit their options for having a child. A couple wishing to follow these options would be further disenfranchised from the Muslim way of life. Like Islam, Catholicism, and Mormonism, the Jewish faith also communicates the importance of childbearing to its followers.

## Judaism[1]

In Ancient Israel, a woman's motherhood was seen as her primary role in Jewish society. "Childbearing and raising children were highly regarded functions and were seen as essential to the survival of the Jewish people" (Kaufman, 1993, p. 46). The stories of Rachel and Elizabeth in the Old Testament are told in the Jewish religion, as well as in the Catholic and Mormon religions. For the Jewish follower, "fertility is associated with blessing, barrenness is associated with punishment for transgressions" (p. 46). Although there are many different sects of Judaism, all Jews accept the "importance of family and entry into marriage as a religious and social obligation" (Hyman, 1986, p. 7). In the Jewish wedding ceremony, an officiant praises God for "fashioning woman in the likeness of man, preparing for man a mate, that together they might perpetuate life" (Hertzberg, 1991, p. 114). These views are similar to those of the Catholic Church. However, in the Jewish religion the pressure of fertility and procreation is placed on the man rather than the woman.

Generally, Jewish teachings view marriage as the bond that makes two incomplete beings whole (Kaufman, 1993). Sexual relations in marriage are acceptable even when the purpose is not procreation (Lauterbach, 1970; Schneider, 1984). It is part of the bond of husband and wife. Marriage is considered optional and voluntary for the woman under the reasoning that seeking a mate is an aggressive act, more suited for the man than the woman. It must be noted, however, that "Judaism regards the deliberate intent to remain single as unforgivable selfishness" (Kaufman, 1993, p. 16). For the woman, the release of having to seek out a mate lessens some of the pressure to bear children. In addition, the Jewish religious text, the

---

[1]Judaism is comprised of three dominant branches: reform, conservative, and orthodox. This discussion attempts to address commonalities about infertility within, rather than differences between, these branches.

Torah, does not require a woman to bear children if it might endanger her health (Kaufman, 1993; Schneider, 1984). A commitment to having children must be made by a woman's "free will" and not by order of an outside source (Kaufman, 1993).

The command to procreate is directed toward the man more than toward the woman (Hertzberg, 1991; Kaufman, 1993). Lauterbach (1970) cited the "duty of propagation" as central to a man's role, "a man must fulfill the duty of propagation of the race" (p. 218). However, Lauterbach described many situations where marriage and sexual relations were acceptable even when having children was impossible. For the infertile couple, marriage is not seen as demanding childbearing, yet the emphasis placed on procreation might seem contradictory.

Today the pressure for Jewish couples to bear children might be even more intense (Schneider, 1984). It is seen as positive that American men and women are marrying later and having few children. However, Schneider asserted that the Jewish population level is cause for alarm: "We're not even *at* replacement level! The goals of the Jewish community are clear: at the same time that Zero Population Growth is urging high school students to plan for one-child families, the Task Force on Jewish Population in New York is advocating that Jewish schools put up posters showing families with five children" (p. 371).

Feminism, contraceptives, and work have all been blamed for the falling Jewish birthrate. Couples who cannot conceive are caught in the crossfire between these ideals. Schneider recounted a letter received in a Jewish magazine where a woman wrote: "You write about the pressures on Jewish women to have babies. My husband and I can't conceive, but we want very much to bring children into our home and raise them as Jews. Where is the community which cries out for families to have more children when it comes to setting up a support system for those Jewish families who are trying to adopt?" (p. 396).

Longing to respond to the cry to have children, infertile couples feel left without resources. As a result, Schneider listed the names and addresses of several Jewish adoption agencies and counseling centers. In addition, artificial insemination is encouraged for couples who are fertile but cannot conceive, as long as the husband's sperm is used (Schneider, 1984). Although these options offer some relief, these strongly pronatalistic messages continue to disenfranchise the infertile couple.

## The Centrality of Religion

Religion is an important part of the lives of many individuals. Messages received in religious institutions often alienate people from their faith and their perceptions of their roles within the religion. The four religions examined here—Catholicism, Mormonism, Islam, and Judaism—are certainly not exhaustive, either of the specific religion or religions as a whole. However, delineating their messages on marriage, family, and childbearing allows us to explore the possible meanings of these messages for infertile couples. In an infertile couple's life, religion is one contact point that communicates to them about their infertility. Another contact point is the health care system.

## INFERTILITY AND HEALTH CARE

The health care system plays an extremely powerful role in communicating disenfranchising messages to infertile couples. For some couples, the first words to confirm their pregnancy are spoken by a medical professional. And medical professionals often are the ones to report, explain, and offer advice about the end of a pregnancy through miscarriage, stillbirth, or Sudden Infant Death Syndrome (SIDS). And when couples fail to conceive or give birth, medical professionals are the ones who speak of hope by offering alternatives for treating infertility. The elation and devastation of pregnancy, loss, and potential infertility are often discussed with and treated by medical professionals during medical visits.

The origins of disenfranchising messages from the medical community can be traced to diagnosis and treatment of the condition labeled as infertility. The traditional medical model leads medical professionals to treat infertility like an illness. Patients who often are not really ill, who have no physical symptoms, but instead desire to have a child, are subject to a highly technological industry of diagnosis and treatment (Greil, 1991).

Inevitably, infertility is becoming increasingly medicalized and industrialized. As Greil (1991) pointed out, American life, in particular, has become medicalized, relying to a greater extent on medical experts to solve problems such as infertility. However, the solutions offered by most medical professionals focus on the technical aspects of infertility, often ignoring social, emotional, and cognitive aspects (Daniluk, Leader, & Taylor, 1985; Greil, 1991; Mazor & Simons, 1984; Phoenix, Woollett, & Lloyd, 1991; Stanton & Dunkel-Schetter, 1991).

The process of being treated for infertility has a profound impact on the couple. Couples often feel powerless, as if they have turned their lives over to physicians (Abbey, 1992; Mahlstedt, 1985). Relational difficulties are not uncommon as couples experience emotional and psychological stress (Daniluk, 1988; Daniluk et al., 1985; McEwan, Costelli, & Taylor, 1987), personal, interpersonal, and ethical dilemmas (McDaniel et al., 1992; Valentine, 1986), and dysfunctional and unsatisfying sexual relations (Berger, 1980; Link & Darling, 1986; Morse & Dennerstein, 1985). The family system is, in a sense, dismantled from without by professional fertility experts as couples seek guidance in exchange for the commodified goods and services of infertility treatment (Deetz, 1992; Luke, 1989). Not surprisingly, in the process, these men and women may experience depression (Hynes, Callan, Terry, & Gallois, 1992), stress (O'Moore & Harrison, 1991), lowered self-esteem (Abbey, Andrews, & Halman, 1992), and feelings of loss of control over their everyday lives (Daniluk et al., 1985).

Although the number of medical visits for fertility problems nearly tripled between 1968 and 1984, only half the people who seek assistance overcome their infertility problem (Elmer-DeWitt, 1991a). However, it is important to note that the medical community's definition of infertility has changed over time. Currently, the medical community defines a couple as infertile if they are unable to conceive after 1 year, or if they have experienced three or more miscarriages. Not so long ago, the definition of infertility was set at 5 years:

> [T]he twelve month [infertility] rule is a recent development, inspired by "infertility specialists" marketing experimental and expensive new reproductive technologies. . . . The one year cut-off is widely challenged by demographers who point out that it takes young newlyweds a mean time of eight months to conceive. In fact, only 16 to 21 percent of couples who are defined as infertile under the one-year definition actually prove to be, a congressional study found. (Faludi, 1991, p. 28)

As Faludi pointed out, time is the greatest and the cheapest cure for infertility. In her view, the so-called "infertility epidemic" has led to a great deal of needless anxiety and costly medical treatment for couples who would in time become pregnant without medical advice or intervention.

One major dilemma regarding infertility diagnosis and treatment is that although infertility problems can be attributed to women in 50% of the cases, to men in 40% of the cases, and to both in 10% of cases, the primary recipients of infertility treatment are women (DeWitt, 1993). Frequently, women and their bodies are the target of diagnosis and treatment (Becker & Nachtigall, 1991), in some cases without checking the sperm count of the husband (Corea, 1985a, 1985b). As McDaniel et al. (1992) pointed out, "it is not unusual for a poorly trained physician to schedule advanced infertility treatments—even surgery—on a woman without first checking her partner's sperm count" (p. 114). Low sperm count, as one of the principal causes of infertility, has been understudied. And surprisingly, the government does not include men in its national fertility survey (Faludi, 1991).

More recently, problems have developed in the governmentally unregulated business of infertility medicine. One case in particular has opened our eyes to the disturbing kinds of fraud that are possible with infertility treatment. Dr. Cecil Jacobson, one of the geneticists who founded the amniocentesis procedure, faces 53 felony charges for giving patients hormone treatments that simulated the effects of early pregnancy. Women testifying at the hearings indicated that "Jacobson would show them sonograms of what he said was their fetus, pointing out nonexistent heartbeats, fetal movements and thumbsucking. He would give them fetal snapshots to take home—only later to announce several weeks later that their baby had died" (Elmer-DeWitt, 1991b, p. 27). More recent charges and genetic testing reveals that Jacobson has fathered some of the babies of the patients he treated. The indictment indicates that "Jacobson conned patients into thinking he had an elaborate system for matching sperm donors to particular physical, mental and social characteristics. But in some cases, says the government, he was the sole donor" (p. 27). What we are discovering in cases like Dr. Jacobson is that because there is no board certification and little regulation, "doctors can claim to be experts on the basis of scant experience or training" (p. 27).

The medical community's powerful role in diagnosing, treating, and even defining infertility affords them what other contemporary corporations are developing—greater control, often unnecessary standardization, and industrialization (Deetz, 1992). The woman's body as a place of gestation is medicalized and the woman as a person is detached from the structures, practices, and discourses of infertility (Tubert, 1992). According to Spallone and Steinberg (1988), "Feminists see a future in which women are used as 'mother machines' and 'living laboratories' of reproduction and becoming available as ever expanding material for sexual and reproductive biomedical research and experimentation" (p. 64). Feminists see the biomedical industry using infertility research as just another vehicle for male expansionism cloaked behind a moralistic facade—helping people to bear children (Overall, 1987).

The medicalization of reproduction is one in the same with its industrialization as it has become "an enterprise of mass production, supervised by trained specialists, dependent upon expensive and sophisticated equipment, and managed according to principles of rational efficiency" (Greil, 1991, p. 37). And in fact, the medicalization of reproduction in some cases has contributed to infertility because of the effects of DES, intrauterine devices (IUDs), Caesarean sections, and birth control pills (Clarke, 1988; Greil, 1991).

For the approximately 20% of American couples who are infertile, infertility is a crisis with no resolution (Butler & Koraleski, 1990). The inability to conceive and bear children is a deeply serious psychological crisis—for many it means not achieving one of life's milestones and it symbolizes a failure to live up to one's own or others' expectations (Butler & Koraleski, 1990; Pines, 1990). And for many couples the only resolution is negotiating an empowered identity through any number of avenues.

## NEGOTIATING EMPOWERED IDENTITIES

The disenfranchisement of infertile people contributes to their sense of powerlessness and emotional upheaval. At different stages of coping with the pain of infertility, individuals are faced with an emotionally charged decision-making process about the options they want to pursue to either remedy or accept their childlessness. Many individuals escape their disenfranchisement by negotiating empowered identities through a number of other avenues. Some continue to build a sense of comfort and hope through alternative medicine or through infertility clinics offered by traditional medicine. Others turn to adoption to ease and overcome the pain of infertility. And still others regain or strengthen identities through their participation in groups such as the National Association for the Childless, RESOLVE, or local support groups such as Empty Cradle. We close this chapter with a brief examination of some of the options for negotiating empowered identities.

### Social Support

At the same time that the demand for infertility services has expanded dramatically, so too have the numbers of women and men who have sought social support from groups who meet weekly or monthly to share information, emotions, and friendship with others who have experienced infertility, either through a loss or the inability to conceive. For example, RESOLVE, the national infertility group providing counseling and support for infertile couples, has grown from 16,000 to 25,000 in 4 years (Minton, 1992).

Support groups provide opportunities for personal insight, peer support, and education (Menning, 1984; Shapiro, 1988). In this safe refuge, individuals can express feelings, receive empathy and understanding, and examine options for resolution (Harkness, 1987). The vital role of support groups cannot be understated; infertile individuals are susceptible to feelings of social isolation, misunderstanding, and lack of belonging with peers, "many of whom are beginning families and unable to understand the pain of infertility" (Shapiro, 1988, p. 68).

Support groups vary in their mission and individuals may find one more appropriate than another, depending on their stage in decision making about their infertility. The National Association for the Childless (NAC) is a national advocacy organization that provides education on infertility treatments, contacts for adoption, sympathetic correspondence regarding infertility dilemmas, and general advice on dealing with the bureaucratic and complicated processes of infertility decision making. NAC described its objectives in the following way: "to determine policy at the national level, to focus awareness on the need for improved medical treatment of infertility, for better adoption and fostering services and for an acceptance of the childless as valued members of society with a unique contribution to make" (Houghton & Houghton, 1984, p. 7). At the local level NAC encourages the formation of self-help groups, improvement of services for advice and comfort, and activities of common interest for individuals experiencing infertility.

Another advocacy support group, RESOLVE, provides counseling, support, and encourages infertile people to educate themselves so they can make informed decisions about their own health care (Menning, 1984). RESOLVE is not an acronym but a word that states what individuals in the group hope to achieve: ". . . resolution of the state of longing to have children and being unable to. The state is not always resolved by pregnancy—in fact, only about half of infertility is 'cured' by medical intervention. We try to help people resolve their feelings and get on with their lives; this can mean selection of an alternative way of family building, acceptance of life without children, or successful pregnancy and childbirth" (p. 54). Getting on with one's life often means coming to terms with the specific nature of infertility the individuals are experiencing.

Empty Cradle, although not affiliated with NAC or RESOLVE, serves the community by offering emotional support to parents who have experienced the loss of a baby through miscarriage, stillbirth, or infant death. Although these individuals may not be defined by the medical community as infertile, their concerns about childlessness are very similar. Empty Cradle offers monthly support group meetings, education through a lending library, and focused discussions on avenues for copying with infertility and the emotional turmoil surrounding infertility treatments and subsequent pregnancy.

### Subsequent Pregnancy

Subsequent pregnancy seems like the ideal solution to infertility. "Most of us think that bearing a child will banish the specter of infertility. In fact pregnancy and childbirth don't always erase infertility scars and often raise sensitive issues of their own" (Harkness, 1987, p. 246). Individuals who become pregnant may have difficulty believing that they actually are pregnant, and as a result, move back and forth between emotions: excitement over being pregnant and frightened about what lies ahead. In addition, the pregnancy may create difficulty in interacting with the infertile people who have been supportive:

> Every time I heard of a fellow infertile's pregnancy, I remember thinking, "Hurray, there's one for our side" and a feeling of hope would come over me. So when I learned I was pregnant, why did I sit in the back of our

support group meeting, wringing my hands, heart pounding, afraid to share the good news? How could I tell all these people that I had something we all wanted so badly? I worried that this meant leaving a group of people I had learned to love and cherish for their never-ending support and encouragement. What would happen now that things had changed? (p. 249)

Individuals who do not naively assume that pregnancy resolves the emotional traumas of infertility and gain the support they need throughout the subsequent pregnancy can begin to feel a sense of empowerment with the birth of their child. When pregnancy is clearly not an option, some couples will turn to surrogacy.

## Surrogacy

Surrogacy is the process whereby a woman contracts with an infertile couple (or in some cases, a single man) to be artificially inseminated with the man's sperm. The surrogate mother carries and delivers the child, and relinquishes it to the couple (Harkness, 1987; Overall, 1987). "Usually, the husband's name will be listed on the infant's birth certificate; the infertile wife, however, must formally adopt the child in order to become its legal mother" (Overall, p. 112). Surrogacy is regarded by some as a form of "collaborative reproduction" (p. 113). Clearly, surrogacy is one avenue for empowerment. However, infertile couples need to consider carefully the cost of surrogacy, the importance of finding an acceptable surrogate, the complex legal issues, and the possible outcomes (Harkness, 1987). These same issues, and others, are part of adoption as another alternative for empowering infertile couples.

## Adoption

Adoption is considered the best approach when "social" parenthood is more important than "biological" parenthood (Crowe, 1987). It has been suggested that, "the decision to try to adopt may mark the first stage of acceptance by a couple that they may not be able to have their own child" (Houghton & Houghton, 1984, p. 99). Adoption focuses the infertile couple on roles as nurturers rather than genitors (natural parents). Although the odds against successfully completing the adoption process are high, these odds decrease if the couple is willing to adopt an older child, a child of another race, or a child with a handicap (Houghton & Houghton). For couples who discover the bond they can create with their adopted child, this option can be as fulfilling as biological parenthood.

## Summary

Regardless of the decisions individuals make to remedy or accept their childlessness, both partners need to agree about the option they choose (Crowe, 1987). Support groups, subsequent pregnancy, surrogacy, and adoption are avenues of empowerment that infertile individuals may choose to pursue. Each option carries with it important, emotional, relational, financial, and medical considerations. Parenthood should be considered *one* of many lifestyle choices.

## THE RESPONSIBILITY OF SOCIETY TO ALLEVIATE DISENFRANCHISEMENT

We must embrace the diversity of our society. Childlessness is not a disease or a condition to be scorned. Infertility, medical therapy, and adoption become problematic for infertile people largely because they are problematic in American culture (Sandelowski, 1993). After 7 years of formal study with infertile women and couples, Sandelowski indicated that:

> The struggles of the infertile people in my studies reprise larger themes in Western culture: the tendencies to view as opposite and conflicting the natural and the artificial, the biological and the technological, and to value one over the other. The infertile people described here sought and succeeded (more or less) to reconcile these cultural oppositions. Through their encounters with and experiences of the paradox and "liminality" of artificial conception and artificial family, they often concluded that "artificiality" is part of the "natural" condition of the world, not separate from it. (p. 3)

Alleviating or eliminating disenfranchisement necessitates lifting the cultural taboo surrounding motherhood: the pronatalism of our society that sanctifies a woman's desire to have children as natural and the choice not to have children or not to have them "naturally" as illegitimate (Firestone, 1970; Sterney, 1994). For those who are childless, disenfranchisement may be reduced if they are allowed to see themselves as valued and contributing members of society with or without children.

Individuals and couples who reported coping best with the infertility experience were those who maintained ongoing supportive relationships. These relationships were found among family, friends, and other infertile persons. But caregivers as well need to provide the support infertile couples need by communicating in ways that allow the couple to feel "normal" when they do become pregnant—like other childbearing couples (Sandelowski, Harris, & Black, 1992). In essence, supportive relationships provide infertile individuals with opportunities to "tell their stories," thereby facilitating the grieving process and their sense of control.

At the societal level, infertile individuals and couples can be enfranchised in a number of ways, such as including men in infertility studies and changing media portrayals that give credence to parenthood obsession. Increased government funding of research also is needed to increase our understanding of the profound effects that the medicalization of infertility has on individuals, couples, their friends, and their families as they experience, and deal with, the pain of infertility.

## REFERENCES

Abbey, A., Andrews, F. M., & Halman, L. J. (1991). Gender's role in responses to infertility. *Psychology of Women Quarterly, 15*, 295–316.

Abbey, A., Andrews, F. M., & Halman, L. J. (1992). Infertility and subjective well-being: The mediating roles of self-esteem, internal control, and interpersonal conflict. *Journal of Marriage and the Family, 54*, 408–417.

Aral, S. O., & Cates, W., Jr. (1983). The increasing concern with infertility. *Journal of the American Medical Association, 250*, 2327–2331.

Becker, G., & Nachtigall, R. D. (1991). Ambiguous responsibility in the doctor-patient relationship: The case of infertility. *Social Science and Medicine, 32*, 875–885.

Berg, B. J., Wilson, J. F., & Weingartner, P. J. (1991). Psychological sequelae of infertility treatment: The role of gender and sex-role identification. *Social Science and Medicine, 33*, 1071–1080.

Berger, D. M. (1980). Couples' reactions to male infertility and donor insemination. *American Journal of Psychiatry, 137*, 1047–1049.

Boszormenyi-Nagy, I., & Sparks, G. (1973). *Invisible loyalties*. New York: Harper & Row.

Burns, L. H. (1987). Infertility as boundary ambiguity: One theoretical perspective. *Family Process, 26*, 259–371.

Butler, R. R., & Koraleski, S. (1990). Infertility: A crisis with no resolution. *Journal of Mental Health Counseling, 12*, 151–163.

Charles, M. M. (1987). Precedents for Mormon women from scriptures. In M. U. Beecher & L. F. Anderson (Eds.), *Sisters in spirit: Mormon women in historical and cultural perspective* (pp. 37–63). Chicago: University of Illinois Press.

Clarke, A. (1988, April 9). *The industrialization of human reproduction, c. 1890–1990*. Plenary address of annual conference of the University of California system-wide Council of Women's Programs, Davis.

Coates, D., & Wortman, C. B. (1980). Depression maintenance and interpersonal control. In A. Baum & J. Singer (Eds.), *Advances in environmental psychology: Applications for personal control* (Vol. 2, pp. 149–182). Hillsdale, NJ: Lawrence Erlbaum Associates.

Corea, G. (1985a). *The hidden malpractice: How American medicine mistreats women* (2nd ed.). New York: Harper & Row.

Corea, G. (1985b). *The mother machine: Reproductive technologies from artificial insemination to artificial wombs*. New York: Harper & Row.

Corea, G., Hanmer, J., Hoskins, B., Raymond, J., Duelli-Klein, R., Holmes, H. B., Kishwar, M., Rowland, R., & Steinbacher, R. (1987). *Man-made women: How new reproductive technologies affect women*. Bloomington: Indiana University Press.

Crowe, C. (1987). Women want it: In vitro fertilization and women's motivations for participation. In P. Spallone & D. L. Steinberg (Eds.), *Made to order: The myth of reproductive and genetic progress* (pp. 84–93). New York: Pergamon.

Daniluk, J. C. (1988). Infertility: Intrapersonal and interpersonal impact. *Fertility and Sterility, 49*, 982–990.

Daniluk, J. C. (1991). Infertile couples. *Journal of Counseling & Development, 69*, 317–319.

Daniluk, J., Leader, A., & Taylor, P. J. (1985). The psychological sequelae of infertility. In J. H. Gold (Ed.), *The psychiatric implications of menstruation* (pp. 77–85). Washington, DC: American Psychiatric Press.

Deetz, S. A. (1992). *Democracy in an age of corporate colonization: Developments in communication and the politics of everyday life.* New York: State University of New York Press.

DeWitt, P. M. (1993). The pursuit of pregnancy. *American Demographics, 15*, 48–51.

Dunkel-Schetter, C., & Lobel, M. (1991). Psychological reactions to infertility. In A. L. Stanton & C. Dunkel-Schetter (Eds.), *Infertility perspectives from stress and coping research* (pp. 29–57). New York: Plenum.

Elmer-DeWitt, P. (1991a, September 30). Making babies. *Time*, pp. 56–63.

Elmer-DeWitt, P. (1991b, December 2). The cruelest kind of fraud. *Time*, p. 27.

Faludi, S. (1991). *Backlash: The undeclared war against American women.* New York: Crown.

Firestone, S. (1970). *The dialectic of sex.* New York: Morrow.

Greil, A. L. (1991). *Not yet pregnant: Infertile couples in contemporary America.* New Brunswick, NJ: Rutgers University Press.

Harkness, C. (1987). *The infertility book: A comprehensive medical and emotional guide.* San Francisco: Volcano Press.

Hertzberg, A. (1991). *Judaism: The key spiritual writings of the Jewish tradition.* New York: Simon & Schuster.

Honea-Flemming, P. (1986). Psychosocial components in obstetric gynecologic conditions with a special consideration of infertility. *Alabama Journal of Medical Sciences, 23*, 27–30.

Houghton, D., & Houghton, P. (1984). *Coping with childlessness.* Boston: Allen & Unwin.

Hyman, P. E. (1986). Introduction: Perspectives on the evolving Jewish family. In S. M. Cohen & P. E. Hyman (Eds.), *The Jewish family: Myths and reality* (pp. 3–13). New York: Holmes & Meier.

Hynes, G. J., Callan, V. J., Terry, D. J., & Gallois, C. (1992). The psychological well-being of infertile women after a failed IVF attempt: The effects of coping. *British Journal of Medical Psychology, 65*, 269–278.

Kaufman, M. (1993). *The woman in Jewish law and tradition.* Northvale, NJ: Aronson.

Klein, R. D. (1989). *Infertility: Women speak out about their experiences of reproductive medicine.* London: Pandora.

Lauterbach, J. Z. (1970). *Studies in Jewish law, custom and folklore.* New York: Ktav Publishing House.

Link, P. W., & Darling, C. A. (1986). Couples undergoing treatment for infertility: Dimensions of life satisfaction. *Journal of Sex and Marital Therapy, 12*, 46–59.

Lorber, J., & Bandlamudi, L. (1993). The dynamics of marital bargaining in male infertility. *Gender and Society, 7*, 32–49.

Luke, T. (1989). *Screens of power: Ideology, domination, and resistance in information society.* Urbana: University of Illinois Press.

Mahlstedt, P. P. (1985). The psychological component of infertility. *Fertility and Sterility, 43*, 335–346.

Mahmood, T. (1977). *Family planning: The Muslim viewpoint.* New Delhi, India: Vikas.

Marshner, C. (1982). *The new traditional woman.* Washington, DC: Free Congress Research and Education Foundation.

Mazor, M. D., & Simons, H. F. (Eds.). (1984). *Infertility: Medical, emotional and social considerations.* New York: Human Sciences.

McDaniel, S. H., Hepworth, J., & Doherty, W. (1992). Medical family therapy with couples facing infertility. *The American Journal of Family Therapy, 20,* 101–122.

McEwan, K. L., Costelli, C. G., & Taylor, P. G. (1987). Adjustment to infertility. *Journal of Abnormal Psychology, 96,* 108–116.

Menning, B. E. (1977). *Infertility: A guide for the childless couple.* Englewood Cliffs, NJ: Prentice-Hall.

Menning, B. E. (1984). RESOLVE: Counseling and support for infertile couples. In M. D. Mazor & H. F. Simons (Eds.), *Infertility: Medical, emotional and social considerations* (pp. 53–60). New York: Human Sciences.

Miall, C. E. (1985). Perceptions of informal sanctioning and the stigma of involuntary childlessness. *Deviant Behavior, 6,* 383–403.

Minton, T. (1992, October 31). Childless—Touchy topic out in open. *San Diego Union Tribune,* pp. E1, E11.

Morse, C., & Dennerstein, L. (1985). Infertile couples entering an in vitro fertilization program: A preliminary survey. *Journal of Psychosomatic Obstetrics and Gynecology, 4,* 207–219.

O'Moore, M. A., & Harrison, R. F. (1991). Anxiety and reproductive failure: Experiences from a Dublin fertility clinic. *The Irish Journal of Psychology, 12,* 276–285.

Omran, A. R. (1992). *Family planning in the legacy of Islam.* New York: Routledge.

Overall, C. (1987). *Ethics and human reproduction: A feminist analysis.* Boston: Allen & Unwin.

Phoenix, A., Woollett, A., & Lloyd, E. (Eds.). (1991). *Motherhood: Meanings, practices and ideologies.* Newbury Park, CA: Sage.

Pines, D. (1990). Emotional aspects of infertility and its remedies. *International Journal of Psychoanalysis, 71,* 561–568.

Poston, D. L., & Kramer, K. B. (1984, May). *Patterns of childlessness among Catholics and non-Catholics in the United States.* Paper presented at the annual meeting of the Population Association of America, Minneapolis.

Sandelowski, M. (1993). *With child in mind: Studies of the personal encounter with infertility.* Philadelphia: University of Pennsylvania Press.

Sandelowski, M., Harris, B. G., & Black, B. P. (1992). Relinquishing infertility: The work of pregnancy for infertile couples. *Qualitative Health Research, 2,* 282–301.

Schneider, S. W. (1984). *Jewish and female: Choices and changes in our lives today.* New York: Simon & Schuster.

Schwartz, D., & Mayaux, M. J. (1982). Female fecundity as a function of age. *The New England Journal of Medicine, 306,* 424–426.

Schwartz, J. (1993). *The mother puzzle: A new generation reckons with motherhood.* New York: Simon & Schuster.

Shapiro, C. H. (1988). *Infertility and pregnancy loss: A guide for helping professionals.* San Francisco: Jossey-Bass.

Shipps, J. (1987). Foreword. In M. U. Beecher & L. F. Anderson (Eds.), *Sisters in spirit: Mormon women in historical and cultural perspective* (pp. vii–xii). Chicago: University of Illinois Press.

Spallone, P., & Steinberg, D. L. (1988). *Made to order: The myth of reproductive and genetic progress.* New York: Pergamon.

Stanton, A. L., & Dunkel-Schetter, C. (Eds.). (1991). *Infertility: Perspectives from stress and coping research.* New York: Plenum.

Stanworth, M. (1987). *Reproductive technologies: Gender, motherhood and medicine.* Minneapolis: University of Minnesota Press.

Stenhouse, T. B. H. (1872). *A lady's life among the Mormons: A record of personal experience as one of the wives of a Mormon elder.* New York: American News Company.

Sterney, L. M. (1994). Feminism, ecofeminism, and the maternal archetype. Motherhood as a feminine universal. *Communication Quarterly, 42,* 145–159.

Thompson, I. E. (1984). The medical workup: Female and combined problems. In M. D. Mazor & H. F. Simmons (Eds.), *Infertility: Medical, emotional, and social considerations* (pp. 3–12). New York: Human Sciences.

*The Thompson chain-reference Bible: New international version.* (1983). Indianapolis: B. B. Kirkbride, & Grand Rapids, MI: Zondervan.

Tubert, S. (1992). How IVF exploits the wish to be a mother: A psychoanalyst's account. *Genders, 14,* 33–49.

U.S. National Center for Health Statistics. (1985). *The 1985 National Survey of Family Growth Cycle III.* Washington, DC: U.S. Government Printing Office.

Valentine, D. P. (1986). Psychological impact of infertility: Identifying issues and needs. *Social Work in Health Care, 11,* 61–69.

Webster, B. (1982, February 18). Study shows female fertility drops sharply after age of 30. *The New York Times,* p. A1.

Wilcox, L. P. (1987). Mormon motherhood: Official images. In M. U. Beecher & L. F. Anderson (Eds.), *Sisters in spirit: Mormon women in historical and cultural perspective* (pp. 208–226). Chicago: University of Illinois Press.

Wortman, C. B., & Dunkel-Schetter, C. (1979). Interpersonal relationships and cancer: A theoretical analysis. *Journal of Social Issues, 35,* 120–155.

Young, K. (1954). *Isn't one wife enough.* New York: Holt.

# 10 Coping With Alienation, Fear, and Isolation: The Disenfranchisement of Adolescents With Cancer and Their Families

Deborah S. Ballard-Reisch
*University of Nevada, Reno*

A diagnosis of cancer in an adolescent is a crisis that leads to the disenfranchisement of the entire family through alienation, fear, and isolation. Alienation is caused by the social stigma surrounding cancer, which is characterized by a pervasive, historically based cancerphobia. Fear results from uncertainty about the disease, treatment, and prognosis, as well as from the need of families to relinquish control of their lives and put their trust in an often impersonal, disease-oriented medical establishment. The demands of cancer treatment lead to isolation from other family members and friends as the pattern of the family's day-to-day life is disrupted to meet the demands of treatment, and cancer management becomes the main focus of the family's energies. Isolation is also common within the family as the individual needs of the adolescent, siblings, and parents are subsumed to the demands of treatment.

This chapter explores disenfranchisement through the themes of alienation, fear, and isolation as they impact families of adolescents coping with cancer. First, the alienation of families is grounded historically in the social response to cancer. Then, fear and isolation of adolescents and family members are examined through the phases of disease management.

## CANCER DYNAMICS IN THE UNITED STATES

With the exception of AIDS, no disease in U.S. history has been as feared and its victims as stigmatized as those who suffer from cancer (Patterson, 1987; Tross, 1989). In order to understand the nature of this nationwide cancerphobia, it is first necessary to explore the prevalence of cancer in the United States, the evolution of the cultural response to cancer throughout the 20th century, and the development of the cancer establishment, the cancer counterculture, and alternative cancer treatments.

## Cancer Prevalence

To date, over 200 types of cancer, characterized by the uncontrolled growth and spread of abnormal cells (American Cancer Society, 1994) have been identified (Patterson, 1987). According to current estimates, one in three Americans will develop cancer at some time in their lives. In 1994, over 2,008,000 people in the United States were diagnosed with cancer, 8,200 of them children, making cancer the most common cause of death by disease in children under 15 (American Cancer Society, 1994).

From 1973 to 1990, the incidence rate for all types of childhood cancer increased, with significant increases in acute lymphocytic leukemia and brain cancer for children under age 15 and non-Hodgkin's lymphoma for those under 20 (Miller et al., 1993). The prognosis for those suffering from childhood cancer has changed radically. Mortality rates have declined 60% since 1950, and cancers that were almost universally fatal now have 5-year survival rates ranging from 57% to 88%. The overall survival rate for childhood cancers is 68%, 57% for neuroblastoma, 58% for bone cancer, 60% for brain and central nervous system cancers, 72% for acute lymphocytic leukemia, 88% for Wilms' tumor (kidney), and 88% for Hodgkin's disease (American Cancer Society, 1994).

The rapid decrease in mortality rates for most types of childhood cancer has led some to argue that the nature of cancer should be redefined. For example, because most patients can look forward to long periods of remission and good health following cancer treatment, and because long-term survival and cure are real possibilities for many, childhood cancers should now be regarded as "life threatening chronic" illnesses rather than "acute, almost invariably fatal" diseases (Slavin, 1981, p. 1). With the increase in long-term survival rates, the orientation of medical care has changed. Previously geared toward assisting children and their families in facing death, care now centers around preparing the child and family for coping with life in the face of the chronic adversity of the disease and its treatment (Hathorn & Pizzo, 1991).

## The Cultural Response to Cancer

Traditionally, the cultural response to cancer in the United States has been highly negative and has adversely impacted both patient and family functioning. An historical overview of the U.S. cultural response to cancer indicates that although advances have been made in treatment and most can look forward to long-term remission, remaining uncertainty about cancer causes and increased incidence rates have maintained the cancerphobia characteristic of the opening decades of this century (Holland, 1989a; Patterson, 1987).

In the early 1900s, a cancer diagnosis was a death sentence. Patients could look forward to little in the way of pain management or treatment. For those who could not undergo surgical removal of tumors or affected limbs, the prognosis included the likelihood of pain, diminished capacity, disfiguring tumors or painful lesions, and ultimately, death. As little was known about the causes of cancer, the pain suffered by patients was compounded by societal fears regarding communicability and contagion (Holland, 1989b; Patterson, 1987).

Many "cures" for cancer were touted in the popular press ranging from faith healing and tonics to salves, ointments, and leeches. Drugs and patent medicines were easily available to everyone, and the fear of cancer mounted (Patterson, 1987). Simultaneously, a number of theories about the causes of cancer arose. One theory was that cancer was hereditary. Some thought cancer was caused by individual personality characteristics like moodiness and melancholy. Others thought cancer was caused by the stress of increased urbanization, which led to a host of ills including class distinctions, poverty, and pollution, as well as luxurious living, little exercise, and rich foods (Patterson, 1987).

The most popular theories were the irritation theory and the germ theory. The irritation theory advanced that any irritant to the body could cause cancer. Both physical irritants like bruises, infections, bumps, and sores, and environmental irritants, some ingested like tobacco, others ingested passively like coal dust and soot, were believed to cause cancer (Patterson, 1987). At a time when infectious diseases like tuberculosis, cholera, yellow fever, and the like were widely feared (Holland, 1989b), the theory that germs caused cancer was extremely popular (Patterson, 1987). A reasonable correlate was that cancer was contagious. It shared many of the symptoms of other communicable diseases; for example, cancer lesions were similar to lesions caused by syphilis. Consequently, many people thought cancer was related to venereal disease (Holland, 1989b; Patterson, 1987).

Society was gripped with a growing cancerphobia. Disease phobias generally arise around illnesses about which individuals have excessive fears but little knowledge (Brandt, 1985; Holland, 1989b). Cancer's almost certainly fatal outcome, the absence of known causes, the lack of successful treatments or cures, and the association with pain, disfigurement, and often rapid deterioration made it particularly frightening and loathsome (Lederberg, Holland, & Massie, 1989).

## The Rise of the Cancer Establishment

From 1900 through the 1920s, medical advancements led to the control of a number of communicable diseases while the life expectancy of many Americans was increasing (Holland, 1989b). An appreciative public put their faith in physicians at an unprecedented rate, especially the upper middle, professional classes who valued scientific solutions to medical problems and the middle classes who were increasingly fearful of death (Patterson, 1987).

Physicians responded that cancer could be conquered. This was the start of the "alliance against cancer" (Patterson, 1987, p. viii). In 1913, the American Society for the Control of Cancer, later called the American Cancer Society (ACS), was formed (Holland, 1989b). Its efforts to make the public aware of early warning signals for cancer and prevention and its theory testing regarding cancer causation gave the "cancer establishment" more credibility and institutionalized it within mainstream society. The successful removal of some cancers through surgery and the use of radiation as a palliative treatment increased the hope of many. The biggest boost to the cancer alliance was the establishment by Congress in 1937 of the National Cancer Institute (NCI; Holland, 1989b) and by the mid-1940s, well-financed research empires arose for scientists working under the auspices of the NCI (Patterson, 1987). Within the public domain and the medical community, however, the 1930s and 1940s were still characterized by pessimism regarding cancer treatment. The outcome of treatment by surgery and irradiation was still bleak (Holland, 1989b). In the 1930s, fewer than one in five cancer patients were alive 5 years after diagnosis (ACS, 1994).

The establishment of the NCI led to increased research in the 1940s. Simultaneously, the ACS focused attention on the need for emotional support for cancer patients. These were two parallel but unrelated efforts. The NCI and physicians were reluctant to acknowledge the need to deal with the personal, emotional responses of cancer patients, viewing such aid as interference in the doctor–patient relationship (Holland, 1989b). The research of the 1940s led to major breakthroughs in cancer treatment in the 1950s, and a grateful public responded. Federal funding for cancer increased rapidly during these decades (Patterson, 1987). Among the breakthroughs, nitrogen mustard, developed from World War II research on chemical warfare, induced remission in acute leukemia patients. This led to the development of chemotherapy, and in 1951, methotrexate became the first chemotherapeutic agent to arrest cancer (Holland, 1989b). In 1959, Dr. John Heller of the NCI appeared on the cover of *Time* magazine; the headline read "The New War on Cancer via Virus Research and Chemotherapy."

The 1960s led to the development of multimodal therapies and by the end of the decade, one in three patients diagnosed with cancer could expect to survive at least 5 years (ACS, 1994). The increased emphasis on technology did not come without costs, however. Particularly problematic was the growing distance between patients and physicians and the negative side effects of treatment. As Lederberg et al. (1989) noted: "As physicians came to depend more on laboratory data and spent less time at the bedside, patients complained increasingly about the diminished closeness to their new, more technologically oriented doctors" (p. 2192).

Those who underwent cancer treatment prior to the 1960s had to contend with the side effects of surgery and amputation. With the increased emphasis on radiation and then chemotherapy, a host of new and often toxic side effects confronted cancer sufferers. Hair loss, anorexia, fatigue, anemia, sore throat, diarrhea, weight gain, nausea, and vomiting were, and continue to be, common side effects. Long-term side effects of radiation and chemotherapy include permanent damage to reproductive organs, the liver, kidneys, and lungs, as well as secondary malignancies (Haskell, 1990).

The 1970s and 1980s led to further development and refinement of chemotherapeutic drugs and claims that some types of cancer could be cured. The potential for long-term survival necessitated that the emotional needs of cancer patients and their families be considered in treatment (Holland, 1989b). The growing number of cancer survivors led to the development of the National Coalition of Cancer Survivors (NCCS) in 1986, as well as other groups. These organizations act as information resources for the more than 8 million cancer survivors living in the United States (ACS, 1994) and in the case of the NCCS, act as political advocates.

The growing patient-as-consumer movement during the 1980s contributed to increased concern for the personal aspects of medical treatment, including informed consent and quality of life. The move toward patient self-determination and away from medical paternalism (Ballard-Reisch, 1990) also led to greater influence by the "cancer counterculture" and increased interest in alternative cancer treatments (Patterson, 1987).

## The Cancer Counterculture

Since the turn of the century, a wide variety of people have stood in opposition to the cancer establishment. Called the "cancer counterculture," they are "skeptical about orthodox medical notions of disease and about the claims to expert knowledge by the Cancer Establishment" (Patterson, 1987, p. ix). Even as the supporters of the cancer establishment grew, the cancer counterculture grew as well. Patterson observed:

> . . . especially in times of cultural disarray, such as the late 1970s, they boldly challenged the research emphasis of the Cancer Establishment. Some insisted that the best weapon against cancer was not high-tech research and therapy,

but prevention: control pollution, eat carefully, drink less, above all stop smoking. Others deplored exaggerated claims in the media, the commercialization of the research establishment, the flaws of the medical profession, and the deterioration of the environment. (p. x)

The cancer counterculture perceived the close-knit medical establishment as closed to ideas emanating from outside the ACS and NCI (Patterson, 1987). The significance of the "cancer counterculture" as a force was clearly indicated in the 1970s when, bowing to public pressure, the NCI began trials on laetrile (Whorton, 1987) in the absence of any empirical evidence of its efficacy (Lederberg et al., 1989).

## Alternative Cancer Treatments

One particularly vexing characteristic of the cancer counterculture for the medical establishment has been the proliferation of unorthodox and alternative cancer treatments. The economic impact of alternative therapies is estimated at over $4 million per year (Cassileth, Lusk, Strouse, & Bodenheimer, 1984). Alternative therapies range from those that improve a patient's well-being and enhance the body's ability to fight the cancer to outright frauds that are dangerous to health. The former reflect the growing interest in patient participation in health care as well as the popularity of naturalistic approaches to medicine (Holland, Geary, & Furman, 1989).

Alternative treatments have varied widely throughout the century. Balms, tonics, and electrical waves were popular at the turn of the century, krebiozen in the 1960s, laetrile in the 1970s and, most recently, natural holistic approaches that enhance the body's defenses (Holland, 1993). Conventional medical practitioners explain patient interest in alternative treatments in a number of ways: as an understandable defense mechanism against dying, a response to pressure from family members, and an effort to avoid pain, discomfort, and the side effects of conventional treatment. Often, simple explanations of cancer causation, poor eating habits, elimination problems, and emotional and spiritual stress appeal to patients who are desperately searching for answers (Bond & Wellisch, 1990).

Myths about the people who seek alternative treatments have proliferated. At the turn of the century, members of the cancer counterculture were characterized as uneducated and poor (Patterson, 1987), and it is often assumed that patients in the later stages of illness with the poorest prognosis are most likely to seek alternative treatments. Results of a study of over 1,000 alternative treatment patients and 138 alternative therapy practitioners contradicted much of this conventional wisdom (Cassileth et al., 1984). Of the patients interviewed, one third indicated that they had participated in conventional therapy alone, close to one half took part in both conventional and alternative treatments, and one tenth reported participating in only alternative therapies. Eventually, 40% of those who had used both conventional and alternative treatment abandoned mainstream medical therapy in favor of alternative treatment. The characteristics of these patients were particularly interesting. The interviews indicated that patients chose alternative treatments early in therapy as often as they did when their condition was considered terminal. Patients who sought alternative treatments were better educated than those who used conventional therapy alone. Additionally, 60% of the 138 alternative therapy practitioners interviewed were physicians.

## Summary

In the early part of the 20th century, the cultural response to cancer in the United States was based on fear and ignorance. A diagnosis of cancer was a death sentence hidden from friends and neighbors, whispered among family members, and withheld from children and patients (Holland, 1989b; Patterson, 1987). The anguish of having cancer was compounded by the social stigma (Sontag, 1978). Social reaction to a cancer diagnosis led the cancer patient "to be stigmatized, isolated, and humiliated, a fate similar to that of persons with leprosy and syphilis" (Holland, 1989b, p. 3). Although it is far more treatable today, fear persists and impacts current attitudes toward cancer. The disenfranchisement of adolescents with cancer and their families continues beyond the alienation caused by the social stigma of cancer. It is perpetuated as well through the fear and isolation caused by the process of cancer management.

## THE PHASES OF CANCER MANAGEMENT

When the cultural mythology and social stigma surrounding cancer are combined with an actual cancer diagnosis, the overwhelming reaction is fear. Fear of loss of control, disfigurement, debilitation, economic hardship, and death impact the adolescent and every family member, pervading every aspect of their lives throughout the process of cancer management (Gogan & Slavin, 1981; Hersh & Wiener, 1993).

Cancer management occurs within three predictable phases of the disease: the diagnostic phase; the exploration of treatment alternatives phase; and the treatment decision, implementation, and evaluation phase (Ballard-Reisch, 1990). The following section examines the impact of adolescent cancer on parents, the adolescent, and well siblings throughout these phases, as well as the possibilities for long-term survival, relapse, and death. As family needs differ throughout the cancer management process, diagnosis, ongoing treatment, remission, relapse, deterioration, and long-term survival all present the family with special requirements for patient care and support (Rait & Lederberg, 1989).

## Diagnostic Phase

The diagnostic phase involves exploring the patient's condition and the characteristics and capabilities that affect the patient's ability to deal with the illness (Ballard-Reisch, 1990, 1993). A cancer diagnosis has an immediate and lasting impact on the family. It is a crisis that transforms their accepted roles, relationships, and expectations for the future (Chanock, Kundra, Johnson, & Singer, 1993; Rait & Lederberg, 1989). Responses to this crisis are characterized by hopelessness, loneliness, helplessness, and a sense of isolation (Schnaper, Kellner, & Panitz, 1991). The psychological pressures on cancer patients and their families are intense and do not fully subside even when the disease is considered cured. Koocher and O'Malley (1981) compared these ongoing pressures to the sword of Damocles, hanging over the family's future.

*Parents.* In the case of most adolescents with cancer, it is their parents who first hear the diagnosis. As parents generally view themselves as responsible for keeping their children safe from fear, hurt, and pain, a cancer diagnosis assaults their identity and perceptions of their adequacy as guardians. They often feel numb and may feel guilt over what they view as their responsibility for the illness as well as anger at those who diagnosed it, physicians and hospital staff (Hathorn & Pizzo, 1991; Hersh & Wiener, 1993).

Common parental responses include denial, panic, shock, disbelief, helplessness, confusion, and fear (Hathorn & Pizzo, 1991; Hersh & Wiener, 1993; A. S. Levine & Hersh, 1982). In the first few weeks following diagnosis, parents may experience depression, distress, and an inability to function (A. S. Levine & Hersh, 1982). Early denial is an appropriate response as it allows the reality of the illness to be integrated at a rate that does not overwhelm defenses (see Holland, 1993; Kubler-Ross, 1969), reducing what might otherwise be intolerable anxiety, guilt, and anger (Hersh & Wiener, 1993).

Denial is often followed by a need to seek all available information, either as a means of disconfirming the diagnosis or as a method of mobilizing resources to confront the demands of treatment. This latter purpose can be seen as a vigilant approach to coping with stress (Janis & Mann,

1977). Accurate information in the diagnostic phase is critical in assisting the family as they move from an affective to an effective response.

*Adolescent.* A cancer diagnosis poses a unique set of problems for adolescents; "probably at no other age is illness as shameful as it is during adolescence" (Schowalter, 1977, p. 505). At a time in life when adolescents are striving for independence and self-determination, they are confronted with an illness that requires dependence and a lack of control. When body image and peer relationships are of foremost importance, they must cope with hospitalization and medical treatments that alter their bodies, sometimes in frightening ways, and keep them out of school and away from peers. Developmental issues of peer identification and acceptance, body image and sexuality, self-identity, and self-esteem are all significantly impacted when an adolescent is diagnosed with cancer (Hathorn & Pizzo, 1991; Orr, Hoffman, & Bennetts, 1984). Additionally, long-term plans about career and family may need to be reevaluated in consideration of physical limitations, academic difficulties, and questions related to fertility and parenthood (Lansky, Ritter-Sterr, List, & Hart, 1993). Concerns about mortality become significant, often for the first time in the adolescent's life (Hathorn & Pizzo, 1991).

As with parents, the adolescent's first reaction to the diagnosis is usually denial, often followed by anger and rebellion. Initial hospitalization provides a disruption in the adolescent's social life as plans regarding school functions and peer relationships are superseded by treatment demands (Hathorn & Pizzo, 1991; Lansky et al., 1993). Illness, loss of independence, and loss of privacy result in feelings of helplessness, leading to distrust, alienation, anger, acting out, and uncooperativeness during the diagnosis and early treatment phases (Zeltzer, LeBaron, & Zeltzer, 1984).

*Siblings.* Well siblings often feel a sense of isolation and deprivation as hospitalization and treatment lead to recurrent separation from the sibling with cancer as well as one or both parents (Chanock et al., 1993; Nir & Maslin, 1981). The realities of treatment, including the amount of time parents spend with the ill child, may lead to a variety of responses, including jealousy and resentment over the extra attention their sibling receives (Gogan & Slavin, 1981; Nir & Maslin, 1981). They may feel guilty that their sibling was afflicted but they were spared and they may fear for their own health. They may feel that no one has time for them and that they are no longer important members of the family. They may even feel that something they did caused their sibling to contract cancer (Gogan & Slavin, 1981; Hersh & Wiener, 1993). Siblings feel "acute and painful disturbances in the sibling relationship that, given the potential for strong identification and severe rivalry, cut very deeply" (Rait & Lederberg, 1989, p. 589).

## Exploration of Treatment Alternatives Phase

The exploration of treatment alternatives phase involves the generation of alternatives, the establishment of criteria for an effective decision, and the process of weighing alternatives against criteria established (Ballard-Reisch, 1990). Within the context of family management of cancer, this phase also includes initial treatment designed to produce cancer remission.

One of the most difficult tasks for families following a diagnosis is giving up control and putting themselves in the hands of professionals (Chanock et al., 1993; Hersh & Wiener, 1993). Within the context of adolescent cancer, the family and patient often have little choice and little input into treatment decisions, especially if they participate in a clinical treatment trial (Ballard-Reisch & Ballard, 1991).

The degree of uncertainty the family, and particularly parents, experiences is compounded by their need to assimilate the diagnosis, the advantages and disadvantages of treatment alternatives, the recommended treatment plan, implementation schedules, prognosis, and side effects of treatment, in a short period of time. In addition, they are expected to sign informed consent documents authorizing treatment (Hersh & Wiener, 1993; A. S. Levine & Hersh, 1982).

Family dynamics and routines change, both to encompass the illness itself and to accommodate the adolescent's treatment (Hersh & Wiener, 1993). Initial treatment typically takes place in a hospital and often families must travel great distances to cancer centers for treatment. Adolescent cancer patients and their families are often isolated from those who would typically offer support in times of crisis, both because of the rigor of treatment demands and the social stigma associated with cancer. Further, the often impersonal nature of modern cancer treatment may make them feel isolated from physicians and hospital staff as well. As Thomas (1989) noted:

> . . . the treatment of cancer has come to be an extremely technical undertaking, based almost entirely within the busiest and most active wards of the hospital, and involving the strenuous efforts of highly specialized professionals, each taking his or her responsibility for a share of the patient's problem, but sometimes working at a rather impersonal distance from the patient as an individual. To many patients, stunned by the diagnosis, suffering numerous losses and discomforts, moved from place to place for one procedure after another, the experience is bewildering and frightening; at worst, it is like being trapped in the workings of a huge piece of complicated machinery. (p. v)

During this second phase, therapeutic and social support systems become increasingly important. Mobilizing a strong support system can have a significant impact on the patient's and family's ability to cope with the illness and disease (see Dunkel-Schetter, 1984; Sullivan & Reardon, 1986).

*Parents.* During this phase, parents often continue their vigilant information search, soliciting and receiving opinions from other family members and friends (Wellisch & Cohen, 1985). Many parents pursue contacts with alternative treatment practitioners in the hope that they will be able to achieve a cure for their child's cancer and at the same time avoid the damaging side effects of conventional treatment (Hersh & Wiener, 1993). This vigilant information search has the potential to stress the relationship between parents and physicians.

Traditionally, medical professionals have been reluctant to discuss alternative, nontraditional treatments with patients and their families. Families have often feared hostility or treatment refusal if they questioned physicians about nontraditional alternatives (Holland et al., 1989). Negative sanctions can go much further. Some theorists have even indicated that, in extreme cases, if parents pursue nontraditional therapies, "the juvenile court can be enlisted" (Lansky et al., 1993, p. 1134). They admonished that "such measures should be taken only after all efforts have been exhausted to secure the parents' willing participation in the treatment regimen" but concluded that "use of the child abuse and neglect statutes may be the only way to ensure that a child with a treatable disease receives appropriate therapy" (p. 1134). This view is not one that encourages open, frank communication about alternatives between parents and practitioners.

*Adolescent.* The importance of social support in assisting cancer patients with coping cannot be overstated. When managing an illness, we look to others for reassurance that we are acting appropriately, so the reactions of others can seriously impact a patient's decisions about how to cope with illness. Without satisfactory communication and support from others, patients may feel unsure, helpless, isolated, and rejected (Sullivan & Reardon, 1986).

Adolescents with cancer tend to rank their most valuable support as first from their mothers, followed by their fathers, medical staff, and siblings (Tebbi, Stern, Boyle, Mettlin, & Mindell, 1985). Peers, who play a significant part in identity formation and esteem in adolescence, are an especially powerful support system. However, patients tend to report support from their friends as distant and disappointing (Tebbi et al., 1985). Unfortunately, hospitalization, the physical limitations caused by illness and treatment side effects, and the separation from peers caused by intensive or prolonged periods of illness and treatment put the adolescent at risk of feeling isolated (Rowland, 1989a).

As treatment progresses, increasing uncertainty about their appearance and functioning, as well as fatigue, may lead patients to withdraw from friends (Slavin, 1981). Similarly, socialized fears and the stigma surrounding cancer may make friends feel uncomfortable as they find themselves at a loss for words, uncertain how to behave, and fearful about the possibility of contagion (Van Eys, 1977). Fear of death may be the biggest threat to adolescent friendships as both patient and peers avoid one another due to mutual discomfort (Slavin, 1981).

During this phase, patients also have to adjust to the loss of control over their bodies and the normal pattern of their lives (Hathorn & Pizzo, 1991). Physicians and parents make treatment decisions for them; they are required to stay in the hospital, and they cannot attend school or spend time with friends. In short, total disruption in their lives is the legacy of illness and treatment management (Orr et al., 1984).

Adolescents who feel they no longer have control over their lives may act out in a variety of ways. They may challenge the authority of medical professionals and parents, they may refuse to comply with treatment regimens; in short, they may do anything in their power to regain some control (Chanock et al., 1993; Hersh & Wiener, 1993).

*Siblings.*  Healthy sisters and brothers of sick children may be especially vulnerable to the stress created by life-threatening illness in the family (Cairns, Clark, Smith, & Lansky, 1979; Carpenter & Sahler, 1991; Gogan & Slavin, 1981). Siblings who have reported difficulty adapting to their brother's or sister's cancer also tended to feel that the illness significantly disrupted family functioning. They also felt overwhelmed with their feelings and unable to talk to their parents about how the cancer was affecting them. In short, they felt interpersonally isolated (Carpenter & Sahler, 1991). As studies have found, "comparisons between patients, siblings and controls have shown siblings to fare as badly or worse than the patients on selected measures such as self-esteem, social isolation, and fear of confronting family members" (Rait & Lederberg, 1989, p. 589).

Although numerous hospitals have attempted to organize sibling support groups, they have been almost universally ineffective (S. Delipco, personal communication, November 1993). One problem may lie in the fact that siblings are expected to voice their concerns and feelings about the disruption cancer has caused in their lives in the very environment in which their sibling is being treated. To get organized support, they must further enmesh themselves in the hospital environment where the primary concern is treating their sibling with cancer.

## Treatment Decision, Implementation, and Evaluation Phase

This phase involves the selection of the treatment protocol, the implementation of the treatment regimen, and the evaluation of the effectiveness of treatment. This phase requires clear understanding and communication on the part of adolescent, parents, and the medical team. The family must be thoroughly prepared for the specifics of the treatment regimen; they must know what to expect from treatment and what to do if, and when, unexpected outcomes occur (Ballard-Reisch, 1990).

The family must now reestablish some sense of normalcy as the adolescent returns home and extended treatment is integrated into daily life. Families must coordinate the needs of the patient, parents, and well siblings. Frustration over changes in family routines, roles, and responsibilities may lead family members to show anger, jealousy, and neediness (Rait & Lederberg, 1989). When the adolescent is confined to home due to fatigue, pain, or treatment side effects, stress within the family increases considerably (Hersh & Wiener, 1993).

At a time when the family may need increased support, other family members, friends, and coworkers may be less supportive, further isolating the family (Rait & Lederberg, 1989). The family may feel that they can no longer relate to people who provided valuable emotional support in the past. This may lead to anger, disappointment, and feelings of isolation, which may evolve into family withdrawal (Hersh & Wiener, 1993). In fact, the family faces paradoxical reentry problems. They may remain overprotective or they may push for the reestablishment of normal activity before the adolescent feels ready.

*Parents.* Parents are often confronted with conflicting demands at this time. They feel the need to continue to protect their child and avoid unnecessary expectations. At the same time, the return to normalcy demands the reassertion of the adolescent's roles and responsibilities within the family. Chores, expectations, and discipline need to be renegotiated (Hersh & Wiener, 1993; Lansky et al., 1993).

Because their child has just gone through an exhausting physical ordeal, both with the cancer itself and the treatment necessary to induce remission, parents commonly want to protect them from any negative psychological experiences. Now the course of curative treatment is underway and troubling side effects, as well as fear about long-term risks, create additional stress. It is not uncommon for an overdependence to develop between parents and the adolescent that leads to separation anxiety for both (Hersh & Wiener, 1993; Lansky et al., 1993; A. S. Levine & Hersh, 1982).

*Adolescent.* The adolescent's goal during this phase is often to return to normal activities. This desire may be hampered by changes in physical capacity and intellectual functioning due to illness and treatment. This can lead to increased frustration and anxiety (A. S. Levine & Hersh, 1982), as "shame, guilt, and shyness are the legacy of their physical malady" (Schowalter, 1977, p. 505).

Often the biggest challenge for adolescents is the return to school. Many find this an unpleasant experience, where they are teased or treated as outcasts (Wasserman, Thompson, Wilimas, & Fairclough, 1987). Although some problems are directly related to the cancer, many others result from the attitudes and behaviors of teachers and peers (Zwarnes, 1978). Teachers and classmates may view the returning student as different, which may lead them to isolate the adolescent out of embarrassment, fear, or admiration (Lederberg et al., 1989).

Whereas one of the early difficulties faced by the adolescent when diagnosed was the involuntary disruption of school and social lives, return to school and adequate attendance may be hampered by physical limitations and feelings of isolation (Lansky et al., 1993). As Hathorn and Pizzo (1991) noted: "Amputation, hair loss, persistent nausea and vomiting, weight loss, and the absence from school and social activities all serve to ostracize adolescent patients at a time when they most need to be accepted by their peers. This leads to a loss of self-esteem and feelings of inadequacy, sometimes severe enough to result in overt depression" (p. 1596).

Some forms of cancer and treatment affect the patient's intellectual functioning. Radiation, chemotherapy, and multimodal therapies can all negatively affect the central nervous system and reduce perceptual, motor, sensory, reasoning, and other intellectual activities (Tross & Holland, 1989), limiting the student's abilities in the classroom.

*Siblings.* The effects of adolescent cancer on well siblings during this phase are often adverse, including depression, fear, separation anxiety, antisocial behavior, withdrawal, guilt, and poor school performance (Binger, 1973; Cairns et al., 1979).

Family life disruptions are often felt most acutely by well siblings (Carr-Gregg & White, 1987). During initial hospitalization, they are separated from their sibling and, typically, at least one of their parents. Healthy siblings often feel a sense of isolation and deprivation and respond with anger toward their parents and jealousy or hostility toward their sick sibling (Hersh & Wiener, 1993). In addition, well siblings are expected to continue living their everyday lives, attending school, doing chores, and so forth, as if nothing has changed.

The social stigma regarding cancer may lead siblings to withhold the information of their sibling's illness from teachers and friends at the same time that their own performance is being seriously impacted by the disruption the illness is causing in the family (Adams & Deveau, 1987; Bluebond-Langner, 1989). Fear of the disease and treatment, as well as the family's isolation from others, furthers the disenfranchisement they experience. Even after the cancer is considered cured, however, the family's concerns do not end.

## COPING WITH LONG-TERM SURVIVAL, RELAPSE, AND DEATH

After initial adaptation and the return to normalcy in the family, long-term survival, relapse, and death are possible outcomes that cause their own unique stresses and concerns for the adolescent and family. Family members struggling with these stressor events may emerge less healthy and more vulnerable than before, or they may move toward increased health, maturity, and growth (McCubbin, Cauble, & Patterson, 1982). The conclusion of treatment may be met with a sense of accomplishment at having "made it," combined with anxiety over fear of relapse (Hersh & Wiener, 1993). Concern about recurrence and difficulty getting back to normal are natural reactions. The family has been through a crisis and needs to readjust to health. Their individual coping patterns (Rowland, 1989b) and communication within the family (Ballard-Reisch & Ballard, 1991) are strong determinants of the family's ability to manage the crisis.

### Long-Term Survival of Adolescents With Cancer

The crisis of childhood cancer affects every parent's marriage (Hersh & Wiener, 1993), with a fluctuation between closeness and distance as treatment progresses. Marital stability is strained during the acute phase (immediately after diagnosis and during initial treatment), consolidated during the chronic phase (the extended treatment period), and then strained again during the resolution phase (post-treatment as the family comes to terms with life following the illness) (Rait & Lederberg, 1989). As with parents, the longer the adolescent remains in remission, the more confidence siblings have in cure and the more they allow their lives to return to normal. There are both positive and negative long-term effects for siblings. Positive effects include enhanced closeness to the former patient, enhanced emotional growth, and the development of personal coping skills. Most siblings tend to resolve any anger or jealousy toward the patient once the treatment has ended and they return to normal sibling relationships (Gogan & Slavin, 1981).

All family members gain more faith in cure and worry less about relapse as time goes on, but the experience of coping with cancer remains with them (Koocher & O'Malley, 1981). The impact of the experience changes the family no matter what the outcome, for once cancer has occurred in a family, the family is never the same (Rait & Lederberg, 1989). In addition to adjustment issues, significant physical risks also exist for cancer survivors. Among them are second malignancies and relapse of the original cancer.

With the increasing number of cancer survivors, 8 million currently living in the United States (ACS, 1994), an interest has developed in studying the long-term effects of cancer on quality of life. To this point, most of these studies have been conducted on survivors of childhood and adolescent cancers. Significant issues include psychological effects; intimacy, fertility, and sexual functioning; social functioning; and work performance and insurance.

*Psychological Effects.*    Both positive and negative psychological effects of cancer have been identified in long-term survivors. Positive effects include an increased appreciation of life, enhanced goals, and an absence of psychological problems in those who were psychologically healthy prior to diagnosis (Holland, 1993). The negative effects of long-term survival include heightened anxiety, depression, a greater sense of vulnerability, uncertainty about the future, and lower self-esteem (Koocher & O'Malley, 1981). Even after cure has been achieved, cancer survivors may still view their situations as tenuous, with lingering fears of relapse, death and long-term consequences of treatment producing anxiety, depression, and damaged body image (Tross & Holland, 1989). Anxiety seems to decrease over time. However, it re-emerges in anticipation of periodic medical examinations and with the emergence of any symptoms associated with cancer (Holland, 1993).

*Intimacy, Fertility, and Sexual Functioning.*    A wide variety of intimacy and sexual functioning problems have been identified in long-term cancer survivors, including infertility due to radiation, chemotherapy, and surgical treatment, decreased sexual desire and poorer sexual functioning (Tross & Holland, 1989), resulting in lower self-confidence in intimate settings (Holland, 1993).

In adolescents, fears about infertility and the implications of cancer and treatment for their future offspring are common (Lansky et al., 1993; A. S. Levine & Hersh, 1982). The impact varies widely depending on age at diagnosis, type of cancer, and the type and duration of treatment. However, this concern has not been reinforced in the literature, with studies finding no increased incidence of birth defects, morbidity, or mortality in progeny of childhood cancer survivors (e.g., Li & Jaffe, 1974).

*Social Functioning.*    Research has been mixed regarding difficulties survivors may have in establishing and maintaining interpersonal relationships. In early studies, which relied primarily on demographic data, no significant differences were found between cancer survivors and the population at large in terms of rates of marriage, work performance, and school achievement (Holmes & Holmes, 1975). An ongoing study of adolescent cancer survivors found that, as a group, they functioned well in school and social settings but that individuals had significant problems in peer and family relationships (Cella & Smith, 1987).

Several factors seem to predict effective functioning following childhood cancer. They include the onset of disease—younger children seem to suffer fewer developmentally based problems than do older children and adolescents—a short treatment course, no relapse or recurrences of the disease, early use of denial as a coping strategy, and supportive and open communication in the family.

*Work Performance and Insurance.* The continuing disenfranchisement of adolescents with cancer is perhaps most prevalent in the public sphere, with numerous problems related to job and insurance discrimination. Employers fear that cancer survivors will be unable to work, will have low productivity, and high absenteeism. Coworkers may view survivors as victims, avoid them because of social stigma, or because they fear contagion. Survivors may experience uncertainty about their ability to work up to their precancer abilities, they may fear rejection by coworkers and negative attitudes of supervisors, they may feel uncertain about their ability to get another job should they lose their current one, they may feel uncertain about how future health and the possibility of recurrence may impact their job performance, and they may fear loss of health and life insurance. These concerns are not unfounded. Over half of the survivors surveyed in various studies reported discrimination on the job and trouble getting health and life insurance (Tross & Holland, 1989).

## Second Malignancies and Relapse

Although multimodal therapies have improved the 5-year survivor rate following treatment, the prospect of death due to recurrence, second malignancies, organ dysfunction or failure, and infections due to immune system suppression has also increased. Highest risk of recurrence, organ dysfunction, and failure and infection occurs between 5 and 9 years following diagnosis, with second malignancy rates being highest between 15 and 19 years (Li, Myers, Heise, & Jaffe, 1978).

*Second Malignancies.* Adolescents considered cured of one malignant disease develop second malignancies 20 times more often than expected in the population at large (Byrd, 1983). It is likely that the treatment that resulted in arresting the first malignancy is a major factor in the development of the second malignancy (Schwartz, 1991), with a latency period ranging from several years to several decades (Schwartz, 1991; Tucker, Coleman, Cox, Varghese, & Rosenberg, 1988).

Radiation therapy can cause acute nonlymphocytic leukemia, which is highly resistant to treatment, malignant and nonmalignant thyroid tumors, soft tissue and brain sarcomas, breast, brain, colon, and renal cancers, and a variety of other neoplasms (Schwartz, 1991). The most common types of radiation-induced malignancies are breast and thyroid tumors, osteogenic sarcoma, and leukemia (Tross & Holland, 1989).

Chemotherapy also results in a greater incidence of second malignancies. Acute leukemia and urinary tract carcinoma have been identified as linked to treatment with alkylating agents and cyclophosphamide respectively (Schwartz, 1991; Tross & Holland, 1989). Patients who receive both radiation and chemotherapy are more likely to develop leukemia (Tucker et al., 1988).

*Relapse.* Relapse is an especially difficult experience. Often treatment has been progressing well, family life has returned to normal, and the recurrence of the cancer sends the family back into the crisis they experienced upon initial diagnosis (Chanock et al., 1993; Hersh & Wiener, 1993).

Effective coping with relapse is complicated by several factors, among them poorer likelihood of survival, increased likelihood of toxicity and long-term negative consequences from treatment, as well as knowledge of what is to come (Chanock et al., 1993). The difficulty of coping with the recurrence is compounded further by the fact that the family is now different from other families undergoing treatment for adolescent cancer. As a result of their new circumstances, they are isolated from those with whom they previously shared similar treatment protocols.

At this point, families are likely to reconsider, or consider for the first time, alternative treatment (Cassileth et al., 1984). Additionally, physicians may recommend families seek treatment at another cancer center and participate in a clinical treatment trial. Although both of these approaches may be vigilant methods of dealing with the relapse, they may also isolate the family from their familiar medical team (R. J. Levine, 1986).

Most families adapt effectively to the new crisis. They develop a new family routine within the constraints of treatment demands, side effects, and outside pressures (Hersh & Wiener, 1993). Some families, however, develop an overly pessimistic attitude, withdraw physically or emotionally from the child, refuse treatment, or have difficulty stabilizing their lives. Some adolescents refuse treatment out of anger at the failure of the first treatment, feelings of hopelessness regarding the outcome, or as an attempt to reassert control over their lives (Lansky et al., 1993).

Results of relapse can either be successive remissions and ultimately cure, or degeneration and death (Hersh & Wiener, 1993). Successive relapses offer a more limited prognosis and greater likelihood of significant adverse side effects of the treatment. Effective family coping becomes increasingly difficult. At some point the decision may need to be made to shift from curative to palliative treatment and this is a significant crisis for the patient and family (Chanock et al., 1993).

## Coping With Death

The decision to end cure-based treatment and shift to symptom and pain management alone is a difficult one for the patient and family. As Hersh and Wiener (1993) noted, "Once it is clear that treatment is no longer effective, hope ebbs and parents begin the process of accepting that their child will die" (p. 1150). Many parents have difficulty or find it impossible to discuss the imminence of death with their child (Kubler-Ross, 1969; see Thompson, chap. 20, for a discussion of communication with the terminally ill).

Two communication styles have been identified in families at the terminal stage of childhood illness (Share, 1972). The first, a protective approach, avoids direct discussion of death in the hope of making it easier for the child. This approach often results from a parental belief that the child is unaware that death is imminent. The second approach is one of open communication where the child and family members are encouraged to discuss their fears and feelings about death. Children encouraged to communicate openly about illness and death adapt more effectively than those discouraged from discussing their feelings (Rait & Lederberg, 1989). In addition, siblings experience acute separation anxiety at the imminent death of their sister or brother (Cairns et al., 1979; A. S. Levine & Hersh, 1982).

As the child's death becomes imminent, families may become more isolated if the medical staff avoid the child. This avoidance may occur because medical professionals often have difficulty dealing with the death of a child, and out of their own discomfort, physicians may avoid the family and patient, so that "at a time when most needed, the professional often assumes a neutral or even negative role in contacts with the family of the dying child" (Binger et al., 1969, p. 415).

In addition, the absence of familiarity with death and its rituals in our society makes grieving even more difficult. Families who lose a child to cancer have few social supports for their grief and are consequently isolated at a time when support is needed. Parents and siblings experience significant short- and long-term reactions to the death of an adolescent from cancer. Adaptive family responses during the course of the illness, including open, responsive communication, an adaptive philosophy of life, and for parents, the strong support of a partner, lead to better adaptation of both parents and siblings to the child's death (Spinetta, Swarner, & Sheposh, 1981).

Active participation in the care of the child throughout the illness, as well as active participation in the dying process, help family members cope with feelings of guilt and anger (Hersh & Wiener, 1993). Acute grief, characterized by waves of distress, reduced concentration, preoccupation with the deceased, and difficulty functioning, typically last about 6 weeks but can be prolonged in parents who lose a child. Coming to terms with the loss is the second period of grief and can last from 6 weeks to 5 years or longer (Chochinov & Holland, 1989; Hersh & Wiener, 1993). The longer the duration of grief, the greater the risk of chronic grief characterized by social withdrawal, anxiety, decreased concentration, and depression. Physical symptoms include weight loss, sleep disturbances, and greater susceptibility to illness (Hofer, 1984).

Bereavement reactions in children include anger, guilt, sadness, anxiety, a sense of vulnerability, insecurity, and behavioral and disciplinary problems (Chochinov & Holland, 1989). Because parents are also grieving, siblings may continue to feel isolated and their needs for encouragement, support, and understanding may not be met (Pollack, 1985). Additionally, it is common for siblings to attempt to replace the dead child in an effort to ease the parents' pain. Parents may contribute to negative sibling adjustment by becoming overly vigilant about the health of surviving children (Chochinov & Holland, 1989).

## CONCLUSION

Adolescent cancer is a crisis that affects all members of the family. Coping is made more difficult by the disenfranchisement of the adolescents and their families caused by the social stigma surrounding cancer in the United States. This cancerphobia results in the social alienation of the adolescent and other family members. The fear and isolation that pervade all aspects of treatment and rehabilitation intensify the family's disenfranchisement by cutting them off from family and friends, as well as one another. Even in the 1990s, when a growing number of adolescents are surviving cancer, society is ill equipped to make their reintegration a smooth one. Unanswered questions regarding long-term consequences of treatment on fertility, offspring, second malignancies, and relapse plague adolescent survivors. These concerns, along with continuing discrimination in both the private and public spheres, continue the isolation that characterize adolescents' experiences with cancer.

## ACKNOWLEDGMENT

The author would like to thank Sherry Cushman for her research assistance throughout the preparation of this manuscript.

# REFERENCES

Adams, D. W., & Deveau, E. J. (1987). When a brother or sister is dying of cancer: The vulnerability of the adolescent sibling. *Death Studies, 11*, 279–295.

American Cancer Society. (1994). *Cancer facts & figures: 1994.* Atlanta: Author.

Ballard-Reisch, D. (1990). A model of participative decision making for physician-patient interaction. *Health Communication, 2*(2), 91–104.

Ballard-Reisch, D. (1993). Health care providers and consumers: Making decisions together. In B. C. Thornton & G. L. Kreps (Eds.), *Perspectives on health communication* (pp. 66–80). Prospect Heights, IL: Waveland Press.

Ballard-Reisch, D., & Ballard, J. (1991, October). *Separation and oncology: Coping strategies of a family dealing with leukemia.* Paper presented at the annual meeting of the Speech Communication Association, Atlanta.

Binger, C. M. (1973). Childhood leukemia: Emotional impact on siblings. In E. J. Anthony & E. Koupernick (Eds.), *The child and his family* (pp. 195–209). New York: Wiley.

Binger, C. M., Ablin, A. R., Feuerstein, R. C., Kushner, J. H., Zoger, S., & Mikkelson, C. (1969). Childhood leukemia: Emotional impact on patient and family. *The New England Journal of Medicine, 280*(8), 414–418.

Bluebond-Langner, M. (1989). Worlds of dying children and their well siblings. *Death Studies, 13*, 1–16.

Bond, G. G., & Wellisch, D. K. (1990). Psychosocial care. In C. M. Haskell (Ed.), *Cancer treatment* (3rd ed., pp. 893–904). Philadelphia: Saunders.

Brandt, A. (1985). *No magic bullet: A social history of venereal disease in the United States since 1980.* New York: Oxford University Press.

Byrd, B. L. (1983). Late effects of treatment of cancer in children. *Pediatric Annual, 12*, 450–460.

Cairns, N. U., Clark, G. M., Smith, S. D., & Lansky, S. B. (1979). Adaptation of siblings to childhood malignancy. *Journal of Pediatrics, 95*, 484–487.

Carpenter, P. J., & Sahler, O. J. Z. (1991). Sibling perception and adaptation to childhood cancer: Conceptual and methodological considerations. In J. H. Johnson & S. B. Johnson (Eds.), *Advances in child health psychology* (pp. 193–205). Gainesville: University of Florida Press.

Carr-Gregg, M., & White, L. (1987). Sibling of pediatric cancer patients: A population at risk. *Medical and Pediatric Oncology, 15*, 62–68.

Cassileth, B. R., Lusk, E. J., Strouse, B. A., & Bodenheimer, B. J. (1984). Contemporary unorthodox treatments in cancer medicine. *Annual of Internal Medicine, 101*, 105–112.

Cella, D. F., & Smith, K. (1987, January). *Sexual and reproductive problems in cancer survivors.* Paper presented at the workshop on psychosexual and reproductive issues in cancer survivors, American Cancer Society, San Antonio, TX.

Chanock, S. J., Kundra, V., Johnson, F. L., & Singer, M. D. (1993). The other side of the bed: What caregivers can learn from listening to patients and their families. In P. A. Pizzo & D. G. Poplack (Eds.), *Pediatric oncology* (2nd ed., pp. 1157–1169). Philadelphia: Lippincott.

Chochinov, H., & Holland, J. C. (1989). Bereavement: A special issue of oncology. In J. C. Holland & J. H. Rowland (Eds.), *Handbook of psycho-oncology: Psychological care of the patient with cancer* (pp. 612–627). New York: Oxford University Press.

Dunkel-Schetter, C. (1984). Social support and cancer: Findings based on patient interviews and their implications. *Journal of Social Issues, 40*, 77–98.

Gogan, J. L., & Slavin, L. A. (1981). Interviews with brothers and sisters. In G. P. Koocher & J. E. O'Malley (Eds.), *The Damocles syndrome: Psychosocial consequences of surviving childhood cancer* (pp. 101–111). San Francisco: McGraw-Hill.

Haskell, C. M. (Ed.). (1990). *Cancer treatment* (3rd ed.). Philadelphia: Saunders.

Hathorn, J. W., & Pizzo, P. A. (1991). Pediatric supportive care. In A. R. Moossa, S. C. Schimpff, & M. C. Robson (Eds.), *Comprehensive textbook of oncology* (2nd ed., Vol. 2, pp. 1595–1614). San Francisco: Williams & Wilkins.

Hersh, S. P., & Wiener, L. S. (1993). Psychosocial support for the family of the child with cancer. In P. A. Pizzo & D. G. Poplack (Eds.), *Pediatric oncology* (2nd ed., pp. 1141–1156). Philadelphia: Lippincott.

Hofer, M. A. (1984). Relationships as regulators: A psychobiologic perspective on bereavement. *Psychosomatic Medicine, 34,* 481–507.

Holland, J. C. (1989a). Historical overview. In J. C. Holland & J. H. Rowland (Eds.), *Handbook of psycho-oncology: Psychological care of the patient with cancer* (pp. 3–12). New York: Oxford University Press.

Holland, J. C. (1989b). Fears and abnormal reactions to cancer in physically healthy individuals. In J. C. Holland & J. H. Rowland (Eds.), *Handbook of psycho-oncology: Psychological care of the patient with cancer* (pp. 13–21). New York: Oxford University Press.

Holland, J. C. (1993). Principles of psycho-oncology. In J. C. Holland, E. Frei III, R. C. Bast, Jr., D. W. Kufe, D. L. Morton, & R. R. Weichselbaum (Eds.), *Cancer medicine* (pp. 1017–1033). Philadelphia: Lea & Febiger.

Holland, J. C., Geary, N., & Furman, A. (1989). Alternative cancer therapies. In J. C. Holland & J. H. Rowland (Eds.), *Handbook of psycho-oncology: Psychological care of the patient with cancer* (pp. 508–516). New York: Oxford University Press.

Holmes, H. A., & Holmes, F. F. (1975). After ten years, what are the handicaps and life styles of children treated for cancer? *Clinical Pediatrics, 14,* 819–823.

Janis, I., & Mann, L. (1977). *Decision making: A psychological analysis of conflict, choice, and commitment.* New York: The Free Press.

Koocher, G. P., & O'Malley, J. E. (Eds.). (1981). *The Damocles syndrome: Psychosocial consequences of surviving childhood cancer.* San Francisco: McGraw-Hill.

Kubler-Ross, E. (1969). *On death and dying.* New York: Macmillan.

Lansky, S. B., Ritter-Sterr, C., List, M. A., & Hart, M. J. (1993). Psychiatric and psychological support of the child and adolescent with cancer. In P. A. Pizzo & D. G. Poplack (Eds.), *Pediatric oncology* (pp. 1127–1139). Philadelphia: Lippincott.

Lederberg, M. S., Holland, J. C., & Massie, M. J. (1989). Psychologic aspects of patients with cancer. In V. T. DeVita, Jr., S. Hellman, & S. A. Rosenberg (Eds.), *Cancer: Principles and practice of oncology* (pp. 2192–2205). Philadelphia: Lippincott.

Levine, A. S., & Hersh, S. P. (1982). The psychosocial concomitants of cancer in young patients. In A. S. Levine (Ed.), *Cancer in the young* (pp. 367–387). New York: Masson.

Levine, R. J. (1986). Referral of patients with cancer for participation in randomized clinical trials: Ethical considerations. *CA, 36,* 95–99.

Li, F. P., & Jaffe, N. (1974). Progeny of childhood cancer survivors. *Lancet, 2,* 707–709.

Li, F. P., Myers, M. H., Heise, H. W., & Jaffe, N. (1978). The course of five-year survivors of cancer in childhood. *Journal of Pediatrics, 93,* 185–187.

McCubbin, H. I., Cauble, A. E., & Patterson, J. M. (1982). *Family stress, coping and social support.* Springfield, IL: Thomas.

Miller, B. A., Reis, L. A. G., Hankey, B. F., Kosary, C. L., Harras, A., Devesa, S. S., & Edwards, B. K. (Eds.). (1993). *SEER cancer statistics review 1973–1990* (Publication No. 93-2789). Bethesda, MD: National Institutes of Health, National Cancer Institute.

Nir, Y., & Maslin, B. (1981). Psychological adjustment of children with cancer. In J. G. Goldberg (Ed.), *Psychotherapeutic treatment of cancer patients* (pp. 263–272). New York: The Free Press.

Orr, D. P., Hoffman, M. A., & Bennetts, G. (1984). Adolescents with cancer report their psychosocial needs. *Journal of Psychosocial Oncology, 2*(2), 47–59.

Patterson, J. T. (1987). *The dread disease: Cancer and modern American culture.* Cambridge, MA: Harvard University Press.

Pollack, G. H. (1985). Childhood sibling loss: A family tragedy. *Psychiatry Annual, 16,* 309–314.

Rait, D., & Lederberg, M. (1989). The family of the cancer patient. In J. C. Holland & J. H. Rowland (Eds.), *Handbook of psycho-oncology: Psychological care of the patient with cancer* (pp. 585–597). New York: Oxford University Press.

Rowland, J. H. (1989a). Intrapersonal resources: Coping. In J. C. Holland & J. H. Rowland (Eds.), *Handbook of psycho-oncology: Psychological care of the patient with cancer* (pp. 44–57). New York: Oxford University Press.

Rowland, J. H. (1989b). Interpersonal resources: Social support. In J. C. Holland & J. H. Rowland (Eds.), *Handbook of psycho-oncology: Psychological care of the patient with cancer* (pp. 58–71). New York: Oxford University Press.

Schnaper, N., Kellner, R. K., & Panitz, H. L. (1991). Emotional and psychologic aspects of cancer management. In A. R. Moossa, S. C. Schimpff, & M. C. Robson (Eds.), *Comprehensive textbook of oncology* (pp. 1789–1795). San Francisco: Williams & Wilkins.

Schowalter, J. E. (1977). Psychological reactions to physical illness and hospitalization in adolescence. *Journal of the American Academy of Child Psychiatry, 16,* 500–516.

Schwartz, A. D. (1991). Cancer in children: An overview. In A. R. Moossa, S. C. Schimpff, & M. C. Robson (Eds.), *Comprehensive textbook of oncology* (pp. 1469–1475). San Francisco: Williams & Wilkins.

Share, L. (1972). Family communication in the crisis of a child's fatal illness: A literature review and analysis. *Omega, 3,* 187–201.

Slavin, L. A. (1981). Evolving psychosocial issues in the treatment of childhood cancer: A review. In G. P. Koocher & J. E. O'Malley (Eds.), *The Damocles syndrome: Psychosocial consequences of surviving childhood cancer* (pp. 1–30). San Francisco: McGraw-Hill.

Sontag, S. (1978). *Illness as metaphor.* New York: Farrar, Straus & Giroux.

Spinetta, J. J., Swarner, J., & Sheposh, J. (1981). Effective parental coping following the death of a child from cancer. *Journal of Pediatric Psychology, 6,* 251–263.

Sullivan, C. F., & Reardon, K. K. (1986). Social support satisfaction and health locus of control: Discriminators of breast cancer patients' styles of coping. In M. L. McLaughlin (Ed.), *Communication yearbook 9* (pp. 707–722). Beverly Hills, CA: Sage.

Tebbi, C. K., Stern, M., Boyle, M., Mettlin, C. J., & Mindell, E. R. (1985). The role of social support systems in adolescent cancer amputees. *CA, 56,* 965–971.

Thomas, L. (1989). Foreword. In J. C. Holland & J. H. Rowland (Eds.), *Handbook of psycho-oncology: Psychological care of the patient with cancer* (pp. v–vi). New York: Oxford University Press.

Tross, S. (1989). Acquired immunodeficiency syndrome. In J. C. Holland & J. H. Rowland (Eds.), *Handbook of psycho-oncology: Psychological care of the patient with cancer* (pp. 254–272). New York: Oxford University Press.

Tross, S., & Holland, J. C. (1989). Psychological sequelas in cancer survivors. In J. C. Holland & J. H. Rowland (Eds.), *Handbook of psycho-oncology: Psychological care of the patient with cancer* (pp. 101–116). New York: Oxford University Press.

Tucker, M. A., Coleman, C. N., Cox, R. S., Varghese, A., & Rosenberg, S. A. (1988). Risk of second cancers after treatment for Hodgkin's disease. *The New England Journal of Medicine, 318,* 76–81.

Van Eys, J. (1977, March). The outlook for the child with cancer. *Journal of School Health,* pp. 165–169.

Wasserman, A. L., Thompson, E. I., Wilimas, J. A., & Fairclough, D. L. (1987). The psychological status of survivors of childhood/adolescent Hodgkin's disease. *American Journal of Disabled Children, 141,* 626–631.

Wellisch, D. K., & Cohen, R. S. (1985). Psychosocial aspects of cancer. In C. M. Haskell (Ed.), *Cancer treatment* (pp. 948–962). Philadelphia: Saunders.

Whorton, J. C. (1987). Traditions of folk medicine in America. *Journal of the American Medical Association, 257,* 1632–1635.

Zeltzer, L., LeBaron, S., & Zeltzer, P. (1984). The adolescent with cancer. In R. W. Blum (Ed.), *Chronic illness in childhood and adolescence* (pp. 375–395). New York: Grune & Stratton.

Zwarnes, W. J. (1978, September). *Education of the child with cancer.* Paper presented at the National Conference on the Care of the Child with Cancer, American Cancer Society, Boston.

# 11  *Divorce Mediation:*
## *One Step Forward or*
## *Two Steps Back?*

Jill E. Rudd
*Cleveland State University*

It was estimated that more than 1 million marriages would end in divorce in 1994, with more than 75% involving children (Mathis & Yingling, 1990). For many, the marriage was terminated through litigation, an approach steeped within the patriarchal structure that perpetuates the traditional gender-biased power imbalance. Others, however, chose a nonadversarial process, such as divorce mediation. This approach is designed to counter the problems inherent in the adversarial process, particularly balancing power differentials. Although this is a worthy goal, the extent to which this is possible must be critically examined. In other words, does divorce mediation, in fact, correct the inequities of the traditional adversarial court system or does it function to maintain the hegemonic distribution of power inherent in a patriarchal society. This chapter addresses this concern by examining divorce from an historical perspective, what divorce mediation is, and its advantages and disadvantages as it attempts to operate within existing societal and political constraints.

## History of Divorce in the United States

U.S. divorce laws were strongly influenced by the laws of England. In the 1700s, English divorce laws did not grant divorces to women, even when they had been brutally beaten by their husbands. Typically, during this time, a husband who wanted to end his marriage either deserted his wife, agreed to an informal separation, or sold his wife at a wife sale (Phillips, 1988). Marriage was a permanent union unless the husband chose to end it, with the double standard set in place until the late 1800s. During this period, for example, the Plymouth Colony granted divorces to husbands whose wives had been unfaithful but not to wives whose husbands had committed adultery (Weitzman, 1985).

Heading into the 19th century, women were still considered property of their husbands. This began to change with the passage of the Married Women's Property Acts of the 1900s, which allowed women to file for divorce on grounds of infidelity. By the early 1900s most of the United States permitted divorce, although obtaining one was subject to certain restrictions. The major requirement was proving fault of either spouse. By 1930, statutory grounds for divorce in the United States were primarily acts such as adultery, desertion, cruelty, and imprisonment (Phillips, 1988; Weitzman, 1985).

As the 1900s progressed, the law reinforced the division of traditional family roles. As Weitzman (1985) noted, "The traditional law defined the basic rights and obligations of husbands and wives on the basis of gender, creating a sex-based division of family roles and responsibilities" (p. 2). This was exemplified in divorce settlements, as the wife was legally responsible for the children's care, the care of her home, and devotion to her husband whereas the husband was responsible for the financial support of his wife and children. Thus, the law encouraged women to stay home and not secure financial stability outside the home and discouraged husbands to take a nurturing role with their children (Weitzman, 1985).

There was a shift in the early 20th century. Divorce laws began to punish those who had been found guilty by conferring financial gain on the other spouse. For example, if a woman was found guilty of adultery, she would be denied alimony, and if a husband was guilty of adultery he would be obligated to pay alimony and child care. The innocent spouse was therefore rewarded, at least financially, for his or her spouse's guilty behavior (Weitzman, 1985). This system continued until 1970 when California introduced the "no-fault" divorce (Shaffer, 1988).

*No-Fault Divorce.*  No-fault divorce laws created a system that no longer reimburses one spouse for another's wrongful acts. Rather, it grants divorces without cause or placing blame. All a person needs to claim is "irreconcilable differences" to obtain a divorce. With no-fault laws came what advocates contend is a more equitable marriage termination process, allowing increased opportunities for couples to negotiate their own settlement.

A result of these increased opportunities was the development of alternative methods for terminating marriages. Currently, there are three methods commonly utilized by divorcing couples. The first is traditional litigation in court. Couples who cannot or will not resolve disputes amicably can present their respective arguments to a court referee or judge. The court then decides the issues in a written opinion or divorce decree. Thus, in litigation, the couple place their fate, and the fate of their children, in the hands of a stranger (the judge) who is part of the court system. The second method is negotiation. If couples can resolve all issues through negotiation, the judge makes the negotiated settlement part of their divorce decree, provided that the agreement complies with basic legal requirements. The third method is divorce mediation. If couples cannot resolve differences through direct negotiation, a neutral third party mediates the dispute and helps them arrive at a settlement to avoid litigation. Mediation has gained popularity, with, as of 1993, at least 33 states mandating its use to resolve contested custody and visitation matters. Although mediation has been touted by some as a promising mechanism for balancing the gender-biased scales, it may, in fact, be little more than a wolf in sheep's clothing. A discussion of divorce mediation and its strengths and weaknesses follow.

## Divorce Mediation

Divorce mediation is "the process in which divorcing spouses negotiate some or all of the terms of their settlement agreement with the aid of a neutral and learned third party" (Kressel, 1985, p. 179). The mediation process usually occurs over a period of three to ten 1-hour meetings, bringing the couple together face-to-face to work out a mutually agreeable settlement. The emphasis is on achieving a win–win solution. There are many variations of divorce mediation models (Coogler, 1978; Cramer & Schoeneman, 1985; Haynes, 1978; Moore, 1986; Volkema, 1986), with most describing the process in terms of a series of steps or phases. One example is the five-stage model presented by Cramer and Schoeneman:

1) *initiation*: The mediation process and the mediator's role are explained. Groundwork issues such as entering the process in the spirit of cooperation, full disclosure by participants and the option of declaring an impasse if a participant no longer wishes to continue are agreed upon;

2) *orientation*: The spouses agree on issues to be resolved;

3) *exploration*: This includes arrangement of issues to be discussed. Anger is often expressed at this stage as issues arise. This point in the mediation is often an opportunity to restructure communication patterns;

4) *formulation*: The mediator begins with the least complicated issues to foster a feeling of success and movement. The process moves from a "this is what I demand" to "this is what will be most beneficial to the family";

5) *finalization*: A written memorandum is prepared. (p. 45)

Advocates of divorce mediation promote several important benefits of the mediation process such as: (a) It is more cost effective for the couple both emotionally and monetarily, (b) spouses are given an opportunity to be heard, thus they feel a sense of empowerment, and (c) mediation provides an opportunity for participants to learn more productive communication skills, which can then be used if necessary for future postdecree conflicts, and (d) it decreases the backlog of cases currently on our court dockets. It is estimated that one half of individuals using the adversarial system will return to court after their divorce for resolution of spousal disputes (Neumann, 1989). Divorce mediation proponents argue that more mediation and less litigation provides a savings to our society and yields a more efficient legal system, which can then be available for cases better suited for adjudication. However, opponents argue that although the process may differ, the results of mediation are the same as those reached through litigation and investigations into how gender-related power inequality is manifested in the mediation process are needed (e.g., Shaffer, 1988).

## DIVORCE MEDIATION ISSUES

The ongoing debate between proponents and opponents of divorce mediation can be illustrated through the following discussion of several key concerns, those of fairness and power, economics, and relational issues.

### Fairness and Power Issues

Research suggests that couples who use divorce mediation feel a sense of fairness (Neumann, 1989), with both parties reporting "the decision-making process as fair, most apt to see both parties as equally influential in determining the outcome, and most likely to perceive their decrees as complete and thorough" (Pearson & Thoennes, 1984, p. 254). This is probably because mediation allows the agreement to reflect the individuals' needs and values. Issues not admissible in the courts can be included in mediation. For example, a wife may feel entitled to some type of compensation (i.e., financial, keeping the house) because her husband had an affair with her best friend. The traditional legal system currently does not recognize the husband's betrayal as a direct issue in divorce litigation. However, in mediation the wife may negotiate some remuneration in the settlement for the unfaithful acts. Thus, she is likely to feel a sense of empowerment having been able to have her feelings and wishes reflected in the divorce settlement.

However, feminists have recently questioned the ability of mediation to shift the power imbalance as it is a process embedded in a patriarchal social context (Lipman-Blumen, 1994; Ricci, 1985; Shaffer, 1988; Weitzman, 1984). As Shaffer noted, "Most often, because the structure of our society and our social norms and values have been shaped by centuries of patriarchy, women find themselves in a disadvantageous position vis-à-vis men" (p. 181). Although mediation advocates claim that mediators are the balancing component of unequal power balance, one cannot help to question whether mediators can do more than reflect their culture or represent the norms and values of their community (Merry, 1982).

As Crouch (1982) noted, "mediation is a device which can facilitate exploitation by a shrewder or otherwise dominant party" (p. 223). Negotiating the balance of power between spouses is critical because mediation lacks the same checks and balances offered by the adversarial system. Two people usually do not have the same level of knowledge, skill, or experience in negotiating for their own best interest. One of the parties, typically the woman, is often not equally equipped to deal with the emotional or financial costs, and it is probable that these inequities undergird the mediation. Thus, the "bargaining chips" each spouse brings into the mediation process is a critical component of the final agreement, and most often the reality is that women have fewer "chips" to bargain with (Shaffer, 1988).

As long as patriarchal values and peer structure remain strong, mediation will not produce results that are in the best interest of women. In fact, mediation may actually cause women harm if the process lacks the safeguards that are necessary to ensure them an equitable settlement. For example, there is little, if any, right to appeal or reopen for amendment a previous mediation settlement, under the rationale that it was a freely bargained agreement between equals (Shaffer, 1988). Within its patriarchal context, the removal of safeguards built into the traditional system results in a more informal and less protected system. Bottomley (1985) posited that this new form of informal justice (divorce mediation) is in reality reproducing the existing power relationships more effectively than the traditional adversarial system; thus the manipulation, oppression, and inequality continue to the detriment of all women.

The fact that mediation allows each party to voice their needs and feelings is a unique difference from the traditional litigious system. From a societal perspective, divorce mediation may correct some of the cultural gender biases. However, as postmodern feminists argue, caution is essential given that divorce mediation was created within the confines of the traditional patriarchal structure.

## Economic Issues

Many researchers report that mediation is a cost-effective method for terminating marriages (Bahr, 1981; Grossen, 1984; Pearson & Thoennes, 1982), with both the couple and the public saving money. McIsaac (1981) asserted that "$181.7 million per year could be saved in the United States if all child custody cases were mediated" (p. 4). California alone could save 75% of their current costs if conflicts over child custody and visitation were resolved through mediation. On an individual level, the costs of litigation in a child custody suit can easily range from $60,000 to $70,000 (Neumann, 1989).

It is not only the initial costs of divorcing but also the significant relitigation costs that warrant consideration. Several mediation advocates report that couples who successfully mediate are less likely to relitigate than couples using the adversarial method (Bahr, 1981; Milne, 1978; Pearson & Thoennes, 1982). Mediated agreements result in better personal and spousal compliance than those reached through litigation. For example, McEwen and Maiman (1981) found that 70.6% of the mediation agreements with a monetary settlement were paid in full, whereas the same was true for only 33.8% of the adjudicated cases. The question remains, however, if either partner in the mediated couples settled for less financially than couples who used adjudication.

Some opponents of divorce mediation argue that, in general, women are worse off economically than men and are even more economically deprived when they divorce under the traditional system (Davis, 1991; Weitzman, 1985). For example, it is estimated that fewer than 13% of divorcing women in the 1980s received any type of alimony and that women who did receive it were restricted to a maximum of 3 years of compensation (Davis, 1991). Some also argue that women typically fall far behind economically immediately after the divorce than men, with some estimating husband's standard of living rising by about 42% and falling about 73% for his exwife and children (Davis, 1991; Weitzman, 1985). However, other researchers find much less of a dramatic decline, with only a 10% to 15% increase for men and 30% decline for women. They further argue that the initial decline is temporary and that 5 years postdivorce, the average woman's standard of living is actually slightly higher than when she was married (see Faludi, 1991). Thus, the argument regarding postdivorce economic deficiency must be made with great caution.

Divorce mediation also raises the concern of economic entitlement for women. Women may be willing to settle for less than they are entitled to because mediation is more expedient, or because a mother sees the children suffering emotionally from the unstable and temporary situation, or perhaps because she just wants to be rid of the past. Reasons other than a realistic outlook of their economic future may cost the women a great deal financially. Women are not paid equal wages, have less opportunity to make up lost career years and often times incur more of the child expenses than originally planned (Beer & Stief, 1985). And whereas judges will often take into consideration issues such as a woman's interrupted career while married, mediation may not. One can only hope women seek outside legal advice before reaching a settlement because the degree to which mediation considers wage inequity remains unclear.

Clearly divorce mediation is initially a cheaper method of marriage termination for both the individuals and society. Individuals benefit by spending less in attorney fees as they may choose to use attorneys in limited ways or not at all. This cost alone can be a significant savings at a time when money may be scarce as couples stretch their budget to accommodate two households. Mediation also provides a significant saving to society. The cost of backlogs in court dockets has created a very slow and ineffective method of judicial process. Divorce cases that do reach trial put a significant drain on the judicial system. In general, most would agree that courts are not the efficient place to deal with the termination of marriage.

## Relational Issues

Increased communication is considered one of mediation's benefits and lays the foundation for future conversations (Neumann, 1989; Saposnek, 1983). Advocates (e.g., Blades, 1985; Coulson, 1983) contend that mediation improves the relationship between parties by trying to establish and maintain a positive bond between spouses. For example, Pearson and Thoennes (1984) found that 69% of mediated couples, compared to 14% of those adjudicated, reported better understanding and communication with their exspouse. Mediated couples were also generally more optimistic about their ability as a couple to resolve future issues, such as property and custody with their ex-spouse and more likely to enjoy joint custody and more visitation with their children.

Any process that encourages harmony is indeed a welcome alternative to our traditional system. However, the concern of many is that mediation may in reality not help couples develop more productive communication patterns but, rather, continue the manipulation of power by one spouse over the other in a new context (Rifkin, 1984). Furthermore, joint custody, which is often the outcome of mediated divorce, may increase women's financial problems. In these situations, most often children continue to live with their mothers but the courts set child support payments at less than the norm assuming fathers will contribute equally to the financial living expenses of the children (Davis, 1991). Not only can the joint custody work to the financial disadvantage of women but it can also weaken their position in negotiations, especially if husbands use custody as part of the power struggle to get, for example, women to settle for less financially (Davis, 1991). Faced with the threat of losing their children, women may agree to a less than equitable settlement.

When mediation works well, couples may indeed learn to communicate more constructively. As one mediator observed, "The traditional divorce process transforms couples from spouses to ex-spouses but the mediation process helps couples to make the transition from spouses to your children's parent and that can make all the difference in their future discussions" (Haynes, 1988, p. 9). However, mediation does not assure this kind of transformation. In fact, it may be that communicative manipulation by the more powerful spouse further ensures an unequitable agreement. Thus, the risk involved in achieving a more constructive communication pattern with one's spouse has, potentially, a very high cost for many women.

## CONCLUSION

Divorce mediation appears to offer numerous benefits to society, in regard to saving time and money for the beleaguered court systems and the people involved. The statistics regarding the extent to which mediated settlements are adhered to without the parties returning to the courts, and the high degree of participants' satisfaction, is impressive (Pearson & Thoennes, 1984).

It is clear that the neutrality of divorce mediators is critical for these outcomes to be achieved. Although all mediators bring their personal biases to their work, it is essential that they are able to accurately assess and monitor their biases, determine if and how these are influencing their impartiality, and then take appropriate action to keep their prejudices from spilling over into the mediation. However, there are several reasons this may not occur. First, divorce mediator training varies a great deal. Some trainers offer a more legal perspective, others emphasize counseling, and still others take a financial orientation. Second, certification of mediators deviates across states. Florida, for example, certifies accountants, social workers, or attorneys, whereas other states, such as Ohio, have no requirements concerning who can act as a mediator. This lack of consistent regulations sets the stage for a less than ideal situation that is likely to have major ramifications on the outcome of the mediation.

Whereas some may consider divorce mediation a potential panacea for the problems with the adversarial divorce process others contend that although different in form, the content of mediation is remarkably similar to adjudication. The critical question becomes to what extent does divorce mediation balance the gender inequality scales. Although any movement toward allowing those involved to resolve their issues and make their own decisions is admirable, there are also risks. Whereas the mediation process, at least on the surface, promises a more equitable way for couples to participate in reaching their own agreement, one cannot help but wonder whether, in some cases, patriarchal hierarchy has donned new clothes named "divorce mediation."

# REFERENCES

Bahr, S. J. (1981). An evaluation of court mediation: A comparison in divorce cases with children. *Journal of Family Issues, 2*, 39–60.

Beer, J., & Stief, E. (1985). Mediation and feminism. *Conflict Resolution Notes, 2*, 27–28.

Blades, J. (1985). *Family mediation: A cooperative divorce settlement.* Englewood Cliffs, NJ: Prentice-Hall.

Bottomley, A. (1985). What is happening to family law? A feminist critique of reconciliation. In J. Brophy & C. Smart (Eds.), *Women-in-law* (pp. 12–187). London: Routledge.

Coogler, O. J. (1978). *Structured mediation in divorce settlement.* Boston, MA: Lexington.

Coulson, R. (1983). *Fighting fair.* New York: The Free Press.

Cramer, C., & Schoeneman, R. (1985). A court mediation model with an eye toward standards. *Mediation Quarterly, 8*, 33–45.

Crouch, R. (1982). Divorce mediation and legal ethics. *Family Law Quarterly, 16*, 219–223.

Davis, F. (1991). *Moving the mountain.* New York: Simon & Schuster.

Faludi, S. (1991). *Backlash: The undeclared war against American women.* New York: Crown.

Grossen, J. M. (1984). Agreements regarding the financial aspects of divorce: How free/how binding? In J. M. Eekelaar & S. Katz (Eds.), *The resolution of family conflict* (pp. 313–321). Toronto: Butterworths.

Haynes, J. (1978). Divorce mediator: A new role. *Social Work, 23*, 5–9.

Haynes, J. (1988). Power balancing. In J. Folberg & A. Milne (Eds.), *Divorce mediation* (pp. 277–296). New York: Guilford.

Kressel, K. (1985). *The process of divorce.* New York: Basic Books.

Lipman-Blumen, J. (1994). The existential bases of power relationships: The gender role case. In H. L. Radtke & S. J. Henderikus (Eds.), *Power/gender: Social relations in theory and practice* (pp. 108–135). London: Sage.

Mathis, R. D., & Yingling, L. C. (1990). Family functioning level and divorce mediation outcome. *Mediation Quarterly, 8*, 3–14.

McEwen, C., & Maiman, R. (1981). Small claims mediation in Maine: An empirical assessment. *Maine Law Review, 33*, 237.

McIsaac, H. (1981). Mandatory conciliation custody/visitation matters: California's bold stroke. *Conciliation Courts Review, 19*, 73–81.

Merry, S. (1982). The social organization of mediation in non-industrial societies: Implications for informal justice in America. In R. Abel (Ed.), *The politics of informal justice* (Vol. 2, pp. 17–42). New York: Academic Press.

Milne, A. (1978). Custody of children in a divorce process: A family self-determination model. *Conciliation Courts Review, 16*, 1–10.

Moore, C. (1986). *The mediation process: Practical strategies for resolving conflict.* San Francisco: Jossey-Bass.

Neumann, D. (1989). *Divorce mediation.* New York: Holt.

Pearson, J., & Thoennes, N. (1982). The benefits outweigh the costs. *Family Advocate, 4*, 26–32.

Pearson, J., & Thoennes, N. (1984). Custody mediation in Denver: Short and longer term effects. In J. M. Eekelaar & S. Katz (Eds.), *The resolution of family conflict* (pp. 248–267). Toronto: Butterworths.

Phillips, R. (1988). *Putting asunder.* New York: Cambridge University Press.

Ricci, I. (1985). Mediator's notebook: Reflections on promoting equal empowerment and entitlement for women. *Journal of Divorce, 8*, 49–61.

Rifkin, J. (1984). Mediation from a feminist perspective: Promise and problems. *Law and Inequality, 2*, 21–31.

Saposnek, D. T. (1983). *Mediating child custody disputes.* San Francisco: Jossey-Bass.

Shaffer, M. (1988). Divorce mediation: A feminist perspective. *University of Toronto Faculty of Law Review, 46,* 162–200.

Volkema, R. (1986). Training disputants: Theory and practice. *Mediation Quarterly, 13,* 43–51.

Weitzman, L. J. (1984). Equity and equality in divorce settlements: A comparative analysis of property and maintenance awards in the United States and England. In J. M. Eekelaar & S. Katz (Eds.), *The resolution of family conflict* (pp. 461–487). Toronto: Butterworths.

Weitzman, L. J. (1985). *The divorce revolution.* New York: The Free Press.

# 12 The Institutionalized Elderly: Interactive Implications of Long-Term Care

Jon F. Nussbaum
University of Oklahoma

Mark Bergstrom
University of Utah

Lisa Sparks
University of Oklahoma

Robert Butler, founder of the National Institute on Aging and widely regarded as the foremost expert on the aging process, stated in a recent talk to communication and aging researchers that it is now quite common for individuals to live well into their 80s. Dying before one's 80th birthday is considered a premature death. The great majority of individuals beyond their 65th birthday are happy, healthy, active individuals who each day make meaningful contributions to society. However, as we age into our eighth decade, our lives do slow down and the possibility that professional care is needed increases quite significantly. One dominant location for this care is within nursing homes (Butler, 1994).

Many Americans will spend some portion of their lives institutionalized. At any one time, approximately 5% of individuals over the age of 65 reside in nursing homes. In 1994, this represented about 1.5 million to 2 million people. Because the older population is the fastest growing segment of our society, this number is expected to increase to as many as 5 million by the year 2030. The numbers are a bit misleading considering that approximately 43% of people who are currently 65 are expected to enter a nursing home for a significant period of time at some point before their death (Kemper & Murtaugh, 1991). Of those who enter a home, 55% will live there for at least 1 year, with the typical resident being "female, widowed, white, age 81, who has a disease of the circulatory system as a primary diagnosis, and who depends on assistance to bathe, dress, use the bathroom, and get about" (Van Nostrand, 1981, p. 403).

Although nursing homes are a necessary choice of care for many, this care is not without costs. Nursing homes structurally segregate residents from family and friends and limit interaction within and outside the home. This may be especially problematic because, whereas many residents have physical limitations, a majority are still capable of maintaining interpersonal relationships. The curtailment of these relationships, combined with physical health problems and psychological concerns with aging and approaching death, further segments residents from their former community. This chapter examines the impact of these forces as they are manifested in the interactive life of nursing home residents and how they promote the disenfranchisement of this elderly population.

## THE NURSING HOME INDUSTRY

The nursing home industry owes its existence to the fact that life expectancy has increased by 35 years during the 20th century. At the turn of the century, life expectancy was just under 50 years, whereas for those born in 1990 expectancy is just under 80 years (American Association of Retired Persons, 1991). The federal government reacted to the ever increasing life span by passing the Social Security Act of 1935, which created the for-profit system of nursing homes now operating across the United States (Moss & Halamandaro, 1977). The Medicaid and Medicare legislation of the mid-1960s changed the nursing home industry from a family enterprise to a multibillion dollar business. Currently, large multinational corporations specializing in everything but health care are investing in nursing homes, speculating that large profits can be made in the future. It is important to note that the United States has no long-term care policy or national plan to deal with the ever increasing number of frail elderly individuals who will one day reside in a nursing home.

### International Comparisons

The lack of a long-term care policy in the United States is in stark contrast to many other industrialized countries with similar population demographics. Countries with a national health system (e.g., the United Kingdom, Canada, Australia) have more highly developed standards for long-term care, which produce a higher standard of living for their institutionalized residents than countries such as the United States or Germany. As Alber (1992) noted, "A national health system of the British type links political decision makers via the election mechanism more closely to the concerns of the public" (p. 929). The British National Health Service covers all of the country's residents and considers nursing homes to be part of the national health service. It is interesting to note that geriatrics is a legitimate specialty area of medicine in the United Kingdom but is not a recognized specialty area in the United States (Alber, 1992).

The German health care system is quite different from both the United Kingdom and the United States. Alber (1992) observed, "Germany relies predominantly on a compulsory sickness insurance scheme financed by contributions from employees and employers" (p. 931). The German system funds sickness that needs medical care quite differently than frailty that requires long-term care. When older individuals need long-term care, they must often rely on public welfare to help pay for their room within one of the voluntary nonprofit associations that provide nursing home care.

As previously mentioned, the United States provides for its nonemployed citizens with two government programs, Medicare and Medicaid. Medicare is a federally operated insurance program that provides benefits, including the cost of skilled nursing care within nursing homes, for up to 150 days for individuals over the age of 65 and for persons with disabilities. Medicaid is a federally regulated, public welfare program of basic health services for low-income persons. The great majority of nursing home costs in the United States are financed from private resources (by the older individuals or by family members) or from the state-administered Medicaid program.

Recent research comparing long-term care for the elderly within the United States, the United Kingdom, and Germany provides evidence that a system such as the British National Health Service produces much higher levels of satisfaction with care among those institutionalized (Alber, 1992; Kayser-Jones, 1982). The British system recognizes the special needs of the elderly, emphasizes geriatric care within the medical field, provides more independence to the frail elderly for a longer period of time, and gives the elderly who desperately need to be institutionalized more choices for their nursing home care. It would be fair to conclude that the British system of financing health care is more sensitive and marginalizes the elderly far less than the health system within the United States.

## THE DISENFRANCHISEMENT OF NURSING HOME ELDERLY

### Nursing Home Admission

In the United States, admission to a nursing home is rarely viewed as a positive life transition either by the individual moving into the home or by family members. The transition from independent to dependent living is often brought about because of a severe physical problem that can no longer be cared for at home or in a hospital. The actual decision to enter a home is often made by family members, who may or may not consult the individual to be admitted (Nussbaum, 1993).

The federal and state regulations that cover the majority of nursing home admissions require facilities to provide basic information on services and financial obligations to potential residents or to designated family members. Regulations are also in place that require a physical assessment of the incoming resident prior to admission (Ambrogi, 1990). The "nuts and bolts" of the admissions process have been reviewed and criticized by Ambrogi and reforms are underway in many states to uphold the civil rights of individuals as they enter nursing homes.

Beyond the legal and ethical problems potential residents must confront are the communicative difficulties associated with the admissions process that reinforce the notion that they are being removed from the community and entering a sanitized place to die. Nussbaum (1993) highlighted the communicative impact of this process by following one elderly woman and her daughter as they moved through the system to enter a nursing home in Oklahoma City. He noted:

> The overwhelming feeling that I as an observer had once the admission process was complete centered on the quick, professional nature of the process. Within a period of two weeks, an elderly woman had made a major transition from living at home with her daughter and son-in-law to life within a nursing home with total strangers. (p. 244)

At no time during the admissions process did nursing home staff direct questions toward the future resident, even though her physical difficulties did not prevent her from understanding or answering the questions. Information was given to the future resident concerning meals, visits, and therapy. However, negotiations as to which room the woman would live in, who her roommate would be, or even what foods she liked or disliked were never held. As Nussbaum observed, "One communicative outcome of the resident-staff interactions prior to admission was a clear message that a move to a nursing facility is a move into total dependence" (p. 244). The ease with which incoming residents may be treated as invisible, and the fact that this behavior is allowed to occur unchallenged (i.e., family members typically do not refuse to answer and tell the staff to ask questions directly to the elderly person) formally begins the new resident's disenfranchisement.

This disenfranchisement is central to the success of nursing homes. Nursing homes are institutions and require conformity. Although relationships with family and friends may be considered important, they cannot be allowed to interfere with resident compliance. The institution must foster dependency so that the home, not the residents, are in control. This is achieved structurally and relationally within the home.

## Structural Marginalization

Life within a nursing home can lead to "interactive starvation" (Nussbaum, 1983), a complete lack of meaningful communication for residents. The physical environment, for example, is often constructed to impede interaction. Many nursing homes are purposely located away from the heart of the community and are designed for medical efficiency. Nursing stations are located at the ends of long hallways, individual rooms are lined up next to one another down the hallways, and recreation rooms are filled with semicomfortable chairs all pointed to an elevated television. These architectural features are reinforced by the institution's rules and regulations, which have very little regard for personal freedoms or individual desires for interaction. All meals are served at one time, informal interaction must take place within designated areas, and sustained interaction with individuals who are not one's roommate is all but impossible (Nussbaum, 1983).

## Relational Marginalization

Despite evidence that positive relationships between nursing staff and residents appears to increase longevity, improve residents' quality of life, decrease physical pain, and provide residents with more verbal praise and attention (Miller & Lelieuvre, 1982; Noelker & Harel, 1978), nursing homes are structured to minimize resident-staff interaction and maximize staff control. Staff reinforce dependency behaviors while simultaneously extinguishing independence (Baltes, Neumann, & Zank, 1994; Baltes, Wahl, & Reichert, 1991). Staff control residents' daily activities and tend to keep interaction with them efficient and professional (Nussbaum & Robinson, 1990).

However, these staff behaviors appear to be interpreted differently by residents. Research by Nussbaum and his colleagues (e.g., Nussbaum, 1990, 1993; Nussbaum, Holladay, Robinson, & Ragan, 1985; Nussbaum & Robinson, 1984; Nussbaum, Robinson, & Grew, 1985) indicates residents perceive closer relationships with nursing home staff than staff perceive them to be. As Nussbaum (1990) found, "The residents simply stated that since 'I am interacting with this individual quite frequently, it is normal for us to be "friends" ' " (p. 164). Staff, however, rarely use the term "friend" to identify their relationship with residents (Patterson, Bettini, &

Nussbaum, 1993). Residents also perceived staff as controlling the level of relationship, as it was staff's prerogative to initiate relational development.

Although there may be idiosyncratic factors that prevent staff from pursuing relationships with residents, the reality is that nursing home institutions are dependent on maintaining the division between resident and staff. This can only be done by sacrificing the *individual* elderly for the collective residents. The result is institutional support for the disenfranchisement of its residents. It is within this framework that all intrahome relationships are embedded. A strong counterinfluence to the institutional behaviors may be provided by residents' family and friends.

## ENFRANCHISING THE ELDERLY

There are a number of ways the elderly can be enfranchised. For those living in nursing homes, relationships with family and friends are important deterrents to the institutional disenfranchisement. For elderly outside nursing homes, the availability of alternatives to institutionalized care foster independence and enable them to remain active in mainstream society.

### Relationships Within Nursing Homes

*Interaction With Family.*   Family members often work hard to keep residents enfranchised within the family unit. Contrary to the belief some have that nursing homes allow families to abandon their elderly, research provides no evidence of abandonment or family alienation. From the admissions process to an average of 12 visits a month, the family is involved regularly with their elderly nursing home residents (York & Calsyn, 1986).

One important predictor of family involvement is the visitation pattern prior to admission. Adult children who visited their elderly parent twice a week prior to admission are likely to visit them twice a week after admission (York & Calsyn, 1986). In addition, families with denser ties are more likely to maintain close interpersonal contact with the resident and residents who phone and/or write their family are also likely to find these behaviors reciprocated (Bear, 1990).

Resident–family contact is also related to the duration of the stay in the nursing home. The sense of responsibility felt toward residents is most intense at the time of admission until about 1 year. It surfaces again after 3 years, possibly because after 3 years the move is perceived as permanent and the acceptance of responsibility for the care of the family member resumes (Schwartz & Vogel, 1990). It is also quite possible that, after 3 years, responsibility issues such as financial strains continue to increase.

Close resident–family communication, however, may be paradoxical (Nussbaum, 1990). Observations from nurse aides and nurses suggest many elderly become depressed following a family visit. It is possible that visits may be guilt-driven and residents can detect feelings of resentment and frustration from the visitors. However, it is more likely that, because visits bring the outside world into the residents' isolated world, they are temporarily nonresidents. They become reintegrated into the family and are respected by family members just because of their age and relationship. Once the visit ends, residents are abruptly thrust back into their isolated world, where control over their own lives is minimal, where they are not treated respectfully, and where their feelings and opinions are perhaps heard but not listened to. The visits, by upsetting the status quo, may underscore their dependence and their segregation from mainstream society.

*Interaction With Friends.* Social gerontologists have repeatedly found a positive relationship between close friendship relationships in old age and psychological well-being (see Nussbaum, 1994, for a review of this research). Friendships allow the elderly to remain socially active and stay in touch with society, offer an opportunity for self-disclosure without sanctions, and provide informal support. In addition, the sense of obligation and guilt associated with familial relationships usually does not exist within friendships (Nussbaum, 1990). In other words, friendships are an important vehicle for enfranchising the elderly.

Although their importance within nursing homes has not been investigated, Nussbaum (1983) speculated that friendships may be an important predictor of psychological well-being for nursing home elderly. Although residents maintain prior friendships after admission (Bitzan & Kruzich, 1990), many also report friendships within the nursing home (Gutheil, 1991; Restinas & Garrity, 1985). For those who desire, and are able to remain socially active after admission, the environment has the potential to be a rich arena for social interaction and friendship formation. Similarity of age, life situation, and the forced proximity can become positive forces in the formation of new friendships. The home's homogeneous environment is so overpowering that factors such as social class and ethnicity, which are predictors of friendship outside nursing homes, do not seem to matter within the home. As Restinas and Garrity noted, "For residents who are able to communicate, the nursing home may offer new friendships. Indeed, withdrawing from the larger world may enable residents to enter a new social world" (p. 380).

Positive relationships with family and friends decrease isolation and loneliness, provide companionship and support, and allow life within the home to parallel some aspects of pre-nursing-home life. Family and friends remind residents of their individuality in a setting that emphasizes the collective. However, these relationships can only do so much once the individual has been institutionalized. Alternatives to nursing homes must be found to restructure care so that independence, individual control, and individuality are emphasized.

## ALTERNATIVES TO NURSING HOMES

The lack of a national long-term policy in the United States, combined with the Medicaid/Medicare financing of care, has produced a society that places many individuals in nursing homes who do not need that extent of care. Knight and Walker (1985) estimated that as many as 55% of all nursing home admissions are inappropriate. At the individual level, most elderly prefer to remain independent and live in their own homes as long as possible (Nussbaum, Thompson, & Robinson, 1989). At the societal level, the cost of institutionalizing all frail elderly will shortly bankrupt both state and federal government. Motivated primarily by cost savings, several alternatives for frail elderly have been pioneered in the 1980s and deserve attention as alternatives to institutionalization.

Services such as respite care, adult day care, sheltered workshops, senior centers, group and congregate care homes, and intergenerational centers have emerged as viable options to nursing home placement. Although there is controversy regarding the effectiveness of these programs, singularly or in some combination, Holt (1986–1987) noted that home care remains the cornerstone of a community-based approach to long-term care and provides the best opportunity to combat the marginalization of the institutionalized elderly. This can be seen in the specific examples of successful programs that follow.

### Hartford House

For individuals who are experiencing the inevitable normal changes in vision, hearing, and mobility and simultaneously having manageable acute health problems, modifications of their living environment may enable them to remain home for a significant period of time. The Hartford House is an exhibit home developed by the ITT Hartford Insurance Group and the American Association of Retired Persons that incorporates a variety of architectural and design features to enable the elderly to live longer at home with comfort and security. Custom-designed features such as extra lighting, temperature controls that prevent scalding water, grab bars in bathrooms, color contrasts that are easier to detect, glare-reducing shades, large cabinet door handles, and large numbers on the thermostat make life much easier for elderly who have difficulty managing in an unadapted home.

## Nursing Home Without Walls

An excellent example of a home care program for those who need more than home design changes is the Nursing Home Without Walls Program, first introduced into the New York state legislature in 1976. This program provides "long term care custom-tailored to the needs of the patient at home, without unnecessary services and without requiring the patient to fit into a fixed routine of an institution" (Lombardi, 1986–1987, p. 21). Well-trained formal care providers visit the elderly in their own homes to supplement the care provided by family members. The program has grown to include more than 10,000 frail elderly throughout New York who remain either at home or live with family or friends. The major benefits of the program include the positive effects of living at home as well as a significant savings in total costs for the state (Lombardi, 1986–1987).

## Adult Foster Care

The state of Oregon has a history of progressive health programs. One example is the Adult Foster Care Program, which permits Oregon to use Medicaid funds earmarked for nursing homes for community-based care settings. An adult foster home is a private residence licensed under Oregon law to provide care for up to five elderly or persons with disabilities on a 24-hour basis. These homes are single-family residences located in residential areas with a noninstitutional appearance. Trained foster caregivers assist residents with meal preparation, housekeeping, various activities of daily living, and individual health maintenance needs. Depending on the services provided and the health status of the resident, individuals can remain in the home until death. Although there are some problems with this program, it remains very popular with residents and family members who view adult foster care as a viable alternative to placement in a nursing home.

## CONCLUSION

The three programs just discussed are only a fraction of options available to the elderly. However, because of the lack of a national long-term care policy, each is dependent on private initiatives. The overwhelming majority of frail elderly who are discharged from a hospital or whose family can no longer manage their health problems are routinely admitted to nursing homes regardless of their ability to remain noninstitutionalized with minimal assistance.

The alternatives are enfranchising, allowing the elderly to remain physically present in mainstream society and to continue to contribute to their community and maintain some level of independence. They are in marked structural and relational contrast to institutional life. These programs promote inclusion rather than segregation. Although some elderly require the full-care service provided by nursing homes, many do not. For them, placement there only serves to expedite the inevitable while increasing their isolation. The existence of options other than nursing homes reflects an unwillingness to automatically disenfranchise the elderly through institutionalization. The more choices available to meet the varying needs of the elderly, the greater the likelihood that institutionalization will become just one more selection and will be used more selectively. The more the elderly can continue to live within mainstream society, the less chance that they will live their final years as outsiders.

# REFERENCES

Alber, J. (1992). Residential care for the elderly. *Journal of Health Politics, 17,* 929–957.

Ambrogi, D. M. (1990). Nursing home admissions: Problematic process and agreements. *Generations, 15,* 72–74.

American Association of Retired Persons. (1991). *A profile of older Americans: 1990.* Washington, DC: Author.

Baltes, M. M., Neumann, E. M., & Zank, S. (1994). Maintenance and rehabilitation of independence in old age: An intervention program for staff. *Psychology and Aging, 9,* 179–188.

Baltes, M. M., Wahl, H. W., & Reichert, M. (1991). Institutions and successful aging for the elderly. *Annual Review of Gerontology and Geriatrics, 11,* 311–337.

Bear, M. (1990). Social network characteristics and the duration of primary relationships after entry into long-term care. *Journal of Gerontology, 45,* 156–162.

Bitzan, J. E., & Kruzich, J. M. (1990). Interpersonal relationships of nursing home residents. *The Gerontologist, 30,* 385–390.

Butler, R. (1994, April). *Keynote address.* Presented at the Communication, Health, and Aging Conference, Hamilton, Ontario, Canada.

Gutheil, I. A. (1991). Intimacy in nursing home friendships. *Journal of Gerontological Social Work, 17,* 59–73.

Holt, S. W. (1986–1987). The role of home care in long term care. *Generations, 11,* 9–11.

Kayser-Jones, S. J. (1982). Institutional structures: Catalysts or barriers to quality care for the institutionalized aged in Scotland and the U.S. *Social Science and Medicine, 16,* 935–944.

Kemper, P., & Murtaugh, C. M. (1991). Lifetime use of nursing home care. *The New England Journal of Medicine, 324, 9,* 28, 595–600.

Knight, B., & Walker, D. L. (1985). Toward a definition of alternatives to institutionalization for the frail and elderly. *The Gerontologist, 25,* 358–363.

Lombardi, T. (1986–1987). Nursing home without walls. *Generations, 11,* 21–23.

Miller, C., & Lelieuvre, R. (1982). A method to reduce chronic pain in elderly nursing home residents. *The Gerontologist, 22,* 314–323.

Moss, F. E., & Halamandaro, V. J. (1977). *Too old, too sick, too bad: Nursing homes in America*. Germantown, MD: Aspen Systems.

Noelker, L., & Harel, Z. (1978). Predictors of well-being and survival among institutionalized aged. *The Gerontologist, 18*, 562–567.

Nussbaum, J. F. (1983). Relational closeness of elderly interaction: Implications for life satisfaction. *Western Journal of Speech Communication, 47*, 229–243.

Nussbaum, J. F. (1990). Communication and the nursing home environment: Survivability as a function of resident-nursing staff affinity. In H. Giles, N. Coupland, & J. Wiemann (Eds.), *Communication, health, and the elderly* (pp. 155–171). Manchester, England: Manchester University Press.

Nussbaum, J. F. (1993). The communicative impact of institutionalization for the elderly: The admissions process. *Aging and Society, 7*, 237–246.

Nussbaum, J. F. (1994). Friendship in older adulthood. In M. L. Hummert, J. Wiemann, & J. F. Nussbaum (Eds.), *Interpersonal communication in older adulthood: Interdisciplinary research* (pp. 209–225). Hillsdale, NJ: Lawrence Erlbaum Associates.

Nussbaum, J. F., Holladay, S., Robinson, J., & Ragan, S. (1985, November). *The communicative world of the nursing home resident: A preliminary analysis of in-depth interviews concentrating upon friendship*. Paper presented at the annual meeting of the Speech Communication Association, Denver.

Nussbaum, J. F., & Robinson, J. (1984, November). *Nursing staff communication as a predictor of affinity with nursing home residents and satisfaction with work*. Paper presented at the annual meeting of the Speech Communication Association, Chicago.

Nussbaum, J. F., & Robinson, J. D. (1990). Communication within the nursing home. In D. O'Hair & G. Kreps (Eds.), *Applied communication theory and research* (pp. 353–370). Hillsdale, NJ: Lawrence Erlbaum Associates.

Nussbaum, J. F., Robinson, J., & Grew, D. (1985). Communication behavior of the long-term health care employee: Implications for the elderly resident. *Communication Research Reports, 2*, 16–22.

Nussbaum, J. F., Thompson, T., & Robinson, J. D. (1989). *Communication and aging*. New York: Harper & Row.

Patterson, B., Bettini, L., & Nussbaum, J. F. (1993). The meaning of friendship across the life-span: Two studies. *Communication Quarterly, 41*, 145–160.

Restinas, J., & Garrity, P. (1985). Nursing home friendships. *The Gerontologist, 25*, 376–381.

Schwartz, A. N., & Vogel, M. E. (1990). Nursing home staff and residents' families role expectations. *The Gerontologist, 30*, 49–53.

Van Nostrand, I. F. (1981). The aged in nursing homes: Baseline data. *Research on Aging, 3*, 403–416.

York, J. L., & Calsyn, R. J. (1986). Family involvement in nursing homes. In L. Troll (Ed.), *Family issues in current gerontology* (pp. 178–188). New York: Springer.

# PART IV

# ISSUES RELATED TO ABUSE

# 13 Feminist Approaches to Sexual Violence: A Discursive Analysis

Anne Eckman
Maria Mastronardi
*University of Illinois at Urbana-Champaign*

*For feminism is not a fixed state. It is an evolving and changing charter for a way of living.*
—Cheris Kramarae and Dale Spender (1992, p. 6)

*The world is a bigger, meaner, more complicated place than they ever told us, and . . . the tools for dealing with it are real but we have to make them up as we go along. One of the reasons I write is to show my sisters a few of the things I've learned and to take back from them the things that they can teach me.*
—Dorothy Allison (1993, p. 110)

Understanding and intervening in the contexts in which women encounter violence has been a central preoccupation for feminists. Over the years, feminists have challenged a variety of social systems—legal, economic, familial, representational—that have been implicated in fostering violence against women. Even though feminists have approached this issue from a variety of different perspectives and have utilized many different theoretical tools and methods for analysis, we would suggest that one of the common themes that unifies feminist analyses involves questioning the ways that myths work to reproduce gender-based systems of inequality (see Bullis & Bach, chap. 1 of this volume, for an in-depth discussion of feminist issues).

Myths constitute perhaps one of the most central communication practices that disenfranchise women who experience sexual violence. Williams (1985) explained that myths perpetuate beliefs in "fundamental expressions of certain properties of the human mind, and even of basic mental or psychological human organization. These expressions are 'timeless' (permanent) or fundamental to particular periods or cultures" (p. 212). In short, myths work by stripping a situation of the conditions that produced it. More specifically, when historical, economic, and political contexts are removed from discussions of sexual violence, women are often blamed for violence that is inflicted on them as well as silenced from articulating their experiences in meaningful ways. Vance (1989) explicated:

> A rag bag of myths and folk knowledge that the contemporary feminist movement opposed depicted male lust as intrinsic, uncontrollable, and easily aroused by any show of female sexuality and desire. The main features of this ideology have been roundly critiqued by feminists, primarily for blaming the female victim while letting men off the hook, but its corollaries are equally pernicious. If female sexual desire triggers male attack, it cannot be freely or spontaneously shown, either in public or in private. (p. 3)

Myths of an intrinsic female sexuality, which we explore further in our section Social Construction, have been, and continue to be, used to punish women who have been victims of sexual violence. Even today in Iraq and a number of Middle Eastern countries, a man can "with impunity kill any female relative he feels is 'dishonoring' him by unchaste behavior; in Pakistan, the jails are full of women and girls, some only 9 years old, whose crime was to be victims of rape" (Pollitt, 1994, p. 441). And, analysis of even more "progressive" societies similarly reveals a sustained reliance on perpetuating and reproducing these myths, as well as the tremendous force these myths exert on the lives of women (e.g., J. D. Hall, 1983; hooks, 1984; Morrison, 1992; Scholder, 1993). We have only to look at the spate of narratives mobilized around two recent examples we explore later in this essay—the Clarence Thomas–Anita Hill debacle or the amount of media space devoted to Katie Roiphe's attacks on rape prevention programs—to show the continued power with which myths work to deny women the legitimized spaces and resources to articulate their experiences of violence in satisfying, productive ways.

Feminist analysis, as this chapter shows, has been a crucial force in contextualizing sexual violence. The critiques that feminists have carved out work largely the way that Allison's (1993) quote suggests: that we make up our tools and our strategies as we go along, creating spaces in which we articulate our felt experiences and resist our oppression. More particularly, though, we create these tools because the available ones often work to render women's experiences invisible, legitimating ongoing inequalities—inequalities that are both the condition and the result of sexual violence's perpetration. We understand feminism, then, as a theory of contexts for understanding the complexities of women's lives. This grounding in the real relations of everyday life speaks to feminism's history as both a political movement as well as an epistemology. Like any discursive formation, feminist theory has a number of histories—in the academy, in the streets, in the home, wherever there are women—which has shaped its context for understanding women's experiences. (Theory is, after all, a way of explaining experience.) As a result of these multiple histories, feminism is more a dynamic ensemble of complex and often contradictory discourses than a monolithic body of knowledge.

Although the project of feminist analysis is inherently political, feminists have nonetheless taken many "necessary detours into theory," as S. Hall (1992, p. 283) called them, in order to help us to better comprehend our experiences. These detours are crucial steps for scholars who are committed to social change, as they help to get us farther down the road toward more successful interventions. Feminists realize, however, that much traditional theory is based more on myth than history, which makes appropriating theories a speculative endeavor indeed. As this chapter shows, when feminists appropriate existing theoretical tools, what results is often a reconfiguration so radical that the resulting theory is vitually unrecognizable from its predecessor. As Kramarae and Spender (1992) posited, "How could there be more than one truth in a system that admits only one without the system being undermined?" (p. 6). As we explore later, some feminists co-opted Marx's base/superstructure model, supplementing the economic base with patriarchy. This move, characteristic of American radical feminism of the late 1960s and early 1970s, significantly transformed Marx's analysis as it created new spaces for a political analysis of gender relations, with particular attention to violence against women.

Turning to feminism and sexual violence, it is important that we explicitly acknowledge that feminist analysis, like all analyses, can also produce its own myths. Analysis that claims that patriarchy alone—by which we mean, "a sexual system of power in which the male possesses superior power and economic privilege" (Eisenstein, 1979, p. 17)—can adequately account for sexual violence, has been a central site of contestation within feminist thought. Rubin (1993), whose work we consider when we discuss prosex feminism, argued that in fact sexual violence may be better explained via a theory of sexuality that, although intertwined with gender, constitutes a separate category of analysis. She would thus argue that feminist analysis that focuses on masculinized systems of power constructs its own myths about sexual violence.

Such self-reflexivity and self-critique is a hallmark of feminist thought. The results, as far as analytic tools provided, suggest that feminism affords a remarkably rich set of techniques and well-delineated questions for ongoing research on sexual violence. In order to make the most powerful use of feminism's tools, we need to clarify the different theories and practices that different feminist analyses have brought to bear on sexual violence. For the sake of convenience, we have appropriated Echols' (1989a) history and terminology to distinguish between radical feminism and cultural feminism, which forms the theoretical base for our section on social-constructionist feminism. We also include our commentary on antifeminism, which is not a feminist discourse, but that has, historically, positioned itself in opposition to its own reductive and opportunistic definition of feminism.

In order to address sexual violence as systematically as possible, we have asked of each perspective:

- How is sexual violence defined?
- What forms does it assume?
- What are identified as its causes?
- What effects of sexual violence are claimed and privileged?
- What are the key strategies for change?

Inevitably, by using these categories, we ourselves have forced generalizations that are not absolute. Although we have tried to indicate some of the tensions within these categories, we have inevitably glossed some. We recognize this tendency, hoping that these analyses provide an invitation, and perhaps a guide, for reading more deeply and using more thoroughly the tools that these critiques offer—a process that should reveal further tensions and, with luck, generate new ones.

Given the rich and complex theorizing, and the magnitude of work that feminists have produced over just the past 20 years, our history is necessarily incomplete and fraught with oversimplifications. We hope, however, that our approach will allow us to trace out, with some thematic consistency, the contexts from which different feminist perspectives on sexual violence emerged. As all discourse has more than one history, we encourage readers to explore these more comprehensive histories of feminism (Donovan, 1992; Echols, 1989a; Kauffman, 1993; Kramarae & Spender, 1992).

Because of the limited focus of this essay, our project begins with Second Wave Feminism, which is the name given to the 1960s revitalization of the feminist movement in Europe and the Americas (Kramarae & Treichler, 1985, p. 403).[1] The categories we are using to delineate feminist approaches

---

[1]We acknowledge the problematic ethnocentrism of this term. In fact, there have been many waves of feminism in many locations. Sarah (1982) reflected on the short-sightedness with labeling First Wave Feminism, which is often assumed to have begun with the Seneca Falls, New York, convention of 1848: "What does the brutal murder of nine million witches suggest to us about the scale of feminist resistance in the sixteenth and seventeenth centuries? Are we justified in fixing the 'first wave' between the mid-nineteenth century and the first two decades of the twentieth century? Timing the 'first wave' in this way, presupposes a particular political and economic context—the development of liberalism, capitalism and socialist movements in this period—which is only relevant for the feminist movements which developed in the western world. India, for example, subjected to British colonial rule and characterized by a different set of political and economic factors, experienced the 'high point' of her 'first wave' later" (p. 521).

to sexual violence emerged during this historical period. Many of the differences among current strands of feminist analysis involve either divergent approaches to theories or variance among which theoretical components to privilege. This first section addresses radical feminism and cultural feminism, and their impact on liberal feminism in the United States, as well as each strand's positioning with respect to violence against women. These feminisms provide a theoretical base for exploring more current feminist approaches, including social construction.

## RADICAL FEMINISM

This section discusses American radical feminism of the 1960s, whose extension of Marx's economic base resulted in conceptualizing gender as a class. This theoretical move politicized the unequal social relations between women and men as well as the social institutions that manifest this inequality, and allowed feminists to focus on the family as a site of social struggle. Millett's (1970) book, *Sexual Politics*, considered by many to be the tour de force of radical feminism, outlines its theory and political possibilities. In terms of theory, radical feminists insisted that biological differences between the genders do not adequately explain women's subordinate status. Asserted Millett, "Whatever the 'real' differences between the sexes may be, we are not likely to know them until the sexes are treated differently, that is, alike" (p. 39). Instead, radical feminists focused on politics, which Millett defined as "power-structured relationships, arrangements whereby one group of persons is controlled by another" (p. 31). With this emphasis on social relations, radical feminists created a space for assessing how violence against women is woven through the fabric of everyday life. Redstockings, a feminist group that was prominent in New York City, delivered the "First Manifesto" in 1969, from which this excerpt is taken:

> Women are an oppressed class. We are exploited as sex objects, breeders, domestic servants, and cheap labor. . . . Our prescribed behavior is enforced by threat of physical violence. Because we have lived so intimately with our oppressors, in isolation from each other, we have been kept from seeing our personal suffering as a political condition. This creates the illusion that a woman's relationship with her man is a matter of interplay between two unique personalities, and can be worked out individually. In reality, every such relationship is a *class* relationship, and the conflicts between individual men and women are political conflicts that can only be solved collectively. (Redstockings, 1969, in Kramarae & Treichler, 1985, p. 164)

By conceptualizing women's oppression as a political issue, Redstockings asserted the need for women to join together and resist. The "Manifesto" continues:

We regard our personal experience, and our feelings about that experience, as the basis for an analysis of our common situation. We cannot rely on existing ideologies as they are all products of a male supremacist culture. We question every generalization and accept none that is not confirmed by our experience. We identify with all women. We define our best interest as that of the poorest, the most brutally exploited woman. In fighting for our liberation, we will always take the side of women against their oppressors. We will not ask what is 'revolutionary' or 'reformist,' only what is good for women. (p. 164)

In order to fully grasp the significance of this manifesto, and of radical feminism in general, we need to take a brief detour into leftist politics, with particular attention to Marxism as it was experienced by women of the time. Radical feminists of the 1960s were responding to the sexism they experienced in what was commonly referred to as the "new left." Marx's approach to class analysis was useful for understanding economic relations that structure men into relationships with the means of production and therefore, with one other. However, radical feminists objected to Marx's neglect of women and their relationship to labor.

Marx had focused on how society's economic base (i.e., capitalism) structures human relationships. As Nicholson (1987) pointed out, ". . . Marx appears to be making the claim that the ways in which we produce food and objects in turn structures the manner in which other necessary human activities are performed" (p. 14). Marx's attention to food and objects, however, ignores much traditional female labor, such as raising children or nursing the sick. Because these activities did not contribute to the accumulation of capital, traditional Marxist theory had found them incidental at best. "Thus, if in capitalist society such activities as raising children or nursing the sick had been as easily conducive to making a profit, as became activities concerned with the production of food and objects, we might in turn believe that the manner in which human societies raise children or nurse their sick structure all other life activities in which they engage" (p. 20).

Many feminists found that by extending Marx—who never attended to gender as a significant factor in a person's relation to the economy—they could explore the relationship between gender and class. Whereas Marx maintains that social relations are determined by an economic base, radical feminists asserted that patriarchy, the system by which men exert power over women, should be relegated its own position as a base, and its own power to determine relationships between the sexes. Therefore, radical feminist analysis locates patriarchy as the outcome of divisions between men and women in the workforce and in the family. This move characterizes the beginnings of what later feminist theory refers to as a dual systems approach, in which patriarchy and capitalism exist as two interdependent systems (Hartmann, 1981; Nicholson, 1987).

In view of this theoretical positioning, the radical feminist analysis of sexual politics has consistently stressed that the sexual abuse of women is symptomatic of a wider oppression and control of women by men. Millett (1970) described sexuality, with variations along a continuum of masculine aggression (from the celebration of penetration to the brutality of rape) as the site in which male power and male supremacy are expressed. J. D. Hall (1983) elaborated on the project of radical feminism: "From the beginning flowed both an analysis that held rape to be a political act by which men affirm their power over women and strategies for change that ranged from feminist self-help methods of rape crisis centers to institutional reform of the criminal justice and medical care systems" (p. 341). Furthermore, because violence against women is only a part of a gender-based system of oppression, radical feminists took up a variety of political struggles around issues pertinent to sexual freedom and self-determination—including fighting for abortion rights, marital rape laws, and contraception.

The radical feminist offensive against rape and violence against women has opened spaces for current redefinitions of rape and for allowing women new sexual freedoms:

> We have redefined rape to include many sexual encounters that nineteenth-century feminists would have considered mere seduction, and for which they might have held the woman responsible; we have included in our definition of rape what was once normal marital intercourse. We have denied impunity to all men: we will bring charges against boyfriends, fathers, and teachers; we will label as sexual harassment what was once the ordinary banter of males asserting their dominance. We declare our right—still contested, viciously—to safety not only in our homes but in the streets. (DuBois & Gordon, 1989, p. 42)

Despite its hard-won political legacy, Echols (1989a) emphasized that the multitude of contradictory perspectives within the radical feminist movement eventually resulted in its decline and cultural feminism's ascendance. By the time Brownmiller's *Against Our Will: Men, Women and Rape* gained national attention in 1975, radical feminists were already irreparably fragmented. Although radical feminism had succeeded in pulling the National Organization of Women (NOW), the bastion of liberal feminism, to the left, inciting its current preoccupation with legal reform (Echols, 1989a), the movement itself had become increasingly unable to manage its contradictory elements.

The major contradiction involved interpretations of male supremacy, which some radical feminists insisted was rooted in biology. Although most radical feminists would agree that patriarchy was a gender-based system of power, they differed over the origins of male privilege. Firestone (1970) for instance, argued that the nuclear family is one development from a basic "biological family." She characterized the biological family as a reproductive unit and asserted that it rests on the following four "facts": (a) Women are at the mercy of their reproductive biology and are therefore dependent on men for survival, (b) human infants are dependent on adults for a long period, (c) a basic mother/child interdependency is universal, and (d) the natural reproductive division between the genders is the origin of all divisions of labor, economic and cultural classes, and possibly of castes. Similarly, this contradiction reveals itself in Millett (1970), who characterized men as a group who rule by "birthright"—in the same work in which she claimed, as we mentioned earlier, that we cannot know the differences between the genders, if there are any, until they are treated equally. Clearly, even radical feminism's early works contained the elements of its unraveling.

In contrast, Barrett (1988) has consistently maintained that male supremacy is not an essential characteristic of all societies. The facts of which Firestone (1970) spoke are "culturally and historically variable," she pointed out (p. 196). Barrett took issue with this biologic reduction as she critiqued the essentialism implicit in this use of the "family": "The 'family,' however, does not exist other than as an ideological construct, since the structure of the household, the definition and meaning of kinship, and the ideology of 'the family' itself have all varied enormously in different types of society" (p. 213). Hence, the categories of men and women (as opposed to males and females) are socially and ideologically constructed, rather than naturally given, but they are in a real sense historically "there" as "concrete collectivities" (p. 213). Here, Barrett noted biological determinism's ahistorical reliance on myths, which has come to be a defining feature of cultural feminism. By emphasizing the differences between males and females, and linking these differences to biology, this line of thought leads to an inevitable focus on intrinsic and distinct male and female systems of value.

This emphasis on biological determinism shifted the ground from defining sexual violence against women as a political expression to an essential characteristic of masculinity. Barrett (1988) explained, "An analysis of sexuality in terms of male supremacy, with no real understanding of the construction and meaning of heterosexual femininity as it is experienced by a majority of women today, can lead to a political position of radical lesbian separatism" (p. 47). It is here that cultural feminism, with its focus on separate male and female "cultures," becomes a dominant paradigm. In the next section, we explore cultural feminism, which, for a number of reasons whose explication are beyond the scope of this chapter, had become the dominant paradigm for American feminists by the late 1970s. Cultural feminism, as we show, departed from radical feminism's call for active political opposition to patriarchy as it created its own female counterculture.[2]

## CULTURAL FEMINISM

Cultural feminism seems to be at one end of the current polarization of discourses we would consider feminist, with prosex feminists situated at the opposite end. Feminist historians generally agree that this polarization occurred around debates over pornography, which grew out of an early 1970s antirape movement. In order to best contextualize this debate, which is crucial for understanding current feminist positionings with respect to sexual violence, we shift the ground of our critique for a brief history of the antiporn movement.

In the early 1970s, the first rape crisis centers and rape hotlines opened across the country, materializations of the rapidly growing antirape movement.[3] Although providing a needed service to women, when the Feminist Alliance Against Rape gained prominence in 1974, feminists acknowledged the additional need to confront cultural attitudes about women that perpetuate rape. The antirape movement, then, inspired politically motivated attention to representations of women, especially sexual representations. In 1976, Women Against Violence Against Women (WAVAW), a Los Angeles-based group, forced Warner Brothers to remove the infamous Rolling Stones billboard ("I'm black and blue from the Rolling Stones and I love it."). This victory, which secured a discursive space for feminist groups critical of mass media, allowed such groups to define their project as the "eradication of rape" (Lentz, 1993, p. 389).

After 1976, feminist antipornography groups became an increasingly powerful political force as they solidified their claim that popular representations of women and pornography cause rape. This move resulted in shifts in meaning and practice among feminists, which can be exemplified in the changing role of the "Take Back the Night" march. Hunter (1986) pointed out that "Take Back the Night" marches originated with an antirape/antiviolence theme: "The march sought to dramatize women's insistence on the right to enjoy public space in safety" (p. 27), which was a central preoccupation of radical feminism. Lederer (1980) further illustrated this point: " 'Take Back the Night' was a profound symbolic statement of

---

[2]For a more detailed account of the decline of radical feminism and the ascent of cultural feminism, see Echols (1989a).

[3]Lentz (1993) provided an excellent history and analysis of these debates in her article, "Female Revenge and Guns," from which we borrow heavily.

our commitment to stopping the tide of violence against women in all arenas—and our demand that the perpetrators of such violence—from rapists to batterers to pornographers—be held responsible for their actions and made to change" (p. 5). By the late 1970s, however, antiporn groups appropriated the "Take Back the Night" theme: In 1978, 5,000 feminists attending a conference on "Feminist Perspectives on Pornography," marched through San Francisco's porn district (Hunter, 1986).

Cultural feminists began constructing causal linkages between representations of women in pornography and real acts of violence against women. MacKinnon (1989) maintained that the "objectification" of women in pornography both reveals and promotes male sexuality's inherent brutality:

> To be sexually objectified means having a social meaning imposed on your being that defines you as to be sexually used, according to your desired uses, and then using you that way. Doing this is sex in the male system . . . If sex is a social construct of sexism, men have sex with their image of a woman. Pornography creates an accessible sexual object, the possession and consumption of which is male sexuality, to be possessed and consumed which is female sexuality. (p. 140)

As this passage indicates, cultural feminists have forged a causal correlation between pornographic representations and the social practice of male sexual violence. This theoretical move has engaged cultural feminists in tireless battles to censor pornography. Over the past 10 years, cultural feminists have fought for legislation that would criminalize pornography production and distribution, in the belief that these laws would prevent rape. Dworkin and MacKinnon, for example, cosponsored an amendment to the Minneapolis Civil Rights Ordinance in 1983. This amendment would have included pornography as gender discrimination on the grounds that pornography promotes violence against women. Although the Minneapolis city council passed the ordinance, Mayor Donald Fraser later vetoed it (Lentz, 1993, p. 392). A similar amendment was passed in Indianapolis in 1986, although later declared unconstitutional.[4] Bright (1994) cautioned on the far-reaching implications of the recently passed obscenity statute in Canada: ". . . thousands of books and magazines [are] being banned, including authors like me, Kathy Acker, David Leavitt and even . . . Andrea Dworkin. (A Canadian customs official took one look at Dworkin's title, *Woman Hating*, and, dumbly using MacKinnon's criterion of banning anything that 'degrades women,' refused the book entry.)" (p. 39).

Aside from censorship's potential implications, Lentz (1993) pointed out that "the anti-porn position . . . constructs 'men', 'women', 'sexuality', and

---

[4]Part of this ordinance was used in a Senate bill called the Pornography Victims Protection Act, introduced in a 1985 Congressional Session by Senator Arlen Specter (R-PA).

'male power' in static, reified ways" (p. 390). These constructions tend toward binary oppositions, with women as victims and men as brutalizers. In order to prevent men from inflicting violence on them, women submit to the laws of patriarchy, which involves participating in marriage, child-bearing, and childrearing—and ultimate deference to male authority in all social practices. Dworkin (1983) asserted that women submit to male authority in order to gain protection:

> From father's house to husband's house to a grave that still might not be her own, a woman acquiesces to male authority in order to gain some protection from male violence. She conforms, in order to be as safe as she can be. Sometimes it is a lethargic conformity, in which case male demands slowly close in on her, as if she were a character buried alive in an Edgar Allan Poe story. . . . Women know, but must not acknowledge, that resisting male control or confronting male betrayal will lead to rape, battery, destitution, ostracization or exile, confinement in a mental institution or jail, or death. (pp. 14–15)

So, women's fear of men's potentially violent behavior renders them mystified, incapable of articulating their oppression because of patriarchy's absolute stranglehold on their physical and mental comportment. Despite this somewhat pessimistic construction of women, by the late 1970s cultural feminism had evolved into a distinct theoretical approach, and as such it began to develop its own epistemology, which was made manifest in Daly's (1978) book, *Gyn/Ecology*. Morris (1988) pointed out that "*Gyn/Ecology* is probably the most important and influential single work to come out of the women's movement since Kate Millett's *Sexual Politics*" (p. 28). Dis-cursively aligned with the work of Dworkin and MacKinnon, Daly asserted that women are subordinated by a "State of Rapism," and *Gyn/Ecology* attempts to trace out its historical and mythic roots. Her work inverts many of Western civilization's sacred tropes, which she reconfigured through the lens of the "State of Rapism." Hence, all social structures and cultural products can be understood through their direct link with the universal male urge to subjugate females. For example, in an inversion of Freud, *Gyn/Ecology* maintains that men have constructed elaborate systems that oppress women because they envy women's reproductive capacity, which they, of course, lack: "The male sense of barrenness, then, breeds hierarchical structures of violence, epitomized in war. . . . Such organized aggression/violence of males filled with fear of their own emptiness and weakness is carried out against women in concrete acts of rape, dismem-berment and murder" (p. 361).

Ironically, Daly (1978) supported her thesis of an ahistoric, universal "State of Rapism," through an attempt at historical analysis, locating wars as the ultimate manifestation of men's attempts to compensate for their biological dearth. In addition, she maintained that rape stories in ancient Greek and Roman myths further substantiate her view—that patriarchy has always violated women: "The rape of the goddess in all her aspects is an almost universal theme in patriarchal myth" (p. 84). Rape, she continued, has been a tool men have always used in order to maintain social structures that constrain women. Daly authenticated this claim by reading a number of Western civilization's myths, including Christianity, via the lens of this "State of Rapism": "In the charming story of the 'Annunciation,' the angel Gabriel appears to the terrified young girl, announcing that she has been chosen to be the mother of god. Her response to this sudden proposal from the Godfather is total nonresistance: 'Let it be done to me according to thy word.' Physical rape is not necessary when the mind/will/spirit has already been invaded" (p. 85). The effect of locating rape within one of the most sacred myths of the Christian tradition is undeniably heretical. Yet, given the causal premise of her argument—that women submit in order to prevent rape—for Daly, it is impossible to interpret this story any other way. Rape has moved out of the realm of physical violence and here, as with Dworkin earlier, it can be used as theory.

This perspective, as we mentioned previously, is the site of bitter contestation and rigid polarization within American feminism today. Although we align ourselves with the theoretical and political project of prosex feminists, we do believe that cultural feminist work is important for several reasons. First, cultural feminists have consistently emphasized structures through which women are oppressed. Whether or not their premises are accurate, violence against women is structurally enforced by discourses and practices that constrain our ability to resist in meaningful ways. Finding and using more sophisticated analytic tools to assess the complexity of these structures is an ongoing project for feminist social constructionists, whose work we explore throughout the rest of this chapter. Second, cultural feminists have also maintained that rape is never a woman's fault. Even though men are demonized in this discourse, removing all blame for sexual violence from women is a subversive and necessary move, as our next section's feminist historians show. And third, although we find their strategies and tactics misdirected for the most part, cultural feminists have exhibited a passionate activism that we find inspiring. In addition, it is not commonly recognized among prosex feminists that some work by cultural feminists has resulted in significant legal gains for women. MacKinnon's (1979) legislative efforts to curtail sexual harassment in the workplace have resulted in legal precedents that we tend to take for granted today.

Nevertheless, cultural feminism has been soundly critiqued by women who have expressed alienation from its core beliefs. According to hooks (1984), the basis for this movement is a common oppression, which obscures the role that many women have in perpetuating racism and classism:

So far feminist movement has primarily focused on male violence and as a consequence lends credibility to sexist stereotypes that suggest men are violent, women are not; men are abusers, women victims. This type of thinking allows us to ignore the extent to which women (with men) in this society accept and perpetuate the idea that it is acceptable for a dominant party or group to maintain power over the dominated by using coercive force. It allows us to overlook or ignore the extent to which women exert coercive authority over others or act violently. (p. 118)

Here, hooks challenged feminists to explore the complexities of sexual violence, which necessitates a critical look at our own participation in narratives that promote violence against one another. She continued: "While we need not diminish the severity of the problem of male violence against women or male violence against nations or the planet, we must acknowledge that men and women have together made the United States a culture of violence and we must work together to transform and recreate that culture. Women and men must oppose the use of violence as a means of social control in all its manifestations" (p. 130). It is this call for complex analysis, for analysis that can account for the contradictions of oppression, that has led some feminists to social construction.

## SOCIAL CONSTRUCTION

Since the woman's movement began its analysis of sexual violence in the early 1970s, feminist criticism has developed another set of analytic perspectives that rely on the theoretical concept of the social construction of meaning. The social construction of meaning, although an umbrella term for a variety of approaches and perspectives, can be broadly taken as an understanding that systems of meanings shape the possibility of people's actions and that people's actions, in turn, shape these meanings. In Fisher's (1987) words, "The world as we know it is a set of stories that must be chosen among in order for us to live life in a process of continual recreation" (p. 65). To interpret these interpretations, then, today's social constructionist feminists make use of a variety of sophisticated theoretical tools, many of which have been appropriated from critical theory. One of the most important interpretive practices for feminists today involves exploring the complex and contradictory ways that women are constructed in discourse. Discursive analyses have offered profound insights into the historical and contextual complexity of women's experiences of violence.

By discursive, we mean, in a general sense, any regulated system of statements (Henriques, Holloway, Urwin, Venn, & Walkerdine, 1984). This definition can, of course, apply to everything that can be said and runs the risk of being too all-inclusive and too imprecise.[5] However, we can say that discourse is a body of ideas that is regulated by its own set of rules for what can and what cannot be said, and for what counts and what does not count as knowledge. "In practice, discourses delimit what can be said, whilst providing the spaces—the concepts, metaphors, models, analogies—for making new statements within any specific discourse" (Henriques et al., 1984, p. 106). These rules, or ideologies, often appear as "natural" extensions of a society's common sense, and therefore they are difficult to pinpoint, difficult to resist and contest, and even more difficult to change. Morris (1988) commented that, "If the politics of language debates seems invisible, it is in part because verbal language is the most intensely naturalized—i.e., transparent—mode of social control at work in our culture" (p. 34). Eagleton (1991) expanded on this naturalizing function of ideology: "Ideology is language which forgets the essentially contingent, accidental relations between itself and the world, and comes instead to mistake itself as having some kind of organic, inevitable bond with what it represents" (p. 200). Language's relation to social control is transparent because we, for the most part, consent to the way language structures us as subjects. Thus, this "forgetting" stems from social forces, or power, that structure our conceptions of ourselves and our world, usually without our realizing it. Teresa de Lauretis (1984) expanded on Foucault to explore the role of power in shaping discourse: ". . . power is a productive force that weaves through the social body as a network of discourses and generates simultaneously forms of knowledge and forms of subjectivity, or what we call social subjects" (p. 35). These forms of knowledge, power, and subjectivity become sites of analysis when we explore the connection between women and sexual violence.

In particular, many narratives that deny sexual violence are deployed so that women are not even permitted to articulate their experience of sexual violence. Feminist analyses of the social construction of violence, therefore, are interested in what discourses define rape, and how these definitions vary in different contexts. In shifting the focus of analysis to discourse, feminist analyses are not denying the concrete physical and emotional effects that sexual violence inflicts on women. These analyses do, however, privilege analyzing the discursive processes that structure how sexual violence is communicated about. Critical theorists will often position "the discursive" and "the material" as distinct cultural arenas, with discursive referring to cultural texts and products, and material referring to

---

[5]Part of the difficulty in precisely delimiting discourse has to do with its theoretical history stretching from semiotics to Derrida to Deleuze and to the histories of knowledge that Foucault has attempted in examining the emergence and functioning of the human sciences. For a thorough and reader-friendly discussion of the use of discourse in the social sciences and critical theory, see Henriques et al. (1984, pp. 105–118).

the practices whereby people physically act out their relation to the real conditions of their existence. Clearly, though, at some point it becomes difficult to differentiate between the two, as they are so complexly inter-related. Whereas most critical theorists would agree that changes in one terrain are often reflected by changes in the other, we hesitate to imply that there is a necessary correspondence between the discursive and the material. The relations between the two are constantly changing (Eagleton, 1991). Cultural feminists, as we have discussed, tend to elide any distinction between the two, which results in their contention that physical acts of violence against women can be reduced to representations of violence against women. Although discursive analyses are necessarily complex, we believe that the practice is crucial because it allows us to examine relations of power contextually, or as they are constructed through language. Given that sexual violence, and the power to define it as such, operates within a political field, its definition has been used to discipline women and others who are disenfranchised, often in ways that further restrict the linguistic capital needed to produce alternate accounts to gain the material conditions necessary to oppose sexual violence. Discursive processes thus regulate access to changing the meanings of sexual violence, so to better acknowledge and cohere with the needs and experiences of women. And thus, changing discursive practices are a necessary condition for changing human actions.

Feminists who use social construction to analyze sexual violence do build upon radical and cultural feminist analyses of sexual violence. They take as their starting point these claims so fiercely fought for by the woman's movement: that sexual violence is pervasive, that it is structured by and perpetuates social inequality, and that this resulting inequality systematically silences women's ability to contest sexual violence. The goals of feminists who use social construction to analyze sexual violence thus are also similar to those of cultural and radical feminists: to analyze the systems that allow the domination necessary for sexual violence to continue in order to (a) recognize and explore women's experiences of sexual violence, and (b) work to redefine institutions and systems so that they legitimate, rather than elide, the reality of women's experiences.

Social construction analysis of sexual violence, however, directs its attention to analyzing the *different* discursive structures that interlock to produce sexual violence. Social constructionists thus do not attribute sexual violence to any one underlying cause. Rather, they argue that different discursive structures intersect to produce specific constructions of sexual violence and ways of communicating about them. Despite their shared commitment to the goals of eradicating oppression and sexual violence, feminists who use social construction nevertheless critique assumptions central to radical and cultural feminism. Social constructionists argue that, contrary to the theories proposed by cultural and radical feminists, sexual violence cannot be sufficiently explained by one underlying system that is universal and ahistorical. Hennessy (1993) noted, "The challenge is to find ways to anchor feminist analysis in our recognition of the continued brutal force certain social totalities like patriarchy and racism still exercise, at the same time acknowledging that the social construction of 'woman' is never monolithic" (p. xi). In theoretical terms, many social constructionist perspectives rely on linking a Marxist-influenced assessment of the ways women are positioned with respect to the means of economic production with a poststructuralist emphasis on the importance of language as a socializing tool that has, historically, constructed "woman" as a discursive category.

In this emergent understanding of sexual violence, the work of feminist social historians has been key to substantiating that, in fact, different discursive practices have produced different conditions for different women. Concurrently, this body of work seeks to excavate these practices, many of which still structure current discussion of sexual violence. So, for example, historical analysis challenges Brownmiller's (1975) thesis that, since the time of the first men and women, rape has been used to secure male patriarchy through the myth that women's safety depends on male protection. It instead reveals that this myth was invented at a particular point in history. Specifically, historian Anna Clark (1987) shows in her analysis of late 18th- and early 19th-century Britain that "the protection racket of rape only became privileged when sexual danger increasingly became used to restrict women's freedom" during the early 1800s (p. 2). Although women were undeniably the victims of sexual violence prior to the early 19th century, it was only in the early 1800s that newspapers read by middle-class women first reported rape and, thus, it was only in the early 1800s that rape started functioning as a myth warning women to stay at home where their man would keep them safe. Such analysis concludes, therefore, that patriarchy has not produced the same effects over time and, more germane to our discussion of sexual violence, that rape has not always served the same mythic functions.

Social construction leads to a second important conclusion: that the history of rape is driven not just by the motor of patriarchy, but also by the gears and sprockets of other oppressions. For instance, Clark's (1987) work shows that the invention of rape as a myth of warning depended on a very particular social and class formation—the emergence of private and public spheres with the rise of the bourgeoisie. In the early 1800s, with the development of urbanization and industrialization, middle-class city women had the leisure time to engage in activities not related to domestic work. For rape to keep these middle-class women from pursuing activities other than traditional domestic work, the invention of the private sphere provided a place to contain these women where their potential independence could not threaten middle-class male feelings of authority—feelings themselves being challenged by a labor system in which most men now were no longer their own bosses. In addition, as narratives of popular middle-class newspapers represented the lower class as "teeming masses" of urbanization, the protection myth relied on a specific narrative of class—that of the lower class as potentially violent.

Historical studies of the social construction of sexual violence also show that, far from sexual violence universally silencing women, feminists have organized against sexual violence; feminists have—depending on the time and place—engaged in transformative contests for meaning in order to redefine how sexual violence was labeled and responded to. At the same time, these actions are circumscribed by the particular conditions constructing sexual violence and communication about it. For instance, not only was sexual violence against women different for women of different classes, but the possibility of women opposing sexual violence also varied with class. Clark (1987) showed that working-class radicals who opposed capitalism during the late 1700s popularized accounts of rich factory owners raping working-class women. This strategy did successfully rehabilitate the image of the working class. However, this narrative of rape was driven by the drama of class war—a drama that afforded working-class women little opportunity to distinguish between coercion and seduction in their relationships with factory owners, much less to articulate the reality that most working women's rapes were perpetuated by working men.

These analyses reveal a marked similarity over time, then, in the conclusion that women have been directly affected physically and mentally by the perpetration of sexual violence, and have had their space and resources in society consistently curtailed via direct sexual violence and the myths that surround it. They reveal, even more critically though, that the processes by which these patterns have been determined depend on the social, political, and economic conditions at the time, and that the effects of these constructions also vary with these different conditions both within and over time. In light of the multiple systems of domination that interlock to produce and sustain when, where, and how, and by whom rape is communicated about, social constructionists argue that analysts who reduce the causes of sexual violence to one underlying force do more than make a theoretical error. Social constructionists, in showing that Brownmiller's (1975) understanding of patriarchy omits identifying other systems that maintain and gain power through the perpetration of sexual violence, would charge her analysis with perpetuating a myth that itself can help to perpetuate sexual violence. Although her analysis allows for difference in laws over time, and raises issues of race, it ultimately approaches these as "variables" that can be subsumed under one underlying cause of all sexual violence—the ability for men to gain control over women's bodies by virtue of the biological fact that they possess penises.

Effective strategy for change thus depends on analyzing the discourses at work based both on historical patterns and on contemporary politics; the historians offer the means by which to better understand the complexities in the past and, in so doing, to suggest the outlines of the present. In particular, they have also laid the groundwork for two other approaches to sexual violence that rely on social construction to analyze sexual violence—that of women of color and prosex feminists.


## WOMEN OF COLOR


Women of color[6] emphasize that the dominant understanding of sexual violence has been based on the experiences of middle-class White women. Given that White women's experiences are necessarily also a narrative of race, White women's formulations of sexual violence have themselves served to legitimate, or at least leave unexamined and unchallenged, the dynamics of sexual violence in the lives of women of color. To do so, women of color specifically analyze the ways that narratives of race and gender have been woven together to produce sexual violence, especially in ways that sexual violence is used to legitimate and perpetuate racism and sexism. Women of color thus emphasize, in their definition of sexual violence, that "rape was not simply an act of violence, but a sexual story that men [and White women, too] told that legitimated other forms of violence" (Snitow, Stansell, & Thompson, 1983, p. 328).

By not understanding the way that race has interlocked with narratives of sexual violence, feminists have often perpetuated the racism central to the sexual violence perpetuated against women of color. Brownmiller's (1975) feminist analysis of the Black male rapist as having a stronger drive to rape than most White men because he is more disenfranchised and therefore has a greater need to display his masculine power relies upon, and perpetuates, the racist mythology invoked to justify lynching. By ignoring the way that racism structures sexual violence, White feminists have ignored that constructions of sexual violence against White women—con-

---

[6]We acknowledge the potential problems with this term. In 1984, the Modern Language Association's Commission on the Status of Women reported that some women suggest that "women of color" obscures diversity and specificity and lumps all racial and ethnic groups together, thus facilitating the tendency in language to universalize and to position discourses with respect to a mythic White experience (in Kramarae & Treichler, 1985, p. 499). We use the term, however, to demonstrate the significance of critiques made against feminism's tendency to refer to its subject as a White, middle-class woman. As Moraga and Anzaldua (1981) pointed out in their edited collection, "We are women from all kinds of childhood streets: the farms of Puerto Rico, the downtown streets of Chinatown, the barrio, city-Bronx streets, quiet suburban sidewalks, the plains, and the reservation" (p. 5).

structions in which women participated—have often fueled violent racist acts against Black men and continued sexual violence against Black women.[7]

For this reason, women of color who address sexual violence do so with reference to the lynching perpetuated by White men against Black men. As Snitow et al. (1983) noted in their introduction to "The Mind That Burns in Each Body: Women, Rape and Racial Violence," women of color insistently ground their analyses in the fact that "in the post-Reconstruction South, rape—an act of violence against women's bodies—was inseparable from lynching—an act of terror against men's. Both were necessary to a society that upheld not just men's control over women, but white men's control over white and black men and women" (p. 328). In the words of J. D. Hall (1983), understanding lynching allows us to begin "to understand the web of connections among racism, attitudes toward women, and sexual ideologies. The purpose of looking more closely at the dynamics of repressive violence is not to reduce sexual assault and mob murder to static equivalents but to illuminate some of the strands of that tangled web" (p. 331).

The practice of lynching became widespread, as the preceding quote indicates, at precisely the time that Black men and women were free for the first time in U.S. history (Davis, 1981). Between 1882 and 1946, almost 5,000 people died of lynching. At the point that Black men were legally empowered to self-determination, White Southerners began a new regime of systematic mob terror against Blacks that inflicted obscene physical and psychic damage on Black people. Violence thus served materially and symbolically to disempower Black men and women, who could now lay legal claim to enfranchisement. And a Black man did not experience sexual violence solely as one accused of having perpetrated it. For instance, the gruesome, sexually explicit details of a 1934 lynch mob's actions against a Black man were graphically described in the press at that time. J. D. Hall (1983) thus noted that "such incidents did not have to occur often, or to be witnessed directly, to be burned indelibly into the mind" (p. 329).

Lynching successfully restricted Black people's access to public space and power in the Reconstruction South. It also furnished a host of images that, condensed in the myth of the Black male rapist, continue to be deployed against Black men. Davis (1981) noted that accusing a Black man of raping a White woman anchored the justification of lynching, even though a study published by the Southern Commission on the Study of Lynching shows that between 1889 and 1929 only one sixth of the mob victims were actually accused of rape. By reviewing newspaper accounts and public records, Davis argued that the specter of a Black man raping a White woman continued to provide the cultural fuel necessary to con-

---

[7]See, especially, Angela Davis' "Rape, Racism and the Myth of the Black Rapist," in her 1981 edited collection.

tinuing legitimating such violence. As of 1967, of the 455 U.S. men put to death for rape between 1930 and 1967, 405 of them were Black (Davis, 1981). When looking at the fact that today more identified rapists are Black than White, Davis noted that we must question the identity of the remaining 80% of rapists who go unapprehended—especially given the relative empowerment of Black and White men, both in access to institutional power and discursive structures (such as the culturally constructed role of the protector of a White woman vs. that of her rapist).

That sexual violence against people of color has been the result of racism as well as sexism may explain, argued Davis (1981), why most Black women have not joined the women's movement antirape organizing that has privileged patriarchy as its theoretical frame. The conjunction of the two also explains the form of organizing that the earliest organized Black women's groups engaged in. Given that, as Lerner (1972) wrote, "the myth of the black rapist of white women is the twin of the myth of the bad black woman—both designed to apologize for and facilitate the continued exploitation of black men and women—black women perceived this connection very clearly and were in the forefront against the fight against lynching" (p. 174). Mary Church Terrell organized the National Association of Colored Women (NACW) in 1896 and it took as one of its main missions the cessation of lynching. At the same time, "at the core of essentially every activity of NACW's individual members was a concern with creating positive images of black women's sexuality"—images, already negatively constructed through the structures of slavery, which lynching further compounded (Hine, 1990, p. 295).

Under slavery, the ritual sexual abuse of Black women had been maintained—and maintained via not only the legal argument that Black women were property of White men, but under the essentialization of Black women as naturally "promiscuous." Constructing Black men as sexually dangerous to White women produced the corollary that their "usual" Black female partners were automatically promiscuous and available to any sexual advances, thereby further reinforcing the assumption that Black women were sexually promiscuous and thus legitimately available to any White man who so desired. In addition, Black women were themselves often the object of the rape and then lynching by White men—another dimension of lynching's context elided by the overriding image that lynching was about Black men's sexual transgressions against White women.

Such history, in addition to illuminating the way that racism and sexism combined to oppress Black men and women to the advantage of White men, indicates the degree to which the construction of middle-class White women as sexually innocent rested on, and perpetuated, racist ideology. The option to stay inside a domestic space—ideologically coded as safe—was not an option for African-American women. Most African-American women worked outside the sphere of their own home; ironically, in fact, many African-American women worked inside the homes of White people[8] under whose roof White men's (the father as well as his son's) access to Black women was considered part and parcel of her employment. In addition, the narrative grounds upon which claiming oneself had been the victim of sexual violence rested on the image of a besmirched madonna. To have access to this image White women needed to adhere to the dictates of middle-class domesticity, circumstances not only undesirable but also unavailable to many White women; Black women, however, by virtue of their essentialized sexuality, were assumed by definition to never be able to meet this category.[9] In the process, an ideology of race as a naturalized essence resulted (Giddings, 1992). And this process continues today:

> That respectable journals would make connections between green monkeys and African women, for example, or trace the origins of AIDS to African prostitutes—the polluted organs of black women—reveals our continued vulnerability to racist ideology. It tells us that concepts of racial difference (in this situation, sexual practices) can still be used as weapons of degradation, and that the idea turns on sexuality, and sexuality, in this culture, is loaded with concepts of race, gender, and class. (p. 457)

The positioning of Black women's sexuality as fundamentally unvirtuous and fundamentally central to securing racial difference has, and continues to, make access to discursive spaces to discuss either sexuality or sexual violence very difficult for Black women. In addition to the directly repressive effects of sexual violence on Black men and women, Hine (1990) explored the discursive strategies that Black women developed to contest sexual violence. With regard to the NACW, "to counter negative stereotypes, many black women felt compelled to downplay, even deny, sexual expression" (p. 295). Hine saw this desexualized discourse as part of a larger "culture of dissemblance . . . that created the appearance of openness and disclosure but actually shields the truth of their inner selves from their oppressors" (p. 292). Hine continued, "Only with secrecy, thus achieving a self-imposed visibility, could ordinary women accrue the psychic space and harness the resources needed to hold their own and often one-sided and mismatched resistance struggle" (p. 295).

Thus, argued Hine (1990), many of the experiences of sexual violence have gone unreported by Black women. Hine cited White (1985) in support of her argument that purposefully little about Black women's lives has been

---

[8]Angela Davis (1981) noted that on the eve of World War II, 59.5% of employed Black women were in domestic service (p. 98).

[9]For a detailed analysis of this discursive history, see the work of Gilman (1985) on the Venus of Hottentot, and Collins' (1991) subsequent commentary.

revealed: "Black women have also been reluctant to donate their papers to manuscript repositories. This is in part a manifestation of the black women's perennial concern with image, a justifiable concern born of centuries of vilification" (p. 294). Hine concluded that "undoubtedly, these fears and suspicions contribute to the absence of historical discussion of the impact of rape (or threat of rape) and incidence of domestic violence on the shape of black women's experiences" (p. 294).

Within the literature that has addressed lynching, this dissemblance has often resulted, argued Hine (1990), in a "misplaced emphasis" on the effects of lynching on Black men—noting their emasculation as the central effect of both lynching and the rape of Black women, and that White men's access to Black women was thus primarily a way to destroy Black men's sense of manhood. Although important, these accounts ignore questioning the effects of lynching and sexual violence on Black women. The larger discursive framework in which Black men and women are so persistently vilified—and whereby much of this vilification continues to employ the myths of the Black male rapist for racist ends—has also severely limited discussion of the sexual violence that Black men perpetuate against Black women. Women of color who have spoken out on such issues bear the censure of the Black community (Giddings, 1992), as well as the disbelief of White audiences who will not grant Black women the moral status necessary to be raped.

The consequences of so little articulated space for Black women were writ large in the confirmation hearings of Clarence Thomas. In the words of Crenshaw (1992), "as television, the Clarence Thomas/Anita Hill hearings played beautifully as an episode right out of 'The Twilight Zone' " (p. 402). "But," she elaborated:

> it was no "Twilight Zone" that America discovered when Anita Hill came forward. America simply stumbled into the place where African-American women live, a political vacuum of erasure and contradiction maintained by the almost routine polarization of "blacks and women" into separate and overlapping camps. Existing within the overlapping margins of race and gender discourse and in the empty spaces between, it is a location whose very nature resists telling. (p. 403)

Crenshaw's analysis of discourses of feminism and race solidarity shows that not only did neither adequately represent Anita Hill's testimony, but ultimately they worked against each other and the possibility of Anita Hill articulating her own experiences: "Because she was situated within two fundamental hierarchies of social power, the central disadvantage that Hill faced was the lack of available and widely comprehended narratives to communicate the reality of her experiences as a black woman to the world" (p. 404). The central tropes through which the hearings became read, and into which Hill's testimony was fit, were those of "rape" offered by White feminists and "lynching" offered by the Black community. Crenshaw showed that although the rape motif adequately portrayed Hill's experience of sexual harassment and certainly her experiences of having the burden of proving her virtue put on trial, feminist narratives could not account for the extra burden of proof put on Hill by virtue of her race. Similarly, within the Black community, lynching has so great a resonance and connection with Blacks' oppression by Whites that Black women's experiences of sexual violence are subsumed under this narrative. Noted Crenshaw:

> To the limited extent that sexual victimization of black women is symbolically represented within our collective memory, it is as tragic characters whose vulnerabilities illustrates the racist emasculation of black men. . . . Hill, had she been so inclined, could have invoked only vague and hazy recollections in the African-American memory, half-digested experiences of black female sexual abuse that could not withstand the totalizing power of the lynching metaphor. (p. 418)

We are left with the conclusion, then, that we must understand the "intersections" of race and class and gender and whatever else is at work in sexual violence so that these oppressions are recognized and responded to in total. When we do not, analyses work against each other. And all those who do not fit into a dominant trope, or who might fit into more than one, remain out in "The Twilight Zone": "When feminism does not explicitly oppose racism, and when anti-racism does not incorporate opposition to patriarchy, race and gender politics end up being antagonistic to each other and both interests lose" (p. 405). And so, too, does the woman lose: "In this sense, both feminist and anti-racists told tales on Anita Hill, tales in which she was appropriated to be everybody's story but her own" (p. 406).

## PROSEX FEMINISTS

Prosex feminists select as the particular pattern and narrative of disenfranchisement an examination of the intersection of, primarily, pleasure and danger in ways such that (a) narratives of women's sexual desires have consistently been silenced via an emphasis on sexual danger for all acts not anchored in White, middle-class monogamous marital heterosexuality, and (b) how such narratives of sexual desire are key to disrupting the myths that perpetuate sexual violence. More specifically, within the narrative of sexual violence popularly articulated by cultural feminists, prosex feminists have contested the assumed linkage of sexuality with "restriction, repression, and danger" (Vance, 1989, p. 1). Instead, they argue, "sexuality is simultaneously

... a domain of exploration, pleasure and agency. To focus only on pleasure and gratification ignores the patriarchal structure in which women act, yet to speak only of sexual violence and oppression ignores women's experiences with sexual agency and choice and unwittingly increases the sexual terror and despair in which women live" (Vance, 1989, p. 1).

In so opposing the restriction of female sexuality through an emphasis on danger to the exclusion of possible pleasure, prosex feminists argue against cultural feminist assumptions about sexuality. Stated Echols (1989b):

> Cultural feminist sexual politics really offer us nothing more than women's traditional sexual values disguised as radical feminist sexual values. Moreover, these values derive . . . from our powerlessness. . . . Rather than develop a feminist understanding of sexual liberation, cultural feminists reject it as inherently anti-feminist and instead endorse a sexual code which drastically circumscribes the sort of sexual expressions considered acceptable. And, in demanding "respect," rather than challenging the terms upon which women are granted "respect," cultural feminists reinforce the distinction between the virgin and the whore. . . . More importantly, this view suggests that sexual repression is a satisfactory solution to violence against women. (p. 65)

Instead of accepting cultural feminists' proscription that safety for women exists in repression of sexuality, Vance (1989) suggested that feminism must speak to sexuality as a site of oppression, not only through sexual violence but also through the repression of women's sexual desires.

The key to opposing a reified construction of both male and female sexuality, and thus to opening up exploration of pleasurable sexuality, is the belief that sexuality, like sexual violence, is socially constructed. As Vance (1989) elucidated:

> Much feminist work on sexuality starts from the premise that sex is a social construction, articulated at many points with the economic, social, and political structures of the material world. Sex is not simply a "natural" fact, as earlier, essentialist theories would suggest. Although sexuality, like all human cultural activity, is grounded in the body, the body's structure, physiology, and functioning do not directly or simply determine the configuration or meaning of sexuality. . . . Without denying the body, we note that the body and its actions are understood according to prevailing codes of meaning. (pp. 7–8)

Theorists who rely on social construction to analyze women's sexuality thus argue that although both gender and sexuality overlap and reinforce each other, "sexuality is not a residual category, a subcategory of gender; nor are theories of sexuality fully adequate to account for sexuality. [Rather,] the task is to describe and analyze how cultural connections are made between female bodies and what comes to be understood as 'women' and 'female sexuality' " (Vance, 1989, pp. 9–10).[10]

Prosex feminists focus on women's desires first to help empower women to explore that which has been denied via dominant constructions of sexuality—"that female desire should be restricted to zones protected and privileged in culture: traditional marriage and the nuclear family" (Vance, 1989, p. 3). Outside of these bounds, women's sexuality has been portrayed as morally corrupt and medically unsafe. Cultural feminist discourse, in its focus on male sexuality as inherently violent and female sexuality as inherently whole and passive, has precluded women from themselves exploring the complexity and contradictions that structure our desires. To quote Echols (1989b) again:

> The solution is not to reprivatize sexuality or eschew a critical analysis of sexuality. . . . Instead, we need to develop a feminist understanding of sexuality which is not predicated on denial and repression, but which acknowledges the complexities and ambiguities of sexuality. Above all, we should admit that we know far too little to embark upon a crusade to circumscribe it. Rather than foreclose on sexuality, we should identify what conditions will best afford women sexual autonomy, safety and pleasure, and work towards their realization. (p. 66)

In addition to the self-muting that has limited women's access to exploring their sexuality—both in the dominant matrix of good and bad girl sexuality and in the essentialized sexuality presented by cultural feminists—prosex feminists also show that specific constructions of female sexuality often work to produce narratives that justify other ongoing oppressions. Narratives of sexuality constitute a vector of oppression that interlock with other oppressions and, in the process, produce and perpetuate sexual violence. Therefore, exploring female sexuality—and reclaiming the public space to do so—is an important means to contesting mechanisms of oppression. For instance, Vance (1989) noted that "although the boundaries of the safe zone have been somewhat renegotiated since the nineteenth century to include relatively respectable forms of unmarried and non-procreative heterosexuality, gross and public departures from 'good' woman status, such as lesbianism, promiscuity, or non-traditional heterosexuality still invite—and are thought to justify—violation" (p. 4).

Prosex feminism, specifically, takes as its cause a very specific conjunction in which cultural feminist notions of sexuality were, they feared, too easily

---

[10]Gayle Rubin (1993) elaborated very thoroughly both the common false assumption that prohibit fully understanding and using a cultural construction approach to sexuality and the problematic tendencies of assuming that systems of gender, sexuality, capital, and so on, can be collapsed into each other. See, especially, pages 11–20, 35–45.

appropriated by conservative politics. In support of this claim, prosex feminists have both inspired and used the work of social historians who investigate the social construction of sexuality and, in particular, the discourses that feminists in the past have used to contest sexual violence. In particular, prosex feminists draw a parallel between the strategies of contemporary cultural feminists who rely on narratives of women's sexuality as solely constituted in and through male violence as a way to enact legislation and late 19th-century feminists who argued against prostitution.

In the late 19th century, prostitution formed the privileged site for feminist analysis of male sexual coercion where "the symbolic emphasis in prostitution is on ownership, possession, purchase by men" (DuBois & Gordon, 1989, p. 33). In terms of conceptualizing this danger, Walkowitz (1986) noted that the first feminists who organized against prostitution emphasized the material conditions that contributed to their use of sex work for money. However, noted Walkowitz, in order to get widespread public support these feminists focused their narratives on tales of prostitutes' victimization by male vice to the detriment of noting "the artificial constraints placed on women's social and economic diversity" that caused women to take up prostitution as "the best paid industry" (p. 422).

Such an emphasis denied the "prostitutes" a position as agents making the best choices possible in a set of oppressive conditions and, for the feminists who produce this plot of sexual victimization, such a focus on male lasciviousness rested on their denying women's sexual expression in a public sphere. As a result, when feminist arguments to regulate the conditions that resulted in prostitution became institutionalized, institutions used their power to seek out and discipline women's displays of sexuality in public. More often than not, these transformed meanings were often rearticulated to justify disciplining working- and lower-class women, often immigrants or African Americans and often young, who, by virtue of using public spaces for work and for leisure, were by definition in need of regulation. Organizations that originally emphasized the social and economic conditions that necessitated women's work as prostitutes gave way to a series of institutionalized laws and reform programs that further disenfranchised women.[11] Concluded Walkowitz (1983):

---

[11]Prostitution, once a temporary occupation for women as they moved on whether to other employment and/or marriage, became a permanent profession because increased police scrutiny caused working-class people to avoid regular socializing/contact with these now surveyed women (Walkowitz, 1983, 1986). Similarly, age of consent laws that raised the legal age of intercourse in order "to protect" young women's virtue were used both by authorities and families to regulate young women's sexual activities (Odem, 1995) and the spaces within cities that young women occupied were sites that could justify the "search and seizure" of any woman who frequented them (Odem, 1995; Peiss, 1983; Schlossman & Wallach, 1978; Stansell, 1987).

> In their defense of prostitutes and concerns to protect women from male
> sexual oppression, feminists were limited by their own class bias and by their
> continued adherence to a separate sphere ideology that stressed women's
> purity, moral supremacy, and domestic virtues. Moreover, they lacked the
> cultural and political power to reshape the world according to their own
> image. Although they tried to set the standards of conduct, they did not
> control the instruments that ultimately enforced these norms. (p. 434)

Given that constructions of vice and virtue, even (especially) by feminists, are themselves contingent upon social, political, and economic forces, two conclusions emerge. First, the narratives that feminists use are susceptible to being rearticulated to conservative ends, especially given that most feminists lack institutional power. Second, in light of this, feminists need to be especially careful that the narratives of sexuality they construct work to contest sexual repression as well as oppression, given that sexual repression lends itself so well as a site onto which other oppressions latch.

Contemporary prosex feminists specifically argue against what they view as a replay of earlier "social purity" politics of sexuality.[12] Specifically, prosex feminists oppose the anti-pornography movement. As we discussed in our section on cultural feminism, the anti-pornography movement grew out of the early seventies anti-rape movement. As rape crisis centers became established, feminists expanded their interventions to include opposing cultural attitudes against rape. In the process, antiporn feminists began to focus on sexual representations of women and increasingly argued that the root of sexual violence lay in pornography and the pornographers who produced it. Prosex feminists find several faults with the assumptions behind antipornography feminists' construction of sexuality. First, antiporn feminists' arguments rest on a notion of sexuality totally controlled by male aggression and domination and, as a corollary, on the assumption that women can not have a relationship to sexual representations, porn or otherwise, that might include pleasure as well as danger. Lentz (1993) noted that this assumption rests on false premises that absolutely disavow women's implication in, and use of, violence:

> The anti-porn position attempted to convince us that women have nothing
> to do with violence; that they have no access to violent practice—whether
> that "violence" be consensual and playful (as in S/M practices), actual physical
> brutality, or discursive violence directed towards others (as in the elision of
> women of color from critiques of rape). But, . . . the feminist critiques of
> the anti-porn position have had a profound and positive effect upon the
> politics of feminist theory and practice precisely because they have shown us

---

[12]For one of the most complete and aggressive challenges by prosex feminists, see the interventionist collection by Ellis, Hunter, Jaker, O'Dair, and Tallmer (1986).

that women cannot be conveniently removed from positions of violence by being women. (p. 394)

Prosex feminists further argue that such a construction of sexuality has afforded a rich set of images for scapegoating the New Right which, too, has an interest in a passive victimhood construction of sexuality and, in the process, has elided the consideration of other areas that contribute to sexual violence. Vance (1990) commented on the Meese Commission on Pornography's construction of sexuality:

> Although they presented their program under the guise of feminist language and concerns, their abiding desire was to reestablish control by restricting women—and their desires—within the ever-shrinking boundaries of the private and the domestic. . . . Unmasked, too, was the commission's primary aim: not to increase safe space for women, but to narrow what can be seen, spoken about, imagined, and—they hope—done. . . . In the face of false patriarchal protections embedded in shame and silence, feminists need to assert their entitlement to public speech, variety, safety, and bodily and visual pleasures. (p. 131)

In addition, the Meese Commission constructed deviance in the form of pornographers to deflect investigation and regulation by the state of male perpetrators within the family. The Meese Commission worked to keep the White middle-class family man positioned as a bastion of moral rectitude among multiple, violent perversities. Early in the hearings, the Commission was considering enforcing stringent laws to prosecute those who sexually abused youths. The Commission, however, promptly dropped provision for such enforcement and turned its attention, instead, to targeting child pornographers for indictment. The cause of this sudden change of heart? The Commissioners realized that "the perpetrator was often grandpa" (Vance, 1992).

Thus, not only do narratives of sexual danger preclude women's explorations of a significant set of experiences, but these narratives provide easy scripts with which to legitimize other vectors of oppression.[13] In terms of intervening against sexual violence, per se, prosex feminists who rely on the cultural construction of sexuality still are left with a few more don'ts than dos. For, having noted the multiple ways that sexual violence is constructed and deployed, it becomes much more difficult to unite women's rage successfully into political opposition to sexual violence:

---

[13]Other instances where narratives of sexual abuse are deployed to deflect other perpetrators are detailed both by Nathan (1991), who argued that current focus on ritual sexual abuse at day-care centers have as a subtext that these children would be safe had they been left at home, thus reinscribing the myth that child sexual abuse is perpetrated by all but the father, and by Warren (in progress), who examined the recent spate of media coverage of patient-therapist sex where the perpetrator-therapists exposed have been women.

Feminists have not yet found a form of political activism against rape which is both emotionally satisfying and which avoids a dangerous reliance upon the fantasy of perfect agency, sexual panic, and a centralized white experience. . . . In order to have a successful political movement, we must not only mobilize theories of women's oppression, but we must also mobilize women's pleasures. Political subjects cannot find the necessary and sufficient motivation and optimism to effect political change without them. (Lentz, 1993, p. 398)

To be able to identify and oppose sexual violence, while at the same time not essentializing it, is the struggle that feminists need to continue to engage in. In the process of this struggle, argue prosex feminists, we must not give up our exploration of sexual pleasure in hopes that it will provide some clarity or more solid grounds from which to oppose sexual violence. Contemporary and past incidents suggest that, instead, such ceding of grounds results in further fuel for oppression. These incidents, only a few of which we have described, also provide the outlines of unresolved tensions that feminists still struggle to intervene in and understand. As historians DuBois and Gordon (1989) illuminated:

It would be easier if we could progress towards sexual liberation without sufferings, if we could resolve the tension between seeking pleasure and avoiding danger by simple policy; but we cannot. We must conduct our sexual politics in a real world. For women this is like advancing across a mined field. Looking only to your feet to avoid the mines means missing the horizon and the vision of why the advance is worthwhile; but if you only see the future possibilities, you may blow yourself up. (p. 42)

The tentative conclusion to be drawn from these feminist analyses that draw upon social construction thus is not that radical and cultural feminists who have emphasized the pervasive nature of women's domination through sexual violence were wrong. They are right—especially for the important space opened up for addressing the structural inequalities that are the conditions of, and are in turn sustained by, sexual violence. But they are not right enough—to capture the ways that systems interlock to make sexual violence and sexual pleasure much more far reaching and complex in its effects in women's lives and in the strategies needed, in turn, to challenge such dominations. Just as significantly, understanding the various systems brought to bear in perpetuating and maintaining sexual violence hints at the various and nuanced experiences women have had with regard to sexual violence—nuances not allowed via the categories dominantly inherited and, arguably, via the categories that other feminists have offered. It also reveals the outlines of the multiple strategies, discursive and material, that regulate such exploration and expression of "subordinated" experiences.

## ANTIFEMINISM

In this chapter we have emphasized that discourse has a political history that structures our ability to intervene in productive ways. With regard to sexual violence, each step feminists have made toward creating discursive spaces and improving material conditions has been fraught with opposition. Feminists and their political agenda have been caricatured, co-opted, misrepresented, and demonized by much of the mainstream press. As American studies scholar Cynthia Kinnard (1986) observed in her bibliography of American antifeminist literature, journalistic attacks against women's rights "grew in intensity during the late 19th century and reached regular peaks with each new suffrage campaign" (p. xiii). The arguments were always the same: Equal education would make women spinsters, equal employment would make women sterile, equal rights would make women bad mothers. With each new historical cycle, the threats were simply updated and sanitized, and new "experts" enlisted (in Faludi, 1991).

In more recent times, Phyllis Schlafly and the conservative right fueled public hysteria over their hyperbolized consequences of the Equal Rights Amendment. Women, they threatened, would be hurt more than helped by equal rights. Women would be drafted and would be forced to share public bathrooms with men (e.g., see Amiel, 1980). Ironically, the bathroom scare seemed to be articulated with women's fears of sexual violence, and feminists were blamed for putting women's lives in danger. These scenarios served to shift the discursive terrain from useful discussions of the hard-won and well-deserved benefits of equal rights as feminists were forced to defend themselves against allegations that they were trying to harm women. Instead of the possibilities that this amendment would provide, feminists were forced to defend their very existence. In this way, discursive spaces were closed down.

With respect to feminism, the conservative tendencies of the mass media follow structural patterns. Faludi (1991) pointed out that what she called the antifeminist trend in the mass media displays certain key features: "The trend story is not always labeled as such, but certain characteristics give it away: an absence of factual evidence or hard numbers; a tendency to cite only three or four women, typically anonymously, to establish the trend; the use of vague qualifiers like 'there is the sense that' or 'more and more' . . ." (p. 81).

It is in this context that we turn to current attacks on feminism. In the past year, Katie Roiphe's (1993) book, *The Morning After: Sex, Fear and Feminism on Campus*, has been a media sweetheart, garnering covers on *Time* and *Newsweek*, as well as innumerable favorable reviews in much of the mainstream press.

Briefly, Roiphe (1993) maintained that feminist "propaganda" on rape serves to disempower women as it emphasizes women's vulnerability and weakness, rather than choice and strength. Her argument offers a conservative articulation of a feminist antivictim perspective by using rhetoric that sounds eerily similar to that of prosex feminists. However, her "antivictim" rhetoric serves to shut down spaces that feminists have fought for, whereas prosex feminists have consistently struggled to make even more spaces available for women in which to articulate their sexualities. Specifically, Roiphe asserted that date-rape prevention purportedly squelches sexual inquisitiveness, that seminars and pamphlets on date rape generate a hysterical amount of fear and self-censorship among women students, and that feminism on campus closes off more discussion than it opens up. She maintained that women in powerful places should not have problems with discrimination; rather, they should get a sense of humor.

Needless to say, this attack on feminism dovetails with the discursive history of the representation of feminism in the mass media. Many feminists have already taken Roiphe (1993) to task for her "slapdashery of research" (Pollitt, 1993) and for her failure to adequately explore feminist research on sexual violence. Roiphe's overarching claim that, "The crisis is not a rape crisis, but a crisis in sexual identity" (p. 27) contradicts women's own reports of sexual violence. The National Women's Study, conducted by the Crime Research & Treatment Center at the Medical University of South Carolina, working under a grant from the National Institute of Drug Abuse, found that 13% of adult American women—one in eight—have been raped at least once, 75% by someone they knew. This study used the conservative legal definition of rape: "an event that occurred without the women's consent, involved the use of force or threat of force, and involved sexual penetration of the victim's vagina, mouth or rectum" (Pollitt, 1993, p. 222). Faced with these brutal statistics, how can the threat of sexual violence not be a serious concern for all women?

We do not plan on refuting each of Roiphe's (1993) claims;[14] however, we do want to emphasize that her work shifts the discursive terrain in much the same way that Phyllis Schlafly's did in 1978, even though many of her claims are based on impressionistic reflections that contradict the facts about women and violence. Her arguments are that rape education makes women paranoid, that speak-outs make women weak, that feminist theory makes women ugly.

Roiphe's (1993) historical vacuity manifests itself most clearly in her discussion of the "Take Back the Night March and Speak-Out." As we

---

[14]For a detailed analysis of Roiphe's (1993) "uncritical use of self, agency and desire," see Ring (1994).

emphasized earlier, these marches were fueled by women's demands for public safety. Nevertheless, not only did Roiphe imply that women lie when they describe their experiences of sexual violence, she also displayed a complete lack of understanding about the historical need for such events:

> A girl tells of being raped by a Frenchman when she was traveling in Europe. Several girls describe sexual violence in distant lands and foreign languages. A few tell of being molested by a relative. Someone tells of being raped in another country *and* (sic) being molested by a relative.
> The strange thing is that as these different girls—tall and short, fat and thin, nervous and confident—get up to give intensely personal accounts, all of their stories begin to sound the same. Listening to them, I hear patterns begin to emerge. The same phrases float through different voices. Almost all begin "I wasn't planning to speak out tonight but . . . ," even the ones who had spoken in previous years. They talk about feeling helpless, and feeling guilty. Some talk about hating their bodies. The echoes continue: "I didn't admit it or talk about it." "I was silenced." "I was powerless over my own body." (p. 33)

Roiphe's callous dismissal of the legitimacy of these stories simply because they follow a pattern reveals a shocking lack of context for understanding the significance of this event. First, narrative consistency does not imply that the stories are not true. Rather, as this chapter has argued, consistency points to the limited descriptive and narrative strategies available to women to describe their experiences of sexual violence. Second, without the gains made by feminism, the contexts in which women can collectively speak about their experiences would be much more circumscribed today. As de Lauretis (1984) pointed out, feminism, "the historical practice of the women's movement and the discourses which have emerged from it—such as collective speaking, confirmation, and reconceptualization of a female's experience of sexuality" (p. 34) has created spaces for women to transform their experiences. Speak-outs provide women with an institutionalized space to speak out about their experiences, and, more important, to transform these experiences into expressions of power.

Roiphe's (1993) dismissal of the empowerment women gain from participating in speak-outs reveals more about her active ignorance of feminist interventions. In addition, her book conveys the message that many people—especially men—want to hear, "that sexual violence is anomalous, not endemic, to American society, and appearances to the contrary can be explained away as a kind of mass hysteria, fomented by man-hating fanatics" (Pollitt, 1993, p. 220). Women, however, do need more creative outlets for expressing their sexuality without fear. As many feminists have already cautioned, part of the power of danger discourse is that it prohibits women from creating a subjective space to discuss sexual pleasure.

## ACTION AND ACTIVISM

In terms of communication about women's health and sexual violence, then, feminist analyses suggest the following. The challenge, and call to action, is to expose, deconstruct, and reconstruct the seemingly awesome set of narratives that rely on—and constitute—women's subordination. More particularly, it involves understanding how these narratives mutually reinforce one another. Our examples forcefully show that when we have sexual violence perpetuated against us, the range of narrative possibilities available to voice such violence are incredibly circumscribed. To be recognized and allowed to author anything close to a women's own story, one needs to fit within the bounds of acceptable narratives for a plethora of categories—such as gender, race, ethnicity, sexuality, class, age, and whose wife or daughter you are—each contingent upon interpretive strategies that women, themselves, have historically had little access to shape. These acceptable narratives are further determined by who perpetuates sexual violence and whether available interpretive frameworks will permit such a perpetrator to be held culpable for his actions.

In terms of empowering women, perhaps this is both the most sobering and exciting task opened up by a feminist analysis of sexual violence. That of knowing to listen to what may be remembered but not always articulated in all its contradiction and complexity—and of developing the tools to begin to subvert more publicly the discursive structures that would preclude hearing these other knowledges. In keeping with the chapter's emphasis on communication practices about sexual violence, we want to remind readers that what has not been public is not necessarily not there—that women, indeed, have been engaging in many actions to empower themselves. Women have developed multiple strategies for communicating about sexual violence in ways that may resist (without directly challenging) the conditions of their violation. We, therefore, want to offer an admittedly cursory look at the ways that women have publicly subverted, or at least interrupted, narratives.[15]

For many women writers, the act of writing itself breaks one of the most profound narratives that perpetuates sexual violence: that because a woman is by definition "sullied" by the sexual violence done to her, she may not speak of it without legitimately expecting further sexual violence. Allison (1993) wrote of her experience of transgression—and danger—as she began to write even for an audience of one:

---

[15]These textual productions work similarly to the AIDS activist art that Douglas Crimp (1989) commented on. Specifically, Crimp argued that AIDS activist art gains its value from neither of two commonly assumed "political uses of art"—those of raising money for research or of representing some transcendent truths about AIDS. Rather, AIDS activist art is comprised of "Cultural practices actively participating in the struggle against AIDS" (p. 7).

I was taught never to tell outside the family what is going on, not just because it's shameful but because it is literally physically damaging and dangerous to you. . . . I didn't start writing, or at least I didn't start keeping the writing, until 1974 when I published a poem. Everything I wrote before then—ten years of journals, ten years of poems and short stories—I burned because I was afraid someone would read them. And always in the back of my mind there were my mother's whispers: They'll send you to detention, you'll wind up in the county home. You don't want to do that. (p. 108)

Other narratives outline the profound disruption that speaking these experiences pose to the dominant myths of sexual violence. Living in a home where both she and her cousin are sexually abused by their grandfather, Carla Kirkwood related how the kidnapping, rape, and murder of Donna Marie—a young woman who epitomized the image of wholesome girlhood—reconfigured *her* understanding of the split between home and public: " 'I wonder if Grandpa did it? What do you think?' Then she laughed. I told her to shut up. I didn't want to talk about it. And, no, I didn't think grandpa did it. 'Yeah, you're right, lots of people could have done it.' . . . I wanted to cry, but I didn't. I was scared. Now, going outside would never feel like being free, like being safe from the inside, safe from this house" (in Scholder, 1993, p. 10).

Other women who have opposed narratives of sexual violence have done so by employing different strategies—depending on how, where, and who regulates these spaces—to reclaim spaces deemed unsafe or unlegitimate arenas for the displays of female sexuality. Carby (1990) elaborated on the space that Black women's blues carved out for narratives of Black women's sexuality. With regard to the actual performances that Black women gave, Carby commented, "the women blues singers occupied a privileged space; they had broken out of the boundaries of the home and taken their sensuality and sexuality out of the private into the public sphere" (p. 247). She illustrated this point with singer Bessie Smith's "Young Woman Blues":

Woke up this morning when the chickens were crowing for day.
Felt on the right side of my pillow, my man had gone away.
On his pillow he left a note, reading I'm sorry you've got my goat.
No time to marry, no time to settle down.

I'm a young woman and ain't done running around.
I'm a young woman and ain't done running around.
Some people call me a hobo, some call me a bum,
Nobody know my name, nobody knows what I've done.
I'm as good as any woman in your town,
I ain't no high yella, I'm a deep killa brown.

I ain't gonna marry, ain't gonna settle down.
I'm gonna drink good moonshine and run these browns down.
See that long lonesome road, cause you know its got a end.
And I'm a good woman and I can get plenty men. (p. 247)

Similarly, women today continue to demand a safe public space for expressing their sexualities. "Sluts Against Rape," a grass-roots group in Champaign-Urbana, Illinois, marches in sexually provocative clothing at "Take Back the Night" rallies—in order to claim sexual pleasure publicly while, at the same time, demanding an end to sexual violence against all women. Their "Manifesto" reads, in part, "We are feminists. We call ourselves 'Sluts Against Rape' because we believe that a woman has the right to be sexual in any way she chooses and that she is never at fault for rape. We choose to focus on promiscuity—straight or queer—as a positive assertion of sexual identity and to focus on women as sexual agents as opposed to sexual victims" (Sluts Against Rape, 1991).

Artist Carla Kirkwood's public art project conveys a similar interventionary spirit. Her project began in February, 1992, with the unveiling of two billboards bearing the enlarged photograph of Donna Gentile with the letters "N. H. I." Gentile, a sex worker as well as a police informant, was the second victim in a string of murders in San Diego. The letters, "N. H. I.," stand for "No Humans Involved," a term law-enforcement officials use to label sexual assaults that result in the murder of a prostitute. In San Diego, from 1985 to 1992, 45 women who were sexually assaulted and murdered were given such a label, and the crimes against them were ignored by law-enforcement authorities. "These were misdemeanor murders, biker women and hookers . . . we'd call them N. H. I.'s—no humans involved," a San Diego police officer explained to *The Sacramento Bee* (in Scholder, 1993, p. 43). In a grass-roots attempt to carve out a discursive space in this extremely dense terrain, Carla Kirkwood displayed a billboard-size enlarged photograph of what could be Donna Gentile's high school yearbook picture. Two days after this billboard went up, a group of public artists rented a storefront gallery in downtown San Diego in order to display portraits representing the 45 women. The title of the exhibition was M. W. I.—Many Women Involved.

Elizabeth Sisco, one of the participating artists, commented, "Since we are conditioned to believe that violence and death are known occupational hazards for sex workers, we respond to their demise with apathy or a resigned willingness to blame the victim, to accept the murder of a prostitute as one of life's harsh realities. At the same time, we are relieved that such brutality could never be visited upon those of us who comply with social mores" (in Scholder, 1993, p. 43). By focusing on the faces of the women, this group of activist-artists attempted to humanize the victims and demonstrate that violence against any woman is unacceptable. By waging a discursive battle, or a battle at the level of representation, they attempted to redefine the terms of the discourse that would, ultimately, create possibilities for changing material conditions. As the hijackings by these and other feminist activist artists such as Barbara Kruger reveal, such subversion depends centrally on taking back narrative practices—be they the usual purposes of billboards or the existing language of advertisements—in order to challenge their naturalized narratives and to open the space for new ones.


## NOTES FOR A FUTURE RESEARCH AGENDA

> Yet we know that the fear of rape is real; it is the illusion of safety that is false. Understanding the myth of rape as warning as a historical creation helps us to defy it; defying the reality of sexual violence is a more difficult, but necessary, endeavor.
> —Anna Clark (1987, p. 134)

In this chapter, we have taken as our focus feminist analyses of sexual violence. These analyses, regardless of their profound differences, consistently and collectively delineate how those who are disenfranchised lack access to both material and discursive resources. These analyses also show how fundamental sexual violence is to disenfranchisement. Women's unequal access to material and discursive resources provide the conditions that perpetuate sexual violence. In turn, sexual violence, both in the material and psychic damage done directly to women and in the effects of its myths, perpetuates women's marginalization.

Almost all the aforementioned feminists would thus agree that Roiphe's (1993) argument, and the mass media's coverage of it, have given new life to a traditionally debilitating myth of sexual violence: If women would just "lighten up" and not be duped by feminist analyses, women would not need to be afraid of sexual violence. Such a myth ignores feminist analyses that have worked to claim sexual pleasure for women. Perhaps more important, it ignores the history of actions taken against women who have sought pleasure. In so doing, Roiphe seems unaware of how much her argument discredits the feminist claim, made simultaneously with women's claiming of sexual agency, upon which her legitimated space of sexual agency rests: that we need to expose and fight the sexual violence used to deny women access to spaces—including sexual pleasure—in which women have traditionally been exiled or, at least, subordinate.

Thomas (1994) noted a similar problematic within a different area—the gains fought for and by women journalists, gains often unrecognized, but relied upon, by younger women in the newsroom. She remarked on Molly Moore who "on the face of it is one of those lucky young women" (p. 139). Thomas said, with regard to Moore's book *A Woman at War*, much of what we would like to say about Roiphe:

> I wanted more about the woman and less about the war, especially at moments such as the one in which Moore, as a journalist, was allowed to go to the battlefield while the soldiers who had to share their tent with her were obliged, because they were women, to stay behind. I wanted more introspection and reflection. In this, I was disappointed.
>
> As she left to ride to the front lines with the commanding general, Moore remarked to her tent mates: "It just doesn't seem fair, does it?" (p. 235)
>
> The women soldiers gave her the same response I would: "Watch yourself. Be careful out there." (p. 325)

As we consider communication and sexual violence, we need to be especially careful to delineate the structures that produce danger, while encouraging that all women who want to go to the front lines can. To approach this task, it is crucial that we avoid, as Fine (1993) argued, "the individualistic research bias that extracts women and men from their social contexts" (p. 278)—a bias that "has inadvertently invaded the study of violence against women, yielding unfortunate consequences for social theory and social movements" (p. 278). If, as Fine further suggested, "the most basic knowledge we need is of how social and economic institutions sustain and multiply the kinds of violence women experience" (p. 286), feminist analyses of sexual violence offer analytic tools central to doing so.

## ACKNOWLEDGMENTS

We would like to thank our advisor, Larry Grossberg, for his thoughtful feedback on this chapter, and for his continuing support of our work. We would also like to acknowledge the scholars we have been privileged to work with at the University of Illinois: Jesse Delia, Lisa Duggan, Cheris Kramarae, Leslie Reagan, and Paula Treichler. Finally, we thank Noshir Contractor for taking the time to read through this chapter and for helping us to make it accessible to a more general audience.

## REFERENCES

Allison, D. (1993). Forum III: Self-revelation: The art of rewriting personal history. In A. Scholder (Ed.), *Critical condition: Women on the edge of violence* (pp. 107–110). San Francisco: City Light Books.

Amiel, B. (1980, July 14). Let's raise the spectre of unisex washrooms—and all that implies. *MacLeans*, p. 49.

Barrett, M. (1988). *Women's oppression today: Problems in Marxist feminist analysis.* London: Verso.

Bright, S. (1994, March 7–20). The prime of Miss Catharine MacKinnon. *In These Times*, pp. 38–39.

Brownmiller, S. (1975). *Against our will: Men, women and rape.* New York: Bantam.

Carby, H. (1990). It jus be dat way sometimes: The sexual politics of women's blues. In E. C. DuBois & V. L. Ruiz (Eds.), *Unequal sisters: A multi-cultural reader in U.S. women's history* (pp. 238–249). New York: Routledge.

Clark, A. (1987). *Women's silence men's violence: Sexual assault in England, 1770–1845.* London: Pandora Press.

Collins, P. (1991). *Black feminist thought: Knowledge, consciousness, and the politics of empowerment.* New York: Routledge.

Crenshaw, K. (1992). Whose story is it, anyway?: Feminist and anti-racist appropriations of Anita Hill. In T. Morrison (Ed.), *Race-ing justice, en-gendering power: Essays on Anita Hill, Clarence Thomas and the social construction of reality* (pp. 402–440). New York: Pantheon.

Crimp, D. (Ed.). (1989). *AIDS: Cultural analysis/cultural activism.* Cambridge, MA: MIT Press.

Daly, M. (1978). *Gyn/ecology: The metaethics of radical feminism.* Boston: Beacon Press.

Davis, A. (1981). *Women, race and class.* New York: Random House.

de Lauretis, T. (1984). *Alice doesn't: Feminism, semiotics, cinema.* Bloomington: Indiana University Press.

Donovan, J. (1992). *Feminist theory: The intellectual traditions of American feminism.* New York: Continuum.

DuBois, E. C., & Gordon, L. (1989). Seeking ecstasy on the battlefield: Danger and pleasure in nineteenth-century feminist sexual thought. In C. S. Vance (Ed.), *Pleasure and danger: Exploring female sexuality* (2nd ed., pp. 31–49). London: Pandora.

Dworkin, A. (1983). *Right-wing women.* New York: Perigee.

Eagleton, T. (1991). The (body) politics of feminist theory. *Phoebe, 3,* 56–63.

Echols, A. (1989a). *Daring to be bad: Radical feminism in America 1967–1975.* Minneapolis: University of Minnesota Press.

Echols, A. (1989b). The taming of the id: Feminist sexual politics, 1968–1983. In C. S. Vance (Ed.), *Pleasure and danger: Exploring female sexuality* (2nd ed., pp. 50–72). London: Pandora.

Eisenstein, Z. (Ed.). (1979). *Capitalist patriarchy and the case for socialist feminism.* New York: Monthly Review Press.

Ellis, K., Hunter, N. D., Jaker, B., O'Dair, B., & Tallmer, A. (Eds.). (1986). *Caught looking: Feminism, pornography and censorship.* New York: Caught Looking, Inc.

Faludi, S. (1991). *Backlash: The undeclared war against American women.* New York: Crown.

Fine, M. (1993). The politics of research and activism: Violence against women. In P. B. Bart & E. G. Moran (Eds.), *Violence against women: The bloody footprints* (pp. 278–287). Newbury Park, CA: Sage.

Firestone, S. (1970). *The dialectic of sex: The case for feminist revolution.* New York: Morrow.

Fisher, W. R. (1987). *Human communication as narration: Toward a philosophy of reason, value and action.* Columbia: University of South Carolina Press.

Giddings, P. (1992). The last taboo. In T. Morrison (Ed.), *Race-ing justice, en-gendering power: Essays on Anita Hill, Clarence Thomas and the social construction of reality* (pp. 441–470). New York: Pantheon.

Gilman, S. (1985). Black bodies, white bodies: Toward an iconography of female sexuality in late nineteenth-century art, medicine, and literature. *Critical Inquiry, 12*(1), 205–243.

Hall, J. (1983). "The mind that burns in each body": Women, rape, and racial violence. In A. Snitow, C. Stansell, & S. Thompson (Eds.), *Powers of desire: The politics of sexuality* (pp. 328–349). New York: Monthly Review Press.

Hall, S. (1992). Cultural studies and its theoretical legacies. In L. Grossberg, C. Nelson, & P. Treichler (Eds.), *Cultural studies* (pp. 277–295). New York: Routledge.

Hartmann, H. (1981). The unhappy marriage of Marxism and feminism: Towards a more progressive union. In L. Sargent (Ed.), *Women and revolution* (pp. 1–41). Boston: South End Press.

Hennessy, R. (1993). *Materialist feminism and the politics of discourse.* New York: Routledge.

Henriques, J., Holloway, W., Urwin, C., Venn, C., & Walkerdine, V. (1984). *Changing the subject: Psychology, social regulation and subjectivity.* New York: Methuen.

Hine, D. C. (1990). Rape and the inner lives of women in the Middle West: Preliminary thoughts on the culture of dissemblance. In E. C. DuBois & V. L. Ruiz (Eds.), *Unequal sisters: A multi-cultural reader in U.S. women's history* (pp. 292–297). New York: Routledge.

hooks, b. (1984). *Feminist theory: From margin to center.* Boston: South End Press.

Hunter, N. (1986). The pornography debate in context. In K. Ellis, N. D. Hunter, B. Jaker, B. O'Dair, & A. Tallmer (Eds.), *Caught looking: Feminism, pornography and censorship* (pp. 26–29). New York: Caught Looking, Inc.

Kauffman, L. (Ed.). (1993). *American feminist thought at century's end: A reader.* Cambridge, MA: Blackwell.

Kinnard, C. D. (1986). *Antifeminism in American thought: An annotated bibliography.* Boston: G. K. Hall.

Kramarae, C., & Spender, D. (Eds.). (1992). *The knowledge explosion: Generations of feminist scholarship.* New York: Teachers College Press.

Kramarae, C., & Treichler, P., with Russo, A. (1985). *A feminist dictionary.* London: Pandora.

Lederer, L. (1980). Theory and practice: Pornography and rape. In L. Lederer (Ed.), *Take back the night: Women on pornography* (pp. 1–16). New York: Bantam.

Lentz, K. M. (1993). The popular pleasures of female revenge. [Rage bursting in a blaze of gunfire]. *Cultural Studies, 7*(3), 374–405.

Lerner, G. (Ed.). (1972). *Black women in White America: A documentary history.* New York: Vintage.

MacKinnon, C. A. (1979). *The sexual harassment of working women.* New Haven, CT: Yale University Press.

MacKinnon, C. A. (1989). *Toward a feminist theory of the state.* Cambridge, MA: Harvard University Press.

Millett, K. (1970). *Sexual politics.* New York: Ballantine.

Moraga, C., & Anzaldua, G. (Eds.). (1981). *This bridge called my back: Writings by radical women of color.* Watertown, MA: Persephone Press.

Morris, M. (1988). *The pirate's fiancee: Feminism, reading, postmodernism.* New York: Verso.

Morrison, T. (Ed.). (1992). *Race-ing justice, en-gendering power: Essays on Anita Hill, Clarence Thomas and the social construction of reality.* New York: Pantheon.

Nathan, D. (1991). *Women and aliens: Essays from the U.S.-Mexican border.* El Paso, TX: Cinco Puentos Press.

Nicholson, L. (1987). Feminism and Marx: Integrating kinship with the economic. In S. Benhabib & D. Cornell (Eds.), *Feminism as critique: On the politics of gender* (pp. 16–30). Minneapolis: University of Minnesota Press.

Odem, M. E. (1995). *Delinquent daughters: Protecting and policing adolescent female sexuality in the United States, 1885–1920*. Chapel Hill: University of North Carolina Press.

Peiss, K. (1983). Charity girls and city pleasures: Historical notes on working-class sexuality, 1880–1920. In A. Snitow, C. Stansell, & S. Thompson (Eds.), *Powers of desire: The politics of sexuality* (pp. 74–87). New York: Monthly Review Press.

Pollitt, K. (1993, October 4). Review of book *The morning after: Sex, fear and feminism on campus*. *The New Yorker*, pp. 220–224.

Pollitt, K. (1994, April 4). Subject to debate. *The Nation*, p. 441.

Ring, L. (1994). And if morning never comes?: Roiphe, resistance and the subject of women. *Radical America, 25*(2), 57–64.

Roiphe, K. (1993). *The morning after: Sex, fear and feminism on campus*. Boston: Little, Brown.

Rubin, G. (1993). Thinking sex: Notes for a radical theory of politics of sexuality. In L. S. Kauffman (Ed.), *American feminist thought at century's end: A reader* (pp. 1–64). Cambridge, MA: Blackwell.

Sarah, E. (1982). Editorial: Toward a reassessment of feminist history. *Women's Studies International Forum, 5/6*, 519–524.

Schlossman, S., & Wallach, S. (1978). The crime of precocious sexuality: Female juvenile delinquency in the progressive era. *Harvard Educational Review, 148*, 65–94.

Scholder, A. (Ed.). (1993). *Critical condition: Women on the edge of violence*. San Francisco: City Light Books.

Sluts Against Rape. (1991). *Manifesto* [Brochure]. Urbana, IL: Author.

Snitow, A., Stansell, C., & Thompson, S. (1983). Introduction. In A. Snitow, C. Stansell, & S. Thompson (Eds.), *Powers of desire: The politics of sexuality* (pp. 9–50). New York: Monthly Review Press.

Stansell, C. (1987). *City of women: Sex and class in New York 1789–1860*. Urbana: University of Illinois Press.

Thomas, J. (1994). Sagas of women journalists: A review essay. *Journal of Communication, 44*(1), 128–139.

Vance, C. S. (1989). Pleasure and danger: Towards a politics of sexuality. In C. S. Vance (Ed.), *Pleasure and danger: Exploring female sexuality* (2nd ed., pp. 1–28). London: Pandora.

Vance, C. S. (1990). Negotiating sex and gender in the Attorney General's Commission on Pornography. In F. Ginsburg & A. L. Tsing (Eds.), *Uncertain terms: Negotiating gender in American culture* (pp. 118–134). Boston: Beacon Press.

Vance, C. S. (1992, February 27). *Reframing domestic danger in the attorney general's commission on pornography*. Paper presented at the second annual Wilbur Schramm Lecture for the Institute on Communication Research, University of Illinois, Urbana-Champaign.

Walkowitz, J. (1983). Male vice and female virtue: Feminism and the politics of prostitution in nineteenth-century Britain. In A. Snitow, C. Stansell, & S. Thompson (Eds.), *Powers of desire: The politics of sexuality* (pp. 419–438). New York: Monthly Review Press.

Walkowitz, J. (1986). *Prostitution and Victorian society: Women, class and the state*. New York: Cambridge University Press.

Warren, C. A. (in progress). *Institutional power as silence: The case of medical sexual abuse*. Doctoral dissertation in progress, University of Illinois, Urbana-Champaign.

White, D. G. (1985). *Ar'n't I a woman?: Female slaves in the plantation south*. New York: Norton.

Williams, R. (1985). *Keywords: A vocabulary of culture and society* (rev. ed.). New York: Oxford University Press.

# 14 Challenging the Stigmatizing Messages: The Emerging Voices of Adult Survivors of Incest

Eileen Berlin Ray
*Cleveland State University*

*I was about nine years old when it happened. They put a towel around my head. Then one of them pinned my arms down while the other two raped me. They took turns raping me for about 30 minutes. I just tried to think about other things while they were doing it. That was the first time but it wasn't the last.*
—Sandy, describing her abuse by her two brothers and a cousin

*I adored him. He used to buy me presents and said I was his special daughter. When I was about ten, things changed. He said we had a bond like no one else had but that we had to keep it between us because if we told, my sisters and my mother would be jealous. He never hurt me physically. But he would come into my bedroom about once a week, climb into bed with me, and tell me it was his job to teach me how to act with men. Then he'd do things to my body and make me do things to him. I still can't talk about the specifics.*
—Linda, who was abused by her father

Incest is a violation of a child's body and spirit. It happens in the best and worst of homes. No one is immune, regardless of race, socioeconomic status, occupation, religion, or any other demographic variable. Incest happens often. Statistics claim 20% of females have had an experience of incestuous abuse at some time in their lives, 12% before the age of 14, 16% before the age of 18 (Russell, 1986), with estimates of 1,000 per million annually for father–daughter incest alone (Summit, 1982) to 38

273

## THE STIGMA OF INCEST

According to Goffman (1963), stigma is "an attribute that is deeply discrediting" (p. 3). Stigma does not reside in an individual but rather in relationships. Persons can only be stigmatized if they are defined by the dominant culture as the "other." Stigma essentially divides people into those who are acceptable and those who are not, forcing the groups into a superior–subordinate dichotomy. It is necessary for the dominant group to exclude the "others" from membership and to objectify and stereotype them so that the subordinate group cannot infiltrate or overtake the dominant culture (see Bullis & Bach, chap. 1 of this volume, for a more detailed discussion).

Incest is understood as potentially traumatic to most victims due to the dynamics of traumatic sexualization and betrayal within a trusted relationship and the helplessness and stigmatization that ensue (Finkelhor & Browne, 1985). Adult incest survivors feel stigmatized because of their loneliness and isolation, intense feelings of shame and guilt, the pressure of keeping the secret, feelings of powerlessness, and the reaction of others experienced by some when they tell of the abuse. They may feel stigmatized if they are blamed or asked to keep the "secret" within the immediate family (Finkelhor & Browne, 1986). Their stigmatization is compounded if they are also members of other stigmatized groups because of behaviors such as drug or alcohol abuse, prostitution, or suicidality.

Survivors are further stigmatized when they are portrayed as helpless victims who are likely to continue abusive behavior or when their survival skills are labeled as pathological (i.e., their depression is classified as a psychiatric illness) rather than labeled as adaptive behaviors that enabled the adult to survive as a child. When the focus is on the destructive outcomes of the abuse, rather than on the resilience and creativity of the survivors, stigmatization is further sustained (Driver, 1989).

Until recently, the patriarchal societal structure has successfully disenfranchised adult survivors by actively participating in the "conspiracy of silence" (Butler, 1978), encouraging survivors to keep their abuse secret, subsequently reinforcing their isolation (Dinsmore, 1991; Summit, 1982). However, the roots of the patriarchy's power to perpetuate feelings of isolation, shame, and guilt among adult survivors can be found, in large part, in the field of mental health. The result has been a reinforcement and institutionalization of the incest stigma.

## THE INSTITUTIONALIZATION
## OF THE INCEST STIGMA

In-depth discussions regarding the religious and cultural roots of the incest taboo can be found in numerous reviews (see, e.g., Armstrong, 1978; Crewdson, 1988; Donat & D'Emilio, 1992; Meiselman, 1979; Rush, 1980).

For the purposes of this chapter, the historical focus is on the roots of the incest taboo from within the mental health community. A review of this history provides revealing insights into the perpetuation of the incest taboo for adult survivors.

*Psychiatric Perspective.* Virtually all discussion about the incest taboo begins with the influence of Sigmund Freud (Dinsmore, 1991; Goodwin, 1993; Haugaard & Reppucci, 1988; J. H. Herman, 1981; Meiselman, 1979; Russell, 1986; Summit, 1983; Waldby, Clancy, Emetchi, & Summerfield, 1989). In the 1890s in Vienna, in the midst of the Victorian era, Freud was treating a group of upper-class, well-educated women who were, in his opinion, suffering from hysteria. Their symptoms parallel those today diagnosed as neurosis: hypochondria, anxiety, hallucinations, unfounded fears, and uncontrollable impulses (Crewdson, 1988). They had more than their symptoms in common. All reported being sexually abused, most by their fathers but some by other male relatives. After much consideration, Freud concluded that the women were telling the truth and, in 1896, presented a paper titled "The Aetiology of Hysteria" to the Viennese Society for Psychiatry and Neurology. In this paper he proposed his seduction theory, using case studies from his patients, stating that childhood sexual abuse was the cause of hysteria. Freud quickly found himself ostracized by his peers. In 1924, he revised his thinking and proposed his oedipal theory, claiming that adult neurosis was not cause by actual sexual experiences but by the unconscious desire for sexual experiences and the repression of that desire. Thus, large numbers of children were not having sex with their parents but unconsciously wished to (Crewdson, 1988; Summit, 1982; Waldby et al., 1989). Essentially, Freud was the frontrunner to the long history of denial of women's reality (Dinsmore, 1991) by invalidating the reality of incest (Courtois, 1988). The oedipal theory was received favorably by his peers and Freud took his place as the father of psychiatry.[1]

The abandonment by Freud of seduction theory in favor of the oedipal theory has had serious ramifications for survivors of sexual abuse. The oedipal theory ". . . denied any incidence of real child molestation within the family, and it created disbelief of any child or woman who complained.

---

[1]Interestingly, Sandor Ferenczi, one of Freud's closest colleagues, observed a difference with his female patients who reported being sexually abused by family members. Several of them also reported to Ferenczi that, as adults, they had sexually molested children. As Ferenczi saw it, although fantasizing about being sexually abused may be possible, it was unlikely that patients would fantasize about doing the molesting. Based on his data, Ferenczi resurrected the seduction theory in a paper he delivered to the Twelfth International Psycho-Analytic Congress in 1932. He received the same ostracism Freud had received decades earlier. When Ferenczi died soon after presenting the paper, his refutation of Freud's oedipal theory died with him (Crewdson, 1988).

And where the girl was dangerously persistent in her story, it rendered her the culprit, the seductress" (Armstrong, 1982, pp. 112–113). Today, the impact is still felt, as women's reality is still often denied. Those seeking psychiatric help are often told they are fantasizing the events and are not believed. The oedipal theory ". . . insured that the complaint was treated as a childhood fantasy and not as reality. It had the additional effect of exonerating the involved adult while allowing for both the continuation of the incest and society's denial of it" (Courtois, 1988, p. 7). Some of the more current perspectives continue critical elements of the psychiatric perspective with adaptations. One example is family systems theory.

*Family Systems Perspective.* Family systems theory posits that incest is the result of a dysfunctional family and emphasizes the interdependencies among all the family members. There is an emphasis on shared responsibility and often the incest is seen as a symptom of underlying deeper problems within the family. This has the danger of minimizing the incest. Within the framework of a dysfunctional family, the underlying problems are commonly attributed to the mother for failing to be adequately nurturing and protective. This blame may be manifested in several ways, including:

> the mother is dysfunctional as a wife, in that she fails to meet her husband's sexual demands and/or pursues interests outside the home; the mother is dysfunctional as a mother—the mother who does not want sex with her husband and pursues interests outside the home is also the mother who fails to give adequate nurturing to her children; the mother is dysfunctional as an adult and as a parent. Both mother and father are accused of seeking to turn their child into their parent and themselves becoming like children. (Waldby et al., 1989, p. 93)

It is the family relationships, rather than the incest, that is the focus of family systems therapy, removing responsibility from the perpetrator. By blaming the mother, the perpetrator becomes the victim and the other family members are considered complicitous in the incest. According to this perspective, each member of the family, including the incested child, is responsible for the incest (Dinsmore, 1991; Haugaard & Reppucci, 1988; Waldby et al., 1989).

*Feminist Perspective.* The most current shift of perspectives regarding incest comes from feminism. From this framework, incest must be considered within the power relationships that are sustained culturally. The dominant culture is patriarchal, a "political system in which the balance of power and authority between men and women favours men" (Vickers, 1994, p. 37). How society is structured and functions is evidence of the dominance of patriarchal values (i.e., legal, welfare, religious, judicial systems). Because these values have infiltrated every realm of society, male perception is accepted as reality and hegemony is sustained (Dinsmore, 1991; Waldby et al., 1989), as "they" retain power and control by silencing "others." Their institutionalized power privileges them over the powerless and attempts of the powerless to change this are "thwarted by the very institutions which have power over them" (Waldby et al., 1989, p. 102).

From the feminist perspective, the mother is culturally bound by her powerlessness. Incestuous families are typically traditional ones, where the mother has been socialized into the traditional female role of subservience and economic and social dependence on her partner to the extreme (Driver, 1989; J. H. Herman, 1981). As Ward (1984) observed: "Mothers have many reasons for not being able to 'see' or 'hear' incest . . . All the cultural baggage about marriage, motherhood and Happy Families contains absolutely no information about the possible need to protect children from men within the family" (p. 116).

This perspective offers an explanation for the collusion of some mothers or their ability to deny its occurrence or disbelieve or blame their child. She is as powerless as her daughter to challenge the perpetrator. It is her survival mechanism within the patriarchal structure (Dinsmore, 1991; Waldby et al., 1989). However, it should be underscored that many mothers do not have knowledge of the incest while it is occurring and, once told, put the child's safety above all other constraints.

Feminism expands the conceptualization of incest from not only an individual, but a societal issue as well. It validates the survivor's reality and puts the blame on the perpetrator. From a feminist perspective, sexual assault is seen as "a means of enforcing gender roles in society and maintaining the hierarchy in which men retain[ed] control" (Donat & D'Emilio, 1992, p. 14). In a number of ways, feminism has moved discourse about incest from the private to public arena, beginning the process of destigmatization for adult survivors. However, it is very slow and arduous because of the strongly ingrained messages from the perpetrator, significant others, and society. Attempting to replace years of stigmatizing messages with enfranchising ones, especially within a patriarchal culture, makes destigmatization even more difficult. It is the proliferation of these messages, when vocally unchallenged, that function to maintain the stigma for incest survivors.

## MAINTAINING THE STIGMA

When someone is in a position of power or authority, a breaking of boundaries and trust can wreak havoc on a child's perception of herself and her world. When a child is given the message that the older people who know her will love her and protect her, and then instead an older, trusted member of her family abuses her, the child's sense of reality becomes distorted. She begins to doubt her understanding of reality because she is experiencing one thing (sexual abuse) but is told that she is actually experiencing something else (love, care, protection, etc.). This mistrust of her perception often follows her into adulthood. (Dinsmore, 1991, p. 23)

The volume of academic research on incest has increased over the past 15 years. Although theoretic frameworks and methodologies have shifted over time, there remains a consistency in the findings of behavioral and psychological outcomes for adult survivors. The child has been violated physically and emotionally. Children seeking love and affirmation are instead forced into an adult sexual agenda. The message they get is that what they need or feel makes no difference (Poston & Lison, 1989), and that they are to blame. The destructive results of the incest are likely to set into motion a life of self-fulfilling prophecies (Summit, 1982), as it is essential that the perpetrator invoke so much fear and terror in the child that the messages function to maintain their emotional power so that the secret is kept, even long after the incest has stopped. Thus, the effects of the incest are likely to be evident in both childhood coping strategies and adult behaviors.

This section draws from both extant academic literature and the voices of survivors. Excerpts from the author's interviews with adult incest survivors (all women) are included, providing one more move toward enfranchisement through an opportunity for their voices to be heard.

## Effects of Incest

The results of incest are multidimensional. In addition to the physical and psychological trauma, victims also experience apprehension, guilt, terror, and fear between sexual encounters, the loss of a trusted relationship with an emotionally significant person, the loss of their childhood, and an overwhelming sense of powerlessness (Briere & Runtz, 1988; Cole & Putnam, 1992; Finkelhor, 1978; Finkelhor & Browne, 1985, 1986; Poston & Lison, 1989). They are also faced with the paradox of support, for the people whom they should be able to talk to about the abuse are, in fact, the abusers. As J. H. Herman (1992) observed:

The child trapped in an abusive environment is faced with a formidable task of adaptation. She must find a way to preserve a sense of trust in people who are untrustworthy, safety in a situation that is unsafe, control in a situation that is terrifyingly unpredictable, power in a situation of helplessness.

Unable to care for or protect herself, she must compensate for the failures of adult care and protection with the only means at her disposal, an immature system of psychological defenses. (p. 96)

Survivors develop a variety of behaviors to manage their confusion, pain, and fear. Summit (1983) provided a useful model for how children adapt and interested readers are referred to his work. For the purposes of this chapter, the focus is on the long-term manifestations of the effects of the incest (Meiselman, 1979). Most common are emotional and behavioral effects such as isolation, guilt, shame, depression, hypervigilance, lack of trust, high need for control, substance abuse, self-mutilation, and suicidality (these and other effects can be found in, e.g., Briere, 1989; Browne & Finkelhor, 1986; Liem, O'Toole, & James, 1992; Meiselman, 1979; Price, 1992). Physical complaints are also common, including headaches, stomach ailments, and other psychosomatic pains (these and other effects can be found in, e.g., Armstrong, 1978; Butler, 1978; Dinsmore, 1991; Gelinas, 1993; Meiselman, 1979; Tsai & Wagner, 1978). Although these effects are "normal responses to abnormal childhoods" (Dinsmore, 1991, p. 23), they often continue to be played out in the survivors' adult lives and relationships (Finkelhor & Browne, 1986; Nelson, 1978; Poston & Lison, 1989). Yet the same strength that enabled the incested child to survive can enable the adult survivor to change her destructive behaviors and overcome the negative effects of the incest. However, the perpetrator's and societal messages are so firmly ingrained that it is very difficult for many survivors to reconcile what they know with what they feel. As interviewees commented:

The abuse made a mess of my relationships with other people. Not just with lovers but with friends and definitely with my kids. I couldn't trust anyone, I kept testing them because I couldn't believe they could really love me. (Donna, abused by her stepfather)

I always feel like I have to be in control of everything and everyone. I can't trust other people so I have to do everything myself. (Louise, abused by her mother and father)

Incest is about the misuse of power by the abuser and the powerlessness of the child. Incest is about betrayal and manipulation by a trusted adult whom the child depends on for her or his safety and well-being. The impact of the trauma is often exacerbated when combined with ongoing interpersonal and societal stigmatizing messages from the perpetrator, family, friends, the mass media, and/or messages sanctioned within formal organizational structures. Their ability to marginalize survivors and perpetuate disenfranchisement is evident in an examination of some of these messages.

## Interpersonal Stigmatizing Messages

The messages heard by the child from the perpetrator and/or her family often function in several ways to maintain the incest stigma. These functions include ensuring the secret is kept, perpetuating feelings of powerlessness, and invalidating the survivor's reality. It is virtually impossible to discuss these functions separately, as most messages serve multiple functions. However, for purposes of discussion they are treated separately.

*Ensuring the Secret Is Kept.* The perpetrator must make sure his victim will not tell the secret. He does this in a number of ways. Although some may use force, it is typical that all that is needed is the implied threat of negative repercussions. Fear of what will happen if she tells is enough to keep the abused child quiet, typically for many years:

> People ask me why I didn't tell what was happening to me. It was because I perceived no way out. A young child tells on her father and what happens? She's taken away from her family. Her father goes to jail. The family is destroyed, and the message is, "It's all your fault." (Marilyn Van Derbur, 1957 Miss America)

These themes were shared by interviewees:

> He said if I told my mother, it would kill her. (Barbara, abused by her maternal grandfather)

> He said he would kill me if I ever told anyone. (Carolyn, abused by her stepfather)

> He said if I told, I would destroy the family. That he would go to jail and I would have to live with strangers. (Marsha, abused by her father)

Some interviewees received similar messages when, as adults, they told their families about their abuse:

> My parents believed me. But they made it very clear they didn't want me to tell anyone else, not even my brother or sister. (Denise, abused by her uncle)

> My mother tried to get me to promise I wouldn't tell anyone else, not even my father. What she didn't know was that she was about the last person I told. (Suzanne, abused by her brother)

Essentially, incest is about turning the truth into a lie and a lie into the truth. Victims are faced with a huge moral dilemma. To maintain the lie is the ultimate virtue whereas telling the truth is the ultimate sin (Goodwin, 1990; Summit, 1983).

*Perpetuating Feelings of Powerlessness.*   It is no wonder that incest survivors experience much confusion. They are powerless to stop the abuse but had the power to destroy the family and the responsibility to keep it together. And because the incest often occurs during a critical period of the child's emotional development (most incest begins at 8 years old; Summit, 1983), the child is especially vulnerable to the ploys of the abuser. As a result, many survivors feel responsible for the incest and feel guilty for not having done something to stop it. As some interviewees recalled:

> I still believe I could have stopped him. If I had just screamed or kicked him or something. I still believe it's my fault, at least some of it, because if I didn't want it, why didn't I stop him? (Wendy, abused by her stepfather)

> It has taken me years of therapy to finally believe, I mean really believe, that it wasn't my fault. That there was nothing I could do. That I really was helpless. (Jean, abused by her father)

> I felt powerful. I let him abuse me because he said if I didn't, then he would start with my younger sisters. So I felt like I was protecting them and actually controlling the situation. When I found out as an adult that he had been doing the same thing to them, I realized how powerless I really had been. It's taken me a long time to come to terms with that. (Nancy, abused by her father)

Adult survivors feel overwhelming terror because of their helplessness and powerlessness at a time when they were dependent on the abuser for their survival. It is not surprising that power and control are central issues for many survivors in their subsequent relationships, manifesting itself both as a strong desire to exert power over other people and situations, and as a continuing fear of others' power (Liem et al., 1992). For incest survivors, "basic feelings of powerlessness create paradoxically both the fear of control by others and compensatory striving for power" (Olarte, 1994, p. 468).

*Invalidating the Survivor's Reality.*   In keeping with Freud's view of incest, the messages also function to deny that what survivors experience is real. This often takes the form of blaming the victim and/or focusing on the veracity of the victim's claims rather than focusing on the perpetrator. From the perspective of the interviewees, messages they recalled included:

> He said no one would believe me, that I wanted it and made him do it, that I was nothing but a slut and if I told, then everyone would know that. (Alison, abused by her stepbrother)

> He said that I wanted it or else he wouldn't have done it. (Bonnie, abused by her maternal grandfather)

> When I was young, I did confront him. He called me a liar. He said I was making it all up or had dreamt it. (Joanne, abused by her father)

These messages were not constrained to perpetrators. When adult survivors confronted family members, they often heard similar comments:

> My mother said, "How could you say such horrible things about your stepfather? If he really did that to you, why did it take you until now to tell me?" (Margaret)

> My mother was furious. She just kept saying, "You're lying. You've always been a liar. You just want to get attention. I won't let you ruin our lives with your lies." (Michelle, abused by her father and uncle)

> When I told my mother that I had been raped by my stepfather and gang raped by my brother, cousin, and some of their friends, she told me I was crazy and should see a psychiatrist. (Annette)

When these types of messages from the most significant others in a child's life are dominant, they perpetuate the isolation, self-blaming, and guilt necessary to continue disenfranchisement. When combined with their simultaneous reinforcement at the societal level, the power of these messages is further intensified. One vehicle for the widespread dissemination of these stigmatizing messages is the mass media.

## Mass-Media Stigmatizing Messages

Attempts to publicly blame the incest survivor are reinforced in volumes of non-incest-specific self-help books that proclaim we are each responsible for our own happiness, with titles such as *You Can Heal Your Life* (Hay, 1987), *You Can Be Happy No Matter What* (Carlson, 1992), and *Toxic Parents: Overcoming Their Hurtful Legacy and Reclaiming Your Life* (Forward & Buck, 1989; see Simonds, 1992, for a critique of this genre). It follows, then, that we are also responsible for our own unhappiness. This suggests we have choices and only ourselves to blame if we "choose" unhappiness. For example, survivors who "choose" to abuse alcohol and/or drugs or be in abusive relationships can easily change the course of their lives by making different choices. It is her own fault she is in her predicament (Alcoff & Gray, 1993). It should be noted, however, that although this theme is common in the generalized self-help popular press, incest-specific self-help books vociferously disagree with the claim that the survivor has freely chosen to adopt destructive behaviors. Rather, these behaviors are a logical outcome of the social and political context of the childhood abuse and have been continued within the confines of patriarchy. These books urge those who were abused to acknowledge they were victims as children, refute the stigmatizing messages, and move on to survivorship (e.g., Bass & Davis, 1995; Dinsmore, 1991; Poston & Lison, 1989), urging survivors to understand the contextual confines of incest and its aftermath.

However, public blaming messages continue to be prevalent, as supported by the psychiatric community's labeling of many survivor-adaptive behaviors as intrapersonal and pathological, excluding the impact of the social context (Caplan, McCurdy-Myers, & Gans, 1992). For example, the American Psychological Association's bible, the *Diagnostic and Statistical Manual of Mental Disorders (DSM),* includes a diagnosis of masochistic personality disorder, clearly directed toward behaviors that typify stereotypic female roles (i.e., self-sacrificing and self-deprecating behavior), which labels as masochistic people who choose "people who 'disappoint' or 'mistreat' them" and choose to remain "in relationships in which others exploit, abuse, or take advantage" (Faludi, 1991, p. 358). These messages attempt to maintain the incest stigma by blaming the survivor, not the perpetrator, and labeling the survivor as deviant.

This has been further highlighted by the debate regarding the veracity of repressed memories (see Comment, 1994, for one example). The purpose of this chapter is not to engage in an academic debate regarding the reality of repressed memories. What is of concern here is how these debates are interpreted via the media to the lay public and how these interpretations are then used to attempt to discredit the adult survivor. In the hands of the public, challenging the veracity of adult survivors' memories recalls Freud's refutation of his seduction theory and all of the ramifications of his oedipal theory for incest survivors. This is further exemplified by the formation of groups of alleged perpetrators claiming to have been unjustly accused, evidenced by the establishment in 1992 of the False Memory Syndrome Foundation. As in all crimes, there is likely to be some percentage of misidentification. However, incest is not the exceptionally rare occurrence many would like to believe (Meiselman, 1979) and showcasing false reports diverts attention from the central issues surrounding incest.

Despite the profusion of interpersonal and societal stigmatizing messages heard by survivors since childhood, the past two decades has brought incest from a taboo topic to one making regular appearances on TV talk shows, workshops, bookshelves, and becoming a focus of research among academicians and mental health professionals. These changes are direct challenges to the incest stigma and owe their genesis to the feminist movement.

## CHALLENGING THE INCEST TABOO

The feminist movement deserves the credit for raising public awareness about incest and is responsible for this movement toward enfranchisement and away from stigmatizing adult incest survivors as the "other" (see

Eckman & Mastronardi, chap. 13 of this volume, for an historical review of feminism and violence against women). In the early 1970s, consciousness-raising groups provided a forum for women to begin talking to each other about sexual violence. In 1971, the first rape speakout was held in New York City (Dinsmore, 1991) and in 1972, the first rape crisis center was established (J. H. Herman, 1981). The term *child sexual abuse* was first used in the federal Child Abuse Prevention and Treatment Act of 1974 (Haugaard & Reppucci, 1988). The feminist movement has encouraged women to end their silence about all types of abuse, and provided safe havens for them to do so. In this context, women, a few at first and then increasingly more, began to share their secret, only to find out that they were not alone. As they have banded together, they have gained not only personal, but political strength. The feminist movement has thus enabled adult incest survivors to become enfranchised by speaking out, thereby moving the topic from unspeakable and private into the public sphere.

The media has also played a role in removing the stigma. For example, the 1984 made-for-TV movie *Something About Amelia* focused on father–daughter incest in an upstanding middle-class home. This groundbreaking movie had a huge impact, as indicated by the tens of thousands of phone calls to child-abuse hotlines across the nation immediately following its airing (Crewdson, 1988).

Public figures have also spoken publicly about their experiences. Among the most influential was Marilyn Van Derbur, the 1957 Miss America. From the outside, her family was the American ideal, enjoying status, wealth, and the image of the perfect family. In fact, her father had been molesting her from the time she was 5 until she was 18. She later learned he had also molested her older sister. Van Derbur made her incest public through interviews in TV and print media. Because of her courage, other celebrities came forward, further lifting the shroud of secrecy. Rape crisis centers began including incest survivors as part of their domain and centers such as the Adult Incest Survivors Program at Denver's Kempe National Center for Prevention of and Treatment for Child Abuse and Neglect, started with a $240,000 donation from the Van Derbur family, helped move incest to center stage. Thus, the incest taboo was being confronted and supports were being put in place to help adult survivors deal with the repercussions of their abuse.

Incest has also found its place on the popular press bookshelves. The plethora of self-help books for adult survivors of incest serves an important function by further reinforcing that the survivor is not alone and that there is help and support. Books discuss common behavioral outcomes of incest, further validating the survivor's experiences. Just the fact that incest has been "universalized" helps remove the incest stigma. The high volume of sales of these books further attests to the prevalence of incest and the shared reactions of survivors to the trauma.

The secret is out and for adult survivors of incest this is particularly good news, because as children they had no one to talk to and nowhere to go. There were no available outlets to challenge the perpetrator's reality or to have their experiences validated. Today, help is available is a wide variety of forms, including individual counseling from professionals trained in incest-related issues, rape crisis centers, self-help groups, group therapy, support groups (Courtois, 1988; Goodwin, 1990; J. L. Herman & Schatzow, 1984; Paddison, Einbinder, Maker, & Strain, 1993; Summit, 1982). Thus, a positive by-product of the media's jumping on the incest bandwagon has been to raise public awareness, resulting in a conscious emphasis on protecting children by making incest speakable (Berliner & Conte, 1990).

Some would argue, however, that the media's overindulgent attention to incest also acts to uphold the existing culturally defined power dimensions (e.g., Alcoff & Gray, 1993). In effect, it is little more than a superficial nod toward enfranchisement designed to give the illusion of destigmatization. Examples abound in all media, where incest has been sensationalized and survivors have been exploited. Referring to such formats as talk shows (i.e., Geraldo Rivera, Phil Donahue), Alcoff and Gray observed "The media often use the presence of survivors for shock value and to pander to a sadistic voyeurism among viewers, focusing on the details of the violations with close-ups of survivors' anguished expressions. They often eroticize the depictions of survivors and of sexual violence to titillate and expand their audiences" (p. 262).

The proliferation of incest-related talk shows, radio shows, popular press books, and debates regarding the veracity of repressed memories threaten to turn survivors into caricatures and present incest as a popular culture icon. Although the topic may drive ratings upward, the mass marketing of incest minimizes survivors' trauma, downplays the perpetrator's responsibility, and directs attention away from society's accountability. As long as survivors can be grouped together and characterized as stereotypes, they continue to be divided into "us" and "them." And the "us" remains privileged with the dominant discourse whereas "they" remain outside and hegemony, under the guise of empowerment, continues.

## CONCLUSION

Incest denial and incest myths seem to have three purposes: (a) to silence the survivor; (b) to protect the attacker; and (c) to comfort the community member or professional worker with the idea that she or he is totally removed from the experience of the people in the "case," and free from any implication of responsibility or collusion; thereby to reinforce the illusion that incest is an isolated aberration rather than a fundamental pattern of societal abuse. (Driver, 1989, p. 27)

The incest taboo pendulum has swung from the extreme of silence to loud voices staking a claim in the dominant discourse. However, when the privileged are threatened, they fight back and confronting those with a vested interest in perpetuating the status quo is extremely difficult. As survivors become more vocal, they gain power and strength. As their numbers and voices swell, they become even more of a threat. It is evident how the historical roots of the incest stigma have woven their threads within society and been perpetuated through patriarchal discourse. It was not until the feminist movement that the myths of sexual abuse were challenged. As these voices have increased, a new version of the patriarchal discourse has emerged. It takes the form of groups such as the False Memory Syndrome Foundation, an overabundance of media attention to false accusations, attacks on the integrity of therapists as a profession, and the continued focus on *what* happened rather than on *why* it happened. In essence, there is a discursive tug-of-war between survivors and neo-taboo groups as survivors fight to make their discourse privileged.

Removing the stigmatization of incest is clearly rooted in issues of communication. It is a process of negating the messages told to the child by the perpetrator, significant others, and society. It is a process of changing the self-destructive messages victims tell themselves. It is a process of breaking the silence by telling the secret. It is a process of ending the isolation by sharing memories of the abuse with others. It is a process of stating the truth as the truth and the lie as a lie. It is the process of ensuring that legislation is passed and enacted to hold perpetrators, not mothers or children, responsible for incest. It is a process of passing laws and then imposing severe penalties for those convicted of incest. It is a process of becoming vocal advocates for "others." It is the process of forcing the public to hear the individual and collective voices of adult survivors that can end the stigmatization and disenfranchisement for adult incest survivors.

However, moving incest discourse into the public arena is the first, not final, step toward removing its stigma. It must also be incorporated into formal societal discourse through structural changes, a very difficult and political process. As Crewdson (1988) observed:

> The Child Abuse Prevention and Treatment Act of 1974 established the National Center on Child Abuse and Neglect (NCCAN) to coordinate federal funding for treatment and research . . . When Carter was president, the agency's four-year budget totalled $79 million; during the first Reagan Administration, it fell to $71 million total. In 1986, after two years of intensive publicity on the subject of child abuse, NCCAN's annual budget was increased to $26 million—less than half the amount of foreign aid given during the same period to the government of Haitian dictator Jean-Claude Duvalier. (p. 213)

It is incumbent upon survivors to make the personal political and use their collective voice for structural change. Those who control the resources have the power and the privilege. Survivors and their supporters must infiltrate the patriarchal structure and play an active role in determining how much funding will be allocated and to whom, propose and enact stringent legislation for offenders, and ensure that they, politically, financially, and discursively, are no longer the "other."

## REFERENCES

Alcoff, L., & Gray, L. (1993, Winter). Survivor discourse: Transgression or recuperation? *Signs*, pp. 260–290.

Armstrong, L. (1978). *Kiss daddy goodnight: A speakout on incest.* New York: Hawthorn.

Armstrong, L. (1982). The cradle of sexual politics: Incest. In M. Kirkpatrick (Ed.), *Women's sexual experience* (pp. 109–125). New York: Plenum.

Bass, E., & Davis, L. (1994). *The courage to heal: A guide for women survivors of child sexual abuse* (3rd ed.). New York: Harper & Row.

Berliner, L., & Conte, J. R. (1990). The process of victimization: The victims' perspective. *Child Abuse & Neglect, 14,* 29–40.

Briere, J. (1989). *Therapy for adults molested as children: Beyond survival.* New York: Springer.

Briere, J., & Runtz, M. (1988). Symptomatology associated with childhood sexual victimization in a nonclinical sample. *Child Abuse & Neglect, 12,* 51–59.

Browne, A., & Finkelhor, D. (1986). Impact of child sexual abuse: A review of the research. *Psychological Bulletin, 99,* 66–77.

Butler, S. (1978). *The conspiracy of silence: The trauma of incest.* San Francisco: New Glide.

Caplan, P. J., McCurdy-Myers, J., & Gans, M. (1992). Should "premenstrual syndrome" be called a psychiatric abnormality? *Feminism & Psychology, 2*(1), 27–44.

Carlson, R. (1992). *You can be happy no matter what.* San Rafael, CA: New World Library.

Cole, P. M., & Putnam, F. W. (1992). Effect of incest on self and social functioning: A developmental psychopathology perspective. *Journal of Consulting and Clinical Psychology, 60*(2), 174–184.

Comment (1994). *American Psychologist, 49*(5), 439–443.

Courtois, C. A. (1988). *Healing the incest wound: Adult survivors in therapy.* New York: Norton.

Crewdson, J. (1988). *By silence betrayed.* Boston: Little, Brown.

Dinsmore, C. (1991). *From surviving to thriving: Incest, feminism, and recovery.* Albany: State University of New York Press.

Donat, P. L. N., & D'Emilio, J. (1992). A feminist redefinition of rape and sexual assault: Historical foundations and change. *Journal of Social Issues, 48*(1), 9–22.

Driver, E. (1989). Introduction. In E. Driver & A. Droisen (Eds.), *Child sexual abuse: A feminist reader* (pp. 1–68). New York: New York University Press.

Faludi, S. (1991). *Backlash: The undeclared war against American women.* New York: Crown.

Finkelhor, D. (1978). *Sexually victimized children.* New York: The Free Press.

Finkelhor, D. (1984). *Child sexual abuse: New theory and research.* New York: The Free Press.

Finkelhor, D. (1990). Early and long-term effects of child sexual abuse: An update. *Professional Psychology: Research and Practice, 21,* 325–330.

Finkelhor, D., & Browne, A. (1985). The traumatic impact of child sexual abuse: A conceptualization. *American Journal of Orthopsychiatry, 55,* 530–541.

Finkelhor, D., & Browne, A. (1986). Initial and long-term effects: A conceptual framework. In D. Finkelhor, S. Araji, L. Baron, A. Browne, D. Peters, & G. Wyatt (Eds.), *A sourcebook on child sexual abuse* (pp. 180–198). Beverly Hills, CA: Sage.

Forward, S., & Buck, C. (1989). *Toxic parents: Overcoming their hurtful legacy and reclaiming your life.* New York: Bantam.

Gelinas, D. J. (1993). Relational patterns in incestuous families, malevolent variations, and specific interventions with the adult survivor. In P. L. Paddison (Ed.), *Treatment of adult survivors of incest* (pp. 1–34). Washington, DC: American Psychiatric Press.

Goffman, E. (1963). *Stigma: Notes on the management of spoiled identity.* Englewood Cliffs, NJ: Prentice-Hall.

Goodwin, J. (1990). *Rediscovering childhood trauma: Historical casebook and clinical applications.* Washington, DC: American Psychiatric Press.

Goodwin, J. (1993). The seduction hypothesis 100 years after. In P. L. Paddison (Ed.), *Treatment of adult survivors of incest* (pp. 135–142). Washington, DC: American Psychiatric Press.

Haugaard, J. J., & Reppucci, N. D. (1988). *The sexual abuse of children.* San Francisco: Jossey-Bass.

Hay, L. L. (1987). *You can heal your life* (rev. ed.). Santa Monica, CA: Hay House.

Herman, J. H. (1981). *Father–daughter incest.* Cambridge, MA: Harvard University Press.

Herman, J. H. (1992). *Trauma and recovery.* New York: Basic Books.

Herman, J. L., & Schatzow, E. (1984). Time-limited group therapy for women with a history of incest. *International Journal for Group Psychotherapy, 34,* 605–616.

Liem, J. H., O'Toole, J. G., & James, J. B. (1992). The need for power in women who were sexually abused as children: An exploratory study. *Psychology of Women Quarterly, 16,* 467–480.

Meiselman, K. C. (1979). *Incest: A psychological study of causes and effects with treatment recommendations.* San Francisco: Jossey-Bass.

Nelson, B. K. (1978). Setting the public agenda: The case of child abuse. In J. V. May & A. Wildevsky (Eds.), *The policy cycle* (pp. 81–109). Beverly Hills, CA: Sage.

Olarte, S. W. (1994). Discussion of "incest and the idealized self: Adaptations to childhood sexual abuse." *American Journal of Psychoanalysis, 54*(1), 37–39.

Paddison, P. L., Einbinder, R. G., Maker, E., & Strain, J. J. (1993). Group treatment with incest survivors. In P. L. Paddison (Ed.), *Treatment of adult survivors of incest* (pp. 35–53). Washington, DC: American Psychiatric Press.

Poston, C., & Lison, K. (1989). *Reclaiming our lives: Hope for adult survivors of incest.* Boston: Little, Brown.

Price, M. (1992). The psychoanalysis of an adult survivor of incest: A case study. *American Journal of Psychoanalysis, 52*(2), 119–136.

Renshaw, D. C. (1982). *Incest: Understanding and treatment.* Boston: Little, Brown.

Rush, F. (1980). *The best kept secret: Sexual abuse of children.* Englewood Cliffs, NJ: Prentice-Hall.

Russell, D. E. H. (1986). *The secret trauma: Incest in the lives of girls and women.* New York: Basic Books.

Simonds, W. (1992). *Women and self-help culture: Reading between the lines.* New Brunswick, NJ: Rutgers University Press.

Steele, B. F. (1986). Notes on the lasting effects of early child abuse throughout the life cycle. *Child Abuse & Neglect, 10,* 283–291.

Summit, R. (1982). Beyond belief: The reluctant discovery of incest. In M. Kirkpatrick (Ed.), *Women's sexual experience* (pp. 127–150). New York: Plenum.

Summit, R. (1983). The child sexual abuse accommodation syndrome. *Child Abuse & Neglect, 7,* 177–193.

Tsai, M., & Wagner, N. N. (1978). Therapy groups for women sexually molested as children. *Archives of Sexual Behavior, 7,* 421–425.

Vickers, J. (1994). Notes toward a political theory of sex and power. In H. L. Radtke & H. J. Stam (Eds.), *Power/gender: Social relations in theory and practice* (pp. 174–193). London: Sage.

Waldby, C., Clancy, A., Emetchi, J., & Summerfield, C. (1989). In E. Driver & A. Droisen (Eds.), *Child sexual abuse: A feminist reader* (pp. 88–106). New York: New York University Press.

Ward, E. (1984). *Father–daughter rape.* London: Women's Press.

# 15 Communication and Abused Women: Empowering Their Voices and Exposing the Ideological Constraints

James T. West
*Honolulu, Hawaii*

O. J. Simpson's trial (which began in 1994) for the brutal murder of his ex-wife, Nicole Simpson, along with the discovery that he had beaten her at least eight times during their marriage, focused national attention on the problem of intimate violence. The unprecedented amount of media attention on the Simpson drama gave experts on abusive relationships an opportunity to educate the American public about the magnitude of the problem. They often cited a 1992 report by the American Medical Association that said 4 million women are beaten by an intimate partner each year. What was not examined closely by either the experts or the media was how these women are disenfranchised by institutional authorities who sometimes ignore their cries for help.

All disenfranchised groups are impacted by ideological forces and nowhere are these forces more transparent than in violent relationships. Individuals in violent relationships are often so afflicted by ideological pressure to stay in their marriages that they often feel they have no means of escape from their violent partners. Lorena Bobbitt's trial for cutting off her husband's penis is the most well-known example of a woman who stayed in her marriage for years despite being repeatedly abused. Although tragic, these types of violent relationships are pervasive in American society.

In order to provide insights into the issues surrounding how women are disenfranchised by violent relationships and by institutional authorities, this chapter is divided into four areas: (a) the basic framework of scholarship on communication and ideology, (b) a brief historical overview of the social problem of violent relationships, (c) a description of how the narratives of violence between intimates complicate conventional understandings of communication processes by the significance they place on ideological constraints as a source of the problem, and (d) how abused women might be empowered.

## THE IMPORTANCE OF UNDERSTANDING
## HOW IDEOLOGY WORKS

Abused women describe ideological constraints as the main source of their continuing disenfranchisement (West, 1992, 1995). Consequently, it becomes vital to understand how ideology works. Yet, the study of ideology as it relates to communication and disenfranchised groups is a relatively new area of study (Wander, 1983). Communication researchers have studied a wide variety of relationships and groups, but only recently have they begun to recognize that although many groups are not overtly concerned with power as an issue of control, *all* groups are enacted within relations of power (West, 1993).

Unfortunately, many of the past and present communication research studies concerning disenfranchised groups have taken a "structuralist" approach that attaches meaning to these groups based on the personality or pathological traits of the individuals in the group. A structuralist approach centers, or structures, the actions of a group around one factor, usually a behavioristic trait the researcher says is common to all the individuals in the group. For instance, 1960s psychological reports said women stayed in violent relationships because they were masochistic and enjoyed the beatings (Ferraro & Johnson, 1983). By focusing on just one factor this reduces the group's actions to a fixed set of binary oppositions: cause or effect, hereditary or environment, masochistic or nonmasochistic, normal or pathological. The structuralist focus on individual factors has kept macropractices and other cultural meanings hidden in the margins.

Dissatisfied with the limitations and biases of the structuralist approach, scholars from many disciplines have created a number of new approaches for studying groups that have come to be known collectively as "poststructuralism." One vein of the poststructuralist movement is the study of ideology. Ideology is a complex and dynamic concept defined as the interwoven and inseparable nexus of: (a) the production of knowledge, (b) relations of power, and (c) institutional practices (West, 1992).

Using this nexus as its core, research on ideology brings a three-pronged strategy to the understanding of communication by triangulating the three dynamics that comprise it. First, it deconstructs—that is to say, opens up—the ways in which institutions and institutional authorities produce knowledge (Eagleton, 1983). This deconstruction examines the multiple meanings and voices that have been silenced by the singular, linear, cause–effect, and fixed meaning that an institution attempts to have the public reproduce and "know" about a group. It shows how all groups are dynamic, in process, inherently multidimensional, and open to various interpretations. Second, an ideological approach examines the relations of power in which all groups are embedded. Third, it does a close reading of how specific institutional practices are used by authorities as a means to maintain their power to produce knowledge about these groups.

Beginning with the production of knowledge, I briefly clarify and describe each of these three prongs, show how they are interconnected, and how ideology impacts all communication processes.

## THE PRODUCTION OF KNOWLEDGE

In the first prong of its examination, research on ideology deconstructs how institutions, and the individuals who are in positions of authority to speak for institutions, are involved in the production of knowledge. It questions how institutional authorities structure knowledge in a way that reflects most favorably on their institution's viewpoint. It opens up how they use their resources to tell others how to think (know) about groups in one way and not in other ways.

For example, after the Vietnam War ended, Vietnam veterans were disenfranchised. They were marginalized because they were viewed as a painful reminder of a war that America had lost. They were given no parades, no memorials, often had their claims of posttraumatic stress disorders ignored, and illnesses related to Agent Orange dismissed. Their viewpoint was silenced. Initial mass-media productions telling the public how we should think about this group reflected the old established military views associated with World War II veterans. The first wave of movies produced about the Vietnam War sanctioned the position that Vietnam veterans worked together harmoniously in a noble battle to help fight for democracy and to stop the so-called "domino effect" of communism. However, when actual Vietnam combat soldiers, such as Oliver Stone (*Platoon* & *Born On The Fourth of July*), began making movies about the war, their images deconstructed the institutionalized and noble versions of the war.

For instance, notice how American soldiers in the movie *Apocalypse Now* provide a very different meaning about the wary than does John Wayne's relationships with his infantrymen in the movie *The Green Berets*. Francis Ford Coppola's *Apocalypse Now* shows war as selfish, chaotic, insane, racist, and murderous. *The Green Berets* portrays the Vietnam War as a noble battle of all-American boys working together to stop the "yellow" communist hoards.

## RELATIONS OF POWER

Whereas the first prong of the ideological approach deconstructs how institutional authorities produce a self-enhancing and structured meaning regarding a group, the second prong of the ideological approach examines how the production of knowledge is inextricably connected to relations of power. As Foucault (1980) pointed out, the production of knowledge always involves power, and he referred to this inseparable combination as power/knowledge. He went on to establish that all forms of communication are caught up in the production and (re)presentation of power/knowledge. By producing a fixed and one-dimensional meaning regarding an event or group, institutions communicate to their audiences the "correct" manner in which relations of power should be ordered.

Institutions maintain relations of power and the production of knowledge through what Foucault (1972) called "discursive fields." Discursive fields are sets of institutional practices that prescribe who may speak (or write) in specific locations and how they may speak under different types of conditions (Foucault, 1972). S. Foss, K. Foss, and Trapp (1985) described how discursive fields:

> impose conditions on the individuals who speak so that only those deemed qualified by satisfying these conditions may engage in discourse on a specific subject. Among these conditions are legal requirements that give the right to speak in certain ways; lawyers, for example, must pass the bar examination in order to practice law. . . . For example, we listen to medical doctors speak about issues involving health because our society attributes competence to them in this area. (pp. 196–197)

Institutions create and maintain discursive fields as "strategies" (de Certeau, 1984) to maintain the centripetal force of their institutional practices. Through discursive fields, institutions regulate relations of power and the production of knowledge for anyone who comes in contact with them. This allows institutions to form an ideology that tells individuals how to order their relationships with various groups.

For example, the psychological community maintains a discursive field that produces specific ways of classifying and objectifying individuals. Individuals who exhibit certain traits are classified as part of a "normal" group. However, individuals falling outside the "normal" boundaries are defined by psychologists as "insane." Notice how in the English language we do not have any positive words for people who think or act differently. All the words are negative: insane, mad, crazy, mental illness, psychotic, and so on.

To find a positive connotation we have to turn to Native Americans' descriptions of shamans. Shamans are tribe members who have mystical visions, healing power, and who are able to communicate with the spirit world. They are not viewed as people to be scorned or given electric shock treatments, but as valuable members of the tribe who should be honored for their special gifts.

However, psychologists view such "gifted" individuals as "crazy." Through the communication patterns of the discursive field of psychology, anyone considered "mentally ill" is completely disenfranchised and has his or her most basic rights taken away. This disenfranchisement has been the subject of numerous plays and movies, such as *One Flew Over the Cuckoo's Nest.*

Institutions do their utmost to maintain and increase their power over their discursive fields. For example, religious institutions had for many centuries been the primary sites of confessional power. One of Freud's political ventures was to move confessional practices away from institutionalized religions and toward a group of medical practitioners (Rieff, 1987). But as decades have gone by and Freud's views have been increasingly attacked as sexist, psychology's relations of power have moved away from Freudian confessional practices that focused on parent-child sexuality (i.e., an Oedipus or Electra complex) and have moved toward relations of power with the psychologist-as-parent and the patient-as-child.

The psychological community's management of the relations of power has focused more and more on providing the proper written classification of the conduct of individuals. The number of classifications has proliferated over the last several decades. Currently, the specific classifications of individual pathologies are listed in the *Diagnostic and Statistical Manual of Mental Disorders* (3rd ed.), also known as the *DSM–III.* This book organizes the discursive field of the psychological community.

## INSTITUTIONAL PRACTICES

After using the first prong of the study of ideology to examine the production of knowledge and the second prong to analyze how this production of knowledge establishes relations of power, the third prong illustrates how institutions maintain their authority and power/knowledge through four interconnected techniques I refer to collectively as "institutional practices." The four techniques are: monopolizing, normalizing, constituting, and reproducing. Institutional practices constitute and normalize the way we think of ourselves and others by monopolizing our view of the world to one "correct" representation.

For example, when we first go to school around age 5 we are not given a menu. We do not emerge from the yellow school bus and request to learn how to speak Tagalog and worship as a Hindu. Our experience is monopolized and normalized to speak the language of our parents and of the school, to eat what they eat, to pray as they pray, and to reproduce knowledge in the way they tell us. Our history is constituted and represented in one way and not in other ways.

For instance, generations of U.S. schoolchildren have been taught that October 10 is a national holiday because Columbus "discovered" America. They are not taught that he landed in Jamaica and never saw what is now the United States, or that he murdered and enslaved the people already living there because they would not worship his Pope's god. Children are not taught to question this institutionalized holiday, but to celebrate it and reproduce the false consciousness about its meaning. They are taught that Western European people are superior to "primitive" indigenous groups. Institutional practices produce knowledge that establishes the relationships between groups of people in one way and not in other ways.

## OVERVIEW OF THE HISTORY OF ABUSED WOMEN

To further illustrate how ideology impacts all disenfranchised groups and how an ideological research perspective enhances our studies of such groups, I focus specifically on one disenfranchised group, namely abused women. The history of how women have been abused cuts across many centuries and most world cultures (Bersani & Chen, 1988; Gordon, 1988). For centuries, women have been considered men's property (Pahl, 1985; Yllo, 1988). And like other pieces of property they could be sold, married off, beaten, or enslaved. This legacy is still with us today. For instance, the saying, "a rule of thumb," traces its origins back to 19th-century English common law when the "rule" was that a man should not beat his wife and children with any stick larger than his thumb. Gordon's historical investigation of family violence in Boston from 1880 to 1960, illustrates how the rule of thumb was carried out in the American family. Her study implicates the American family as having a long history of violence, and institutional authorities as having an equally long history of reinforcing the violence.

A review of the last 20 years (1970–1990) provides an understanding of how abused women are still disenfranchised today. In the 1970s, some social researchers began focusing their attention on violence between intimates and how to best address it. Psychologists linked "the cause" of the problem to certain types of personalities (Ball, 1977; Elbow, 1977; Faulk, 1977; Hamberger & Hastings, 1986; Rosenbaum & O'Leary, 1981; Shainess, 1977). However, these attempts to correlate relational violence to personality types without examining other factors was soon recognized as problematic. Gelles and Cornell (1985) stated:

The earliest publications on the subject of wife abuse took a distinctively psychiatric view of both offender and victim. Women who were abused were believed to suffer from psychological disorders as did the men who abused them. Research conducted in the 1970s and 1980s found this view of wife battery too simplistic. There are a number of individual, demographic, relational, and situational factors related to violence toward wives. These factors are probably all interrelated. (p. 71)

Recognizing the limitations of an approach that mirrored the psychological institution's focus on the individual, interpersonal communication researchers, as well as marriage and family counseling workers, began a series of studies that attempted to capture the relational factors associated with family violence. These studies highlighted the interactional patterns of couples as the locus of the problem (Berk, Berk, Loseke, & Rauma, 1983; J. Foss, 1980; Gulotta & Neuberger, 1983; Hotaling & Sugarman, 1986; Rogers & Millar, 1988; Weitzman & Dreen, 1982). They used a pragmatic approach that focused on the couple as a system in which the husband and wife were constantly defining and redefining the relationship (Courtright, Millar, & Rogers, 1979; Giles-Sims, 1983; Manderscheid, Rae, McCarrick, & Silbergeld, 1982; Watzlawick, Beavin, & Jackson, 1967). The couple negotiated the relational pattern through their interaction. The pragmatic perspective outlined how an abusive relationship may be either symmetrical or complementary. Either of these patterns may lead the relationship to become violent if one or both people in the relationship demands constant control of the relational patterns.

The central examination for this type of communication research focused on whether violence within an intimate relationship was reflected in a series of redundant patterns within the couples' conversations. Millar and Rogers (1981) remarked: "The concept of redundancy is of primary importance in the clinical literature where it is posited that overly redundant or rigid interaction patterns are related to various individual and family pathologies" (p. 16).

While family, marriage, and communication researchers were concentrating on verbal patterns, psychological and sociological researchers turned their attention to measuring the frequency of physical violence in marriages (Dutton, 1988; Huggins & Straus, 1980; Straus, 1979; Straus & Gelles, 1986). The results of the earliest frequency studies varied greatly. Some suggested that violence between intimates occurred in only 5% of married households, whereas other studies suggested a rate as high as 45% (McNeely & Robinson-Simpson, 1989). However, the accuracy of statistical studies and the implications that could be drawn from these results was disputed. One of the unfortunate consequences of the preoccupation and debate over the frequency of violence in the home was that violence between intimates was "discussed as if all battered women were similar and all battering relationships were alike" (Follingstad, Laughlin, Polek, Rutledge, & Hause, 1991, p. 187). Follingstad et al. argued: "Recognizing the variability among these women begins to reduce stereotypes and forces researchers to abandon the idea that one cause produces battered victims" (p. 200).

As frequency studies, psychological trait studies, and causal models were increasingly being seen as problematic, one of the most significant developments in the history of understanding relational violence was a shift toward feminist research and research on ideology. In "Sociological Perspectives in Family Violence," Bersani and Chen (1988) argued:

> For this perspective, the core principle in accounting for pervasive spouse violence is that the traditional family reflects an arrangement of domination by males. The social structure supports gender inequality, and this inequality is rooted in the history and in the traditions of Western societies. Marriage is viewed as the central element of a patriarchal society. (p. 73)

One of the most significant feminist responses to the violence was the creation of "shelters" so that women had a safe place to escape the violence. It also offered a place to provide "real" help because many women found when they attempted to leave violent relationships and/or seek justice their efforts were often thwarted by the ideological practices of their families and institutions.

The best attempts to end intimate violence over the last two decades were directly tied to the feminist movement. The patriarchal system created barriers that prevented women from obtaining political positions that would allow them to change their status as second-class citizens and as subjects of abuse (Yllo, 1984). Yllo (1984, 1988) has shown how relational violence is immersed in both societal and interpersonal sexist practices that saturate and constitute women's experiences. Gelles and Straus (1989) also described sexism as a primary contributor to the disenfranchisement of abused women: "Examination of family violence over the years has consistently found that socially structured inequality is a prime contributor to violence in the home. We cannot over emphasize the preventative value of promoting sexual equality and eliminating sexism" (p. 203).

It is important to point out that sexism is not only a contributing factor to violence against women; it also permeates the manner in which researchers construct women as research subjects. For instance, psychological literature on intimate violence has sometimes depicted women as being unwilling to help themselves. As Spitzack and Carter (1987) explained:

> Simply pointing to women as a disadvantaged Other falsely implies that women are passive victims, trapped in sex-typed communication constraints with no hope of escape, when in fact they can be viewed as active agents. Valid investigations of female communication behavior require a noncom-

parative approach which, by implication, not only questions the normative power of male experience, but views women as self-conscious actors, as co-producers of their communicative climates. (p. 410)

Feminist and ideological critiques add a valuable poststructuralist turn to the understanding of abused women by highlighting the discursive and cultural systems in which the violence is subsumed. For instance, Pahl (1985) described how the rhetorical choice of the term *domestic violence* indicates that violence against a woman "by a husband within their family home, is somehow seen as a different sort of crime from violence against a stranger in a public place" (p. 13). As narratives of violence between intimates illustrate, no one should minimize the violence in a private home as "domestic." This term, applied to violence in a home, provides an image of the violence in a family as somehow less severe than violence between strangers. It also implies relations of power that are suggestive of a slave-holder hitting a domestic servant. Consequently, most discussions now refer to the problem as "intimate violence" and emphasize that violence in an intimate relationship is as brutal and debilitating as any other form of violence, perhaps more so.

Feminist and ideological understanding of the problem have slowly begun to move the focus away from a violent "pathological" individual who hits a "victim," and toward the complex ideological processes that constitute violent practices. These ideological practices are still widely reproduced today in many places because wife abuse is thought of as a private affair and there is little institutional intervention or assistance for women who are abused because they are viewed as being subordinate to their husband's authority.

Certainly, academic researchers are also implicated in reproducing the ideological structures that disenfranchise abused women. Their dominant research format favors a structuralist approach that greatly curtails and marginalizes this disenfranchised group's ability to speak about the problem for themselves. Even though a poststructuralist view of intimate violence is beginning to find a place in an academic world still dominated by structuralist views, researchers from both view points rarely allow these women to have a direct voice in their research documents. Just as abused women are marginalized to shelters, their voices have also been marginalized and silenced by the way researchers report their findings within the standard journal format.

## THE REPRODUCTION OF VIOLENT RELATIONSHIPS

This section expands on the framework of the previous two sections by offering a description of how abused women's narratives complicate conventional understandings of intimate violence by the significance they place on ideological constraints as a source of the problem. In conventional studies of disenfranchised groups, individuals in the group are viewed as autonomous, almost completely independent of forces outside this group. They are confined within the narrow limits of a quantitative survey form that uses a Likert scale that privileges the researcher's opinions and position. However, when researchers throw away their questionnaires and empower the voices of the people being studied, they discover that "their subjects" describe a set of complex ideological practices that work to keep them silent and disenfranchised. Nowhere is this more apparent than in that group we refer to collectively as abused women.

For example, when Lilia told her husband that she was thinking about leaving the relationship his response was to severely beat her. After recovering in a Salt Lake City hospital and in a shelter for abused women, she decided she would seek legal help and press charges against him. She described her experience with the legal system:

> The city prosecutors would never explain anything to me. I would go in there and virtually cry because I didn't know what was happening, no one would talk with me, they were very rude to me. Many times I heard, "Oh, she's just a spouse abuse." And they would send me out the door until one day I made a big scene, told them I was going to tear apart the office if they did not come and speak to me. And they sent me this lawyer who was very rude to me from the beginning and when he would talk to me, he would point his finger at me and he would tell me, "Oh, 75% of you women just drop charges. You are just going to do the same thing. You are probably already talking to him, this is already a honeymoon stage, you are just doing this because you are pissed off."

Jenni tells a similar story. After being beaten by her husband, she turned to her church and family for help, but everyone encouraged her to act out the role of the long-suffering wife. She described how her priest instructed her to return to her husband:

> And I said, "I can't. What am I supposed to do if he's cheating on me and hits me?" He [the priest] said, "You should forgive him." And I said, "What if he continues to do it?" Then he said, "You should pray that he'll stop." [She laughed sarcastically.] I said, "I'm sorry, I'm sorry, I've waited for a long time for him to stop and he hasn't and I'm not going back." Then he told me that I was very selfish and all I cared about was myself and what I was doing. You know, so it was really hard. The priest was mad, my parents were mad, my brother [who was best friends with her husband] didn't talk to me for a long time, I mean he would say, "Hi, how's it going." Once in a while, he would make rude comments. I mean here I was brought up believing, I mean my parents always said you come from a large family, you work together, there's no one like your family, only your family does things

for you, you know, really ingrained, the family, the family, the family, and all of a sudden to have part of my family not just pissed but totally sided with my ex was tough.

As in Lilia's and Jenni's narratives, the narratives of women who have been in violent relationships often emphasize the importance of understanding how ideological practices attempt to regulate their sense making of the problem by suggesting that they stay with their husbands. Institutional voices of authority—judicial, legislative, religious, family, clinical—form an overlapping normative set of communication practices that constitute and constrain how violent relationships are adjudicated, regulated, and anesthetized.

As more and more of the millions of American women who are beaten in their homes each year turn to community institutions for help, these community agencies, especially the judicial system, are being forced to make crucial decisions about these cases. For instance, lawyers have begun to use the "battered woman syndrome" as a means to overturn or dismiss charges against women who have killed their violent partners. In 1991 and 1992, women who killed their husbands, but could prove they did so because of years of abuse, have been pardoned from prisons by the governors of several states. In some communities, police departments and court officials have responded to the problem by initiating domestic violence sensitivity training sessions.

Unfortunately, many abused women's narratives regarding their experiences seeking help from institutional authorities are similar to Lilia's and Jenni's narratives. They describe how they experience physical and verbal violence in their marriages, and then experience ideological repression from legal officials and other institutional authorities. In this manner, institutional practices not only perpetuate the disenfranchisement and marginalization of abused women, but in some cases these practices are implicated in the deaths of these women.

Barbara is another woman I interviewed during a 7-year ethnographic study of 123 women and men in violent relationships.[1] Her emphasis on how she experienced ideological pressure to remain in her violent relationship was the most common theme voiced by all the women.[2] It is a theme

---

[1]Six women were interviewed at Utah's Correctional Facility for Women; five examples of these 123 open-ended interview sessions are fully transcribed in chapter 2 of West (1992).

[2]My examination of the narratives of individuals with direct experience of intimate violence and the narratives of counselors focuses on the emergent components in these narratives. I examine how these personal experience narratives create meanings and reproduce or resist political practices. This does not focus on the referential functions of the narratives (i.e., details of the action and/or setting), but on the evaluative function of the narratives (i.e., how the speaker interprets her or his experiences). I also examine how these narratives privilege specific meanings as embedded within relations of political praxis.

that cuts across economic, educational, and racial demographics. For example, whereas Lilia is African American and owns a successful company, and Jenni is a secretary from a middle-class Mexican-American family, Barbara is a professor from a wealthy White family whose members are part of the elite of the Mormon church. She said:

> There is a lot of ideological pressure to stay in the marriage, you have to stay married. My parents applied it, and my husband said, "You can't leave, you are breaking your covenant." That argument is, of course, fallacious. By hitting me, I could argue that he broke his covenants, but there was all that pressure and just people wanting us to stay married. They didn't want to see another relationship crumble, but I realize there was nothing real, there is no material support for doing that. There hasn't been any material support since I've been single and raising the five kids by myself. There is no material help, it's really all ideological. No one really helps out. They just don't want you to upset the apples. I think I felt that as a real heavy burden that I needed not to blow my marriage. I had to keep up the picture even though mine was in pieces.

Although Jenni and Lilia resisted the ideological pressures applied by legal, church, and family authorities and did not return to their husbands after being beaten, many women such as Barbara spend years in their violent marriages before breaking through the institutional pressures that tell them to stay in their relationships. The fact that many women stay in violent marriages illustrates why the (re)production of relations of power is one of the key components to understanding how some women submit to continual subordination.

Abused women are repeatedly encouraged to stay in the violent relationship by both family members and institutional authorities, that is, judges, prosecutors, and family counselors. In cases where women followed this advice they often ended up being severely injured, or, in a few cases, killed. These injuries and deaths could be prevented if family members and institutional authorities would stop encouraging women to stay in these relationships.

For instance, in describing why she stayed in her violent marriage for 8 years and was repeatedly hospitalized, Pat said:

> His grandmother told me, "Be patient. He'll change." See, I was Catholic then and his family were strong Catholic and they said if I ever got married again it would be adultery, you know, and all this stuff. And I was just naive to it. And I figured it wouldn't be fair for our daughter not to have her father. And so I hung around and took it.

As in Pat's story, many individuals learn that speaking about the problem to other family members or to community authorities does little to help.

Barbara described how her attempt to obtain help from various authorities was marginalized by sexist practices:

> A lot of times he would use physical force to make me do something. And a lot of times where he would use his economic clout to keep me from doing things. When I think back on it now, this Mormon psychologist, who is really a brilliant man was just so amazingly arrogant. They never said, "Has anything like this ever happened before? What brought it on." I don't think they even asked very many questions about it. They just told me it wouldn't happen again. Like they didn't even interview Ty [her husband] and say, "Will you promise never to do it again?" They were sure it wouldn't. Apparently the Stake President called this therapist, which was probably a violation of confidentiality, but he called him and said, "Do you know what is going on here," because he knew he had counseled us. "Do you know what is going on, is this going to be okay?" And they reassured him that it would be okay. I think that is a collusion, not that anybody was trying to hurt me. I don't think they thought I was at risk. It wasn't that, it was just more their male way of thinking. They didn't think about my safety as an issue and that they saw it as somebody under stress. Just the fact that they didn't look at all the other issues, the issue of safety, issue of controlling, why is he doing this? They didn't go into it very deeply. Even in the therapy they were always focusing on me. I went into therapy originally to say that my husband doesn't love me and he makes me feel sort of insecure. What should we do? It was never that they trusted my judgment and say, oh, she thinks that, I wonder why she thinks that. It was oh, she's wrong so how can we help her quit thinking like this. It was never a trusting my judgment. I mean I think that was that male collusion, just trusting more in their male instinct and the male voices and feeling more familiar with Ty's voice, Ty's explanation than mine. So I was always dealing with men. But I don't see it as a conscious collusion, the conspiracy fear, them sitting around smoking cigars saying how can we keep these women down. It was just a lack of knowing, a lack of interest.

Barbara's statements about how her voice was silenced depict some of the ideological and sexist practices interwoven within the problem of violence between intimates. This silencing process was reiterated by many other abused women in the ways they described the nonsupportive and sexist environment they encountered when they sought help.

As more and more women speak out against their abusers and against the lack of institutional support, institutional authorities are slowly recognizing how some of their organizational settings work against women's attempts to communicate their needs. For instance, a director of one of the three counseling centers where I did part of my ethnographic fieldwork described how professional counselors sometimes keep women within the violent relational process:

Realistically, I mean one of the worst offenders, of keeping those women coming back [to the abusive relationship] are people from my own profession. Because there are many people from my profession that are willing to see a couple co-jointly. They are literally setting the woman up, because frequently what a perpetrator will do is that they will say to the woman, "If you weren't so crazy, if you weren't so sick, I wouldn't have to beat you. I wouldn't have to hurt you. I wouldn't have to show you the right way to behave." Frequently, the abuser will also say, "Well then let's go see a marital therapist. Let's go see somebody." Or sometimes the victim will say, "Let's go see a marital therapist." But they get into that therapy room and they realize that if they open up and tell the therapist what is really going on, that they are being hurt by their partner, that he is going to beat her up as soon as she gets out of that room. The therapist doesn't see that the perpetrator is manipulative, but instead what they see is this person who is very congenial, very willing to tell the therapist what he sees is wrong with the relationship. Well, the victim sits there and doesn't talk, doesn't say anything, is very sullen, withdrawn and quiet. The therapist takes the perpetrator aside and says, "I'm really concerned about the signs of depression that I'm seeing in your wife. So what I would like to do is see your wife for a while individually before I see you as a couple." They leave and the husband says, "See, I told you. He thinks you are crazy too." And he's just been given a clear bill of health never to come back again. There are many therapists out there who still carry that on. That are still willing to see families, to see couples co-jointly before they get a clear picture of what they are dealing with. The message that that gives the victim at that point is that it is useless. She might as well just stay. The same message that she gets from the police.

When the reproduction and retrenchment of institutional practices is seen as a major stumbling block to women being able to leave their violent relationships, this casts a spotlight on how relational violence is entrenched within ideologies. Viewing the problem as complex and as connected to ideological systems points to institutions as sometimes being part of the problem and not the solution. This sense of institutions sometimes being unhelpful is articulated in numerous narratives.

Another force that contributes to the disenfranchisement of abused women is the romantic image we are sold of the happy American family. Discussions of the family as a violent social unit struggle against institutional and media myths that picture the family as the embodiment of all that is good about life in America. America's cultural traditions position the family as a sacred institution and women describe leaving their family as an unthinkable act. Gelles and Straus (1989) wrote:

We want to believe that the family is a safe, nurturant environment. We also do not want to see our own behavior, the behavior of our friends, neighbors, and relatives as improper. Thus, most people want to envision family violence as terrible acts, committed by horrible people against innocents. This allows us to construct a problem that is carried out by "people other than us." (p. 42)

Deferring violence to a position where it occurs to people other than us helps perpetuate the complex set of ideological processes that create an atmosphere for the violence to take place. Women's narratives about this problem acknowledge that one of the primary reasons the violence continues is because they are ashamed to tell anyone that they are trapped within a violent home. And added to this sense of shame are the terrors of the actual physical brutality and repeated threats that they will be killed if they tell anyone.

This is why it is vital for institutional authorities to not turn away women who seek help. Unfortunately, abused women still face the very real possibility of being marginalized. For example, Barbara described how after the first time her husband beat her she went to the police station and the officers said there was nothing they could do. In retrospect, she is able to understand how she was subsumed within a "patriarchal scheme," and how she slowly liberated herself, but at the time of the violence she could not comprehend the social and ideological forces influencing her life. She said:

Well I was still really in the structure. I just said, [in response to the police not helping] "Oh, well, I guess that's how the world was." I didn't see it as a big patriarchy, or a big collusion against women, I didn't ever think of anything like that. I just thought that's how the system is and it didn't seem fair to me, but I was already sort of getting that life wasn't fair. You know it's really sort of amazing that it took me so long to come to a feminist consciousness after that experience. I think it was because of my whole way of viewing the world was really based within the patriarchal scheme. I mean it was really important to me that things were like that because I did have five kids by now. And I needed to believe that a man was going to protect me and that I wasn't going to have to work outside the home. I had bought in so far into that that it was important for those things to keep being true. So I remember even in the therapy, sort of resisting having those basic fundamental beliefs upset because I wanted them to be like that.

Barbara's description of how she had "bought in" to her role as wife and how this role kept her from leaving her violent marriage provides a good summary of the personal experience narratives of most individuals who have survived their violent marriages. Their narratives describe how ideological forces discourage them from leaving their relationships and why intimate violence is the leading cause of death for women between the ages of 24 and 49 (Browne, 1987).

## HOW TO EMPOWER ABUSED WOMEN
## AND OTHER DISENFRANCHISED GROUPS

We gain a better understanding of the communication patterns of disenfranchised groups by realizing that ideology impacts *all* of these groups. If
disenfranchised groups are to be empowered, then the organizational culture
of groups designed to help them will need to change. Disenfranchisement
implies that there is an unequal balance of power. The first way we need
to begin empowering disenfranchised groups is by giving them the opportunity to have their voices heard. What do they say they need? What do
they feel are the best steps for balancing the unequal relations of power
they find themselves subjected to?

An ideological analysis offers a valuable method of empowering the
voices of the disenfranchised and not reproducing the voice of the researcher
as is so common in almost all academic writing. Scholarship on ideology
unearths how communication between disenfranchised groups and institutional authorities are contextualized within issues of power that urge individuals in these groups to articulate a system of meaning that privileges
institutional interests over other interests (Mumby, 1987). For instance,
abused women will continue to struggle through their abusive marriages
if prosecutors, psychologists, police officers, judges, and priests do not
change their flawed institutional practices that encourage women to stay
in the violent relationships.

Of course, personal responsibility is an important form of empowerment,
and women and men must take responsibility for their dysfunctional dyadic
patterns and learn to change these. Empowerment also occurs by the creation of early educational programs that make teenagers aware of how to
*prevent* a violent relationship before it starts. In this way they will never
become a part of this disenfranchised group.

The narratives of abused women dramatize how violence is often enacted
within scripted roles where ideologies attempt to dominate their decisions.
These complex cultural and ideological practices tend to severely limit the
ways women think about their violent relationships. These ideological forces
also limit the way institutional authorities and researchers formulate their
sense making of the problem. Consequently, it becomes important for
researchers of disenfranchised groups to understand the ideological forces
that ask people in these various groups to give their active consent to forms
of continual subordination.

The way that individuals think about disenfranchised groups is not just
a matter of idiosyncratic measures. Individuals approach disenfranchised
groups through various levels of cultural production and multiplicities of
power. A thorough examination of these groups and their problems requires
that these multiple connections be taken into consideration.

For example, a frequently asked question is, "Why don't these women who are in violent marriages simply leave their abusive relationships?" This often repeated question reveals that many people reproduce relations of power that follow the cultural practices of examining a problem by locating its source at the level of a dysfunctional individual or a dysfunctional couple. Many people locate the problem almost exclusively as a problem of "those women" or "those marriages." They want to reduce the problem to a few misguided individuals, to a group of "others."

However, this question misses the complexity of the problem, does not address dyadic relational patterns, and avoids examining cultural relations of power. The question would address the problem of violence between intimates more accurately if it asked: "What cultural practices teach men that it is acceptable to hit women?" Another way to rephrase the question would be: "*How* (not why) and under what set of communication and ideological conditions is it possible that the majority of individuals involved in violent relationships see no alternative but to stay in those relationships?" The answer to these questions seems clear at least as far as can be gathered from the personal experience narratives of many women (Ferraro & Johnson, 1983; West, 1992). What these women say is that they thought the violence was their fault, that they deserved it, that they never thought of leaving or calling the police, and that they were ashamed to ask for help. Women describe how they are socialized to believe that their primary roles are that of wife and homemaker. They are taught that marriage and the family are sacred. To flee from the violence also means to flee from these roles and these sacred vows. Some women are capable of making an immediate transition, however most women say they are not. To help women break the cycle of violence, they must be given support that shows them that no sacred vows and no cultural practices require them to tolerate violence.

Can we make a difference in reducing violence and violent relationships? In recent years, new laws and new support centers have been making positive changes in the way abused women are treated. However, it is important to emphasize that these changes are not uniform and they are not always quick to take hold. They vary greatly from one local to another. Consequently, the narratives of abused women take on more importance for they serve as a gauge to tell us exactly how the new laws are enforced or unenforced, effective or ineffective, and they serve as a reminder as to how institutions directly impact the social actions of individuals in violent relationships.

The narratives also give us insights into how ideologies impact all communication processes and how institutions avoid implicating themselves as part of a problem by focusing on a set of dysfunctional individuals. It is through this strategy of having the individual as the center of the problem that law enforcement officers, judicial officials, counselors, and other institutional groups attempt to exempt themselves from any type of self-examination. However, if we listen closely, and give voice to the narratives of members of these disenfranchised groups, we will learn how they are greatly impacted by the ideological practices of various institutions and how these institutions may be part of the problem.

In the narratives of disenfranchised groups we find the nexus of ideology. We discover the link between discourses about marginalized groups and the institutions that tell us both consciously and unconsciously how to make sense of those groups. The narratives should also be viewed as open texts that not only show how people are repressed, but also how they create forms of resistance and thereby can potentially reach a sense of liberation.

In examining how ideology impacts abused women we find mostly a repressive force. However, in other disenfranchised groups we may find the opposite, or a mixing of both repression and liberation. And one of the potential benefits of research on ideology is that we discover how some people are liberated by becoming aware for the first time that they have been unconsciously following a set of ideological practices that is detrimental to them.

For future studies of disenfranchised groups, it is important to understand how the concept of ideology is a constitutive force that suggests to people how they "should" enact their lives. Attempts to understand various groups are mediated through ideology. To study disenfranchised groups is to study the relations of power that give them form and substance. Hopefully, future research will make more use of poststructuralist and ideological approaches that allow us the ability to unearth the structures of power and knowledge that have made America such a violent culture.

In learning to focus on groups as constituted by ideology, we need to articulate the institutional practices that suggest to individuals how they should "interpellate" themselves or constitute their interactions in accordance with institutional rules (Althusser, 1976; Belsey, 1980). As Williams (1989) argued, we must learn to understand hegemonic social forces by analyzing "the central, effective and dominant system of meanings and values, which are not merely abstract but which are organized and lived" (p. 383). This type of analysis focuses on the multidimensional sense making that occurs when people transact relationships. The researcher emphasized how people reproduce or resist ideologies and how they articulate meanings about their relationships (Conquergood, 1991). With this focus on ideologies—the production of knowledge, relations of power as established through discursive fields, and institutional practices—we will be better able to understand the roles institutions play in defining disenfranchised groups. It will also open up our thinking to the ways we are connected and constituted by ideologies such as patriarchy, colonialism, rationalism or capitalism. Certainly, there are numerous ways that the communication of disenfranchised groups may be analyzed, but by understanding how ideologies contextualize *all* groups, we will facilitate our understanding of disenfranchised groups.

## REFERENCES

Althusser, L. (1976). *Essays in self-criticism* (G. Locke, Trans.). London: New Left Books.

Ball, M. (1977). Issues of violence in family casework. *Social Casework, 58*, 3–12.

Belsey, C. (1980). *Critical practice.* London: Methuen.

Berk, R., Berk, S., Loseke, D., & Rauma, D. (1983). Mutual combat and other family violence myths. In D. Finkelhor, R. Gelles, G. Hotaling, & M. Straus (Eds.), *The dark side of families: Current family violence research* (pp. 197–212). Beverly Hills, CA: Sage.

Bersani, C. A., & Chen, H. (1988). Sociological perspectives in family violence. In V. B. Van Hasselt, R. L. Morrison, A. S. Bellack, & M. Hersen (Eds.), *Handbook of family violence* (pp. 57–86). New York: Plenum.

Browne, A. (1987). *When battered women kill.* New York: The Free Press.

Conquergood, D. (1991). Rethinking ethnography: Toward a critical cultural politics. *Communication Monographs, 58*, 179–194.

Courtright, J., Millar, F., & Rogers, L. E. (1979). Domineeringness and dominance: Replication and expansion. *Communication Monographs, 46*, 179–192.

de Certeau, M. (1984). *The practice of everyday life* (S. Randall, Trans.). Berkeley: University of California Press.

Dutton, D. G. (1988). *The domestic assault on women.* Boston: Allyn & Bacon.

Eagleton, T. (1983). *Literary theory.* Minneapolis: Minnesota Press.

Elbow, M. (1977). Theoretical considerations of violent marriages (personality characteristics of wife abusers). *Social Casework, 58*, 515–526.

Faulk, M. (1977, October). Sexual factors in marital violence. *Medical Aspects of Human Sexuality*, pp. 30–43.

Ferraro, K. J., & Johnson, J. (1983). How women experience battering: The process of victimization. *Social Problems, 30*, 325–339.

Follingstad, D., Laughlin, J., Polek, D., Rutledge, L., & Hause, E. (1991). Identification of patterns of wife abuse. *Journal of Interpersonal Violence, 6*, 187–204.

Foss, J. (1980). The paradoxical nature of family relationship and family conflict. In M. Straus & G. Hotaling (Eds.), *The social causes of husband-wife violence* (pp. 115–135). Minneapolis: University of Minnesota Press.

Foss, S., Foss, K., & Trapp, R. (1985). *Contemporary perspectives on rhetoric.* Prospect Heights, IL: Waveland Press.

Foucault, M. (1972). *The archaeology of knowledge* (S. Smith, Trans.). New York: Pantheon.

Foucault, M. (1980). *Power/knowledge* (C. Gordon, Ed.). New York: Pantheon.

Gelles, R. J., & Cornell, C. P. (1985). *Intimate violence in families.* Beverly Hills, CA: Sage.

Gelles, R., & Straus, M. (1989). *Intimate violence.* New York: Simon & Schuster.

Giles-Sims, J. (1983). *Wife-battering: A systems theory approach.* New York: Guilford.

Gordon, L. (1988). *Heroes of their own lives.* New York: Viking.

Gulotta, G., & Neuberger, L. (1983). A systemic and attributional approach to victimology. *Victimology, 8*, 5–16.

Hamberger, L., & Hastings, J. (1986). Characteristics of spouse abusers: Predictors of treatment acceptance. *Journal of Interpersonal Violence, 1*(3), 363–373.

Hotaling, G., & Sugerman, D. (1986). An analysis of risk makers in husband to wife violence: The current state of knowledge. *Violence and Victims, 1*(2), 101–124.

Huggins, M., & Straus, M. (1980). Violence and the social structure as reflected in childrens' books from 1950 to 1970. In M. Straus & G. Hotaling (Eds.), *The social causes of husband-wife violence* (pp. 51–67). Minneapolis: University of Minnesota Press.

Manderscheid, R., Rae, D., McCarrick, A., & Silbergeld, S. (1982). A stochastic model of relational control in dyadic interaction. *American Sociological Review, 47*, 62–75.

McNeely, R. L., & Robinson-Simpson, G. (1989). The truth about domestic violence: A falsely framed issue. In N. Davidson (Ed.), *Gender sanity* (pp. 163–176). New York: University Press of America.

Millar, F. E., & Rogers, L. E. (1981, May). *A pragmatic approach to relational communication: A case study.* Paper presented at the annual meeting of the International Communication Association, Minneapolis.

Mumby, D. (1987). The political function of narrative in organizations. *Communication Monographs, 54*, 113–127.

Pahl, J. (Ed.). (1985). *Private violence and public policy.* London: Routledge & Kegan Paul.

Rieff, P. (1987). *The triumph of the therapeutic.* Chicago: University of Chicago Press.

Rogers, L. E., & Millar, F. E. (1988). Relational communication. In S. W. Duck (Ed.), *Handbook of personal relationships* (pp. 289–306). New York: Wiley.

Rosenbaum, A., & O'Leary, K. (1981). Marital violence: Characteristics of abusive couples. *Journal of Consulting and Clinical Psychology, 49*, 63–71.

Shainess, N. (1977). Psychological aspects of wife battering. In M. Roy (Ed.), *Battered women* (pp. 111–119). New York: Van Nostrand Reinhold.

Spitzack, C., & Carter, K. (1987). Women in communication studies: A typology for revision. *Quarterly Journal of Speech, 2*, 401–423.

Straus, M. (1979). Measuring intrafamily conflict and violence: The conflict tactics (CT) scales. *Journal of Marriage and Family, 41*, 75–88.

Straus, M. A., & Gelles, R. (1986). Societal change and change in family violence from 1975 to 1985 as revealed by two national surveys. *Journal of Marriage and Family, 48*, 465–479.

Wander, P. (1983). The ideological turn in modern criticism. *Central States Speech Journal, 34*, 1–18.

Watzlawick, P., Beavin, J., & Jackson, D. (1967). *Pragmatics of human communication: A study of interaction patterns, pathologies, and paradoxes.* New York: Norton.

Weitzman, J., & Dreen, K. (1982). Wife beating: A view of the marital dyad. *Social Casework, 63*, 11–18.

West, J. (1992). *Discursive practices and relations of power: A qualitative study of intimate violence.* Unpublished doctoral dissertation, University of Utah, Salt Lake City.

West, J. (1993). Ethnography and ideology: The politics of cultural representation. *Western Journal of Communication, 57*, 209–214.

West, J. (1995). Understanding how the dynamics of ideology influence violence between intimates. In S. Duck & J. Wood (Eds.), *Confronting relationship challenges* (pp. 129–149). Thousand Oaks, CA: Sage.

Williams, R. (1989). Base and superstructure in Marxist cultural theory. In R. C. Davis & R. Schliefer (Eds.), *Contemporary literary criticism* (pp. 378–390). New York: Longman.

Yllo, K. (1984). The status of women, marital equality and violence against wives. *Journal of Comparative Family Studies, 14*, 67–86.

Yllo, K. (1988). Political and methodological debates in wife abuse research. In K. Yllo & M. Bograd (Eds.), *Feminist perspectives on wife abuse* (pp. 28–50). Newbury Park, CA: Sage.

# 16 Discourse and Disenfranchisement: Targets, Victims, and Survivors of Sexual Harassment

Robin P. Clair
*Purdue University*

The term *sexual harassment* was spotlighted by the media when Anita Hill appeared before Congressional members and charged Clarence Thomas, then Supreme Court nominee, with subjecting her to offensive behavior that included discussing pubic hairs and pornography. Americans became more familiar with the term sexual harassment when the Navy's Tailhook convention was revealed for its less than conventional and professional practices. Ninety individuals, civilians and Navy personnel, reported being verbally or physically assaulted in a sexual manner at the Tailhook convention in 1991. Although these two events were considered spectacular media stories, sexual harassment is an everyday occurrence and far too many people have their own stories of sexual harassment.

Researchers estimate between 42% of women and 15% of men working in government-related jobs have encountered sexual harassment (U.S. Merit Protection Board [USMSPB], 1981, 1988). Women in the private sector face sexual harassment at an alarming rate. Studies vary in their estimation from 48% (Clair, 1993b) and 50% (Loy & Stewart, 1984) to 75% (Lafontaine & Tredeau, 1986), depending partly on the type of employment.

Society may be familiar with the term *sexual harassment* and in general we may be growing more comfortable in our talk about it, but we have not as yet figured out how to talk to, or about, the thousands of victims who suffer the ridicule, anguish, and despair so often associated with sexual harassment. As Wood (1992) suggested we have just begun to "name" sexual harassment. What is not named is invisible (Spender, 1984). Now

313

we must ask, "How are we to name those who struggle with sexual harassment?" For in naming there is power (Wood, 1992).

A rhetorical debate is quietly being waged among scholars over the labeling of individuals who encounter sexual harassment. Labels such as "target," "victim," and "survivor" have been proposed. Denotations of these terms may seem less problematic than the connotations. However, a feminist perspective suggests that both denotations and connotations carry patriarchal implications.

The present chapter discusses women as a disenfranchised group who are the primary "targets," "victims," and "survivors" of sexual harassment. Sexual harassment is explained as a discursive practice that promotes patriarchy and disenfranchises those who are subjected to it. Disenfranchisement is explained in terms of patriarchal privilege, a means of oppressing women and other marginalized individuals. Finally, an analysis of the patriarchal implications embedded in the terms "target," "victim," and "survivor" are discussed.

## SEXUAL HARASSMENT

Although sexual harassment has a lengthy history, definitions of the term have been debated more recently. Farley (1978) provided a general definition of the term that limited sexual harassment to a practice imposed upon women by men in positions of power. That definition has been expanded over the years. MacKinnon's (1979) classic analysis of the subject was instrumental in leading women activists to refine the definitions of sexual harassment. Crocker (1983) provided an excellent overview of the definitions of sexual harassment and challenged the most widely accepted definition supplied by the Equal Employment Opportunity Commission (EEOC). Although the EEOC's definition is not without flaws, it is the most widely accepted definition and has been upheld by the Supreme Court. It is described as follows:

> The 1980 EEOC guidelines for the legal definition of sexual harassment suggests that unwelcome sexual advances, either verbal or physical, constitute sexual harassment when (1) submission to the advances is a term or condition of employment, (2) submission to or rejection of the advances is used as basis for making employment decisions, or (3) such conduct interferes with a person's work performance or creates an intimidating, hostile, or offensive work environment. (Konrad & Gutek, 1986, p. 422)

The Civil Rights Act of 1991 upheld the right of individuals subjected to sexual harassment to claim both compensatory and punitive damages for the emotional, physical, and economic suffering incurred. Those who are subjected to sexual harassment can now rely on legal definitions as well as federal statutes to compensate them financially. However there is a cap on the amount of money that can be claimed and money does not take away the long-lasting effects of sexual harassment.

Sexual harassment affects the emotional and physical health of those subjected to it; and, it impedes their economic and sociopolitical welfare. Although men have been sexually harassed, little research exists on the effects that sexual harassment incurs upon male victims (see, for exceptions, Clair, 1994; Department of Defense Inspector General, 1993; Gutek, 1985; USMSPB, 1981, 1988). Thus, the following review of the impact of sexual harassment is limited to reports from women.

In terms of emotional and physical health, women report symptoms including headaches, loss of appetite, insomnia, and depression (McKinney & Maroules, 1991). They also suffer from increased nervousness, irritability, uncontrolled anger and crying, loss of motivation, weight loss, and stomach problems (Loy & Stewart, 1984). Victims of Tailhook report symptoms of posttraumatic stress disorder, plagued by nightmares and nightsweats months after the assault occurred (Castaneda, 1992; also see Koss, 1990).

Emotional and physical suffering are often compounded by economic privation. Women are frequently transferred, fired, or forced to quit due to the unbearable working environment. Furthermore, it is not uncommon for college women to alter their career choices to avoid sexual harassment in the classroom (see Dziech & Weiner, 1990; Paludi, 1990). "Our Stories" (1992), a collection of women's accounts of sexual harassment, is replete with examples of emotional, physical, and economic hardships endured by the sexually harassed.

Sexual harassment negatively impacts those subjected to it in emotional, physical, and economic ways. These effects may be long-lasting. Furthermore, victimage may spread through subtle socializing practices to those not directly harassed. Victims of sexual harassment are far too often isolated and disenfranchised.


## DISENFRANCHISEMENT

Women have a long and uninterrupted history of disenfranchisement. In the classic sense of the term, disenfranchise or disfranchise refers to depriving a person of rights as a citizen. Although the women's U.S. suffrage movement is a classic example of women overcoming disenfranchisement, disenfranchisement is not limited to voting. To be disenfranchised is to be denied equal status as a citizen. Women have been denied equal access not only to political decision making, but also to equal employment, and equal participation in social, religious, and academic arenas.

Although women's suffrage may come to mind when the term disenfranchisement is used, women's disenfranchisement is neither limited to the United States or even to this century. Without a doubt woman's oppression can be traced to preindustrial and precapitalist eras. Misogynistic practices cross ancient cultures and modern societies, communist and capitalist alike (Jagger, 1983). Although Engels (1884/1983) offered the development of private ownership as the link to women's oppression, these Marxist explanations have left many feminists dissatisfied (Daly, 1973; de Beauvoir, 1974; MacKinnon, 1989). Oppression of women, most feminists agree, predates the development of capitalism (see Tong, 1989). Furthermore, modern communist social systems have failed to free women from the domination of men. Subsequently, most feminists accept that capitalism may well be an exploitive system that perpetuates gender oppression, but it is not the sole driving force behind women's disenfranchisement.

It is more than a socioeconomic system that maintains the domination of women; rather, it is patriarchy. Patriarchy permeates socioeconomic systems, political systems including the state and cultural institutions (e.g., religions, education, and popular entertainment), and even interpersonal relationships.

## PATRIARCHY AND DISENFRANCHISEMENT

Both Engels (1884/1983) and Foucault (1976/1978) traced patriarchy to early Roman law, specifically *patria potesta* that gave the father the right to kill his children, servants, and wife. Whether this is the origin of patriarchy or not may be debatable, but it certainly characterizes the principles of patriarchy.

Cockburn (1991) provided several definitions of patriarchy ranging from "a system of social structures and practices in which men dominate, oppress and exploit women" (p. 7) to a shifting system of control changing throughout history in an interrelated fashion with the modes of production yet not necessarily tied to those economic systems. After providing a series of definitions, Cockburn concluded that "today father-right as such is giving way to more generalized male sex-right, that might better be termed 'fratriarchy'. However, 'patriarchy' has come to be a popular shorthand term for systematic male dominance" (pp. 7–8). It is this systematic male dominance that keeps men from voting women into political positions, hiring women for certain jobs, appointing them to higher positions within the workplace, and accepting their knowledge and expertise within unions (Cockburn, 1991). In other words, fratiarchy-patriarchy contributes to the disenfranchisement of women.

Patriarchy is guided by the principle of privilege; disenfranchisement has been described as being deprived of privileges, of rights. For women and other marginalized individuals, disenfranchisement could be described as being *subjected to privilege*—male privilege.

Women are particularly subjected to male privilege through gender discrimination. Sexual harassment, a form of gender discrimination, is a discursive practice that reinforces patriarchy through its insidious use of power. Thus, sexual harassment supports patriarchy in both direct and indirect ways by announcing, through discursive practices, the inferior role of women in society and throughout history.

## THE DISCOURSE OF PRIVILEGE AND SEXUAL HARASSMENT

Ferguson (1984) defined *discourse* as "the characteristic ways of speaking and writing that both constitute and reflect our experiences" (p. 6). Extending this definition, Deetz (1992) explained discourse as "a signifying, representational practice" (p. 260). *Discursive practices* combine to create *discursive formations*. Discussions of discourse in this theoretical vein can be attributed to the work of Foucault (1972), who described discourse as "a group of statements and conceptual configurations brought together in a discursive formation" (pp. 116–117). These discursive formations exist within discursive fields that consist "of alternative ways of structuring the world and organizing social processes" (Deetz, 1992, p. 263). Certain discourses are privileged, whereas others are marginalized. Marginalized discourses are often "dismissed by the hegemonic system of meanings and practices as irrelevant or bad" (Weedon, 1987, p. 35).

Patriarchy is a discursive formation brought together by a series of discourses that undermine alternatives. Although women have been disenfranchised through their exclusion from educational (e.g., limited opportunities in certain fields), social (e.g., excluded from membership in male clubs and limited participation in sports), religious positions (e.g., the Catholic Church still forbids women from becoming priests), and organizational opportunities (e.g., the glass ceiling), their entrance into some of these arenas is still met with sexual intimidation intended to remind women of their inferior status. As such, sexual harassment is a discourse intended to promote patriarchy and disenfranchise women.

Cockburn (1991) explained that sexual harassment is a clear means for men to marginalize women and maintain control. Cockburn provided numerous examples from the junior office worker who must deal with men commenting upon her "boobs" and ogling her legs to the successful senior female executive who was "pinched [on] her bottom" by a male colleague as she climbed the stairs on her way to an executive meeting (pp. 140–142). The female executive explained that she already felt marginalized in a male world of executives, after being pinched she felt "stunned" and "mortified" (p. 142). In these two cases, sexual harassment is a discursive practice that "tells" the individual women that they should not forget their inferior status nor should they forget that men, in general, are privileged in our society and see it as their right to subject women to these practices.

Challenges to the dominant discourse of patriarchy are often met with further humiliating discourses. Complaints against sexual harassment, for insistence, are often answered with the attitude: "Can't she take a jock/joke?" (Daly, 1984, p. 209; also see Clair, 1993b; MacKinnon, 1979, for examples of the trivialization of sexual harassment). Often times, harassed individuals encounter further harassment from colleagues, peers, management, and even courtroom judges (see MacKinnon, 1979).

In order not to perpetuate the status quo, people must be careful not to inadvertently label the harassed person in ways that make them feel further victimized by society. It is important that we maintain a sensitivity to the discourse we use to describe people who have suffered sexual harassment. In other words, how we respond to, and talk about, people who have been subjected to sexual harassment can have powerful effects and far-reaching implications. Subsequently, the remaining sections of this chapter address the patriarchal and disenfranchising aspects of the terms "target," "victim," and "survivor," as they relate to the sexually harassed.

## CRITICAL ANALYSIS OF "TARGET," "VICTIM," AND "SURVIVOR"

Relying on the expertise of several well-known feminists, Wood (1992) asserted that:

> Those who have power have the prerogative to name the world. Invariably ... they name it from their perspective ... Recognizing the central consequence of naming sheds light on the long history of silence surrounding sexual harassment—the not naming of it: Because it is experienced primarily by women. (p. 352)

Naming sexual harassment allows us to claim both rights and responsibilities with regard to these practices. Wood was equally careful to note that how we name or label people who have been sexually harassed is also a matter for sensitive scrutiny. Specifically, Wood stated:

> Currently, there is a controversy about the use of the term "victim" since, some argue, it is disempowering. As an alternative "survivor" has been suggested as a more empowering term that encourages someone who experienced sexual harassment [or rape or abuse] to see herself or himself as having

control. Because the term "victim" is widely understood and describes perhaps accurately the feelings of someone at the time of the incident, I use that term in this essay. (p. 349)

Whether describing self or others who have been sexually harassed, the terms "target," "victim," and "survivor" may come to mind. At certain times or in certain cases, one term may seem more appropriate than another. At other times or in other cases, the differences among the terms may seem irrelevant. Nevertheless, the terms are not without both denotative and connotative histories. Each of the terms carries implications through its general definition and the general interpretation of that definition. As noted earlier, naming sexual harassment has provided those subjected to it with a new sense of power. Naming the individuals as "targets," "victims," or "survivors" should receive equally serious consideration.

Potentially any person is a "target" of sexual harassment, when target implies a "person or thing made an object of attack." "Victim" refers to one who is "subjected to suffering." Thus, for a "target" of sexual harassment to be labeled a "victim," he or she must have experienced what can be labeled sexual harassment (by patriarchal logic). Most "victims" of sexual harassment can be considered "survivors" of harassment (although exceptions do exist), where "survivor" denotes the ability "to remain alive."

Denotative delineations among "target," "victim," and "survivor" seem straightforward, yet they invoke patriarchal metaphors. Baudrillard (1982/1988) suggested that denotations and connotations are embedded with political and economic meanings. Extending this concept, Clair (1993a) argued that the sign is "patriarchally imprisoned." The following analyses focus on uncovering patriarchal implications of the three terms.

## Patriarchal Implications of "Target"

The term "target" reinforces the objectification of the harassed individual conjuring images of a dart board or military mark. Sports and military metaphors adequately present the attack, the violence, the invasion; however, they fail to represent the living, feeling human being as the recipient of these assaults.

In spite of these patriarchal implications, studies investigating the "targets" of sexual harassment have been helpful in developing the case that sexual harassment is both pervasive and directed primarily toward women by men (Tangri, Burt, & Johnson, 1982). Concomitantly, studies of "targets" have led to myopic views of sexual harassment as seduction that can obscure patriarchal implications of sexual harassment and stifle the development of feminist-oriented theories. Furthermore, focus on the primary "targets" of sexual harassment can marginalize individuals who do not fit the stereotypical portrait of a "target."

Research addressing who the "targets" of sexual harassment are emphasizes the demographic distinctions that make some "targets" more or less *vulnerable* to sexual harassment. Findings have been helpful in providing descriptions of primary "targets" and frequency of assaults. For example, researchers have confirmed that women are the primary targets of sexual harassment (USMPB, 1981, 1988). Unmarried women are more susceptible to sexual harassment than married women (USMPB, 1981). In addition, both younger and more economically dependent women are more apt to report being sexually harassed than older or more economically independent women (Tangri et al., 1982). According to Fain and Anderton (1987), minority ethnic status also increases vulnerability to sexual harassment. Finally, women in nontraditional jobs report more sexual harassment than women in traditional jobs (Gutek, 1985; Lafontaine & Tredeau, 1986).

Demographic data have been of benefit in building the case that sexual harassment is a pervasive condition and not isolated to a few individuals. Furthermore, it has spawned several useful explanations (Fain & Anderton, 1987; Gutek, 1985; Tangri et al., 1982). However, an overemphasis on the "targets" of sexual harassment can stifle theories.

Under the assumption that young single women (rather than unmarried women) are at highest risk, several scholars focus their efforts exclusively on the "seduction" scenario. For example, Pryor (1987) investigated men's proclivities to touch attractive women. Pryor's work reveals that harassers are insensitive, dominance-seeking individuals who are more apt to harass when they think they can get away with it. These are important findings, yet the limitations of this approach need to be addressed. Heterosexual seduction scenarios can lead to viewing sexual harassment as inept romantic overtures or attempts to develop an affair. Although unsolicited touching is an aspect of sexual harassment, it does not tell the whole story. For example, one might question why Pryor employs attractive women; attractiveness has never been a criterion for sexual harassment.[1] Further, one might question why the studies are limited to touching when most sexual harassment comes in the form of degrading remarks (MacKinnon, 1989); for example, the boss who ends a conversation with his secretary by saying, "Now take your nice ass and get out of here" (Clair, 1993b, p. 127) or the surgeons who humiliate a nurse by asking if her pubic hair matches the color of the hair on her head. Although studies of unsolicited touching of attractive women are important and offer knowledge about sexual harassment, they may also limit our perceptions of the problem.

---

[1] To the best of my knowledge, the only case study of sexual harassment that specifically points out that only attractive women were targeted for harassment is that of Tailhook 91 (see Department of Defense Inspector General, 1993).

Also, an overemphasis on who the "targets" are falls prey to the patriarchal practice of marginalizing others. For example, after reporting that between 1% and 21% of men reported being sexually harassed in ways ranging from insulting remarks to quid pro quo sexual harassment, Gutek and Cohen (1987) concluded that "men *might* experience some of the *less severe* [italics added] social-sexual behaviors" (p. 105). This conclusion may have been rooted in the need to establish that women are the primary "targets" of sexual harassment, which was crucial to building legal arguments of sexual harassment as a form of gender discrimination. Feminists, however, *are* able to account for the sexual harassment of men without destroying gender discrimination arguments. For example, Clair (1994) provided an analysis of one man's story of sexual harassment that indicates some women sexually harass men in order to keep them from joining a female-dominated work group (i.e., nursing assistants). Although an unlikely target, the man claims he is sexually harassed. The female nursing assistants seem to participate in the sexual harassment of the man in order to maintain their control in the workplace, yet their control is limited to the lowest level of the medical hierarchy. Furthermore, they question his heterosexual prowess and invoke racial discrimination by suggesting that he may not be "man enough" to handle having sex with a Black woman. This story of sexual harassment and ones like it are ignored by researchers primarily because men are rarely sexually harassed. In other words, men are not the stereotypical "targets" of sexual harassment.

As mentioned previously, the term "target" reinforces the objectification of the person subjected to it—objects, rather than thinking, feeling human beings. MacKinnon (1989) argued that objectification is unique to women and is the "fundamental motive force" (p. 130) in the construction of sexuality as a system of patriarchal domination. Objectification allows researchers to more easily quantify the experiences of sexually harassed individuals, rather than listening to their stories. In addition to marking down demographics, it is imperative that researchers recognize the human beings involved and document their suffering. Furthermore, members of society need to recognize the consequences of stereotyping certain people as the "targets" of sexual harassment.

## Patriarchal Implications of "Victim"

"Victims," according to Holstein and Miller (1990), are viewed as people unjustly subjected to harmful behavior that is outside of their control. The term "victim" provides an outlet for the suffering human being, but it fails to empower that individual. "Victim" constructs the person as isolated and powerless.

Although "victim" has limitations in terms of empowerment, Koss (1990) pointed out that women often blame themselves for the sexual harassment. For women subjected to sexual harassment to acknowledge their status as "victims" is to realize that they are not to blame, that in fact they have been victimized. Thus, accepting a "victim" status can be empowering.

"Victims" of harassment should never be blamed for the harassment in · the sense that they "deserved such treatment" or "brought it upon themselves," yet women must be aware of their hegemonic complicity (Clair, 1993b). For example, "victims" who trivialize the harassment, fail to label it as sexual harassment, or privatize the experience tend to support the status quo. In other words, although these actions may keep women safe from further sexual harassment or ease their emotional or economic situations, they perpetuate the reign of patriarchy by minimizing sexual harassment. MacKinnon (1989) pointed out that:

> Women often find ways to resist male supremacy and to expand their spheres of action. But they are never free of it. Women also embrace the standards of women's place in this regime as "our own" to varying degrees and in varying voices ... just to make it through another day. This, not inert passivity, is the meaning of being a victim. (p. 138)

The Department of Defense Inspector General (1993) recently released paraphrased versions of the sexual harassment experienced by Navy personnel and civilians at the infamous Tailhook convention. The government document lists the stories of the "victims." Several women objected to being called "victims." For example, a 29-year-old female Navy lieutenant who preferred not to be called a "victim" is nevertheless referred to in this manner. She is listed as "Victim 1." The following quote exemplifies the reluctance of this woman to take on the label of "victim" and the insensitivity of the researchers:

> According to the victim, she entered the third floor hallway ... As she walked up the hallway, she was bitten on the buttocks. The victim turned, kicked her assailant in the shins and threw her drink on him ... The victim felt that she handled the incident and objected to being labeled as a "victim" despite the fact that the bite caused a bruise on her buttocks. (p. F-1)

In this case, under patriarchal guidance those writing the document impose their label—victim—upon the woman. Quina (1990) suggested that the term "victim" should be used "to refer to the dynamic, and survivor to refer to the individual after the assault" (p. 101). "Victim" is a complex term that should not be tossed about in academic or bureaucratic text without sensitivity to the people who are being labeled.

## Patriarchal Implications of "Survivor"

Finally, "survivor" as a term is not without its share of problems, metaphorically painting images of bruised and battered people surrounding a crashed Boeing 747 or determined individuals who rebuild following natural catastrophes. On a more political note, "survivor" evokes images of disenfranchised Jews who lived to see their release from concentration camps.

"Survivor" evokes the image of having overcome extreme difficulties especially during a crisis situation. Sexual harassment does not always take on the salient characteristics of a crisis. It may be easier to refer to one who mentally and physically overcomes the violence of physical assault and/or rape (one form of sexual harassment) as a survivor than it is to think of people who are continually and subtly assaulted as survivors.

A useful analogy might be to substitute racial discrimination for gender discrimination to see how the word parallels. Thus, would we call African Americans survivors of racism? Oddly enough it sounds as if racism has disappeared and Blacks have survived to see the proverbial dawning of a new day. Neither racism nor sexism has been eliminated; marginalized individuals do not survive the aftermath of racism and sexism—they survive in it, with it, and through it.

What does it mean to survive sexual harassment? The following story provided by Quina (1990) sheds some light on sexual harassment survival:

> Faye spent months being "tough" about her lawsuit—she described it as having to block out all emotions in order to survive (denial). When her mother called and accused her of shaming the family, her well crafted armor came crashing down. . . . Her therapist wisely recognized the signs of mourning . . . Faye did not feel strong enough to pursue the lawsuit, her therapist helped her mourn that loss as well, appreciating that she had done all she could, and helping her feel like a survivor rather than a victim. (p. 100)

Although Quina offered several excellent activist strategies for dealing with sexual harassment, "mourning" the loss "in order to achieve that peace" (p. 100) condemns this particular survivor to a state of complacent defeat. Unless this is considered a temporary recourse, this form of therapy may encourage a silent submission to the current system and discourage progressive counteractivities. Certainly, women grow tired of the constant battles they face; they need time to rest and regroup, but they must not give up. For social transformation to occur, we need to listen to the words of Michelle Vinson: "If I fight, some day some woman will win" (see MacKinnon, 1989, p. 237). Had the therapist given strength through activism rather than defeatism, more might be achieved. When Faye's strength wore thin, why didn't the therapist go to court with her, file a law suit on her behalf, or direct her toward other women or men who would? Maybe the therapist did not "wisely recognize" the problem, not of mourning, but of patriarchy, and the continuing disenfranchisement of women.

In "Our Stories" (1992) a woman, who was teaching at a small liberal arts college, tells of being sexually harassed nearly 10 years prior. She survived the incident. Two years after the incident occurred, a student came to her reporting that she had been sexually harassed by the same man. Although the woman had taken no legal action against the harasser when he harassed her, she felt it was urgent that something now be done. Both she and her student registered formal complaints. Several other complaints followed and the man was eventually terminated from his position. Both of these women were the "targets" of sexual harassment, they were the "victims," and they are the "survivors." In this case, they survive now knowing that their mutual support helped to bring some justice to their situation.

Being a "survivor" of sexual harassment does not necessarily ensure empowerment, but neither does it have to mean passive acceptance. Another woman reflected upon her experiences in the following way:

> While I don't believe that feminism can provide a complete account of why sexual harassment takes place in the academy, feminist literature has provided me with an extremely valuable analytic language, and a systematic way to reflect upon my experiences . . . Seven years after the ordeal, I think that I am finally able to recall the events with some sympathy for myself . . . I would like to think that my sympathy for myself is complemented by my commitment to help less senior graduate students succeeded [sic], to contribute to a climate of diversity, and to promote the better parts of academic life. . . . Yet, some residue remains inside . . . At times I feel like a boxer, miraculously in the ring after a whopper of a punch in the first round, still reeling, still trying to steady one's feet. ("Our Stories," 1992, p. 368)

More than likely, as this woman's story suggests, being a "survivor" contains elements of empowerment as well as confusion and pain.

## CONCLUSION

Sexual harassment, itself, is a discourse of disenfranchisement, a discourse of the strife perpetuated by a patriarchal society. The point is not to argue whether we can or cannot call sexually harassed people "targets," "victims," or "survivors"; rather, it is that discourse constructs a sociopolitical reality. Discursive practices are not neutral, innocent symbolic exchanges. They are embedded with patriarchal implications. Thus, we must make ourselves aware of the ramifications, theoretically and pragmatically, when we embrace a discourse.

Today, as in the past, a discourse dominates that ensures the disenfranchisement of women—that discourse is patriarchy. It is substantiated through discursive practices such as sexual harassment. Recently, a challenge has been waged against the dominant discourse, especially against sexual harassment. Voices are being heard that were never heard before, stories are being told that were never told before, and we need to do more than listen.

We must recognize and affirm the realities that women encounter in a patriarchal society. We must continue efforts to expose the dominant discourse as patriarchal, not as a neutral or apolitical practice. We must develop and enact counterstrategies—with concrete goals in mind. We must reach out a hand to women like Faye who are exhausted from the fight, and when we grow tired, we must remember that it is only temporary.

From research to everyday resistance, we must recognize that no discourse we choose will be without limitations. Only the naive would think otherwise. We must recognize that whatever words we choose to guide our discussions, whatever practices we employ to counter sexual harassment can be co-opted. Yet, we cannot let this overwhelm us or preoccupy us. From time to time, we need to step back and assess our strategies and our discourse, especially drawing out patriarchal implications, in hopes of ending the disenfranchisement of women.

Sexual harassment is a discursive practice that has been used to remind certain "targets" of sexual harassment, especially women, of their inferior status. The disenfranchisement of women is perpetuated by acts of sexual harassment that condemn the "victims" to a hostile environment that often keeps them from enjoying the privileges that most White men enjoy. Sexual harassment has far too often blocked the efforts of these individuals to enter political, social, religious, academic, and economic arenas with the same rights that most men pursue these opportunities. In the past, surviving this inequitable situation generally meant that "survivors" learned to live with it. Today, "survivors" can pursue more activist strategies, albeit they are still limited by patriarchal institutions and ideology.

We must not fall prey to the patriarchal stereotypes embedded in our terminology concerning those who are sexually harassed. "Targets" are not always voluptuous women. "Harassers" are not always middle-aged White men looking for a romantic encounter. "Victims" should not be viewed as naive participants who brought this upon themselves, nor should they be viewed as helpless. More important, the term "victim" must be expanded to include friends, relatives, and coworkers of the person who has been sexually harassed, as the impact of sexual harassment is never isolated to one person. Nor can we neatly divide the world into "victims," "harassers," and "everyone else," as though "everyone else" were not responsible in some way. We cannot categorically label and thereby once again isolate and disenfranchise the "targets," "victims," and "survivors" of sexual harassment. To the contrary, we must be aware of how discourse perpetuates an oppressive situation and work together to end it.

## REFERENCES

Baudrillard, J. (1988). For a critique of the political economy of the sign. In M. Poster (Ed.), *Jean Baudrillard selected writings* (pp. 57–97). Stanford, CA: Stanford University Press. (Original work published 1982)

Castaneda, C. J. (1992, August 3). Tailhook investigation "no help." Women go public, may file suit. *USA Today*, p. 3A.

Clair, R. P. (1993a). The bureaucratization, commodification, and privatization of sexual harassment: A study of the "Big Ten" universities. *Management Communication Quarterly, 7*, 123–157.

Clair, R. P. (1993b). The use of framing devices to sequester organizational narratives. *Communication Monographs, 60*, 113–136.

Clair, R. P. (1994). Resistance and oppression as a self-contained opposite: An organizational communication analysis of one man's story of sexual harassment. *Western Journal of Communication, 58*, 235–262.

Cockburn, C. (1991). *In the way of women*. Ithaca, NY: ILR Press.

Crocker, P. L. (1983). An analysis of university definitions of sexual harassment. *Signs, 8*, 696–707.

Daly, M. (1973). *Beyond God the father*. Boston: Beacon Press.

Daly, M. (1984). *Pure lust*. Boston: Beacon Press.

de Beauvoir, S. (1974). *The second sex* (H. M. Parshley, Ed. & Trans.). New York: Vintage.

Deetz, S. A. (1992). *Democracy in an age of corporate colonization*. Albany: State University of New York Press.

Department of Defense Inspector General. (1993, February). *Tailhook 91 part 2: Events at the 35th annual Tailhook symposium*. Washington, DC: U.S. Government Printing Office.

Dziech, B. W., & Weiner, L. (1990). *The lecherous professor* (2nd ed.). Urbana: University of Illinois Press.

Engels, F. (1983). Origin of the family. In M. B. Mahowald (Ed.), *Philosophy of women* (pp. 101–116). Indianapolis: Hackett Publishing. (Excerpted from *Origin of the family, private property and the state*, original work published in 1884)

Fain, T. C., & Anderton, D. L. (1987). Sexual harassment: Organizational context and diffuse status. *Sex Roles, 5/6*, 291–311.

Farley, L. (1978). *Sexual shakedown: The sexual harassment of women on the job*. New York: McGraw-Hill.

Ferguson, K. E. (1984). *The feminist case against bureaucracy*. Philadelphia: Temple University Press.

Foucault, M. (1972). *The archaeology of knowledge* (A. Sheridan, Trans.). New York: Pantheon.

Foucault, M. (1978). *The history of sexuality, an introduction: Vol. I* (R. Hurley, Trans.). New York: Vintage. (Original work published 1976)

Gutek, B. A. (1985). *Sex and the workplace*. San Francisco: Jossey-Bass.

Gutek, B. A., & Cohen, A. G. (1987). Sex ratios, sex role spillover, and sex at work: A comparison of men's and women's experiences. *Human Relations, 40*, 97–115.

Holstein, J. A., & Miller, G. (1990). Rethinking victimization: An interactional approach to victimology. *Symbolic Interaction, 13*, 103–122.

Jagger, A. M. (1983). *Feminist politics and human nature*. Totowa, NJ: Rowman & Allanheld.

Konrad, A. M., & Gutek, B. A. (1986). Impact of work experiences on attitudes toward sexual harassment. *Administrative Science Quarterly, 31*, 422–438.

Koss, M. P. (1990). Changed lives: The psychological impact of sexual harassment. In M. A. Paludi (Ed.), *Ivory power: Sexual harassment on campus* (pp. 73–92). Albany: State University of New York Press.

Lafontaine, E., & Tredeau, L. (1986). The frequency, sources, and correlates of sexual harassment among women in traditional male occupations. *Sex Roles, 15*, 433–442.

Loy, P. H., & Stewart, L. P. (1984). The extent and effects of sexual harassment of working women. *Sociological Focus, 17*, 31–43.

MacKinnon, C. A. (1979). *Sexual harassment of working women.* New Haven, CT: Yale University Press.

MacKinnon, C. A. (1989). *Toward a feminist theory of the state.* Cambridge, MA: Harvard University Press.

McKinney, K., & Maroules, N. (1991). Sexual harassment. In E. Grauerholz & M. Koralewski (Eds.), *Sexual coercion: A sourcebook on its nature, causes and prevention* (pp. 29–44). Lexington, MA: Lexington.

"Our stories": Communication professionals' narratives of sexual harassment. (1992). *Journal of Applied Communication Research, 20*, 363–391.

Paludi, M. A. (Ed.). (1990). *Ivory power: Sexual harassment on campus.* Albany: State University of New York Press.

Pryor, J. B. (1987). Sexual harassment proclivities in men. *Sex Roles, 17*, 269–290.

Quina, K. (1990). The victimizations of women. In M. A. Paludi (Ed.), *Ivory power: Sexual harassment on campus* (pp. 93–102). Albany: State University of New York Press.

Spender, D. (1984). Defining reality: A powerful tool. In C. Kramarae, M. Schultz, & W. M. O'Barr (Eds.), *Language and power* (pp. 194–205). Beverly Hills, CA: Sage.

Tangri, S. S., Burt, M. R., & Johnson, L. B. (1982). Sexual harassment at work: Three explanatory models. *Journal of Social Issues, 38*, 33–54.

Tong, R. (1989). *Feminist thought.* Boulder, CO: Westview.

U.S. Merit Protection Board. (1981). *Sexual harassment in the federal workplace: Is it a problem?* Washington, DC: U.S. Government Printing Office.

U.S. Merit Protection Board. (1988). *Sexual harassment in the federal government: An update.* Washington, DC: U.S. Government Printing Office.

Weedon, C. (1987). *Feminist practice and poststructuralist theory.* New York: Basil Blackwell.

Wood, J. T. (1992). Telling our stories: Narratives as a basis for theorizing sexual harassment. *Journal of Applied Communication Research, 20*, 349–362.

# PART V

# ISSUES RELATED TO HEALTH CONCERNS

# 17 Gay Men and Their Physicians: Discourse and Disenfranchisement

Frederick C. Corey
*Arizona State University*

Historically, medical views of same-sex attraction have been marked by disease, perversion, and psychiatric illness (Bullough, 1974; Foucault, 1976/1978; Katz, 1976). The desire to be in intimate personal relationships with someone of the same gender was seen by the medical establishment as something in need of a cure. In contemporary medical practices, same-sex desire is no longer treated as an inherent disease, but problems still exist in both public discourse and private dialogue. Through discourse, the medical industry marginalizes those with same-sex desire. In interpersonal contexts between physicians and patients with same-sex desire, the patients are confronted with the enduring history of same-sex desire as disease, stigmatization, and perceived disenfranchisement. In this chapter, I explore several of these issues as they relate to communication between gay men and their physicians. I offer four principal arguments: (a) The history of gay men in medical science is defined by illness, (b) the advent of HIV disease has introduced not only a further stigmatization of gay men in the health care system, but also a social construct that reinscribes the gay man's body with illness, (c) gay men are adept at avoiding disenfranchisement by keeping their sexual orientation invisible, and (d) relationships between gay men and medical physicians are characterized by negotiations of power. I begin the exploration of these issues with a discussion of the theoretical perspective I employ in this essay.

## THEORETICAL PERSPECTIVE

Throughout the 1970s and 1980s, scholars in lesbian and gay studies concerned themselves with a theoretical debate that created a dichotomy between an essentialist view of same-sex desire and the social construction of gay culture.[1] Essentialists believe that sexual orientation is not a choice, per se, but a natural, culture-independent property intrinsic to an individual's biological constitution. Social constructionists, by contrast, believe that being gay, lesbian, or bisexual is culture-dependent, developmental, and based not in the biology of an individual, but in the social production of sexuality. To some extent, the debate is that of nature versus nurture. Whereas essentialists believe same-sex desire is a part of nature, social constructionists believe people define what it means to be "gay" through cultural practice (Stein, 1990).

In recent years, the debate between social constructionism and essentialism has been reframed.[2] From a pragmatic perspective, no one knows if sexual orientation is biological or cultural. No irrefutable proof exists to support either claim. Further, the quest to understand what "causes" sexual orientation has, at its center, a positivistic aim to predict and control human behavior. The aim to predict behavior and control human lives raises a host of ethical questions. If we knew what "caused" same-sex desire, would we engage in genetic engineering (if the essentialists are correct) or social engineering (if the constructionists are correct) in an effort to produce a completely heterosexual world? Would we "cause" people to be gay, lesbian, or bisexual? Is a passive, benign understanding of sexual orientation all we want? Would information about the "cause" of same-sex desires liberate gays, lesbians, and bisexuals from the tyranny of moral chastisement? The answers to these questions are, at best, speculative. We do not know the answers to these questions because we have no experiential proofs, no data. We can only guess what would happen if we discovered a necessary and sufficient causal explanation of same-sex desire.

In this chapter, I ground my arguments in social constructionist theory, but I answer Warner's (1993) call to reapproach the traditions of theory in the process. Specifically, I do not want to make the claim that same-sex desire is a social construct. Instead, I want to argue from the position that although we do not know what "causes" same-sex desire, we do know that public and

---

[1]For overviews of social constructionism and essentialism, see Edward Stein (Ed.), *Forms of Desire*; David Greenberg, *The Construction of Homosexuality*; and David Halperin, *One Hundred Years of Homosexuality*.

[2]A wide range of contemporary social theorists have addressed issues facing gays, lesbians, and bisexuals. See, for example, Frank Browning, *The Culture of Desire*; Teresa de Lauretis' introduction to *Queer Theory: Lesbian and Gay Sexualities*; Diana Fuss (Ed.), *Inside/Out: Lesbian Theories, Gay Theories*; Larry Gross, *Contested Closets*; and Bad-Object Choices (Ed.), *How Do I Look? Queer Film and Video*.

private discourse create contextual meanings that construct a reality within which gay men negotiate for power in health care systems. My theoretical basis, then, is informed by social constructionism, historicism, and queer politics. I offer the following tenets in which I ground my essay:

1. Inquiry is determined by available concepts, words, and systems of communication (Gergen, 1985). In the present study, for example, the categorization of people into the heterosexual/homosexual binary is not a map of reality, but instead a manifestation of the historical words used to define cultural practice.

2. Meanings of words are socially constructed and vary across cultures and eras (Gergen, 1985). Words such as *gay, queer, straight,* and *political* are not fixed. Their meanings shift between locale, generations, and societies.

3. Systems of inquiry are privileged over other systems not based on their validity but on the evolutions of social processes (Gergen, 1985). Historically, inquiries into same-sex desire have focused on scientific "causal" explanations, not because scientific studies are more valid than rhetorical, literary, or ethnographic studies, but because science has been constructed as a preeminent epistemology.

4. Language is itself a form of social action that constructs meanings and has consequences (Gergen, 1985). Language used to describe same-sex desire—abnormal, deviant, variant, inverted—places heterosexuality as the norm from which others differ and are, as a result, marginalized.

5. The social production of discourse is controlled in an effort to exclude and prohibit adversarial discourses (Foucault, 1972). In popular and academic cultures, discourse from the queer perspective is limited not because it lacks merit, but because it disrupts the normalization of heterosexuality.

Throughout this chapter, I avoid essentialism at all of its levels. I address issues facing gay men, for example, and not lesbians. That gay men and lesbians are essentially the same because they both have same-sex desires is not my position. I contend that the social construction of lesbianism is different than the construction of gay men. Likewise, intersecting cultural constructs of race, religion, geography, and ethnicity are critical factors worthy of explication. In this study, however, I acknowledge the impact of my position as a gay, White male.

## HISTORICAL OVERVIEW

When Michel Foucault (1976/1978) published the first volume of *The History of Sexuality* in 1976, he set the stage for the social constructionist view of same-sex desire. In this volume, Foucault traced the history of discourse about human sexuality and presented the argument that legal, religious, and medical constructions of same-sex desire led to concepts of "perverse," "inverted," and "unnatural" acts. The effect upon the gay man was the "psychiatrization of perverse pleasure" (Foucault, 1976/1978, p. 105). The words used to construct discourse about gay men—unnatural, deviant, and abnormal—marginalized gay men by using language that normalized heterosexuality.

The history of homosexuality as sick and wrong has a rich and omnipotent history. The most absurd proponents of homosexuality-as-a-disease created household legacies, Graham crackers and Kellogg's cereals (Bullough, 1974). Both contended that nonprocreative sex was detrimental to a person's health. Semen, the argument goes, is precious, and semen expended for anything but procreation causes anything from languor and genital disorder (Graham, cited in Bullough, 1974) to acne and epilepsy (Kellogg, cited in Bullough, 1974). To help men not waste their semen, Graham encouraged men to eat unbolted "graham" wheat flour, a dietary substance he believed would cut down on their sexual desires. Similarly, John Harvey Kellogg founded the Battle Creek Sanitarium, where cereals were developed to help males cease activities such as masturbation and homosexual activity.

Historically, then, the family physician treated homosexuality as a medical disorder, and homosexual clients were referred to the psychiatrist. Between 1874 and 1974, psychiatric treatment of homosexuality was based on the premise of same-sex attraction as illness, and the physician's aim was to find a "cure" for the patient (Katz, 1976). The cures were vicious: castration, vasectomy, LSD, shock therapy, and, as late as 1951, lobotomy (Katz, 1976). In *Gay American History*, Katz, using field notes written by physicians, documented 36 cases of medical oppression of homosexuals. The accounts are horrific. In spite of the fact that the accounts are written from the physicians' point of view, the field notes provide portraits of the patients as living, breathing human beings who appear not to be sick at all. That is, not sick before treatment. Take, for example, the case of castration performed by Dr. Charles Hughes (Katz, 1976). Dr. Hughes described his patient as "a gentleman of ordinary moral, intellectual and physical parts" (p. 153) who was tired of dietary treatment. The patient wanted surgery to end his desire for same-sex "handpressing, kissing, and embracing" (p. 154). The physician performed two operations, the first an excision of the dorsales penis nerve, and the second an entire excision of the testes. In the end, this 28-year-old bookkeeper "lost his erotic inclinations toward his own sex but showed a social inclination towards asexualized ladies" (p. 155).

Has the social construct changed? In 1973, the American Psychiatric Association (APA) declassified homosexuality as a disease or mental disorder. And then what? Overnight, medical practitioners suddenly adjusted their beliefs about same-sex attraction? Of course not. Schwanberg (1985) analyzed health sciences literature between 1974 and 1983 and classified the image of gay men and lesbians. In 32 articles from psychiatric medicine, 10 presented positive images, 7 were neutral, and 15 perpetuated the image of homosexuality as a disease that was "caused" by something and could be cured. General medicine fared much better, where of 14 articles, 5 presented positive images, 8 were neutral, and only 1 was negative. In a follow-up study, Schwanberg (1990) discovered little improvement. From 1983 to 1987, 61% of the empirical studies, letters to the editor, policy statements, and opinion papers expressed negative views of homosexuality. Other studies provide similarly mixed reviews of changing attitudes about homosexuality in the medical professions (Douglas, Kalman, & Kalman, 1985; Scherer, Wu, & Haughey, 1991; Schmidt, 1984; Smith, 1993). In an effort to build new constructs of medical discourse, Schwartz (1994) edited a forum on attitudes toward gays and lesbians in medical schools, but Suppe (1984) argued that the entire classification system of sexual disorders by the APA is more a codification of sexual mores than a medical taxonomy. In sum, it would seem the gay man is taking a chance when seeking medical care, for the view of homosexuality as a disease still exists. A gay man could well find himself in the office of a physician who wants to "treat" same-sex affections.

The notion that the academic tradition of stigmatizing homosexuality has passed and we are in a new era is enticing but untrue. In the Library of Congress cataloging system, for example, the HQ section contains, in sequential order, books about: marriage and the family, the history of sexuality, sexuality in various nations, sexual abuse, sex crimes, incest, pedophilia, rape, raping children, child pornography, homosexuality, sadomasochism, prostitution, child prostitution, adult pornography, and then the topic returns to the family. The Library of Congress provides a useful construct for the signification of the company queers keep. They have placed us in the neighborhood of child pornography and sadomasochism, and in so doing, have constructed a stigmatized margin from which gays and lesbians speak.

Inroads to the center are in progress, though, and the advent of Human Immunodeficiency Virus (HIV) and Acquired Immune Deficiency Syndrome (AIDS) have been major forces in the resituation of the relationship between gay men and the medical industry.[3] AIDS activists, in both practice and theory, resist the construction of gay men as disenfranchised. The minori-

---

[3]The literature on AIDS and gay men is vast. Some key works that address issues of activism include Douglas Crimp (Ed.), *AIDS: Cultural Analysis/Cultural Activism*; Cindy Patton, *Sex and Germs*, and *Inventing AIDS*.

tizing logic of marginalization is replaced with an activist view of gay men as angry, not disenfranchised, and the difference is critical. From a social constructionist perspective, the difference between saying, "I am disenfranchised," and, "I am angry," is one of power. Whereas the former bestows the center with authority to construct territories of who stands where in relation to whom, the latter is an act of self-definition and empowerment. Activist organizations such as ACT UP and Queer Nation have constructed themselves as angry, not disenfranchised. Likewise, queer theorists are marked by self-determination, and the construction of marginalization, like the construction of victimization, is detrimental to the cause. The very use of the word *queer* becomes a statement of self-definition and revolution. Through the use of the word *queer*, the oppressed appropriate the language of oppression. Queer activists take control of one of the weapons used to keep gays and lesbians in the margins. By analogy, gays and lesbians using the word *queer* is like a person being held at gunpoint gaining control of the gun. AIDS, as a matter of life and death, has played a major role in queer activism and the shift from disenfranchisement to anger.

## GAY MEN = AIDS

HIV and AIDS have had multiple effects upon gay men and health care. Radical activism, as discussed earlier, is one effect. Another effect, one that is less progressive, has been the conterminous construction of gay men and HIV disease. The gay man's body has been inscribed, once again, with illness. Historically, the gay man's body was equated with illness because same-sex desire was viewed as perverse. Throughout the 20th century, the construct of homosexuality as illness was being questioned and disassembled. In the 1980s, however, a new equation between gay men and illness was being constructed. Gay-Related Immune Deficiency (GRID), as AIDS was called initially, reconstructed the gay man's body as a house of disease.

The equation between gay men and AIDS has had dangerous effects on relationships between gay men and their physicians, and one of the problems occurs when the patient fails to resist the social practice of assuming AIDS is a "gay disease." If, for example, I have a sore throat that will not go away (it lingers beyond its "normal" 2 weeks), I enter a secret panic. "It must be AIDS." If I have an unusual rash, an enduring fatigue, or diarrhea, it must be AIDS. If I have night sweats, God forbid, it must be AIDS. *It must be AIDS.*

To utter the phrase is to privilege the power of the language of AIDS. The constructs are dramatic. First is the drama of mortality, or death as a certainty, looming over future, perhaps a year, perhaps a decade, but, in any case, looming. Second is the drama of illness as a way of life, of being sick off and on forever, of treating symptoms rather than seeking cures. Third is the drama of T-cell counts, of tracking the number and comparing notes with friends who are seropositive. Fourth is the drama of AZT, the toxic relief. AZT is poison, and although it provides solace from the advance of HIV disease, it kills. If I do not die from complications of AIDS, I will die from the toxicity of AZT. Hence, the moment I decide to go on AZT, I acknowledge that, for me, there will be no cure. Fifth is the fear of changing jobs, or losing my job, and being without health insurance. Sixth is the drama of sexual relationships, of the change in the carnal formula. Now, my bodily fluids are lethal, and my sexual satisfaction is a weapon. Sex will never be the same. Seventh is the drama of guilt. Why did I have unsafe sex? I could cut the drama by not being tested. The angst of the test is overwhelming. My name is shrouded in secrecy. I cannot go to my personal physician, but instead must go to a public health clinic. I must wait, in agony, for the results. Maybe the sore throat will go away. I will wait.

And if I go to my physician? Physicians, too, participate in the equation between gay men and AIDS. This construct gives the physician relief from the responsibility of curing the sore throat or rash. The cause of the problem might be HIV, after all, and whose fault is that? How can I, the physician ponders, be responsible for treating the symptoms of this illness when I do not know for certain what the illness is? The indirection abounds. A patient may be in the physician's office describing a symptom in great detail, look at the floor, look at the wall, and finally make eye contact with the physician to ask, nervously, "What do you think it is?" What the patient wants to ask is, of course, "Does this sound like AIDS?" Likewise, the physician may be with a patient and ask, with the eyebrows raised ever so slightly, "Might there be a systemic problem?" The word *systemic* reverberates throughout the office, and both parties fall into an abyss of silence. The physician has played into the patient's greatest fear, and without a definitive answer, the physician is simply not responsible for a comprehensive analysis of the ailment.

The conterminous construction of gay men and HIV disease is perilous. Physicians who assume the gay man who is sick has HIV disease puts the patient at risk. Gay men are susceptible to the full range of illnesses, from cancer and heart disease to nonfatal viruses and infections. A delay in treatment of common illnesses can be detrimental to the patient's health, though, and when a physician wants to rule out HIV before investigating other illnesses, the patient is in danger. Ideally, a physician would ask the patient, "Have you been tested for HIV?" If the patient says yes, and if the test is positive, then treatment can proceed in the context of HIV disease. If the patient says no, the physician might suggest going to a clinic for the HIV test, but then the patient is in limbo until the test results are received; this can take up to 2 weeks. The period of uncertainty can become particularly troubling if a physician, playing into the conterminous construction of gay men and HIV disease, delays further investigation of symptoms until test results are received. The trouble increases if, after a first negative test, a physician wants a second test in 6 months, to account for the "window period" between possible infection and positive test results.

The positionality of gay men and AIDS can be viewed as a paradox. The incidence of HIV disease among gay men is high, and AIDS activists have challenged the health care system to address the needs of this marginalized segment of the population. It would be incorrect, then, to suggest that gay men and AIDS are not related. AIDS is not, however, a "gay disease." Not everyone with AIDS is gay, and not all gay men have AIDS. Thus, when gay men are sick, it is not safe to assume that the cause of the problem is HIV infection. The challenge is to deconstruct the gay men/AIDS equation, to resist the tendency to inscribe the gay man's body with illness.

## SILENCE: THE CONSTRUCTION OF INVISIBILITY

Some gay men are adept at moving in and out of visibility in an effort to avoid the construct of stigmatized marginality. The military policy of "Don't Ask, Don't Tell" is a strategy used well by gay men with their physicians. In this communicative construct, the physician never asks about sexual orientation and the patient does not resist the assumption of heterosexuality. The entire topic of personal relationships is left as a question mark; perhaps the patient has checked the box "single," or "married," two heterosexual categories, and the physician speculates but never asks directly.

"Why," the patient rationalizes, "is it important for the doctor to know about my being gay?" In this model, the patient views his body as nothing more than an automobile, and the physician as an auto mechanic. If, in fact, the human body is a biological organism that can be examined in objective terms, then knowledge of the organism's affective characteristics is extraneous. A ruptured appendix, for example, is what it is, regardless of the life of the body housing the rupture. Cancer is cancer, and a sore throat is a sore throat. The physician does not need to know what has been in the throat any more than an auto mechanic needs to know what has happened in the back seat of a broken car.

Both physician and patient can avoid the topics of sex and sexuality, but physicians are recognizing the need to address issues of sex with their patients. In a two-part essay, David Schnarch (1988a, 1988b) talked to physicians about the importance of taking a sexual history. Schnarch engaged in a persuasive strategy first to convince the reader that taking a history is important. Second, he acknowledged the awkwardness of taking such a history, and finally, he offered a pragmatic strategy for taking a sexual history. In no way do I censure Schnarch for the content of his essays. What I want to do is take his prescription and show how the language of the questions and answers could be coded so that the physician and patient could talk past each other and establish heterosexuality as an assumed norm. Schnarch offered five sequential questions the physician may ask the patient, but for our purposes only four are relevant (the fifth concerns the menstrual cycle). Unless otherwise indicated, the physician's questions are verbatim from Schnarch. The questions use nonspecific gender classifications and apparently avoid heterosexism. Let us create scripts, though, and show how indirection can be counterproductive:

Doctor:   Are you satisfied with your sex life? If not, why not?
Patient:  Oh, well, no, I would not say I am satisfied—
Doctor:   And why not?
Patient:  I think what I am missing is love. I mean, sex without love is just not very satisfying.

The doctor would probably agree, but the patient has avoided the aspect of sexuality successfully. Let's look at Schnarch's next question:

Doctor:   Are you currently active with a sexual partner? If so, what is the approximate frequency of sexual activity? How often do you have difficulty becoming sexually aroused?
Patient:  Oh, I don't have any problem being aroused. I get aroused. And yea, I am with someone, and we've been together, for 5 years, and sometimes we have sex, I don't know, maybe once a week, if work is not too much—

Here, the patient is answering the questions, but both the doctor and the patient are avoiding sexuality. They are negotiating their way through the discussion with an implication of heterosexuality. Notice, too, how the patient is making an attempt to shift the conversation away from sex and toward work, but the physician, suspecting the problem with the prostate (for example) is not due to work, pursues with Schnarch's third set of questions:

Doctor:   How often do you have difficulty obtaining or maintaining an erection? How often do you have difficulty with control of ejaculation?
Patient:  Sometimes it's hard. I mean, sometimes it's hard to get an erection. And yea, sometimes I can't come at all, but I think I am trying too hard. I mean, I get distracted, self-conscious, you know? Why do you ask?
Doctor:   Oh, well, the prostate problems may be related to sex, not cancer, because the tests are all negative and everything looks normal [my words for the doctor here].

Patient:   Normal? Great!

The doctor, with all good intentions, has arrived at a dead end, for the patient has heard the one word most of us want to hear in the doctor's office, *normal*. Schnarch appears to anticipate this as he offers his final primary question:

Doctor:   What questions or problems related to sex would you like to discuss?

Patient:   Nothing. Maybe we should just give it a week and see if the pain goes away.

What doctor would not be glad to agree? The conversation was going nowhere. Throughout the dialogue, the words were defined contingently, and meanings were based in the absence of specificity rather than the presence of clear referents.

The communication indirection of "Don't Ask, Don't Tell" is troubling. The relationship between physician and patient is based on deceit. The patient is not being honest with the physician, and when lying is a mode of operation, the ramifications can permeate the entire diagnostic process. As the gay man does not mention sexuality, the gay man might not mention rectal pain, urinary discomfort, or anything else that may trigger a connection between the body, sexual behavior, and AIDS. This lack of open communication prevents analysis of relationships between personality, behavior, and sexually related diseases (Ma & Armstrong, 1989; Ross, 1986). The web of deceit has stress as an additional ramification. Stress, based in the shame of homosexuality or lying about sexual activity, could lead to a host of medical problems, ranging from ulcers to rashes to fatigue. Thus, when a patient makes his sexual orientation invisible in an effort to avoid the marginality of homosexuality, he sacrifices his health care.

## THE NEGOTIATION OF POWER

To this point, we have looked at the production of discourse involving gay men and their physicians, and to some extent, we have considered both the personal and social significance of the discourse. What I want to address now are power relationships between gay men and their physicians. In this discussion, I borrow widely from Foucault, who wrote extensively about the struggle between the individual and medical science (1972, 1976/1978), sexuality in the context of medicine (1976/1978), and the uncomfortable trade-off between power and knowledge (1972, 1977, 1982). Further, Foucault was himself a gay man, and the Foucault reader need not have a vivid imagination to see how so much of what Foucault writes applies directly to the medical subjection of gay men.

In this light, I note at the outset a universal power struggle between the medical profession and the individual, the medical institution's "uncontrolled power over people's bodies, their health, and their life and death" (Foucault, 1982, p. 780). At this macrolevel, gay men are in company with all humans as subjects of medical treatment. More specifically, though, gay men are left to personal devices in the struggle against a history of subjection. One way to resist the oppression is to avoid the construct of marginality by being silent about sexuality. When a gay man does not tell the physician he is gay, the patient uses silence, or absence of meaning, in an effort to escape disenfranchisement. He suppresses the institution of homosexuality. By concealing his sexual activity with other men, the patient does not give the physician more power than the history of medicine already gives the physician. The physician has control over the patient's body, but the patient has, as an individual, freedom to bracket the historical struggle between homosexuality and medicine, and focus instead on the more common struggle between the individual and medical science. Why fight two battles when it is possible to fight only one?

Physicians need patients as much as patients need physicians. This mutually dependent relationship creates a context for a prototypical power struggle, one in which subjects are not slaves; they are instead "faced with a field of possibilities in which several ways of behaving, several reactions and diverse comportments, may be realized" (Foucault, 1982, p. 790). By remaining silent, by choosing not to talk about sexuality, the patient and physician avoid a bevy of problems. The physician will not be afraid to touch the patient's body. The diagnosis will not be assumed HIV related. The physician will not be able to use as a weapon the violent social discourse used against gay men and what ails them: "Whatever disease you have, you have brought upon yourself."

Gay men are promiscuous and therefore prone to Hepatitis B, HIV, syphilis, gonorrhea, and crabs. "We must conceive discourse as a violence that we do to things," wrote Foucault (1972, p. 229). And indeed, the heteroconstruct of homosexuality is one of bath houses, anonymous sex partners, and carnal bedlam, regardless of the individual. Again turning to Foucault (1972), "in every society the production of discourse is at once controlled, selected, organised and redistributed according to a certain number of procedures, whose role is to avert its powers and its dangers" (p. 216). Sexuality is dangerous enough, but homosexuality is particularly dangerous, strangled in constructs of illness, deviance, and, in religious discourse, sin.

The discourse is changing. Health care professionals are recognizing the need for medicine free of shame and stigma (Taravella, 1992). In large

American cities, physicians are advertising in gay newspapers. The physicians are appealing to gay men with a wide range of slogans and advertising copy: "You're a person, not a statistic. Isn't it about time you had a doctor that realized that?" "A general practice devoted to the medical conditions of gay men." "As a gay man, you put your body through a lot of extra stress.... Dr. X's concern goes deeper than just a doctor–patient relationship. This is a man who truly understands and cares about his community." "Gay men suffer unique problems." Although HIV treatment is prevalent in many of the messages, it is not an exclusive appeal. Physicians include appeals to other cultural values—the latest in hair-growth treatments, Retin A, and collagen—but perhaps most important, the physicians are appealing to safety and sensitivity.

At the surface level, these "new doctors" help their patients develop new levels of honesty, reduce stress-related illnesses, and increased self-confidence. These physicians may have more experience diagnosing HIV and treating HIV-related illnesses. They would be likely to accept relational partners as spouses and include the relational partners in medical matters, in the same way husbands and wives are included when appropriate. These new doctors do not have the inclination to treat same-sex attraction as a disorder, and this is particularly important within the realm of psychiatric medicine (Taravella, 1992). Perhaps most important, a primary physician who attends to gay youth can help the patient deal with sexuality and avoid suicide (Cwayna, Remafedi, & Treadway, 1991).

At a deeper, more insidious level, physicians who appeal to the gay community are reformulating power relationships between gay men and their physicians. The gay man who goes to the new doctor needs the physician more than he might need the traditional physician. That is, the physician has the patient in something of a bind, creating an environment of "Where else are you going to go?" This message can be sent by the physician, consciously or unconsciously, or constructed in the psyche of the patient. In any case, when a gay man carefully selects a physician because that physician is sensitive to gay issues, then the patient is trapped. If the gay man is unhappy with his treatment, his decision to change physicians is complicated by the fear that if he changes physicians, he will have to risk falling into the hands of a physician who views homosexuality as illness. The "field of possibilities" has been constricted for the patient. To make matters worse for the patient, a physician who is sensitive to gay issues and has a large clientele of financially lucrative HIV-infected patients may well be able to sacrifice an unsatisfied patient; thus, the physician does not "need" a patient who complains or demands too much. The patient is rendered virtually powerless and, in extremity, becomes a slave to the master/physician.

Ideally, many physicians would be sensitive to gay issues, and a patient would be able to select from a host of physicians. Toward this end, the

American Association of Physicians for Human Rights wanted to place an advertisement in *The Journal of the American Medical Association*. The advertisement warned of negative consequences of homophobia in medical care ("Health Hazard?," 1993). The journal rejected the advertisement, saying it was political, not scientific. Recent issues of the journal are replete with nonscientific advertisements encouraging physicians to lobby against health care reform, work for the U.S. military, and recognize the nutritional value of McDonald's fast food. The problem with the advertisement encouraging a shift in attitudes regarding gays and lesbians is that it represents a disenfranchised group of people negotiating for power within an exclusive social institution. The essence of the struggle is not located in what constitutes political, but rather in how power is negotiated. The institution of medicine is slow to give gay men and lesbians control over the language of sexuality. The rejected advertisement represents an effort by gay men and lesbians to enter the marketplace of medical discourse with language that comes from the lesbian/gay perspective, and this effort represents a threat to the heteronormativity of institutional medicine. Thus, the word *political* has been used by the journal to mean "an effort to control discourse," and the effort was rejected by those who hold power.

## CONCLUSION

Throughout this chapter, I have employed a social constructionist perspective to explore issues facing gay men and their physicians. My goal has been to address key issues in the historical construction of same-sex desire as illness, the equation between gay men and HIV disease, the construction of silence as a means of avoiding stigmatization, and the negotiation of power between the institution of medicine and the marginalized gay population. The sum total of the gay male experience has been one of disenfranchisement. Heteronormativity in medical discourse places the male–female couple as the center from which all else defers.

The promotion of sensitivity to issues confronting gay men in the health care system is a formidable challenge. The institutional constructs of medical discourse place gay men in the margins. The use of words such as *perversion*, *deviance*, *inversion*, and *abnormal*—words that are central to historical discussions of gay men—create margins that make gay men different from "normal" people. The words mark the gay man's body as a house of illness. In contemporary contexts, the discourse of AIDS reinvents the gay man's body as a site of disease. Although health educators make efforts to deconstruct the idea that AIDS is a "gay disease," the efforts are, to some extent, in vain. The public discourse about AIDS, implicitly or explicitly, places gay men at the center of the disease. The resulting conterminous constructions of gay men and HIV disease further disenfranchise gay men from "normal" health care through the stigmatization of the means of transmission of the virus that causes AIDS. The social text that informs gay men's health care—gay men get sick and die because they have sex with other men—is impossible to erase.

Adding to the formidability of cultural sensitivity is that gay men are complicitous in the disenfranchisement of gay men from the health care system. At times, it appears we are our own enemies. When we do not identify ourselves as being gay, for example, we construct an invisible closet that perpetuates heteronormativity. Can a physician who does not know a patient is gay be held accountable for being insensitive to gay issues? Certainly not. Likewise, gay men are quick to buy into the conterminous constructions of being gay and having HIV disease. Our fears overtake our better judgment.

Perhaps the most formidable challenge facing the understanding of what constitutes gay sensitivity is within the discourse of understanding itself. Here I refer to the language of education, academia, and scholarship. In *Fear of a Queer Planet*, Warner (1993) and the contributors discussed, among many other issues, the heteronormativity of social theory. Their attacks on academic traditions are at times pithy and at other times angry, but always, their arguments are framed from a queer perspective. They wrote for queer readers, and I wonder if their arguments would be rejected by traditional theorists—gay, lesbian, bisexual, and straight—as being not "theoretical," but merely a perspective from which gays and lesbians write. Part of the challenge facing people in health communication may well be to bracket the traditional concepts of "theory" and participate in "queer talk" about health care.

In any case, I hope the views presented in this essay spur interest, debate, and further research. Numerous key issues remain unaddressed. What are the dynamics between intersecting cultural vectors of sex, sexuality, race, ethnicity, and religion? How does the lesbian's body become subject to heteronormativity? How does geography create perspective? How does heteronormativity impact the gay physician? How does transexuality shift cultural production of power? These are but a few of the questions that linger, ready to explode.

## REFERENCES

Bullough, V. (1974). Homosexuality and the medical model. *Journal of Homosexuality, 1*(1), 99–110.

Cwayna, K., Remafedi, G., & Treadway, L. (1991). Caring for gay and lesbian youth. *Medical Aspects of Human Sexuality, 25*(7), 50–54.

Douglas, C., Kalman, C., & Kalman, T. (1985). Homophobia among physicians and nurses: An empirical study. *Hospital and Community Psychiatry, 36*, 1309–1311.

Foucault, M. (1972). *The archaeology of knowledge/The discourse on language* (A. M. Sheridan Smith & R. Swyer, Trans.). New York: Pantheon.

Foucault, M. (1977). *Power/knowledge* (C. Gordon, L. Marshall, J. Mepham, & K. Soper, Trans.). New York: Pantheon.

Foucault, M. (1978). *The history of sexuality* (Vol. 1, R. Hurley, Trans.). New York: Random House. (Original work published 1976)

Foucault, M. (1982). The subject and power. *Critical Inquiry, 8*, 777–795.

Gergen, K. J. (1985). The social constructionist movement in modern psychology. *American Psychologist, 40*(3), 266–275.

Health hazard? (1993, June 29). *Advocate*, p. 7.

Katz, J. (1976). *Gay American history*. New York: Harper.

Ma, P., & Armstrong, D. (Eds.). (1989). *AIDS and infections of homosexual men* (2nd ed.). Boston: Butterworths.

Ross, M. W. (1986). *Psychovenereology: Personality and lifestyle factors in sexually transmitted diseases in homosexual men*. New York: Praeger.

Scherer, Y. K., Wu, Y. W., & Haughey, B. P. (1991). AIDS and homophobia among nurses. *Journal of Homosexuality, 21*(4), 17–27.

Schmidt, G. (1984). Allies and persecutors: Science and medicine in the homosexuality issue. *Journal of Homosexuality, 10*(3/4), 127–139.

Schnarch, D. M. (1988a, May). Talking to patients about sex: Part I. *Medical Aspects of Human Sexuality*, pp. 66–73.

Schnarch, D. M. (1988b, June). Talking to patients about sex: Part II. *Medical Aspects of Human Sexuality*, pp. 97–106.

Schwanberg, S. L. (1985). Changes in labeling homosexuality in health sciences literature: A preliminary investigation. *Journal of Homosexuality, 12*(1), 51–73.

Schwanberg, S. L. (1990). Attitudes toward homosexuality in American health care literature 1983–1987. *Journal of Homosexuality, 19*(3), 117–136.

Schwartz, G. R. (Ed.). (1994). Gay and lesbian patients and colleagues. *Journal of the American Medical Association, 9*, 712–717.

Smith, G. B. (1993). Homophobia and attitudes toward gay men and lesbians by psychiatric nurses. *Archives of Psychiatric Nursing, 7*, 377–384.

Stein, E. (Ed.). (1990). *Forms of desire: Sexual orientation and the social constructionist controversy*. New York: Garland.

Suppe, F. (1984). Classifying sexual disorders: The *Diagnostic and Statistical Manual* of the American Psychiatric Association. *Journal of Homosexuality, 9*(4), 9–28.

Taravella, S. (1992, November 9). Healthcare recognizing gay and lesbian needs. *Modern Healthcare*, pp. 33–35.

Warner, M. (Ed.). (1993). *Fear of a queer planet: Queer politics and social theory*. Minneapolis: University of Minnesota Press.

# 18 Coping With HIV and AIDS: The Social and Personal Challenges

Sandra Metts
Heather Manns
*Illinois State University*

Few groups in America today are so vividly and consistently disenfranchised as those persons who are HIV positive or living with AIDS. Theirs is a life of progressive physical deterioration endured within a social climate of fear and hostility. Not only is death, at present, inevitable, but so too is eventual loss of job and job-related health benefits, and rejection by the noninfected community, including many public schools and health care providers (Franzini, 1993). Infected persons are avoided for fear of contamination and rejected for their association with a stigmatized disease (Weitz, 1990). Although infected individuals are more likely now than in the early years of the epidemic to take legal steps against discrimination, the battles are costly to their health, their finances, and their personal comfort (Gostin & Curran, 1987; Terl, 1992). In short, persons who are HIV positive or have AIDS are in every sense of the word a marginalized group who are denied access to the resources of society at a time when economic, medical, and psychological resources are essential.

Remarkably, in this unlikely environment, despair is often transformed into tranquility, and social rejection is transformed into network cohesion (Schaefer & Coleman, 1992; Vandevyer, 1993). The consequence of disenfranchisement, in these cases, is empowerment, both for the individual and for the community of HIV- and AIDS-infected persons. This chapter explores the influence of these transformations on the individual's ability to cope with HIV or AIDS infection.

We set the stage for that discussion in the first half of the chapter by summarizing the research on both the social and the personal consequences of HIV/AIDS infection. Although it is virtually impossible to separate these two arenas in the daily lived experiences of an HIV-positive or AIDS person, we do so here for the purpose of clarity and focus. We describe how living with HIV or AIDS is a *social condition* with problems and consequences unlike any other chronic and debilitating disease. Among the problems we foreground is its unique stigma; among the consequences we foreground is the network strain associated with the disease. We also describe how living with HIV or AIDS is a *personal condition,* with special emphasis given to the sense of loss experienced by the person with HIV or AIDS in almost every aspect of his or her life.

In the second half of the chapter, we explore the factors associated with coping when one is HIV positive or diagnosed with AIDS. Although the social and personal conditions associated with HIV/AIDS constrain many aspects of the lives of infected individuals, they do not necessarily lead to isolation or despair. Many individuals learn to cope successfully, in fact, productively with the consequences of the disease. We give special emphasis to the role of social support (both formal and informal) and relationship networks as they have been studied in HIV/AIDS populations. This literature reveals a trend over the last decade toward a more positive and functional approach to treatment, counseling, and support for the HIV/AIDS-infected person. We close this chapter with the results of a survey study we conducted that illustrate and extend many of the trends noted in the literature on coping.

## HIV AND AIDS AS A SOCIAL CONDITION

It is impossible to talk about the social implications of being HIV positive or having AIDS without talking about the stigma associated with the disease. It is a powerful frame through which the experience of the infected person and his or her social network are inevitably viewed. Many of the unique personal, relational, and social problems associated with HIV infection and AIDS stem from the negative tenor of the stigma, as much as from the medical condition itself. Indeed, Pryor and Reeder (1993) argue that AIDS is a "socially constructed," "symbolic" disease that was stigmatized by the medical, political, ethical, and scientific forces operating in its early history (see, e.g., Shilts, 1987).

### Stigma

A stigma is a visible or assigned attribute or marking that in some way discredits a person. It might be a *feature of the body* such as a physical impairment, a *blemish of character or morality*, a socially construed *devaluation of one's lineage* such as race, social class, nationality, religion, or sexual orientation, or an *association* ("courtesy" stigma) with some person or group who is stigmatized (Goffman, 1963). Persons who are HIV positive or living with AIDS, or who are providing care to persons living with AIDS may experience any or all of these types of stigmatization.

The stigma associated with AIDS can be traced to several sources. Because AIDS made its first appearance among gay males and intravenous drug users (IDUs), it came to be associated with these disenfranchised groups. Thus, the disease acquired the stigma associated with the groups of origin and early disparaging references emerged such as the "gay plague" (see Corey, chap. 17, for a discussion of this issue). In addition, the visible manifestations of the illness in its advanced stages (e.g., Kaposi's sarcoma) contribute to its negative perception and, in many cases, end the secret of its diagnosis (Bor, 1993). As Field and Shore (1992) observed, "the idea of moral decay appearing as external physical deterioration is common in myth and fantasy. AIDS, with its cachexia and purple sarcomatous sores, qualifies as a condition capable of provoking nightmarish fantasy in the observer" (p. 159). Finally, initial lack of medical clarity about how the disease was spread contributed to a generalized fear of those who are HIV positive or have AIDS. Very often, the communicable nature of the virus not only keeps others at a distance during the times of greatest need for the infected person, but caregivers who are associated with infected persons are also avoided by others because of the associative stigma.

The extent of stigmatization for AIDS is reflected in a number of national and international surveys of attitudes toward AIDS and those persons afflicted with the disease. For example, Blendon and Donelan (1988) reviewed 53 such opinion surveys. They found five general trends: (a) Half of Americans surveyed believed that the AIDS epidemic has set off a wave of antihomosexual sentiment, (b) 81% of respondents believed that it was more important to identify those who are infected and control the spread of AIDS than to protect the personal privacy of people who were tested, (c) many respondents considered AIDS to be a punishment for immoral behavior and therefore favored visible public sanctions (e.g., 29% favored a tattoo for infected persons, 17% believed infected persons should be treated as lepers, and 21% to 40%—depending on the study—favored isolating persons with AIDS from public places), (d) nearly half said they would refuse to work with someone who had AIDS and would support employers' rights to fire such workers, and (e) 18% said they would take their child out of school if they had an infected classmate.

It is no surprise that persons afflicted with AIDS still prefer to conceal their condition as long as possible. As Goffman (1963) noted about stigma, once it is known to other people, the target is not merely "discreditable" but, in fact, "discredited." Thus, at-risk people often do not seek testing or delay inquiry about the results for long periods of time. For example, in 1980 a team of medical researchers in San Francisco, in one of five so-called Clinic Studies, drew blood from at-risk groups of homosexual men. These blood samples were frozen until a test could be devised to reliably isolate the virus causing the immunological deficiency. Many of these men still have not contacted the center to learn of their test results. Even those individuals who do seek information as to their status and avail themselves to various treatments often avoid explicit disclosure about their condition. Infected persons often explain their physical problems or weight loss as the result of socially acceptable conditions; for example, weight loss is attributed to stress or exercise, medication to chronic sinus infections, and fatigue to long hours at work.

The intensity and consequences of stigmatization are even more pronounced for minorities. Despite the fact that in 1991 minority gay and bisexual men represented 17% of all adult cases of AIDS in the United States (Centers for Disease Control [CDC], AIDS Hotline, personal communication, August 1991), there has been little systematic study of their experience. This is unfortunate given the relatively greater impact of the stigma within these groups. Homosexuality is even less accepted and/or openly discussed in African-American, Asian, and Hispanic communities than in European-American communities. As a result, the minority person who is homosexual *and* seropositive faces a complicated situation. If he reveals his HIV status (and implicitly his homosexuality), he may lose the support systems that bolstered his racial/ethnic identification and affirmed his worth within a culture that marginalizes ethnic groups (Morales, 1990). On the other hand, to not reveal his HIV status (and thereby avoid revealing his homosexuality) raises the prospect of increasingly poor health and debilitation without the care of those closest to him.

The experience for women who are HIV positive or have AIDS is also not comparable to that of the dominant gay White male who is typically studied. Although not assigned the stigma of sexual immorality associated with the gay lifestyle, these women do acquire the stigma of the disease's communicability and the stigma of the disease's etiology (e.g., intravenous drugs, promiscuity, rape, bisexual partners, etc.). Moreover, these women are often a single parent who has the added responsibility of children. As is the case with ethnic minorities, there has been little systematic effort to formalize appropriate support functions for women who are infected (Green, 1993; see Cline & McKenzie, chap. 19, this volume, for a detailed review of women who have HIV/AIDS).

As we close this discussion of the stigma associated with HIV and AIDS, it is important to emphasize that it combines with the communicability of the disease in producing complicated social ramifications. In the absence of widespread public support and responsive health care facilities, social networks are forced to assume a major role in the long-term care of infected persons. Few families or friends are prepared to accept such a responsibility and the strain is enormous. We turn now to a more detailed discussion of the impact of seropositivity and AIDS on social networks.

## Network Strain

As it becomes increasingly difficult to keep doctor's visits, medication, and progressive physical and mental deterioration from one's social network, infected persons eventually face the decision of how and when to reveal their condition. In many cases, the revelation is compounded by the fact that employers, parents, and even friends may have been ignorant (or in denial) of other elements of an infected person's lifestyle (e.g., homosexuality, promiscuity, or drug use) or personal history (e.g., being raped). Thus, network members who learn of HIV or AIDS infection may be hit with two blows at once.

Evidence suggests that the initial revelation is costly. Weitz (1990), for example, found that all of the 23 informants she interviewed had been rejected by at least one family member when news of their condition was revealed to the family. Several families insisted that the information be kept within the family and not shared with other network members. Of the seven men who had lovers, two reported they were abandoned by their lover and most were asked by nonromantic roommates to move out. Those individuals who were employed were fired or encouraged to quit when they revealed that they had AIDS.

Even when the infected person is not rejected, he or she soon realizes the difficult role that his or her caregivers must assume. The strain on parents, in particular, has been carefully studied (e.g., Takigiku, Brubaker, & Hennon, 1993; Tiblier, Walker, & Rolland, 1989). In part, the fact that parenthood is not an optional or voluntary role and one not easily terminated at any point in the life cycle evokes mixed feelings in a parent. Particularly with adult children, there is "little cultural prescription about when the authority and obligations of a parent end" (Rossi, 1968, p. 30). Some parents respond to a felt sense of responsibility when an "ethos of affection," others with an "ethos of obligation." As might be expected, caregivers who feel high levels of obligation feel greater caregiver stress than those who feel high levels of affection. The unhappiness experienced by obligated caregivers is often communicated to the care recipient, increasing his or her sense of guilt and frustration. In addition, because fathers typically have somewhat less tolerant attitudes toward homosexuality, their strain from caring for a homosexual son with AIDS may be even greater than that felt by mothers.

In a summary of the reasons why revelation of HIV/AIDS infection causes family strain, Bonuck (1993) listed a number of problems, including but not limited to social stigma:

1. Social stigma and isolation from other social networks.
2. Fear of contamination (members fear contracting the disease and this influences their interaction with the infected member).
3. Fear of infection (the infected person fears passing on the disease and this influences his or her interaction with other family members).
4. Fear of abandonment (the infected person fears that he or she will extract too great a toll and caregivers will eventually fail, especially during critical times when intensive care is most necessary).
5. Guilt felt by family members if they had previously rejected the infected person's lifestyle, or guilt because they are healthy.
6. Psychological and physical fatigue associated with care and support of the infected person.

It is important to note that the term "family" need not apply exclusively to groups that are biologically determined. That is, social relationships that fulfill attachment needs, identity needs, and daily maintenance functions are a type of family as well (Anderson, 1988). In the gay community, for example, friends commonly function as an extended family. Thus, each of the sources of strain listed by Bonuck (1993) is relevant to the "chosen family" as well. Even guilt is a concern—not because the infected person had been rejected previously for his or her lifestyle, but because the surviving friends or partner may have lived an almost identical lifestyle and yet be seronegative. In addition, when symptoms of illness become visibly apparent (e.g., extreme weight loss, Kaposi's sarcoma and other skin lesions), emotional strain within the chosen family intensifies: Those who are seronegative feel greater guilt for avoiding contamination and greater fear of becoming contaminated; those who are seropositive face their own mortality in the continued deterioration of the care recipient, and the entire network feels sorrow for the imminent loss of the visibly infected friend.

As great as the strain may be for the social network, the strain of being HIV positive or having AIDS is immeasurably greater for the individual who is infected. We turn now to a discussion of the personal condition associated with the disease.

## HIV AND AIDS AS A PERSONAL CONDITION

### Loss

The stigmatized nature of HIV/AIDS exacerbates the sense of loss felt by infected persons. However, that sense of loss is not quite the same thing as feeling stigmatized. Many of the areas where loss is felt most keenly would still be problematic even if the stigma were somehow reduced. As Hoffman (1991) described the experience:

Every aspect of a person's life is affected. The progression of HIV infection is associated with deterioration (physical and neurological), changes in day-to-day function, loss of employment, stigma and in many cases, exposure of one's life-style around the issues of sexuality and/or drug use. At its simplest, AIDS is about loss. It is about the loss of one's health, vitality, sensuality, and career—and most profoundly, the letting go of the future as one had envisioned it. (p. 468)

Three areas of loss experienced by an HIV/AIDS person are especially problematic: off-time transitions, loss of self-efficacy and self-esteem, and loneliness.

*Off-Time Transitions.*  In all societies, life transitions are anticipated and marked. The adjustment of the individual is facilitated by the continuity of the larger collective. Social norms and rituals are established for adult children leaving home, marriage, childbirth, widowhood, retirement, and so forth.

When a transition is "off-time," it occurs at an unexpected point in the normal process of growth and development. An off-time transition is difficult to deal with because no norms of behavior or social rituals exist to guide the person experiencing the change. AIDS is an off-time transition for several reasons. First, it tends to involve young people who would not otherwise be facing the end of their career, physical deterioration, and imminent death for several decades. In 1988, 39% of all AIDS patients were 15–34 years of age and 54% were 34–54 years of age (Christ, 1988). In the past 6 years, these figures have increased. In May of 1994, the Centers for Disease Control (CDC) AIDS hotline reported that of the 12,520 diagnosed cases of AIDS (by definition, T-cell counts below 400), 64% were between the ages of 13 and 39 years (CDC, personal communication, August 9, 1994). These figures do not include the thousands of symptomatic HIV patients who do not evidence a T-cell count low enough to be officially diagnosed as having AIDS. Thus, thousands of young people who would ordinarily be experiencing personal growth and financial productivity are unexpectedly transitioned into debilitating dependence characteristic of the infirmed elderly.

AIDS is an off-time transition in a second sense as well. The latency period for the virus means that the appearance of symptoms tends to occur long after the behaviors were performed that transmitted the virus. By the time a person learns that he or she is HIV positive or has AIDS, he or she may well be into a phase of life far removed from the one during which the virus was initially contracted. Thus, a person's current lifestyle may include no risk behaviors; he or she may have been "clean and sober," sexually responsible, or sexually monogamous for years. Unexpectedly, the results of an AIDS test reveal that the actions performed in "another time and another place" of his or her life have deadly consequences in the present. Seldom do actions performed at 18 have so much impact on a person at 30. This dissociation between action and consequences is a key feature of AIDS as an off-time transition.

*Loss of Self-Efficacy and Self-Esteem.* Bandura (1977) defined self-efficacy as "the conviction that one can successfully execute the behavior required to produce outcomes" (p. 193). It is associated with a person's sense of control over internal and external factors that influence daily functioning, meeting goals, and achieving desired ends. For persons who are HIV positive or have AIDS, an exceptional degree of control is turned over to medical technicians, caregivers, and fate. The uncertain nature of the disease leaves infected persons wondering when HIV infection will become AIDS, and what particular health issues will arise as the disease progresses (Schneider, Taylor, Hammen, Kemeny, & Dudley, 1991).

Weiss (1988) identified a number of constraints on HIV/AIDS persons that contribute to the loss of self-efficacy. These constraints include daily monitoring of bodily changes and reactions to medication, organizing one's life around hospital visits, diarrhea, fatigue, and increasing physical limitations. For as long as employment is possible, work patterns have to be modified to minimize exertion and stress. In later stages of the disease, when neuropathy and/or retinitis have taken their toll, the person with AIDS must depend more and more on other people for transportation and basic care. Because there is almost no way for the infected person to return these favors in kind, he or she must find alternative ways to repay caregivers, a burden that is greatest when resources (physical, emotional, and financial) are at their lowest.

Self-esteem is an individual's sense of worth. It is based on perceptions of the traits that he or she possesses and the value of these traits to oneself and others. Although the extent to which self-esteem is affected by the AIDS stigma varies as a function of network support, it is nonetheless a prevalent influence on self-esteem. So too is the loss of self-efficacy. As the ability to exert control over one's daily life diminishes, one's sense of worth declines as well.

In addition, for infected persons who continue to work, self-esteem is linked to the reaction of coworkers. Even in cases where there is no intentional animosity, working at a slower pace and requesting frequent absences for treatment tend to move the infected person to the periphery of his or her occupational hierarchy. For many people in the age bracket most likely to be touched by AIDS infection, self-esteem is heavily dependent on employment success and recognition. Loss of job success, and eventually loss of the job, contribute to the global sense of loss that persons with AIDS experience.

*Loneliness.* Loneliness is a term that refers to perceived deficiencies in one's interpersonal relationships, deficiencies that make a person feel isolated and alone. According to Weiss (1973, 1982), the source of these deficiencies might be primarily social (i.e., less participation in social groups than is desired) or primarily emotional (absence of an attachment figure or significant other). Peplau and Perlman (1982) argued that the basis for a person's loneliness may lie both in the *number* of social contacts available (e.g., fewer than desired) as well as in the *quality* of connection they provide (e.g., extent of needs not met).

For persons living with HIV or AIDS, social loneliness is a common, although certainly not inevitable, condition. The group of friends and lovers who often function as the "chosen family" tends to shrink. Some people withdraw from the infected person, others simply move away, and still others have died from AIDS-related illness. Although attrition in any social network is a common phenomenon, for persons who have lost their self-esteem, their mobility, and their health, finding new friends is a taxing process. Thus, the maintenance of social networks that most people do with little awareness is accomplished only with great effort by the HIV/AIDS person (Weiss, 1988).

In addition, research indicates that a frustrating dilemma faces the HIV/AIDS person with regard to emotional loneliness. As would be expected for any traumatic event, the knowledge that one is seropositive or has AIDS promotes a strong need for attachment to a "special" other, as indicated in this excerpt from an interview with an AIDS patient referred to as William:

> It seems as though I have wanted somebody more since I have been sick. Before, I really didn't want to be tied down. Now I want somebody there. I have friends. I just don't know if there is that special person out here for me. In a way I'm searching just like many single people do. Now that I'm sick you want to hurry, make things happen quicker. (Cherry & Smith, 1993, p. 200)

Unfortunately, establishing or maintaining an intimate relationship with someone who could satisfy the need for attachment expressed by William is problematic. Meeting new partners is hampered by loss of income, lowered self-esteem, ill-health, and lowered feelings of sexual attractiveness, especially when disfiguring conditions such as Kaposi's sarcoma are apparent (Bor, 1993).

Moreover, the health status of the potential mate is a difficult issue. A partner who is seronegative risks infection and the prospect of being a care provider throughout the duration of the relationship, followed inevitably by the death of his or her loved one. On the other hand, a partner who is already seropositive might develop AIDS, or if AIDS is already present, become increasingly ill. Providing care when both members of the couple are ill can be difficult or impossible. Whatever the health status of a potential new partner, the person who is seeking an attachment figure has to deal with the knowledge that he or she will leave a loved one in great pain at his or her death, or will be left in great pain if preceded in death. Needless to say, emotional involvement is not taken lightly by the potential new partner or the person seeking the relationship.

Indeed, even for persons who are in committed relationships at the time of their diagnosis, relationship deterioration often results. This occurs in part because seronegative partners abandon their infected lovers (Weitz, 1990). It also, however, results from the actions of seropositive patients who sometimes "deliberately antagonize their partner or create a rift in the relationship whether as a way of ending the relationship or testing the commitment of the partner to the relationship" (Bor, 1993, p. 97). In short, at a time when the HIV/AIDS person most needs emotional connection, emotional isolation is often the outcome.

Fortunately, alternatives to traditional models of social connection—for example, support groups and buddy programs—provide emotional resources for the HIV/AIDS person. They augment or replace the family, the significant other, and the social network when the strain is too great. These sources of support, in conjunction with the individual's own psychological strength, contribute to the coping process. We turn now to a discussion of factors that contribute to successful coping for the HIV/AIDS person.

## COPING WITH HIV AND AIDS

The movie *Philadelphia* was an important milestone in the public history of AIDS. The portrayal of a man whose fighting spirit won the admiration of those who joined his cause represents an accomplishment among persons with AIDS that is rarely seen by the public. Contrary to stereotypes, not all of those who are infected by the disease allow it to consume their life before it is physically over. Hoffman (1991) phrased the issue as a question: "Why do some people rapidly deteriorate in all aspects of their lives, whereas others create a quality of life that in some ways surpasses what they have previously achieved?" (p. 469). Although we have no simple answer to this question, we can say with some degree of confidence that those who remain psychologically, and sometimes physically, stronger are those who are coping better (Nicholson & Long, 1990).

Coping is the process of managing stressful situations. Stressful situations are events, conditions, and problems that a person judges to be personally significant to his or her well-being but that strain or exceed his or her resources (Lazarus & Folkman, 1984). In order to manage the situation, a person tries to minimize, reduce, or somehow control the internal or external causes of stress. Thus, in some cases, coping will consist of primarily "problem-solving strategies" (e.g., resolving a conflict, changing jobs, etc.), but at other times of primarily "emotion-regulating strategies" (e.g., having a positive attitude, seeking social support, etc.). In general, people use problem-solving strategies when they feel they have some degree of control over the outcomes of the situation and use emotion-regulating strategies when they feel they have little or no control over outcomes.

Some people have better coping skills than others. They seem to know how to attack and solve a problem, and they know how to feel and express emotions productively. In times of severe stress, such people are able to draw on these skills. A number of studies have found that coping ability is strongly related to how individuals respond to the possibility of becoming HIV infected or to the fact that they are HIV infected or have AIDS. For example, in a study of gay and bisexual men who were either seronegative or seropositive, the seropositive men were, as expected, more worried about getting AIDS compared to the seronegative men. However, they also reported greater use of emotion-regulating strategies, such as maintaining a positive attitude compared to the seronegative men (Taylor, Kemeny, Schneider, & Aspinwall, 1993). Similarly, Namir, Wolcott, Fawzy, and Alumbaugh (1987) found that active and positive coping strategies were associated with lower depressive mood states and higher self-esteem among seropositive gay men, whereas avoidance coping was related to higher depressive mood states. Finally, in a longitudinal study of HIV-positive and HIV-negative gay men, Folkman, Chesney, Pollack, and Coates (1993) found that depressive moods were less severe over time for men who coped actively by problem solving (seeking advice and information) and reappraising the situation in a positive light. Those men who tried to "detach" themselves emotionally from their stress and keep their feelings to themselves had higher depressed moods a year later.

Interestingly, even an act so typically associated with despair as suicide has been transformed by some AIDS sufferers into an act of control. HIV-positive and AIDS-infected individuals report that they think about (envision) suicide at some point, but consider it a way to exert control over an uncontrollable end, rather than as a response to sadness. As one such patient observed:

> My suicidal thoughts were centered around what I would do if I developed AIDS. . . . I guess I would do it if there was no other option and I was in a lot of pain . . . I think that thinking about suicide alternatives is a way for me to cope, or deal with the "what I would do" question, if I were to develop AIDS. (Schneider et al., 1991, p. 785)

Fortunately, individuals do not have to rely entirely on their own resources in the coping process. Social support is often available from friends, family, and community groups (Berger & Mallon, 1993). We turn now to a more extended discussion of social support and its role in coping.

## Social Support

According to Barrera and Ainlay (1983), social support can be conceptualized in three ways: (a) social embeddedness (i.e., connections to significant others), (b) perceived social support (i.e., perceptions that support is available when needed and satisfying when received), and (c) enacted social support (i.e., helping behaviors actually performed). All three types of support are useful to persons living with HIV and AIDS (Green, 1993).

For example, there is evidence that people who are satisfied with the support they receive (both interpersonal and institutional) report higher psychological adjustment to HIV infection and AIDS-related syndromes (Namir, Alumbaugh, Fawzy, & Wolcott, 1989) and lower levels of psychic distress and depression (Turner, Hays, & Coates, 1990). There is also evidence that social support is correlated with higher "subjective" measures of physical well-being (Green, 1993) as well as with the number of HIV symptoms (Turner et al., 1990). And finally, satisfaction with social support received is associated with positive coping strategies (Namir et al., 1987).

*Support Groups and Organizations.*    Ironically, the stigma associated with HIV has been a blessing and curse for the gay community. Initially, institutions that have traditionally provided support services, such as churches and governmental agencies, were reluctant to affiliate with the groups of greatest need, IV drug users and homosexuals. Their resistance was especially costly in the early years of the epidemic because family and friends were ill prepared for the problems they faced and were as much in need of support as were the care recipients. Thus, the gap created by institutional disregard and governmental underfunding necessitated novel approaches to a nationwide epidemic. Incredible efforts by the gay community marshaled thousands of volunteers to provide immediate care as well as to plan long-range strategies for gaining institutional and governmental support (Lindhorst & Mancoske, 1993).

Currently, support groups are widely available, though more numerous in larger cities. Chicago, for example, has 31 recorded support groups, San Francisco has 72, and New York has over 100. Churches are now providing material, as well as spiritual, support and hospitals are providing psychotherapy as well as medical treatment.

Unfortunately, the rapidly expanding caseload for paid care providers necessitates increasing dependence on volunteers (Lindhorst & Mancoske,

1993). In some cases, because minority groups represent an increasing proportion of patients needing care, volunteers must confront their own sexism, racism, and classism (Lindhorst & Mancoske, 1993). They must also face the "courtesy stigma" (Goffman, 1963) they acquire by being associated with infected groups.

The ability to meet these challenges is enhanced by the fact that volunteers are self-motivated. Unlike "formal" motivation, which arises out of one's role in an organizational structure (e.g., United Way agencies), informal motivation is a spontaneous response to a social need. No formal reward or payment is received. Satisfaction is internally, rather than externally, derived. In a study of AIDS volunteers, Omoto, Snyder, and Berghuis (1993) found that respondents reported high levels of satisfaction and over 80% reported that they had actively approached their AIDS organization.

One special type of volunteer who brings a very high level of informal motivation to service in the AIDS community is the "buddy." Buddy programs match volunteers on a one-to-one basis with AIDS patients who have similar demographic and sociographic backgrounds. The purpose of this arrangement is to provide a companion for persons in need of support and care when a family member or friend is unable or unwilling to provide them. The key element in the remarkable success of these programs is that the buddy volunteers his or her time rather than feeling obligated to provide it. The buddy enters the relationship *after* the AIDS diagnosis is known, with full knowledge that the AIDS person will be seeking emotional and instrumental support. Thus, the AIDS person is free of the guilt that might accompany similar demands made of friends and family (Weiss, 1988).

In sum, individuals who cope successfully with the onset of seropositivity and AIDS seem to have support mechanisms available to them and seem able to draw upon these mechanisms. The support received strengthens individual coping resources while at the same time avoiding some of the guilt that might be associated with exclusive dependence on family and network caregivers.

## A Preliminary Study of Social Support and Coping

Although the literature reviewed to this point is extensive, it leaves several questions unanswered. First, we know that family members, partners, friends, and support groups figure prominently in support functions, but we do not know what their *initial* reactions are, nor do we know the relative contribution of each over time. Second, although we know that general self-efficacy is associated with successful coping, we do not know whether self-efficacy regarding one's health is also associated with successful coping.

We explored these questions as part of an ongoing research agenda concerned with the experience of persons living with HIV and AIDS. Eighty-seven people responded to a questionnaire distributed through support groups in various states and through an open call on e-mail bulletin boards. The sample was primarily male (male = 72; female = 15), and homosexual (63%) (bisexual = 7%; heterosexual = 24%). The average age was 37 years with a range of 23–63 years, and most respondents were White (70%) although minorities were also represented to some degree (African American = 11%; Hispanic = 10%; Native American = 4%). Thirty-six percent of the respondents were HIV asymptomatic, 14% were HIV symptomatic, and 49% had AIDS.

*Who Is Told First and What Is Their Reaction?* Our results indicated that the people most likely to be told first about an HIV or AIDS diagnosis are, in rank order, close friends, mothers, romantic partners, sisters, brothers, and another HIV-positive person. Close friends were told first by 57% of the sample (i.e., 43% did not tell friends first), and mothers were told first by 46% of the sample (i.e., 54% did not tell mothers first). Fathers, ministers, and support groups, however, were less likely to be told initially, with only about 20% of the sample indicating they were told first (i.e., about 80% did not tell them first). As might be expected, given the stigmatized nature of the disease, bosses and coworkers were not often told initially (less than 20%).

Overwhelmingly, the reactions from the initial targets were supportive, although the greatest *proportion* of nonsupportive responses came from family members: children, mothers, fathers, and brothers. The generally positive response of initial targets seems to have made subsequent disclosures easier, with only 20% of the sample reporting that initial reactions made subsequent disclosures more difficult.

However, the fact that an initial conversation is supportive does not necessarily mean that there is no cost in revealing that one is HIV positive or has AIDS. As many scholars have stressed (e.g., Goldsmith, 1992), the need to "save face" of the distressed person is a constraint in conversations where social support is required. Thus, positive affect may be expressed initially, with more negative responses arising later.

With this in mind, we came at the question of reaction to initial self-disclosures of HIV/AIDS diagnosis from a second perspective. We asked respondents who were in a significant romantic relationship at the time of their diagnosis whether the relationship had since terminated and the extent to which revealing the diagnosis contributed to the termination. Of the 48 respondents who were in such a relationship, 37 reported that it had ended since their diagnosis. Although approximately 60% reported that the diagnosis was not the sole reason for the termination (death of partner, e.g., was also a factor), 40% of the sample reported that revealing their HIV/AIDS status contributed to the end of the relationship.

### What Is the Source of Social Support Over Time?

When asked to whom they go for support currently, respondents once again ranked a close or best friend as the person who is sought for continued support (61% talked to a close friend and 39% did not). However, beyond this category, the rank ordering shows significant change from the list of initial disclosure targets. The second and third most important sources of support over time were another person with HIV/AIDS (53%) and support groups (47%). Family members are relatively less important in the long-term support network. Mothers provided support for approximately 35% of all respondents (i.e., 65% did not seek support from mothers), and sisters, brothers, and fathers were used as support providers by only about 20% of the respondents (i.e., 80% did not use them for support).

It appears, then, that initial disclosure is made to those persons who "should" know because they are connected to the infected person, either as close friend, family member, or significant other. However, sustained support seems to be drawn most often from nonfamily members—specifically those people who can provide both *information* for problem-solving coping, and *empathy* for emotional coping (i.e., friends, other infected persons, and support groups).

*Are People Who Feel in Greater Control Less Likely to Be Depressed?* As expected, both social self-efficacy (measured as Social Locus of Control) and health self-efficacy (measured as Health Locus of Control) were negatively correlated with depression. That is, the more a respondent felt that he or she had control over health matters and social events, the less depression he or she reported. But more important, a test of the difference between the correlation coefficients revealed that the association between social efficacy and depression was significantly higher than that for health efficacy and depression.

This finding suggests that, even more than feeling in control of one's health, feeling confident about social interactions predicts lowered depression, perhaps because a strong internal locus of control facilitates participation in groups and relationships that reduce loneliness and provide support. In addition, one's confidence in the ability to control one's health is no doubt moderated by the inconsistent findings in medical research regarding treatment effectiveness.

## CONCLUSION

The medical, social, and personal conditions for individuals who are HIV positive or who are living with AIDS are historically unique. This medical community is not uniformly knowledgeable about the disease nor uniformly unbiased in their attitudes toward those who need care. Not surprising, these problems are reflections of similar conditions in the larger society. Ignorance about HIV and its transmission, as well as deeply felt stigmatization associated with the disease, contribute to the hostile social climate encountered by persons living with HIV and AIDS as well as by their social networks. The consequences of the medical and social reality of HIV and AIDS infection exacerbates the painful reality of the person who attempts to live with pride, dignity, and independence for as long as possible. The difficulty of coping with any debilitating disease is increased tenfold for persons attempting to cope with HIV and AIDS. These individuals experience loss in every aspect of their life from a loss of growth and development resulting from off-time transitions, to a loss of self-efficacy and self-esteem. The ability to cope with these conditions is fundamental to both survival and quality of life for a person who is HIV or AIDS infected.

Fortunately, many individuals do cope successfully with their HIV and AIDS-related condition. They draw on available social support and their own emotional resources. This is possible, in large measure, because the homosexual community responded to the AIDS crisis when other groups did not. What remains to be done is empowerment for other marginalized groups as well, minorities and women particularly. Until all persons who are afflicted with HIV and AIDS have access to such basic resources as medical treatment, education, counseling, and support, the disease will remain the nightmare of the 20th century.

## REFERENCES

Anderson, E. A. (1988). AIDS public policy: Implications for families. *The New England Journal of Public Policy, 4,* 411–427.

Bandura, A. (1977). Self-efficacy: Toward a unifying theory of behavioral change. *Psychological Review, 84,* 191–215.

Barrera, M., & Ainlay, S. L. (1983). The structure of social support: A conceptual and empirical analysis. *Journal of Community Psychology, 11,* 133–143.

Berger, R. M., & Mallon, D. (1993). Social support networks of gay men. *Journal of Sociology and Social Welfare, 20,* 155–174.

Blendon, R. J., & Donelan, K. (1988). Discrimination against people with AIDS: The public's perception. *The New England Journal of Medicine, 319,* 1022–1026.

Bonuck, K. A. (1993). AIDS and families: Cultural, psychosocial, and functional impacts. *Social Work in Health Care, 18*, 75–89.

Bor, R. (1993). Counselling patients with AIDS-associated Kaposi's sarcoma. *Counselling Psychology Quarterly, 6*, 91–98.

Cherry, K., & Smith, D. H. (1993). Sometimes I cry: The experience of loneliness for men with AIDS. *Health Communication, 5*, 181–208.

Christ, H. (1988). Psychological issues for patients with AIDS-related cancers. *Recent Results in Cancer Research, 112*, 84–92.

Field, H. L., & Shore, M. (1992). Living and dying with AIDS: Report of a three-year psychotherapy group. *Group, 16*, 156–164.

Folkman, S., Chesney, M., Pollack, L., & Coates, T. (1993). Stress, control, coping, and depressive mood in Human Immunodeficiency Virus-positive and -negative gay men in San Francisco. *The Journal of Nervous and Mental Disease, 181*, 409–416.

Franzini, L. R. (1993). The paradox of accurate information increasing the fear of AIDS. In S. C. Ratzan (Ed.), *AIDS: Effective health communication for the 90s* (pp. 71–90). Washington, DC: Taylor & Francis.

Goffman, E. (1963). *Stigma: Notes on the management of a spoiled identity.* Englewood Cliffs, NJ: Prentice-Hall.

Goldsmith, D. (1992). Managing conflicting goals in supportive interaction: An integrative theoretical framework. *Communication Research, 19*, 264–286.

Gostin, L., & Curran, W. (1987). AIDS screening, confidentiality, and the duty to warn. *American Journal of Public Health, 77*, 361–365.

Green, G. (1993). Editorial review: Social support and HIV. *Aids Care, 5*, 87–104.

Hoffman, M. A. (1991). Counseling the HIV-infected client: A psychological assessment and intervention. *The Counseling Psychologist, 19*, 467–542.

Lazarus, R., & Folkman, S. (1984). *Stress, appraisal, and coping.* New York: Springer.

Lindhorst, T., & Mancoske, R. (1993). Structuring support for volunteer commitment: An AIDS services program study. *Journal of Sociology and Social Welfare, 20*, 175–188.

Morales, E. (1990). HIV infection and Hispanic gay men. *Hispanic Journal of Behavioral Sciences, 12*, 212–222.

Namir, S., Alumbaugh, M. J., Fawzy, F. I., & Wolcott, D. L. (1989). The relationship of social support to physical and psychological aspects of AIDS. *Psychology and Health, 3*, 77–86.

Namir, S., Wolcott, D., Fawzy, F., & Alumbaugh, M. (1987). Coping with AIDS: Psychological and health implications. *Journal of Applied Social Psychology, 17*, 309–328.

Nicholson, W. D., & Long, B. C. (1990). Self-esteem, social support, internalized homophobia, and coping strategies of HIV+ gay men. *Journal of Consulting and Clinical Psychology, 58*, 873–876.

Omoto, A. M., Snyder, M., & Berghuis, J. P. (1993). The psychology of volunteerism: A conceptual analysis and a program of action research. In J. B. Pryor & G. D. Reeder (Eds.), *The social psychology of HIV infection* (pp. 263–286). Hillsdale, NJ: Lawrence Erlbaum Associates.

Peplau, L. A., & Perlman, D. (1982). Perspectives on loneliness. In L. A. Peplau & D. Perlman (Eds.), *Loneliness: A sourcebook of theory, research and therapy* (pp. 1–20). New York: Wiley.

Pryor, J. B., & Reeder, G. D. (1993). Collective and individual representations of HIV/AIDS stigma. In J. B. Pryor & G. D. Reeder (Eds.), *The social psychology of HIV infection* (pp. 263–286). Hillsdale, NJ: Lawrence Erlbaum Associates.

Rossi, A. S. (1968). Transition to parenthood. *Journal of Marriage and the Family, 30*, 26–39.

Schaefer, S., & Coleman, E. (1992). Shifts in meaning, purpose, and values following a diagnosis of Human Immunodeficiency Virus (HIV) infection among gay men. *Journal of Psychology & Human Sexuality, 5*, 13–29.

Schneider, S., Taylor, S., Hammen, C., Kemeny, M., & Dudley, J. (1991). Factors influencing suicide intent in gay and bisexual suicide ideators: Differing models for HIV+ and HIV– men. *Journal of Personality and Social Psychology, 16*, 776–788.

Shilts, R. (1987). *And the band played on: Politics, people, and the AIDS epidemic.* New York: St. Martin's Press.

Takigiku, S. K., Brubaker, T. H., & Hennon, C. B. (1993). A contextual model of stress among parent caregivers of gay sons with AIDS. *AIDS Education and Prevention, 5,* 25–42.

Taylor, S. E., Kemeny, M. E., Schneider, S. G., & Aspinwall, L. (1993). Coping with the threat of AIDS. In J. B. Pryor & G. D. Reeder (Eds.), *The social psychology of HIV infection* (pp. 263–286). Hillsdale, NJ: Lawrence Erlbaum Associates.

Terl, A. H. (1992). *AIDS and the law: A basic guide for the nonlawyer.* Washington, DC: Hemisphere.

Tiblier, K. B., Walker, G. S., & Rolland, J. S. (1989). Therapeutic issues when working with families of persons with AIDS. In E. D. Macklin (Ed.), *AIDS and families* (pp. 81–128). New York: Harrington Park Press.

Turner, H. A., Hays, R. B., & Coates, T. J. (1990). *Determinants of social support among gay men.* Abstract SB380 from the VIth International Conference on AIDS, San Francisco.

Vandevyer, C. (1993). Homosexual and AIDS: A new approach to the illness. *Journal of Homosexuality, 25,* 319–327.

Weiss, R. S. (1973). *Loneliness: The experience of emotional and social isolation.* Cambridge, MA: MIT Press.

Weiss, R. S. (1982). Attachment. In C. M. Parkes & J. Stevenson-Hinde (Eds.), *The place of attachment in human behavior* (pp. 171–184). New York: Basic Books.

Weiss, R. S. (1988). The experience of AIDS: Hypothesis based on pilot study interviews. *Journal of Palliative Care, 4,* 15–25.

Weitz, R. (1990). Living with the stigma of AIDS. *Qualitative Sociology, 13,* 23–28.

# 19 HIV/AIDS, Women, and Threads of Discrimination: A Tapestry of Disenfranchisement

Rebecca J. Welch Cline
*University of Florida*

Nelya J. McKenzie
*Auburn University at Montgomery*

*I often wonder how society would have responded if AIDS had initially been identified as a woman's disease. I wonder how those whose lives have been lost to this disease will be remembered.*
—Wiener (1991, p. 377)

More than a decade into the epidemic, AIDS is emerging as a disease of women. In the United States, cases of AIDS in women are growing faster than among any other group. Worldwide, AIDS is an "equal opportunity" disease with regard to gender (Cline & McKenzie, 1996), as the World Health Organization noted that since 1992 women have been becoming infected with HIV as often as men (Altman, 1992). But the failure to identify women with AIDS has resulted in the acute disenfranchisement of women with HIV disease. The gender socialization of women is particularly problematic in the context of HIV/AIDS as it adds to women's demise in relational, cultural, and economic contexts. The result is a tapestry of disenfranchisement woven from their many threads of stigma.

## DISENFRANCHISEMENT ROOTED IN STIGMA

AIDS has been socially constructed in the United States as a disease that has both gender and sexual orientation. The early and single-most influential identifying construction of AIDS was to label it a gay man's disease (see Corey, chap. 17, for a discussion of this issue). Ironically, that label functioned as a disservice to women with HIV disease as they were rendered "invisible" in the epidemic in the mind of the public. The association of the disease with an already stigmatized group (gay men) served to divide the world of AIDS into "us" and "them," with "them" conceived of as the individuals at risk for infection. Thus, the initial social construction of AIDS dissociated women from the disease.

Women with HIV disease have been disenfranchised by virtue of the failure, not only of the public but of researchers and educators, to recognize the vulnerability of women to HIV infection. Numerous critics have argued that that failure has taken the form of a dearth of literature (both clinical and psychosocial research) on women and AIDS (e.g., Anastos & Marte, 1989; Campbell, 1990; Cline & McKenzie, 1996). In fact, the first studies focusing primarily on signs of HIV in women did not begin until 1991. Most of what is known currently about HIV comes from studies of White, gay men. Thus, intervention and treatment efforts designed for women have crossed barriers of both race and gender in order to apply current knowledge to women with HIV, most of whom are Black or Latina. As a result of the lack of research, educators were denied the rationale and knowledge base by which to develop efficacious educational programs targeting women. Further, critics contend that the limited scientific literature on women and AIDS is flawed qualitatively by its failure to address women qua women (vs. women as mothers and caretakers) and its failure to address women's social roles in the contexts specifically relevant to HIV (Cline & McKenzie, 1996). An analysis of literature on women and AIDS by Cline and McKenzie reveals several factors that contributed to women's invisibility in the literature that are rooted directly in the defining of AIDS as a disease with both gender and sexual orientation. Those factors include homophobia that contributed to slowness in recognizing AIDS as a threat to heterosexuals (particularly women), controversy regarding heterosexual transmission of HIV, and the prevalence of a male-centered research paradigm that virtually eliminated women from research protocols.

Denying women scientific attention with regard to HIV is just one small step removed from their loss of rights to adequate education, diagnosis, and treatment. Among the many direct implications of the failure of researchers to attend to women in the AIDS epidemic are the following:

- The failure of women to see themselves at risk (Mantell, Schinke, & Akabas, 1988). Even women taking the greatest behavioral risks for HIV infection (e.g., partners of IV drug users) fail to accurately assess their vulnerability (e.g., Harrison et al., 1991; Nyamathi & Vasquez, 1989).
- The failure of providers to diagnose women with HIV disease. Until 1992, the Centers for Disease Control's diagnostic criteria failed to

account for differences in how the disease manifests itself in men versus women. Further, practitioners, directly influenced by the scientific literature, tend to misdiagnose women with HIV disease (Carovano, 1991; Wiener, 1991) as they do not "expect" women to contract HIV. Not only do stereotypes of women in general sometimes preclude their diagnoses, stereotypes of particular groups of women may be even more blinding. Tichy and Talashek (1992) noted that the incidence of AIDS in women over age 50 is increasing, yet stereotypes of older women's sexuality may interfere further with recognizing the disease.

- The failure to treat women with HIV disease adequately. Because of misdiagnoses and late diagnoses, women may not be treated adequately. For example, research by Lemp et al. (1992) found that the median survival period for men with AIDS exceeded that for women; however, no difference existed when treatment consisted of antiretroviral therapy. They concluded that the fact that women less often received this treatment (or received it later in the course of the disease) accounted for the difference in longevity.

Increasingly, HIV prevention in women is seen as a "matter of female empowerment" (Goldsmith, 1992, p. 1814). However, as Hanley and Lincoln (1992) noted, "Women at the greatest risk for HIV disease are not likely to form coalitions and advocate for services, dollars, and education" (p. 934). The resulting disenfranchisement ultimately has taken the form of misdiagnoses, delayed diagnoses, inadequate treatment, loss of longevity, and loss of quality of life. Those implications are rooted in the profound stigma associated with HIV/AIDS in general and in the magnification of that stigma in the case of women.

## STIGMA AND HIV/AIDS

Goffman (1963) defined stigma as "an attribute that is deeply discrediting" (p. 3). Goffman conceived of stigma, however, as less a characteristic of individuals and more a characteristic of relationships. That is, stigma functions to discredit one type of person whereas it can "confirm the usualness of another" (p. 3). Thus, stigma functions to divide and label the world into "us" and "them." In short, AIDS is conceived of as "a scourge of the underclass, the have-nots, and the undesirables" (Hall, 1992, p. 189).

Conceptualizing HIV/AIDS as an "us" and "them" disease is based not only in the association of the disease with gay men but in associations with multiple stigmatizing features. Numerous stigma are associated with the disease (e.g., the stigma of dying) and with the transmission of the virus (e.g., intravenous drug use, promiscuity, prostitution) as well as with populations disproportionately affected by the disease (e.g., gay men, minority groups, the poor).

Homosexuality may well be one of the most stigmatizing characteristics in contemporary American society. Pryor and Reeder (1993) contended that the social construction of AIDS has created an unconscious cognitive connection for most people between homosexuality and the disease. As a result, people experience negative affect in response to someone with HIV/AIDS even when the person is not homosexual.

Likewise, our society stigmatizes the terminally ill. The effect of being terminally ill is two-fold and in tension. First, the patient's need for social support is intensified (Wortman & Dunkel-Schetter, 1979). His or her ability to cope is tied directly to the provision of social support. At the same time, the dying person may be shunned or avoided (unless he or she denies the condition) and thus experiences pressure to function as the supporter of others and to deny his or her own needs. Research indicates that the dying (regardless of the particular illness) are stigmatized in their interactions with others, with both family and friends and professional caregivers (e.g., physicians, nurses). Results of those stigma include a lack of opportunity to talk about life's meaning, a magnified sense of abandonment and helplessness, and the inability to remain fully informed about their medical status (Cline, 1989; see Thompson, chap. 20, for an in-depth discussion of the stigmatization of the terminally ill).

Given the powerful effects of being stigmatized as homosexual or as dying, we should not be surprised that the stigma of AIDS reflects all of that rejection and judgment plus more. So stigmatized are people with AIDS that both family members and friends, as well as those whose professional responsibility it is to care for persons with AIDS (PWAs), hold many of the same stigmatizing stereotypes as does the general public, and therefore may withhold care. Family members and friends who hold the PWA responsible for his or her illness may be unwilling to provide care (McDonell, Abell, & Miller, 1991). But in part, they may be concerned that they too will be shunned by virtue of association with someone who is stigmatized. Thus, although the family network may be a "logical source of social support" (McDonell et al., 1991, p. 50), PWAs may be disinclined to seek that support or may have been estranged as a result of other discrediting features (i.e., drug use, homosexuality). (See Metts & Manns, chap. 18, for a discussion of social support issues for persons with HIV/AIDS.)

Professionals as well as family members may abandon PWAs in need. Research has shown that physicians and nurses (J. A. Kelly, St. Lawrence, Smith, Hood, & Cook, 1987), as well as psychologists (e.g., St. Lawrence, J. A. Kelly, Owen, Hogan, & Wilson, 1990), respond so negatively to PWAs as to characterize them as guilty of "outright intolerance when giving care" (Hall, 1992, p. 190). These professional caregivers are less willing to interact with PWAs than with others with terminal illnesses in both professional and social contexts.

Misperceptions and misinformation about various groups of "them" who are stigmatized have threatened the well-being of people with AIDS, "impaired society's ability to provide treatment," and serve as barriers to HIV prevention (Herek & Capitanio, 1993, p. 574). As several observers note, PWAs often belong to more than one of the stigmatized groups (e.g., women, gay men, Blacks, Hispanics, poor) (e.g., Croteau, Nero, & Prosser, 1993; Herek & Glunt, 1988). Thus, often they are the victims of multiple stigma, multiple sources of discrimination, and multiple forces of disenfranchisement. This is particularly true of women with HIV/AIDS.

Because many people with AIDS already are stigmatized prior to contracting the disease, they have some experience and expectations regarding their social treatment. However, heterosexual women may not *expect* to be stigmatized by the disease. In fact, Crandall (1991) found that those who were infected with HIV homosexually (men) actually *felt* less stigmatized than those who were infected heterosexually (women). The result is that perceptually and psychologically women may feel a magnified impact of their stigmatization. Moreover, the very nature of gender socialization may render women with HIV disease even more vulnerable to the disenfranchisement already associated with HIV/AIDS.

## THE ROLE OF GENDER IN MAGNIFYING STIGMA

Gender socialization does more than provide a set of behavioral expectations for men and women; it also shapes people's self-identities (Wood, 1994). Due to the cultural presumption of differences between the sexes, people tend to expect different behaviors of men and women. For example, men are expected to be adventurous, competitive, dominant, and decisive, whereas women are expected to be compassionate, submissive, and emotional (Rosen & Jerdee, 1974). Eagly (1987) suggested, "Many of these expectations are normative in the sense that they describe qualities or behavioral tendencies believed to be desirable for each sex" (p. 13). Consequently, most people anticipate substantial differences in behavior based on gender. In turn, these anticipated differences influence evaluations. Thus, to a substantial degree, the stigmatization of women with HIV disease is manifested in gender stereotypes.

According to Eagly (1987), "People act to confirm the stereotypic expectations that other people hold about their behavior" (p. 15). When social norms are violated (i.e., unexpected behavior is exhibited), negative sanctions may be imposed. For example, social acceptance of a double standard of sexual conduct encourages men to have multiple sex partners, but stigmatizes women who exhibit similar behavior. Consequently, evaluations of women, by both themselves and others, may be influenced strongly by expectations derived from gender stereotypes.

Social scientists claim that people have different social roles based solely on their gender (i.e., a gender role). Gender roles define shared expectations for behavior of individuals. For women, the behaviors associated with their gender role frequently focus on their relationships with others.

## Women in Relationship With Others

Gender stereotypes form the basis for numerous norms associated with gender roles (Eagly, 1987). In contrast to men, women's gender role often places them in positions where they are valued primarily "in relation to" others rather than in their own right. Such devaluation of women in their own right may be the most insidious factor contributing to the disenfranchisement of women with HIV disease.

Women's gender role, as opposed to men's, tends to be more familial and concerned with personal, affective ties (Chodorow, 1993). Consequently, women are defined primarily in relation to someone else as either a wife or a mother (Chodorow, 1993). Chodorow suggested, "ideology about women and treatment of them in this society . . . tend to derive from this familial location and the assumptions that it is or should be both exclusive and primary for women" (p. 417). For women, the "familial location" encompasses their relationship with partners and children and their labor as family caretaker.

*Women as Partners.* Gender stereotypes and their related gender roles commonly view men as the initiators of sex and women as compliant with that initiative. From this perspective, men are considered less able to control themselves sexually (Richardson, 1990), leaving women solely responsible for protecting their reputations as "good girls" and for avoiding pregnancy and protecting themselves against HIV infection.

Richardson (1990) suggested that in relationships between men and women, sex often is "part of the bargain" (p. 170). That is, in their relationships with women, men expect sex almost as a right and believe it is the woman's duty to comply. Given that men and women tend to share the same behavioral expectations relative to gender roles, women also come to believe they should comply with their partners' sexual demands. Consequently, sex is not always a matter of individual choice for the woman. In many contexts, the woman is powerless to change her (or her partner's) sexual practices without fear of being beaten or raped for refusal of sex or insistence on safer sex (Bell, 1989; Carovano, 1991; Richardson, 1990).

Thus, the potential negative sanctions imposed on a woman for failure to comply with the sexual demands of her partner pit compliance with her gender role (i.e., sexually submissive) against her ability to protect herself from HIV disease.

Perhaps nowhere is the double standard of sexual conduct more evident than in the practice of safer sex. According to Efantis (1991), the practice of safer sex often is more the responsibility of women than men. As Richardson (1990) explained, women are seen as the gatekeepers of male sexuality and "good girls" are expected to "just say no" (Carovano, 1991). Because men are viewed as being less able to control themselves sexually, women, by contrast, are expected to keep their wits about them and insist on use of a condom or abstinence. The irony is that, although women are more likely than men to be held responsible for safer sex by a social double standard, women who carry condoms risk their reputations due to that same standard (i.e., risk becoming marked as "easy" or promiscuous or appearing to be infected themselves).

Women's long-standing responsibility for contraception has expanded to include protection against HIV infection and blame for HIV transmission (Keppel, 1993). Historically women have been blamed for unplanned pregnancies because they failed to initiate contraception or abstinence; now, in the AIDS epidemic, women are seen as blameworthy because they failed to initiate safer sex or practice abstinence. However, for women who see motherhood as part of their gender role, protection against HIV through either safer sex or abstinence is incongruent with attempts to become a mother.

*Women as Mothers.* A traditional and strongly presumed aspect of women's gender role is that of mother. In fact, Allen (1993) and Carovano (1991) contended that women's capacity to bear children is their *defining* characteristic, and that activities and character traits termed "natural to women" (Allen, 1993, p. 381) tend to be deduced from the marking of "mother." However, AIDS in women, due to its association with perinatal transmission, has generated political, ethical, and moral debate regarding women's reproductive rights (Cline & McKenzie, 1996).

The majority of women who are HIV infected are among the most politically powerless and disenfranchised members of society. They are four times discriminated against: They are predominantly minorities, they are female, they are poor, and they have HIV disease. Their powerlessness makes them especially vulnerable to politics and practices imposed by others. Primarily because of their relationship to a fetus, HIV-infected women face the threat of losing the right to one of the most basic aspects of gender role—the role of mother.

Historically, women have been accorded reproductive rights as a matter of common law. However, the dynamics of the AIDS epidemic pits women's reproductive freedom against fetal and societal rights. Consequently, women find themselves the object of AIDS interventions as the primary means of preventing HIV disease in infants, rendering the well-being of women themselves a secondary concern (Cline & McKenzie, 1996). The Centers for Disease Control (CDC, 1985) guidelines, recommending that women who are HIV infected or "at risk" for HIV infection "delay pregnancy," ignore the profound meaning of childbearing to some women (Cohen, 1991; Richardson, 1990). Thus, being HIV infected jeopardizes not only a woman's health, but also one of her most identifying characteristics—that of mother.

For women who exist on the margins of society because of race or poverty, having a child and becoming a mother can define self-worth (Chavkin, Coates, Des Jarlais et al., 1990; Cohen, 1991). Having a child "may represent one of the few creative options open to women who are or feel deprived of economic and educational opportunities (Chavkin et al., 1990, p. 101). For some, a child provides a source of love that otherwise is lacking (Levine & Dubler, 1990; Williams, 1990). To forego pregnancy on the *chance* that the child will be infected is to forego control of perhaps the only thing in life about which these women have a choice: motherhood. For many women even a 50% chance of having a healthy child (and, according to some figures, 80%) is preferable to a 100% chance of not having a child at all (Anastos & Marte, 1989; Levine & Dubler, 1990).

There is widespread sentiment that giving birth to HIV-infected babies is unjustifiable and immoral, particularly when a woman knows she is HIV infected and takes the risk anyway (Levine & Dubler, 1990; Murphy, 1988). Images of women victimizing their children through the "selfish act of procreation" (Juhasz, 1990, p. 36) have resulted in the practice of directive approaches to reproductive counseling for women who are HIV infected (Carovano, 1991). This directive counseling goes beyond providing options and attempts to persuade a woman to pursue a particular course of action (Marte & Anastos, 1990). Most counselors do not believe women who are HIV infected should have a child who might be born with a terminal illness; this belief is stronger regarding women who might transmit HIV disease than for other terminal illnesses (e.g., Tay-Sachs disease or cystic fibrosis; Levin, cited in Bayer, 1990). In addition, that bias is stronger regarding women of color and women from lower socioeconomic classes who, in turn, are advised more strongly to abort (Marte & Anastos, 1990).

*Women as Caregivers.* The sexual division of labor puts women in the position of caretaker for other family members. As Weedon (1987) explained, being a *good* wife and mother calls for qualities thought to be "naturally feminine, such as patience, emotion and self-sacrifice" (p. 3). These expectations lead both women and men to anticipate that women should, and will, "deny their own needs to meet the needs of others" (Shaw, 1991, p. 507).

Because women have been so strongly socialized to put the needs of others first, it is difficult for many women to focus on their own needs or put themselves first (Hanley & Lincoln, 1992).

In the role of family caretaker, women, including those who are HIV positive, are likely to attend to the health needs of other family members while neglecting their own needs. For example, public health clinics often serve either adults or children, but not both. So women often use their limited resources (time, energy, and money) to seek medical care for their children rather than for themselves (Carovano, 1991; J. K. Kelly & Holman, 1993). As a result, when a woman with HIV complies with her role of caregiver, she may actually exacerbate the progress of HIV/AIDS by denying health care for herself while providing care for others.

From the beginning, women's place in the AIDS epidemic has placed them in the role of caregiver (Campbell, 1990). From the early days of the epidemic, women have been caring for their adult sons, partners, and children who have AIDS. Often these women have become isolated and disenfranchised, providing social support to others, but denied such support themselves. As Wiener (1991) explained, because of the stigma and fear associated with AIDS, both family members and friends are likely to abandon the caregiver.

In summary, the normative behavioral expectations associated with women's gender role set the stage for both their vulnerability and disenfranchisement in the AIDS epidemic. These gender roles are particularly significant in the interpersonal, cultural, and economic contexts in which women find themselves coping with HIV disease.

## WOMEN AND AIDS: THE MANY LOST CONTEXTS

Critics widely recognize the need for AIDS education and prevention programs that target specific audiences and thereby are able to be adapted to the numerous differential qualitative aspects of those audiences. Because very little attention has been paid to women in the AIDS literature in general, there has been virtually no focused attention to gender as a factor that interacts with interpersonal relationships, culture, and economic conditions as contexts for understanding women and AIDS. Despite the lack of both focus and depth, roadsigns in the literature, when considered as a whole, begin to inform us of, if nothing else, the significance of these features in understanding the AIDS epidemic as it touches women.

### Gender and Interpersonal Relationships as Context

Fundamentally, AIDS prevention advice consists of imperatives to be carried out in the context of interpersonal relationships. Advice related to sexual contexts specifically calls for self-disclosure and assertiveness for the purposes of sharing sexual histories and negotiating condom use. The interpersonal context of efforts to prevent AIDS is virtually ignored in the literature on women and AIDS, despite cumulative evidence that compels the conclusion that gender is an important determinant of communication behavior (e.g., Bresnahan, 1993; Coates, 1986; Quina, Wingard, & Bates, 1987; Smith-Lovin & Robinson, 1992).

Like other neglected issues, interpersonal relationships are addressed as a significant issue primarily by critics of the women and AIDS literature. For example, Mays and Cochran (1988) claimed the interpersonal decision-making framework as "the most appropriate context" for addressing educational interventions. They recognized that individuals do not engage in preventive action alone, but that the advice is carried out in a social context of interdependence. Specifically, HIV prevention directives involve intimate relationships governed by gender role norms, gender, economics, and culture. Thus, changes in behavior to follow such directives require changes in the interpersonal relationships in which they occur (Mays & Cochran, 1988). Likewise, Cochran (1989) contended that "Although HIV is a biological, and not a social entity, its transmission from one person to another, for the most part, occurs within the social context of interpersonal relationships" (p. 309).

Relational power, risk of damaging the relationship, and peer group norms are just three examples of interpersonal factors that may interfere with engaging in AIDS prevention behavior for women differently than for men.

*Relational Power.* Traditional gender roles cast the man as the superior, the woman as the subordinate. However, AIDS prevention advice targeted to women requires women to reverse these roles and influence the men in their lives (Conti, Lieb, Spradling, & Witte, 1993; Stein, 1990). This advice to abstain or demand condom use assumes that the situation is under a woman's control (Cohen, 1991; Richardson, 1990). For those in traditional role relationships, the advice expects women to assume new and unfamiliar roles "in an intensely emotional and private situation" (Cohen, 1991, p. 105; see also Stein, 1990). In many cultures, these attempts will be associated with trying to control a man's sexuality (Cohen, 1991). Family power structure constitutes one important barrier for women and AIDS prevention (Kelly & Murphy, 1991). Traditional gender socialization teaches males greater assertiveness than females. One result is that when decision-making situations arise in mixed-gender dyads (e.g., the decision to have sex, the decision to use a condom), men tend to be more assertive than women (Stake & Stake, 1979). Research indicates that women are highly cognizant of the role demand to be submissive (Osmond, Wambach, Harrison, Byers et al., 1993). For example, focus groups of African-American women whose behavior placed them at highest risk for HIV explicitly identified their need to be passive and submissive in sexual negotiations as a factor impeding their ability to insist on condom use (Shervington, 1993).

In some ethnic groups, women may experience verbal and physical abuse for merely advocating condom use (Cochran & Mays, 1989). In this context, North and Rothenberg (1993) explored the ethics of partner notification programs (i.e., programs that encourage or require an infected person to notify his or her partners of their own HIV status) when the infected woman is at high risk for domestic violence. The authors warned that connections between domestic violence, drug abuse, and AIDS suggest that thousands of women may be vulnerable to physical harm if their partners are notified: "We are aware of two women who were shot and many others who were injured or abandoned after revealing" (p. 1195) their HIV status to partners. Thus, the risk of violence is an important factor contributing to the failure of AIDS-prevention programs for women.

*Risk of Damaging the Relationship.*   Ironically, sex may be a means for a woman to overcome her sense of powerlessness by defining herself as part of a relationship (Cochran, 1989). Sex can be a means of "establishing proprietary rights" and a means of gaining emotional and tangible social support (Mays & Cochran, 1988). In this context, practicing AIDS prevention requires women to jeopardize the very interpersonal relationships in which the prevention occurs.

For women, sex often is defined as "the consummation of a relationship" rather than simply a pleasurable act (Fullilove, Fullilove, Haynes, & Gross, 1990). For many women, sex may be the only way for them to experience intimacy (Ybarra, 1991). The woman who is HIV positive may already feel unloved and is likely to fear both rejection and abandonment (Ybarra, 1991).

In a developing relationship, sex may be a means of transforming a dating relationship into a serious and committed one; sexuality becomes a "component in generating attachment" (Cochran, 1989, p. 314). And thus, for a woman to insist on condom use, particularly when competing partners may not, "could destroy her hold on a developing relationship" (Cochran, 1989, p. 314). In corollary fashion, then, prevention behaviors can function to express dissatisfaction with the relational partner. Thus, prevention turns on the issues of trust and commitment (Kenen & Armstrong, 1992).

Where women are "committed" to those relationships, requesting safer sex from a partner is viewed as conveying a message of distrust (e.g., Anastos & Palleja, 1991; Caravano, 1991; Shayne & Kaplan, 1991). In this context, the interpersonal elements are key to understanding women's behavior. For example, in-depth interviews of women drug users and partners of IV drug users revealed that these women saw initiating condom use as a risk to the relationship (Williams, 1991). They feared rejection as they believed their partners would assume *they* were infected and thus would terminate the relationship. At a minimum they saw attempted condom use as arousing suspicion regarding past or current behavior, and thus as an indicator of a violation of trust. Likewise, in a focus group of African-American women, Fullilove et al. (1990) found that where there was "deep trust, women were willing to 'take a chance' " (p. 55) but where trust was not yet established or had eroded they asked for condom use. One woman reported demanding that her husband use a condom as punishment for coming home late. Some of the women indicated fear of asking a man to use a condom, showing an awareness of marital and date rape.

As a result of defining the negotiation of safer sex as an issue of interpersonal trust, "the least successful rates of behavior change to reduce risk occur in prolonged relationships," (Cohen, 1991, p. 106). Women are more likely to succeed to practicing safer sex in casual situations and with multiple partners (Cohen, 1991; Harrison et al., 1991). In fact, the most extensive use of condoms reported are among prostitutes, but like other women they tend to not use condoms with their steady partners, even if they always use them with customers (CDC, 1987; Cohen, 1991; Cohen, Alexander, & Wofsy, 1988; Mantell, Schinke, & Akabas, 1988). Thus, many women are fearful of losing their relationships, afraid that the demand for safer sex will drive the man away (Mays & Cochran, 1988). In this context, engaging in unsafe sex may seem to require "a woman to demonstrate her love for her partner by sacrificing her own health as a romantic symbol of commitment" (Murphy, 1988). Recognition of this choice has prompted some researchers to call for prevention interventions that are controlled by the female partner, such as the female condom (e.g., Golub & Stein, 1993).

Beyond risking the relationship itself, the woman who demands safer sex may risk damage to her identity in the relationship, which may in turn risk the relationship itself. The request to demand abstention, monogamy, or condom use functions to deny the woman's need for love and support; and the request for condom use may be associated with infidelity and may invoke suspicion (Cohen, 1991; Shayne & Kaplan, 1991; Stuntzner-Gibson, 1991). Women who attempt to negotiate condom use may be seen as promiscuous, unfaithful, or even HIV infected (Caravano, 1991). Beyond the risk of violence, women demanding safer sex may be met with sexual rejection and, potentially, the termination of the relationship (Cohen, 1991). In sum, women's behavior with regard to condom use is driven less by health issues and personal beliefs than by her meta-perceptions of her partner's attitudes regarding prevention. For example, McCusker, Stoddard, Zapka, and Zorn (1993) found that women's behavior was predictable from their perceptions of their sex partner's attitudes about condoms rather than from their own beliefs about condoms.

*Peer Group Norms.* For the drug-addicted woman, engaging in AIDS prevention requires a lifestyle change relative to the norms of her peer group (Mays & Cochran, 1988). Such a change requires the ability to negotiate safer sex and safer drug works, non-normative behaviors, in a subculture that the woman relies on for emotional and tangible support. In addition, compared to men, women who are IV drug users are more likely to have as their sexual partners other IV drug users. Thus, for women IV drug users, the "shooting partner" may be the most significant relationship in the woman's life as they are often also sexual partners (Des Jarlais, Friedman, Casrield, & Kott, 1987). As a result, women fail to negotiate "safe drug use" for the same reasons they fail to negotiate condom use (Williams, 1991). Sharing drug works is a relational bond, and as one female drug-using interviewee put it, "You don't think your best friend has this" (Williams, 1991, p. 211).

## Gender and Culture as Context

Culture only adds to the difficulty of understanding male–female interpersonal relationships in the context of AIDS prevention issues. Generally, minority women at high risk for HIV infection tend to be less concerned about their risk than nonminority women engaging in the same risk behaviors (Kalichman, Hunter, & Kelly, 1992). The following discussion provides examples to illustrate the need to sensitize AIDS prevention efforts to cultural norms.

There has been "minimal development of prevention efforts geared to the needs of black women" (Fullilove et al., 1990, p. 47). The literature does suggest that the need for education may come earlier for Black girls as Blacks tend to initiate sexual intercourse at an earlier age than Whites (Zelnick & Kanter, 1980), know less about contraception (Zelnick & Kim, 1982), and tend to wait longer between initiating sex and initiating contraception (Zabin & Clark, 1981).

At the same time Black women tend to value fertility more than White women and thus are less likely to have partners use contraception (Cochran, 1989). Anastos and Palleja (1991) pointed out that having children may be the only means of obtaining a sense of identity or status for many women: "We are, in fact, only one generation away from the time when bearing children was the most important contribution a woman could make to her community, no matter what her class or color" (p. S42). This remains true for many women whose opportunities are limited by poverty and racism. Among Blacks in particular, reproduction is seen as a powerful tool against racism (Mays & Cochran, 1988). Thus condom use conflicts with a cultural value.

Developing efficacious AIDS prevention programs for Black women requires knowledge of differences in cultural values, normative behavior, and appropriate adaptations. Although imploring women to "take charge" and negotiate safer sex in relationships may challenge women in general, it is particularly problematic for Black women who do not tend to use methods of birth control that depend on their partners' behavior (Wyatt, Peters, & Guthrie, 1988). Thus the AIDS prevention advice mandates women to give up control as well as to counter a cultural value.

Research indicates that Hispanic women, relative to White women, tend to be less likely to believe that they can avoid AIDS (Marin, Tschann, Gomez, & Kegeles, 1993). Hispanic women who do perceive risk and who attempt to practice AIDS prevention advice are faced with a multitude of barriers related to culture-based gender roles (Amaro, 1988). The cultural norm for Hispanic women is to be modest, faithful, and virginal (Mays & Cochran, 1988). She is supposed to be naive with regard to sex, having sex only in the context of marriage (Anastos & Palleja, 1991). The man is responsible for knowledge about sex and controls contraceptive decisions. At best, Hispanic men tend to be ambivalent toward women who suggest using condoms (Forrest, Austin, Valdes, Fuentes, & Wilson, 1993). The cultural norm is to not discuss sexual matters; the woman who does often will be judged negatively. The culture emphasizes respect for authority, with the man "in charge." In this context, asking a man to use a condom likely will result in the attribution that the woman is "loose" or "bad" (Anastos & Palleja, 1991; Mantell et al., 1988).

Some Hispanic women have reported abuse in response to requests for partners to use condoms (Mays & Cochran, 1988). Hispanic men may believe that using a condom is acceptable but not with a "good woman" (i.e., wives or steady partners). The request to use condoms is interpreted as a message of distrust. Not only can Hispanic women not talk about sex, as it would violate their virgin image, Hispanic men cannot propose condom use as women may then see them as merely desiring sex for pleasure rather than intending it to lead to marriage and pregnancy (Worth & Rodriguez, 1987).

AIDS threatens Hispanic women most as it jeopardizes their maternal role, their ability to care for their children (Nyamathi & Vasquez, 1989). AIDS threatens their abilities to carry out a provider role which in turn jeopardizes their self-esteem. Hispanic women who are diagnosed with HIV often are stripped of their very identities as their families reject them and they are "thrust into a cycle of rejection, isolation, and homelessness" (Stuntzner-Gibson, 1991, p. 25).

## Gender and Economic Factors as Context

Critics recognize the need to address women and AIDS in the context of "powerlessness" with regard to social and economic barriers. However, little literature has focused on researching these issues and developing appropriate interventions. Poverty and AIDS go hand in hand.

In the United States, socioeconomic status is related to ethnicity. Thus, not only are many women at risk faced with managing difficult interpersonal relationships within the confines of cultural norms but they do so in a context of few resources. Minority women often are coping with poverty, large families, low education, and limited social support systems in their everyday survival (Amaro, 1988). Many women who are at risk or who become HIV infected are "overwhelmed with survival issues" (Zuckerman & Gordon, 1988, p. 619). Once diagnosed, they have desperate needs for legal and social services and "many of these individual patients and their families are disempowered, disenfranchised, and alienated from traditional sources of help and support" (Zuckerman & Gordon, 1988, p. 619).

Poor women often see their risk to HIV infection differently than do their middle-class counterparts. Sexual involvement may be a means to improve a woman's economic position and access to social support (Cochran, 1989). Sharing of needles and syringes emanates from economic factors (Stuntzner-Gibson, 1991). In the context of poverty, a woman's "decisions surrounding behavioral choices are motivated primarily by the immediacy of her current life concerns. For some individuals, prevention behaviors can be a luxury afforded only if they do not conflict with other primary needs" (Cochran, 1989, p. 317). Faced with the issue of survival versus health risks, survival comes first. The threat of AIDS is diminished when one is coping with "homelessness, joblessness, starvation, and abandonment" and may even become irrelevant (Nyamathi & Vasquez, 1989, p. 300).

The extant literature on women and AIDS has functioned to make women invisible in the epidemic despite current epidemiological trends that project that AIDS is rapidly becoming a disease of women, and particularly poor minority women in this country. Women in general, and particular populations of women, are devalued by their treatment (or absence thereof). Moreover, the very psychosocial factors that likely enhance women's risk and result in their differential responses to the epidemic are virtually ignored by researchers (i.e., interpersonal relationships, culture, economic factors). Rosser (1991) contended that "the uncritical acceptance of sexism, racism, and classism in our society and the consequent incorporation of those biases into AIDS research has led to the current . . . failure to understand the disease's progression, complications, treatment, and complex transmission patterns" (p. 238). This conclusion points directly to the threads of stigma that have woven a tapestry of disenfranchisement of women in the AIDS epidemic.

## BLAMING THE INVISIBLE VICTIM:
## EFFECTS OF STIGMA ON COMMUNICATION
## AND SOCIAL SUPPORT

The social construction of AIDS has made women invisible "victims." Because of their invisibility, in conjunction with the construction of AIDS as a gay male and drug user disease, and the tendency to treat AIDS as a moral problem rather than a health problem, women who are diagnosed with HIV encounter a uniquely high level of stigma. In effect, when the invisible become visible, the impact of their presence is magnified. In fact, Shayne and Kaplan (1991) contended that women with AIDS may be more stigmatized than their male counterparts by the association of AIDS with prostitution. They are further stigmatized often by being members of a minority group and by being IV drug users (Wiener, 1991). As a result they are less likely to get parental support upon diagnosis (Shayne & Kaplan, 1991). Further, the stigma associated with AIDS is exacerbated when applied to women in part by a "pervasive double standard applied to sexual behavior" (Buckingham & Rehm, 1987, p. 8). The result is a magnified "blame-the-victim" response.

Women with HIV disease face all of the ramifications of the stigma associated with AIDS in general, and more. Researchers have noted that "alienation and ostracism can proceed directly from infection with HIV" (Crandall & Coleman, 1992, p. 174). Typically, PWAs feel anxious, depressed, alienated, in emotional distress, and estranged in their relationships (Crandall & Coleman, 1992). However, the degree of the negative affect *felt* is directly related to *how* stigmatized one feels (Crandall & Coleman, 1992). Generally, heterosexual women feel more stigmatized by AIDS than do their gay male counterparts. Thus, women may feel a relatively more profound psychological impact from an HIV diagnosis. In fact, women with AIDS in support groups have described themselves as "feeling alone with the illness, a feeling intensified by public discourse that describes AIDS as a gay male disease" (Chung & Magraw, 1992, p. 892).

As with stigma in general (Goffman, 1963), women with AIDS may well come to blame themselves (Nichols, 1989). Those who are stigmatized tend to hold the same beliefs about the stigma as do the nonstigmatized (Goffman, 1963). Thus, the stigmatized incorporate the larger society's view and essentially come to discredit themselves (Bennett, 1990). Self-blame is particularly strong among women with AIDS when they have children (Nichols, 1989) as they feel the failure of being unable to provide for their children, experience the grief of their children, and often witness the illness and death of their also-infected lovers, spouses, and/or children (Anastos & Palleja, 1991). In addition, women with HIV disease often come to question their identities as women (in terms of femininity and adequacy) and may condemn themselves for being unable to have a child or being unable to "compete" for a lover's exclusive attention (Buckingham & Rehm, 1987, p. 8).

As with stigma in general, PWAs experience stigma most strongly in its impact on their interactions with others (Laryea & Gien, 1993). Most PWAs report being lonely and experience disruption of family and peer relationships. They live in constant fear of disclosure of their illness and the accompanying rejection by society. At the same time, most suffer from not always being able to discuss these fears openly with family and friends (Laryea & Gien, 1993).

The rejection that women diagnosed as HIV infected encounter is typical of the tendency to avoid, reject, and treat as "not quite human" those who are stigmatized (Goffman, 1963, p. 5). The most devastating consequences of stigma often are found in interpersonal contexts; as social contact is avoided, the possibilities for social support evaporate. Thus, the health benefits associated with socially supportive communication (e.g., offering tangible assistance, expressing acceptance, and listening) are denied to women with AIDS. Although the effect of being stigmatized may be paramount for all people with AIDS, the impact is particularly devastating for women because they tend, more than men, to define themselves in terms of their relationships with others. The pragmatic implications of being stigmatized and thereby losing social support are particularly troublesome as women with AIDS already tend to have few personal and economic resources available and often are the sole providers for other family members. Being blamed and stigmatized simply drains an already limited supply of support.

Beyond the effects of stigma in general, and the effects of the stigma of AIDS in particular, women stigmatized by AIDS experience losses specific to their gender. These include loss of self-esteem as they are cast as endangering significant others: "Women with HIV are presumed to be promiscuous and dangerous" (Chung & Magraw, 1992, p. 892), a feeling reinforced by characterizations of women as "vehicles for AIDS transmission" (p. 892). Additional losses experienced include:

> profound grief for the loss of . . . body image, sexuality, and childbearing potential; the burden of making decisions about initiation, continuation, and termination of pregnancy; the lack of a natural community . . . the abruptness of diagnosis, which may be disclosed at the birth of an infected baby . . . feeling unwanted and unloveable; the feeling of guilt from watching a child die; lack of male responsibility and the societal assumption that women have the responsibility for control of sex and contraception. (Pizzi, 1992, p. 1024)

Women with AIDS face a reality in which they tend to be "tangled in a web of poverty, illness, and oppression; by the dictates of racism and poverty, they are disempowered, disenfranchised, and alienated from traditional sources of help and support" (Wiener, 1991, p. 377; see also Zuckerman & Gordon, 1988). Compared to gay men, women with AIDS lack a community of support desperately needed. The multiple stigma experienced by women with AIDS functions to preclude them from the very social support requisite to their coping and survival. As a result of becoming "invisible participants" in the epidemic (Wiener, 1991, p. 375) they tend to be "forgotten" in general, but when "remembered" to be stigmatized.

## REFERENCES

Allen, J. (1993). Motherhood: An annihilation of women. In A. Jaggar & P. Rothenberg (Eds.), *Feminist frameworks: Alternative theoretical accounts of the relations between women and men* (3rd ed., pp. 380–385). New York: McGraw-Hill.

Altman, L. K. (1992, July 21). Women near men's AIDS infection rate. *The Gainesville Sun*, pp. 1A, 6A.

Amaro, H. (1988). Considerations for prevention of HIV infection among Hispanic women. *Psychology of Women Quarterly, 12*, 429–443.

Anastos, K., & Marte, C. (1989). Women—The missing persons in the AIDS epidemic. *Health/PAC Bulletin, 19*(4), 6–13.

Anastos, K., & Palleja, S. M. (1991). Caring for women at risk of HIV infection. *Journal of General Internal Medicine, 6* (January–February supplement), S40–S46.

Bayer, R. (1990). AIDS and the future of reproductive freedom. *The Milbank Quarterly, 68*(2), 179–204.

Bell, N. K. (1989). AIDS and women: Remaining ethical issues. *AIDS Education and Prevention, 1*, 22–30.

Bennett, N. J. (1990). Stigmatization: Experiences of persons with acquired immune deficiency syndrome. *Issues in Mental Health Nursing, 11*, 141–154.

Bresnahan, M. I. (1993). Gender differences in initiating requests for help. *Text, 13*, 7–27.

Buckingham, S. L., & Rehm, S. J. (1987). AIDS and women at risk. *Health and Social Work*, 5–11.

Campbell, C. A. (1990). Women and AIDS. *Social Science and Medicine, 30*, 407–415.

Carovano, K. (1991). More than mothers and whores: Redefining the AIDS prevention needs of women. *International Journal of Health Services, 21*, 131–142.

Centers for Disease Control. (1985, December 6). Recommendations for assisting in the prevention of perinatal transmission of human T-lymphotropic virus type III/lymphadenopathy-associated virus and acquired immunodeficiency syndrome. *Morbidity and Mortality Weekly Report, 34*(48), 721–732.

Centers for Disease Control. (1987). Antibody to immunodeficiency virus in female prostitutes. *Morbidity and Mortality Weekly Report, 36*, 158–161.

Chavkin, W., Coates, T., Des Jarlais, D., Ehrhardt, A. A., Miller, T., Stryker, J., & Worth, D. (1990). Prevention: The continuing challenge. In H. Miller, C. Turner, & L. Moses (Eds.), *AIDS: The second decade* (pp. 81–146). Washington, DC: National Academy Press.

Chodorow, N. (1993). Gender personality and the sexual sociology of adult life. In A. Jaggar & P. Rothenberg (Eds.), *Feminist frameworks: Alternative theoretical accounts of the relations between women and men* (3rd ed., pp. 414–424). New York: McGraw-Hill.

Chung, J. Y., & Magraw, M. M. (1992). A group approach to psychosocial issues faced by HIV-positive women. *Hospital and Community Psychiatry, 43*, 891–894.

Cline, R. J. W. (1989). Communication and death and dying: Implications for coping with AIDS. *AIDS & Public Policy Journal, 4*(1), 40–50.

Cline, R. J. W., & McKenzie, N. J. (1996). Women and AIDS: The lost population. In R. L. Parrott & C. M. Condit (Eds.), *Evaluating women's health messages: A resource book* (pp. 382–401). Newbury Park, CA: Sage.

Coates, J. (1986). *Women, men, and language: Studies in language and linguistics.* London: Longman.

Cochran, S. D. (1989). Women and HIV infection: Issues in prevention and behavior change. In V. M. Mays, G. W. Albel, & S. F. Schneider (Eds.), *Primary prevention of AIDS* (pp. 309–327). Newbury Park: Sage.

Cochran, S. D., & Mays, V. M. (1989). Women and AIDS-related concerns: Roles for psychologists in helping the worried well. *American Psychologist, 44,* 529–535.

Cohen, J. B. (1991). Why women partners of drug users will continue to be at high risk for HIV infection. *Journal of Addictive Diseases, 10,* 99–110.

Cohen, J. B., Alexander, P., & Wofsy, C. B. (1988). Prostitutes and AIDS: Public policy issues. *AIDS and Public Policy Journal, 3*(2), 16–22.

Conti, L., Lieb, S., Spradling, T., & Witte, J. J. (1993). AIDS epidemic among Florida women. *Journal of the Florida Medical Association, 80,* 246–249.

Crandall, C. S. (1991). AIDS-related stigma and the lay sense of justice. *Contemporary Social Psychology, 15,* 66–67.

Crandall, C. S., & Coleman, R. (1992). AIDS-related stigmatization and the disruption of social relationships. *Journal of Social and Personal Relationships, 9,* 163–177.

Croteau, J. M., Nero, C. I., & Prosser, D. J. (1993). Social and cultural sensitivity in group-specific HIV and AIDS programming. *Journal of Counseling and Development, 71,* 290–296.

Des Jarlais, D. C., Friedman, S. R., Casrield, C., & Kott, A. (1987). AIDS and preventing initiation into intravenous (IV) drug use. *Psychology and Health, 1,* 179–194.

Eagly, A. H. (1987). *Sex differences in social behavior: A social-role interpretation.* Hillsdale, NJ: Lawrence Erlbaum Associates.

Efantis, J. (1991). The impact of HIV infection on women. In J. Durham & F. Cohen (Eds.), *The person with AIDS: Nursing perspectives* (2nd ed., pp. 300–315). New York: Springer.

Forrest, K. A., Austin, D. M., Valdes, M. I., Fuentes, E. G., & Wilson, S. R. (1993). Exploring norms and beliefs related to AIDS prevention among California Hispanic men. *Family Planning Perspectives, 25,* 111–117.

Fullilove, M. T., Fullilove, R. E., Haynes, K., & Gross, S. (1990). Black women and AIDS prevention: A view towards understanding the gender rules. *The Journal of Sex Research, 27,* 47–64.

Goffman, E. (1963). *Stigma: Notes on the management of spoiled identity.* Englewood Cliffs, NJ: Prentice-Hall.

Goldsmith, M. F. (1992). Specific HIV-related problems of women gain more attention at a price—Affecting more women. *Journal of the American Medical Association, 268,* 1814–1816.

Golub, E. L., & Stein, Z. A. (1993). Commentary: The new female condom—Item 1 on a women's AIDS prevention agenda. *American Journal of Public Health, 83*(4), 483–503.

Hall, B. A. (1992). Overcoming stigmatization: Social and personal implications of the human immunodeficiency virus diagnosis. *Archives of Psychiatric Nursing, 6,* 189–194.

Hanley, E., & Lincoln, P. (1992). HIV infection in women: Implications for nursing practice. *Women's Health, 27,* 925–936.

Harrison, D. F., Wambach, K. G., Byers, J. B., Imersshein, A. W., Levine, P., Maddox, K., Quadagno, D. M., Fordyce, M. L., & Jones, M. A. (1991). AIDS knowledge and risk behaviors among culturally diverse women. *AIDS Education and Prevention, 3*(2), 79–89.

Herek, G. M., & Capitanio, J. P. (1993). Public reactions to AIDS in the United States: A second decade of stigma. *American Journal of Public Health, 83*, 574–577.

Herek, G. M., & Glunt, E. K. (1988). An epidemic of stigma: Public reactions to AIDS. *American Psychologist, 32*, 886–891.

Juhasz, A. (1990). The contained threat: Women in mainstream AIDS documentary. *The Journal of Sex Research, 27*(7), 25–46.

Kalichman, S. C., Hunter, T. L., & Kelly, J. A. (1992). Perceptions of AIDS susceptibility among minority and nonminority women at risk for HIV infection. *Journal of Consulting and Clinical Psychology, 60*, 725–732.

Kelly, J. A., & Murphy, D. A. (1991). Some lessons learned about risk reduction after ten years of the HIV/AIDS epidemic. *AIDS Care, 3*, 251–257.

Kelly, J. A., St. Lawrence, J. S., Smith, S., Hood, H., & Cook, D. (1987). Stigmatization of AIDS patients by physicians. *American Journal of Public Health, 77*, 789–791.

Kelly, J. K., & Holman, S. (1993). The new face of AIDS. *American Journal of Nursing, 93*(3), 26–34.

Kenen, R. H., & Armstrong, K. (1992). The why, when and whether of condom use among female and male drug users. *Journal of Community Health, 17*, 303–317.

Keppel, B. (1993). The impact of sexism, racism and classism on HIV-infected women. In A. Jaggar & P. Rothenberg (Eds.), *Feminist frameworks: Alternative accounts of the relations between women and men* (3rd ed., pp. 54–59). New York: McGraw-Hill.

Laryea, M., & Gien, L. (1993). The impact of HIV-positive diagnosis on the individual. *Clinical Nursing Research, 2*, 245–263.

Lemp, G. F., Hirozawa, A. M., Cohen, J. B., Derish, P. A., McKinney, K. C., & Hernandez, S. R. (1992). Survival for women and men with AIDS. *Journal of Infectious Disease, 166*, 74–79.

Levine, C., & Dubler, N. (1990). Uncertain risks and bitter realities: The reproductive choices of HIV-infected women. *The Milbank Quarterly, 68*(3), 321–351.

Mantell, J. E., Schinke, S. P., & Akabas, S. H. (1988). Women and AIDS prevention. *Journal of Primary Prevention, 9*, 18–40.

Marin, B. V., Tschann, J. M., Gomez, C. A., & Kegeles, S. M. (1993). Acculturation and gender differences in sexual attitudes and behaviors: Hispanic vs. non-Hispanic White unmarried adults. *American Journal of Public Health, 83*, 1759–1761.

Marte, C., & Anastos, K. (1990). Women—The missing persons in the AIDS epidemic: Part II. *Health/PAC Bulletin, 20*(1), 11–18.

Mays, V. M., & Cochran, S. D. (1988). Issues in the perception of AIDS risk and risk reduction activities by Black and Hispanic/Latino women. *American Psychologist, 43*(11), 949–957.

McCusker, J., Stoddard, A. M., Zapka, J. G., & Zorn, M. (1993). Use of condoms by heterosexually active drug abusers before and after AIDS education. *Sexually Transmitted Diseases, 20*, 81–88.

McDonell, N. R., Abell, N., & Miller, J. (1991). Family members' willingness to care for people with AIDS: A psychosocial assessment model. *Social Work, 36*, 43–53.

Murphy, J. S. (1988). Women and AIDS: Sexual ethics in an epidemic. In I. B. Corless & M. Pittman-Lindeman (Eds.), *AIDS: Principles, practices, and politics* (pp. 65–79). New York: Hemisphere.

Nichols, M. (1989). The forgotten seven percent: Women and AIDS. In C. Kain (Ed.), *No longer immune: A counselor's guide to AIDS* (pp. 77–92). Alexandria, VA: American Association for Counseling and Development.

North, R. L., & Rothenberg, K. H. (1993). Partner notification and the threat of domestic violence against women with HIV infection. *The New England Journal of Medicine, 329*, 1194–1196.

Nyamathi, A., & Vasquez, R. (1989). Impact of poverty, homelessness, and drugs on Hispanic women at risk for HIV infection. *Hispanic Journal of Behavioral Sciences, 11*, 299–314.

Osmond, M. W., Wambach, K. G., Harrison, D. F., Byers, J. et al. (1993). The multiple jeopardy of race, class, and gender for AIDS risk among women. *Gender and Society, 7,* 99–120.

Pizzi, M. (1992). Women, HIV infection, and AIDS: Tapestries of life, death, and empowerment. *The American Journal of Occupational Therapy, 46,* 1021–1027.

Pryor, J. B., & Reeder, G. D. (1993). Collective and individual representations of HIV/AIDS stigma. In R. Pryor & G. Reeder (Eds.), *The social psychology of HIV infection* (pp. 263–286). Hillsdale, NJ: Lawrence Erlbaum Associates.

Quina, K., Wingard, J. A., & Bates, H. G. (1987). Language style and gender stereotypes in person perception. *Psychology of Women Quarterly, 11,* 111–122.

Richardson, D. (1990). AIDS education and women: Sexual and reproductive issues. In P. Aggleton, P. Davies, & G. Hart (Eds.), *AIDS: Individual, cultural, and policy dimensions* (pp. 169–179). London: The Palmer Press.

Rosen, B., & Jerdee, T. H. (1974). Effects of applicant's sex and difficulty of job on evaluations of candidates for managerial positions. *Journal of Applied Psychology, 59,* 511–512.

Rosser, S. V. (1991). Perspectives: AIDS and women. *AIDS Education and Prevention, 3,* 230–240.

St. Lawrence, J. S., Kelly, J. A., Owen, A. D., Hogan, I. G., & Wilson, R. A. (1990). Psychologists' attitudes toward AIDS. *Psychology and Health, 4*(4), 357–365.

Shaw, N. S. (1991). Preventing AIDS among women: The role of community organizing. In N. McKenzie (Ed.), *The AIDS reader: Social, political, ethical issues* (pp. 505–521). New York: Penguin.

Shayne, V. T., & Kaplan, B. J. (1991). Double victims: Poor women and AIDS. *Women and Health, 17,* 21–37.

Shervington, D. O. (1993). The acceptability of the female condom among low-income African-American women. *Journal of the National Medical Association, 85,* 341–347.

Smith-Lovin, L., & Robinson, D. T. (1992). Gender and conversational dynamics. In C. Ridgeway (Ed.), *Gender, interaction, and inequality* (pp. 122–156). New York: Springer-Verlag.

Stake, J. E., & Stake, M. N. (1979). Performance: Self-esteem and dominance in mixed sex dyads. *Journal of Personality, 47,* 71–84.

Stein, Z. A. (1990). HIV prevention: The need for methods women can use. *American Journal of Public Health, 80,* 460–462.

Stuntzner-Gibson, D. (1991). Women and HIV disease: An emerging social crisis. *Social Work, 36*(1), 22–28.

Tichy, A. M., & Talashek, M. L. (1992). Older women. Sexually transmitted diseases and acquired immunodeficiency syndrome. *Nurse Clinician in North America, 27,* 937–949.

Weedon, C. (1987). *Feminist practice and poststructuralist theory.* New York: Basil Blackwell.

Wiener, L. S. (1991). Women and human immunodeficiency virus: A historical and personal psychosocial perspective. *Social Work, 36,* 375–378.

Williams, A. B. (1990). Reproductive concerns of women at risk for HIV infection. *Journal of Nurse-Midwifery, 35,* 292–298.

Williams, A. B. (1991). Women at risk: An AIDS educational needs assessment. *Journal of Nursing Scholarship, 23,* 208–213.

Wood, J. T. (1994). *Gendered lives: Communication, gender, and culture.* Belmont, CA: Wadsworth.

Worth, D., & Rodriguez, R. (1987, January–February). Latino women and AIDS. *SIECUS Report,* pp. 5–7.

Wortman, C. B., & Dunkel-Schetter, C. (1979). Interpersonal relationships and cancer: A theoretical analysis. *Journal of Social Issues, 35,* 120–155.

Wyatt, G. E., Peters, S. C., & Guthrie, D. (1988). Kinsey revisited Part II: Comparisons of the sexual socialization and sexual behavior of Black women over 33 years. *Archives of Sexual Behavior, 17,* 289–332.

Ybarra, S. (1991). Women and AIDS: Implications for counseling. *Journal of Counseling and Development, 69,* 285–287.

Zabin, L. S., & Clark, S. D., Jr. (1981). Why they delay: A study of teenage family planning clinic patients. *Family Planning Perspectives, 13,* 181–185.

Zelnick, M., & Kanter, J. F. (1980). Sexual activity, contraceptive use and pregnancy among metropolitan-area teenagers: 1971–1979. *Family Planning Perspectives, 12,* 231–237.

Zelnick, M., & Kim, Y. J. (1982). Sex education and its association with teenage sexual activity, pregnancy and contraceptive use. *Family Planning Perspectives, 14,* 117–126.

Zuckerman, C., & Gordon, L. (1988). Meeting the psychosocial and legal needs of women with AIDS and their families. *New York State Journal of Medicine, 88,* 619–620.

# 20 Allowing Dignity: Communication With the Dying

Teresa L. Thompson
*University of Dayton*

In years gone by, our ancestors did not need to worry much about communication with the terminally ill. Medical technology had not advanced to the point of being able to identify pending terminality as adequately as can now be done. Nor could medicine or technology prolong impending death to the degree that is presently possible. Our ancestors' experiences with communication with the terminally ill were much more focused. Such experiences were more likely to include being called to the bedside of a dying relative, who probably died later that same day or week. As a result of this, dying individuals were not terribly likely to be disenfranchised—there was not much opportunity to interact with them. In some past cultures, dying was seen as a part of life rather than something to be feared and avoided.

In contrast to the past, many individuals today know of impending terminality many weeks, months, or years before it actually occurs. Both early diagnosis and the ability to prolong life have impacted this. Dying individuals are frequently given much time to accept that reality—and others have ample opportunity to interact with those who are dying before the death occurs. Thus, a topic that had previously been fairly irrelevant to most people's interaction patterns has now become potentially problematic for many. As opportunities for interaction with the dying, and as medical technology prolonging dying have increased, so have our fears of dying.

Interacting with dying individuals forces us to confront our own impending terminality (Ezell, Anspaugh, & Oaks, 1987). Such confrontation is not easy. Over 300 years ago, the philosopher La Rochefoucauld wrote,

"The human mind is as little capable to contemplate death for any length of time as the eye is able to look at the sun" (cited in Kalish, 1981, p. 6). The fear of death has been prominent historically across many cultures (Ezell et al., 1987). The early Greeks alternatively conceptualized death as hateful and cleansing (Kalish, 1981). Our own culture is characterized as death defying (Ezell et al., 1987)—we do whatever we can to avoid death.

Because interaction with the dying forces confrontation with terminality, the dying, too, are typically avoided by both loved ones and others (Epley & McCaghy, 1977–1978; Smith, Lingle, & Brock, 1978–1979). Sudnow (1967) even documented avoidance of individuals who deal with dead bodies as an example of our reaction to dying. The disenfranchisement of the terminally ill may be even stronger than the disenfranchisement of many other groups, because we all know that we will sometime die. Although we may *fear* that we will be in the shoes of individuals in other disenfranchised groups, we *know* that we will sometime be in the position of dying.

This chapter examines much of the research that has been conducted on communication between terminally ill individuals and others beyond what this author has reviewed in past writing (see chap. 12 in Nussbaum, Thompson, & Robinson, 1989; Thompson, 1989). Research from both medical and social science journals is discussed, although much of the writing on this topic in medical journals is more anecdotal than empirical. This research also tends to simplistically conceptualize communication with guidelines such as, "you should communicate more." For the most part, the present review focuses on empirical research and excludes most, although not all, of the "how to communicate with the dying" pieces. The decision to exclude these pieces has been made not because the pieces are unimportant, as they may have strong and pragmatic impacts on readers, but because they are typically untested and should, thus, be shared in the social science context only with care. One interesting point must, however, be mentioned about the writing on this topic in medical journals—the existence of a common theme of "You can communicate with dying patients and their families in a way that won't take a lot of your time" in several of the articles (e.g., Fuller & Gels, 1985; Harris, Hartner, Linn, & Linn, 1979).

## THE NEED

Concern over interaction between dying individuals and their family, friends, and health care providers has been argued from many directions, including medicine, law, ethics, therapy, and social science (cf., Crispell & Gomez, 1987; Gotay, Crockett, & West, 1985; Walsh & Kingston, 1988). Numerous explanations have been offered about why communication between the dying and other individuals is an uncomfortable experience and should, thus, be examined by researchers. Some have noted that technology comes between patients and doctors, and high levels of medical technology are particularly likely to be used with individuals who are seriously ill (Bertman, Wertheimer, & Wheeler, 1986; Bryant, 1986; Holman, 1990). Others have suggested that the organizational power structure (Holman, 1990) and institutional policies (Strauss, Glaser, & Quint, 1964) come between doctors and patients. Our heroic measures to save lives further help develop our fear of death (Potter, Schneiderman, & Gibson, 1979)—if we work so hard to avoid it, it must be really awful!

This fear of death is one of the factors that has been linked to the difficulty people experience interacting with the terminally ill, as have changes in people's appearances as they near death and the "funeralese" euphemisms that accompany death (Bryant, 1986). The stress generated by that fear inhibits open communication (Delvaux, Razavi, & Farvacques, 1988). The fear itself also helps lead to avoidance of the dying (Peters-Golden, 1982)—few of us are comfortable confronting our fears.

In addition to this fear and inhibition of communication, research has documented a construct labeled communication apprehension regarding the terminally ill (CA-dying; Hayslip, 1986–1987). Hayslip found that those high on CA-dying are less likely to repress fears about their own death, more likely to express concerns over their own or another's dying, and more likely to have negative attitudes toward aging and death. These findings, however, are not consistent with those of Reisetter and Thomas (1986). They found a positive correlation between death anxiety and communication with the terminally ill.

Concerns about their abilities to communicate effectively with the terminally ill are frequently expressed by medical students (Field & Howells, 1985) and social workers (Tobin & Gustafson, 1987). That a fear of death is taught to students in medical school is substantiated by the qualitative research of Williams (1992). Williams' research took place in the gross anatomy lab, where she studied medical students' initial and later experiences with the dissection of human cadavers. She observed:

> medical faculty's tacit prohibition against discussion of their own and their student's attitudes and anxieties about illness, dying and death. A two-fold strain is observed in the laboratory: the difficulty professors encounter handling their own discomfort with this yearly ritual, and the anxiety of students for whom this is a first experience. The parallel tension is exacerbated by a conspiracy of silence between professors and students and between students and their fellow students. (p. 65)

This conspiracy of silence extends far beyond the anatomy lab, and seems to affect interaction between care providers and humans who are not yet, but soon to be, cadavers. Such avoidance and lack of communication is also not unique to care providers. We return to issues relevant to this topic in later portions of this chapter. To provide a context for that discussion, however, we first discuss the needs of the dying person.

## THE TERMINALLY ILL INDIVIDUAL

Several researchers have described the needs of the dying patient. Harris et al. (1979) articulated the following as major concerns for dying individuals: (a) their emotional responses to the physical limitations of the illness, (b) communication with significant others in their lives, including physicians, (c) their self-concepts from a life-review perspective, and (d) coming to some resolution regarding impending death. In a thorough review of the research, Northouse and Northouse (1987) identified four related concerns: (a) maintaining a sense of control, in light of the fear, uncertainty, helplessness, and dependence that the patient is experiencing, (b) seeking information to help reduce uncertainty and interpret what is happening to them, (c) disclosing feelings to help adjustment and lessen depression, and (d) searching for meaning. That the tendency to disclose feelings is not universal regardless of context, however, is indicated by the research of Hunt and Meerabeau (1993). Terminally ill British patients being visited in their homes by nurses rarely responded to invitations to talk about their feelings. This led Hunt and Meerabeau to note that patients who are not willing to talk about their feelings are labeled "denying." If pressed to do so, they may become "angry." Both denial and anger are stages that have been described in the acceptance of terminality. Hunt and Meerabeau speculated about the extent to which this reality is socially constructed. Jones (1990) suggested the use of diaries for those terminally individuals who are reluctant to talk about their feelings.

Other issues facing dying individuals may also impact communication. For instance, pain makes communication more difficult (Brena, 1987). It is also not easy for individuals who are dying to communicate their logic and emotion at that time (Potter et al., 1979). Potter et al. articulated other communication problems for the dying, including restriction of contact with others, withdrawal of support by others, people "talking for" them instead of "to" them, impatience on the part of others when the terminally ill person has difficulty expressing him or herself, people talking to the person like a child, and others talking about the person in their presence but as if they were not there. Potter et al. argued that such behaviors isolate the person, reduce dignity, and remove the person from the decision-making process. The patient becomes an object in the therapy paradigm instead of a team member.

Other communication dilemmas have also been described. Longhofer (1980) noted possible double-binds for patients. Examples include a patient being told that a procedure is safe and routine, but then observing anxiety among staff members about it. Even more subtle are the times when the patient is verbally given reason to believe that there is hope, but the non-verbals of those with whom the patient interacts indicate impending terminality.

A less-studied need of the dying is their desire to bid farewell to significant others. Kellehear and Lewin (1988–1989) found that 81% of the dying patients they interviewed reported a desire to say farewell, most of them late in the course of dying. Three styles of farewell were mentioned most frequently: gifts, conversations, and letters.

One of the major concerns of dying individuals mentioned earlier is a loss of control caused by feelings of dependence and helplessness. Harris et al. (1979) provided some additional insight into this issue with their suggestion of casting the patient in the role of teacher to others who have not experienced death. The researchers noted that some patients complain incessantly because they feel that they have not been heard by others—acknowledgment of communication can help lessen this problem. Patients, fearing abandonment by others and that they are abandoning others as terminality approaches, are extremely sensitive to the slightest hesitation from interactants.

Patients' feelings of helplessness and lack of control are affected by the predictability of the interpersonal environment (Northouse & Northouse, 1987). However, even when, according to observers, patients are frequently offered control by nurses, the patients still report feeling a lack of control (Pepler & Lynch, 1991). Pepler and Lynch coded relational control sequences in nurse-terminal patient interactions. Their focus on control was chosen because being offered control affirms an individual's worth, and is associated with death with dignity. They found that relational bids were usually accepted by both nurses and patients, and that patients took or requested control more often than did nurses. The most frequent behavior observed was the nurse offering control to the patient. Patients bid for control by giving directions to the nurse about their care or environment, asking for help with their care or environment, or seeking information. These bids varied, however, in the degree of hesitancy, confidence, and directness they evidenced. Nurses usually agreed to control bids. When a nurse rejected a control bid, a rationale was usually provided, or control was returned to the patient shortly thereafter. Nurses only took control frequently in those situations when patients took or requested it infrequently. Rarely did a nurse do something to a patient that the patient had refused. The least frequently observed behavior was the patient asking the nurse to take control. Despite all this, however, patients complained about a lack of control.

Feeling out of control and helpless is intensified when the patient is excluded from communication (Cable, 1991). This notion of exclusion from communication and decision making leads us to our next topic of discussion—truth telling about terminality.


## TRUTH TELLING

The notion of "truth telling" is debated vigorously in regard to terminally ill individuals and has a special meaning in this context. It is used to refer to telling a terminally ill patient and his or her family that the individual is, indeed, dying. Although truth telling used to be uncommon, it is now the norm in our culture, although that is not the case in all cultures (Kai, Ohi, Yano et al., 1993). Graham-Pole, Wass, Eyberg, and Chu (1989) nicely summarized the arguments for truth telling: (a) Not telling patients is likely to lead to distrust, (b) caregivers are not "wise" (p. 466) enough to judge who should and should not be told the truth (although Adler, 1989, argued that social workers are competent to make such assessments), (c) it is immoral to deny a dying person the opportunity to survey his or her life, and (d) withholding such information is likely to be caused by the care provider's reluctance to acknowledge failure or deal with grief rather than by concern for the patient or family. Research has also indicated higher levels of job satisfaction when health care providers are allowed to communicate more openly with patients who are dying and their families (Parry, 1987; Parry & Smith, 1987). Additionally, open communication was associated with more effective symptom control in the Parry and Smith study.

Writing about Japan, where truth telling is rare even though data indicate that patients want to know the truth, Kai et al. (1993) argued that a lack of candid communication restricts the spectrum of therapeutic options, and frequently leads to an extended hospital stay and superfluous treatment. Data from within both the United States and Great Britain also indicate that patients do want to know of impending terminality, and are usually told (Seale, 1991). In a 1984 small-sample study, however, Todd and Still found three out of four British physicians withholding a diagnosis of terminality from their patients. The researchers noted that withholding the diagnosis prevented the physician from having to acknowledge helplessness. Other research has examined the use of medical terminology and medical slang to reduce the emotional impact of distressing situations (e.g., "expire" instead of "die"). Coombs, Chopra, Schenk, and Yutan (1993) noted that the purposes of medical slang include softening tragedy, discharging strong emotions, increasing feelings of control, and dealing with frustration. They wrote that, "slang terms deflect feelings that are incompatible with those formally defined as appropriate" (p. 996), and also observed that medical prognosis jargon refers almost exclusively to patient deterioration rather than improvement.

Despite some of the findings just mentioned, most hospitals now expect truth telling regardless of circumstances (Adler, 1989). Armstrong (1987) likened the process to a medical interrogation, so strong is the pressure on patients to avoid denial and confront impending terminality.

Consistent with Armstrong's (1987) reasoning, others have cited examples of insensitive truth telling that may harm already vulnerable people. An example provided by Adler (1989) exemplifies such behavior:

> Not waiting for a patient's wife to return from the ladies' room, the physician blurts out, "We found a malignancy in the lung." Bewildered, the patient responds, "Malignancy? That means I don't have long to live." Sharply, the doctor responds, "Are you asking me or telling me? *You* are going to die. I am going to die. We *all* are going to die. Did you think you were going to live forever?" When the patient's wife returns, the doctor repeats the diagnosis in technical terms and quickly mentions some referrals for treatment. When the wife asks if the doctors to whom he had referred were good, the physician responds, "No, they are not. I'm sending you to my uncle, because he needs the money.... Do you get it all now? Or do you want to go through it all again?" (p. 159)

Another instance, reported by Seale (1991), included a nurse telling family members, "You know your wife is dying, don't you, and the doctor wants to see you tomorrow" (p. 949). Most of the reports by patients and family members, however, indicated sensitivity on the part of the truth teller (Seale, 1991). Researchers have stressed two keys when communicating bad news to patients: being sensitive enough to find out how much patients want to know and realizing that often people do not hear bad news when it is communicated to them (Lloyd, 1991).

One study indicated that, although physicians were supposed to break the news to terminally ill patients, nurses typically were more effective at doing so (Field, 1989). This study also found that relatives had more trouble accepting a terminal prognosis than did the patients themselves. The nurses reported finding rewards in their work with patients, but not with families.

Although Field (1989) found consensus that nurses were more effective at death telling, Helm and Mazur (1989) determined that patients prefer to receive this news from physicians. They also want their physician to begin the dialogue about advanced directives (e.g., living wills).

Patient satisfaction with the communication surrounding a diagnosis has been associated with a less severe reaction to that diagnosis (Jacobsen, Perry, & Hirsch, 1990). McCann (1992), too, reported more negative responses among patients who felt their diagnosis had been poorly communicated or that they had been given little opportunity to discuss the diagnosis. Patients' perceptions of poor communication were associated with use of medical language during the diagnosis and having the care provider blurt out the diagnosis. Those patients who received more information reacted more positively. Similarly, those who perceived the staff as more understanding and kinder were more accepting of the diagnosis. Acceptance was also greater if the implications of the diagnosis were explained at the time it was communicated or soon afterward. Maguire and Faulkner (1988) also stressed the importance of how a diagnosis of terminality is communicated.

## PROVIDER COMMUNICATION WITH DYING PATIENTS

Beyond the communication of the diagnosis of terminality, additional research has focused on other aspects of how health care providers interact with terminally ill individuals. Blanchard et al. (1983) coded interactions between oncologists and their patients during rounds and factor analyzed the results. The first factor, accounting for 23.3% of the variance, included informational behaviors; the second (16.1%) focused on behaviors such as addressing patients by name and introducing themselves. The third factor (10.5%) was examining patients and establishing privacy, whereas the fourth (8.8%) involved psychosocial support. Not a great deal of time, then, is spent providing the support that the terminally ill desperately need.

Nurses typically concentrate on providing support more than do physicians, however. Hunt (1991), for instance, found that nurses attempted to be friendly and informal in their interactions with terminally ill patients and their families. This included behaviors such as using first names, offering cups of tea, engaging in small talk prior to and following procedures, and giving appropriate leave-taking cues. The nurses' communication also indicated little urgency, as it included comments like, "You're not holding me up." Although there was some reciprocal story telling, there was little self-disclosure by the nurse. When self-disclosure was communicated by a nurse, it typically did not receive as lengthy a response as did self-disclosure from a patient. This finding about self-disclosure is interesting in light of the suggestion offered by Cable (1991) that care providers *should* self-disclose to the terminally ill and in light of the oft-replicated finding of the reciprocal nature of self-disclosure. Overall, the conversations observed by Hunt (1991) were more like informal, friendly talk than like characteristic professional-client interaction.

Another frequently researched aspect of interaction between health care providers and terminally ill individuals is discussion about "Do Not Resuscitate" (DNR) orders—an important ethical consideration in this context.

Bryant (1986) cited data indicating that 17% of DNR orders and 78% of decisions to code (to actively fight for the patient's life) are made without consultation with the patient or the family. Sixty-eight percent of the time when the patient is near death, there is no discussion of DNR decisions, so no decision is reached. Although there are some who argue that communication about DNR orders should not involve the patient because of the pain it causes them, Loewy (1991) suggested such arguments are based on anecdotal data, and that allowing others to make such decisions for competent adults, "is likely to decrease communication with the dying patient and to introduce an atmosphere of suspicion and fear and to exclude the competent patient from his/her rightful place in the community" (p. 156). Even when DNR discussions do involve the patient, the physician's presentation of options is not likely to be neutral—it is typically loaded toward the physician's desires (Ventres, Nichter, Reed, & Frankel, 1992).

The major concerns of health care providers about interacting with the terminally ill were summarized by Northouse and Northouse (1987). Unlike the concerns of the patient, mentioned earlier, providers focus on: (a) imparting information, (b) communicating hope, and (c) sharing control. The first of these is difficult because of different levels of comprehension and preferences for information among patients, because physicians typically spend little time with patients, and because providers have varying levels of comfort with such communication. Sharing control, too, providers typically find difficult and energy consuming (Northouse & Northouse, 1987).

Other differences in priorities have also surfaced. Whereas providers typically are concerned about ethical and legal issues regarding the terminally ill, patients and their families focus more on emotional and communicative problems (Bronstein & Jones, 1986). Similarly, care providers rate symptom and pain control as more important and communication as less important than do patients (Doyle, 1989). However, cancer patients rank minimizing side-effects of treatment as a major priority, whereas nurses focus more on dealing with feelings (Lauer, Murphy, & Powers, 1982).

In addition to differences in priorities, physicians and patients demonstrate disparities in other perceptions. Physicians estimate higher levels of fear and dissatisfaction with choices of tests and treatment and less understanding of procedures than patients themselves report (Pfefferbaum, Levenson, & van Eys, 1982). And patients and their families also perceive things differently. Family members of individuals receiving palliative care perceive more problems of all sorts, but especially communication problems, than do the patients (Higginson, Wade, & McCarthy, 1990). The patients report no communication problems with members of the support team, but frequent communication problems with hospital physicians and nurses. The most serious concern of these patients was communication of the diagnosis, which tended to be abrupt and given with little detail.

When the issue of communicating with terminally ill patients is concerned, the role of the family also becomes a crucial factor. We turn now to the research that has focused on this issue.

## FAMILIES OF THE TERMINALLY ILL

One notable development can be observed in the literature on terminal illness as it discusses the family of the dying person—a suggestion to treat the family as a unit and in addition to the patient (Bonjean, 1989; Hall & Kirschling, 1990; Parry & Smith, 1985). Although such a notion is not new to those who have written about and studied families in other arenas, it is new in this area of study. It exemplifies a growing concern with, and awareness of, the difficult experience through which a family goes as a member of the family is dying. Quite a bit of research is now emphasizing this concern. Our focus within this chapter is on the communicative aspects of this issue, but the interested reader may turn to such sources as Hall and Kirschling for a more extensive discussion of the topic.

The interpersonal needs of relatives of terminally ill individuals have been summarized in several studies. These include: (a) being honest with the family, (b) providing a clear explanation of what is being done to/for the patient and why it is being done, (c) keeping the family informed, and (d) showing interest in answering questions from family members (Irwin & Meier, 1973). The subjects in this study also noted that they did *not* desire the following from hospital or hospice staff members, all of which are behaviors sometimes performed by staff members: (a) leaving the family alone, (b) taking the family away from the dying person, and (c) being told not to think about themselves or not to discuss death around the terminally ill individual. Similarly, Truglio-Londrigan and Hayes' (1986) examination of family caregivers of the dying found a focus on developing assertive communication skills, coping with guilt, finding time to talk about their own needs so that they could get the strength to go back and help the dying person, and insecurity about asking questions of health professionals. Freihofer and Felton (1976) found that family members did *not* want nurses to hold their hands, encourage them to cry, cry with them, or remind them that the patient's suffering will soon be over. Again, all of these behaviors are sometimes observed in nurses.

Family caregivers of dying people who have been in hospice for a longer time report more communication tasks than if the patient has been in hospice a shorter time (Yang & Kirschling, 1992). These tasks include monitoring visitors and keeping others informed about the dying person's condition. The researchers speculated that these results may be an artifact of the fact that with longer stays a person's condition is likely to worsen, or it may be because the environment of the hospice encourages discussion of death and terminality. These family caregivers reported many positive outcomes, including becoming closer to the patient and finding new meaning in life. They especially appreciated being able to hold the person, just sit with him or her, and engage in activities with the dying individual. These behaviors are also important to the dying person, of course, who is likely to fear withdrawal of affection from family members (Farkas, 1992).

Northouse and Northouse's (1987) summary of the research on families of cancer patients indicated that they have three main concerns: (a) concealing feelings, (b) acquiring information, as the family is rarely with the patient in the hospital at the time the physician comes by, physicians do not seek the family out, and the family feels awkward about approaching busy doctors, and (c) coping with helplessness, because the family frequently receives even less social support or opportunity to talk about their experiences than does the patient. The first of these is primarily a concern when the patient and family have been given different information by the care provider. If the patient does not know the diagnosis, communication becomes very difficult. Family members try to conceal their feelings so that the patient does not find out. Because the patient usually figures out that he or she is dying anyway, such behavior frequently communicates to the patient that family members do not care. Even if the patient has been told, family members frequently try to be brave so as to help the dying person remain cheerful. Research also indicates, however, that patients frequently try to conceal their feelings so as not to burden the family (Harris et al., 1979). Some families even claim that the key to their successful handling of terminal illness has been never talking about dying (Northouse & Northouse, 1987)!

Other research has also substantiated a lack of communication about dying among family members and even between spouses. Cooper (1982) found lung cancer patients and their spouses rarely discussing the diagnosis except superficially. Hinton (1981) described three patterns of restricted communication between spouses coping with the terminal phase of cancer. One group of couples avoided any discussion to prevent their own levels of distress from rising. A second set avoided discussion to maintain the positive attitude that they felt was necessary to cope. The third group rarely talked about important emotional events anyway, so their behavior was merely a continuation of this pattern.

Farber (1990) also observed much restricted communication, which, each spouse claimed, occurred so as to not upset the other person. However, this may really have been done more to protect themselves from the anxiety of the other person. Farber advocated more open communication, noting that forewarning helps determine recovery and that open communication helps the dying person feel less alone, maintains self-esteem, and helps the surviving partner fortify the relationship to protect him or her against the difficult times ahead.

Other researchers, too, have noted that interaction with a dying person helps a spouse cope with the death. Hampe (1975) described the following needs of a grieving spouse: (a) be with the dying person, (b) be helpful to the dying person, (c) be assured of the comfort of the dying person, (d) be informed of impending death, (e) be able to ventilate emotions, and (f) receive comfort, support, and acceptance from care providers and other family members. Couldrick (1992) found a strong impact of the last weeks, days, and hours spent with a dying person on adjustment to bereavement.

Couldrick's (1992) research also indicated that preparation for death helps adjustment during bereavement. Many who have experienced the death of a loved one have wondered about which is easier to handle—a quick death or a slow death. The data are consistent in this regard. Field (1989) found that a quick death is easier for medical providers to handle, but more difficult for the family. Helm and Mazur (1989) also found poorer outcomes in loved ones of those who had died suddenly.

Other factors beyond the quickness of death are also likely to impact grieving, of course. Many individuals are concerned about what to say to bereaved family members after a loss. Research has indicated that the appropriateness of particular comments varies based on the type of death, but comments about personal willingness to help or listen are consistently regarded as helpful and comments about the funeral home doing a good job are consistently rated as not helpful (Range, Wallston, & Pollard, 1992). Permission to talk about the deceased also helps a survivor (Farber, 1990).

Hall and Kirschling's (1990) research identified changes in family communication patterns during stressful times, such as the death of a family member. They noted that some people's communication tends to become irrelevant at such times. Their discomfort is so intense that they do not dare acknowledge what the patient is saying. Thus, they change the subject to distract the patient. Others try to intellectualize and appear unusually reasonable, and others chatter incessantly. All approaches serve to block the kinds of open communication that have been advocated by the authors mentioned previously, such as addressing death in a straightforward, non-euphemistic manner (Farber, 1990).

Communication problems are not, of course, confined to family members; staff members also experience problems when communicating with the family. Nurses rate doctors very low on such communication (Bakemeir, 1990), but coding of audio tapes indicates a poor level of facilitative communication when nurses communicate with dying patients (Wilkinson, 1991) and their families. This is especially true when patients are experiencing a recurrence. Researchers have suggested some issues about which it is particularly important to communicate with family members: (a) social unacceptability of presenting symptoms (edema, incontinence), (b) helplessness, anger, and guilt, (c) sexual feelings and expectations, (d) financial and legal preparation for death, and (e) bereavement.

## DEATH OF A CHILD

When a child dies, the needs of other family members become even more focused. Helmrath and Steinitz (1978) studied parental grieving of infant death. Husbands in this research felt that they had to be "strong" for their wives, and that they could not break down and cry. They felt frustrated that they could not help their wives resolve grief and that they received no support from wives for their own grief. Wives, however, could not understand why their husbands were not grieving intensely. These findings are also consistent with those found in research by Cook (1983, 1988) and Schwab (1992). Additionally, Schwab found a temporary halt in communication, loss of sexual intimacy, and general irritability between the spouses. Klass (1986–1987) concluded that marriages do not end because of a child's death, but parents in such a situation frequently feel that it is no longer worth struggling with marital problems that they have always had.

Communicating with siblings about a child's death helps the bereaved mother cope with the experience (Graham-Pole et al., 1989). Coping is also affected by how hospital staff members communicate with the parents (Johnson & Mattson, 1992). Johnson and Mattson and Korth (1988) both provided suggestions about therapeutic versus nontherapeutic messages for care providers.

The importance of communicating with children about a family death is evidenced by research relating such experiences to how one looks at life and death as an adult (Dickinson, 1992), to perceived vulnerability to future losses (Mireault & Bond, 1992), and to adult depression (Mireault & Bond, 1992; Saler & Skolnick, 1992; see also Graham-Pole et al., 1989, for other research on the importance of handling death in childhood and its impacts). Adult depression is a particularly likely outcome of childhood death experiences if a surviving parent is less warm, empathic, or promoting of autonomy and if the child is not allowed to participate in mourning (Saler & Skolnick, 1992). Most parents, however, do not even talk with their pediatricians about concerns related to their child's adjustment to the death of a family member (Triggs & Perrin, 1989). This behavior is perhaps inconsistent with the data indicating that communicating with children about death is even more important than communicating with adults about it (Couldrick, 1992) and that the experience of a child's serious illness is at least as intense for siblings as it is for the dying child. It is a myth that children cannot understand and could be harmed by communication about death (Graham-Pole et al., 1989). Children's conceptions about death, of course, change developmentally (see Gibbons, 1992, for a summary of these stages). These conceptualizations of death apply to both one's own death and to the death of others.

Techniques for helping dying children cope with pain through imagery have been described (LeBaron & Zeltzer, 1985), as have dying children's reactions to their treatment by care providers. LeBaron and Zeltzer, for instance, reported children feeling that they were fighting to stay alive whereas the doctors kept trying to make them die. These children also frequently felt that the staff did not believe that the children were in the pain they were. The children discussed by LeBaron and Zeltzer often knew that they were dying even when they had not been told, and needed to be reassured that they were not being abandoned or punished.

In addition to these problems, other problems must be confronted when the dying child is an adolescent. Terminally ill adolescents experience anger, frustration, and a conflict between independence and dependence (LeBaron & Zeltzer, 1985). They report friends staying away, and particular anger at the preferential treatment the dying child him or herself receives from teachers and family members (Byrne, Stockwell, & Gudelis, 1984). However, the adolescents do not want to ask too many questions, express anger, or "make waves," because they fear retaliation by health care personnel (Orr, Hoffmans, & Bennetts, 1984).

Munro-Ludders (1992) pointed out that all these problems are exacerbated when a deaf child is dying or is experiencing the death of a sibling. Physical degeneration makes signing more difficult, and other individuals may lose their focus on communication when they become wrapped up in the multitude of other concerns certain to be encountered when a family member is dying.

## CONCLUSION

Training programs in medical and nursing schools as well as within hospitals and hospices are beginning to address some of the issues described in this chapter (Bertman et al., 1986; Calman & Donaldson, 1991; Knox & Thomson, 1989; Lister & Ward, 1985). Additionally, researchers have begun to develop this area of study by such attempts as theoretical formulation (Nimocks, Webb, & Connell, 1987) and the qualitative research described herein. These efforts will provide an important foundation for future work. Perhaps most important, however, researchers are providing practical, empirically based, suggestions for people about communicating with the terminally ill. In addition to some of the suggestions that have been implicit or explicit in the preceding paragraphs, those writing on the topic have encouraged others to follow the patient's lead, not to force communication, not to argue with denial, to accept the patient's feelings, not to talk too much, to allow the patient to talk, to use open questions, to reflect feelings, to accept silence (Cable, 1991), and not to communicate despair (Rhymes, 1991). Rhymes also reminded us that availability—being there—is the most important thing we can do to allow dignity and avoid disenfranchisement for a dying person.

# REFERENCES

Adler, S. S. (1989). Truth-telling to the terminally ill: Neglected role of the social worker. *Social Work, 34*, 158–160.

Armstrong, D. (1987). Silence and truth in death and dying. *Social Science and Medicine, 24*, 651–658.

Bakemeir, A. H. (1990). Hospice nurses' perceptions of their patients' physicians. *The Hospice Journal, 6*(3), 79–90.

Bertman, S. L., Wertheimer, M. D., & Wheeler, H. B. (1986). Humanities in surgery, a life threatening situation: Communicating the diagnosis. *Death Studies, 10*, 431–439.

Blanchard, C. G., Ruckdeschel, J. C., Blanchard, E. B., Arena, J. G., Saunders, N. L., & Malloy, E. D. (1983). Interactions between oncologists and patients during rounds. *Annals of Internal Medicine, 99*, 694–699.

Bonjean, M. (1989). Solution focused psychotherapy with families caring for an Alzheimer's patient. *Journal of Psychotherapy & the Family, 5*, 197–210.

Brena, S. F. (1987). Management of pain in the terminally ill patient. *Issues in Law & Medicine, 2*, 379–390.

Bronstein, J. M., & Jones, C. A. (1986). Ethics, technology, and the high cost of dying: A public forum. *Southern Journal of Medicine, 79*, 1485–1488.

Bryant, D. D. (1986). The doctor and death. *Journal of the National Medical Association, 78*, 227–235.

Byrne, C. M., Stockwell, M., & Gudelis, S. (1984). Adolescent support groups in oncology. *Oncological Nursing Forum, 11*(4), 36–40.

Cable, D. G. (1991). Caring for the terminally ill: Communicating with patients and families. *Henry Ford Hospital Medical Journal, 39*, 85–88.

Calman, K. C., & Donaldson, M. (1991). The pre-registration house officer year: A critical incident study. *Medical Education, 25*, 51–59.

Cook, J. A. (1983). Death in the family: Parental bereavement in the first year. *Suicide and Life-Threatening Behavior, 13*, 42–61.

Cook, J. A. (1988). Dad's double-binds: Rethinking father's bereavement from a men's studies perspective. *Journal of Contemporary Ethnography, 17*, 285–308.

Coombs, R. H., Chopra, S., Schenk, D. R., & Yutan, E. (1993). Medical slang and its functions. *Social Science and Medicine, 36*, 987–998.

Cooper, A. (1982). Disabilities and how to live with them—Hodgkin's disease. *Lancet, I*, 612–613.

Couldrick, A. (1992). Optimizing bereavement outcome: Reading the road ahead. *Social Science and Medicine, 35*, 1521–1523.

Crispell, K. R., & Gomez, C. F. (1987). Proper care for the dying: A critical public issue. *Journal of Medical Ethics, 13*, 74–80.

Delvaux, N., Razavi, D., & Farvacques, C. (1988). Cancer care—A stress for health professionals. *Social Science and Medicine, 27,* 159–166.

Dickinson, G. E. (1992). First childhood death experiences. *Omega, 25,* 169–182.

Doyle, D. (1989). Education in palliative medicine and pain therapy: An overview. In R. G. Twycross (Ed.), *Edinburgh Symposium on Pain Control and Medical Education* (pp. 165–174). London: Royal Society of Medicine.

Epley, R. J., & McCaghy, C. H. (1977–1978). The stigma of dying: Attitudes toward the terminally ill. *Omega: Journal of Death and Dying, 5,* 287–298.

Ezell, G., Anspaugh, D. J., & Oaks, J. (1987). *Dying & death: From a health and sociological perspective.* Scottsdale, AZ: Gorsuch.

Farber, R. S. (1990). Widowhood: Integrating loss and love. *The Psychotherapy Patient, 6*(3–4), 39–48.

Farkas, C. G. (1992). Neglected issues in the care of dying patients: Nonverbal communication and sexuality. In C. G. Farkas (Ed.), *Loss, grief and care* (pp. 125–129). New York: Hawthorn.

Field, D. (1989). Nurses' accounts of nursing the terminally ill on a coronary care unit. *Intensive Care Nursing, 5,* 114–122.

Field, D., & Howells, S. K. (1985). Medical students' self-reported worries about aspects of death and dying. *Death Studies, 16,* 147–154.

Freihofer, P., & Felton, G. (1976). Nursing behaviors in bereavement: An exploratory study. *Nursing Research, 25,* 332–337.

Fuller, R. L., & Gels, S. (1985). Communicating with the grieving family. *Journal of Family Practice, 21,* 139–144.

Gibbons, M. B. (1992). A child dies, a sibling survives: The impact of sibling loss. *Journal of Pediatric Health Care, 6*(2), 65–72.

Gotay, C. C., Crockett, S., & West, C. (1985). Palliative homecare nursing: Nurses' perceptions of roles and stress. *Canada's Mental Health, 33*(2), 6–9.

Graham-Pole, J., Wass, H., Eyberg, S., & Chu, L. (1989). Communicating with dying children and their siblings: A retrospective analysis. *Death Studies, 13,* 465–483.

Hall, J. E., & Kirschling, J. M. (1990). A conceptual framework for caring for families. *The Hospice Journal, 6*(2), 1–28.

Hampe, S. O. (1975). Needs of the grieving spouse in a hospital setting. *Nursing Research, 24,* 113–120.

Harris, R., Hartner, R., Linn, M. W., & Linn, B. (1979). The importance of the doctor to the dying patient. *Southern Medical Journal, 72,* 1319–1324.

Hayslip, B. (1986–1987). The measurement of communication apprehension regarding the terminally ill. *Omega, 17,* 251–261.

Helm, A., & Mazur, D. J. (1989). Death notification: Legal and ethical issues. *Dimensions of Critical Care Nursing, 8,* 382–385.

Helmrath, T. A., & Steinitz, E. M. (1978). Death of an infant: Parental grieving and the failure of social support. *Journal of Family Practice, 6,* 785–790.

Higginson, I., Wade, A., & McCarthy, M. (1990). Palliative care: Views of patients and their families. *British Medical Journal, 301,* 277–281.

Hinton, J. (1981). Sharing or withholding awareness of dying between husband and wife. *Journal of Psychosomatic Research, 25,* 337–343.

Holman, E. A. (1990). Death and the health professional: Organization and defense in health care. *Death Studies, 14,* 13–24.

Hunt, M. (1991). Being friendly and informal: Reflected in nurses' and terminally ill patients' and relatives' conversations at home. *Journal of Advanced Nursing, 16,* 929–938.

Hunt, M., & Meerabeau, L. (1993). Purging the emotions: The lack of emotional expression in subfertility and in the care of the dying. *International Journal of Nursing Studies, 30,* 115–123.

Irwin, B. L., & Meier, J. R. (1973). Supportive measures for the relative of the fatally ill. In M. V. Batey (Ed.), *Communicating nursing research: Collaboration and competition* (pp. 119–128). Boulder, CO: Western Interstate Commission for Higher Education.

Jacobsen, P., Perry, S., & Hirsch, D. (1990). Behavioral and psychological responses to HIV antibody testing. *Journal of Counseling & Clinical Psychology, 58*, 31–37.

Johnson, L., & Mattson, S. (1992). Communication: The key to crisis prevention in pediatric death. *Critical Care Nurse, 12*(8), 23–27.

Jones, B. (1990). Dear Diary.... *Nursing Times, 86*(22), 31–33.

Kai, I., Ohi, G., Yano, E. et al. (1993). Communication between patients and physicians about terminal care: A survey in Japan. *Social Science & Medicine, 36*, 1151–1159.

Kalish, R. A. (1981). *Death, grief, and caring relationships*. Monterey, CA: Brooks/Cole.

Kellehear, A., & Lewin, T. (1988–1989). Farewells by the dying: A sociological study. *Omega, 19*, 275–292.

Klass, D. (1986–1987). Marriage and divorce among bereaved parents in a self-help group. *Omega, 17*, 237–249.

Knox, J. D. E., & Thomson, G. M. (1989). Breaking bad news: Medical undergraduate communication skills teaching and learning. *Medical Education, 23*, 258–261.

Korth, S. K. (1988). Unexpected pediatric death in the emergency dept.: Supporting the family. *Journal of Emergency Nursing, 14*, 302–304.

Lauer, P., Murphy, S., & Powers, M. (1982). Learning needs of cancer patients: A comparison of nurse and patient perceptions. *Nursing Research, 31*, 11–16.

LeBaron, S., & Zeltzer, L. K. (1985). The role of imagery in the treatment of dying children and adolescents. *Developmental & Behavioral Pediatrics, 6*, 252–258.

Lister, L., & Ward, D. (1985). Youth hospice training. *Death Studies, 9*, 353–363.

Lloyd, A. (1991, March 20). Stop, look & listen. *Nursing Times*, pp. 30–32.

Loewy, E. H. (1991). Involving patients in Do Not Resuscitate (DNR) decisions: An old issue raising its ugly head. *Journal of Medical Ethics, 17*, 156–160.

Longhofer, J. (1980). Dying or living?: The double bind. *Cultural Medical Psychiatry, 4*, 119–136.

Maguire, P., & Faulkner, A. (1988). Communicating with cancer patients: 1. Handling bad news and difficult questions. *British Medical Journal, 297*, 972–974.

McCann, K. (1992). The impact of receiving a positive HIV antibody test: Factors associated with the response. *Counseling Psychology Quarterly, 5*, 37–45.

Mireault, G. C., & Bond, L. A. (1992). Parental death in childhood: Perceived vulnerability and adult depression and anxiety. *American Journal of Orthopsychiatry, 62*, 517–520.

Munro-Ludders, B. (1992). Deaf and dying: Deaf people and the process of dying. *Journal of the American Deafness and Rehabilitation Association, 26*(1), 31–41.

Nimocks, M. J. A., Webb, L., & Connell, J. R. (1987). Communication and the terminally ill: A theoretical model. *Death Studies, 11*, 323–344.

Northouse, P. G., & Northouse, L. L. (1987). Communication and cancer: Issues confronting patients, health professionals, and family members. *Journal of Psychosocial Oncology, 5*(3), 17–46.

Nussbaum, J. F., Thompson, T., & Robinson, J. D. (1989). *Communication and aging*. New York: Harper & Row.

Orr, D. P., Hoffmans, M. A., & Bennetts, G. (1984). Adolescents with cancer report their psychosocial needs. *Journal of Psychosocial Oncology, 2*(2), 47–59.

Parry, J. K. (1987). The significance of open communication in working with terminally ill clients. *The Hospice Journal, 3*(4), 33–49.

Parry, J. K., & Smith, M. J. (1985). The significance of the patient/family as a unit of care in working with terminally ill patients. *The Hospice Journal, 1*(3), 37–49.

Parry, J. K., & Smith, M. J. (1987). A study of social workers' job satisfaction as based on an optimal model of care for the terminally ill. *Journal of Social Science Research, 11,* 39–48.

Pepler, C. J., & Lynch, A. (1991). Relational messages of control in nurse-patient interactions with terminally ill patients with AIDS and cancer. *Journal of Palliative Care, 7,* 18–29.

Peters-Golden, H. (1982). Breast cancer: Varied perceptions of social support in the illness experience. *Social Science and Medicine, 16,* 483–491.

Pfefferbaum, B., Levenson, P., & van Eys, J. (1982). Comparison of physician and patient perceptions of communication issues. *Southern Medical Journal, 75,* 1080–1083.

Potter, R. E., Schneiderman, C. R., & Gibson, G. M. (1979). Understanding death, dying, and the critically ill: A concern for speech-language pathologists. *Journal of Communication Disorders, 12,* 495–502.

Range, L. M., Walston, A. S., & Pollard, P. M. (1992). Helpful and unhelpful comments after suicide, homicide, accidents, or natural death. *Omega, 25,* 25–31.

Reisetter, K. H., & Thomas, B. (1986). Nursing care of the dying: Its relationship to selected nurse characteristics. *International Journal of Nursing Studies, 23,* 39–50.

Rhymes, J. A. (1991). Clinical management of the terminally ill. *Geriatrics, 46,* 57–67.

Saler, L., & Skolnick, N. (1992). Childhood parental death and depression in adulthood: Roles of surviving parent and family environment. *American Journal of Orthopsychiatry, 62,* 504–516.

Schwab, R. (1992). Effects of a child's death on the marital relationship: A preliminary study. *Death Studies, 16,* 141–154.

Seale, C. (1991). Communication and awareness about death: A study of a random sample of dying people. *Social Science and Medicine, 32,* 943–952.

Smith, R. J., Lingle, J. H., & Brock, T. C. (1978–1979). Reactions to death as a function of perceived similarity to the deceased. *Omega: Journal of Death and Dying, 9,* 125–138.

Strauss, A., Glaser, B., & Quint, J. (1964). The nonaccountability of terminal care. *Hospitals, 38,* 73–80.

Sudnow, D. (1967). *Passing on.* Englewood Cliffs, NJ: Prentice-Hall.

Thompson, T. (1989). Communication and the dying: The end of the life span. In J. F. Nussbaum (Ed.), *Life-span communication: Normative processes* (pp. 339–354). Hillsdale, NJ: Lawrence Erlbaum Associates.

Tobin, S. S., & Gustafson, J. D. (1987). What do we do differently with elderly clients? *Journal of Gerontological Social Work, 10,* 107–121.

Todd, C. J., & Still, A. W. (1984). Communication between general practitioners and patients dying at home. *Social Science and Medicine, 18,* 667–672.

Triggs, E. G., & Perrin, E. C. (1989). Listening carefully: Improving communication about behavior and development—Recognizing parental concerns. *Clinical Pediatricians, 28,* 185–192.

Truglio-Londrigan, M., & Hayes, P. M. (1986). Carers learn to cope. *Geriatric Nursing, 7,* 310–312.

Ventres, W., Nichter, M., Reed, R., & Frankel, R. (1992). Do Not Resuscitate discussions: A qualitative analysis. *Family Practice Research Journal, 12,* 157–169.

Walsh, S., & Kingston, R. D. (1988). The use of hospital beds for terminally ill cancer patients. *European Journal of Surgical Oncology, 14,* 367–370.

Wilkinson, S. (1991). Factors which influence how nurses communicate with cancer patients. *Journal of Advanced Nursing, 16,* 677–688.

Williams, J. L. (1992). Don't discuss it: Reconciling illness, dying and death in a medical school anatomy laboratory. *Family Systems Medicine, 10,* 65–78.

Yang, C. T., & Kirschling, J. M. (1992). Exploration of factors related to direct care and outcomes of caregiving: Caregivers of terminally ill older persons. *Cancer Nursing, 15,* 173–181.

# 21 Communicating With Alcoholics: A Strategic Influence Approach to Personal Intervention

Richard W. Thomas
*Central Michigan University*

David R. Seibold
*University of California, Santa Barbara*

The 1990s have witnessed a growing awareness of the harmful effects of alcohol use and abuse on both those who consume alcohol and those affected by the actions of drinkers. As society's most socially sanctioned, most commonly accepted, and most abused legal drug (Blair, 1983; Denzin, 1987b), 60% to 70% of the general American population consume alcoholic beverages on a regular basis (Taylor & Chermak, 1993; U.S. Census Bureau, 1992). At least 10% of those who consume alcohol will develop alcohol dependency problems at some point in their drinking career (Denzin, 1987a; Johnson, 1980), and alcohol use and abuse is even more pervasive among younger populations. Studies reveal that in some groups of youths, 80% to 90% consume alcoholic beverages. Between 18% and 25% of these individuals can be classified as problem drinkers now (Berkowitz & Perkins, 1986; Hanson & Engs, 1992; Margolis, 1992; Quindlen, 1994; Seay & Beck, 1984; Seibold & Thomas, 1994; Thomas & Seibold, 1993a, 1993b, 1995a) and will experience alcohol-related problems as adults (Massey & Neidigh, 1990).

This pervasive and excessive use of alcohol has resulted in a myriad of problems, both for drinkers and for those surrounding drinkers. An estimated 15% to 40% of all hospital admissions are associated with alcohol, and approximately 200,000 deaths occur each year because of alcohol abuse (Dumerauf, 1987). Alcohol is involved in about 50% of all traffic accidents, claiming 18,000 to 20,000 lives each year (Carroll, 1989) and injuring another 1.5 million people. Alcohol abuse costs society $116 billion each year due to costs associated with crime, violence, absenteeism, low worker production, and medical care (Carroll, 1989; Dumerauf, 1987). Alcoholism has been characterized as the third greatest health problem in America, behind cancer and heart disease respectively (Carroll, 1989; National Council on Alcoholism, 1987). In addition, alcohol abuse affects one out of every four American homes (American College Health Association, 1989; Carroll, 1989), and contributes to such relational problems as physical violence and sexual abuse (Gomberg, 1993; Raffaeli, 1990), and marital distress (Leonard & Senchak, 1993; Paolino & McCrady, 1977; Womack, 1990). Children of alcoholics, estimated to exceed 30 million (Carroll, 1989), are two to four times more likely to develop alcohol abuse problems, twice as likely to marry alcoholics, more likely to abuse other drugs or to develop other patterns of compulsive behaviors such as eating disorders, and more apt to attempt and to commit suicide (American College Health Association, 1989; Carroll, 1989; Quindlen, 1994).

One "social injury" that has not received much attention is the stigmatizing effect alcohol abuse brings with it, both to the abuser and to others affected by the drinkers' abuse of alcohol. People who fall prey to alcohol dependency problems find themselves separated from themselves (Denzin, 1987a) and mainstream society, and cast as individuals who are weak, irresponsible, and immature (Denzin, 1987a). Those who have overcome addiction are seen as one step away from "falling off the wagon." Too, even those who are associated with alcohol abusers find themselves caught in a vicious cycle of denial, enabling, and codependence from which they cannot escape (Bennett, 1990; Cermak, 1986; Denzin, 1987c; Klingman & Takala, 1992; LePoire, 1992).

Despite continued efforts to deal with alcohol abuse problems and to overcome the prejudices associated with alcohol abuse, many individuals (based on their own perceptions or those of others) find themselves on the margins of society. Throughout this chapter, we argue that alcohol use/abuse encompasses a disenfranchising *process,* a process that involves not only the drinker, but those who attempt to respond to the drinking situation as well. Furthermore, we argue that public programs focused on dealing with alcohol-related problems—either through education or restriction—do not provide sufficient means with which to deal with alcohol problems. In addition to these programs, *interpersonal* communication skills (particularly interpersonal influence skills) are required to provide the impetus for interrupting the dynamics of disenfranchisement. After a brief review of the history of alcohol use, we discuss the disenfranchising process involved in alcohol use and develop a model relevant to communication with individuals involved in the alcohol abuse cycle. Finally, we explicate the interpersonal communication requirements relevant to communication with alcoholics.

## ALCOHOL AND DISENFRANCHISEMENT

Alcohol has always played an integral role in America. Introduced in the 1600s by the early European immigrants, alcohol became the beverage of choice. Individuals of all ages drank alcohol, typically with every meal, and it was not uncommon for individuals to consume large quantities of alcohol. In fact, during this period, Americans averaged 3½ gallons per year per person, a consumption amount twice the level it is today. For the most part, excessive use of alcohol was condoned, particularly for men, and strong social forces emerged to make alcohol use acceptable. Only small segments of society defined excessive use as "sinful" (Rorabaugh, 1991).

It was not until the 18th century that antialcohol use sentiments (particularly against public drunkenness) began to emerge. At that time, several antialcohol movements developed. Driven primarily by moral concerns and secondarily by health concerns, groups such as Protestant ministers, the Women's Crusade, the Women's Christian Temperance Union, and the Anti-Saloon League demonstrated against alcohol consumption. Although they received much resistance, they were able to muster successfully both social and political pressure to limit alcohol use (Gottheil, McLellan, Druley, & Alterman, 1979; Rorabaugh, 1991). In fact, these groups provided the impetus for the passage of the 18th Amendment to the Constitution, which instituted Prohibition. More significant for this chapter, these movements provided the foundation upon which alcoholics were seen as morally deficient and seeking to escape problems and responsibilities. Hence, these movements began to marginalize individuals entrenched in the founding "alcohol-oriented" culture and to begin the moralistic separation of those who were "strong" enough to overcome the temptation of alcohol from those who were not, a perception that still exists today (Denzin, 1987a).

The prohibition movement was short lived for, with growing social, legal, and economic pressures after World War I, Congress passed the 21st Amendment repealing Prohibition. In the aftermath of WWI and with improved economic recovery, alcohol consumption again took a central role in the lives of individuals. From 1933 through the 1980s, alcohol consumption increased. Changes in styles (greater acceptance of women drinking) and changes in laws (lowering of the drinking age in some states) made alcohol consumption attractive and socially acceptable, particularly with respect to certain populations (professional White males between the ages of 25 and 35; Rorabaugh, 1991).

During this period, alternative views of alcohol abuse problems also emerged. In contrast to the moral model predominant up until this point, alternative perspectives on alcohol abuse problems attempted to negate the disenfranchising element of the moral model. For example, 1935 saw the birth of Alcoholics Anonymous, which attempted to counter the moralistic conception of alcoholism with a disease perspective, a perspective that saw alcoholism as a biologically (or genetically) based *disease* resulting in the inability of individuals to control their drinking. The disease perspective placed the locus of control of alcoholism beyond the moral fabric of the individual and attempted to remove the moral stigma already attached to alcohol abuse problems (see Blume, 1984; Johnson Institute, 1972). With help from the Yale Center for Alcohol Studies, and subsequently from the National Committee for Education on Alcoholism (now the National Council on Alcoholism), enough pressure was put on the American Medical Association that in 1956 they officially accepted the disease concept (Cahalan, 1988; Jellinek, 1960; Roman, 1988; Wallace, 1983), which provided the first steps toward destigmatizing the alcohol abuser.

The 1980s and 1990s has witnessed somewhat of a reversal of this trend toward demarginalization. With the increase of alcohol-related problems (e.g., drunk driving accidents, fetal alcohol syndrome), the onset of these problems in young people at a much faster rate, and the increased social costs related to alcohol abuse, a growing *intolerance* of alcohol abuse is emerging (Rorabaugh, 1991). Currently, a paradox exists with respect to public acceptance of alcohol problems. On the one hand, due to both mass media campaigns and an increase in the number of programs designed to educate people about the harmful effects of alcohol, there is growing acceptance of the disease model. Although alcohol consumption remains at high levels (especially for younger populations), evidence suggests that it is beginning to decrease (U.S. Census Bureau, 1992). In addition, greater acceptance of the disease model of alcoholism is becoming evident in the public at large; more individuals see the alcohol abuser as a sick person, unable to help him or herself, and who needs professional help to overcome the affliction (Marlatt & Tapert, 1993). On the other hand, because of the increase in severity and prevalence of consequences associated with alcohol abuse (particularly among young people), intolerance for excessive and "irresponsible" alcohol use has grown. Witness the emergence of such groups as Mothers Against Drunk Driving (MADD), Students Against Drunk Driving (SADD), the increased penalties associated with alcohol abuse, and the development of programs such as Designated Drivers and Substance Free Living Environments to help circumvent and/or alleviate problems associated with alcohol abuse.

## Dynamics of Disenfranchising

The excessive use of alcohol creates dynamics disenfranchising both drinkers and individuals concerned with drinkers' behaviors. According to *Webster's New World Dictionary* (1970), to be disenfranchised is to be deprived of a privilege, a right, or a power. The abuse of alcohol can be very disenfranchising. Individuals who abuse alcohol run the risk of losing certain privileges (e.g., losing their license for driving under the influence of alcohol) and, in chronic cases, being stigmatized as an individual who does not "measure up" to the standards of society (e.g., being cast as an "alcoholic").

The disenfranchisement associated with alcohol abuse is even more complex when one considers the psychological and communicative implications of admitting to, or being cast as, having an alcohol-related problem. On one hand, strong social pressures exist to participate in the drinking culture. In fact, in many circles, the person who drinks, and drinks heavily, is valued (Ablon, 1983). Drinking can mark a "passage" from adolescence to adulthood, especially among men, college students, and young adults (Baer, Stacy, & Larimer, 1991; Brennen, Walfish, & AuBuchon, 1986a, 1986b). These individuals may be seen as strong, powerful, and mature (Denzin, 1987a), and even as role models. On the other hand, society frowns upon persons who cannot control their drinking and succumb to intoxication. These individuals are perceived as weak, immature, and irresponsible (Denzin, 1987a). Paradoxically, then, if one *chooses not* to participate in a drinking event, he or she runs the risk of being disenfranchised—of being seen as a person who does not measure up to the social standards of the culture; if one *chooses* to participate but does not maintain control over his or her drinking, disenfranchisement also can occur.

A similar paradox exists for persons seeking to stand against or to intervene in an alcohol-related situation. In one respect, intervention can be seen as the act of disenfranchising someone—of depriving that individual of certain privileges or powers, such as the privilege to drive (as in a drunk driving intervention situation) or their power to drink (as in the case of alcoholism intervention). Intervention also enacts the situational disenfranchisement process, in that it makes public the stigmatizing behavior. Choosing to intervene also may put one at risk of becoming disenfranchised. The intervention attempt may be viewed negatively, and the intervener may subsequently be deprived of inclusion in future events with the drinker or the power to comment on another's drinking behavior. Depending on the reaction from the drinker and others in the same proximity, intervention may result in self-stigmatization (Thomas & Seibold, 1995a, 1995b).

Thus, communicating with individuals involved with alcohol is neither a simple nor unequivocal task. The diverse problems associated with alcohol use, coupled with the variety of situations in which concerns over someone's alcohol-related behavior exist, present communicators with a multitude of challenges (LePoire, 1992; Seibold & Thomas, 1994; Thomas & Seibold, 1993b). These challenges can range from what to say to a child about how to live and survive in a world in which alcohol exists, to how to deal with an employee or loved one who has succumbed to an alcohol dependency problem, or to how to communicate with someone who has recovered from alcohol addiction but who has not yet come to terms with the disenfranchising dynamics of alcohol abuse. In the next section, we explicate a model to illustrate the different challenges and difficulties associated with alcohol-related communication.

## TAXONOMY OF ORIENTATIONS TO ALCOHOL RISK REDUCTION

Central to understanding the role of communication in alcohol problems is a person's perception of the *type* of alcohol problem to be confronted. Many explanations for alcohol abuse problems and/or alcoholism exist in a variety of fields (cf. Blume, 1984; Cahalan, 1988; Gottheil et al., 1979; Jellinek, 1960; Kissen, 1977; Marlatt & Tapert, 1993; Siegler, Osmond, & Newell, 1968; Wallace, 1983; also see Thomas & Seibold, 1993b, for a comparison of these perspectives). Although these approaches differ, researchers agree on several facets of dispositional and situational excessive alcohol use. First, all agree that the effect of alcohol is progressive in nature. As the amount an individual consumes increases, physiological and psychological effects increase (Blume, 1981; Ewing, 1983; Premer, 1982). Second, researchers concur that some persons are able to tolerate increased amounts of alcohol. However, ultimately even this leads first to psychological reliance, and then to physical dependence, or what we call alcoholism (Denzin, 1987b; Johnson, 1980; Marlatt, Larimer, Baer, & Quigley, 1993; Pattison & Kaufman, 1982; Schuckitt, 1981). Third, researchers agree that excessive use of alcohol is manifested both cognitively and behaviorally, and that these effects become apparent to those surrounding the drinker at some point (see Geller, 1984; Johnson Institute, 1972; Mann, 1958; Wiseman, 1983). Hence, alcohol problems develop progressively and are evidenced by the effects alcohol has on the drinker. Because of the nature of the problem, the severity of the problem usually is not seen by the drinker, but by those surrounding the drinker (Johnson, 1980).

The progressive nature of problems associated with alcohol, or what we term the *problem type*, is depicted in Fig. 21.1 on the horizontal axis and is divided into two areas: situational problems and dispositional problems. *Situational problems* are those alcohol-related problems that occur (or will occur) within a single drinking episode (e.g., a person gets drunk and wants to drive). Whether they drink or not, many individuals experience situational problems relevant to alcohol use at *one time or another*. These problems may be self-oriented (e.g., someone becomes intoxicated and has to adapt his or her behavior to his or her level of intoxication) or other-oriented (e.g., someone has a friend who has drunk too much but wants

Risk Reduction Orientation

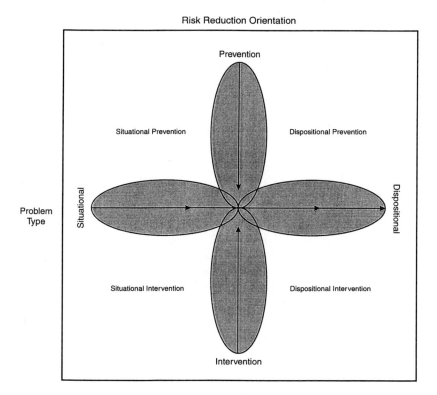

FIG. 21.1.   Taxonomy of orientations to alcohol risk reduction.

to drive while intoxicated). In contrast, *dispositional problems* encompass those situations in which a person experiences (or will experience) alcohol-related problems that *persist* over a long period of time and are seen as a relatively permanent component of the person's personality and behavior. Perceptions of a dispositional problem is usually termed a "drinking problem." As with situational problems, dispositional problems may be self-oriented (knowing whether or not one has a drinking problem) or other-oriented (perceiving an alcohol dependency problem in another person and wanting to do something about it).

The shading around each dimension (see Fig. 21.1) serves to highlight the uncertainty that is associated with knowing whether or not a problem exists (or will develop). As mentioned previously, evidence of a drinking problem is typically determined by the cognitive and behavioral manifestations of alcohol use, manifested progressively but often slowly. The progression of the severity of the problem is indicated by the arrows that move along this dimension: As one continues to drink greater quantities of alcohol (situational) or the number of episodes in which intoxication occurs increases and/or more negative consequences associated with drinking manifest themselves (dispositional), the problem becomes more severe. However, both the drinker and surrounding others typically are uncertain about the extent of the alcohol-related problem. In fact, one of the cognitive effects of alcohol abuse is denial; individuals who consume excessive amounts of alcohol typically deny that a problem exists (Johnson Institute, 1983; Ness, 1985; Rohan, 1982; Thorton, Gottheil, Skoloda, & Alterman, 1979). Too, because of the social acceptance of drinking behavior in general and the stigmatization associated with excessive drinking behavior, many individuals are hesitant to define symptomatic problems such as excessive intoxication, driving while intoxicated, and mood swings as alcohol related (Blair, 1983; Johnson Institute, 1982). Thus, the uncertainty about the severity of the problem increases—up to a point. After that point (e.g., obvious intoxication or the inability of the drinker to stop drinking), uncertainty about the severity of the problem decreases. It is this uncertainty curve that activates communication.

A second aspect of the alcohol situation focuses on the primary communication goals, or *risk reduction orientations*, of those who want to affect alcohol-related behaviors. As mentioned earlier, the effects of alcohol on the drinker are usually seen by those surrounding the drinker. In fact, researchers argue that once these individuals become aware of the problem, they will be motivated to engage in some sort of coping behavior (LePoire, 1992; Rabow, Newcomb, Monto, & Hernandez, 1990; Wiseman, 1983). Generally, these coping behaviors take one of two forms: prevention or intervention. *Prevention* approaches acknowledge the possibility of alcohol-related problems and, through a variety of methods, attempt to dissuade individuals from excessive drinking *prior to* any actual drinking episode. *Intervention* approaches, on the other hand, focus on those situations in which excessive drinking has occurred and on the methods available to deal with the problem *as it is being manifested*. As with the first dimension, a certain amount of uncertainty exists in terms of whether or not action is needed, as is depicted by the shaded area (see Fig. 21.1). This uncertainty parallels the uncertainty associated with the perceptions of the severity of the problem; when only moderate evidence of a problem (or risk of a problem) is available, communicators experience a greater uncertainty about whether or not to engage in risk reduction communication. However, as the evidence of a problem (or risk of a problem) increases, so does the perceived need for communication (as reflected in the arrows).

When combined, these two dimensions define four "orientations" to alcohol risk reduction (and general alcohol risk reduction). The top two quadrants focus on preventative orientations. The first quadrant, which we term *situational prevention* (quadrant 1), focuses on those methods aimed at preventing the occurrence of situational drinking. In these situations, individuals perceive the possibility of an alcohol-related problem occurring and engage in communication behavior prior to the situation in hopes of preventing any problems (Coyne, 1984). For example, many parents who worry about their child's social experiences might talk to the child prior to a party about the dangers of drinking too much. *Dispositional prevention* (quadrant 2), encompasses a variety of approaches for preventing the onset of a long-term drinking problem. Here, individuals acknowledge the potential for an alcohol problem and engage in communicative and noninteractional behaviors that serve to "warn" the person about the impending danger. For example, the "disease" perspective currently dominates thinking concerning the development of alcoholism. Proponents argue that certain individuals are genetically predisposed to alcohol abuse problems (Cahalan, 1988; Johnson Institute, 1972; Marlatt et al., 1993; Purvis, 1990). They propose that children of alcoholics should be told about their potential predisposition so that they may circumvent impending problems with alcohol. Another example would be social support programs for "recovering alcoholics" such as Alcoholics Anonymous. These programs aim at providing supportive messages for individuals who have overcome dispositional problems with alcohol and who run the risk of relapse (Denzin, 1987c; Hickenbottom, Bissonnette, & O'Shea, 1987; Johnson Institute, 1983).

The bottom two quadrants of Fig. 21.1 focus on intervention measures. *Situational intervention* (quadrant 3), deals with those situations in which excessive drinking has occurred and someone deems it necessary to engage in some action that will affect the behavior of the drinker. One of the most common occurrences of this type of situation is when someone desires to drive while intoxicated, leaving the communicator with the goal of intervening in the specific situation in order to prevent that person from driving. The final quadrant, *dispositional intervention* (quadrant 4), includes techniques used to intervene in long-term alcohol-related problems. Again, these situations involve an individual who is presently drinking (although he or she may not be drunk at the time of the intervention) and whose behavior is reflective of a chronic alcohol abuse problem. The major concern of the intervener is to make the person aware of the problem (a task complicated by the denial system that develops from the abuse of alcohol) and to influence the individual to seek treatment for their problem.

## COMMUNICATION APPROACHES TO ALCOHOL PREVENTION AND INTERVENTION

The taxonomy reflected in Fig. 21.1 identifies the general orientations toward alcohol-risk reduction, including both prevention and intervention goals to both situational and dispositional drinking problems. These orientations define the different communication challenges people face when trying to communicate with individuals who have disenfranchised themselves through excessive alcohol use, and include both communicative and noncommunicative approaches. In the following sections, we focus on communication approaches to alcohol prevention in general and intervention in particular. We first examine communication approaches that are *non*-interpersonal in nature and then examine research on *interpersonal* communication strategies.

## Noninterpersonal Approaches

Many approaches to preventing, intervening into, and treating alcohol abuse problems are employed in our society. These approaches attempt to provide direction to individuals in hopes of circumventing and/or dealing with alcohol abuse problems (Thomas & Seibold, 1993b). Although the approaches differ with respect to their etiological underpinnings and their prescribed treatment regimens (cf. Ablon, 1983; Baer et al., 1992; Gottheil et al., 1979; Marlatt et al., 1993; Marlatt & Tapert, 1993), they share several assumptions concerning effective prevention and intervention. First, proponents of each approach imply that if individuals are made *aware* of the potential dangers of excessive alcohol consumption, they will be *motivated* to engage in more "responsible" choices concerning their drinking behaviors. Indeed, many programs and mass-media campaigns focus primarily on educating individuals about the negative consequences associated with excessive alcohol consumption (Montgomery et al., 1989). In doing so, they work to make individuals more aware of the dangers associated with excessive alcohol consumption and to motivate them to adjust their behavior to a level that is "socially acceptable" (Dean & Bryon, 1982; Kivlahan, Marlatt, Fromme, Coppel, & Williams, 1990; Marlatt et al., 1993; Seibold & Thomas, 1994). Second, many approaches incorporate normative, restrictive, and/or punitive measures to control drinking behavior. In doing so, they assume that the power of social norms, the inaccessibility of alcohol, and the fear of sanctions will inhibit excessive use, and the imposition of sanctions (for those for whom fear appeals are not successful) will serve to prevent recidivism and strengthen the fear in others (Klingman & Takala, 1992; Liska, 1992; Peele, 1989).

These approaches to dealing with alcohol-related behaviors are what we termed *noninterpersonal* approaches (Seibold & Thomas, 1994). These are approaches that are societally based (i.e., grounded in organizationally supported institutions), attempt to deal with alcohol-related problems in contexts other than the one in which the drinking occurs, and involve individuals not closely acquainted with the drinker (or potential drinker). These programs underscore society's belief that alcohol problems are too complex and too difficult for the average person. Instead, more valued and/or empowered institutions or individuals are required to affect the behavior of the drinker (e.g., the church, the legal system, organizationally based agencies, professional counselors).

However, despite the amount of effort put into developing programs aimed at affecting both situational and dispositional alcohol-related problems, the ability of these approaches to impact behavior at the individual level has been limited (Kauth, Christoff, Sartor, & Sharp, 1993; Michal-Johnson, 1993). In fact, recent studies of alcohol programs have placed the efficacy of these programs in question. Studies suggest that these programs are not able to alter consumption behavior or produce change at the individual level; many individuals consume alcohol at levels that are considered excessive, and the harmful effects of alcohol continue to occur (Burnham & Nelson, 1984; Kauth et al., 1993; Nichols, Weinstein, Ellingstad, & Struckman-Johnson, 1978). Most problematic is the fact that, because of the denial and rationalization system associated with the abuse of alcohol, those individuals who most need help (e.g., the chronic abuser) are unable to help themselves and unwilling to seek help from these different agencies (Cherry, 1987; Denzin, 1987a; Johnson, 1980; LePoire, 1992; Marlatt et al., 1993). Moreover, in that these programs emphasize the severity of the problem, they, in themselves, contribute to the stigmatization of problem drinkers. Thus, although these programs and processes may be necessary components to dealing with alcohol problems, they are not sufficient to produce the changes required to deal with the problem effectively. The literature strongly suggests that, in addition to the regulative and education programs, more personal forms of attention are needed to sway individuals to alter their drinking behavior and to seek the help of outside agencies if it is deemed necessary. In the next section, we outline the interpersonal communication dynamics associated with personal intervention.

### Interpersonal Approaches

Preventative alcohol-related communication and intervention inherently involves resistance, typically by a target whom Monroe, DiSalvo, Lewis, and Borzi (1990) aptly termed "difficult." According to these researchers, difficult people are those who have low self-esteem and lack critical communication skills (characteristic of many alcoholics and alcohol abusers). Because of this, "difficult people" tend not only to behave in ways that cause distress for others, but also to remain unresponsive to the feedback others offer them to adjust their troublesome behavior. Moreover, when presented with negative feedback, "difficult people" tend to employ one of four responses: (a) They avoid the individual after the negative feedback has been provided, (b) they show apparent compliance to the request of the target, but at a later time revert back to their prior behavior, (c) they construct alibis by refusing to take responsibility for their actions, blaming their behavior on their situation or on others, or (d) they employ the strategy of relational leverage, where they recast the negative feedback as a personal attack on themselves and on the relationship (Monroe et al., 1990).

These characteristics underscore the problems faced by individuals attempting to address alcohol-related problems. The typical response of a difficult person is to promise to change, but to revert back to old behaviors in a very short time. This type of response produces not only frustration on the part of the agent, but also seriously impacts the trust component of the intimate relationship, especially when relational tactics are used. For example, in marital relationships, where the husband is typically the alcoholic, attempts by the wife to control the drinking behavior of the husband is met many times by deceit and resistance, which challenges the intimate foundation from which the original intervention attempt is formed (LePoire, 1992; Roloff & Janiszewski, 1989; Wiseman, 1983). Thus, communicating with individuals under any of the quadrants in the taxonomy becomes very difficult and, in part, explains why noninterpersonal approaches provide only limited potential.

The challenge of impacting the alcohol abuser's (or potential abuser's) behavior, especially in light of the social pressure to participate in the drinking culture and the concomitant resistance that will be encountered, highlights the significance of nonprofessionals (friends and family members) employing more personal influence strategies to accomplish their goals. Personal influence encompasses the interactional strategies employed by interactants closest to the drinker *prior to* any involvement of professional counselors. Unlike noninterpersonal approaches, where those responsible for affecting the drinker's behavior are somewhat removed from episodes in which the problem develops, individuals involved in alcohol-related situations are those who are able to witness (or anticipate) the development of the problem first hand. Often, they are the ones who are in the best position to affect the drinker's behavior owing to their close acquaintance with the problem drinker. Thus, personal influence processes hold the greatest potential for dealing with, limiting, and/or circumventing the disenfranchising process.

The significance of personal intervention processes emanates from our understanding of the effects of alcohol. As discussed earlier, alcohol problems develop in a progressive fashion and manifest themselves cognitively and behaviorally over a period of time. For situational problems, this time period may be only a few hours; the time period may be several years in the case of a dispositional problem. Many researchers contend that, irrespective of the amount of time it takes to manifest itself, individuals associated with alcohol problems progress through a series of stages when dealing with the problem (e.g., Rabow et al., 1990). For example, Throwe (1986) argued that the first response to a developing alcohol problem is that of denial, both on the part of the drinker and those surrounding the drinker. In this stage, individuals fail to see the existence of an alcohol problem and, through the process of rationalization, attribute any "problematic" behavior to factors other than the alcohol. Even in light of increasing evidence of an alcohol-related problem, individuals remain relatively blind to the effect of alcohol on themselves or on others. Thus, even with excessive alcohol consumption, the situation remains defined as relatively normal and nonproblematic.

However, when alcohol problems persist, individuals pass into what Throwe (1986) called the control stage. In this stage, primary others (friends and family members) (a) become aware of the effects of the excessive alcohol consumption, (b) develop an understanding and definition of the problem, (c) formulate a strategy based on their definition of the problem, and (d) engage in a series of influence attempts aimed at controlling or dealing with the problem (cf. LePoire, 1992, 1994, 1995; Wiseman, 1983). Thus, the control phase represents an interaction period that occurs prior to professional intervention in which an influence agent employs a variety of interpersonal strategies aimed at dealing with and/or ending the drinking episode. It is in this stage that the "difficult person" (i.e., resistance) is met.

Based on compliance-gaining research, we have argued that the alcohol prevention/intervention situation is one that "requires an agent to make a series of decisions, to engage in a variety of communicative behaviors, and to coordinate those behaviors with the responses of the target and the demands of the situation in order to accomplish his or her goals" (Thomas & Seibold, 1993a, p. 4; also see Kellermann, 1988; Thomas & Seibold, 1995b). Furthermore, we have advanced a "transactional" reconceptualization of the influence episode and have argued that "it is important not only to examine the specific communication behaviors of an interactant (e.g., the specific compliance-gaining messages [peers] employ in intervening), but also to analyze the factors precipitating the communication behavior and the conjoint influences of each participant's actions on subsequent behaviors that—taken collectively—represent the intervention episode and the influence outcome" (Thomas & Seibold, 1993a, p. 4; also see Garko, 1990; Miller, Boster, Roloff, & Seibold, 1987; Miller & Burgoon, 1978; Newton & Burgoon, 1990).

In terms of transactional influence processes in alcohol-related contexts, one of the first factors that needs to be considered is the influence agent's *decision* to address the alcohol issue. As mentioned earlier, individuals faced with alcohol problems must move from the denial stage to the control stage and overcome the uncertainty associated with understanding the problem. In part, awareness is accomplished by the presence of ever increasingly negative consequences associated with excessive alcohol use. Faced with such problems as obvious intoxication, loss of memory, physical injuries, or any of the other typical problems associated with alcohol abuse, individuals no longer can deny that another's drinking problem does not exist. This awareness constitutes the onset of the control stage.

However, prior to initiating risk reduction communication, communicators must consciously make decisions about how to deal with the problem. Studies have indicated that individuals' decisions to get involved in alcohol-related situations (i.e., to embark on the control stage) are not spontaneous, but involve a series of steps through which agents must pass in order to carry out their influence attempt (Blair, 1983, 1984; Johnson Institute, 1982; Jung, 1986; Rabow et al., 1990; Wiseman, 1983). For example, Dillard (1990b) proposed that influence decisions are affected by a series of approach-avoidance forces. Approach forces are those relevant to what Dillard termed influence goals (not unlike what we have called risk reduction orientations). Influence goals focus on the future state of affairs desired by the influence agent and serve as a motivating device for communication interaction. In other words, influence goals (e.g., the desire of the influence agent to bring about change in the target) support interactants' decisions to engage in influence attempts. In terms of the alcohol context, influence goals relate to the desire of the influence agents to affect the drinking behavior of the target and are based on their perceptions of the negative consequences that might ensue if the behavior continues and/or the amount of risk to which the drinker is subject. Acting as a counterforce, however, are what Dillard called secondary goals. These are goals that inhibit and/or constrain an influence agent's motivation to engage in the influence process. Secondary goals include such factors as the desire of the agent to maintain a positive self-concept, to engage in socially appropriate behavior, to avoid emotional confrontations with the target, or to maintain a positive relationship with the target. From Dillard's perspective, when individuals are faced with the decision to engage in the control stage (i.e., risk reduction communication), a variety of differentially weighted approach and avoidance factors contribute to their decision to engage the target and attempt to control the drinking behavior. Only when approach forces outweigh avoidance forces will influence agents engage the target.

Consistent with this perspective, studies indicate that several factors contribute to agents' decisions to engage in influence attempts in both situational and dispositional contexts. These include: (a) *power* (the agent's belief in his or her ability to affect the behavior of a drinker), (b) *responsibility* (the degree to which the agent feels responsible for the target's behavior), (c) *relational adequacy* (whether the agent feels close enough to the target to say something), (d) *anticipated response of the target* (the degree to which the agent feels confrontation would lead to conflict or emotional anxiety), (e) *competence* (the agent's belief that he or she possesses the skills necessary to affect such a situation), and/or (f) *misperception* (the agent's accurate perception of the problem). Specifically, studies indicate that when individuals feel the safety of the target is in jeopardy and/or the target is a close friend, coupled with their belief that they are able to impact the behavior of the drinker, they choose to engage in influence attempts (Jung, 1986; Rabow et al., 1990; Thomas & Seibold, 1995a). However, when agents do not feel close to, or responsible for, the target, when they feel they are no condition to do anything, when they anticipate a negative response from the target, or when they perceive that intervention will negatively affect their self-image, they choose to avoid confrontation (Jung, 1986; Rabow et al., 1990; Thomas & Seibold, 1995a). Hence, in the decision process, several factors operate to affect participation in the influence process, factors that individuals must overcome in order to influence the disenfranchising process.

Once individuals overcome the barriers to action, they engage in influence attempts aimed at affecting the target's behavior. Thus, a second area relevant to personal intervention involves the *strategies* individuals use to intervene in alcohol-related situations and the factors that affect selection and effectiveness of specific strategies. Strategic communication involves both the verbal and nonverbal strategies individuals choose to influence others in light of the consequences (goals) they want to produce (cf. Conrad, 1994; Dillard, 1990a, 1990b; Goffman, 1969; Johnson, 1986). Specifically, it focuses on the strategies and tactics interactants employ to accomplish primary influence (instrumental) goals, and (as we later argue) on the methods interactants use to integrate their influence goals with their secondary (interpersonal and identity-management) goals (Dillard, 1990a, 1990b).

Specific to these claims, researchers have found that interactants employ a variety of tactics to accomplish their goals and that these strategies vary along a continuum of verbal aggressiveness (Dillard & Burgoon, 1985; Hunter & Boster, 1979, 1987; Lim, 1990; Miller, Boster, Roloff, & Seibold, 1977; Monto, Newcomb, Rabow, & Hernandez, 1992; Newton & Burgoon, 1990; Roloff & Barnicott, 1978; Seibold, Cantrill, & Meyers, 1994; Thomas & Seibold, 1995b; Wiseman, 1983). For example, in examining the influence strategies used in peers' intervention practices, Thomas and Seibold (Seibold & Thomas, 1994; Thomas & Seibold, 1993b, 1995b) have indicated that interactants employ a variety of different *strategy "sets"* when attempting to control the drinking behavior of another (also see LePoire, 1992; Wiseman, 1983) which include: direct positive, direct negative, indirect, and behavioral strategies. *Direct-positive* strategies are those *verbal* strategies interactants employ that directly deal with and acknowledge the alcohol-related problem (e.g., direct requests, gentle nudging or hinting tactics, sympathetic discussions with the drinker, logical persuasion, and negotiation) and that attempt to gain the target's compliance through positive and rewarding behaviors (cf. Hunter & Boster, 1987; Johnson Institute, 1972; Jung, 1986; King, 1986; Mann, 1958; Miller et al., 1977; Wiseman, 1983). *Direct-negative* strategies, in contrast, are those negatively valenced *verbal* strategies delivered directly to a target in an attempt to affect his or her behavior: argumentativeness, where persuasion is attempted but in a hostile manner; aggressiveness, where argumentativeness is coupled with physical aggression, criticism or nagging; guilt appeals; moral lectures; begging and pleading tactics; and verbal threats (Hunter & Boster, 1987; Johnson Institute, 1972; Jung, 1986; LePoire, 1992; Lim, 1990; Mann, 1958; Miller et al., 1977; Wiseman, 1983).

A third set of strategies address the problem in an indirect fashion. Through the use of *indirect strategies* (e.g., enticing the drinker to engage in a behavior other than the intended risky behavior, observing the target's behavior in case he or she gets into trouble, or talking to others about the target's problem), influence agents attempt to affect the behavior of the target verbally but in an indirect fashion (i.e., without identifying the specific alcohol-related behavior in question) (cf. LePoire, 1992; Thomas & Seibold, 1995b).

Finally, with *behavioral strategies*—positively or negatively valenced *nonverbal* tactics employed to affect the behavior of the target—agents attempt to control the drinking behavior without the target knowing about and/or agreeing to it. Although these behavioral strategies can include direct confrontations with the drinker, such as forcibly taking keys away from someone who wants to drive, engaging in physical violence with the target, and physically preventing the target from drinking (as is the case in imprisonment), many of these strategies tend to be behind-the-scenes manipulative tactics in which the target is not aware of the fact that he or she is being manipulated (see LePoire, 1992; Thomas & Seibold, 1993b, 1995b).

Research suggests that strategy use is influenced by a number of factors. One factor is the degree of *message force* the influence agent deems necessary to impact the behavior of the target. As mentioned previously, influence strategies vary in their degree of assertiveness or power. In fact, Garko (1990) argued that exchange and power orientations implicitly undergird the enactment of most compliance-gaining strategies (see also De-Paulo & Fisher, 1980; Marwell & Schmitt, 1967a, 1967b). This power orientation is implicit in the strategies used to intervene into alcohol-related situations: The differences between *asking* someone to drive him or her home, *telling* someone she or he will be driven home, and *taking* a person's keys so he or she cannot drive home exhibits increasing use of more forceful strategies to ensure compliance and potentially reflects differing power orientations. Hence, selection of a more forceful strategy suggests that agents place a higher priority on accomplishing their influence goals (as opposed to their secondary goals) and/or feel the need for stronger messages to make the target more aware of his or her condition and/or impact the target's behavior.

Studies also indicate that situational and individual difference factors operate to affect the enactment process (Newcomb, Rabow, Monto, & Hernandez, 1991). Rabow, Hernandez, and Watts (1986) found that women tended to avoid intervention more than men, especially when the target was male; that when women did intervene, they employed, on the average, more influence attempts per situation than men; and that both men and women preferred less assertive (prosocial) strategies.

Finally, research suggests that strategies differ in terms of their likelihood of being used and in their potential for success. Specifically, studies indicate that although positively valenced strategies tend to be preferred first choices in all situations (Lim, 1990; Miller et al., 1977; Rabow et al., 1986; Thomas & Seibold, 1995b; Wiseman, 1983), these strategies tend to be indicative of interpersonal rather than noninterpersonal relationships (Miller et al., 1977), and are especially likely to be employed when the agent is less dominant in the relationship (Dillard & Burgoon, 1985). In contrast, negatively valenced strategies have a higher probability of use after prosocial attempts fail (Hunter & Boster, 1987; Lim, 1990; Miller et al., 1977), when the target faces aggressive resistance (Lim, 1990; Newton & Burgoon, 1990), and when the agent feels that he or she has a legitimate right to ask for compliance, perceives that compliance will bring about self-benefit, and when compliance is seen in the best interest of the target (Dillard & Burgoon, 1985).

Thus, it seems that the *most likely* strategies to be employed by both men and women in alcohol prevention/intervention situations are those that are the least intrusive and involve verbal messages, such as telling the individual he or she was too drunk to drive, asking to drive him or her home, or suggesting that he or she had (or will have) a problem with alcohol. Those strategies that are least likely to be employed are the more intrusive, less verbal, and more negatively valenced strategies, such as preventing the other from driving and threatening the other person. Hence, individuals appear to prefer the more positive, less intrusive strategies when confronting alcohol-related situations (Hernandez & Rabow, 1987; Rabow et al., 1986).

However, the strategies that appear to be *most successful* are the most intrusive strategies (e.g., driving the other person home, preventing the other person from driving by taking the keys away from him or her). Thus, in contrast to the likelihood of use of any particular strategy, there appears to be a *positive relationship* between the assertiveness of the strategy and the perceived/reported success of the intervention: Strategies reported as most successful are strategies that are most assertive or forceful (see Seibold & Thomas, 1994; Thomas & Seibold, 1995b). In view of the previous findings, it is ironic that strategies most likely to be used in these situations are the strategies that have the lowest probability of being successful (Hernandez & Rabow, 1987; Rabow et al., 1986).

These findings (in concert with the principles associated with the "difficult person" outlined earlier), point to a need to understand the influence process as it unfolds. Specifically, they suggest that a transactive understanding of the influence episode is obtained when one examines the *sequence* of strategies employed to accomplish instrumental goals, especially when resistance is offered from a target (DeTurck, 1985; Hunter & Boster, 1987; Lim, 1990; Monroe et al., 1990; Newton & Burgoon, 1990; also see Cantrill & Seibold, 1986, for a brief review of relevant findings). As stated earlier, intervening in alcohol-related situations typically requires the agent to engage in influence attempts in the face of strong resistance. Under normal situations, this resistance might be sufficient to motivate the agent to disengage from the influence attempt (Dillard, 1990b). However, if the agent cares about the safety of the target (i.e., if compliance is seen as being in the best interest of the target) and/or the agent either gains compliance or risks being hurt (e.g., if compliance will bring about self-benefit), then continued attempts are essential (Dillard & Burgoon, 1985; Hunter & Boster, 1987; Lim, 1990; Miller et al., 1977; Newton & Burgoon, 1990). In other words, the ability to overcome the challenges associated with alcohol prevention or intervention requires persistent influence attempts.

This unfolding pattern of interaction was examined in a study by Thomas and Seibold (1995b). Studying the sequential strategy structure employed by college students when attempting to intervene in either a situational alcohol-related problem (a drunk driving situation) or a dispositional alcohol-related problem (a chronic abuse problem), they found that influence agents (both men and women) preferred employing positively valenced strategies in *initial* influence attempts, especially when facing dispositional problems. However, in *subsequent* intervention attempts, both male and female respondents reported using an increasingly higher amount of negatively valenced strategies, and reported greater success with these strategies than with the use of positively valenced strategies.

The importance of a transactional view of the strategy construction process is underscored by inclusion of two additional communication principles. First, this view emphasizes agents' choices to accomplish, either simultaneously or sequentially, *multiple* goals within the influence episode. As mentioned previously, interpersonal interaction can be conceptualized as goal directed (see Craig, 1986, 1990; Dillard, 1990a, 1990b, Seibold et al., 1994; Wilson & Putnam, 1990). As Clark and Delia (1979) and Newton and Burgoon (1990) argued, richer insight into the influence process is obtained if one examines not only how interactants pursue instrumental goals, but also the manner in which they simultaneously accomplish interpersonal (relational) and identity management objectives.

In fact, the results reported by Thomas and Seibold (1995b) indicate that not only are these multiple communication objectives relevant to the alcohol influence process, they are also differentially weighted in the inter-action situation. For example, in both intervention situations, respondents reported preferences for positively valenced strategies in initial attempts. In essence, this reflected a concern not only for the agent's instrumental objective, but also for interpersonal objectives (wanting to maintain a posi-tive relationship with the target) and identity-management objectives (not wanting to embarrass the target or to appear as an "inconsiderate" indi-vidual). However, analysis of subsequent strategy use suggested that agents "reweighed" these objectives, depending on the outcome they wanted to achieve. In the drunk driving situation, for example, strategic moves were toward increasingly more assertive and intrusive strategies. In terms of communication objectives, this suggests that agents placed greater weight on their instrumental objectives (stopping the target from driving while intoxicated) and decreased the importance of accomplishing interpersonal objectives (not caring if the target got angry) and/or identity-management objectives (not caring if the target "looked bad" by having to be forcibly restrained). Although similar results were obtained in the alcohol abuse situation, strategy use in subsequent intervention attempts revealed that agents maintained a balance between these objectives more so than in the drunk driving situation. Movement toward negatively valenced strategies was more restrained here and the most intrusive strategies (behavioral) were not employed. Hence, in this drunk driving situation, the data seem to suggest that agents were concerned with instrumental objectives (as evidenced by use of persuasion and complex request strategies), but inter-personal objectives (staying friends with the target) and identity manage-ment objectives (not stigmatizing the target) maintained a high priority throughout the interaction episode.

Second, examination of the sequential structure of the influence episode also lends insight into agents' use of "metagoals." Kellermann (1988) pro-posed that tactical message choices are constrained by, and contingent upon, how socially "appropriate" and how "efficient" actors judge them to be in achieving social goals. She and colleagues (Kellermann & Cole, 1994; Kellermann & Kim, 1992) have reported empirical support for these metagoal dimensions as determinants of actors' compliance-gaining tactics. An important implication of this research is that situational, relational, and/or personal factors' effects on message selection are explicable insofar as they affect the importance of being efficient and/or appropriate in par-ticular influence situations. Hence, in alcohol-related interventions, strate-gies that appear to be antisocial and assertive may be demonstrably effective. But, from a metagoal perspective, it is neither the relational or situational factors that explains effectiveness. Rather, the probability is that situational immediacy (i.e., preventing drunk driving) makes the *efficiency* of messages selected more salient to message choosers in these situations than concerns with the (in)*appropriateness* of messages that threaten the relationship with the alcohol abuser.

Particularly in the face of noncompliance, results from studies suggest that agents' definition of the situation and the target are altered; the target is seen as more hostile and/or nonrational and the situation is seen as more "crisis oriented." In light of resistance, then, situational immediacy makes the strategic efficiency of messages selected more salient to message choosers than concerns with the (in)appropriateness of messages (which threaten the relationship with the target and the identity of the agent). This interpretation might help explain the less frequent use of negatively valenced strategies in chronic abuse situations (Thomas & Seibold, 1995b). In that noncompliance does not place the target in immediate danger (as it does with situational problems), and in that the agent may perceive that maintaining positive relationships with the target might allow assistance at a later point in time, the more efficient strategies may remain defined as socially inappropriate, and thus their use is inhibited. Only when the abuse problem becomes crisis oriented will the more efficient and inappropriate strategies be employed (cf. LePoire, 1992; Wiseman, 1983).

## CONCLUSION

Throughout this essay, we have emphasized the significance and harmfulness of the problems associated with alcohol abuse, and have underscored the significance of personal communication practices in dealing with these problems, particularly with respect to how involvement with these issues (potentially) exposes *both* the drinker and the concerned party to a disenfranchising process. Moreover, we have argued that the pervasiveness and seriousness of this problem, coupled with the limitations of present alcohol programs to impact behavior at the individual level, emphasizes the importance of everyday interactants' skills at intervening in these potentially dangerous situations. Most important, we have emphasized the need to view communication (particularly interpersonal communication) with a disenfranchised person from a transactional perspective. In doing so, we have tried to highlight significant issues relevant to communicating *with* a disenfranchised person, as well as communicating *as* a disenfranchised person.

The disenfranchising process associated with alcohol dependency is, in part, a result of the historical beliefs generated out of individuals' reactions to, and lack of understanding of, the problems associated with alcohol abuse. Although these beliefs produced the stigma associated with alcohol abuse we face today, they also identify a central leverage point for dealing with the disenfranchising process. As we have argued throughout this chapter, individuals' beliefs about the problem of alcohol abuse and their perceptions of the alcohol abuser significantly contribute both to their decision to communicate in alcohol-related situations and to the way in which they approach these situations. Past moralistic and stigmatized perceptions of alcohol abuse have led individuals to attribute alcohol problems to the personal inadequacies of the alcohol abuser and, hence, to limit their involvement with (to disenfranchise) these individuals. Thus, increased awareness and understanding of alcohol dependency problems, the ways in which these problems develop and manifest themselves, and the consequences associated with noninvolvement constitute the first step in dealing with this affliction and overcoming the disenfranchising dynamics associated with alcohol abuse. The noninterpersonal efforts (mass-media campaigns, education programs) aimed at increasing society's awareness of the seriousness and the extensiveness of the affliction provide an effective means to create this awareness. With continued efforts, these programs should lead to greater *social acceptability* of the affliction as one over which individuals do not have control. This, in turn, should demarginalize alcohol abusers to the point that individuals are more willing to communicate with them. By providing individuals the ability to see potential problems at an earlier stage and the knowledge that these problems are not associated with a moral defect, individuals will be able to more readily accept the problem and act more quickly to get involved.

However, as we have argued, these noninterpersonal efforts are not sufficient to impact behavior at the individual level. In fact, as we have shown, many people feel that they do not have the appropriate skills to be effective in these types of situations, and those who do choose to intervene do so in ways that are not always effective. Thus, a second set of issues relevant to communicating with alcoholics emphasizes the need for interpersonal methods to impact drinkers' behavior at the interpersonal level. In that alcohol abusers are typically unaware of their own problems, these issues focus on the motivations of individuals surrounding the drinker and on their ability to enact interpersonal strategies to either prevent and/or intervene in alcohol-related situations. To some degree, increased awareness of the affliction should create greater motivation to get involved; more awareness of the symptoms of alcohol-related problems (accomplished through noninterpersonal methods) should result in more willingness to overcome the barriers to intervention and to engage in the influence process. However, individuals need to acknowledge the fact that, even though communication about (situational or dispositional) alcohol-related problems likely will result in an anxiety-producing interaction, may cast a negative image on the influence agent, and may even threaten the relationship that the agent has with the target, the risks associated with nonintervention far outweigh these negative consequences associated with intervention.

To develop these skills, we feel that individuals need (a) to understand how an alcohol intervention situation communicatively develops and progresses, (b) to develop a basic strategic repertoire relevant to intervention techniques—especially in the face of resistance to initial attempts, and (c) to appreciate how multiple communication objectives can be achieved simultaneously in strategy choices. Also, by understanding the typical resistance response of targets, agents will be better able to engage in tactics that may not be the most "socially appropriate" ones (thereby lessening the chances of disenfranchisement), but because of their persistence, be able to impact the drinker's behavior. In doing so, peers will be better able to guide the drinker to professional agencies or programs that will help deal with the problem over the long term.

However, we would be remiss if we did not consider this process from the alcohol abuser's perspective. In doing so, several issues become relevant. To begin with, individuals must realize that just because the drinking stops, the drinking problem is not over (Blair, 1984; Denzin, 1987c). As mentioned earlier, influencing someone's drinking behavior is a disenfranchising event for the drinker—that person's identity is put at stake. This is particularly problematic in long-term dispositional problems where self-concept and self-esteem have been "constructed" and "validated" within an alcohol-centered environment (Denzin, 1987b; Goffman, 1959). Thus, when control of the drinking behavior is finally achieved—when a person admits to having an alcohol dependency problem—much of the person's identity is destroyed (Denzin, 1987a); the drinker is no longer the "good" person he or she thought he or she was. Hence, the drinker's identity must be reconstructed.

The reconstruction of the drinker's identity requires two objectives. First, the drinker must learn that he or she can succeed in life without alcohol (Denzin, 1987a). In other words, the drinker must have the ability to successfully accomplish goals and regain his or her self-esteem in a world without alcohol. Many professional programs now in existence allow for this. For example, programs such as Alcoholics Anonymous provide support and validation for the recovering alcoholic and help him or her regain self-esteem. In addition, many organizations sponsor employee assistance programs that allow individuals the time they need to deal with their alcohol problem without risking loss of employment (Johnson, 1980; Johnson Institute, 1983). Too, with the acceptance of the disease model of alcoholism, society in general has developed a more accepting view of the alcohol dependency problem and therefore does not "penalize" someone as greatly as they have in the past (Marlatt et al., 1993).

During the recovery period, alcoholics lack much of the confidence they need to be successful. They have left their "comfort zone" and now operate in a world that is unfamiliar and frightening to them. In fact, until they build up their self-confidence, any type of stress can send them back to their old patterns of behavior. Hence, it is important to plan for "small wins" in order to rebuild the drinker's identity; they cannot be expected to change overnight. Only when the drinker gains confidence in his or her abilities without the assistance of alcohol—only when he or she has built up a catalogue of small wins—will he or she be able to manage stress without resorting to the use of alcohol (Denzin, 1987b).

Just as important as accomplishments, however, is supportive communication from others. Alcohol dependency usually results in a lot of negative feelings from those who have been adversely affected by the drinker (Le-Poire, 1992; Paolino & McCrady, 1977). Once the drinker realizes the full extent of the problems that he or she has caused, he or she experiences a significant amount of guilt. Part of the recovery from alcohol dependency, as practiced in the 12-step program, is the purging of this guilt; members are asked to make amends to those they have injured in the past. In doing so, they strive to rebuild relationships that have been torn apart by the alcohol and to regain a certain degree of self-respect. In order for this to be successful, those who work with alcoholics must realize the important role supportive communication plays in this rebuilding process. Unlike other adults, recovering alcoholics need significantly more reassurance that their new way of life is appreciated by those around him or her. Combined with accomplishments, supportive communication will allow the recovering alcoholic to regain a sense of self-control and self-esteem and to lead a healthier life—reversing both the situational and dispositional cycle of "disenfranchisement" we have described throughout this chapter.

# REFERENCES

Ablon, J. (1983). The significance of cultural patterning for the "alcoholic family." In D. H. Olson & B. C. Miller (Eds.), *Family studies review yearbook* (Vol. 6, pp. 361–378). Beverly Hills, CA: Sage.

American College Health Association. (1989). *Adult children of alcohol abusers*. Rockville, MD: Author.

Baer, J. S., Marlatt, G. A., Kivlahan, D. R., Fromme, K., Larimer, M. E., & Williams, E. (1992). An experimental test of three methods of alcohol risk reduction with young adults. *Journal of Consulting and Clinical Psychology, 60,* 974–979.

Baer, J. S., Stacy, A., & Larimer, M. (1991). Biases in the perception of drinking norms among college students. *Journal of Studies on Alcohol, 52,* 580–586.

Bennett, M. J. (1990). Stigmatization: Experience of persons with Acquired Immune Deficiency Syndrome. *Issues in Mental Health Nursing, 11,* 141–154.

Berkowitz, A. D., & Perkins, H. W. (1986). Problem drinking among college students: A review of recent research. *Journal of American College Health, 35,* 21–28.

Blair, B. R. (1983). *Supervisors and managers as enablers.* Minneapolis: Johnson Institute.

Blair, B. R. (1984). *The supervisors role in early recovery.* Minneapolis: Johnson Institute.

Blume, S. B. (1981). *Drinking and pregnancy.* Minneapolis: Johnson Institute.

Blume, S. B. (1984). *Alcoholism and depression.* Minneapolis: Johnson Institute.

Brennen, A. F., Walfish, S., & AuBuchon, P. (1986a). Alcohol use and abuse in college students: I. A review of individual and personality correlates. *International Journal of the Addictions, 21,* 449–474.

Brennen, A. F., Walfish, S., & AuBuchon, P. (1986b). Alcohol use and abuse in college students: II. Social/environmental correlates, methodological issues, and implications for intervention. *International Journal of the Addictions, 21,* 475–493.

Burnham, R. B., & Nelson, S. J. (1984, October). When "alternatives" aren't. *Association of College Unions-International Bulletin, 52*(5), 15–17.

Cahalan, D. (1988). Implications of the disease concept of alcoholism. In B. Segal (Ed.), *Alcoholism etiology and treatment: Issues for theory and practice* (pp. 49–68). New York: Haworth.

Cantrill, J. G., & Seibold, D. R. (1986). The perceptual contrast explanation of sequential request strategy effectiveness. *Human Communication Research, 13,* 253–267.

Carroll, C. R. (1989). *Drugs* (2nd ed.). Dubuque, IA: Brown.

Cermak, T. L. (1986). *Diagnosing and treating co-dependence: A guide for professionals who work with chemical dependents, their spouses, and children.* Minneapolis: Johnson Institute Books.

Cherry, A. (1987). Undergraduate alcohol misuse: Suggested strategies for prevention and early detection. *Journal of Alcohol and Drug Education, 32,* 1–6.

Clark, R. A., & Delia, J. G. (1979). Topoi and rhetorical competence. *Quarterly Journal of Speech, 65,* 187–206.

Conrad, C. (1994). *Strategic organizational communication: Toward the twenty-first century* (3rd ed.). Fort Worth, TX: Harcourt Brace.

Coyne, R. K. (1984). Primary prevention through a campus alcohol education project. *Personnel and Guidance Journal, 62,* 524–528.

Craig, R. T. (1986). Goals in discourse. In D. G. Ellis & W. A. Donohue (Eds.), *Contemporary issues in language discourse processes* (pp. 257–273). Hillsdale, NJ: Lawrence Erlbaum Associates.

Craig, R. T. (1990). Multiple goals in discourse: An epilogue. *Journal of Language and Social Psychology, 9,* 163–170.

Dean, J. C., & Bryon, W. A. (1982). *Alcohol programs for higher education.* Carbondale: Southern Illinois University Press.

Denzin, N. K. (1987a). *The alcoholic self.* Newbury Park, CA: Sage.

Denzin, N. K. (1987b). *The recovering alcoholic.* Newbury Park, CA: Sage.

Denzin, N. K. (1987c). *Treating alcoholism.* Newbury Park, CA: Sage.

DePaulo, B. M., & Fisher, J. D. (1980). The costs of asking for help. *Basic and Applied Social Psychology, 1,* 23–35.

DeTurck, M. A. (1985). A transactional analysis of compliance-gaining behavior: Effects of noncompliance, relational contexts, and actor's gender. *Human Communication Research, 12,* 54–78.

Dillard, J. P. (1990a). A goal-driven model of interpersonal influence. In J. P. Dillard (Ed.), *Seeking compliance: The production of interpersonal influence messages* (pp. 41–56). Scottsdale, AZ: Gorsuch Scarisbrick.

Dillard, J. P. (1990b). The nature and substance of goals in tactical communication. In M. J. Cody & M. L. McLaughlin (Eds.), *The psychology of tactical communication* (pp. 70–90). London: Multilingual Matters.

Dillard, J. P., & Burgoon, M. (1985). Situational influences on the selection of compliance-gaining messages: Two test of the predictive utility of the Cody–McLaughlin typology. *Communication Monographs, 52,* 289–304.

Dumerauf, J. R. (1987, November). *The detection of alcoholism: Directions for communication research.* Paper presented at the annual meeting of the Speech Communication Association, Boston.

Ewing, J. A. (1983). *Today's biomedical research on alcoholism.* Minneapolis: Johnson Institute.

Garko, M. G. (1990). Perspectives on and conceptualizations of compliance-gaining. *Communication Quarterly, 38,* 138–157.

Geller, A. (1984). *Alcohol and sexual performance.* Minneapolis: Johnson Institute.

Goffman, E. (1959). *The presentation of self in everyday life.* Garden City, NY: Doubleday.

Goffman, E. (1969). *Strategic interaction.* Philadelphia: University of Pennsylvania Press.

Gomberg, E. S. L. (1993). Alcohol, women, and the expression of aggression. *Journal of Studies on Alcohol,* (Suppl. 11), 89–95.

Gottheil, E., McLellan, A. T., Druley, K. A., & Alterman, A. I. (1979). Some relationships between experimental, theoretical and clinical approaches to alcoholism. In E. L. Gottheil, A. T. McLellan, K. A. Druley, & A. I. Alterman (Eds.), *Addiction research and treatment: Converging trends* (pp. 1–11). New York: Pergamon.

Hanson, D. J., & Engs, R. C. (1992). College students drinking problems: A national study, 1982–1991. *Psychological Reports, 71,* 39–42.

Hernandez, A. C., & Rabow, J. (1987). Passive and assertive interventions in public and private drunken driving situations. *Journal of Studies on Alcohol, 48,* 269–271.

Hickenbottom, J. P., Bissonnette, R. P., & O'Shea, R. M. (1987). Preventative medicine and college alcohol abuse. *Journal of American College Health, 36,* 67–72.

Hunter, J. E., & Boster, F. J. (1979, November). *Situational differences in the selection of compliance-gaining messages.* Paper presented at the annual meeting of the Speech Communication Association, San Antonio, TX.

Hunter, J. E., & Boster, F. J. (1987). A model of compliance-gaining message selection. *Communication Monographs, 54,* 63–84.

Jellinek, E. M. (1960). *The disease concept of alcoholism.* New Brunswick, NJ: Hillhouse Press.

Johnson, V. E. (1980). *I'll quit tomorrow: A practical guide to alcoholism treatment.* New York: Harper & Row.

Johnson, V. E. (1986). *Intervention: How to help someone who doesn't want help.* Minneapolis: Johnson Institute Books.

Johnson Institute. (1972). *Alcoholism: A treatable disease.* Minneapolis: Author.

Johnson Institute. (1982). *The family enablers.* Minneapolis: Author.

Johnson Institute. (1983). *Intervention: A professional's guide.* Minneapolis: Author.

Jung, J. (1986). How significant others cope with problem drinkers. *International Journal of the Addictions, 21,* 5–22.

Kauth, M. R., Christoff, K. A., Sartor, J., & Sharp, S. (1993). HIV sexual risk reduction among college women: Applying a peer influence model. *Journal of College Student Development, 34,* 346–351.

Kellermann, K. (1988, March). Understanding tactical choice: Metagoals in conversation. Paper presented at the Temple University Discourse Conference, Philadelphia.

Kellermann, K., & Cole, T. (1994). Classifying compliance-gaining messages: Taxonomic disorder and strategic confusion. *Communication Theory, 4,* 3–60.

Kellermann, K., & Kim, M-S. (1992, May). *Working within constraints: Tactical choices in the pursuit of social goals.* Paper presented at the annual meeting of the International Communication Association, Miami, FL.

King, B. L. (1986). Decision-making in the intervention process. *Alcoholism Treatment Quarterly, 3*(3), 5–22.

Kissen, B. (1977). Theory and practice in the treatment of alcoholism. In B. Kissen & H. Begleiter (Eds.), *Treatment and rehabilitation of the chronic alcoholic* (pp. 1–51). New York: Plenum.

Kivlahan, D. R., Marlatt, G. A., Fromme, K., Coppel, D. B., & Williams, E. (1990). Secondary prevention with college drinkers: Evaluation of an alcohol skills training program. *Journal of Consulting and Clinical Psychology, 58*, 805–810.

Klingman, H., & Takala, J-P. (1992). *Cure, care, or control: Alcoholism treatment in sixteen different countries.* Albany: State University of New York Press.

Leonard, K. E., & Senchak, M. (1993). Alcohol and premarital aggression among newlywed couples. *Journal of Studies on Alcohol*, (Suppl. 11), 96–118.

LePoire, B. A. (1992). Does the codependent encourage substance-dependent behavior? Paradoxical injunctions in the codependent relationship. *International Journal of the Addictions, 27*, 1465–1474.

LePoire, B. A. (1994). Two contrasting explanations of involvement violations: Expectancy violations theory vs discrepancy arousal theory. *Human Communication Research, 20,* 560–591.

LePoire, B. A. (1995). Inconsistent nurturing as control theory: Implications for communication researchers of the substance-dependent spousal relationship. *Journal of Applied Communication Research, 23*, 60–74.

Lim, T. S. (1990). The influence of receiver's resistance on persuaders' verbal aggressiveness. *Communication Quarterly, 38*, 170–188.

Liska, A. E. (1992). *Social threat and social control.* Albany: State University of New York Press.

Mann, M. (1958). *New primer on alcoholism: How people drink, how to recognize alcoholics, and what to do about them.* New York: Holt, Rinehart & Winston.

Margolis, G. (1992). Earlier intervention: Confronting the idea and practice of drinking to drunkenness on college campuses: A next step. *Journal of College Student Psychotherapy, 7,* 15–22.

Marlatt, G. A., Larimer, M. E., Baer, J. S., & Quigley, L. A. (1993). Harm reduction for alcohol problems: Moving beyond the controlled drinking controversy. *Behavior Therapy, 24,* 461–504.

Marlatt, G. A., & Tapert, S. F. (1993). Harm reduction: Reducing the risks of addictive behaviors. In J. S. Baer, G. A. Marlatt, & R. J. McMahon (Eds.), *Addictive behaviors across the lifespan* (pp. 243–273). Newbury Park, CA: Sage.

Marwell, G., & Schmitt, D. R. (1967a). Compliance-gaining behavior: A synthesis and model. *Sociological Quarterly, 8*, 317–328.

Marwell, G., & Schmitt, D. R. (1967b). Dimensions of compliance-gaining behavior: An empirical analysis. *Sociometry, 30,* 350–364.

Massey, R. F., & Neidigh, L. W. (1990). Evaluating and improving the functioning of a peer-based alcohol abuse prevention organization. *Journal of Alcohol and Drug Education, 35,* 24–35.

Michal-Johnson, P. (1993, November). *Response to "AIDS, alcohol, and the college student: Competitively selected papers."* Paper presented at the annual convention of the Speech Communication Association, Miami, FL.

Miller, G. R., Boster, F. J., Roloff, M., & Seibold, D. R. (1977). Compliance-gaining message strategies: A typology and some findings concerning effects of situational differences. *Communication Monographs, 44*, 37–50.

Miller, G. R., Boster, F. J., Roloff, M., & Seibold, D. R. (1987). MBRS rekindled: Some thoughts on compliance gaining in interpersonal settings. In M. E. Roloff & G. R. Miller (Eds.), Interpersonal processes: New directions in communication research (pp. 89–116). Newbury Park, CA: Sage.

Miller, G. R., & Burgoon, M. (1978). Persuasion research: Review and commentary. In B. D. Rubin (Ed.), *Communication yearbook 2* (pp. 29–47). New Brunswick, NJ: Transaction Books.

Monroe, C., DiSalvo, V. S., Lewis, J. J., & Borzi, M. G. (1990). Conflict behaviors of difficult subordinates: Interactive effects of gender. *Southern Communication Journal, 56*, 12–23.

Montgomery, S. B., Joseph, J. G., Becker, M. H., Ostrow, D. G., Kessler, R. C., & Kirscht, J. P. (1989). The health belief model in understanding compliance with preventative recommendations for AIDS: How useful? *AIDS Education and Prevention, 1*, 303–323.

Monto, M. A., Newcomb, M. D., Rabow, J., & Hernandez, A. C. R. (1992). Social status and drunk-driving intervention. *Journal of Studies on Alcohol, 53*, 63–68.

National Council on Alcoholism. (1987). *Facts on alcoholism and alcohol-related problems.* New York: Author.

Ness, E. (1985). The identification, confrontation and referral of problem drinkers by resident assistants. *Journal of Alcohol and Drug Education, 31*, 32–40.

Newcomb, M. D., Rabow, J., Monto, M., & Hernandez, A. C. R. (1991). Informal drunk driving intervention: Psychosocial correlates among young adult women and men. *Journal of Applied Social Psychology, 21*, 1988–2006.

Newton, D. A., & Burgoon, J. K. (1990). The use and consequences of verbal influence strategies during interpersonal disagreements. *Human Communication Research, 16*, 477–518.

Nichols, J. L., Weinstein, E. G., Ellingstad, V. S., & Struckman-Johnson, D. L. (1978). The specific deterrent effect of ASAP education and rehabilitation programs. *Journal of Safety Research, 10*, 177–187.

Paolino, T. J., & McCrady, B. S. (1977). *The alcoholic marriage: Alternative perspectives.* New York: Grune & Stratton.

Pattison, E. M., & Kaufman, E. (1982). The alcoholism syndrome: Definitions and models. In E. M. Pattison & E. Kaufman (Eds.), *Encyclopedic handbook of alcoholism* (pp. 31–39). New York: Gardner.

Peele, S. (1989). *Diseasing of America: Addiction treatment out of control.* Lexington, MA: Lexington.

Premer, R. F. (1982). *Medical consequences of alcoholism.* Minneapolis: Johnson Institute.

Purvis, A. (1990, April 30). DNA and the desire to drink. *Time,* p. 88.

Quindlen, A. (1994, June 13). Alcohol an accident waiting to happen to youngsters. *Chicago Tribune,* p. 21.

Rabow, J., Hernandez, A. C. R., & Watts, R. K. (1986). College students do intervene in drunk driving situations. *Sociology and Social Research, 70*, 224–225.

Rabow, J., Newcomb, M. D., Monto, M. A., & Hernandez, A. C. R. (1990). Altruism in drunk driving situations: Personal and situational factors in intervention. *Social Psychology Quarterly, 53*, 199–213.

Raffaeli, R. M. (1990, June). *Discovering relationships between communication patterns, family violence, and alcoholism.* Paper presented at the annual convention of the International Communication Association, Dublin, Ireland.

Rohan, W. P. (1982). The concept of alcoholism: Assumptions and issues. In E. M. Pattison & E. Kaufman (Eds.), *Encyclopedic handbook of alcoholism* (pp. 31–39). New York: Gardner.

Roloff, M. E., & Barnicott, E. F. (1978). The situational use of pro- and antisocial compliance-gaining strategies by high and low Machiavellians. In B. D. Rubin (Ed.), *Communication yearbook 2* (pp. 193–208). New Brunswick, NJ: Transaction Books.

Roloff, M. E., & Janiszewski, C. A. (1989). Overcoming obstacles to interpersonal compliance: A principle of message construction. *Human Communication Research, 16*, 33–61.

Roman, P. M. (1988). The disease concept of alcoholism: Sociocultural and organizational bases of support. In B. Segal (Ed.), *Alcoholism etiology and treatment: Issues for theory and practice* (pp. 5–32). New York: Haworth.

Rorabaugh, W. J. (1991). Alcohol in America. *Organization of American Historians Magazine of History, 6*(2), 17–19.

Schuckitt, M. A. (1981). The genetics of alcoholism. *Alcoholism: Clinical and Experimental Research, 5*, 439–440.

Seay, T. A., & Beck, T. D. (1984). Alcoholism among college students. *Journal of College Student Personnel, 25,* 90–92.

Seibold, D. R., Cantrill, J. G., & Meyers, R. A. (1994). Communication and interpersonal influence. In M. L. Knapp & G. R. Miller (Eds.), *Handbook of interpersonal communication* (2nd ed., pp. 542–588). Newbury Park, CA: Sage.

Seibold, D. R., & Thomas, R. W. (1994). Rethinking the role of interpersonal influence processes in alcohol intervention situations. *Journal of Applied Communication Research, 22,* 177–197.

Siegler, M., Osmond, H., & Newell, S. (1968). Models of alcoholism. *Quarterly Journal of Studies on Alcoholism, 29,* 571–591.

Taylor, S. P., & Chermak, S. T. (1993). Alcohol, drugs, and human physical aggression. *Journal of Studies on Alcohol,* (Suppl. 11), 78–88.

Thomas, R. W., & Seibold, D. R. (1993a, November). *College students' attitudes toward alcohol, alcohol consumption patterns, and decisions to intervene in alcohol-related situations.* Paper presented to the Commission on Health Communication at the Speech Communication Association Convention, Miami, FL.

Thomas, R. W., & Seibold, D. R. (1993b). Interpersonal influence processes in the "home treatment method" of alcoholism intervention. *Journal of Alcohol and Drug Education, 38,* 49–79.

Thomas, R. W., & Seibold, D. R. (1995a). College students' decisions to intervene in alcohol-related situations. *Journal of Studies on Alcohol, 56,* 580–588.

Thomas, R. W., & Seibold, D. R. (1995b). Interpersonal influence and alcohol-related interventions in the college environment. *Health Communication, 7,* 93–123.

Thorton, C. C., Gottheil, E., Skoloda, T. E., & Alterman, A. I. (1979). Alcoholics' drinking decisions: Implications for treatment and outcome. In E. L. Gottheil, A. T. McLellan, K. A. Druley, & A. I. Alterman (Eds.), *Addiction research and treatment: Converging trends* (pp. 12–18). New York: Pergamon.

Throwe, A. N. (1986). Families and alcohol. *Critical Care Quarterly, 8*(4), 79–88.

U.S. Census Bureau. (1992). *Statistical abstracts of the United States.* Washington, DC: U.S. Department of Commerce Economics and Statistics Administration.

Wallace, J. (1983). Our approach to alcoholism: A shift in paradigm is not necessary. *Journal of Psychiatric Treatment and Evaluation, 5,* 479–484.

*Webster's New World Dictionary* (2nd college ed.). (1970). New York: World Publishing.

Wilson, S. R., & Putnam, L. L. (1990). Interaction goals in negotiation. In J. A. Anderson (Ed.), *Communication yearbook 13* (pp. 374–406). Newbury Park, CA: Sage.

Wiseman, J. P. (1983). The "home treatment": The first steps in trying to cope with an alcoholic husband. In D. H. Olson & B. C. Miller (Eds.), *Family studies review yearbook* (Vol. 6, pp. 352–360). Beverly Hills, CA: Sage.

Womack, M. S. (1990, July). *Relational equality in the alcoholic/coalcoholic marriage: A communication rules approach focusing on relational coherence, control, and power.* Paper presented at the annual convention of the International Communication Association, Dublin, Ireland.

# 22 Supportive Structures for Persons With Disability: Smoothing or Smothering the Way?

Gerianne M. Johnson
*San Francisco State University*

Terrance L. Albrecht
*University of South Florida*

Major shifts are occurring in the social and legal constructions of disability in the United States, changing our view of ourselves and one another as abled, disabled, challenged, and differently abled (Berger & Luckmann, 1967; Fine & Asch, 1988). Yet, the prospects for fulfilling competitive employment of people with disabilities remain bleak (G. Miller, 1991), with nearly 66% of U.S. citizens with disabilities unemployed (International Center for the Disabled [ICD], 1986). The 1980 U.S. Census Bureau (Bowe, 1982) estimated the number of Americans with disabilities at 36 million; 27 million were between the ages of 18 and 64. Only 42% of the men and 23% of those women with disabilities were employed,[1] resulting in double stigmatization. Not only are they stigmatized because they are unemployed but also because of their disability (see Braithwaite, chap. 23, this volume, for a discussion on the stigmatization of persons with disabilities). Because they are unemployed, they are deprived of the rights, privileges, and power associated with pulling one's own weight in U.S. culture. Because of their disability, satisfactory employment is more difficult. Thus, their dual membership increases their disenfranchisement from mainstream society.

---

[1]The 1986 ICD survey sampled 1,000 working age U.S. citizens with disabilities and showed about a 34% employment rate. Passage of the Americans With Disabilities Act in 1990 broadened the legal definition of disability, significantly increasing the number of disabled citizens in the United States; the exact size of this increase is not yet known.

However, once employed, people with disabilities are further disenfranchised as they remain in a symbolically low-status position in relation to temporarily abled employees (Roberts, 1993).[2] This relational asymmetry is reflected in lack of internal social support and involvement in supportive communication networks. In this chapter, we explore some implications of communication network involvement and social support for persons with disabilities, within the employment context of the United States.

## TRACING EMPLOYMENT DISENFRANCHISEMENT

Until the middle of this century, individuals in the United States who were diagnosed with a disability were institutionalized—isolated in residential settings with few or no work opportunities (MacGugan, 1993). More recently, sheltered workshop settings were created to keep people with disabilities occupied. These settings are, for example, simulated work organizations usually modeled after a factory production line except that all employees have disabilities. However, the degree of challenge and reward inherent in sheltered work suggests that its purpose was to keep the worker busy and ease the burden of the caretakers rather than to provide mentally and physically meaningful work (Hammel, 1993). Even today, employed people with disabilities are frequently found in sheltered work placements with noncompetitive rewards and opportunities (Fine & Asch, 1988; G. Miller, 1991).

Historical evidence demonstrating the perpetuation of disenfranchisement for persons with disabilities in regard to work can be traced backward from present discussions of unsuccessful school-to-work transitions for disabled youth. Despite years of research and task force inquiries about why this is so, "those labeled disabled do not experience post-school success" (Retish, 1989, p. 36). The failures have been blamed on bad teachers or poor teaching, poor adjustment, a weak economy, and a lack of understanding about why people with disabilities fail—ironically supporting the need for more research on the failures.

Various recommendations to increase the likelihood of successful school-to-work transitions have been offered, including mainstreaming high school students with disabilities into vocational programs, instead of segregating them in special education classrooms (Retish, 1989) and providing internships (Hammel, 1993). However, internships are difficult to implement, mostly due to employer reluctance to participate. In addition, they are often doomed to fail because they enable employers to take advantage of the

---

[2]We borrowed the term *temporarily abled* from Ed Roberts, former president of the World Institute on Disability, located in Berkeley, California.

supported system with no long-term commitment to the intern (Retish, 1989).

One noteworthy strategy suggested is to increase interactions between vocational teachers and the community in regard to job needs, which may predispose potential employers toward hiring a person with a disability (Retish, 1989). Essentially, this strategy would serve to develop strong ties between the teachers and community, which could then aid employment placements of students. When speaking of persons with disabilities, ". . . employment seems contingent upon a friend or relative" (Retish, 1989, p. 37). In communication network terms, people with disabilities must rely heavily upon their strong network links to secure and maintain employment. Ironically, Granovetter's (1982) research suggested the exact opposite: In an able population, weak links were associated with successful job seeking.

Discussions of frustrating school-to-work transitions for disabled youth are echoed in the rehabilitation literature by stories of failed return-to-work transitions after adult onset of disability. Returning to work involves adapting a previously established career path in light of an acquired disability, or alternatively, establishing a new career. Networking and ascertaining specific expectations for job success are commendable strategies for any job seeker, but for adults returning to work with a disability, the correlation with actual job placement is weak (Retish, 1989).

In sum, there is little positive news about the potential for employment of disabled workers from employers, agencies, or people with disabilities (Retish, 1989). Disabled workers get jobs that offer less permanence, security, and stability, and many are working below their potential because of limited opportunities for upward mobility (G. Miller, 1991). The rehabilitation system emphasizes initial job placement, largely ignoring the subsequent challenges of job stability and mobility. Thus, it could be interpreted that the societal structure is giving little more than a nod to persons with disabilities, essentially continuing their marginalization from mainstream society. This is accomplished, in large part, through the traditional social construction of persons with disabilities as low-status members of society. In the next section, we present evidence of the changing social construction of disability in the United States, both in and out of the workplace, and some current responses to this change.


## THE CHANGING SOCIAL CONSTRUCTION
## OF DISABILITY AND WORK

The social construction of disability and work is based on a lifelong process of socialization to occupation. In U.S. culture, personal identity is closely tied to one's profession (Eisenberg & Goodall, 1993). For example, children with congenital disabilities gradually come to know themselves as different because they do not fit the traditional school-to-work model of membership predominant in U.S. culture. Disabled children are given few positive alternatives to consider during the formative school years. Societal marginalization is communicated in daily interactions, when other students, and later, coworkers, do not speak, act, or look like the person with a disability.

People who become disabled after entering the workforce as able adults must reinterpret lifelong socialization-to-occupation in light of the present handicap. New role models must be adopted to emulate successful occupational behavior with the disability. Those who do return to work, whether at the same or a new job, may have to adapt to being an outgroup member in relationship to the career status they enjoyed prior to the onset of disability. Adaptation to these changes, concurrent with the employment disenfranchisement described earlier, can require considerable emotional, financial, and instrumental support.

Outgroup membership, systematic underemployment, and a lack of upward mobility result in part from the low priority given full participation for disabled citizens in U.S. culture (Fine & Asch, 1988; Scotch, 1988). Their limited status in the cultural priority system—more than educational deficits, more than the sensory or physical ability losses, per se, more than the adjustment problems of individuals—accounts for the employment disenfranchisement of persons with disabilities.

The low priority given full participation for people with disabilities in our cultural value system excuses unfulfilled needs whenever time is short, the economy is bad, and so on. As G. Miller (1991) observed, "society often expects disabled individuals to be satisfied just to be employed" (p. 333). Expectations about what people should be satisfied with reflect cultural premises, as do beliefs about what people with disabilities can and cannot do, and what means of accommodating a disability are reasonable.

One potentially empowering response to societal disenfranchisement has been to begin defining disabled as a separate culture. Braithwaite (chap. 23, this volume) argues somewhat more broadly for disability as one cultural category. In this view, interaction between people with disabilities and people without disabilities constitutes an intercultural communication event, and communication differences are attributed to conflicting cultural norms, rather than to skill deficits on the part of the person with a disability.[3]

---

[3]We believe that communication training can be used for something other than the deficit model identified by MacGugan (1993). In that model, people with disabilities are trained to compensate for sensory, motor, or mental handicaps in ways that disguise and deny the differences in capabilities. In our view, helping people with disabilities to advance their own interests may include helping them learn to successfully resist pressures to acculturate and to communicate like able people.

This cultural approach can be juxtaposed with the assimilation model, advising persons with disabilities to assimilate, or learn to behave like those who are able. The prescription is akin to myriad other advice aimed at prompting minority group members to walk, talk, and think like members of the dominant culture. A prescription to acculturate is particularly disturbing and disenfranchising for people who can never regain the physical, sensory, or mental capabilities that differentiate them from members of the dominant able culture. The advice to assimilate is also disenfranchising because it indicates that the advisor views people with disabilities as powerless and needing this kind of support (Augusto & McGraw, 1990).

A final piece of evidence for our claim that disability is socially constructed lies in the fact that there is a hierarchy of preference associated with various types of disability (Hammel, 1993), and this hierarchy is recognized and expressed by people with and without disabilities. For example, individuals without any identified disability will sometimes ask one another, hypothetically speaking, if they would rather be blind or deaf. People with vision or hearing loss may remark, "Well, at least I can still walk" (G. Johnson, 1993).

The criteria for the hierarchy order includes, for example, the perceived degree of impairment. G. Johnson (1995) found that employees with low residual vision were less trusted and trusting, on average, than either sighted or totally blind workers. Another consideration is the perceived level of personal responsibility for the disability, as "applicants who were seen as personally responsible for their disabilities are also viewed as potentially causing work-related problems if hired" (Bordieri & Drehmer, 1988, p. 245).

A preferential hierarchy of disabilities is constructed in social interaction and is associated with difficulty in gaining and keeping employment. For example, architectural accommodations required by the Americans With Disabilities Act (ADA) are easing the entrance of wheelchair riders into the workplace. But the removal of physical barriers does little to address the disenfranchisement of deaf people, whose linguistic differences from hearing workers separate and may disempower them. Nor does the ADA address the disenfranchisement of people with a socially undesirable disability, such as AIDS or drug addiction, beyond making overt job discrimination illegal.

A hierarchy of preference for certain disabilities over others is related to the types and amounts of social support needed (Belgrave, 1991; Greenwood, Schriner, & V. Johnson, 1991). It may be easier for an employer and coworkers to support a person with dyslexia, for example, than to provide the instrumental and emotional support needed by a recovering alcoholic, or adapt to the changing support needs of a person with degenerating sensory, motor, or mental capabilities. In fact, the requisite support needs of people with different types of disabilities is, in part, at the root of the preferential hierarchy (cf. Woelfe, Roessler, & Schriner, 1992).

## THE CHANGING LEGAL CONSTRUCTION
## OF DISABILITY AND WORK

Social and legal constructions of disability overlap, and government legislation of disability and work issues is helping to change these constructions within the United States. In this section, we review four factors related to the changing legal construction of disability in the United States: (a) The mission of rehabilitation agencies charged with formal disability assistance is restricted to initial work placement, (b) disability-related educational assistance is narrowly focused, (c) individuals with disability are accountable for communicating needs for reasonable accommodation, and (d) there is a legitimate fear of litigation regarding reasonable accommodation among employers and organizations.[4]

Some overlap between social and legal constructions of disability is associated with structural characteristics of the rehabilitation system (e.g., education level, vocational tracking, and placement vs. mobility efforts). Educational assistance for persons with disability frequently targets the achievement of a high school or bachelor's degree as the terminal educational objective (G. Miller, 1991; Welsh, 1991). Consequently, rehabilitation professionals who are attempting to deal realistically with the school-to-work transition often track students with disabilities into vocational programs, rather than encouraging a broader liberal arts education. Liberal arts education is negatively associated with salary and degree of control in initial job placement, but positively associated with long-term ascendance into jobs of greater control, permanence, and prestige (Ross & Reskin, 1992; Welsh, 1991), with probable spillover into feelings of employee empowerment and perceived personal control (Greenberger, Porter, Miceli, & Strasser, 1991; G. Johnson, 1993).

Furthermore, most rehabilitation agencies are chartered with a mission to place persons with disability in jobs—not to facilitate their upward mobility. As G. Miller (1991) observed, "No regulation appears to exist which would require a rehabilitation counselor to discuss with an individual employment opportunities beyond the initial placement" (p. 332). Thus, upward mobility is a problem even for employees in sheltered or supported employment programs (G. Johnson, 1995; G. Miller, 1991).

In addition to limiting educational and vocational choices for people with disabilities, traditional rehabilitation models designated able professionals to speak for disabled patients (Fine & Asch, 1988). The positions

---

[4]An NBC evening news story broadcast (Tom Brokaw, anchor) on May 16, 1994, detailed the unexpected consequences of the ADA in U.S. organizations. The financial costs associated with accommodating a greater number and type of disabilities is substantially greater than expected. One group cited by Brokaw estimated the number of ADA-related lawsuits filed during 1993 at 88 million.

of power in the rehabilitation system itself, from designing adaptive technology (vs. producing it) to making decisions about funding allocations, are usually held by able individuals, rather than by members of the disabled community (ICD, 1986). This is a source of bitterness and disenfranchisement among some people with disabilities. In fact, a specific premise of the World Institute on Disability (WID) has been the advancement of persons with disabilities into positions of authority and accountability within the disability civil rights movement (Roberts, 1993).

Consistent with changing social and legal constructions of disability in the United States, a preference has emerged in rehabilitation scholarship for voicing and defining support from the perspective of the person with the disability (Fine & Asch, 1988; Nixon, 1988). This is in contrast to scholarly publications on disability that reflect a "philosophical determinism relative to disability and presuppose disability as negative stigma, then postulate medical solutions for the problems of disability" (MacGugan, 1993, p. 2). This new preference is expressed in the growth of qualitative research methods used to conduct disability studies (cf. Brooks, 1991; Hammel, 1993). The epistemological assumptions of qualitative data and the perspective from which the data originate (i.e., participant points of view) are associated with greater attention being given the communication, advocacy, and political competencies that empower people with disabilities to advance their own interests (see Balcazar, Seekins, Fawcett, & Hopkins, 1990; Scotch, 1988; Scudder & Guinan, 1989) and give them greater accountability.

However, the issue of accountability is a paradoxical one in the legal construction of disability. A disabled job applicant carries the burden of communicating reasonable accommodation to potential employers. The applicant must initiate a conversation about accommodation by disclosing the disability, if it is not already visible to a potential employer. The dilemma is whether to self-identify. As disabled, the applicant will receive the benefit of structured programs like the ADA, but will risk being silently crossed off the list before a first interview can be gained.

Increased legislative pressures on employers, such as the unfunded mandates and compliance dates associated with the ADA, mean that employers are likely to become ever more wary of the political and legal issues associated with hiring a disabled worker. It is difficult for employers in such a defensive communication climate to experience a person with a disability as something other than a potential litigant (Gibb, 1961). Immense face, legal, and emotional issues are involved in confronting employment and disability. Anxiety leads to less open communication, limiting opportunities for employers to become educated about accommodating people with disabilities. In these ways, "the links become chains" (Ray, 1993, p. 106), and a structure designed to help people with disabilities get work places unforeseen constraints on their actions.

Social support should help people with disabilities cope with a variety of stresses related to their economic, social, and medical well-being (Belgrave, 1991). Theoretically, supportive relationships can buffer the stress of economic deprivation and social stigmatization, and bolster the ability to cope with a mental, physical, or sensory handicap (Albrecht & Adelman, 1987; Jackson & Lawson, 1995). In the last part of this chapter, we consider some structural sources of social support in light of the changing social and legal constructions of disability in the United States. Specifically, we focus on the implications of communication network involvement and work-related social support for persons with disabilities.

## IMPLICATIONS FOR SOCIAL SUPPORT, DISABILITY, AND WORK

The present dilemma for working-age persons with disability lies in coping with current constructions of disability and operating within current social structures. To this end, social support may mediate the financial, social, and health-related stressors associated with employment disenfranchisement.

Without work, United States citizens live at poverty level or below, even with government assistance (e.g., Social Security disability income averages about $600 per month, according to ICD, 1986). Unemployed people lack a productive occupation, and too much leisure time spent at home watching television can lead to depression, alcohol and drug dependencies, weight gain, and other deleterious health consequences (Braithwaite, 1993).

Absent the social ties gained in relationships within the work setting, persons with disability are likely to receive little self-esteem-building recognition and validation (Belgrave, 1991; Blitzer, Peterson, & Rogers, 1993). Entitlement programs were created to alleviate financial stress, but they may actually increase emotional stress because of the stigma associated with receiving assistance. Furthermore, individuals with limited social ties are more likely to experience the stress of loneliness.

One consequence of these combined stressors is that persons with disabilities easily can overtax their existing support resources and relationships (Hammel, 1993). In the remainder of this chapter, we consider the implications of communication network involvement and social support interventions for assisting people with disability in coping with employment disenfranchisement.

### Communication Network Involvement

Sheer lack of work-related ties and restricted career mobility render limited opportunities for people with disabilities to become elite group members in any communication network (Albrecht & Hall, 1991). In the United

States, people who do not gain competitive employment remain forever outside the mainstream of society. Institutionalized outgroup status leads to imploded relationships (Krackhardt & Hanson, 1993), so that people with disabilities spend much of their time talking to others who are like themselves (e.g., deaf people talk to other deaf people). In addition, some people with disabilities necessarily have frequent interactions with members of the rehabilitation system, which provides them with access to possible sources of support. For example, the American Foundation for the Blind's (AFB) Career and Technology Information Bank is a resource that could be used to support disabled job seekers. The data bank provides employment information about approximately 1,200 currently employed blind people and 90% of those in the data bank expressed a willingness to share information directly with those interested (G. Miller, 1991). The relationships established through such interactions can be a source of social support, role modeling, and mentoring, as well as information exchange. Yet people with visual impairments who are not clients of a rehabilitation agency are unlikely to know about the existence of the data bank or have access to it. On the other side, however, the tendency of marginalized group members to communicate primarily with similar others means that other sources of support and resources, only available through relationships with elite group members, will be unaccessible (Ibarra, 1993).

Those members of marginalized groups who recognize the tendency for imploded relationships choose to associate primarily with elite group members. If people with disabilities relate only with nondisabled persons, they miss the opportunities for confirmation and validation available in interactions with similar others (Blitzer et al., 1993). One structural result is that cohesion among people with disabilities is decreased, eventually impacting the collective political power of the group. A balance of strong and weak ties (i.e., ingroup and outgroup relationships) seems the best way to ensure receipt of both types of support (Albrecht & Adelman, 1987). Yet greater numbers and diverse types of relationships are stressful to achieve and maintain (Ray, 1991).

## Social Support Interventions

Supportive programs developed to provide financial independence to people with disabilities may actually result in disincentives to work, thereby maintaining their disenfranchisement (Bardwick, 1991). Many government financial assistance programs are discontinued automatically when a person with disability works for 3 consecutive months (ICD, 1986). This results in a disincentive to full-time temporary employment. Other types of assistance provided to enhance independent living, such as transportation subsidies or attendant care funding, are taken away if the person earns more than about $600 per month (Hammel, 1993). The financial assistance needed for daily living becomes a chain that keeps disabled individuals from risking full-time, wage-earning positions. If the full-time job does not work out, they may be unable to regain financial assistance, or it could take months for aid to be reinstated. Any independence the person had gained through an assistance program quickly evaporates as transportation, attendant care, or rent subsidies are withdrawn.

In addition to the stress associated with limited occupational ties, people with spinal cord injuries or other ambulatory impairments (e.g., multiple sclerosis) have role stress associated with recruiting, hiring, managing, and firing attendant caregivers. The attendant care relationship is highly important and tightly coupled, depending on the degree of physical assistance needed. Reliance on caregivers is high, yet detachment is also key. The person with the disability has to maintain supervisory authority and face needs with the attendant(s), despite highly personal interactions and routine violations of privacy boundaries constructed by able society (Braithwaite, 1991; Hammel, 1993). Communication training aimed at increasing perspective-taking skills, conducting selection interviews, and providing feedback could help people with ambulatory disabilities cope with the stress of managing attendant care demands.

Research on the job stress-social support-burnout relationship suggests that participation in decision making and support from coworkers and supervisors reduces perceived work-related stress and burnout, and increases satisfaction with and commitment to work (K. I. Miller, Ellis, Zook, & Lyles, 1990). This research was conducted among able employees, but the marginalized status of people with disability suggests that the communication of support from these organizational sources will be even more important for these workers. However, it is important to recognize that relationships that are developed to give and receive social support in organizations may, over time, constrain the people involved in them. There also may be hidden costs associated with receiving particular kinds of support (Ray, 1993). Applied to persons with disabilities, a deaf person who relies on an interpreter, rather than learning to read lips, will eventually be at the mercy of interpreter schedules, shortages, and salary demands, whereas, a deaf person with lip-reading skills will be able to operate independently, at least in face-to-face interactions.

Just as the relationships developed to provide support are complex and potentially restrictive, support resources that initially appear to empower a disabled employee may eventually be the source of further disenfranchisement. Johnson (1993) discussed the reliance of visually impaired employees on sight as a resource. Eventually, small amounts of residual vision become a liability rather than an asset, as the individual becomes overly reliant on existing sight and fails to learn nonsight mobility or task skills. For employees with deteriorating capabilities such as vision, mobility, or memory, proactive support interventions should be aimed at easing the transition to other coping mechanisms. In this way, the support offered can enable the person to live with the disability, rather than it becoming a liability.

Frequently, even existing solutions to the career dilemmas of people with disabilities are not implemented. The reasons are usually financial: Computer technology for people with vision loss is deemed too expensive, so employees have no access to print materials, even when accommodation is technologically possible (G. Johnson, 1993). Deaf employees could benefit from a requirement for mandatory sign language training for hearing peers at work (Romer & Schoenberg, 1991); however, such training is labeled unfeasible in light of employee turnover, and again, a potentially supportive intervention is not implemented (Augusto & McGraw, 1990; G. Johnson, 1993; Romer & Schoenberg, 1991). The examples of what is impractical, too expensive, or nearly impossible to accommodate are endless (e.g., accommodating a person with an environmental disability such as multiple chemical sensitivity in a university setting is nearly impossible because of the types of carpet and lighting used in institutional settings, and because it is difficult to ensure that others in a public environment do not wear cologne, hairspray, etc.).

Most of the supportive mechanisms available that could reduce the disenfranchisement of persons with disability are interpersonal. Necessary structural changes are often not implemented due to cost factors and a variety of other excuses. Although there is perhaps some legitimacy to these concerns, they also represent the degree of importance society places on bringing persons with disabilities into the mainstream. If this was considered a high priority, cost issues, for example, would be a much less salient concern.

## CONCLUSION

Clearly, those who are alternatively able face numerous challenges related to employment, including limited job opportunities and mobility, as well as the accommodation of special needs. Some of these challenges are inherently related to communication and to supportive interpersonal relationships. It is imperative for communication scholars to begin to address these challenges through additional training and research efforts. Each of these directions is addressed in turn in the subsections that follow.[5]

---

[5]We want to avoid paternalistic prescriptions in the form of "apply X [support intervention] to alleviate Y [stressor]" (Redding, 1985) because we are among the temporarily able and do not presume to know the support needs of people with disabilities in the same way that they know their own support needs. We also feel strongly that choices about support giving and receiving, and judgments of stress levels, are best made in context by the individual with disability, in consultation with others as she or he chooses. However, we recognize the danger of alleviating group and social accountability with this individualistic stance; that is, by

*Training.* Communication training and development in the areas of negotiating reasonable accommodations, resolving conflicts, and providing social support can be of tremendous value to organizational administrators and legal departments, and to individuals with disabilities, all of whom are struggling to make sense of the ADA and other legal support structures. An example of one program is a training project at San Francisco State University that enables students with disabilities to receive content instruction in the ADA, as well as communication training in presentational speaking and group facilitation. The students then conduct ADA training sessions for small-business owners in the surrounding Bay Area communities. In the process, the students gain confidence, visibility, and exposure to a variety of work settings and employers have an opportunity to ask questions about disability and the law in a nonthreatening environment, as well as get referrals to additional sources of information and advice. A more general example might be the application of Gibb's (1961) work on defensive and supportive communication climates to the litigious climate in U.S. organizations regarding legal accommodation of people with disabilities. For example, the expectation that employers and applicants with disabilities will work together to negotiate reasonable accommodations on a case-by-case basis suggests that messages that communicate equality (rather than superiority) on the part of both parties will likely result in more successful negotiations and fewer legal complications.

*Research.* Communication research needs to move beyond the deficit model of disability, which presumes that there is something wrong with a person who has a disability (or that there is something wrong with employers). One promising direction is the elaboration of structuration processes (Giddens, 1979) through the use of aligning communicative actions (Stokes & Hewitt, 1976). Structuration theory concerns relationships among individual conduct and a variety of class, societal, and institutional constraints on action. In other words, structuration deals with relationships between conduct and culture.

Stokes and Hewitt's (1976) work on aligning actions shows how people try to align their behavior within existing cultural norms. Eventually, cultural norms change in order to accommodate the actual behaviors prevalent in a given group. For example, debates about naming, or what to call particular disabilities, have been prevalent in recent years. Individual communication choices about how to identify oneself as disabled (or not) have

---

privileging the views of the person with a disability, we tend to attribute the responsibilities of eliciting support and changing existing structural barriers to support people with disabilities, individually or collectively. The burden of having to do it all alone is familiar and frustrating to people with disabilities and to those who know them well.

larger ramifications at the societal level, such as the identification of particular disabilities in order to allocate government funds. For example, specialized tutoring assistance for university students with learning disabilities, which is funded by the state, lags 1 to 2 years behind the needs assessment process in which students are tested for and identified as having particular learning disabilities. Once college students self-identify, for example, as sophomores, they still may not receive services for 1 to 2 years, due to the lag time between identification and service delivery. Students will likely be juniors or seniors by the time they receive accommodations or other services for their learning disability. If they had self-identified when they first applied to the university, they would have been served sooner but would have risked being denied admission to the university because of their disability.

The eventual structuring effects of individual actions could be empowering or disempowering, and the same is true for individual organizational interventions designed to support disabled workers. Communication research that explores the use of aligning actions by people with disabilities as they cope with, and seek to change, the current disability culture in the United States could shed light on recursive culture-conduct relationships, and could inform the enfranchisement of all people, with and without disabilities.

# REFERENCES

Albrecht, T. L., & Adelman, M. (1987). *Communicating social support.* Newbury Park, CA: Sage.

Albrecht, T. L., & Hall, B. (1991). Relational and content differences between elites and outsiders in innovation networks. *Human Communication Research, 17,* 535–561.

Augusto, C. R., & McGraw, J. M. (1990). Humanizing blindness through public education. *Journal of Visual Impairment and Blindness, 84,* 397–400.

Balcazar, F. E., Seekins, T., Fawcett, S. B., & Hopkins, B. L. (1990). Empowering people with physical disabilities through advocacy skills training. *American Journal of Community Psychology, 18,* 281–296.

Bardwick, J. M. (1991, October). Stemming the entitlement tide in American business. *Management Review,* pp. 54–58.

Belgrave, F. Z. (1991). Psychosocial predictors of adjustment to disability in African Americans. *Journal of Rehabilitation, 57,* 37–40.

Berger, P., & Luckmann, T. (1967). *The social construction of reality.* New York: Doubleday.

Blitzer, R. J., Peterson, C., & Rogers, L. (1993). How to build self-esteem. *Training & Development, 47,* 58–60.

Bordieri, J., & Drehmer, L. (1988). Causal attribution and hiring recommendations for disabled job applicants. *Rehabilitation Psychology, 33,* 239–246.

Bowe, F. (1982). *Disabled adults in America: A statistical report drawn from U.S. Census Bureau data.* Washington, DC: U.S. Government Printing Office.

Braithwaite, D. O. (1991). "Just how much did that wheelchair cost?" Management of privacy boundaries by persons with disability. *Western Journal of Communication, 55,* 254–274.

Braithwaite, D. O. (1993). "Isn't it great that people like you get out?": The process of adjusting to disability. In E. B. Ray (Ed.), *Case studies in health communication* (pp. 149–159). Hillsdale, NJ: Lawrence Erlbaum Associates.

Brooks, N. A. (1991). Self-empowerment among adults with severe physical disability: A case study. *Journal of Sociology and Social Welfare, XVIII*(1), 103–119.

Eisenberg, E., & Goodhall, H. L., Jr. (1993). *Organizational communication: Balancing creativity and constraint.* New York: St. Martin's Press.

Fine, M., & Asch, A. (1988). Disability beyond stigma: Social interaction, discrimination, and activism. *Journal of Social Issues, 44*(1), 3–21.

Gibb, J. (1961). Defensive communication. *Journal of Communication, 2*, 141–148.

Giddens, A. (1979). *Central problems in social theory.* Berkeley: University of California Press.

Granovetter, M. (1982). The strength of weak ties: A network theory revisited. In P. V. Marsden & N. Lin (Eds.), *Social structure and network analysis* (pp. 105–130). Newbury Park, CA: Sage.

Greenberger, D. B., Porter, G., Miceli, M. P., & Strasser, S. (1991). Responses to inadequate personal control in organizations. *Journal of Social Issues, 47*, 111–128.

Greenwood, R., Schriner, K., & Johnson, V. (1991). Employer concerns regarding workers with disabilities and the business rehabilitation partnership: The PWI practitioner's perspective. *Journal of Rehabilitation, 57*, 21–25.

Hammel, J. (1993). *The development of role repertoire competence among persons with spinal cord injury: A grounded theory.* Unpublished doctoral dissertation, joint doctoral program in Special Education, San Francisco State University and University of California, Berkeley.

Ibarra, H. (1993). Personal networks of women and minorities in management: A conceptual framework. *Academy of Management Review, 18*, 56–87.

International Center for the Disabled. (1986). *The ICD survey of disabled Americans: Bringing disabled Americans into the mainstream.* New York: Author.

Jackson, R., & Lawson, G. (1995). Family environment and psychological distress in persons who are visually impaired. *Journal of Visual Impairment and Blindness, 89*, 157–160.

Johnson, G. (1993). *Communication and empowering social networks.* Unpublished doctoral dissertation, University of Washington, Seattle.

Johnson, G. (1995). Vision, education, and employee empowerment. *Journal of Visual Impairment and Blindness, 89*(2), 112–119.

Krackhardt, D., & Hanson, J. (1993, July–August). Informal networks: The company behind the chart. *Harvard Business Review, 71*(4), 104–111.

MacGugan, K. (1993). *A history of the disability civil rights movement: 1945–1978.* Unpublished manuscript, San Francisco State University, San Francisco.

Miller, G. (1991). The challenge of upward mobility. *Journal of Visual Impairment and Blindness, 85*, 332–334.

Miller, K. I., Ellis, B. H., Zook, E., & Lyles, J. (1990). An integrated model of communication, stress, and burnout in the workplace. *Communication Research, 17*, 300–326.

Nixon, H. L., III. (1988). Reassessing support groups for parents of visually impaired children. *Journal of Visual Impairment and Blindness, 82*(7), 271–278.

Ray, E. B. (1991). The relationships among communication network roles, job stress, and burnout in educational organizations. *Communication Quarterly, 39*, 91–102.

Ray, E. B. (1993). When the links become chains: Considering dysfunctions of supportive communication in the workplace. *Communication Monographs, 60*, 106–111.

Redding, W. C. (1985). Stumbling toward identity: The emergence of organizational communication as a field of study. In R. D. McPhee & P. K. Tompkins (Eds.), *Organizational communication: Traditional themes and new directions* (pp. 15–54). Beverly Hills, CA: Sage.

Retish, P. (1989). Education and transition: Is there a relationship? *Career Development for Exceptional Individuals, 12*, 36–39.

Roberts, E. (1993, September). *The employment power of abilities.* Paper presented at the Counseling 674 (Employment and Disability) class at San Francisco State University, San Francisco, by the President of the World Institute on Disability (WID).

Romer, L. T., & Schoenberg, B. (1991). Communication between staff and deaf-blind people in community residences. *Journal of Visual Impairment and Blindness, 85,* 81–84.

Ross, C. E., & Reskin, B. F. (1992). Education, control at work, and job satisfaction. *Social Science Research, 21,* 134–148.

Scotch, R. K. (1988). Disability as the basis for a social movement: Advocacy and the politics of definition. *Journal of Social Issues, 44,* 159–172.

Scudder, J., & Guinan, P. (1989). Communication competencies as discriminators of superiors' ratings of employee performance. *The Journal of Business Communication, 26,* 216–229.

Stokes, R., & Hewitt, J. P. (1976). Aligning actions. *American Sociological Review, 41,* 838–849.

Welsh, W. (1991). Does a degree influence the occupational attainments of deaf adults? An examination of the initial and long-term impact of college. *Journal of Rehabilitation, 57,* 41–47.

Woelfe, K. E., Roessler, R. T., & Schriner, K. F. (1992). Employment concerns of people with blindness or visual impairments. *Journal of Visual Impairment and Blindness, 86*(4), 185–187.

# 23 "Persons First": Expanding Communicative Choices by Persons With Disabilities

Dawn O. Braithwaite
*Arizona State University West*

Persons with physical disabilities have come far from sequestering imposed by self or others to an increasingly active, public role. From attending school and pursuing careers, appearing as characters on television shows and in advertisements, to patronizing businesses, to lobbying in the halls of Congress, persons with disabilities are no longer a silent minority group. Perhaps most significant has been the passage of the Americans With Disabilities Act (ADA), which has focused attention on persons with disabilities, who constitute up to 7% of the American population and who are, in some states, the largest minority group (Wheratt, 1988). Persons with disabilities represent a minority group that is undereducated, underemployed, and among the poorest of American minority groups ("Exceptional Parents," 1992). With all the public and legislative strides forward, however, one source reports that the rate of participation in the workforce by persons with disabilities has been on the decline in recent years, even though employers report that they find persons with disabilities to be good employees ("Exceptional Parents," 1992; see Johnson & Albrecht, chap. 22, for a discussion of persons with disabilities in the workplace).

Even with legislative support, persons with disabilities face considerable hurdles as they seek to overcome physical and social challenges associated with disability, resulting from its effect on all areas of an individual's life: behavioral, economic, and social. Many aspects of disability are limitations for an individual, in that one or more "key life functions," which include self-care, mobility, communication, socialization, and employment, are affected (Crewe & Athelstan, 1985). Individuals can overcome disabilities by means of assisting devices, medical care, or training. For example, mobility problems for a person who has paraplegia may be overcome through the use of a wheelchair, or hearing disabilities may be compensated via the use of sign language. Disabilities will become handicaps, however, when a person's disability interacts with the environment in such a way that the person's functioning is hampered (Crewe & Athelstan, 1985). This could include obstructions of mobility, access, social roles, or relationships. When the environment or community is willing and/or able to help, persons with disabilities are able to achieve increasingly independent lives.

Even when persons with disabilities do overcome their physical barriers, they still face considerable social barriers and disenfranchisement in an ablebodied-oriented world. Communication and relationships between able-bodied and disabled persons can erect great roadblocks for persons with disabilities to overcome. This essay reflects on the communication of disabled and ablebodied persons, focusing on the communicative choices persons with disabilities can make to empower themselves individually and collectively. As with any area of study, the perspective we take becomes the camera lens through which we view the issue. We begin by looking at disability from four different perspectives: as disenfranchisement, as a health issue, as a social stigma, and as a culture. Finally, we discuss the outcomes of these perspectives on the main goal persons with disabilities report for their relationships with ablebodied people: to be treated as "persons first."

## DISENFRANCHISEMENT OF PERSONS WITH DISABILITIES

Historically, persons with disabilities have found themselves treated as victims, as ill, stigmatized, and as dependents to be taken care of (Crewe & Athelstan, 1985; Goffman, 1963). Persons with disabilities were most often institutionalized, sent to special schools, or otherwise sequestered. This custodial view is reflected in such commonly used phrases as being a "polio *victim*," "arthritis *sufferer*," "*confined* to a wheelchair," or "wheelchair *bound*," and as part of the group referred to as "the handicapped." In fact, most of us have been socialized to "*help the handicapped*" and often are asked to support organizations created *for* persons with disabilities, which are most often led and staffed by ablebodied individuals. For many persons with disabilities, these benevolent organizations, although created with good intentions, serve to perpetuate dependence and custodialism of persons with disabilities. One solution has been to form counter-organizations such as the National Federation of the Blind, an organization made up of persons who are blind to work for equality and the integration into society of persons who are blind (National Federation of the Blind, 1970).

More recently, legislation like ADA has created a framework for persons with disabilities to gain enforcement of their right to be able to enter and interact in the workforce and in public places. ADA guarantees physical access for persons with disabilities, viewing this not as an act of benevolence, but a right under the law (Braithwaite & Labrecque, 1994). The passage of ADA has set the stage to empower the long-standing, traditionally viewed disability community (i.e., those with mobility, hearing, vision, speech, and learning impairment disabilities) to take control of their environment, opportunities, and voice. However, this is not now occurring. Unexpectedly, the population making the most of the ADA law, especially the employment component, are previously ablebodied individuals with mild to moderate acquired disabilities (i.e., back injuries, mental illness, alcoholism, heart conditions, diabetes). The *Disability Compliance Bulletin* substantiated this in their report of Equal Employment Opportunity Commission (EEOC) data on the number of cases of employment discrimination charges filed ("ADA Title I Charges," 1992). They reported that back impairments accounted for 17.9% of *all* cases filed, a number well above any other type of disability. This group of people with what some have termed "New-Age disabilities" have recognized the value of the law and are using it as a tool to equalize opportunities.

Conversely, people with what we might term "traditional disabilities" (i.e., cerebral palsy, muscular dystrophy, paralysis, blindness, hearing impairment) have constituted low use of the law. The *Disability Compliance Bulletin* reported EEOC data indicating that spinal impairments and paralysis together account for only .9% of cases of employment discrimination charges filed, cerebral palsy .8%, muscular dystrophy .4%, multiple sclerosis 1.5%, blindness 3.5% and hearing impairment 3.5% ("ADA Title I Charges," 1992). Little change has been noticed in the traditional community of individuals with more severe disabilities regarding assertiveness, motivation, empowerment, and taking responsibility for themselves (Labrecque, 1993). We must ask why persons who are "newly disabled" are quicker to see and seize the opportunities available to them whereas persons with more traditional disabilities do not seem to hear and/or act on ADA violations. It is important for us to recognize, then, that the existence of legislation does not alone accomplish empowerment and equality of persons with disabilities.

The guarantee of physical access is not enough to overcome the disenfranchisement disability creates for individuals. Attention to the research literature and interactions with both ablebodied and disabled persons reveal that it is the prospect of *interacting* with persons who are disabled that is troublesome for many ablebodied persons. Likewise, persons with disabilities are acutely aware that many ablebodied persons seem to be uncomfortable and awkward around them, an experience that can easily lead to defensiveness, strained communication, or the feeling they are not wanted (Braithwaite, 1989, 1993a). As with other human rights-based legislation, although we may enact laws to deal with access and removal of employment barriers, it is not possible to legislate beliefs, attitudes, and, to a large extent, individuals' behaviors toward minority groups. In the case of persons with disabilities, Morrissey (1992) points out that the ADA alone is not enough to facilitate communication between persons who are ablebodied and those with disabilities. She argued that "when interacting with individuals with disabilities, appropriate etiquette and protocol transcend issues of discrimination or compliance" with ADA (p. 3). For many ablebodied people, persons with disabilities may be viewed as dependent, unable, or even sick, a view that can further crystallize stereotypes (Braithwaite, Emry, & Wiseman, 1984; Braithwaite & Labrecque, 1994).

## Disability as a Health Issue

Interestingly, there is a question about whether matters involving persons with disabilities constitute *health* issues at all. A look at several current books on health communication reveals that although we have tackled definitions of "health communication," we have not fully come to grips with what we mean when we talk about "health" (cf. Kreps & Thornton, 1992; Northouse & Northouse, 1992; Thompson, 1986). Kreps and Thornton discussed Americans' acceptance of a machine metaphor when it comes to health. The implication of this metaphor is that the body functions as a machine that can "break down," "malfunction," and "need repair." This view is based on a traditional medical model, which is focused on the health practitioner responding to a patient's set of symptoms in an attempt to fix or restore the body (Morse & Johnson, 1991). This view of health further perpetuates the view of persons with disabilities as broken or unhealthy, searching for a cure to restore their bodies to a healthy state of "normality." When a person's disability is permanent, then, they are forever unhealthy, part of a marginalized group in an American culture that is obsessed with striving for perfect bodies.

Interviews with persons who are visibly physically disabled have revealed that "health" is certainly a *part* of their experience with disability, at least in some points in time. For example, if a person becomes disabled after an accident or illness, there is great involvement with the health care system and issues involving recovery, physical functioning, and their general state of physical and psychological health. However, when and if a person's disability becomes "stabilized," that is, the individual is able to adapt and receive the physical accommodation to be able to function independently, then "health" may not often be an issue for them. In fact, several people who had mobility-related disabilities stressed that they viewed themselves as basically healthy people whose legs did not work well (Braithwaite, 1985).

In contrast to the medical model, this perspective would fit with Morse and Johnson (1991), who took a more comprehensive view of illness, proposing what they called an "illness-constellation model":

> This model views illness as an experience that affects the sick person *and* his or her significant others. In this view, the ramifications of the individual's illness experience cause profound changes in the interactions, roles, and relationships of those involved in the illness experience and result in a loss of normalcy.... The task of *regaining normalcy*, of regaining former roles and relationships with others is a legitimate task that must be resolved before the person gains a high level of wellness. (p. 317)

Morse and Johnson proposed a four-stage model, which ends with the individual "regaining wellness," "in which the ill person *attains mastery* by regaining former relationships and the control of self" (p. 318). It is in this stage that the individual recovers *control* over his or her life and "determines when he or she is better or adjusts to and accepts a changed level of functioning" (p. 318). So, rather than view disability as an inherently "unhealthy" condition, this perspective stresses what it takes for an individual with a disability to adjust to new ways of functioning in an able-bodied world.

## Disability as a Stigmatizing Condition

Whether or not one's disability would categorize them as unhealthy or not, certainly there has been long-standing agreement with Goffman (1963) that persons with disabilities are often stigmatized because of their disability. Goffman defined stigmatized persons as "those persons who possess attributes that are 'deeply discrediting' " (p. 3) and includes persons with disabilities in that group. Goffman went on to say that the stigma represents an "undesired differentness from what we had anticipated" (p. 3) and he discussed attitudes and behaviors toward stigmatized individuals:

> By definition, of course, we believe the person with a stigma is not quite human. On this assumption we exercise varieties of discrimination, through which we effectively, if often unthinkingly, reduce his life chances. ... We tend to impute a wide range of imperfections on the basis of the original one, and at the same time to impute some desirable but undesired attributes

often of a supernatural case, such as a "sixth sense" or "understanding." (p. 5)

DeLoach and Greer (1981) labeled discomfort with persons who are disabled as a "stigma barrier," noting that length of the barrier period varies with the type of disability, the attitude of the ablebodied person, and the context of the interaction. They maintained that the "biggest problem appears to be that one party or the other is frightened away before the barrier can be broken" (p. 229). DeLoach and Greer saw the stigma barrier as one of the major sources of stress in relationships between ablebodied and disabled persons. Additionally, the stigma will have particularly negative effects on the relationship to the extent that it is perceptible and obtrusive (Goffman, 1963). Persons who are stigmatized due to disability find themselves disenfranchised from public activities, such as employment and education, and in their interpersonal relationships as well.

Jones et al. (1984) took an in-depth look at the communication of those persons who are markable, that is, those who bear a "discrediting mark," which is "perceived or inferred conditions of deviation from a prototype or norm that might initiate the stigmatizing process" (p. 8). Marking or stigmatizing a person implies that the "deviant condition has been noticed and recognized as a problem in the interaction or the relationship" and this can discredit or "spoil the identity" of the bearer (p. 8). In fact, early research on disabled persons would seem to support this view, indicating that they have lower self-esteem than most ablebodied persons (Linkowski & Dunn, 1974; Meissner, Thoreson, & Butler, 1967). Others maintain that disabled persons have few opportunities to develop role-taking skills (Gresham, 1983; Ingwell, Thoreson, & Smits, 1967; Kitano, Stiehl, & Cole, 1978) and interpersonal sensitivity (Kelley, Hastorf, Jones, Thibault, & Usdane, 1960).

How does stigma affect interactions with others? Jones et al. (1984) explained that stigmatized individuals indeed participate in relationships with others from a disadvantaged position, a position that is inherently lower in power. When stigmatized individuals are interacting from a lower power position, they will try and change this situation, trying to "bypass or contain the engulfing potential of the stigma" (p. 193). Researchers found that the nonstigmatized person's communication will be ritualized and constrained rather than flexible and open (Belgrave & Mills, 1981; Jones et al., 1984; Weinberg, 1978).

From this perspective, communication is used to cover up a disabled individual's "spoiled identity." Jones et al. (1984) discussed four "self-presentational strategic alternatives" that persons who are stigmatized may use with others (a) withdrawal, (b) concealment, (c) role acceptance, and (d) confrontation and breaking through. For our purposes these four alternatives are applied to the communication of persons with visible physical disabilities. Withdrawal is used when persons with disabilities avoid contact with those who are uncomfortable with them. Concealment describes an attempt by a disabled person to conceal his or her disability, which Goffman (1963) referred to as "passing." This would, of course, be impossible for most persons who have visible physical disabilities, such as those who use assisting devices like wheelchairs or those who have a physical disfigurement. According to Jones et al. (1984), it is more likely that persons with visible physical disabilities would engage in concealment by using what Goffman (1963) called "covering." Covering involves those behaviors used to keep the stigma from "looming large in particular interactions" (p. 204).

Persons using role acceptance learn and comply with the role that is expected of them by the dominant culture. Jones et al. (1984) argued that even when the markable person does not accept the stereotype held of them, it may be easier to act as if the stereotype is true. They went on to say that because the stereotypes are most often not openly discussed, it is hard for a stigmatized person to challenge stereotypes directly. Stigmatized persons may instead find ways to exploit the stigmatizing condition. One way to do this is through supplication, where the stigmatized person appears to accept helplessness and looks to more powerful persons to protect him or her. Or the person may try the behavioral alternative of exploitation, when "handicapped persons can exploit their own fragility in order to control the demeanor of others . . . by arousing fears that their perception of rejection, avoidance, or indifference might bring them to some form of breaking point" (p. 210).

Finally, confrontation and breaking through involves "the open acknowledgment of the mark, plus a variety of attempts to place the mark in a constructive or laudatory context" (Jones et al., 1984, p. 211). Confrontation is one way to "contain" the stigma and keep it from becoming the focus of the relationship. One may use an exemplifier strategy to arouse the guilt in others by demonstrating one's "moral worthiness" (p. 211). A second strategy, augmentation, plays on the significance of the stigma; the disabled person exaggerates his or her accomplishments in spite of the disability. The message behind this strategy is that the disabled individual would have been able to do even better than their already good performance if he or she were not saddled with the disability.

Jones et al. (1984) suggested other ways to "break through" the stigma barrier and went on to discuss at great length self-depreciating humor as an especially useful strategy. They argued that self-depreciating humor allows the disabled person to ingratiate him or herself with others, and that they can "treat it as an amusing affliction" (p. 214). Self-depreciating humor may reduce potential discomfort and "may be especially effective as the markable person displays his [sic] ability to keep the mark in perspective and to inform the marker that it is all right to talk openly about his [sic] condition" (p. 215).

Jones et al. did warn that a stigmatized person would be unwise to focus exclusively on ingratiation "at the expense of any concern about others' respect for his ability or character . . . The disabled or flawed person may become a likable klutz, which is better than a feared and totally discredited deviant, but a klutz nevertheless" (p. 215). "Breaking through" represents the attempt to override the stigma and move into "normal" interaction patterns. Breaking through keeps the stigma "in its place" as a characteristic of the disabled person. According to Jones et al., breaking through is most effective when the stigmatized person is able to focus others' attention away from their stigma and on their positive attributes.

How does the stigma perspective on disability focus our analysis of disabled persons' communication? A review of the literature clearly shows that the research has centered almost exclusively on the perspective of the ablebodied individual, suggesting behaviors that persons with disabilities should use to reduce the discomfort of others. For example, several re-searchers have found that when a disabled person discloses about his or her disability, ablebodied people will feel more comfortable around them (Evans, 1976; Hastorf, Wildfogel, & Cassman, 1979; Mills, Belgrave, & Boyer, 1984). Thompson and Seibold (1978) reviewed previous studies and concluded that disclosure may reduce the levels of tension and uncertainty of ablebodied persons, but does not necessarily increase their *acceptance* of disabled persons. Whether or not certain communication behaviors create increased comfort with, or acceptance of, persons with disabilities, this perspective has not considered the impact of the communication *on the disabled individual*. Braithwaite et al. (1984) questioned the implicit as-sumption in the literature that what is good for the ablebodied person will be good for disabled person as well. One way to try and overcome this tendency has been to study communication between ablebodied and dis-abled individuals *from the perspective of persons with disabilities*. When we have studied the communication of disabled and ablebodied persons from this perspective, we have seen that persons with disabilities are acutely aware of the social stigma attached to being physically disabled (Braith-waite, 1985, 1989, 1990, 1991; Braithwaite et al., 1984). These findings run counter to earlier research that claimed persons with disabilities have poor interpersonal sensitivity and role-taking skills (Gresham, 1983; Ingwell et al., 1967; Kelley et al., 1960; Kitano et al., 1978).

Along with being ablebodied-centered, when we take a stigma perspective on disability, it is clear that the behavioral alternatives discussed are more *reactive* than *active*. The work by Jones et al. (1984) and others relegate persons with disabilities to reacting to the perceived impressions and ex-pectations of ablebodied others. Along with being reactive, these behavioral alternatives may be characterized as more *negative* than *positive*. For ex-ample, the Jones et al. alternatives of supplication, covering, and even humor may be classified as reactive and negatively oriented, as a disabled person might use the disability to produce guilt or sympathy in ablebodied persons. If our goal is to ameliorate disenfranchisement of persons with disabilities and to highlight empowerment of this group, are there other perspectives that might be better suited to help actualize this goal? Another more recent perspective that has been explored is viewing persons with disabilities as a culture.

## Disability as a Culture

Adopting a cultural focus on being disabled highlights "the spoken system of symbols, symbolic forms, and meanings that constitutes and enacts a common sense of ... life" (Carbaugh, 1990, p. 216). This approach is based on a *communicative* definition of culture, by taking the perspective that culture is a historically transmitted system of symbols and meanings (cf. Schneider, 1976). This communication focus is centered around the observation that "social action is a meaningful activity of human beings. Social action requires commonalty of understandings; it implies common codes of communication; it entails generalized relationships among its parts mediated by human understanding" (Schneider, 1976, p. 198).

Adopting this perspective on culture allows us to view the communication of disabled and ablebodied persons as a cultural phenomenon (Braithwaite, 1990, 1993b; Emry & Wiseman, 1987). Embracing this perspective has allowed researchers to differentiate between being physically disabled and being a member of the disabled culture (Braithwaite, 1990, 1993b). This outlook was inspired by the work of Padden and Humphries (1988) who argued that being deaf is more than an audiological and physical condition; being deaf also means that one is part of a deaf culture. Persons with disabilities constitute a culture because, first, they hold a set of beliefs about themselves as disabled and as distinct from the larger nondisabled society, what is labeled the process of becoming a member of the disabled culture (Braithwaite, 1990). Second, they share common communicative codes, or sets of communication strategies used to communicate with ablebodied others (Braithwaite, 1987, 1989, 1991). This views persons with disabilities as enacting a system of symbols and meanings similar to what other scholars have identified as cultural communication (Carbaugh, 1990; Katriel, 1986). There are certainly cocultures within the disabled culture, set apart by different disability types, yet persons with disabilities share certain commonalties in the experience of being disabled, and especially in the marginalization that accompanies being disabled.

When a person becomes disabled they have many physical adaptations as they learn to function with a disability (DeLoach & Greer, 1981). They learn new ways of accomplishing daily physical activities from using assisting devices (i.e., wheelchairs or walkers) to learning to drive a car with hand controls, dressing, and self-care. However, the social adjustments to disability are perhaps even more challenging, as the individual is usually not immediately aware of the relational changes that will accompany becoming a member of the disabled culture. Becoming a member of the new culture entails significant changes in the interpersonal communication of persons with disabilities as they adjust to communicating as a member of a minority group. This is especially challenging for those who experience sudden-onset disabilities, as a person may literally "wake up disabled" from an accident or illness (Braithwaite, 1990). Although awareness of physical changes associated with disability is immediate upon disablement, becoming part of the disabled *culture* is most often not. That is, the process of becoming disabled is one of cultural assimilation, an experience that is analogous to the immigrant who leaves his or her native culture and must adapt to a new culture (Kim, 1988).

An example from a research interview with a woman who is disabled (also reported in Braithwaite, 1990) can help clarify becoming disabled as cultural assimilation, that is, making the distinction between being physically disabled and being part of the disabled culture. This woman, who became paraplegic during her childhood, recounted her experience of becoming disabled:

> When I was growing up, I spent the first nine years of my life on a farm. . . . And the disability didn't exist. But what my brothers and sisters did, I did. It was like everybody had to fend for themselves. . . . And I think that was a very stimulating and very good period of my life. I was just one of the kids. And then when I was nine years old, we moved to the small town of _____ . . . . And when I tried to climb the tree in the front yard, the woman across the street reported my mother to the welfare office because she wasn't watching me. And suddenly I saw all of these walls coming down around me, and I realized I'm being treated differently. And that point in my life when I really, you know, felt really sorry for myself, and cried and cried and cried about being disabled. . . . It just—it was never so clear in my life, you know, since that, and I went from being just a bruised-up, bratty kid one day to being disabled the next. And I really think my disability, in a lot of ways, didn't occur until society made me disabled.

In this example, the woman clearly differentiated between having to use a wheelchair for mobility and a sense of becoming disabled, entering the disabled culture when "society made me disabled." She was clearly aware of her physical differences, but did not describe herself as disabled until she was treated as such by the members of the ablebodied community.

DeLoach and Greer (1981) offered a three-phase model to describe adjustment to disability: stigma isolation, stigma recognition, and stigma incorporation. This model allows us to see the process of adjusting to disability as acculturation (Braithwaite, 1990). DeLoach and Greer's first phase, stigma isolation, describes the period of adjustment following disablement when the person perceives many things that are occurring as separate from their disability. If the person is to successfully socialize in their new role, they enter the stigma recognition phase, and realize that many of the pressures, conflicts, and frustrations they are experiencing are a result of being disabled. It is in this phase that the disabled person will develop ways to evade, resolve, or try to minimize the effects of their disability. Stigma recognition begins the process of becoming part of the disabled culture by first recognizing the culture and by beginning the process of assimilating into it (Braithwaite, 1990).

The third phase, stigma incorporation, involves integration of the disability into the individual's definition of self. The individual comes to recognize both the positive and negative aspects of being disabled and develops ways to cope with the negative aspects of it (DeLoach & Greer, 1981). In this stage of adjustment, persons with disabilities have developed ways of behaving and communicating and are able to successfully function in the ablebodied-oriented culture (Braithwaite, 1990).

In fact, persons who are disabled often describe their communication with ablebodied persons as communicating "with another culture." Being disabled is physically different from being ablebodied, yet they explained that they were "basically the same person as I always was" before their disability (Braithwaite, 1990, 1993b). Stigma incorporation appears to be analogous to what Morse and Johnson (1991) called "regaining wellness," in which the individual regains control of self, his or her relationships, and adapts to a new type of functioning. Although DeLoach and Greer (1981) and Morse and Johnson identified phases in the adjustment to disability and/or illness as that time when coping strategies are developed, they did not place emphasis on the specific *communication* strategies persons with disabilities use with ablebodied others. Researchers have been able to describe specific strategies that persons with disabilities employ, which are indications that these persons demonstrate an awareness of a common identity and have developed communication strategies to function in the majority culture (cf. Braithwaite, 1987, 1991; Braithwaite & Labrecque, 1994). They have developed a repertoire of communication strategies they employ to help reduce discomfort and uncertainty of ablebodied persons (Braithwaite, 1989; Braithwaite & Labrecque, 1994), to manage their own privacy boundaries (Braithwaite, 1991), and to manage situations when they want and/or receive help from ablebodied others (Braithwaite, 1987).

Along with the development of communication and behavioral strategies, a cultural view of disability also provides a framework for viewing disability as a *characteristic* rather than a handicap, a process Goffman (1963) labeled destigmatization. Jernigan (1965) argued that any characteristic we possess is a limitation, whether it be age, gender, race, height, or disability. Each characteristic "freezes us to some extent into a mold; each restricts to some degree the range of possibility, of flexibility, and very often of opportunity as well" (p. 1). When we can view the characteristics of disability culturally, we see that persons in the disabled culture will have *alternate* ways of communicating and behaving. This would include driving with hand controls rather than foot pedals, moving around by using a wheelchair, or using sign instead of spoken language. The behaviors are different, but not necessarily inferior, to those used by the ablebodied majority (Braithwaite, 1985).

## COMMUNICATING AS "PERSONS FIRST"

When we view communication by disabled individuals culturally, being active rather than reactive and more positive than negative in nature, we see them communicating in ways that are empowering. In interviews with persons who are disabled, one central goal of their communication is clear: to be accepted and treated as *"persons first,"* that is, to be seen as a person rather than objectified as a "disability." To accomplish being viewed as persons, interviewees stressed the importance of self-acceptance (Braithwaite, 1989). One participant revealed that "you just got to feel comfortable with it [disability] so they'll feel comfortable with it." Another reported that when he became comfortable with his disability, "I think that other people sense that and it enables them to be more comfortable and open." From what they disclosed in the interviews, these persons with disabilities appeared to have accepted the fact that they have different kinds of abilities and limitations than do ablebodied persons. They recognize that some ablebodied people will perceive that they are in pain, are overly sensitive about their disability, or that they center their lives around their disability (Braithwaite, 1989). This view reduces disability to a characteristic. One interviewee summed up this view, emphasizing, "Persons with a handicapping condition. You emphasize that person's identity and then you do something about the condition" (Braithwaite, 1985). This theme of wanting to be treated as "normal," to be "treated like anybody else" was repeated in *every* interview. The different communication strategies participants reported using with ablebodied others are designed to accomplish this end. For example, persons might use modeling behavior to show ablebodied others how to treat them, as one man who is a quadriplegic would model dancing in a bar to show others he would like to dance with them (Braithwaite, 1989). Interviewees reported that they will establish their normalcy when they meet a new ablebodied person by delaying disclosure about their disability. Using this strategy, they will delay disclosure about their disability by discussing a wide variety of topics, such as politics or sports, that are not centered around disability (Braithwaite, 1989, 1991). Participants who use wheelchairs reported that they will ask ablebodied persons to sit down when they talk with them, recognizing that this strategy will let them communicate "eye-to-eye" rather than from a one-up, one-down position (Braithwaite, 1989). In another study, persons with disabilities reported strategies they use in situations when they receive unwanted help to establish control of how help is enacted (Braithwaite, 1987). Participants sometimes discussed strategies they would use in reaction to the discomfort of ablebodied others, but most often discussed their communication strategies that are "proactive" rather than "reactive," that is, designed to create the desired impression right from the start of the relationship.

There are also important language strategies that both persons who are ablebodied and disabled can use to personify rather than objectify persons with disabilities. Using the phrase "*persons* with disabilities" rather than "handicapped people" or "the disabled" puts the emphasis on an individual rather than their condition. Some people prefer to use the phrases "physically challenged" or "differently abled" rather than calling someone "disabled." Similarly, talking about a "wheelchair user" rather than calling a person "wheelchair bound," recognizes the person with the disability as an actor and relegates the wheelchair to a tool, rather than the object of emphasis. Referring to a "person who has had polio" rather than "polio victim" and a "person who has arthritis" rather than an "arthritis sufferer," focuses on the individual rather than their disability or disease. These linguistic changes are more than an academic exercise. Rather, they help remind the user that they are dealing with a person rather than their disability. This can only help to empower individuals with disabilities and will help ablebodied persons know how to talk with and behave toward a person who is disabled.

It seems important to ask: Is a disabled person's desire to be treated as "normal" or as a "person first" an unrealistic or unhealthy expectation? DeLoach and Greer (1981) discussed the danger of what they called "deifying normality" (p. 41), where persons with severe disabilities become obsessed with trying to appear and behave normally and "become living caricatures who attempt to appear as normal as possible" (p. 41). For these individuals, the compulsion to appear nondisabled circumvents the disabled persons' successful adjustment to living with a disability. DeLoach and Greer cited the example of a disabled college student who wanted to look normal so badly that he would not push his own wheelchair to classes as it would have made his hands and shirtsleeves dirty, which would have appeared "abnormal." Consequently the man flunked out of college because he missed too many classes.

Is the desire to be seen as a "person first" the same as deifying normality? Considering what interviewees have said, the answer would be "no." Unlike the man in the preceding example, the participants do not deny their disability and its effects; however, they do attempt to *proactively exert control* over the effects of disability on their communication with ablebodied others. Participants stated that they realized disability made them different in some ways, but they communicate in ways designed to minimize the differences, when possible, and to communicate in ways that lessen the negative effects being disabled may have on their relationships.

Although legislation like the Americans with Disabilities Act will help create physical and employment access for persons with disabilities, it will be largely up to disabled individuals themselves to create changes in attitudes of, and relationships with, ablebodied persons. Becoming informed about their rights and taking advantage of opportunities and legal protections will assist persons with disabilities to reject old stereotypes and take an active role in society. Assisting with this effort are organizations committed to "independent living" for persons with disabilities. These organizations are providing training, counseling, support groups, and legal advocacy to assist persons with disabilities to be integrated into the community and to lead independent lives. Rejecting the view of persons with disabilities as unhealthy or stigmatized, and promoting the perspective of disability as a culture, reduces disability as one of the characteristics an individual possesses. Communication researchers and trainers can assist persons with disabilities as they empower themselves and expand both their individual and collective goals (Braithwaite & Labrecque, 1994). When persons with disabilities view themselves as persons first and when they are able to assist others to treat them as persons as well, some of the stigmatization of being disabled, and subsequent disenfranchisement, will be diminished.

## REFERENCES

ADA Title I Charges. (1992). *Disability Compliance Bulletin, 3*(24), 9.

Belgrave, F. Z., & Mills, J. (1981). Effect upon desire for social interaction with a physically disabled person of mentioning the disability in different contexts. *Journal of Applied Social Psychology, 11*(1), 44–57.

Braithwaite, D. O. (1985, November). *Impression management and redefinition of self by persons with disabilities.* Paper presented at the annual meeting of the Speech Communication Association, Denver.

Braithwaite, D. O. (1987, November). *If you push my wheelchair, don't make car sounds":On the problem of "help" between disabled and ablebodied persons.* Paper presented at the annual meeting of the Speech Communication Association, Boston.

Braithwaite, D. O. (1989, February). *An interpretive analysis of disabled persons' impression management strategies in response to perceived discomfort and uncertainty of ablebodied others.* Paper presented at the annual meeting of the Western Speech Communication Association, Spokane, WA.

Braithwaite, D. O. (1990). From majority to minority: An analysis of cultural change from ablebodied to disabled. *International Journal of Intercultural Relations, 14,* 465–483.

Braithwaite, D. O. (1991). Just how much did that wheelchair cost? Management of privacy boundaries by persons with disabilities. *Western Journal of Speech Communication, 55,* 254–274.

Braithwaite, D. O. (1993a). Isn't it great that people like you get out?: Communication between disabled and ablebodied persons. In E. B. Ray (Ed.), *Case studies in health communication* (pp. 149–159). Hillsdale, NJ: Lawrence Erlbaum Associates.

Braithwaite, D. O. (1993b). Viewing disabled persons as a culture. In L. A. Samovar & R. Porter (Eds.), *Intercultural communication: A reader* (7th ed., pp. 148–154). Belmont, CA: Wadsworth.

Braithwaite, D. O., Emry, R. A., & Wiseman, R. L. (1984). *Ablebodied and disablebodied persons' communication: The disabled persons' perspective.* (ERIC Document Reproduction Service No. ED 264 622).

Braithwaite, D. O., & Labrecque, D. (1994). Responding to the Americans with Disabilities Act: Contributions of interpersonal communication research and training. *Journal of Applied Communication Research, 22*(3), 282–294.

Carbaugh, D. (1990). *Cultural communication and intercultural contact.* Hillsdale, NJ: Lawrence Erlbaum Associates.

Crewe, N., & Athelstan, G. (1985). *Social and psychological aspects of physical disability.* Minneapolis: University of Minnesota, Department of Independent Study and University Resources.

DeLoach, C., & Greer, B. G. (1981). *Adjustment to severe disability.* New York: McGraw-Hill.

Emry, R., & Wiseman, R. L. (1987). An intercultural understanding of ablebodied and disabled persons' communication. *International Journal of Intercultural Relations, 11,* 7–27.

Evans, J. H. (1976). Changing attitudes toward disabled persons: An experimental study. *Rehabilitation Counseling Bulletin, 19*(4), 572–579.

Exceptional Parents. (1992). Review of the Americans With Disabilities Act: From policy to practice. *Exceptional Parents' Guide for Active Adults with Disabilities, 1*(1), 32.

Goffman, E. (1963). *Stigma: Notes on the management of spoiled identity.* New York: Simon & Schuster.

Gresham, F. N. (1983). Social skills assessment as a component of mainstreaming decisions. *Exceptional Children, 49*(2), 331–336.

Hastorf, A. H., Wildfogel, J., & Cassman, T. (1979). Acknowledgment of handicap as a tactic in social interaction. *Journal of Personality and Social Psychology, 37,* 1790–1797.

Ingwell, R. H., Thoreson, R. W., & Smits, S. J. (1967). Accuracy of social perception of physically handicapped and non-handicapped persons. *Journal of Social Psychology, 72*(1), 107–116.

Jernigan, K. (1965). *Blindness: Handicap or characteristic.* Address to National Federation of the Blind annual meeting, Chicago, IL.

Jones, E. E., Farina, A., Hastorf, A. H., Markus, H., Miller, D. T., & Scott, R. A. (1984). *Social stigma: The psychology of marked relationships.* New York: Freeman.

Katriel, T. (1986). *Talking straight: Dugri speech in Israeli sabra culture.* Cambridge, England: Cambridge University Press.

Kelley, H. H., Hastorf, A. H., Jones, E. E., Thibault, J. W., & Usdane, W. M. (1960). Some implications of social psychological theory for research on the handicapped. In L. Lofquist (Ed.), *Psychological research and rehabilitation* (pp. 172–204). Washington, DC: American Psychological Association.

Kim, Y. Y. (1988). *Communication and cross-cultural adaptation.* Philadelphia: Multilingual Matters, Ltd.

Kitano, M. R., Stiehl, J., & Cole, J. T. (1978). Role taking: Implications for special education. *Journal of Special Education, 12,* 59–74.

Kreps, G. L., & Thornton, B. C. (1992). *Health communication: Theory and practice* (2nd ed.). Prospect Heights, IL: Waveland.

Labrecque, D. (1993, November). *How the law impacts post-secondary options*. Paper presented at the Fourth Annual Conference on Schools to Adult Life Transitions Services, Arizona Department of Education, Phoenix.

Linkowski, D. C., & Dunn, M. A. (1974). Self-concept and acceptance of disability. *Rehabilitation Counseling Bulletin, 18*(1), 28–32.

Meissner, A. L., Thoreson, R. W., & Butler, J. R. (1967). Relation of self-concept to impact and obviousness of disability among male and female adolescents. *Perceptual and Motor Skills, 24*, 1099–1105.

Mills, J., Belgrave, F. Z., & Boyer, K. M. (1984). Reducing avoidance of social interaction with a physically disabled person by mentioning the disability following a request for aid. *Journal of Applied Social Psychology, 14*(1), 1–11.

Morrisey, P. A. (1992). Etiquette, protocol, and the ADA. *Disability Compliance Bulletin, 3*(6), 1–3.

Morse, J. M., & Johnson, J. S. (1991). *The illness experience: Dimensions of suffering*. Newbury Park, CA: Sage.

National Federation of the Blind. (1970). *The first thirty years: A history of the National Federation of the Blind*. Des Moines, IA: Author.

Northouse, P. G., & Northouse, L. L. (1992). *Health communication: Strategies for health professionals* (2nd ed.). Englewood Cliffs, NJ: Prentice-Hall.

Padden, C., & Humphries, T. (1988). *Deaf in America: Voices from a culture*. Cambridge, MA: Harvard University Press.

Schneider, D. (1976). Notes toward a theory of culture. In K. Basso & H. Selby (Eds.), *Meaning in anthropology* (pp. 197–220). Albuquerque: University of New Mexico Press.

Thompson, T. L. (1986). *Communication for health professionals*. New York: Harper & Row.

Thompson, T. L., & Seibold, D. R. (1978). Stigma management in normal-stigmatized interactions: A test of the disclosure hypothesis and a model of stigma acceptance. *Human Communication Research, 4*, 231–242.

Weinberg, N. (1978). Modifying social stereotypes of the physically disabled. *Rehabilitation Counseling Bulletin, 22*(2), 114–124.

Wheratt, R. (1988, August 1). Minnesota disabled to be heard. *Star Tribune*, pp. 1, 6.

# Author Index

# Subject Index

## A

Abused women, *see* Incest, Intimate violence, Sexual violence

Access to Care Model, 127

African-American (Black), *see also* Feminist theories, Poor/minority women, 11, 15–16, 17–18, 82, 95, 96, 87, 98, 104, 108, 110, 111, 117, 369, 377–378

Aid to Families with Dependent Children (AFDC), 81, 87, 89

AIDS, *see* HIV, Gay men, Women of color

Alan Guttmacher Institute, 34, 35

Alcohol abuse, 405–406
    Alcoholics Anonymous, 407, 426
    communication approaches to prevention/intervention, 413–424
    Designated Drivers, 408
    as disease, 408
    and disenfranchisement, 406, 407–410, 413–414, 424–427
    history, 407–408
    Mothers Against Drunk Driving (MADD), 408
    reconstruction of identity, 426–427
    statistics, 405–406
    Students Against Drunk Driving (SADD), 408
    Substance Free Living Environments, 408
    taxonomy, 410–413

Alliance of the North American Man/Boy Love Association (NAMBLA), 70

American Association of Physicians for Human Rights, 343

American Cancer Society, 142, 188, 190

American College Health Association, 406

American Foundation for the Blind's (AFB) Career and Technology Information Bank, 441

American Medical Association (AMA), 34, 104, 293

American Psychiatric Association (APA), 334–335

American Society for the Control of Cancer, 188

## B

Battered women, *see* Intimate violence, Sexual violence

Biological determinism, 240–241

Biological family, 239–240

## C

Cancer, *see also* Communication, Doctor–patient communication, Gay men, HIV/AIDS, Poor/minority women, Terminally ill
    in adolescence, 185
    alienation, 185
    alternative treatments, 190–191
    breast, 150
    cancerphobia, 185, 187, 204
    coping with, 203–204
    counterculture, 189–190
    cultural response, 186–187
    fear, 185, 191, 196
    germ theory, 187
    intimacy, 200
    irritation theory, 187
    isolation, 185, 191, 192, 198
    living with, 39–42
    long-term survival, 199–200
    management, 191–198
    phases, 191–198
    prevalence, 186
    psychological effects, 200
    relapse, 201, 202
    rise of establishment, 188–189
    second malignancies, 201–202
    social functioning, 200–201
    social support, 195, 197
    work performance/insurance, 201

Centers for Disease Control (CDC), 142, 350, 353, 366

Chicana(o), *see also* Feminist theories, Poor/minority women, 17

481